STORIES
BEHIND
EVERYDAY
THINGS

STORIES BEHIND EVERYDAY THINGS

THE READER'S DIGEST ASSOCIATION, INC.
Pleasantville, New York/Montreal

STORIES BEHIND EVERYDAY THINGS

Editor: Jane Polley
Art Director: Vincent L. Perry
Senior Editor: Will Bradbury
Associate Editor: Kaari Ward
Research Editor and Assistant to the Editor: Tanya Strage
Research Editors: Monica Borrowman, Josephine Reidy
Research Associates: Hildegard Anderson, Laurel Gilbride
Picture Researcher: Marion Bodine
Art Assistant: Marlene Rimsky
Project Secretary: Carol Davis

Contributing Writers: Peter Chaitin, Alicia Fortinberry,
        Zane Kotker, Colin Leinster, Alan Linn,
        David Maxey, Wendy Murphy, Mark Strage, Kim Waller
Contributing Copy Editor: Melvin Wolfson
Contributing Picture Researchers: Elizabeth Bird, Tobi Zausner
Consultant:
        Eugene Ostroff
        Curator of Photography, Smithsonian Institution

Library of Congress Catalog Card Number 79-88053

ISBN 0-89577-068-7

Printed in the United States of America

Third Printing, June 1983

Contents

The 300 articles and the special features that accompany them
are arranged in alphabetical order.

Introduction	6	Oil - Orange, Lemon, Lime	233-235
Acronym - Automobile	15-26	Packaging - Purse	236-256
Balloon - Button	28-53	Quiz Show - Quilt	258-260
Calendar - Crossword Puzzle	54-92	Radio - Rug	270-285
Decimal System - Dye	101-131	Safe - Symbiosis	287-341
Elevator - Eyeglasses	133-137	Table Linen - Typewriter	353-380
Fad - Funeral	138-148	Umbrella - Uniform	382-384
Gadget - Guitar	150-163	Vaccine - Vitamins	385-388
Hairstyle - Hypodermic	164-178	Washing Machine - Wine	389-394
Ice Cream - Iron	188-194	X Ray	397-398
Jacket - Jury	194-200	Yawn - Yogurt	398-399
Ketchup - Knife, Fork, Spoon	200-204	Zipper - Zoo	400-402
Lawn - Lock and Key	204-211	Acknowledgments and Text Credits	403
Magazine - Mustard	211-226	Picture Credits	403-405
Nail - Numbers	227-232	Index	406-416

VANTAGE POINTS—An extraordinary look at ordinary things
through the eyes of special groups.

ADVERTISING: rose-tinted images	7-14
DESIGNS: lead into gold	93-100
IMAGES: modern perspectives	179-187
RENDERINGS: the craftsman's art	261-269
TECHNICAL GENIUS: sum of its parts	343-352

Introduction

The expression "everyday things" is broad enough to embrace subjects as diverse as apples and automobiles, doctors and dolls, scandals and shipping. Even something that sounds as scientifically arcane as symbiosis is vital to everyday life, and nature abounds in colorful, little-known stories of those fascinating relationships at work.

After deciding to consider any "thing," tangible or intangible, that figures in our daily life as a potential candidate for inclusion in this book, Reader's Digest editors faced the Sherlockian task of tracking down and uncovering the "secret lives" of things so often taken for granted. Was what is mundane today once exotic, frightening, or forbidden? (Buttons had to be smuggled into England in the reign of Charles II.) Can it be that what seems as modern as the latest dance craze is actually ancient history? (The can-can, which shocked Nikita Khrushchev in Paris, had been performed in Egypt 4,000 years earlier.) Does an everyday thing have bizarre applications and play undreamed-of roles, funny or tragic, history-making or transitory? Have there been obscure versions of what is now commonplace? (In ancient Greece coin-operated machines dispensed holy water.) What human need was each of these things created to fulfill? How did they evolve?

As colorful and unusual answers to these questions emerged, they repeatedly evoked the same involuntary reaction from the editors: "I didn't know that!" Whenever that happened, the subject inevitably earned a permanent place on the list. "Bicycle" gained entry, for example, when the editors (who knew that bicyclists had thronged to the roads when the automobile was still a rarity) also learned that it was the bike that caused the disappearance of tens of thousands of horses from city streets and that cyclists' demands were responsible for better roads, signs, maps, hotels, and taverns.

Not only are there little-known facts behind ordinary things, there are also unique ways of looking at them. A mechanic sees an engine through different eyes than an advertising man; a banana looks different to an artist and a botanist. The picture portfolios, "Vantage Points," examine our familiar surroundings through a variety of lenses.

Finally, and most importantly, the editors approached this book with the premise that what is educational should also be entertaining, a criterion that figured critically in choosing from amongst the thousands of stories behind everyday things.

The Editors

"*They said father didn't keep his Life Insurance paid up!*"

THE PRUDENTIAL INSURANCE COMPANY *of* AMERICA

EDWARD D. DUFFIELD, *President*   HOME OFFICE, *Newark, N.J.*

ADVERTISING: rose-tinted images

Everyday things were advertised in earliest colonial times by handbill, poster, and newspaper. George Washington advertised—and even wrote some of his own copy. So did Paul Revere, who urged Boston residents to purchase his brand of hand-fashioned false teeth. But it was Ben Franklin, purveyor of soaps and owner of the *Pennsylvania Gazette,* who really fostered advertising in America. By 1820 more than 500 newspapers carried ads for snuff and shoes and even slaves.

With the advent of mass-circulation magazines at the end of the 19th century, competition between rival advertisers became intense. Master of the hard sell was Albert Lasker, who joined a Chicago firm in 1898 at $10 a week. Six years later Lasker became a partner, and the modern era of the agency-produced ad was underway. Since then, advertising has applied its own unique lenses to myriad everyday things— often convincing the impressionable everyday buyer to view a product through the proffered rose-colored or tear-stained glasses, as in the 1926 hard-sell Prudential ad above. Some of the copywriters' viewpoints are intimidating, some awful, and some so exactly right that they have become as much a part of our lives as the things themselves.

The Human Preoccupation

Mankind has always worried about the functions and malfunctions, beauties and blemishes, real and imagined, of the human body. And as these historic ads show with shameless candor so has advertising. Yet for all the product names and gaudy designs the industry has created, it has clearly been at its best in making people worry—about being "over-stout" or bald-ugly. And with good reason. Otherwise who would be concerned about having "arches of regret?" And what baby would require nerve pills if it hadn't been confronted by a huge green frog croaking, "Don't be nervous?"

A FACE OF TWENTY

a throat of 40?

DOROTHY GRAY

Dr WILLIAMS PINK PILLS FOR PALE PEOPLE

DENT'S Toothache Gum

Stops the Ache. Cleanses the cavity, prevents decay. Used by Millions for past 25 years. All drug stores, or by mail 15 cents.
C. S. DENT & CO. Detroit, Mich.

A Swell Affair

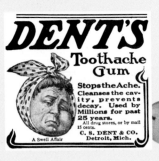

A CLEAR COMPLEXION! USE DR. CAMPBELL'S SAFE ARSENIC COMPLEXION WAFERS!

A Practical Invention
THAT DEVELOPS HAIR GROWTH.

How Men Gain Summer Comfort—

Cool knee-length underwear— And sensible, comfortable

Shir Gar

the **one** really comfortable garter

No binding elastic around your leg. Shir Gar attach to the shirt holding it down while perfectly supporting the socks. Relieves varicose veins.

Put on a pair of Shir Gar today and get a new idea of summer comfort. At all dealers or by mail 50c postpaid. Guaranteed satisfactory.

SHIRT GARTER CO.
Dept. 27   Nashville, Tenn.

Dealers: Order from your jobber, or direct if he can't supply you

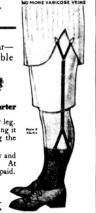

NO BULGING OF SHIRT
NO MORE VARICOSE VEINS

PILE PIPE

Dr BUKER'S KIDNEY PILLS

ALL GOING OUT—NOTHING COMING IN

Cascarets DID IT

THEY WORK WHILE YOU SLEEP

A Matter of Taste

Some people will question the taste of the copywriters and designers who created these ads, as well as the companies that approved and paid for them. Yet at the time of their appearance the ads were generally successful, mostly because the people who dreamed them up, however mercenary, were no less human than the customers they were trying to reach. And if the pitch was sometimes a bit raucous, the products hawked by the ads were occasionally quite useful.

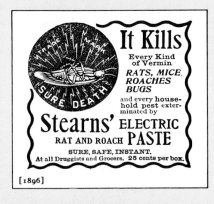

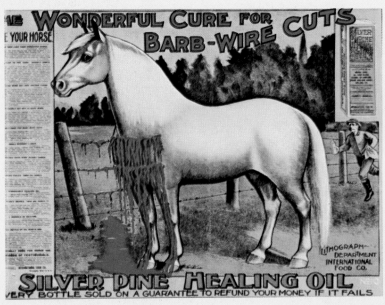

Mozart were alive today, he'd be recording on "Scotch" brand recording tape.

There's deep consolation . . . serene through shower or heavy rain . . . for those who know the casket of a dear one is protected against water in the ground by a Clark Metal Grave Vault

CLARK GRAVE VAULTS

DOOD MORNIN! I HAPPY BABY.

'CAUSE MY MAMMA ALWAYS USES TARRANT'S SELTZER APERIENT.

"Standard" PLUMBING FIXTURES

Slogans That Sell

Some ads and slogans work better than others. A few are so good that they achieve advertising's ultimate pinnacle: they enter the public domain—to be joked about, copied, revered, repeated, and remembered. Words work well, especially those that are unpredictable or outrageous or poke at the human predicament. Pictures are even better, as the familiar symbols cavorting below well indicate; each projects its commercial message as blatantly as if it had scrambled onto the kitchen table and shouted at you.

THERE'S A *Ford* IN YOUR FUTURE

When you get this far into Tabu, there's no turning back
Tabu perfume. One lingering ounce $30

The First Message from Mars

send us up some Pears' Soap

Does she... or doesn't she?

Often a bridesmaid but never a bride

EDNA'S case was really a pathetic one. Like every woman, her primary ambition was to marry. Most of the girls of her set were married—or about to be. Yet she not one possessed more grace or charm or loveliness than

And as her birthdays crept gradually toward that tragic thirty-mark, marriage seemed farther from her life than ever.

She was often a bridesmaid but never a bride.

IVORY SOAP . . . . 99 44/100 % PURE

Unforgettable Pitches

With sound, movement, and a seemingly infinite capacity for repetition, television by the 60's had become the greatest of all advertising media. The ads may have been no worse than their radio predecessors, but they were always there, joking, confiding, jangling—showing famous people doing everyday things and ordinary people doing outrageous things.

Read Serutan Backwards It Spells Nature's

The Flo-Thru Tea Bag ®

Barbasol, Barbasol!
No brush, no lather,
no rub-in

A *The shape but not the sound of our letter "A" derived from the Phoenician sign called* aleph *meaning "ox."*

ACRONYM 1. AWOL. 2. Radar. 3. SWAK. 4. Snafu. 5. ZIP (as in Zip Code). What do these five words have in common? Only that they are acronyms: words composed of the initial letters of a name, title, or saying and pronounced as a single word. An initialism is like an acronym except that it is pronounced letter by letter, as in the prestigious V.I.P., the unmanageable B.L.T. sandwich, and the relieved T.G.I.F. of "Thank God It's Friday."

We see the beginnings of this alphabet soup in the SPQR of Caesar's day (<u>S</u>enatus <u>P</u>opulus<u>q</u>ue <u>R</u>omanus, "the Senate and People of Rome"), then jump to World War I (Anzac for <u>A</u>ustralia and <u>N</u>ew <u>Z</u>ealand <u>A</u>rmy <u>C</u>orps, for example). But the heyday of the acronym, still with us, began with World War II's fractured English: jeep for the G.P. of General Purpose vehicle is perhaps the simplest and most common of all. Waves (<u>W</u>omen <u>A</u>ccepted for <u>V</u>oluntary <u>E</u>mergency <u>S</u>ervice) proved that acronymic creativity was in full flower; it remains so in today's era of supertechnology, as laser (<u>l</u>ight <u>a</u>mplification by <u>s</u>timulated <u>e</u>mission of <u>r</u>adiation) and NASA attest.

The derivations of those first five words? 1. <u>A</u>bsent <u>w</u>ith<u>o</u>ut <u>l</u>eave. 2. <u>Ra</u>dio <u>d</u>etection <u>a</u>nd <u>r</u>anging. 3. <u>S</u>ealed <u>w</u>ith <u>a</u> <u>k</u>iss. 4. <u>S</u>ituation <u>n</u>ormal, <u>a</u>ll <u>f</u>ouled <u>u</u>p. 5. <u>Z</u>one <u>I</u>mprovement <u>P</u>lan.

ADHESIVE BANDAGE The earliest Egyptian medical records mention bandages—soft poultices and harder plasters of myrrh and honey spread on linen (myrrh had a slight antiseptic action, and honey was adhesive). Other early civilizations used similar devices. The Arabs later turned to searing or cauterizing wounds with hot irons and boiling oils. Not until the 16th century did the agonies of cauterization give way to bandaging again.

About 1600, with the development of the microscope, germs were detected and their role in disease first studied. The need to bandage a surgical wound against airborne germs was not fully realized until Joseph Lister proved the value of hygiene in the late 19th century. Before that time doctors had been bandaging surgical incisions with wrappings made from cuttings swept off the floors of textile mills; many patients died.

In the 1920's a Johnson & Johnson employee, Earle Dickson, married a young woman who time and again managed to cut herself while doing housework. Dickson brought his bride gauze and

tape, which his company, heeding Lister, had succeeded in sterilizing, but her bandages usually fell off. Sometimes she cut herself when she was away from home. And so Dickson tried to help again—by folding the gauze into a narrow pad, unrolling the tape, laying the gauze over it, and putting down a band of crinoline to keep the tape from sticking to itself. He then rerolled the tape so that his wife could unwind and scissor off what she needed. Not long after, Dickson mentioned his creation to associates at work, and the Band-Aid adhesive bandage was born. It was precut in 1924, completely sterilized in 1939, and spun out in sheer vinyl in 1958. Other companies soon took to manufacturing similar products, and today the sticky business of covering cuts and scratches turns out some 4 billion bandages a year.

AEROSOL CAN Artificial snow, girdle lubricant, pig-fight preventive, squirt-on–wash-off gloves—a myriad products can be packaged in and dispensed from compact, inexpensive, throwaway spray cans. The immense success of this industry (worldwide sales are more than 150 billion cans a year) is remarkable for the speed with which it occurred. Before 1950, with few exceptions, the hiss of airborne liquids and creams and foams simply was not to be heard. The boom began in 1953 with the creation of a unique sort of crimp-on valve "for dispensing gases under pressure." The inventor was Robert H. Abplanalp, and the world's manufacturers have beaten a path to his door. In the process they have also managed to heap millions of dollars on his doorstep.

Abplanalp, however, was not the first to try his hand at creating a pressure-controlling valve. The concept, in fact, goes back to 1862. Yet relatively little was accomplished until World War II, when an alarming number of U.S. servicemen overseas were stricken with insect-transported diseases such as malaria. The search for a handy spray bug blaster was given immediate and high priority by concerned U.S. government officials, and in 1943 two Department of Agriculture researchers, L.D. Goodhue and W.N. Sullivan, developed a small aerosol can pressurized by a liquefied gas (a fluorocarbon). Within months U.S. servicemen around the world were spraying everything that crawled, flew, or hopped near or on their persons with these new "bug bombs." The nickname was as apt as the application, for the new cans were formed by welding heavy steel halves together and had the heft of hand grenades.

Similar "bug bombs" were first marketed in the United States in 1947, and nearly all sprayed insecticides. Abplanalp's improvements (his valves did not clog, closed tightly, and were fairly cheap to produce) made it possible to design cans that could dispense more exotic substances: foams, powders, and goos. The basic ingredient is compressed by a liquefied gas which, injected into the can under pressure, acts as propellant. A small unfilled space is left to allow some of it to return to its gaseous state. When the button is pressed, the propellant flashes through the liquid and turns it into a mist. Except for paint, all aerosols from shaving cream to barbecue sauce to shark repellent are clear liquids inside the can.

The consumer response was to buy and keep on buying, and within a few years factories around the world were turning out billions of the new cans. The industry's high-pressure bubble seemed likely to pop in the mid-1970's, however, when researchers announced that fluorocarbons might damage the ozone layer that protects us from the sun's ultraviolet radiations. Now Abplanalp has done it again. He has created Aerosol II, or "Aquasol," which uses water-soluble hydrocarbons as the propellant and should keep the industry pressurized for years to come.

AIR CONDITIONING "When Sirius parches the head and knees and the body is dried up by reason of the heat, then sit in the shade and drink." Such was the advice of the Greek poet Hesiod some 3,000 years ago for soothing perhaps the most enervating of all nonfatal human afflictions—submersion in a soup of hot, sticky air. And for the next few thousand years most people did just that. Exceptions were provided by the rich and inventive, who tried, in a variety of ingenious ways, to beat the heat and the humidity. A number of Roman emperors, for example, trucked in mountain snow to cool their summer gardens, and in the 8th century the caliph Al-Mahdi of Baghdad is reported to have had slaves fan blocks of ice as well as pack snow into the double walls of his

Air conditioning became commonplace in 20th-century urban America. In antiquity it was a luxury: (above) slaves fan ice to cool air for an 8th-century caliph.

summer house. Even Leonardo da Vinci tried, devising a foot-powered fan to cool the boudoir of a Milanese duchess. Thick walls, thatched roofs, tree plantings, porches, or a sojourn in the mountains or at the seashore helped, too.

Only about 140 years ago did man actually start doing something on a large scale about the heat. The story begins in Florida, where Dr. John Gorrie developed a machine that blew air over ice to cool malaria and yellow-fever patients. In 1851

Gorrie patented the air compressor, and in France, Ferdinand Carré designed the first ammonia coils, which extracted heat and moisture from air. In 1902 Willis H. Carrier, a founder of today's Carrier Corporation, put these elements together for a Brooklyn printing company. The result was a crude but nonetheless effective modern air-conditioning system—with powered ventilation, moisture control, and refrigeration by mechanical means.

Today air conditioners come in all sizes. The world's largest system—a sprawling giant with 2½ acres of compressors and pumps, 170 miles of pipes, and 124,000 outlets—is housed in New York's World Trade Center.

Yet if the air conditioner is a boon to summer swelterers everywhere, it has also become for many a needless overindulgence, devouring enormous amounts of precious energy. And as any urban dweller who has survived a blackout or brownout knows, there already isn't enough to go around. Some scientists even suggest that air conditioning may be altering our bodily processes, while other experts urge that we switch speedily to OFF, except in crucial medical and industrial situations. And yet when the asphalt oozes, our clothing clings, and our mouths gape, what better relief than "shade and drink"—and a soothing breeze of conditioned air.

AIRPLANE Man's desire to fly is undoubtedly as old as his perceptions of birds and the ease with which they soar through the air and dart away from earthbound predators. Yet it was only when men realized that they were not destined to fly like birds that the history of modern aviation began. "It is impossible," an Italian physicist wrote in the late 17th century, "that men should be able to fly craftily by their own strength." More than 100 years later, in England, George Cayley showed how they might—with a fixed wing.

A Yorkshire baronet, Cayley not only believed in the functional soundness of the fixed wing, he proved it, laying down the mathematical principles of lift and thrust and drag. He also proved it by launching model gliders as early as 1804. Almost 50 years later, in 1853, Cayley built the first man-carrying glider and sent it, with a "pilot," Cayley's reluctant coachman, on a flight across a valley. Finding himself alive on the other side, the coachman-pilot promptly resigned both jobs.

The man credited with the first propeller-driven aircraft was an Englishman, William Henson, who designed an Aerial Steam Carriage. In 1847 he constructed a 20-foot model and launched it down an inclined ramp. The steam engine was not powerful enough, and the craft managed only a brief hop before it flopped into oblivion. Nonetheless, the ship's wings were remarkably like those of modern airplanes.

A 17th-century attempt at flight

By the turn of the century the glider had become a reliable flying structure and the gasoline combustion engine an adequate source of power. Orville and Wilbur Wright, bicycle makers from Dayton, Ohio, proved this and made history in the process. First, they built a biplane kite and experimented with altering its wing contours by means of control wires. Next they built a full-sized glider with controls on the front surfaces of its wings and a rudder for stability. Finally they bolted a 12-horsepower, 4-cylinder engine to an

Aviator Glenn Curtiss in his Gold Bug. *In 1908 he showed doubters that flight is possible.*

even more sophisticated air frame; the engine was connected to a a pair of propellers of their own design. The result was a fragile but flyable biplane of hardwood, cloth, and wire with a wingspan of 40 feet. And on December 17, 1903, on the broad sand flats of Kitty Hawk, North Carolina, the Wright brothers' first *Flyer*, piloted by Orville, lying belly-down on the lower wing, flew 120 feet.

Ironically, though historians later would say that man broke his earthly chains that day,

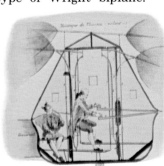

Moving wings and balloon helped lift this 19th-century Swiss craft.

few at the time paid attention. The press was skeptical, the public generally unaware, the army uninterested. In 1907, however, after *Flyer* number three had completed a remarkable 24-mile nonstop flight, President Theodore Roosevelt intervened and induced the army to commission the building of a new type of Wright biplane.

Even so, when World War I began, Zeppelins, or dirigibles, were more important than planes both for observation and for bombing. But as faster, more maneuverable aircraft were developed, along with machine guns that could shoot between rotating propeller blades, planes became effective—if crude—war machines.

French design, 1781: the horn player is designated the "trip companion."

An early French bomber, the Voisin, known as a "chicken coop" because of its struts and wires, carried more than 100 pounds of small bombs on its cockpit floor. When the craft's observer-bombardier found a suitable target, he simply dumped them over the side. The three-engine Italian Caproni, which had three tail rudders, was one of the best bombers of World War I. Nonetheless, it required great heroics on the part of its tail gunners, who stood on open platforms behind the wings as the planes soared over the Alps in the course of making winter raids on Austria.

Barnstorming—stunt flying—was the rage in the 1920's. These high-flying tennis nuts have to be given credit for their temerity even though they were securely wired to the wing—unbeknownst to the awed crowd below.

Unfortunately, after the guns fell silent in 1918, the U.S. government showed little interest in the commercial applications of flying. Out of work, many World War I pilots bought surplus Curtiss Jennies and became barnstormers—goggled gypsy fliers who eked out a glamorous, if dangerous, living selling rides to brave citizens and giving death-defying exhibitions.

The aviator's romantic image was further enhanced by airmail flights, although airmail got off to a very bad start in 1918. The pilot on the first Washington–New York run lost his way, landed in Maryland, and sent his mail on by train. The system overcame that black eye and was firmly established by 1924, the year transcontinental flights began. Like barnstormers, airmail pilots were a hardy breed. They had to be. The flight, for example, between New York and Chicago over the stormy Allegheny Mountains was called the "graveyard run." Pilots flew it in open cockpits, with no radio aids for navigation, no flight instruments, and no weather stations. A shocking statistic: of the first 40 pilots on that run, 31 were killed.

Charles A. Lindbergh, the most famous of all aviation heroes, flew the mails. He was on the St. Louis–Chicago run in 1926 when he decided to compete for the $25,000 prize offered for a nonstop flight from New York to Paris. A year later, on May 20, 1927, at 7:54 A.M., he left Long Island in the *Spirit of St. Louis*, a modified single-engine monoplane crammed with 450 gallons of gasoline, 20 gallons of oil, and very little else. Twenty-eight hours later he sighted the coast of Ireland, and at 9:52 P.M. he touched down at Le Bourget Airport outside Paris. He was welcomed by a cheering crowd, and at age 25 was an international hero.

Commercial aviation came of age in the 1930's. In America the Boeing 247, introduced in 1934 by United Airlines, sparked the revolution. Carrying 10 passengers at a speed of 150 miles per hour, the sturdy twin-engine plane dropped the time of a coast-to-coast flight to below 20 hours. Douglas Aircraft followed with its famous DC series. The first, the DC-2, carried 14 passengers. The DC-3 appeared in 1936, and dominated air travel for more than a decade.

In 1934 the British government decided to fly its mail to the Commonwealth countries. "Empire Boats" started flying to South Africa three years later. Pan American accepted the challenge of the Pacific and ordered a Martin 130, the China Clipper. The great plane made its inaugural mail flight to Honolulu, Midway, Wake, Guam, and Manila in 1935. Four years later, in 1939, Pan American spanned the Atlantic as well. In less than 40 years, aviation had conquered the oceans.

World War II, like World War I, greatly increased the operational capacities of planes—and their ability to destroy. Large sections of London, Berlin, Coventry, Rotterdam, Warsaw, and dozens of other cities were leveled by bombers. Hitler was convinced his Luftwaffe could destroy the Royal Air Force and that London would be "seized by hysteria." He was wrong. For despite hundreds of German sorties a day during August and September of 1940, the RAF, aided enormously by rudimentary radar systems, won the Battle of Britain. Shortly planes were flying the other way. British Lancasters and Halifaxes bombed Germany at night, and American B-17's and B-24's dropped bombloads ranging from 4,000 to 17,600 pounds on factories, bridges, and viaducts. Only three decades earlier, pilots, white scarves streaming in the wind, had lifted bombs off their laps and dropped them overboard.

The American aircraft industry in particular, supplying planes for a war fought far from its shores, concentrated on long-range craft. This turned out to be a bonanza after the war. The B-17 had already spawned the Boeing 307 Stratoliner, and the B–29 Superfortress became the Boeing 377 Stratocruiser. The names dominating postwar flying around the world were Douglas, Lockheed, and Boeing.

The greatest advance of the postwar period was the jet engine. Essentially the engine is an open-ended cylinder that sucks air in at one end; the air is then compressed, mixed with fuel, and ignited. The turbojet dispensed with the propeller, relying on the discharge of a huge volume of high-temperature gases for thrust. American commercial jet operations began in 1958, and the jet's ability to fly high and fast above most turbulence transformed travel habits. The speed of sound (approximately 650 miles per hour at 35,000 feet) remained a barrier, however. The problem was the compressibility of air. When a plane approached such speeds, the molecules of air ahead of it did not have time to move and flow around the craft's body. Thus the plane would shake wildly, its controls frozen. Aeronautical engineers finally broke the barrier by designing planes with swept-back wings and needle noses.

On December 17, 1903, the Wright brothers averaged a little more than 30 miles per hour in four flights in their first *Flyer*. Sixty-four years later, in 1967, North America's X–15 A–2 rocket-powered test plane flew 4,534 miles per hour. Where man is going may not be known, but the pace at which he is traveling has been clearly written in the skies.

AMBULANCE For thousands of years, a soldier downed on the field of battle was likely to lie where he fell until nightfall—or even longer. Then, in the unlikely event he showed signs of life, he might be dragged or carted to a doctor for treatment. This grim situation remained relatively unchanged until 1240, when Italy's Misericordia di Firenze, the first known emergency-care service, was founded. Though rudimentary horse-drawn conveyances for the wounded made sporadic ap-

pearances after that—at the Battle of Málaga in 1487, for example—it was not until 1792 that ambulances became a regular part of the battlefield scene. That was the year Baron Dominique-Jean Larrey, a French army surgeon, organized what he called the *ambulances volantes*, or flying field hospitals. Little more than covered, portable litters filled with equipment, these ambulances were capable of providing front-line medical care.

The first modern ambulance system appeared in the 19th century, during the Civil War, when Dr. Jonathan Letterman, medical director of the Army of the Potomac, assigned two horse-drawn ambulances to every regiment of 500 infantrymen. In 1864 the Geneva Convention recognized military ambulances, declaring that the vehicles, the wounded they carried, and the medics that operated them should be considered neutral.

Even before the Civil War ended, the first nonmilitary ambulance service was organized in Cincinnati, Ohio, by the Commercial Hospital. And less than 10 years later, the first airborne ambulances—hot-air balloons—drifted to the fore in France, during the Siege of Paris (1870–71). Unfortunately, the speed and ultimate destinations of the balloons depended entirely on the whims of the wind—and so did the fate of their wafting wounded.

By the 1930's most of America had some sort of ambulance service, though many were operated by funeral directors, hardly a cheering thought for those being rushed to the hospital. As for the ambulances themselves, they were not much more than "horizontal" taxicabs. Today U.S., state, and local laws require that most ambulances carry vital life-support and emergency-care equipment—oxygen masks, suction devices, intravenous systems—so that emergency victims may be treated and their conditions stabilized even before they reach the hospital. Some of the nation's 28,000 or more ambulances even carry defibrillators to restore the rhythm of the heart and monitors that can transmit beat patterns ahead to hospital experts, so that they can prescribe treatment even while the patient is speeding toward them. Many ambulances, including specially equipped boats, helicopters, planes, and even snowmobiles, carry heavy-duty extrication equipment—hydraulic jacks and cutters for easing the injured out of squashed cars or planes. Emergency care has become so sophisticated that in some cases the vehicle stays home, while paramedics take over, parachuting into forest-fire areas or climbing to crash sites to deliver medical care.

An ambulance dashes through a Washington, D.C., park.

ANESTHETIC Today the science that frees us from pain in the dentist's chair or on the operating table is highly sophisticated. We may still know the numbness of Novocaine and the smell of ether, but the anesthesiologist's world of gases, volatile liquids, barbiturates, muscle relaxants, freezing techniques, and the rest is a far cry from the world of W.T.G. Morton and J.C. Warren, who first popularized the use of ether in surgery.

Through the centuries, men and women lived in terror of the surgeon's knife and often kept their maladies a secret in order to avoid it. There were crude early measures to ease pain: opium, Indian hemp, mandrake, alcohol, hypnotism. People also used diversionary tactics: incantations, ritual dances, fasting, or a bullet or glove between the teeth. But a real breakthrough in the alleviation of pain did not appear until the 19th century.

Around 1800 Sir Humphry Davy did experiments with nitrous oxide. He gathered together some of his friends, including

Dr. James Simpson's equating of anesthetic with the biblical "deep sleep" of Adam, during which Eve was made from his rib, stilled a raging controversy in Scotland over the morality of using painkillers.

Samuel Taylor Coleridge, and asked them to inhale the gas. In short order his guests became giddy and were "feeling no pain." Sniffing the gas became such a fad that people got their "highs" at public demonstrations of this "laughing gas." (Ether parties had been popular just a few years earlier, though no one had thought to use ether with surgery.) Both compounds were first used successfully by a Boston dentist, W.T.G. Morton, who is generally credited with calling attention to the effectiveness of ether for stopping pain.

At Massachusetts General Hospital on October 16, 1846, before a distinguished audience of doubting colleagues, he anesthetized a 20-year-old patient, Gilbert Abbott, then stepped aside to let the surgeon, Dr. J.C. Warren, remove a tumor. "Gentlemen," proclaimed Dr. Warren at the conclusion of the operation, "this is no humbug!"

ANTISEPTIC When the red and painful surprise of a cut makes us reach automatically for an antiseptic and a sterile bandage, we are acting out of comparatively recent "instinct." Though the ancients suspected the existence of invisible disease-bearing agents (which they called vaguely "bad air"), they lacked the magnifiers necessary to detect such infection-producing germs. Nonetheless, many early civilizations adopted elaborate precautions to maintain a relatively high degree of cleanliness: Egyptian priests were required to wash frequently; Persian citizens were under orders to store water in clean copper vessels; lepers were banished entirely from Hebrew cities.

Some knowledge of the germ-killing or antisep-

---

people

Billy "Appleseed"

William Blackstone, the first white settler in Boston and Rhode Island, clearly did not like to be crowded. When John Winthrop arrived in America with a shipload of Puritan settlers in 1630, he found the English eccentric already on hand, living beside an apple orchard he had planted five years earlier on land that would later become Boston's Beacon Hill. Within a few years, the new arrivals made Blackstone feel as crowded as he had in England, so he moved southwest and settled on Indian lands (near what is now Pawtucket, Rhode Island), not far from the site later

occupied by Roger Williams, another nonconformist, and his Providence colony. Of Boston and its theocracy, Blackstone said: "The Lord Brethren are as bad as the Lord Bishops."

Again he planted an orchard, this time developing a sweet apple called Blaxton's Yellow Sweeting, using an earlier spelling of his name. He built a house and stocked it with something almost as rare in the New World as apples—books other than the Holy Bible. Sometimes he filled great bags with his apples and set out on his bull for Roger Williams' trading post. There he preached

his own interpretation of Christianity to Narragansett Indian children, offering apples in return for listening to God's word.

Fortunately, at least for his sense of order and repose, Blackstone died shortly before King Philip's War (1675–76) and was already resting in peace near his orchard when the Indians who lived in that area, enraged by the encroaching presence of the English, burned his house, including all his books. Over the centuries Blackstone's deeds have faded to historical footnotes, but he too deserves the appellation "Appleseed."

tic powers of certain substances is revealed in early medical records. In ancient India, after abscesses were lanced by doctors, the incisions were washed with hot water and covered with a cloth soaked in honey and sesame oil. The Egyptians learned embalming skills that kept the dead from decay, and they used many of the same oils, gums, and spices to protect living tissue.

The Greeks knew the aseptic nature of urine and used it or wine with vinegar on open wounds. During the Dark Ages, logic gave way to magic and doctors rubbed swords with fat and blood instead of putting anything on the wounds they caused. Under Arabic influence, the practice of cauterizing, or searing, a wound replaced balms. During the Renaissance wine was reintroduced as a cleanser, and Italians of the 16th century recommended cold water for washing cuts. With the introduction of the microscope about 1600, the existence of invisible germs was verified, but it took years to make the connection between the germs in the air and the germs in the bloodstream that caused disease and infection.

In France in the mid-19th century, Louis Pasteur finally proved that microscopic airborne germs caused infection within the human body. Through "pasteurization" he worked to keep germs out of food, and through immunization he managed to render them ineffective within the body. He did not try to kill germs outright.

Britain's Joseph Lister did. As a boy he had learned how to use a microscope, and as a grown man and doctor he suspected that some kind of "pollen" caused the infections he noticed when he set broken bones that had pierced the skin. When Lister heard of Pasteur's work in the mid-1860's, he felt that his "pollen" theory was confirmed. After setting a boy's bone, he soaked the ruptured skin in a dressing of phenol, or carbolic acid. The boy went home without infection. Lister turned to his amputee cases, half of whom usually died from infection after operations. He dabbed their surgical wounds with phenol and washed his hands and instruments in it. He even sprayed the operating room with phenol steam. Infections dropped substantially. Other doctors adopted his practices, though the steam spray proved to be unnecessary.

Parents running a needle through fire before taking out a child's splinter are creating an aseptic environment such as Pasteur sought. Parents rushing a cut child to the medicine cabinet are looking for antiseptics or germ killers such as Lister used. Simple hydrogen peroxide is a good, if weak, antiseptic. Red mercurochrome and brown tinctures of iodine are not as common as they once were, because invisible antiseptics that can be sprayed on have grown in popularity.

Adam and Eve's symbolic connection with anesthetic may be a bit obscure; not so their involvement with the fruit of knowledge. Though the Bible does not specify the fruit, the apple has taken the blame for centuries.

Calling something an antiseptic, however, does not necessarily mean that it works, a problem that manufacturers of gargles and mouthwashes seek to antisepticize with regular doses of advertising. The best throat cleanser may still be that recommended by doctors all over the world for years: a solution of warm water and table salt.

APPLE First there were tiny crab apples. By the mountain lakes of Europe's great Alps, prehistoric people plucked and cut and dried these inch-wide fruits, and buried them to store for winter. Then somehow, sometime, in the region of the cool Caucasus Mountains, European crab-apple trees crossbred with Asian crabs and produced the buxom, modern-sized apple. When the people of the Caucasus scattered, they quite naturally took these apples with them.

Many early Indo-European groups worshiped a male sun and a female moon, and in the mythologies of various tribes the apple represented one or the other. The writers of Genesis no longer worshiped celestial bodies. Yet it has long been assumed that Eve handed an apple to Adam, and a possible source for this may be the Indo-

European belief that the sun and the moon produced mankind after Luna gave an apple to her fiery husband.

Classical Greek and Roman literature depicts the apple as golden-hued and mantled with luscious red cheeks when fully ripened. It was a golden apple bearing the inscription "for the fairest" that Eris, goddess of discord, pitched among the guests at a wedding celebration to which she had not been invited. The wifely Hera-Juno, the virginal Athena-Minerva, and the beautiful Aphrodite-Venus squabbled over the apple until Paris, son of the king of Troy, was chosen to award it. He gave it to Aphrodite because she had promised him the fairest woman in all the world, and when she delivered Helen of Troy, the ancient world's great war broke out.

In some European lore the apple was sacred to the moon, symbolizing immortality. Moon-magic in the guise of medical remedy (like drinking ale with apples to cure painful urination) was still practiced in 16th- and 17th-century England, however unconsciously. Even today we say, however great—or slight—our belief, "An apple a day keeps the doctor away."

Englishmen leaving for the New World in the 1620's and 1630's took easy-to-carry apple seeds with them, because they knew they would need cider. In Europe's already crowded cities it was clear that water often carried disease, and very few urbanites drank it. The cider they consumed instead, whether in old England or the New World, was hard. And in the 19th century the journalist-reformer Horace Greeley railed against the dangers of this golden liquid. "Cider was," he wrote, "next to water, the most abundant and the cheapest fluid to be had in New Hampshire, while I lived there—often selling for a dollar per barrel. In many a family of six or eight persons, a barrel tapped on Saturday barely lasted a full week. . . . The transition from cider to warmer and more potent stimulants was easy and natural; so that whole families died drunkards and vagabond paupers from the impetus first given by cider-swilling in their rural homes."

Cider can be made from any apple, even the lowliest, and cider-loving colonists developed many varieties. Those that did not make for good eating were always good for cider. The remainder of the crop was stored in sand in cellars, dried in the rafters, cooked into butter or sauce, or baked in pies. Apple pie, some have said, was served at Yale College every night for a hundred years. The Reverend Henry Ward Beecher rhapsodized on this transfiguring dish, surely more than just dessert to him, urging that it be eaten "while it is yet florescent, white or creamy yellow, with the merest drip of candied juice along the edges (as if the flavor were so good to itself that its own lips watered!)."

Now, though some 1,500 varieties of apples are still grown in the United States, the number of commercially popular brands has dropped to a dozen or so, including Red Delicious, Golden Delicious, McIntosh, Rome, Jonathan, York, Stayman Winesap, and Newtown Pippin. Nonetheless, the crunch, the taste, and the sight of the apple remain supreme, as does apple production. More than 900 million bushels of the lush fruit are grown around the world each year.

ASPIRIN Compressed in little white tablets, an ingredient in hundreds of over-the-counter remedies, tested constantly for new uses, aspirin has been for nearly three-quarters of a century the most widely used and effective, self-administered painkiller in the world. Americans alone buy 50 billion aspirin and aspirin-containing tablets a year, some 20 billion of which are taken to relieve the nag of aching heads. And worldwide production of acetylsalicylic acid—or aspirin—now approaches some 70 million pounds annually.

Despite its enormous success, however, both as a painkiller and a money-maker, scientists don't fully understand how aspirin works. Some believe that it raises the body's threshold of pain, while others think it alters body chemistry. Nonetheless, aspirin works—as an anti-inflammation agent, as a pain reliever (analgesic), and as a fever reducer (antipyretic). Miraculously it brings down the body temperature to the normal point—and not below it—each time it works.

The closest natural substance to acetylsalicylic acid is called salicin, which is found in the leaves, bark, and roots of the willow tree. When primitive man had a toothache, he often went in search of willow bark to chew. In the Middle Ages a concoction of willow leaves and roots was popular for treating all types of pain from headache to gout. It was not until the mid-18th century, however, that natural aspirin or salicin won quasi-official recognition. A highly unlikely theory called the Doctrine of Signatures was in vogue in the medical world at the time. It held that a remedy for an illness could usually be found near its source. Since willows thrived in damp, swampy soil, and such locales were also thought to be the source of fevers, it was likely, therefore, that willows might also embody a cure for fevers. And they did, however circuitous the logic, because of salicin.

How the word changed from salicin to aspirin is a subject of further debate. According to one theory, the word "aspirin" is derived from "spirea," which is the name of a meadow plant that is also rich in salicin. How the world got its first synthetic aspirin is known: it was produced in Germany in the 1890's by a junior chemist for Bayer and Company. The young man, Felix Hofmann, was determined to find a medicine that would ease the pain of his father's arthritis. Using Bayer laboratory facilities, he tested a number of salicylate compounds until he found one that worked. He then developed a technique for making acetylsalicylic acid in powder form, sent samples to physicians, and discovered that he had isolated a remarkably effective painkiller.

Americans were first able to buy mass-produced aspirin over the drug counter in the 1920's, not long after a U.S. firm purchased from the federal government certain Bayer properties that had been seized during World War I. The firm—Sterling Drug, Inc.—soon found that it had acquired, along with everything else, the rights to a little-known medicine called aspirin.

The story of aspirin has no end. Doctors and researchers around the world are looking for new ways to use this old-time remedy. Already under investigation is a remarkable role for it in preventing heart attacks and strokes.

ASSEMBLY LINE Few phrases bring to mind the relentless, grinding thrum of mechanization in the 20th century more vividly than "assembly line." In simplest terms, an assembly line involves a conveyor belt or other system on which parts are moved past stationary workers who perform standardized tasks at a pace dictated by the speed of the belt. The jobs have been broken down into small, repeated movements and arranged in sequence so that the finished product emerges at the end of the line.

Contrary to popular belief, the line and its ultimate by-product—mass production—were not invented by Henry Ford. What Ford did was to "assemble" the assembly line on a grand scale. Many men before Ford had worked on the idea of an endless conveyor belt. An electrically powered belt was used in meat-packing plants in Cincinnati and Chicago during the 19th century. Overhead trolleys moved carcasses from worker to worker. Henry Ford saw this "disassembly line" in operation. He also saw the movement of assemblies from worker to worker in the sequential production of railroad cars in a Detroit factory as early as 1879.

The use of standardized parts had been pioneered in England by James Watt in the second half of the 18th century. The tools and measuring devices to manufacture such parts were developed

soon after. In America, Eli Whitney took up the idea and contracted to make guns for the government, utilizing standardized parts. Enthralled in the esoterics of jigs and tooling, however, Whitney missed his two-year due date for delivery of 10,000 muskets. He had delivered only 500 guns when he appeared at the War Department in 1801 with a large box within which, he said, were 10 muskets. When he opened the box all was chaos inside, a jumble of barrels, stocks, triggers, locks, and other parts. Calmly, Whitney sorted the rifle parts into separate piles and asked an observer to pick a piece from each pile. Using these standardized parts, he assembled a finished musket; the War Department forgave Whitney his delay.

In the 1890's America's bicycle boom sharpened production skills. In 1913 Ford proved at Detroit's Highland Park plant that his workers, using all the elements of mass production, could make and afford—Fords! The assembly line, however, can be dehumanizing. Industrial engineering was developed to study and cut waste movements on the line and thus speed up production. But workers trapped in the grind of such hyperefficiency can easily feel that they have no more individuality than the parts they are tightening. Harsh noise, grimy environments, and lack of communication with other workers all add to the problem, and in some cases workers have actually sabotaged the line—with loose nuts, faulty alignments, and strategically misplaced connections.

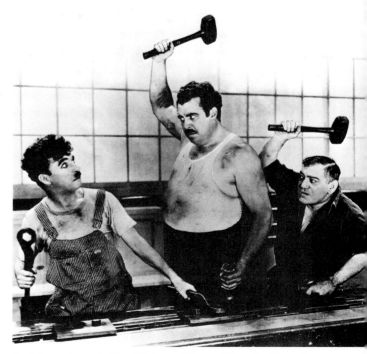

In his poignant film Modern Times, *Charlie Chaplin mocked the dehumanizing aspects of the assembly line.*

Not surprisingly, modern-day studies have found that morale—and consequently production—goes up and absenteeism plunges down when management shows an interest in the company's harried workers and a degree of control is given them. In Sweden, for example, certain automobile companies are returning to teamwork, using groups of workers to complete particular jobs and encouraging team members to rotate the tasks involved. In Japan, manufacturers have taken a bolder step. If a worker wishes to stop the line, he can, simply by tromping on a pedal. The results so far have been better production.

ATTIC If the word "attic" stirs up visions of clutter today, it began with a highfalutin connotation of culture—specifically that of the golden age of Athens, which once held sway over the peninsula of Attica. Skip now to 18th-century London, where architects of the classic revival often modeled buildings on ancient Greek temples, with their peaked roofs on top and pillars out front. The room snugged under the pointed roof became known as the "attic."

From cultural shrine to repository of rummage for bazaars and tag sales, the attic may have had a comedown. But the attic keeper should bear in mind that certain old phonograph records, mechanical banks, presidential campaign buttons, folk art, faded family portraits, baseball cards, and stamp albums can be exchanged for hard cash. The first edition of Theodore Dreiser's *Sister Carrie*, 1900, can bring in $350. Copies of *Action Comics* are rare and can go for something like $2,000 apiece. And that original Ingersoll Mickey Mouse watch (vintage 1932) that sits amid cobwebs in Mother's dusty old sprung jewel box? Treat it very gently, because the asking price of such watches has been known to hit $750.

AUCTION "Every year . . . in each village . . . they gathered together all the maidens that were come to the season of marriage; and round them stood a multitude of men; and an auctioneer caused them to stand up one by one and sold them." This auction—one of the first on public record—took place in Babylon more than 2,500 years ago. And though the marital arts have undergone considerable revision since then, auctions have not. Now as then they are designed to sell marketable items to the highest bidder at public

Stuff too good to throw away, too old to use, may provide entertainment or metamorphose to treasure.

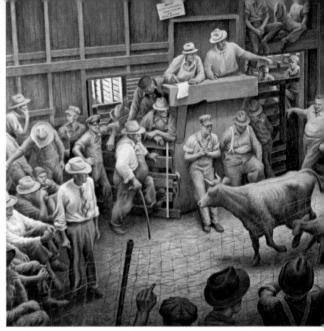

Livestock the world over are sold regularly at auction, Canadians, racehorses to the Japanese, or cattle

sale—"as is" and "all sales final."

That the auction has survived so many centuries without change is really not so surprising, for it has always been one of the quickest and simplest ways of selling something. And it has the unique capability of setting the value of an article that has no standard price. How else to learn how much somebody might pay for an original copy of Lincoln's Gettysburg Address or a glass once drained by W.C. Fields?

Yet auctions do not deal solely with personal possessions. Every day in the world's great agricultural markets and in stock and commodity ex-

changes, sales are made that affect us all—from the price of a pound of hamburger to the success or failure of giant corporations.

The singsong chant of the auctioneer punctuates most types of auctions. Though the chant may be unintelligible at times, it performs the vital functions of acknowledging bids and keeping buyers interested. Styles vary, however, almost as widely as what is for sale.

At an outdoor country auction of farm equipment, for example, the auctioneer may beseech buyers with the fervor of an evangelist, appealing to them directly, "Come on, now. Baby needs new shoes." At one of the prestigious auction houses in New York or London, the chant may be highly sophisticated. An auctioneer at Sotheby Parke Bernet, a New York house specializing in art and antiques, upped a bid of $98,000 on a painting simply by observing, "Now wouldn't it sound a whole lot better . . . if when your friends come into your house, you could say, 'I paid $100,000 for this painting'?" The man from Sotheby Parke Bernet got a big laugh—and a bid of $110,000.

Most often the auctioneer opens the bidding by suggesting a specific amount—for example, "Who'll bid $75?" Once bidding starts, he tries to move the bidders by calling out the bid he has in hand and a higher amount he is seeking, filling in with his chant. Competition between prospective buyers causes the bid price to ascend until all but the highest bidder is eliminated. (The word "auction," in fact, comes from a Latin verb meaning "to increase.") If no buyer bids on an item, the auctioneer may withdraw that item from sale. In some cases the seller may have specified a minimum acceptable price, which is called a "reserve."

The ascending-auction system is almost universal in the United States and England, but other types of auctions are common in other countries. For example, in the Netherlands, where the descending-bid auction is used, the auctioneer starts at a price much higher than he thinks the item is worth. He then reduces the figure step by step until a bidder accepts the price and shouts, "Mine." The bidders compete to be the first to holler at the best price. Normally, the auctioneer does not need to cajole the buyers into action.

Perhaps the oddest auction system of all is the

"Going, Going, Gone"

Don't scratch your nose," auction aficionados warn novices, "or you may find you've just purchased a $10,000 painting." Though the chances of this actually happening are exceedingly rare, many expert buyers do use subtle—often secret—gestures to signal their bids.

A tobacco auctioneer once explained the system this way: "A buyer may touch his nose, brush his ear, lift his hat, wink or signal his bid by glancing at you." Other bid signals in operation at almost any professional auction include nodding, blinking, lighting a cigarette, wiggling the nose, or tugging at an ear lobe.

Such discreet signals serve a number of functions. First, they let the auctioneer know that a buyer is actually bidding. (A good auctioneer can always distinguish between a real bid and an accidental jerk, gesture, or twitch.) In addition, if a signal is subtle enough, it permits a buyer to bid without tipping his hand to competing bidders. At some auctions this can be extremely important, because inexperienced buyers may wait to see what an experienced buyer will do, then bid against him. Signaling also helps reduce the rising verbal pandemonium that prevails at some auctions. And an auctioneer can often distinguish a signaled bid more easily than he can an audible one.

A buyer must arrange his signals with an auctioneer before the auction begins. Sometimes, a buyer will set up a number of different signals for different types of bids. For example, a shrug might signal a bid of $50, while the hiking up of a pant leg might mean the buyer is willing to cuff his bid up to $60. At auctions where the same auctioneers and buyers appear frequently, as in agricultural commodity markets, the transmitting and receiving of signaled bids can be swift. A novice may suddenly see an item "knocked down," or sold, without being aware that the bidding had even opened.

It could be dangerous for a tyro to bid in certain English antique auctions because the auctioneer sets the amount of the increase. The sophisticated buyers understand basically what they are offering—something in the neighborhood of 5 percent more. A newcomer, thinking his bid is a few pounds over the last offer, may find himself with a more substantial treasure than he bargained for.

hether hogs to
ericans (above).

Japanese, or simultaneous-bid, system that is used primarily in Tokyo for selling fish. When the sale opens, the bidders bid at almost the same time, using hand signals to indicate the prices they are offering. The auctioneer reads the bids and awards the sale to the highest bidder.

Nowadays, many auctions have been streamlined by the use of electronic equipment. Some descending-bid auctions, like those in certain Dutch flower markets, employ what are called "Dutch clocks." Such a clock, or dial, has a hand that moves counterclockwise past a series of descending prices. The first buyer to bid presses a button that stops the clock at a particular amount and automatically flashes the bidder's identification number on the clockface. This device has speeded up sales to the point where one transaction takes place every six seconds. An "English clock," indicating ascending prices, works in a similar manner.

In Japanese wholesale fruit and vegetable markets, bidders simultaneously press buttons on their keyboards, indicating the prices they wish to pay. A computer then recognizes the highest bid and flashes it and the buyer's number on a large screen. Computers, in fact, can be used in all three systems to print out sales slips for buyers and sellers as the auction progresses.

Large international auction houses even conduct auctions in two and three countries at the same time. Color slides are normally used along with open, interconnected telephone lines. When the gavel falls on a sale in New York, for example, the lucky bidder may actually be standing in a gallery in Los Angeles or London or Paris.

AUTOMOBILE The automobile is a fairly recent invention, but humans have dreamed of speeding along in self-propelled vehicles for thousands of years. The idea first seems to have been written down about 800 B.C., in Homer's *Iliad*, which mentions 20 marvelous three-wheeled vehicles that were "self-moved." During the Renaissance, Leonardo da Vinci sketched a self-propelled, mechanically powered vehicle, and in 1680 Sir Isaac Newton built a model of a carriage pushed by a jet of steam.

Steam-driven pistons did in fact power the first operating automobile, a three-wheeler built in France by Nicolas-Joseph Cugnot in 1769. It had a top speed of 2.25 miles per hour (m.p.h.), a range of less than a mile, and an unwieldy steering mechanism that ultimately brought the vehicle to grief against a brick wall. Steam also powered the first practical American car, built by identical twins—the Stanley brothers, "Mr. F.E." and "Mr.

"Five Gals to a Mile"

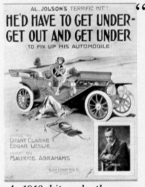

A 1913 hit rode the contemporary car-joke wave.

"Cheap, cheap, cheap, the chicken chirped, having been knocked across the road by a rampaging Ford." Such was the Ford joke—blunt, pithy, rooted in the mule-and-burro stories of European folklore and yet as American as the inexpensive, pioneering machines that the jokes mocked. Henry Ford loved Ford jokes, and offered to pay $100 for any new story that made him laugh. He even made one up; it went like this: "A man, digging an enormous, car-sized hole, was asked what he was doing. The man replied that he was digging the hole for a friend who had died and wished to be buried with his Ford. The car, the dead man had often said, had gotten him out of every hole he had ever gotten into and he thought it might get him out of this one."

Ford jokes poked fun at every aspect of the "people's car." For example, the car's construction produced this rattler: "A lady sent all her tomato cans to Detroit and got back a Model T"; while the assembly line was responsible for: "Model T's are being shipped in asbestos crates because they come off the line hot and smoking." Mass production and reliability were equally provocative, spawning such "tour de Fords" as: "They're making Model T's in yellow next year, so they can sell them in bunches," and "An eastern banker spent $15,000 on a new limousine—but he keeps his Model T right handy in the trunk to pull it out of holes." A parody of the 23rd Psalm stressed the opposite: "The Ford is my auto; I shall not want another. It maketh me to lie down beneath it; it soureth my soul." It ended with what must be the battiest brick ever tossed at a machine: "Surely, if this thing followeth me all the days of my life, I shall dwell in the bug-house forever."

Lizzie, as in "Tin Lizzie," was one of hundreds of names lavished on the Model T. What became known as "Lizzie Labels" were really one-line Ford jokes painted on the outside of the cars. Forerunner of bumper stickers, they touched on everything from mock hauteur ("Henrietta Elizabeth Van Flivver") to cussedness ("Bone Crusher," "Spirit of Jolts") and to girls ("Ten miles to a gal, five gals to a mile"). One stated wistfully: "I would have been a Lincoln but I was born too soon"; and another bragged: "I'm from Texas. You can't steer me." The most profound of all, perhaps, especially for Ford and all his customers, was this one: "Don't laugh, I'm paid for."

F.O." These two cheerfully risked their lives testing their Stanley Steamers—at breakneck speeds. According to a story popular at the time, the Stanleys would gladly give one of their steamers to anyone brave—or foolhardy—enough to drive it with the throttle wide open for at least three minutes. They never had a taker—or speeder—outside the family.

When one of the Stanleys' test drivers did open up the throttle (for less than three minutes) on the hard-packed sands of Ormand Beach, Florida, the steamer set a speed record—at nearly 128 m.p.h. The

1904: A bullfight print shows an odd arena in which the car had to prove itself.

twins finally gave up speed trials, and for good reason: one of their cars, while doing 197 m.p.h., actually became airborne and flew for 100 feet or so. Miraculously the driver survived.

The development of the four-cycle gasoline engine, the kind used in most cars today, was slowed by false starts. A German grocery salesman, Nikolaus August Otto, built one of the first, in the 1870's, but later lost his patent rights in a number of countries because he did not fully understand his engine. Even though it ran fairly well, the gas engine—noisy, temperamental, inefficient, and reeking of noxious fumes—at first seemed a highly unlikely power source for an automobile. Siegfried Marcus, an Austrian, was probably the first man to put such an engine in an auto, in 1865. But his car backfired so vociferously that the police in Vienna, where Marcus lived, banned the vehicle.

The auto business attracted other brother teams besides the Stanleys. Charles and Frank Duryea built the first successful American gasoline auto—in Springfield, Massachusetts, about 1893. A few years later they built and sold 13 improved models, thus becoming the first commercial automakers in the country. Two other brothers, Elmer and Edgar Apperson, built a gas auto a year after the Duryeas' first model, and the Swiss-born Chevrolet brothers—Gaston, Louis, and Arthur—raced automobiles before Louis settled down to design them. The firm founded by the Dodge brothers, John and Horace, was the first to produce and sell a car with an all-metal frame and body.

Not everyone took kindly to the newfangled gas-powered machines. In the late 1800's motoring in England was hampered by, among other things, a modest 4-m.p.h. speed limit and a requirement that every auto be preceded by a flagman flapping a red flag. In some American communities irate townspeople even authorized their police departments to shoot out motorists' tires. In Pennsylvania an anti-auto group proposed a code requiring every motorist meeting a horse-drawn conveyance to "take the machine apart as rapidly as possible and conceal the parts in the bushes." Another law which defied enforcement stated that when a train and a motorcar met at a crossing, each had to stop and wait until the other had passed.

Early automakers faced another critical problem: what to call their machines. They tried "automaton," "oleo locomotive," "motorig," "motor fly," and "electrobat," before finally settling on automobile (a French coinage, 1876, meaning "self-movable").

The modern auto age was ushered in, at least in part, by a raging fire that gutted the Olds Motor Works in Detroit in 1901. Before the fire, the plant had constructed one Oldsmobile at a time. When Ransom Eli Olds went back to work, however, he decided to move the parts of his autos from one group of workmen to another, and thus an early form of the assembly line was born. Henry Ford later perfected the system, so that cars could be mass-produced as cheaply as possi-

The more things change, the more they remain the same: a 1920's auto graveyard (below) differs from a modern one only in depth. Today, however, we know we cannot go on squandering resources like this.

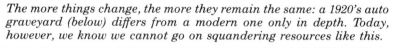

ble. In 1915 Ford was able to assemble a Model T in about 90 minutes and sell it, at a profit, for $440. By the end of the Roaring Twenties, Ford had assembled and sold 15 million "Tin Lizzies" and had quite literally put America on four wheels and a tank of gas.

The impact of the automobilization of America is still being pondered by scholars as well as by motorists themselves. The auto clearly has ended the isolation of rural life and accelerated the exodus of city dwellers and businesses to the suburbs. Today the country sells more than half of all its retail goods in suburbs and shopping centers.

The car has also altered the course of true love in America, allowing young people to move their courtships from the family parlor to the less inhibiting, if more constricting, backseat. Obtaining an auto has become a rite of passage on the route to manhood for many young men. And as adults, many drivers of both sexes actually regard their cars as extensions of their own bodies. "If the car crashes and the driver survives," one psychologist wrote, "he then transcends the death of his mechanical body . . . while a brand new and even more powerful medium of chrome and steel is prepared for his spirit by the angels in Detroit." Yet Americans are generally better at driving than are the citizens of other nations. In the mid-1970's the U.S. fatality rate—3.4 per 100 million vehicle miles—was the lowest in the world.

The American auto-ego was dealt a serious blow in October 1973 when the Arab oil embargo caused severe gas shortages. Smaller cars became necessary, and the federal government imposed a 55-m.p.h. speed limit to save some 200,000 barrels of gas a day. One of the greatest benefits of the new law came almost as a surprise: 9,000 fewer people were killed in accidents the first year.

About 900 B.C. *the Greeks borrowed the Phoenician sign* bĕth, *meaning "house" and changed it to* bēta.

BALLOON Bubbles and balloons are among the first objects to fascinate children, possibly because they appear to disobey nature's great command that all things fall down. Nonetheless, it took a surprisingly long time to build a balloon that would do what it was supposed to do—go up.

In the 2nd century B.C. the Chinese made balloons of paper. We do not know whether children played with balloons, but artwork from the time shows acrobats flying them on the ends of their balancing sticks. Japanese *origami* books still give instructions in the difficult art of turning a sheet of paper into an air-filled globe. But these balloons didn't float. The Indians of Central and South America made balls of rubber much as we make balloons today. They dipped gourds into raw latex taken from rubber trees and smoked the latex over a fire.

It wasn't until 1643, when Evangelista Torricelli, an Italian physicist, showed that air was a good deal more than "mere nothingness," that people really began trying to make balloons go up. A few years later Francesco de Lana, a Jesuit, suggested that if a hollow sphere had the air pumped *out*, it would rise like a bubble. In 1709 Bartholomeu de Gusmão, a Brazilian Jesuit, filled a balloon with heated air, and up it went. Almost three-quarters of a century later the French Montgolfier brothers launched a 33-foot balloon filled with smoke from a straw fire. Soon, toy balloons were on sale, filled, not surprisingly, with hot air.

That same year, 1783, J.A. Charles, a Frenchman, poured sulfuric acid over iron filings and produced the lighter-than-air gas—hydrogen. The toy balloons that became popular following Charles' find were made of taffeta and filled with hydrogen.

In 1839 Charles Goodyear dropped a piece of India rubber infused with sulfur on a hot stove and discovered a way to make rubber thin yet keep it strong and elastic. The process is called

Balloons dotting the summer sky are a familiar sight. They can also be useful: in 1954 balloons carried leaflets to news-starved Czechs.

Bacon

Bacon is one of America's favorite meats. More than a billion pounds are sold here annually. In pioneer days, so the story goes, a covered-wagon driver who hauled bacon from the Missouri River to Denver could trade his load for an entire city block. Bacon was also a favorite of the early Greeks and Romans, who fed it to their wrestlers. They believed the gods favored the altars on which bacon was smoked. In Germany bacon was for centuries the favorite meat of peasant families. Wild pigs, or *Bachen,* roamed the forests, and therein, some believe, lies the derivation of the word "bacon."

The "Precocious Piggy" of Thomas Hood and son pranced through 19th-century London but ended up like all the rest—bacon to bring home.

The origin of the expression "bringing home the bacon" may be ancient. Chaucer, among others, suggested that it came from the English custom, originating about the 12th or the 13th century, of giving young couples a "flitch" of bacon if, after a year of marriage, they were still happy. Some point to the "greased pig" competition at country fairs whence the winner, greasy but exultant, brought home the bacon. Still others suggest that the expression is an attempt at synecdoche, bacon representing all foods. Whatever its origin, "bringing home the bacon" has endured. People still do it everyday.

---

vulcanization, after Vulcan, the Roman god of crafts and the smith's fire. Shortly thereafter, hawkers at parks and circuses were offering balloons of vulcanized rubber for a penny apiece. Today balloons are made by dipping aluminum forms in colored latex. The forms are then oven-cured, the balloons stripped off by air, washed, and, if required, reinflated for printing. The rest is up to the children—and adults—of the world, who send up more than a billion balloons each year.

BAR From the Mermaid Tavern of Shakespeare and Ben Jonson to Maxwell's Plum, a New York singles bar, the barroom has occupied stage center in our social history.

A regular at London's Ye Olde Cheshire Cheese on Fleet Street, Dr. Samuel Johnson, wrote: "There is nothing which has yet been contrived by man by which so much happiness is produced as by a good tavern or inn." One such English tavern, renowned for its yarn-spinning patrons, was the Cock and Bull, a name that came to be associated with any tippler's tall tale.

Taverns have served as a source of inspiration to many writers and offered solace to those who suffered from writer's block. Countless scenes in literature take place in bars. Goethe, as a student, frequented Auerbach's Keller in Leipzig, which he transformed into the setting for his famous Faust and Mephistopheles cellar scene. Chaucer's Friar "knew the tavernes wel in every toun," and so did Shakespeare's Falstaff and Charles Dickens' Pickwickians. They would have felt right at home in *Treasure Island*'s Admiral Benbow inn. But one

has to reach far back, to Aristophanes' play *The Frogs* (405 B.C.), for the first mention of inns in all of literature—a group of roisterers having their fill in a tavern, then running out on the tab. In the United States from one coast to another, writers conjured up stories while sitting in a bar (O. Henry in New York's Pete's Tavern, Jack London in Oakland's First and Last Chance Saloon).

Taverns along the Roman military roads, forerunners of today's bars, had names like the Green Wreath and At the Sign of the Pine, creating the custom of the painted inn sign. Today, throughout Europe, many of the inn signs of old survive. In Britain, artists are often commissioned to restore a sign, and each year there are inn-sign competitions.

The medieval inn—where the genders and classes mixed—was often rough and wild, with chairs and tankards flying, and patrons on occasion were asked to check their weapons at the door.

In colonial America, the tavern was so important that settlers often put one up before they raised the meeting house. It became the scene of the earliest religious services. Warm tavern and unheated church snugged close together so that worshipers could thaw out after a morning-long winter service.

The tavern was the traveler's haven and the

The nonchalant passengers in the First Class bar of the S.S. Leviathan *contrast markedly with roisterers in other bars.*

Many English taverns in the 18th century offered private clubrooms where members gathered to partake of a communal bowl. "A Midnight Modern Conversation" by William Hogarth satirizes the bibulous results.

hub of politics, gossip, and news. The one copy of a newspaper that came to town was kept there and passed from hand to hand until it became unreadable. One taproom posted a sign reading: "Gentlemen learning to spell are requested to use last week's newsletter." There were legal restrictions—no selling to minors, servants, or slaves—and curfews. In 1647 New Amsterdam's Governor Peter Stuyvesant forbade the sale of beer or other liquors on Sunday prior to two o'clock, and if there was to be a sermon that morning, four.

Paul Revere and his compatriots met in Boston's Green Dragon, the Sons of Liberty in New York's Montague's Tavern. George Washington's New York headquarters was in Fraunces Tavern (which still serves customers at its original location), and it was there that he delivered the farewell address to his officers. Thomas Jefferson wrote the first draft of the Declaration of Independence in Philadelphia's Indian Queen. Francis Scott Key, borrowing the melody from a London "drinking club" song, composed the last verses of "The Star-Spangled Banner" in a Baltimore pub. Patriots like John and Samuel Adams were owners or operators of taverns. Abraham Lincoln got his bar license in 1833. In Tombstone, Arizona, saloons played host to the likes of Wyatt Earp, Johnny Ringo, and Doc Holliday.

Overwhelmingly masculine, many U.S. drinking establishments displayed the famous "barroom nude" above the back-bar mirror, a work of high art that came under the hatchet of Carry Nation at the turn of the century. When Prohibition became the law of the land in 1920, tavern business came to an abrupt halt; the era of the speakeasy, hip flask, gangland violence, and bootleg liquor was at hand; and a night at Looie's became coeducational. Texas Guinan welcomed each patron

to her Manhattan club with a cheerful "Hello, sucker!"

Speakeasies often were hard to distinguish from private residences. One New York dowager, irritated by the incessant ringing of her doorbell, posted a sign above the bell: "This Is Not an Illicit Resort.' When revelers took to obliterating the word "Not," she packed up and moved. Her home, of course, became a speakeasy within days.

After Prohibition's 13-year reign the speak's progeny came into their own: the nightclub, "café society," the elevation of the cocktail and the resurgence of jazz, and the disco of the 1970's where customers might order a soft drink and work off their frustrations dancing the hustle.

Throughout history people have gathered in saloons. Decor and manners may change, but not the purpose—to drink and talk. Below, a Dutch tavern c. 1640.

"Here's How"

That particular toast may or may not have derived from the American Indian's greeting, "How!," but it did originate on the U.S. frontier. So did such words for liquor as "joy-water," "firewater," "gut warmer," "rotgut," "red-eye," and "tangle-foot." The Westerners also "bellied up" to the bar and "bent an elbow."

A popular toast the world over is "To your health!"—with variations in French ("*A votre santé!*"), Swedish ("*Skoal!*"), Russian (*Nazdorovje*), German ("*Prosit!*"), among others. Jonathan Swift coined a wry and popular toast: "May you live all the days of your life!" An American Revolutionary officer in a Vermont tavern proposed this toast to the British enemy: "May they have cobweb breeches, a porcupine saddle, a hard-trotting horse, and an eternal journey!"

As for the origin of the toast itself, there are three possibilities. One: after the Danes took the British Isles, the conquered could not drink without their conquerors' permission and therefore waited until the Danes had raised their glasses and uttered the 1000 A.D. version of "Here's how!" Two: it was an old English drinking custom to serve a piece of toasted bread in a goblet of mead; when the saturated toast sank to the bottom, someone would challenge "Toast!" and the drinker would drain the mug so the toast could come sliding after. Three: in the city of Bath in the England of Charles II, a celebrated beauty was immersed in the Cross Bath when an admirer scooped a glass of water from the pool and drank her health; a second admirer, "half fuddled," said he'd jump into the bath "and swore, though he liked not the liquor, he would have the toast, meaning the lady herself."

There's a word for every kind of imbibing, from the last drink of the evening (after our great-grandfather's "nightcap") to the first drink of the morning. In 1789 these were called "anti-fogmatics," as the protectors against the ill effects of morning fogs. Later this drink became a "phlegm cutter," an "eye-opener," and a "fog-cutter."

Between the eye-opener and the nightcap lay that vast time period which the cocktail party helped to fill—but not until the 20th century. Editor and philologist H.L. Mencken, who claimed he himself invented 11 cocktails, could still not pin down the word's real origin after exploring eight different theories. He did not mention an often suggested derivation: in 1776 a drunk in Elmsford, New York, ordered a glass of "those cocktails" which were decorating the bar. The barmaid served him a drink with one of the rooster's feathers as a swizzle stick. The favorite mid-century cocktail-party libation was the dry martini, which James Thurber assessed once and for all in answer to a reporter's question: "One is all right, two is too many, three is not enough."

BARBERSHOP There was a time when a gentleman went to his barber for a haircut, a shave, a manicure, bloodletting, a tooth extraction, or the removal of a wen. The barber-surgeon's dual role goes back as far as Egypt of 1600 B.C. Knives, the earliest of surgical instruments, were used to cut hair, give shaves, and perform minor surgery. Ever since, the barber has left his nick on the jaws of history.

The stripes symbolize barbers' bloody past.

Until about 200 years ago, bloodletting was a remedy for anything that ailed you. Because the bleeding of patients was a regular service of the barber-surgeon, it was appropriate, at that time, for a barber to advertise his trade with a white sign (symbol of the bandage) splattered with touches of red. By the mid-18th century the barbers and surgeons of England had been divided into separate professions, and the barber's sign had become a red-and-white striped pole, from which hung a basin. At one time a patient held onto the pole as he was bled into the bowl.

The barbershop became a social center, a hangout of idlers, who were there for gossip and entertainment, serenaded by lute or viol. The barbershop quartet may well have sprung, in perfect harmony, from just such a setting.

BASEBALL Abner Doubleday did not invent the game of baseball, and the fastest pitch ever recorded was thrown by a second baseman, not a pitcher. Clearly the details and traditions of baseball, the most American of games, are as fascinating as the day-to-day heroics of the sport.

The popular view, for example, is that Abner Doubleday drew the first diagram of the baseball diamond at Cooperstown, New York, in 1839. It comes from a report on the origins of baseball written by A.G. Mills, third president of the National League and chairman of a committee created to settle the controversy over how baseball began. Mills was a close friend of Doubleday's, yet he based his claim that Doubleday invented the game on "a circumstantial statement by a reputable gentleman," as he wrote in 1907. He did not say who the gentleman was, nor did he quote Doubleday himself, an odd fact in view of their friendship. For his part, Doubleday never really claimed to have invented the game. After a distinguished military career, he retired from the army in 1873 and became a writer. The game of baseball was growing rapidly then, but Doubleday never wrote a word about the game he supposedly invented. Nonetheless, Mills' report was used by baseball executives in 1934 and 1935 to announce that baseball was approaching its centennial. There was much ballyhoo, of course, including the establishment of the National Baseball Hall of Fame and Museum at Cooperstown. And responsible or not, Abner Doubleday was enshrined as the father of baseball, although there is doubt about whether he ever played the game.

Baseball probably was not invented at all, but rather evolved from the English games of cricket and rounders, with the help of American variations like one old cat–two old cat–three old cat and town ball. These games were gloriously anarchistic. Any number could play on fields of any size, and rules were variable enough to be argument provoking. In 1845 Alexander J. Cartwright imposed a degree of order by drawing up game rules for his New York Knickerbocker Base Ball Club. He also constructed a diamond 90 feet square, and put the batter at home plate rather than at a distance from it, as was the custom then. In addition, Cartwright ended the dangerous practice known as "plugging," which meant hitting a baserunner with a thrown ball to put him out. Deadly 4-foot-high stakes marking the bases had been replaced earlier with sandbags. In 1841

Mike Kelly executes one of his patented steals during a game in the 1880's. The Philadelphia Keystones' Eddie Cuthbert recorded the first some 20 years before.

they were staked down to frustrate crafty basemen who kicked them away from runners. The rule allowing the imperious batter to call for a high or low ball was abolished in the 1870's.

Early baseballs varied enormously. There were no rules about how balls should be made, so they differed in content, size, and bounce. Each team brought its own ball, and the losing team handed theirs over to the winners, much as in football today. In 1909 the cork-centered ball was put in play, to be followed in 1920 by what was then called the "lively" ball. The use of Australian

customs

"Flip You For It"

In shoe boxes, in shopping bags, even loose and underfoot, hundreds, sometimes thousands, of baseball cards inundate the home of the all-American boy.

The custom of collecting baseball cards began even before half of big-time baseball did, in the 1880's, some 20 years before the American League was established. Printed pictures of players were packed with cigarettes in those days by the Old Judge Tobacco Company to stiffen its packages. Piedmont, Sweet Caporal, Recruits, and Polar Bear cigarettes soon followed suit with sepia cards showing players who had been photographed in a studio catching or batting a ball dangling from a string. These cards survived until the early 1920's.

In 1933 the cards reappeared, but this time they came packed with bubble gum. Printed on heavy cardboard and accompanied by tips on ways to improve your game, these cards were collected avidly until the beginning of World War II. There were other forms of cards, too—pictures of ball players appeared on ice cream containers and in Pepsi Cola cartons. And yet what collector does not most fondly remember his cards dusted with the special chalky powder of the gum? In 1952 the Topps Chewing Gum company added statistics and biographical information to its colored photos. All-Star cards came in 1958 and Record Breakers in 1975.

In 1977 players received $250 plus royalties to pose at spring-training sessions. Photographers

take three shots: with cap; without cap; and with cap angled to hide the team insignia. The second pose is good if a coiffed player is traded; the third is good for bald players who change teams.

Players delight in fooling photographers: the California Angels' batboy posed in place of Aurelio Rodriguez in 1969, and the price of the "incorrect" card zoomed up to $2. When the "record breakers" and "incorrects" cease to interest a boy, it may indicate he's developing an interest in something else—girls.

yarn, which was stronger than American yarn, made the ball harder and enabled it to travel farther. In the year the ball was introduced, Babe Ruth hit 54 home runs.

The cry of "kill the umpire" may have evolved when umpires changed from affable employees to autocratic arbiters. Early in the game's history a referee and two umpires officiated. Each team in a particular game chose one umpire, who tended to be loyal to the team that picked him. The referee, therefore, spent a lot of time settling arguments between umpires over close plays. By 1882 there was but a single umpire, and only team captains were permitted to talk to him. This was the beginning of modern umpiring, since the new rules stated that the umpire would use his own judgment in calling plays. Earlier judges had been more democratic, often consulting players and even spectators before rendering their decisions.

The first professional baseball player was Al Reach. In 1864 he accepted a monied offer to leave the Brooklyn Atlantics and join the Philadelphia Athletics. Others followed, and by 1869 the captain and shortstop of the Cincinnati Red Stockings was earning $1,400 a season. Players were still playing for modest sums in 1946; that year players demanded, and got, a minimum salary of $5,000 per year. Some players now make more than that in a few games.

Attempts to export baseball have met with mixed success. Despite a variety of traveling exhibitions, the English have shown little interest. But baseball is probably more popular in Japan than it is in the United States. In Cuba it is more passion than pastime, with more than 5 percent of the population taking part in some organized form of baseball. It was the Cuban love of baseball that alerted national security adviser Henry Kissinger, in 1970, to the fact that Russians were building a submarine base at Cienfuegos, Cuba. Studying aerial photos of the area, he noticed new soccer fields and decided that they meant Russians were at work—and play.

The fastest pitch ever thrown? Bob Feller, the Cleveland fireballer, had one of his pitches measured at 98.6 miles per hour. Fast indeed, but some years earlier, Mark Koenig, a mere second baseman for the New York Yankees, hurled a pitch through the same electronic measuring device—at a speed of 127 miles per hour.

BATHROOM When you walk into the bathroom of the average American home and shut the door, you are a witness to history. It has taken centuries for toilet and tub to end up in the same room. Those two conveniences plus shower, washbowl, and running water are a grander collection of comfort and ease than even kings knew before the 20th century.

An ad offered "the 'Dolphin' with open seat and back."

What did people do before the bathroom? For bodily functions, ancient Hindus carried brass vessels the distance of an arrow's flight from their houses. But most people used privies, like the Egyptians, or crouched in the great outdoors, like the Greeks, careful not to offend the eyes of their gods and goddesses. Long before the Greeks, the Cretans who occupied the palace at Knossos about 1800 B.C. had special rooms that previewed the future: here were bathtubs remarkably like sarcophagi, and wooden-seated toilets with water piped in and out. But such luxury was only for the privileged few and didn't last.

Bathing was common in ancient Egypt, especially among priests, who were obligated to perform ablutions twice in the morning and twice in the evening. The Greeks oiled their bodies and then wrestled to work up a sweat; they cleaned their pores in a steam bath and finished the ritual with a cool dip. Legendary slaves rubbed down legendary Hellenic heroes and gods, and the upper classes enjoyed the real thing. The Roman version of the Greek bath had much more to do with sensuality than with cleanliness. Using slave labor, the Romans built vast public baths. The Baths of Caracalla covered almost 28 acres, and inside 1,600 Romans could bathe all at the same time. Marble latrines set over the city's sewers were conveniently located inside buildings, and outside tublike urinals were placed over sewer drains at street crossings.

Medieval European cities had public privies on teetering plank arrangements, provided with a communal stick instead of toilet paper. Wealthy barons, however, sometimes had a wooden seat placed over an open shaft in the castle which emptied into the moat.

The Arabs had modified the old Greek steam bath into the so-called Turkish bath, and returning Crusaders restored the public bath to Europe, producing a medieval meeting place where wine and music flowed and the sexes mingled in the water. Sterile women visited baths where others, served by male attendants, were known to have become pregnant. Only fear of the bubonic plague in the 15th century finally shut down the last of the bathhouse-brothels. The 16th and 17th centuries were perhaps the dirtiest in history. Queen Elizabeth did "bathe herself once a month whether she required it or not," but others simply changed their linen and perfumed themselves with grimy hands. Chamber pots were emptied from London's upper stories after dark, and it probably was not over a simple puddle that Sir Walter Raleigh laid down his coat for the queen.

After a long absence of plague, 18th-century doctors began to recommend washing hands, face, and neck daily. People washed in a basin in the bedroom. The chamber pot—unadorned or kept beneath a padded seat or inside a walled stool (called a "close stool")—had long been common in cities. The privy was used in the country.

The flush toilet was patented in England in 1775, and it was eventually installed in a separate "water closet," where European toilets have generally remained. According to a biography of Thomas Crapper, *Flushed with Pride* (which exudes a distinct air of hoax), the Englishman invented a valve in 1882 that made flushing practical.

The French produced a shoe-shaped running-water tub with a drain in the "toe," the first of its kind, which Benjamin Franklin introduced to America in 1790. Franklin sat atub, reading for hours at a stretch, but most of his countrymen did not take to bathing regularly for another hundred years—for a number of reasons. It was not easy to fill a tub, even a relatively small chair-shaped hip tub, and then empty it and clean up afterward. And wooden tubs soon stank. Some people could not face the shock of total immersion, and some of the souls who braved it caught cold.

Nonetheless, bathing for health gradually became the rage in Europe, and the idea spread to America in the 1830's through the good offices of Sylvester Graham, the whirlwind prophet of hygiene. His idea was furthered by contemporary advances in plumbing. In 1829 Boston's Tremont House hotel opened, featuring the nation's first "bathrooms." They were in the basement of the 170-room building—eight water closets and eight

"Rub-A-Dub-Dub"

We all begin life with a nine-month bath in body-temperature fluid. Total-immersion baptism symbolizes new birth for those making a religious commitment. To take a bath is not a simple act, but one layered in the medical, religious, and technological thought of the times.

Paleolithic man bathed for his comfort and pleasure in rivers and lakes. He learned to heat stones for medicinal steam baths, as did the American Indians, Russians, Irish, and Finns after him. Urban dwellers at Mohenjo-Daro about 4000 B.C. bathed in a great city pool—probably for ritual purposes. According to Homer, Greek gods bathed in sweet-smelling ambrosia, and the hero Odysseus was rubbed with oil and gently scrubbed by attending women. Greek athletes after body-building exertion sat in stone, wooden, or marble tubs or in public pools; they also steamed and then took a cool dip before going to mind-stimulating discussion groups.

Athletes in early Rome rid themselves of sweat by jumping into the Tiber; later, wealthy citizens piped water into their villas and heated it for relaxing baths. Nervous emperors built cathedral-like public baths

Some folks are lucky. Bathers at Japan's Funabara Hotel can scrub themselves in this solid gold chicken.

called "thermae" to please and distract their subjects. The Baths of Caracalla were one mile in circumference; New York's old Pennsylvania Station was modeled after them. In most thermae, bathers undressed in one room, anointed themselves with oils and pomades in another, entered a cool bathing pool, then a resting room, and finally the hot bath. At first men and women bathed separately, but in later centuries they bathed together in marble pools where water fell from the mouths of silver lions. Seneca complained: "To such a pitch of luxury have we reached that we are dissatisfied if we do not tread on gems in our baths."

Though most early Christians disapproved of nudity and baths, calling them pagan works, Charlemagne chanced a dip in the sulfur springs at Aix-la-Chapelle. Crusaders loved the Islamic baths described in the story of Abooseer in *The Thousand and One Nights*, and they came home from the wars extolling the pleasures of social bathing.

In Japan public bathing has been popular for centuries. Rooted in Shinto religious practices, which required worshipers to wash, even rinse their mouths, before entering a shrine, the Japanese developed a passion for cleanliness. Today, public bathing is a social event and a popular way to relax after a business day.

bathing rooms. America's first private bathtubs were installed in a row of model houses in Philadelphia in 1832. Tub owners paid $36 a year for water piped from the city's works. In 1852 New York opened public baths for the poor, and by the Civil War most of the city's hotels had bathtubs.

England's flush toilet caught on among the American rich in the 1870's. Foot-operated pedal showers came into use in private homes. In that decade only the super wealthy installed tubs and toilets in the same room. By the 1880's advertisers got into the act, and displays for stationary running-water tubs appeared in plumbers' journals. "Do you bathe?" one company inquired. Another suggested ungrammatically, "Ask your wife if she would like to bathe in a china dish, like her canary does." While the rich continued to install private bathrooms, the poorer folk made do with white enamel chamber pots and washbowls.

Some, like Christian Scientist Mary Baker Eddy, worried that bathing might become a habit. She warned: "The daily ablution of an infant is not more natural or necessary than to take a fish out of water and cover it with dirt once a day, that it may thrive better in its natural element. Cleanliness is next to godliness, but washing should be only to keep the body clean, and this can be done with less than daily scrubbing the whole surface."

By the end of World War I, however, most Americans considered it their inalienable right to have an indoor bathroom with toilet and porcelain-enameled tub. Gradually, the tub bottom reached the floor, the toilet tank was lowered from the ceiling to the back of the toilet, the tub shower appeared, and canvas curtains gave way to vinyl before the shower took to its own stall. Wicker hampers and small scales and designer toilet paper arrived, and America's modern sanctuary was complete. For the luxury-minded few, the bathroom has become a showplace with plants, sun lamp, fireplace, and Oriental rugs.

Having finally got itself together, the American bathroom has begun to show signs of dispersing into its component parts again. New modules put toilets back into a separate compartment in the European way, and chic redwood or teak tubs for heated steaming water have moved into the guest areas of the ultramodern house—for convivial group soaks and conversations.

BATTERY In 1786 an Italian anatomist, Luigi Galvani, found that the legs of a dismembered frog twitched when touched by certain metals and concluded that the frog generated electricity. Galvani's fellow countryman and a physicist, Ales-

Ultramodern bathrooms have come out of the closet. Some, like this, seem bent on returning to nature.

sandro Volta, came to a wiser conclusion. Volta determined that metals did the generating. His "voltaic pile," a stack of copper and zinc discs with brine-soaked cardboard or cloth between each pair, produced the first steady source of electric current.

Those dancing frogs' legs were not the first connection made between animals and electricity. In the 1st century Pliny the Elder noted that certain fish—in particular the electric ray, or torpedo—could give the spear fisherman a nasty shock. Volta compared his invention with the electric eel's structure of living batteries and its capacity for recharging after delivering its shock.

The modern battery is simply a refinement of the voltaic pile. Batteries, even so-called storage batteries, do not store electricity. They produce it through chemical reactions that take place when electrons released from the negative pole flow through the material separating the poles (the electrolyte) to the positive pole. When the poles, or electrodes, are connected by a wire, the current will flow through the wire.

The electrode-electrolyte unit is called a cell. Most flashlight batteries are single cells, and auto and other batteries contain multiple cells. The materials used in the cells and the way the units are connected determine the voltage. An auto battery generates about 2 volts. A flashlight battery produces 1.5 volts. Connecting cells in a series (negative-to-positive) adds their voltage together. Thus a 12-volt auto battery contains six 2-volt cells. Some zinc-manganese batteries used in industrial applications contain 200 cells and produce 300 volts.

Wet-cell batteries contain a liquid electrolyte. Those used to power torpedoes use ordinary seawater as an electrolyte. Many small wet cells occur naturally. The pitting rust that eats away autos in winter is caused by steel-and-saltwater wet cells that form on bare metal surfaces. The metallic taste of new dental fillings is caused by the electricity produced by wet cells in which the filling is an electrode and saliva is the electrolyte.

Dry cells, such as those used in radios and hearing aids, are not actually dry. The liquid electrolyte is contained in a soggy paste that prevents leakage and spillage. Many such pastes are made with wheat flour or cornstarch. The smallest batteries in general use (in wristwatches) are dry cells, about the size of a collar button, and weigh no more than one-twentieth of an ounce. The largest batteries, giant wet cells used to power submerged submarines, are about the size of an office desk and weigh roughly one ton.

Physicist Alessandro Volta displays his voltaic pile at a performance for the prestigious French National Institute. One member, Napoleon Bonaparte, faces Volta.

BEARD One of the earliest symbols of *machismo*, the beard has had its ups and downs through the centuries, being sometimes "in" and sometimes "out." But from Zeus and Adam through King Arthur and Charlemagne and on to the antiestablishment youth of this century, beards have always been serious business.

The Mohammedan swears by the beard of the Prophet, while the most shattering curse a primitive Bedouin can utter is, "May God pluck your beard!" To "beard" a man—to touch, much less pull at, his beard—was in early times a bold and daring insult. In 1185 England's future King John, on a visit to Ireland, infuriated native chieftains by tugging on their flowing beards.

Beards were status symbols, emblems of royalty, in the 2nd millennium B.C. Beards shaped from metal were tied with ribbons or straps to the chins of kings—and queens. In ancient Egypt and Babylonia, men of stature used curling irons, tongs, and dyes on their whiskers and, at festival time, dusted them with perfumed starch and gold. The kings of Persia went even further, plaiting golden threads into their sacred beards.

Beardlessness, as well, has added to history's footnotes. Alexander the Great, having seen that an opponent could seize a soldier by his beard and lop his head off, ordered his troops to shave. In the 12th century the small son of Saladin, sultan of Egypt and Syria, wept in terror at the unaccustomed sight of the Crusaders' envoys' bare chins. It took Queen Elizabeth I to exploit the beard for tax money: anyone with a two-week growth paid the price. The lowest rate, for those of the bottom social rank, was 3 shillings 4 pence a year. Eras in which beards have been "in" have alternated with those in which they have been "out." The French under the bearded Francis I followed the leader. But a century later, under the bare-chinned Louis XIII, they shaved.

In the United States the first 15 presidents, Washington through Buchanan, were clean-shaven, only to have Lincoln introduce the beard to the White House. Since then only four presidents have had real beards—Grant, Hayes, Garfield, and Benjamin Harrison—and none since Taft has sported any facial hair.

BED Life begins and often ends in it; a third of life is spent in it, including some of its better moments. For early man a bed was a pit dug into the earth and lined with palm leaves, reeds, rushes, pine boughs—or anything springy. Members of hunting tribes could cover themselves with animal skins at night.

The bed was simple in early houses: in mild climates, builders made a raised area along one wall and covered it with skins or rush mats; the Eskimos constructed a ledge of ice and covered it with furs for a communal bed. (Communal sleeping is generally related to economic necessity.) In some early houses men slept on a bed on one side of the door and women on the other. Stone pillows were not unknown, though they must have numbed the head and ears.

The use of thongs and ropes probably came about as a result of a desire to be off the ground and away from creeping and slithering night life. Early designers stuck four forked branches into the ground and built a frame of slender tree trunks atop the forks. They latticed the frame with thongs, making a place to deposit a "mattress" of skins. On the Egyptian latticed bed, long linen sheets were folded into a mattress; there was also a wooden headrest to keep coiffures neat overnight.

When Tutankhamen died in the 14th century B.C., his nonlatticed, all wooden royal bed was in the shape of two slender-legged cows (representing Hathor, the goddess of love) attached at the feet by horizontal rails. When the king was still alive, these rails were used to carry him about on his

Convertible furniture, popular in Europe in the 1800's, was widely used in America in the 1870's. This hide-a-bed—"even a woman could lift it"—was shown in 1876.

bed; he even liked to give audiences from this platform. At night the slaves and the poor of Egypt dropped onto nests of palm boughs to rest from their labors.

The Greeks were so knowledgeable about metallurgy that they were able to make bronze beds and wooden ones with silver feet. They used thongs for latticing and filled beautiful pillows with wool, feathers, and vegetable fibers. These they tossed against an innovation of their own: the headboard. Over their bodies they pulled rich coverings and embroidered counterpanes. Alexander the Great occasionally used his bed as a throne. The Greek philosopher Pythagoras liked to have his bed neatened as soon as he arose—for if the impression left by a sleeper's body were stabbed, it was believed, harm could befall him.

The Romans were good farmers and used hay, wool, and feathers to stuff sewn bags and make the first true mattresses. Sheets made of linen from Gaul soothed the bodies of the wealthy. They preferred their beds high and climbed steps to get to them. They ate while reclining, too, but on a different kind of bed. And yet another type was used to display the dead for seven days. Roman slaves slept on pallets or on portable lattice-type beds with sheepskins to cover them.

When Rome fell, the bed collapsed too: German tribesmen often slept on beds of leaves; Saxons stuffed vermin-attracting straw into bags and pil-

lows. Slowly Europe worked its way back to the latticed frame and rush mattress. By the 9th century a Viking queen, Asa, was buried with her wooden slatted bed and down coverlets in a boat to carry her to a happier—and perhaps warmer—world.

Wealth and civilization grew side by side in England, and by the 14th century the rich slept nude under blankets and embroidered, gem-bordered sheets. The poor covered themselves with wool or skins. The Crusaders had returned from the East with the idea of the double bed, but knights, a wary lot, often slept in them sitting up against pillows, their swords hanging ready on the bedpost. Sometimes a bed was surrounded by protective wood paneling, and one medieval model had to be entered by stepping backward through a single hole in the paneling. Canopies, originally designed to keep out dripping water and marauding bugs, rose above beds; lamps hung within and they, together with the cross-shaped design of a sword's handle, kept away the "Evil One." Henry VII sprinkled his bed with holy water before retiring, which was bad for his rheumatism. Beds were already big, 6 feet by 7 feet, but bigger beds were coming—partly as a result of a less worried time.

The cult of the bed flourished on the continent from the Renaissance through the 18th century. Women lay on black satin sheets, which showed off their alluring pallor. Beds often as big as 8 feet by 7 feet were handsomely carved and hung with gorgeous fabrics. Different woods, inlaid stones, shining metals, abundant quilting, and smooth hangings of silk and velvet over mattresses of pea shucks or straw helped make beds beautiful.

In England there were four-posters with tent-like curtains. Queen Elizabeth I worked in such a bed and received ambassadors there. In France Louis XIV ordered his 413 beds, including the great bed at Versailles with its crimson covering, inscribed in gold: "The Triumph of Venus." He even dispensed justice from a bed. Before him, the aging French statesman Cardinal Richelieu had gone about solely by bed, demanding that doorways, house walls, and even city gates be demolished to permit his passage.

Beds have served not only as seats of power but as cradles of creativity. Poor authors often took to their beds to keep warm while writing. Though better off, Milton, Swift, Voltaire, Mark Twain, George Sand, and Elizabeth Browning also wrote in bed. Rossini, Donizetti, and Puccini wrote music in bed. And even Winston Churchill, in better heated quarters, sometimes dictated from his bed.

In the 19th century a maharajah ordered from Paris a silver bed with each of its four posts in the form of a life-size nude woman. The women had

Waiter, there's an artist in my sandwich! Along with pickle pillows, nylon lettuce sheet, and a satin tomato blanket artist Philip Haight decorates his burger bed.

resting on top. With the advent of city apartments, hideaway Murphy beds appeared on living-room walls—and in a good many comedies. The unfolding sofa bed wasn't far behind.

Shortly after World War II, the Duchess of Windsor chose silk printed sheets from Porthault's linens in Paris and liked them so much that she let them show. That began a fad for patterned sheets, which American mills eagerly adopted—to their great relief. For manufacturers were discovering that the new white polyester and cotton blends lasted more than twice as long as plain cotton sheets, and a new gimmick was needed to keep up sales.

Famous designers were hired to produce patterns, and in the 1970's, 90 percent of all sheets sold were in blended prints and gay colors. Some people buy such sheets to make curtains and wall hangings. There is a market, too, for sensual, if slippery, satin sheets. Even waterbeds moved into middle-class stores—and out again.

real hair and blue enamel eyes, and carried fans or fly whisks that moved when the maharajah lay down. His weight also activated a music box that played "God Save the Queen."

In 19th-century Germany another dramatic bed resembled a draped rookery, decorated with life-size carvings of bats, toads, and lizards—all lighted by the eyes of an owl-shaped lamp.

Unusual beds have also been mentioned in literature. The Great Bed of Ware was cited by Shakespeare in *Twelfth Night.* This was originally a canopied Gothic Renaissance giant, 18½ feet by 12 feet, made about 1570. It was later reduced to a 12-by-12 square and ended up in various inns, where 18th- and 19th-century businessmen used it for spectacular, sometimes group, seductions.

In America in the 1850's James Liddy of Watertown, New York, was leaning on a wagon, waiting to go home and tackle the disagreeable task of tightening the ropes of his lattice bed, when he fell against the spring seat of his buggy. At home he designed the American coiled bedspring. By the 1930's machine-made innerspring mattresses were installed on most beds.

The first half of the 20th century gave sleepers the ultimate in comfort but little in style. An estimated 8 out of 10 married couples chose double beds (about twice the width of the average crib), traditionally popular in France but less so in England. Plain white linen sheets, made by the housewife until the 1920's, were mass-produced in the 1930's. They were spread on an innerspring mattress, which rested on outersprings, which in turn were held up by a slatted bed frame. The old "bed," or feather-filled bag, was now the quilt

BEER Ever since December 26, 1620, when the *Mayflower* dropped anchor at Plymouth, Massachusetts—"our victuals being much spent," a passenger's journal noted, "especially our beer"—American history has owed a bit of its effervescence to the malt brew.

The first brewery in Philadelphia was built in 1683 by William Frampton. In the 18th century a number of statesmen were involved with brewing: Thomas Jefferson and James Madison helped to promote the industry; Samuel Adams was a brewer; George Washington maintained a modest brewery at Mount Vernon. And Patrick Henry referred to colonial taverns as "cradles of liberty."

In 1685 Massachusetts put a price ceiling on beer, thus encouraging the citizens to drink the "suds" rather than the stronger stuff—and drink it they did. By 1977 men and women in the United States were guzzling some 4.8 billion gallons of beer, or 22 gallons per person. It should be noted, however, that West Germans down 38.8 gallons apiece and the hardy souls of Australia's Northern Territory about 62.4. Beers elsewhere tend to be stronger than in the United States, where their alcoholic content varies from 3 to 6 percent. The *Guinness Book of World Records* called West Germany's EKU Kulminator Urtyp Hell the strongest—at 13.2 percent.

The story of beer may well have begun 10,000 years ago, when Neolithic man started growing wheat, barley, and millet. From an archeological dig in Mesopotamia, we have stone tablets dating from 7000 B.C. that contain the first recipe for the "wine of grain." In those days breads made from malted cereals became "beer bread," which, when soaked in water and left to ferment, produced the Mesopotamian brew.

The Egyptians—who raised barley—developed pure yeast, refined the art of fermentation, and learned to stopper their beer jars (thus preventing the brew from going sour as the result of a second fermentation). By 1300 B.C. they had made beer a national drink. Considered good for what ails you, it was prescribed for scorpion bite and contributed to a "delicious remedy against death—half an onion in beer foam." The Pharaohs, however, as oppressive as they were greedy, controlled the barley harvest, owned breweries, levied taxes on the sale of beer, and were brutally strict with tavern keepers who dodged payment. A male publican caught at it was drowned, a female buried alive.

The Greeks, who traded with Egypt, came back with barley seeds and the secret of brewing beer, and the European conversion to beer drinking followed. Caesar's armies transported the practice to Gaul and Britain. By the Middle Ages, women were brewing beer at home and were called brewsters. Monasteries took over for a time, to be replaced by commercial breweries. The Weihenstepan Brewery, built in 1040 in Freising, West Germany, is reputed to be the oldest in Europe.

In 1292 Pilsner, the crown prince of beers, made its appearance in Pilsen, a Bohemian town noted for its deep mineral springs. A pleasing concoction, aged gracefully for half a year in limestone caves, Pilsner was paler and lighter than other beers but with a certain tang. It

Beer has long signified hospitality. The little man proffers it in detail from artist's invitation.

is with us still, as are the major varieties of beer: lager, ale, stout, and porter. Bock beer, a dark, heavy brew, is usually made in the spring.

Shortly after Prohibition ended, there were some 700 breweries in the United States. By 1977 the number had dropped to 48, with the top five (Anheuser-Busch, Schlitz, Miller, Pabst, and Coors) producing about 70 percent of the total volume.

Meanwhile, the quarter-million or so Americans who are beer-can collectors (cans were introduced in 1935) continue to seek out rare items: Cloud Nine, Nu Deal, King Snedley's, Kopper Kettle, Olde Frothingslosh, and Soul—the names run on and on. (Soul was a test product that never reached the general market because the brewery was forced out of business by the riots that wracked the Watts area of Los Angeles in 1965.)

Experts estimate that as many as 12,000 domestic labels have been produced in all. Whole collections have brought as high as $25,000, and some single cans have yielded $500.

BELT The belt is probably as old as the first items of clothing worn by early man—leaves or woven vegetable matter or small pieces of animal hides used to protect the body. The first belts undoubtedly did what they do today: they held up and in place garments, tools, even weapons. As loincloths, or breechcloths, evolved, belts were used to secure them, front and back, and perhaps even over closures at the hips.

The belt became a symbol of status and a shaper of fashion and wealth. Egypt's royalty wore handsome aprons suspended from chased gold girdles and belts set with precious colored glass. The Greeks and Romans used thong belts to give their tunics form at the waist or hip, and women tied them below the bust. Athletes and soldiers belted their tunics for action. Agamemnon, the Greek leader in the Trojan War, ordered his men to gird themselves for battle. Both the Greeks and the Romans unbelted their garments to allow them to drag in the dust as a sign of mourning. After the fall of Rome, Charlemagne repopularized the belt by wearing a sword in it.

The Crusaders brought fringes and ornamented belts of silk from the Eastern countries they invaded. Eventually female clothing and male garments were cut to fit more closely, and girdles became a key element in medieval fashion. Belts were used to secure pouches, which in time came to transport books, pens, inkhorns, money, daggers, and keys. After fading in popularity in the 18th and 19th centuries, belts made a comeback in the Gay Nineties. Sportsminded women nipped in their skirts and blouses with belts, and men removed their suspenders, their pants held firmly in place by leather belts and shiny nickel buckles.

The buckle itself has a long, admirable history, dating from the Bronze Age and a variety of subsequent ring and pin arrangements. Its heyday, however, was in the 18th century when silver buckles shimmered on virtually every aristocratic toe in Europe. The humble shoelace finally drove the buckle from the shoe. Yet the buckle remains on the belt, still important to style and fashion.

BICYCLE The dangerous velocipede, known as the "boneshaker," with an enormous front wheel and a tiny rear one, had a maddening penchant for dumping people on their noses. But it had honorable roots, dating from Baron Karl von Drais' 1818 Draisine. A 50-pound vehicle consisting of a saddle between two wooden wheels, it was used for coasting. In 1839 Kirkpatrick Macmillan, a Scotsman, added a brake and treadle-power system to the Draisine's rear wheel. In the 1860's other enterprising inventors attached pedals to the front wheels of their machines and gradually enlarged the forward wheels, so that a single turn of the pedal would advance a bike ever farther.

Finally, in 1885, the first commercially successful "safety bicycle," the Rover, which had equal-size wheels and chain drive, came on the market—and the boom was on. Before long the Vanderbilts and Goulds were riding bikes with friends to band music, and Annie Oakley was shooting at glass balls from her bicycle. The Gay Nineties became the decade of the bicycle.

Unlike the horse, the bicycle did not tire or need food; unlike the train, the bicycle was constantly available. People who theretofore had been content to visit their town's library, go to church, or stop in at the pub or the temperance meeting began to get out of town. Some forswore drinking to save up the $100 or $150 that a bicycle cost. Often the next town didn't even have a sign-post, and the roads were full of mudholes, pits, and humps. Bicyclists demanded better roads, road maps, signs, reports on road conditions, and even lists of approved hotels and taverns. Some went to court to establish that they had as much right to the public thoroughfares as drivers of

Thumbing her nose at pedestrians, an 1890's Parisienne flaunts her machine's virtues: speed and status.

horse-drawn vehicles, and homebound women tossed off their corsets and serge and took to wheeling in shorter skirts and, finally, "bloomers." Ultimately, "bloomer girls" began demanding more than changes in dress: they wanted to vote.

Most doctors acclaimed cycling as a sport that got people six times farther for the same muscular effort they would expend in walking, and strengthened their hearts in the bargain. But some expressed concern that leaning over handlebars would produce a nation of hunchbacks. Dogs barking at silent, speeding cycles were a danger until harmless ammonia-spray pistols sent them scooting away.

By 1895 there were some 300 manufacturers and countless small shops in America supplying bicycles to a million riders. Riverside Drive in New York was thronged with riders out on their wheels. An estimated 50,000 horses disappeared from the streets of Philadelphia, and another 75,000 vanished in Chicago. Blacksmiths and saloon keepers complained that everyone was out wheeling, alone or in club groups, racing a hundred miles, pedaling on a six-day endurance test, or taking lessons on stationary bikes attached to indoor floors. Records were being set: in 1898 the largest bike ever built, a 23-foot, 305-pound monster with seats for 10 riders, whizzed through Walton, Massachusetts, at a reported 40 miles per

Using hand and foot cranks, Dr. Allan Abbott pumped this bike up to a maximum speed of 38.87 m.p.h.

hour. By 1900 the bicycle industry employed 70,000 workers serving 4 million riders.

And then it was over—at least in America—as all the know-how and passion attached to bicycling transferred itself to the fledgling automobile industry. In Europe, however, the bicycle remained supreme. Cycling competition continued as an important part of the Olympic Games, and the 21-day, 3,120-mile Tour de France dominated racing on the continent. In cities, towns, and villages around the world the bicycle was *the* means of transportation.

In America a gasoline shortage during World War II temporarily revived biking. Then came the 1960's and the 1970's with ecological concerns and fuel shortages and renewed interest in physical fitness. (Scientists have learned that a man on a bicycle is the most energy-efficient way of moving body weight, outscoring such travelers as a swimming salmon, a jet fighter, and a horse.) Today 100 million riders are back on the track, asking for better bikeways in urban and suburban settings, better and lighter equipment, and more freedom to race and roam. According to a tire company, bikes may soon outnumber cars on the road. Perhaps one of today's young riders will even break the world speed record of nearly 40 miles per hour.

BIKINI During the 1940's women on the French Riviera dared to expose more of themselves to the sun. Taking this cue, in 1946 a French couturier, Jacques Heim, designed a scanty bathing suit to be sold in his shop in Cannes. The bottom part consisted of two small triangles of cloth riding high above the thigh and low beneath the navel and was joined front and back at the hips by two rings of white bone. The top was a narrow brassiere. Roman women had exercised in a two-piece navel-revealing wool costume about 17 centuries earlier, but its like had not been spotted since. Heim called his suit the *atome* (for atom) and hired a skywriter to fly over Cannes scripting, "*Atome*—the world's smallest bathing suit."

Coincidentally, in July 1946 the United States was conducting atomic bomb tests on Bikini atoll—a bit of land smack in the middle of the Pacific Ocean. Prior to the second blast, announced for July 25, Paris was jangling with rumors that this superbomb would blow up the planet. "Anything goes" parties, called "bikini" parties, became popular among the doomsayers. A copy of Heim's design was dubbed the "bikini," and the rival suit was skywritten up as: "*Bikini*—smaller than the smallest bathing suit in the world." The name stuck. Some writers found similarities between "bikini" and "atomic impact," while others

said it kept the woman as bare as the defoliated Bikini islets after the bomb's destruction.

G.I.'s brought home bikinis for wives and friends, who were thrown off beaches for wearing them. Puritanical America finally accepted the bikini via Mediterranean and Caribbean resorts in the early 1960's.

The form-fitting, neck-to-ankle knit suit introduced in 1910 by Annette Kellerman had been an even greater shocker. Having taken up swimming for her health, the Australian had replaced the bulky sailor-dress suit while the world gasped at her curvaceous daring. Nevertheless, the bathing suit continued thence to lose weight.

Changing styles: in the 1920's the bathing tent provided all-round coverage; today most bathers seek just the opposite.

BINGO The box of numbered cardboard squares and red discs on every child's shelf is but a dusty, domesticated version of America's favorite game of chance—bingo! Played today in crowded halls before huge electric boards, the game is probably as old as man's sense of chance and the ancient art of casting lots to read fate's design. The game's traceable roots lead back to the Italian National Lottery, in operation since 1530.

' Whatever its name of the moment—lotto, housey-housey, lucky, radio, fortune, keno, beano, or pokeno—bingo has become one of the most popular gambling games in the world. Why? Because it is simple and easy to play and somebody wins—and can be seen winning—each and every time. Yet the odds involved are not simple; nor do they indicate that one is more likely to win than not. Chances against winning on the first five numbers called are about 1,700,000 to 1; against winning a particular game—200 to 1; and against winning during an evening's play (about 30 to 35 games)—7 to 1.

In the United States, bingo was first manufactured and sold by a struggling toymaker and salesman, Edwin S. Lowe. Far from home, tired and depressed, Lowe pulled off the road one night in 1929 at a carnival somewhere in Georgia. There he watched for hours as people jostled about a table playing a game called "beano." Two weeks later, Lowe printed his own cards, bought some inexpensive prizes, and tried out the game on friends at his home in Brooklyn. "B-B-B-Bingo," an excited girl cried as she slammed down her final bean—and the modern game was born. Five years later, Lowe was churning out sets on more than 60 presses, all operating 24 hours a day, 365 days a year.

Since then bingo has probably raised more money for more church, fraternal, and social groups than all other types of fund raising combined. New buildings have often been the result, and not without distinguished precedent: if not for lotteries in Philadelphia and Connecticut in the mid-18th century, Princeton might not have been moved from Newark to its present rustic setting.

Some players believe they can "feel it" when they are going to win; others try white magic, sitting in "lucky" seats or wearing "lucky" clothes. Some even play 30 cards at once, risking not only their money—and eyes—but also a preoccupational hazard known as "bingo arm."

BINOCULARS "Compact, Light, Powerful, Stereoscopic Effect," an 1898 advertisement for binoculars proclaimed, adding proudly that they could be taken "Touring, Yachting, Cycling, Racing, Hunting, to the Games, and to War."

The earliest binoculars were anything but light and compact. Devised in the winter of 1608 by a Dutch optician, they consisted of two telescopes placed side by side with a separate set of lenses for each eye. The telescope itself had been assembled just a few months earlier by the same Dutch lens grinder. In 1609 Galileo revolutionized astronomy by aiming a telescope at the heavens; even now a simple twin-telescope instrument is known as the Galilean field glass, or opera glass.

Though field glasses and opera glasses are often referred to simply as binoculars, there is an important difference: binoculars have prisms. In the United States, in fact, the term for sales purposes can be applied without qualification only to prismatic devices. Developed in 1900, the prism binocular is the most popular. Most sets have two prisms in each barrel. Thus the light is bent twice, making it possible to build smaller, more compact instruments. Prisms also make it feasible to set the front lenses farther apart, which creates better

Opera glasses, like those in this painting by Mary Cassatt, are actually twin telescopes.

stereoscopic vision at long range.

Binoculars are classified by a standard system, and the numbers that appear on an instrument casing may read as follows: 6x30, 7x50, 8x30. The first number indicates how many times the device magnifies things; the second figure gives the diameter of the outermost lens in millimeters. The bigger the lens, the more light it will let in, and the better the instrument will perform at dusk or in the dark.

Binoculars enable an observer to advance visually on something that cannot be easily approached physically. A recent development has made binoculars even more accessible for instant bird-watching or neighbor-checking. The new mini model weighs only 4½ ounces and can be stashed in a shirt pocket.

BIRTH CONTROL Sneezing, jumping up and down, swallowing dead bees in honey—the techniques men and women have used over the centuries to block conception are almost as bizarre and varied as the mosaic of human history itself. No one knows for sure when primitive man first guessed the truth about pregnancy—that male sperm helped start it—but the discovery was probably made some 8,000 years ago during Neolithic times. What is certain is that rudimentary attempts to disrupt the process began soon after. An early Egyptian papyrus, now nearly 4,000 years old, suggested for use in the female a crude barrier made of lint and coated with finely ground powder from the acacia tree. This might have been partially effective, for acacia is acidic and thus

"Happy Birthday to You"

Not until men first charted the stars thousands of years ago, and linked their fates with events in the sky, did personal birthdays—indeed, hours of birth—become important. To know one's moment of birth meant that a horoscope could be drawn; the document was considered critical to a good life, which included, of course, a happy marriage.

As with much that is new, the rich and prominent were the first to enjoy birthday celebrations. Egypt's Pharaohs ordered businesses to close on their birthdays and gave enormous feasts for their hundreds of servants. Cleopatra gave Antony a birthday dinner with gifts so plentiful that some partygoers arrived poor and left wealthy. Persian noblemen observed their natal days by barbecuing an ox, a camel, and an ass and serving hundreds of small cakes.

In ancient Greece, a person lucky enough to be born wealthy and male could join a birthday club composed exclusively of men who shared the date. Once a month the privileged group celebrated with a feast. When members died, they even left sums of money to help pay for subsequent parties.

In ancient Rome the emperor gave gigantic parties in honor of his own birthday, which included parades, circuses, and gladiatorial combats. Augustus provided himself with such a celebration every month.

In medieval times, nobles sometimes celebrated their birthdays with raucous parties. Much of Western society's birthday energy, however, went into celebrating the birth of Jesus. The date assigned to his birth—December 25—is the time of the winter solstice and is related to pagan festivals celebrating the rebirth of the sun—when days begin to lengthen. By the 14th century babies born in Christian countries were named after saints, and later on celebrated not their own birthdays but the day on which their special saint had entered heaven.

In some cultures birthdays at the time of puberty receive special attention. Jewish boys traditionally reach manhood on their 13th birthday, which family and friends honor with the bar mitzvah ceremony. Mexican girls are considered ready for marriage on their 15th birthday.

Age has its favors as well. In China the 60th birthday commands respect for the man or woman lucky enough to have finished one sexagenary cycle and started another. India's maharajahs are also honored on reaching that age. The Aga Khan III had himself weighed in public on his birthday because his 20 million Ismaili Muslim followers were prepared to match his weight in birthday treasure—243 pounds worth of diamonds.

Today in America the birthday party is eagerly awaited by every child. Its form comes mainly from Germany, where the birthday child was given gifts, allowed to choose a menu, and provided with a candle-ringed butter or jam cake. Where did the lighted candles come from? Probably from the birthday of the Greek moon goddess Artemis, who was honored by her worshipers with moon-shaped honey cakes surrounded by lighted tapers.

The song "Happy Birthday to You" was composed by two sisters, Mildred and Patty Hill, in 1893, but nobody really paid much attention to it until the original words "Good morning to you" were changed to those that we know so well today, words that are sung in virtually every home across the nation at least once during the year.

Not even a birthday is pure joy: party equipment has not changed much since the 1900's, but new cameras have obviated the command to "Sit still!"

mildly spermicidal. More than 3,000 years later Casanova, the 18th-century Venetian adventurer, advocated the use of half lemons—which may have worked for the same reason.

Other early attempts to create a barrier between sperm and egg involved female use of such alien substances as mustard seeds, crocodile droppings, beeswax, dried figs, and oil-impregnated rock salt. Women also ingested a frightening variety of pills, potions, and powders: some contained quicksilver, others gunpowder, a few arsenic. In North Africa, women swallowed the froth from camels' mouths. "A woman," the Talmud intoned, "is allowed to drink a cup of roots in order to become sterile."

Undoubtedly because they were in charge and it was the female who actually gave birth, men never subjected themselves to such contraceptive indignities. Nonetheless, the Book of Genesis and the Talmud both mention one of the earliest forms of male contraception—withdrawal, or coitus interruptus, as it is known medically. Of all forms, it was probably the most effective and is widely employed throughout the world today. Another early technique involved use of a container (now known as a condom) to trap male sperm. In old Rome goat bladders were used. Today, primitive South American tribes cut the ends of seed pods for the same purpose. Ultimately leather and fabrics, such as linen, were tried, causing Madame de Sévigné, the French aristocrat, to write in 1671 that the devices were "armor against enjoyment and a spider web against danger."

In ancient Greece men and women also sought "safe days," periods when conception might most easily be avoided. Unfortunately, because they knew relatively little about the human reproductive cycle, they often erred, confusing menstrual

words

Black: The Good and the Bad

Darkness, night, fear, evil, death, nothingness—in every culture black is the embodiment of sinister tidings. Why? Undoubtedly early man associated certain colors with particular things and feelings: red with blood and power, yellow with the sun and optimism, green with spring and hope, and black, alas, with things dark, therefore unknown, and often deadly. The world beneath the earth, the world of death, was a black place.

Among the Japanese the soul was seen as a black object that could depart the body. For the Cherokee Indian black meant death. For Hindus it was the color of Siva, the great destroyer. For early Christians it meant death—and regeneration. But black also has had some good connotations. It is the color of rich earth and thus a sign of fertility. In Egypt the black mud of the Nile brought life to the delta each year. Early Egyptians feared red and brown cats; they believed black ones had divine powers. In one African mythology the people who ate the liver of the first ox killed became the forebears of the black race.

Interestingly, expressions and phrases using the word black appear frequently in most languages. The phrase "black-letter day" comes from Roman times, when lucky days were marked on the calendar in white and unlucky ones in black. Christians later marked saints' days in red and ordinary days in black. On

A ride in the infamous Black Maria blackens even the swellest of romps.

"Black Friday," September 24, 1869, James Fisk and Jay Gould tried to corner the gold market, failed, and still made $11 million. In the 14th century the "black death," caused by an organism (*Bacillus pestis*) that produces black sores, wiped out a quarter of Europe's population in three years. A "blackleg" swindled at cards; later, the term was used to describe a nonunion member who worked during strikes. In the word "blackmail," "mail" derives from a 16th-century Scottish word for rent. White mail was paid in silver and black in grain, meat, or base coin. Border farmers paid "blackmail" to marauding gangs to protect their crops. The first "black book" was Henry VIII's list condemning monasteries, so that he might take their lands. Merchants kept "blacklists" of poor credit risks; organizations "blackballed" prospective members in a secret vote, the unwanted receiving a blackball and the desirable a white ball.

Yet for a perceptive few, black is and has always been a color of dignity, elegance, and sophistication. Judicial robes, tuxedos, and the basic little black dress have been proving this for years.

Blind Date

Blind dates—meetings between two people of opposite sex arranged by a third party—have probably existed ever since there were three people on earth. Not all have been successful. The Trojan War resulted from a blind date arranged by Aphrodite between Paris, who had awarded her the prize in a beauty contest, and a girl, Helen, who unfortunately turned out to be already married. In Shakespeare's play, Romeo's helpful friend, Benvolio, offers to "fix him up" with a new girl. Despite such discouraging examples, the custom has persisted.

The term "blind date" seems to have originated in the United States in the 1920's, giving rise to dozens of jokes and puns. Nonetheless, such fate-tempting rendezvous aren't all bad—some people have even met their mates on blind dates. In 1975 *Seventeen* magazine found that 36 percent of those girls who date go on blind dates and that most enjoy them—at least "somewhat."

It remained for American ingenuity to bring the benefits of modern science to what had been at best an uncertain process. The birth of the modern age of blind dating took place in Cambridge, Massachusetts, in 1965, when a Harvard student, Jeff ("We supply everything but the spark") Tarr, started it after a discussion with his roommates on the ineffi-

Always a risk, the blind date faces double jeopardy in this 1960's picture.

ciency of dating girls recommended by third parties. Why not write down one's requirements, he asked, put them into a computer, and mix and match with those of girls who have done the same? Thus the computer would become the third party—a fast and objective one—and provide a large selection of candidates to choose from. Tarr and his friends prepared a questionnaire (which worked in nicely with Tarr's thesis on dating habits) and printed 10,000 to pass out among Boston's student population. Fortunately, computer matching turned out to be relatively inexpensive, costing only a few dollars for two names each month. Soon hundreds, then thousands, tried it. Each day Tarr received mail from far-off places, some sent to fanciful addresses like "Love Ma-

chine, Cambridge, Mass."

"The greatest thing in dating since dancing," as one satisfied customer called it, was duplicated by other computer-dating services across the country. Some companies all but promised marriage, others failed to screen out undesirables (college attendance in itself had been a kind of natural screen), and some took the customer's money and never delivered any names. Still, the price went up and many services prospered as more and more men and women, especially in their late twenties, used them. For as much as $150, a customer could read written profiles and view videotapes of potential dates over a period of three months. That way, as one company stated in its advertising, "the chemistry has already started" and the first date is more like the second.

In the main, matching appears to occur not so much on the basis of psychological values (are you ambitious or contented? philosophical or practical?) as on blunter sociological realities—race, religion, and education level. Slightly behind these precomputer stalwarts are physical condition, alcoholic intake, sexual permissiveness, and job status. Eye color, hair color, height, and weight no longer seem to matter much, perhaps because blind dates are no longer really blind.

activity with heightened fertility, thus enhancing rather than reducing the chances of pregnancy.

Modern techniques reflect many earlier ideas. No longer a noxious potion or poisonous powder, today's pill is effective though it may cause serious problems for some women. Used with spermicidal creams, such barrier devices as the diaphragm and cervical cap work almost as well. The rhythm method, both for moral and religious reasons, is also in wide use today. Aided by special thermometers and careful charting procedures, it has become increasingly effective. Even modern intrauterine devices (I.U.D.'s), have an ancient pedigree. For centuries camel drivers inserted pebbles in the wombs of their camels before long trips to keep *them* from becoming pregnant.

BOARD GAME The earliest kind of "board" was probably dirt: patterns were traced in it, and players moved their men of pebbles or shells or seeds according to the turn of dicelike objects. After that, portable boards appeared: a three-row rectangularly patterned track was found in the royal tombs at Ur in ancient Sumer, accompanied by 7 black and 7 white men and 3 white and 3 lapis-lazuli "dice" shaped like pyramids.

The Egyptians played a similar game, called Senat, with 10 men. The moves of the pieces may have represented the wanderings of the soul in the underworld. On the back of some Senat boards a second, similar, game has 30 squares. The Romans modified this 30-square game and called it Tabula. Roman soldiers took Tabula to Ger-

Human pieces step strategically in living chess game at Marostica, Italy, a tradition about 300 years old.

many, and the Germans transported it to the Scandinavians, who taught it to the English. The game is now called backgammon, and it is probably the oldest track game using dice that is still being played. Some suggest that backgammon's 30 pieces represent the days of the month—its total of 7 spots on the opposite sides of a die the days of the week, and its 24 board points the hours of the day.

Parcheesi, another track game, is laid out in the form of a cross. It originated in India about the 6th century A.D. and has been played there ever since. In the 16th century the Mogul emperor Akbar played it with delightful abandon: he laid out a "board" in his courtyard and dressed harem girls in different colors to serve as his men. Centuries later, Parcheesi was copyrighted in the United States by the founder of Selchoe and Righter, one of the early American game companies.

The path of the track board evokes the days of the hunt. Lattice boards more closely approximated the complex field of war. Indeed, in ancient China a bloody battle was actually suspended—its outcome to be "played" by opposing leaders on a Go board. (On most grid boards, players can move in four directions plus diagonally.) Go is war, with many battles raging simultaneously for possession of territory. Chess, a chivalric and king-oriented game, is but a single battle.

Other games that we think of as board games are actually variations on dice games (dominoes), card games (Mah-Jongg), or alphabet games (Scrabble). Still, scores of true board games are played today, from Candyland, the five-year-old's first game, to Monopoly. The history of board games parallels the history of the world, for many games incorporate changes in cultural and social beliefs.

Not until the 19th century did America get away from its puritanical disapproval of playing cards, dice, and board games. In 1843 Anne Abbott, daughter of a New England clergyman, developed a game called The Mansion of Happiness. To avoid using dice, she employed a spinner. Mansion was essentially a track game, with players proceeding through marked areas, learning as they went that robbers were sent to jail, drunkards to the stocks, and virtue was its own reward. Milton Bradley's Checkered Game of Life appeared in 1860 and provided the same message. It was included in game packs he designed for soldiers, along with chess, checkers, backgammon, and five kinds of dominoes.

Preachy board games weren't much fun, 16-year-old George Parker decided, and left school three weeks early one Christmastime to make something better. His Game of Banking suggested that virtue ultimately rewarded was not nearly as interesting as money shrewdly earned in the present. Eventually Parker set himself up in the games business, which has tracked American interests and history with such games as Klondike; War in Cuba; Lindy; and Polly Pickles, Queen of the Movies. As Milton Bradley's Checkered Game of Life suggests, the tracked board essentially represents a path along which a player's progress is determined as much by chance as by know-how.

With waterproof money and a steel board, California students launch an underwater Monopoly marathon.

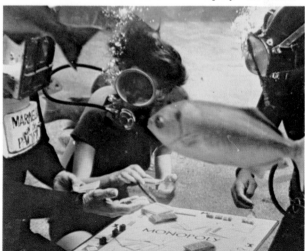

BOTTLE How to store liquid? The gourd and the sewn leather bag of ancient times prepared the way for the clay jar and for the glass bottles on our shelves today. Some 4,000 years ago Egyptian craftsmen made glass bottles by winding liquefied glass threads around a dispersible sand core. Later they dipped bags of sand into vats of glass, which hardened around the sand shape. The invention of glassblowing in the 1st century B.C. led the Romans to produce many different-shaped bottles.

At the turn of the 17th century the English learned to melt glass by using long-lasting, hot-burning coal fires in place of wood and began turning out bottles for pennies apiece. In a few short years the craft became an established profession. Eight glassblowers came as colonists to Jamestown in 1608. They built a factory in the Virginia woods and set to work making window-panes and bottles.

Once bottles were made, the problem was how to keep the contents from evaporating. Usually, bottles were stoppered with oil-soaked hemp or with cork bungs secured by thread or wire. By the late 17th century the corkscrew appeared, allowing vintners to push corks tightly into the necks of bottles and retrieve them. Finally, in the 1890's, William Painter patented the bottle cap or crown seal for pressurized liquids. At first, few people wanted the bother of opening this crimp-edged seal. But because it stayed put and had space for advertising it was common by 1925.

Prime Minister Winston Churchill suggested another use for bottles. In June 1940, after the Allied forces staged their epic retreat from Dunkirk, Churchill's voice boomed over British radio: "We shall fight on the beaches, we shall fight on the landing grounds, we shall fight in the fields and in the streets . . ." and, clamping his hand over the mike, he added in a stage whisper, "and we will hit them over the heads with beer bottles, which is all we have really got."

After World War II disposable metal, plastic, and paper containers began replacing glass. Recognizing that each American uses about 400 bottles or jars per year, today's ecologists want to go back to reusable glass, but scientists, wary of public apathy, are experimenting with plastics that turn to powder, or burn, or can be washed down the drain.

As collectors, bottle buffs fall in line directly behind stamp and coin lovers.

---

people

Mr. Monopoly

Out of work in Philadelphia during the Depression, Charles Darrow supported his family by fixing electric appliances, patching concrete, and walking dogs. He also invented things: puzzles and beach toys and a new bridge score pad, while musing about old times like vacations in Atlantic City.

One night in 1931 Darrow sat down at the kitchen table and sketched the names of various Atlantic City streets on the oilcloth. He colored the name spaces and cut tiny houses and hotels from bits of wooden molding. He typed out title deeds, and added dice and buttons for play money. The family played night after night.

Friends soon joined in. Nothing, it seemed, was better for Depression-battered spirits than an hour or two of buying real estate, even the make-believe kind. Enthusiasts wanted their own sets, and Darrow accommodated them, making and selling the games for $2.50; a friend printed the title cards. In the beginning he made six sets a day. Philadelphia stores demanded more sets; Darrow offered his game to Parker Brothers in Salem, Massachusetts. Parker voted not to buy it.

The game was too complicated, they said, and had 52 errors in it. Darrow persevered and had his printer make up 5,000 sets. Some were sold to Wanamaker's and a few to F.A.O. Schwarz.

Early in 1935, Parker Brothers relented and gave Darrow a contract with royalties on all sets sold. Soon he became a millionaire, gentleman farmer, world traveler, and collector of exotic orchids. Monopoly became Parker's biggest seller and America's favorite game. By the mid-1970's some 80 million sets had been sold.

BOWLING In thousands of large, brightly lit establishments across the United States, some 65 million men, women, and youngsters—bodies coiled, lips tight, eyes intent—at one time or another experience an anxious anticipation as they roll a hard rubber ball down 60 feet of polished runway toward 10 maple pins. Seconds later, if they are practiced and skilled or just plain lucky, the ball will scatter and knock down the pins—all of them—for a strike. Then the pinsetting machine sends the ball back, resets the pins, and the game of bowling is ready to roll once more.

The automation may be new, but the story of bowling, in one form or another, can be traced as far back as the 6th millennium B.C. The unearthed grave of an Egyptian child, dating from 5200 B.C., has yielded a primitive set of bowling implements: nine crude stone "pins" and a stone "ball" used to knock them down. Records show that bowls were a favorite pastime in the Alpine regions of northern Italy about the time of Julius Caesar and involved tossing stones at an object some distance away. That was probably the origin of boccie, a game still played in Italy and the United States today.

In the Middle Ages the course of bowling curved slightly. At that time Germans customarily carried a kegel, a stick or peg that could be used for self-protection or for sport. A religious ceremony evolved in which the kegel, said to represent the heathen, was placed at one end of a cloister. By rolling a stone and knocking the staff

HENRY VIII AND HIS COURTIERS AT WHITEHALL ~1530~

Ultimate in body English: Henry VIII and his courtiers enjoy the delights of bowling at Whitehall in 1530.

down, a parishioner could prove that he was leading a clean, pure life. Thus the origin of the term kegler to mean "bowler."

By the 14th century bowling was an established and popular sport. Rich and poor alike found enjoyment in taking whacks at the pins. Bowling matches even became a part of wedding festivities, and a bride might find herself sitting on the sidelines watching while her groom tested his skill against that of his cronies.

Eventually the stone ball was replaced by a wooden one. The number of pins continued to

vary, depending on the region and the whim of the players. But as one story has it, Martin Luther, an avid supporter of bowling though he had little time to play, favored nine pins, thus making that number the norm.

From Germany the game spread to the Low Countries and on to Austria and Switzerland. While most everyone else was bowling on packed cinders or clay, the British preferred to bowl on lawns. As early as 1299 the town of Southampton formed a bowling club, which still exists today. King Edward III, fearing that such a "useless and unprofitable" game might replace archery, promptly outlawed bowls. (Even so, the game continued to be played by the rich and royal, and the law was repealed in 1845.) About 1450 the English began roofing lanes, an important step in making bowling a year-round, all-weather game.

Just how bowling reached America is a matter of conjecture. Undoubtedly, lawn bowls came with the British settlers. One of the early places to congregate for a game of bowls was an area on the tip of Manhattan Island known to this day as Bowling Green. But there are those who argue that American bowling had its origins in the Dutch game of pin bowling, brought across the Atlantic in the 1600's. In any case, by the early 19th century bowling at pins was flourishing—and gambling with it. The residents of Connecticut refused to tolerate such evils, and in 1841 the state legislature banished ninepins. According to legend, an ingenious Yankee added a tenth pin and circumvented the law.

Regardless of its origin, the game's popularity increased rapidly. By the mid-19th century indoor lanes—pin palaces, as they came to be called—existed in many cities, including Syracuse, Chicago, and Milwaukee. With the formation of the American Bowling Congress in 1895, the game became serious business. And though the rules have changed with time, the basic equipment has remained the same except for technological progress. Lanes, for example, are now constructed with such care that no section deviates from any other by more than forty-thousandths of an inch. Bowling shoes also receive special attention: the sole of the forward or "sliding" shoe is made of leather and the opposite one of rubber.

The automatic pinsetting machine, first introduced in the early 1950's, transformed the already popular sport. These remarkable devices did everything a pinboy could do (except smoke and wear funny hats) but faster and for 24 hours a day. Bowling became a big moneymaker and an important professional sport. Today more than $1 million a year is awarded in prizes to the men and women who knock down pins for a living.

BRASSIERE How to support, conceal or reveal, or minimize or maximize the breasts is a tale as intricate as the twists and turns of human history.

The French claimed they invented the brassiere, a German said he did, and the Chinese had a story all their own. According to the tale, in the 8th century a favorite concubine of T'ang dynasty emperor Hsüan Tsung was having an affair with one of the generals who, overcome by passion, bit her. To conceal the mark, she covered her breasts with red silk, which the emperor found so provocative that all other women at court soon adopted the fashion. In a short time women outside the palace began to wear similar coverings.

Bra lifts a Panamanian Indian into 20th century.

The mother of the modern bra (though it was not called that until 1937) was an American socialite, Mary Jacob. She became the darling of expatriate Paris intellectuals of the 1920's and kept company with such literary luminaries as James Joyce, D.H. Lawrence, and Ernest Hemingway; they called her Caresse.

One evening as Caresse was getting dressed up for a party, she remembered that her rose-garlanded evening gown needed fixing. The last time she had worn it, the embroidery of her corset cover poked between the roses and ruined the effect. She sent her maid for two handkerchiefs, some pink ribbon, and a needle and thread. Before the mirror, Caresse folded and pinned the handkerchiefs on the bias, tied them behind her, and slipped the dress over her head. "I could move much more freely, a nearly naked feeling," she later wrote, "and in the glass I saw that I was flat and proper." She patented her invention and sold the patent to the Warner Brothers Corset Company of Bridgeport, Connecticut, for $1,500.

Soon other corset makers in America and Europe added the brassiere to their stock of waistnippers and corset covers. Then each was faced with the problem of a name. The Americans borrowed brassiere from the French *bracière*, meaning "arm protector," which makes as little sense as the French name for the bra, *soutien-gorge*, which means "throat supporter."

Generally, with each style change in the fashion-frivolous West has come a new line of undergarments. In the 1930's curves were the thing, in contrast to the slender, boyish look of the previous decade. Bra makers advertised such models as "Full Fashion," "Hold Tite," "Over-Ture," and "Accentuate." By the late 1930's and 1940's a big bosom became the ideal, as exemplified by such Hollywood stars as "Sweater Girl" Lana Turner and Jane Russell. As the story goes, millionaire Howard Hughes put his staff of aeronautical engineers to work on a bra for the buxom Miss Russell. The result was called the Outlaw bra, so named because she wore it in a Hughes movie called *The Outlaw*. For "underendowed" women there were inflatable bras, which could be expanded by blowing into a concealed tube, and false bosoms called Gay Deceivers.

The 1950's featured the "pointy" look coveted by schoolgirls, and the 1960's brought in a new stretch-fabric bra for the "no-bra" look. Actually, in only two brief periods in history since the fall of Rome have fashions allowed women's breasts to go unfettered—the era of the French Revolution and early Empire and the decade of the 1970's.

BREAD "Dough" was a widely used slang word for money, before "bread" became the in word. There is a centuries-old connection between bread and money. In ancient Egypt workers at day's end received not coins but bread. They were, one might say, the first "breadwinners."

Bread as the staff of life has always been part of social history and of literature. There is the "daily bread" of the Lord's Prayer and the biblical injunction to "cast thy bread upon the waters" (Ecclesiastes 11:1). Long before that, the Egyptians had been throwing bread in the Nile in tribute to their gods. In the 2nd century A.D., according to Juvenal, Roman emperors hoped that offering the people "bread and circuses" would keep them fed and distracted—and less apt to riot. And in the French Revolution, the story goes, the cry for bread received the now famous reply, "Let them eat cake."

Found in Swiss lake dwellings that go back to the Stone Age were the remains of cakes baked from barley and wheat. The earliest "breads," however, are thought to have been made from acorns and beechnuts, similar to the acorn cakes still eaten by Indians of the Pacific Coast. To this day the peasants in Iraq bake the bread of the ancient Sumerians—a flat bread of barley flour, ground sesame seeds, and onions.

The Egyptians replaced open-air baking with cone-shaped ovens, and they kneaded dough with their feet. They learned that fermenting wheat forms a gas that causes the dough to rise and makes bread lighter and more savory—the first leavened loaves. Over the centuries wheat was made into flour with a grinding stone. Because white bread was made with the highest-quality flour, it became, traditionally, the food of the rich.

By the 2nd century B.C. the Greeks had become the new master bakers and were baking over 50 different breads, including a cheese loaf much like today's. In the Roman Republic, bakehouses were put under the control of the magistrates, with slaves and, later, criminals to pound the grain.

Bakers weren't always in high repute. In the Middle Ages, as they formed guilds, the quality of their product was watched closely by local officials. They were so much distrusted that baker and devil became synonymous. The phrase "baker's dozen" may have evolved from "devil's dozen," a folk expression meaning thirteen. The Turks were harsh with their bakers in the 1700's. When bread prices rose dramatically, they hanged a baker or two. And the baker who stinted on the contents of a loaf was nailed by his ear to his shop's doorpost.

On his second voyage Columbus brought Euro-

Bread was the staff of life even for early man. Made from stone-ground flour, it also contained rock chips.

pean grains to the Caribbean, and subsequent settlers introduced wheat to mainland America. The Pilgrims had a saying, "Brown bread and the Gospel is good fare." And bread had become so important a part of the American diet by the Revolutionary War that the Continental Congress appointed a "Superintendent of Bakers and Director of Baking in the Grand Army of the United States." With the Industrial Revolution came a laborsaving (though mixed) blessing: the roller mill. It took over the job, crushing the grain but also destroying the protein and vitamins in it.

The baking industry of the United States grew to enormous proportions over the years. By the merger of 27 millers in 1929, General Mills became the largest single miller in the world. Eventually, U.S. commercial bakeries came to produce more than 95 percent of all breads in the nation's breadbox.

BREAKFAST CEREAL Though bacon and eggs and griddle cakes have their enthusiastic supporters, the breakfast bestseller is cold cereal and milk. What's more, it is possible to begin each day for 70 days with a different ready-to-eat breakfast cereal. There are such morning noisemakers as Kaboom and Cap'n Crunch, and a myriad of shapes including Flakes, Bits, Stars, and O's. Rather than attack the crossword puzzle, the sleepy-eyed can ponder the spellings of Froot Loops or Krinkles or long for the cereals that did not make it, such as Quake Quangaroos, Pink Panther Flakes, or Baron von Redberry.

What to eat for breakfast was not always a major decision. During most of the 19th century, Americans broke the night's fast with leftover pork, sausage, pies, scrapple, fried potatoes, or hunks of buttered bread—and suffered from dyspepsia and gout. Not until about 1850 when a German immigrant, Ferdinand Schumacher, wondered why Americans fed oats to their horses instead of eating them themselves, as people did in Germany and elsewhere in Europe, was there a change in the breakfast menu. (Samuel Johnson's great dictionary defined oats as: "A grain, which in England is generally given to horses, but in Scotland supports the people.") Schumacher decided that Americans shunned oatmeal because it had to be steamed for hours, and so he developed a kind that did not. Soon the "Oatmeal King of America" was selling 20 barrels a day in his Akron, Ohio, store, and other easy-to-prepare hot cereals began to appear on grocers' shelves.

When miller Tom Avidon of Grand Forks, North Dakota, filled boxes with ground wheat and shipped the homemade containers by railway flour car to brokers in New York City, a telegram came back, "Forget the flour. Send us a car of Cream of Wheat." The day of the unhurried, hot breakfast was coming to an end. One man responsible for the changeover to cold cereals was Henry Perky of Denver. He turned wheat berries into threads by drawing the heat-softened grain through rollers. He didn't sell much "Ceres" in 1892, but some of his airy biscuits (later sold as Shredded Wheat to tourists at Niagara Falls) found their way to Battle Creek, Michigan.

Battle Creek was the home of a fervent group of

Young love and health blossom above the crunch of corn in this 1907 ad.

Seventh-Day Adventists who ran a health institute in a farmhouse on the outskirts of town. The chief cure was a vegetarian diet. The resident doctor was John Harvey Kellogg, and he called his rest home the "Sanitarium." When it was pointed out that the correct word was sanatorium, the young doctor snapped, "Sanatorium means a rest home for wounded soldiers; sanitarium will mean something else." Since Kellogg knew of Perky's little wheat pillows, he too began experimenting with grain foods. John and his brother Will discovered they could flake or flatten wheat, and "Granose" was born. The brothers quarreled, and it was Will who later produced another product, Corn Flakes, under the name of the Kellogg Toasted Corn Flake Company.

Meanwhile, a patient of the Sanitarium, who had arrived there in a wheelchair, left after a few months in not much better health, by some accounts. However, Charles W. Post went on to found a cereal company, also offering the consumer Postum, a coffee substitute made from grain. He wrote a pamphlet, "The Road to Wellville," for enclosure in the box of Grape-Nuts, his other early product. From his endeavors grew General Foods.

Thus were born some of the giants who are almost the only participants in the race to get into America's breakfast spoon.

BRICK Brick is the oldest building material made by man, with a history reaching back 10,000 years. From the first brickmason who got us out of caves and animal-skin tents to the latter-day

wag who called bricks Irish confetti, they have been the building blocks of many civilizations that have stood up staunchly against time. Some early cultures were able to manufacture bricks every bit as strong as we make them today.

Rome's Colosseum is a brick structure. So are parts of the 1,500-mile-long Great Wall of China, built 2,000 years ago. An awesome monument to the art of masonry, it contains close to 4 billion bricks. On the other hand the Tower of Babel, built of sun-dried mud brick, did not last. Archeologists still puzzle over why there are so few remains. One postulates that the nature of the soil and other building materials in that area resulted in unusual erosion; others think that some man-made catastrophe caused its downfall.

The oldest sun-dried mud brick ever found is from the biblical city of Jericho, and the oldest fired brick was discovered at Kalibangan, India. (Both are now in the Museum of Ancient Brick outside Johnson City, Tennessee). There is also a mud brick from the ziggurat at Ur of the Chaldees and another from a fortress of King Solomon. One brick that emigrated to America as ballast on the *Mayflower* later became part of a building foundation in Plymouth Plantation.

Brickmasons were on the first three ships to arrive in Jamestown, Virginia, in 1607. Brickmaking facilities were set up at the sites of most early buildings in the Colonies. Over 150 years later, George Washington had a brick factory at Mount Vernon and Thomas Jefferson one at Monticello.

Long before the days of Jamestown or the *Mayflower*, adobe brick, made of clay and straw and dried in the sun, was important to Central and South American cultures. Among the pre-Inca adobe structures still standing is the ruined and abandoned city of Chan Chan north of Lima, Peru. Some Pueblo brick villages in Arizona date from the early 15th century.

Even today brick is still a widely used building material, made by a process that has changed little over the centuries. Clay is mined, crushed, and mixed with water to form a thick cohesive mass, then shaped, dried, and baked. What was done by hand is now done by machine; what was left in the sun to dry is now baked in ovens. The color of burned clay varies, depending on its chemical composition and the changes in temperature in the burning. Clays containing iron burn red, as the fire oxidizes the iron: thus the traditional "brick red."

Collecting old bricks has become a pastime for some. Officially, these enthusiasts belong to a division of the Wichita Barbed Wire Collectors Association, Inc. A rare or unusual brick has been known to fetch several hundred dollars from an avid "bricksman."

Serpentine wall designed by Thomas Jefferson at U. of Va.

BROOM Some stories tell that Ben Franklin received from a friend in Hungary a whisk made of a plant called broomcorn, which produces stalks with prickly "hairs" that catch and hold dirt. While brushing his hat, Franklin found a seed on a stalk and planted it. The result became a decorative novelty in Philadelphia gardens.

In the 1790's Levi Dickinson raised enough broomcorn in Massachusetts to make 30 brooms, and an American industry was launched. The Shakers later revolutionized the broom by turning the round sweeper (whether of twigs or straws) used for ages the world over into the flat, efficient model used today.

The stiff-branched broomcorn, a 10- to 15-foot-high variety of sorghum, is cultivated in the United States mainly in the Southwest. It is one of the few crops that is not federally subsidized, as the National Broom Council proudly points out.

1937: a New York broom hawker on Lower East Side

BUS In the early 1660's by decree of Louis XIV, eight-passenger carriages traversed fixed routes throughout Paris, offering the poor and infirm a means of getting around at pennies a ride—as much as 40 times cheaper than hiring a cab. In short order, the aristocrats discovered the new method of travel and made it their fad of the moment, thereby setting back the advent of public transportation for a long time because the hoi polloi refused to board the playthings of the rich after the elegantly dressed fun-seekers abandoned the vehicles for a newer thrill.

Paris did not try busing again for another 150 years. The 18-passenger horse-drawn carriages

One-and-a-half decker: this open-topped bus ran between London's Kew Bridge and Surbiton.

that set out in 1827 were carefully marked *Entreprise générale des omnibus* (a general enterprise for all) to indicate that anyone having the fare was welcome. And so the omnibus or "bus," as it was called after its introduction in London a few years later, was born. The first gasoline-powered buses appeared in London in 1904, and within two decades gas replaced hay and coal as fuel in cities from Paris to Los Angeles.

An uncomfortable (albeit with ventilation, lighting, and toilet) transcontinental bus got rolling across the United States in 1928. Diesel engines, air suspension, and express highways made long-distance travel considerably easier on the passenger after World War II.

words

Busman's Holiday

According to author Edwin Radford in his book *Unusual Words*, published in 1946, he learned about the origin of the expression "busman's holiday" from a Mr. Savidge of Middlesex, England:

"Fifty years ago I was a conductor on one of London's horse-buses. The driver and his horses were as one; there was a deep attachment between them. When my driver had a day off, knowing that his horses would miss him, he always came to the terminus to see them off on the journey.

"If he suspected the temporary driver of not treating them well, he would travel throughout the journey as a passenger. He was only one of many such drivers; and when we saw a driver riding on his bus during his day off we always said of him that he was 'taking a busman's holiday.'"

BUTTER "Guns will make us powerful; butter will only make us fat." So said Hermann Goering in a 1936 radio broadcast. But guns-as-necessity versus butter-as-luxury is hardly a modern con-

cept. The Roman encyclopedist Pliny the Elder wrote that butter "is considered as a delicacy in foreign countries, and is one which distinguishes the rich from the lower classes."

Butter has been slathered over more things than the rich man's muffin: the ancient Greeks and Romans used it as a hairdressing, a skin cream, and a medicine; in 16th-century England, doctors prescribed it for growing pains and constipation.

Nor is cow's milk always the base. The Indians churn up a semifluid spread of water buffalo milk called *ghee*. Sheep, goat, horse, and yak milk is also made into butter. According to one educated guess, butter was first created from cream or milk put in leather bags slung over the backs of camels and agitated by their movement across the desert sands. Some Arabs still make a rancid camel-cream butter in a goatskin bag.

A French print depicts the churning of butter.

Many early European settlers in America brought with them a hankering for butter. The Pilgrims had several tubs stored aboard the *Mayflower*. Heading westward on the Oregon Trail, frontier women learned to make butter "by the dashing of the wagon." Until the first commercial creamery was opened in 1856, all butter was hand churned by the blades of a wooden "dasher."

Butter reached its highest level of consumption during the 1920's and 1930's. Gradually, margarine became popular, and by the 1970's it was margarine two to one on U.S. dinner tables.

BUTTON The art of button making goes back to prehistory, but it took an unsung 13th-century genius to make the button a practical object—by inventing the buttonhole. Before that, the button had been ornamental, made of precious metals or stones, and something of a status symbol.

Francis I of France (1494–1547) had a costume for formal occasions adorned with 13,600 gold buttons, and Louis XIV (1638–1715) was said to have buttons worth a million dollars for personal embellishment and ransom insurance—and occasional baubles for his mistresses.

About 1250 the button makers' guild was established in Paris, assuring that the objects would remain symbols of rank because they were fashioned by skilled craftsmen. A honest man 17 years old and of legitimate birth was eligible for apprenticeship: one-fifth of his personal worth had to be paid to the guild for the privilege of learning the art, and one-tenth of his wages went to the king.

Although button production was a recognized trade, employing substantial numbers during the reign of England's Queen Elizabeth (1558-1603), buttons were still too expensive for most people.

In the 18th century the art of button making achieved its apogee; buttons were fashioned of everything from metal to ivory. Between painting portraits, famous artists decorated buttons with pictures of leaders, ladies, and scenes from fable and song. At the same time, buttons became cheap enough for the mass market, owing to the introduction of machinery and of new materials like cattle hooves (horn buttons), and eventually the corozo nut (vegetable ivory) and mollusk shells (mother of pearl).

The Romans converted the Phoenician sign gīmel ("camel") to "C".

CALENDAR When to plant tomatoes, shop for the holidays, pay the rent, or keep a business date in Amsterdam—everything we do is governed by the calendar. This constant, commanding chronicle of time, past, present, and future has a complex history of its own— it was born of astronomy, regulated by various ancient priesthoods, and is grounded in common sense. Nonetheless, this timekeeping system has always been somewhat less than perfect.

That our 24-hour day equates with a single spin of the earth, our month with the phases of the moon, and our year with the earth's annual orbit around the sun seems simple enough. Yet there are problems: the principal one is that a solar year (one orbit) and a lunar year (12 full moons) are out of whack. This is because the lunar year is 354 days, 8 hours, and 48 minutes, whereas the solar year is 365 days, 5 hours, 48 minutes, and 46 seconds. The extra 5 hours and 48 minutes, of course, are why we have an extra day every four years. In Julius Caesar's time, the calendar was already behind, trailing the seasons by more than two months. Caesar's solution: fatten the year 46 B.C. by adding 23 extra days to February and tucking 67 more in between November and December. The "year of confusion," the Romans called it. To prevent future lapses, Caesar created leap year.

Over the centuries, however, other errors cropped up—mainly because Caesar's calendar year was several minutes longer than the solar cycle—and spring gradually slipped backward into

Pigs eat November acorns in this illumination from Duc de Berry's book of hours, a sort of medieval calendar.

winter. As a result Pope Gregory XIII in 1582 lopped 10 days off that year's October. Protestant England and its colonies refused to cooperate—until 1752, when they dropped 11 days from their calendars. London property owners, feeling they were being cheated of 11 days' rent, rioted. But in Philadelphia, Benjamin Franklin calmly advised his readers to be grateful they could "lie down in Peace on the second of this month and not . . . awake till the morning of the 14th."

The names of the months have been no great help in making sense out of the calendar. Since the Roman calendar originally started in March, September (from the Latin for "seven") was the seventh month. Then when things changed, it became the ninth and October (originally the eighth), November (ninth), and December (tenth) were bumped to tenth, eleventh, and twelfth.

January, the time of saying farewell to the old and greeting the new, was named, appropriately, after Janus, the Roman god with two faces. At the Lupercalia festival in February, a time of religious purification (*februum*), two youths with thongs made from the hides of sacrificial goats romped through the city, slapping those women reputed to be barren. Whether this ritual helped make them fertile is not clear, but it did provide the second month with a name. March derives its name from Mars, the god of war; April from *aperio* for "open," referring to the buds of spring; May from Maia, mother of Hermes; June, possibly from Juno; July from calendar repairman Julius Caesar; and August from Emperor Octavian, who bore the title Augustus.

In English the days derived their names

from the Sun and Moon (Sunday and Monday), four Teutonic deities, Tiw, Woden, Thor, and Frigg (Tuesday, Wednesday, Thursday, and Friday), and the Roman god of sowing, Saturn (Saturday).

Though primitive man developed relatively sophisticated methods of calibrating the seasons by observing heavenly

Stonehenge slabs may have measured time.

bodies, the priestly scribes of Sumeria were the first calendar makers, about 5,000 years ago. They gave us 12 lunar months, each with 30 days—and the beginnings of the confusion. The Babylonians succeeded them, and during the Babylonian captivity the Jews adopted the seven-day week and eventually passed it along to the rest of the world.

This Aztec "Calendar Stone" bears signs for the days of the week.

The Egyptians stretched the year to 365 days, adding the 24-hour day as well.

Caesar brought the 365-day year back from Egypt in 46 B.C. and included it in his Julian calendar. Nearly 600 years later, in 525 A.D., a Scythian monk living in Rome, Dionysius Exiguus, played the numbers game again and with considerable impact: he shifted New Year's Day from January 1 to March 25 (Pope Gregory restored it 10 centuries later); he established Christmas as December 25; and he dated events from the birth of Christ, which is why we use B.C. and A.D. The Hebrew calendar begins with the creation of the world, as calculated from Genesis; the Islamic calendar dates from Mohammed's hegira from Mecca to Medina in 622 A.D.

Calendars, however, were not in general use until the Middle Ages. Since then, or at least since Pope Gregory's reforms of 1582, things have been relatively calm. The Gregorian calendar really only misses a day every 3,323 years or so.

July: harvesters gather wheat into sheaves in a book of hours detail.

CAMERA Cameras existed in rudimentary form long before photographers and photographs. Darkened, often oversized, chambers were used to project a single beam of light on an opposing wall and with it an upside-down image of the world outside. As early as the 4th century B.C., Aristotle noted the existence of such devices and studied the optical principles that made them work. Using the holes in a simple strainer, he even projected on the ground the crescent shape of a partially eclipsed sun. The smaller the hole, he wrote, the sharper the image. In the 11th century Arab scholars used their tents as crude cameras for similar experiments, noting again that tiny apertures produced the best pictures.

During the Renaissance an extraordinary array of darkened chambers, enlarged, fitted with trapdoors, portable frames, and special papers for the artists inside were used for everything from public demonstrations to architectural tracings. They came to be known by their Latin name—camera obscura, or "dark room." In the 16th century the "camera" gained two important refinements—a lens and a diaphragm. First mentioned in 1550, Italian lenses were biconvex and resembled the brown lentils used in soup, which is why "lens" is derived from the Latin word for lentil.

Such developments made the camera obscura extremely effective, as Giovanni Battista della Porta, a Neapolitan scientist and writer, discovered some years later. Producing a special show for friends, one that included the use of hired actors, della Porta created such realism in his darkened room that he was charged with sorcery and had to flee Italy.

By 1685 the camera obscura had become a small portable camera, which in principle closely resembled a modern single-lens reflex instrument. As designed by Johann Zahn, a German monk, it consisted of a wooden box about 9 inches high and 2 feet long with an adjustable lens and aperture and an external viewing screen. It was so exacting that British author Laurence Sterne complained in *Tristram Shandy* that the camera was "most unfair of all, because there you are sure to be represented in some of your most ridiculous attitudes."

The camera in which the first recorded picture was exposed—in 1826—wasn't much different. It was a French-made camera obscura and had a prism inside to correct reversal of the image. Joseph Nicéphore Niépce was its owner and operator. Using a pewter plate coated with an asphalt compound, he produced his history-making picture. It still exists today: a dim, fuzzy, but nonetheless recognizable view of his farmyard. Nine years later an English country squire, William Henry Fox Talbot, made the world's first negative—with a quite different version of the camera obscura. To speed up exposure time and sharpen the image, he constructed a tiny camera fitted with lenses from a microscope. "Mousetrap," his wife dubbed his two-and-a-half-inch-square camera. But in 1835 he produced his negative, a ghostly view of a lattice window in his library. Two years later, in Paris, Louis Daguerre completed the cycle of

One of the pesty photographers—a paparazzo—dodges an angry star.

discovery with his first "daguerreotype." In awe the French painter Paul Delaroche said: "From today painting is dead." Yet Daguerre's cameras were little more than refined camera obscuras and his lenses were extremely slow (about f/17).

The first camera with modern lenses, though it looked more like a telescope, was built in 1841 in Vienna. Its lens, designed by Josef Max Petzval, a mathematics professor, admitted 16 times more light than Daguerre's, and its f stop was a more respectable 3.6. Petzval's lens, known as the "German lens," made photography a profession.

Photography developed remarkably during the Victorian period. In 1888 Eastman Kodak introduced the box camera, which came loaded with enough film for 100 pictures. When the film was used up, the owner returned the camera for developing and reloading. Projected motion pictures and color transparencies appeared in the next two decades. Color film arrived in 1935, and instant photography in 1948, when the first Polaroid camera and film, invented by Edwin Land, went on sale. Yet even the most modern camera is related to the camera obscura. Today, however, we put film instead of a picture maker inside the box.

Largest ever built, this 1900's camera was known as the Mammoth and could photograph an entire train. It used quarter-ton plates and made 4½-by-8-foot pictures.

"God," "Man," and Color

With poetic appropriateness, the first simple color-film process—sought in vain by scientists for a hundred years—was invented by two researchers known to their associates as "God" and "Man." Leopold Godowsky, Jr., and Leopold Mannes were unlikely candidates for their role in photographic history. They met as teenagers in 1916 when both attended the Riverdale Country School in New York City. Mannes was studying to be a concert pianist, Godowsky a violinist, and both came from families of successful musicians. What cemented their friendship, however, was a mutual fascination with photography.

Their adventure began in 1917 when they went to see what was advertised as a color movie. Instead, the film they saw was a technical disaster, a muddy mélange of imperfect hues. With the bravado of the young, they set out to create a better color-film process. Their families, charmed by their enterprise, provided $800. During the four years that Godowsky was at the University of California and Mannes was at Harvard, the collaboration continued, resulting finally in color film that required filters and was extremely difficult to project onto the screen.

Undaunted, "Man" and "God" decided to try another approach—to build color into the film emulsion itself. During the 1920's, with technical support from Eastman Kodak and financial aid from a New York investment firm, they made slow and painful progress. Nonetheless, Kodak invited them in 1930 to join their staff. Three years later they produced film for home use that contained two stable color emulsions. Kodak wanted to introduce the film at once, but Godowsky and Mannes pleaded for additional time to achieve what seemed within their grasp—the creation of film having three primary colors. The two researchers finally accomplished their task, and on April 15, 1935, Eastman Kodak introduced Kodachrome film to the world.

CANDY The human craving for something sweet is at least 4,000 years old. The Egyptian tombs of Tutankhamen and Ramses held instructions for making candy from honey, seeds, and sweet herbs. Greek and Roman physicians coaxed vile draughts down their patients' throats by coating the cup with honey. But the casual bonbon—the sweet, tasty tidbit—was not a commonplace item until the last half of the 19th century. In earlier times not everyone could afford sweets. In 1742, for example, sugar was selling in London for $2.75 a pound.

The origin of the word "candy" is not clear. The soldiers of Alexander the Great were fond of a Persian confection, a sweet reed coated with spices, honey, and coloring. The Persians called it *kand*, which is close to *qand*, the Arabic word for sugar; that may be the root.

When man learned to refine sugar from raw cane, the move toward the mass production and consumption of candy began. As early as the 7th century the Chinese possessed crude refining techniques. The Egyptians and Arabs produced a grade of sugar closer to the refined product we know today. In the 13th century Venice became the sugar capital of Europe, and Venetians were the first to purify sugar into fine, uniform crystals. They also pioneered the delicate and delectable art of sugar sculpture, creating enormous statues and intricate castles for royal banquets. Meanwhile, sugarcane was spreading around the world. Columbus, who failed to see the importance of chocolate when he found it in the New World, encouraged the planting of cane on his travels.

Cane grows best in hot, wet climates, most notably in the West Indies, but the world's sugar refineries sprang up in the large cities of Europe and eventually in the English colonies in America. Philadelphia, New York, and Boston were three important sugar cities. Then, in the mid-19th century, automatic candy-making machinery brought sweets to a sweet-toothed public at last.

Most candies start with a mixture of sugar and water called simple syrup. What the manufacturer does to this potion results in one of the three basic kinds of candy. Stick and hard candies are made of simple syrup that has been colored, flavored, and hardened. In the second basic group (nougats and marshmallows, for example) about 95 percent simple syrup and up to 5 percent other ingredients, such as egg white and gelatin, are mixed. These are whipped to produce air pockets in the mixture. Jellies, fudges, chocolates, and the like contain a substantial proportion of ingredients other than the simple syrup. Caramel, one of the third group, contains fat as an important component—to keep it from sticking to the teeth.

The candy bar, an American favorite, was a relatively late arrival, making its appearance in

The caption accompanying this engraving of a well-attended Boston taffy pull describes such events as "a delightful diversion for the Fall and Winter months."

1911, when such bars were first consumer-tested on baseball crowds. World War I, with its military demand for portable energy foods, turned the candy bar into the omnipresent wrapper crackler that it is.

Candy is now firmly embedded in American institutions, as it is occasionally in the teeth of children. Christmas is the top sales period for manufacturers. The traditional curved candy cane was actually an act of desperation, perpetrated by a frantic choirmaster in Germany about 1670. Restless children writhed in agony during his interminable Christmas pageants, so he decided to make sweet pacifiers to soothe them. In honor of the shepherds who visited the Christ child, he put a crook in what until then had been a straight piece of candy. Saint Valentine's Day, which naturally calls for a hearty candy present, may actually be the feast day of a Roman saint. Early Europeans believed that birds selected their mates on that day.

The oldest grocery trademark in America appears on Baker's chocolate. "La Belle Chocolatière," as it is called, is the portrait of a pretty waitress who served chocolate to a prince and later married him. The prince commissioned a work by Jean Etienne Liotard, who depicted the young woman in a Swiss costume serving chocolate. The painting became the trademark for Baker's chocolate in 1877.

In the French village of Montélimar in the 18th century, according to one story, there lived a woman who deluged her friends with special sweets made of sugar, honey, nuts, fruits, and eggs. These holiday gifts were magnificent, so much so that the recipients thanked her by saying, *"Tu nous gâtes"* ("You spoil us"). Thus they provided the nougat with its name, and were nearly right about candy in general. In truth, we all spoil ourselves with it, deliciously.

Unautomated candy vendor: Coney Island, July 4, 1933

CANNING Nicolas Appert, a French candymaker, is credited with inventing the process for preserving foods indefinitely in airtight containers—with an assist from Napoleon. The French emperor, with large and mobile armies to feed, offered a prize for such a discovery, and in 1809, after years of tinkering, Appert won some 12,000 francs, a sum equal to about $250,000 today. Nonetheless, Appert died a poor man without ever having understood why his technique worked. He thought the cause of spoilage was air, perhaps the oxygen in it. It remained for Louis Pasteur, the father of pasteurization, to explain that tiny microorganisms were the villains. Yet canners were slow to progress, mainly because they used ever-larger containers and failed to heat the contents properly. Thus canning dallied, a trial-and-error technique at best, and wise buyers postponed purchase until time and the absence of ominous bulges proved that a particular batch was safe to eat.

Appert himself used bottles and jars, much as home canners do today. But the tin container, known first as a canister and then a "can," appeared in the early 1800's in England and launched the industry. Cans were filled and sealed, except for a small hole in the top. The contents were heated substantially above the boiling point of water, and the hole was closed with a dab of solder. Then the cans were heated again, occasionally with disastrous results. A news report

Filthy working conditions were common in 1900's. These women shuck oysters in Baltimore.

in 1852 offered this account: ". . . steam was generated beyond the power of the canister to endure. As a natural consequence, the canister burst, the dead turkey sprang from his coffin of tinplate and killed the cook forthwith."

From the 1850's on, progress was steady and technological improvement regular, if unspectacular. John L. Mason produced his Mason jar, with its threaded top and rubber gaskets to keep air out. The Mason jar is still extremely popular today, enjoying a boom with collectors as well as canners. Machines to cut, shape, and seal cans were developed as well. Gail Borden learned how to condense and can milk, a breakthrough put quickly to the test by the Union Army in the Civil War. In the 1880's, after Mason's patent expired, the Ball brothers introduced their jar which became the world's most popular. In 1902 Alexander Kerr marketed the Economy lid, with the lid and gasket as a single unit.

Today, 175 billion cans of food are produced in the world each year, and such is the stride of technology that we are capable of opening most of them. The introduction of thin-walled cans made possible the invention of the can opener. One of the earliest, the Sprague Can Opener, was introduced in 1874. Since those early days, the devices have ranged from tiny watch-fob openers to powerful wall-units.

Things were not so complicated in Adm. William Parry's day. When he sailed to the Arctic

Pioneering by Henry John Heinz: each girl had her place in this immaculate dining room at the Heinz company in Pittsburgh. Foreladies were seated at right.

Circle in 1824, he took along a four-pound tin of roast veal. "Cut round on the top near to the outer edge with a chisel and hammer," the directions suggested. Parry didn't use the food, and the tin survived to reappear 114 years later in a military museum. Eager but cautious scientists opened the tin and fed bits of the veal to laboratory rats and a cat, but declined to try it themselves. All the lab animals survived—and thrived—on the 100-year-old meat.

CARBONATED DRINK Somewhere in Virginia toward the end of the 19th century, a doctor named Pepper owned a drugstore, had a beautiful daughter, and employed at his soda fountain an industrious young man given to experimentation.

When love blossomed over the soda fountain, however, the good doctor fired his ardent and creative employee, who went off to Waco, Texas, and took up residence at the soda fountain of the Old Corner Drug Store. One day, while pining for his lost love and whipping up various soft-drink flavors, he hit upon a combination of ingredients that seemed to please his customers. In tribute to the girl he had been forced to leave behind, his customers dubbed the drink "Dr Pepper." Eventually, the young inventor returned to Virginia to win the heart and hand of his sweetheart.

Meanwhile, back in Waco, R. S. Lazenby, a beverage chemist and patron of the Old Corner Drug Store, experimented with the new drink and, in 1885, put Dr Pepper on sale at a number of local soda fountains. Neither he nor the drink's creator, of course, could have guessed that one day Americans would be consuming over a billion bottles and cans of Dr Pepper annually.

A year after Lazenby sold his first Dr Pepper, John S. Pemberton of Atlanta, a pharmacist renowned for his patent medicines, concocted an elixir for the aid of the nervous and those who imbibed too much. The mixture caught on so well at the local soda fountain that Pemberton soon started manufacturing his creation: Coca-Cola. Fourteen of its ingredients—including caramel, coca leaves, cola nuts, caffeine, phosphoric acid, fruit flavors, and various spices—are today generally well known, but the name of the fifteenth, known only as 7X, is one of the best-guarded secrets in industry. So precious is the knowledge that the two or three employees permitted to know the content of 7X are not allowed to travel together.

In 1898 a North Carolina pharmacist, Caleb Bradham, came up with the recipe for Pepsi-Cola. Six years later, he was bottling his new drink for the first of the "Pepsi generations."

The story of carbonated water goes back some four centuries, when men first tried to duplicate nature's bubbling mineral waters. In 1772 Joseph Priestley, an Englishman, succeeded, and within a few years bottling companies began offering "soda water" to the public.

Ginger ale, the first flavor to revolutionize the soft-drink market, was developed by a Dr. Cantrall in Ireland about 1850 and was soon being shipped to the United States in bottles. Canada Dry, with a new, drier ginger ale, cracked the U.S. market in 1921 and soon came to dominate it. Still another innovator, Hyman Kirsch of Brooklyn, in 1952 introduced the sugar-free soft drink with his No-Cal sodas. Today diet sodas claim some 11 percent of the market, and an extraordinary market it is: soft drinks are the second-ranked beverage in the United States, trailing only milk and preceding coffee, which is third.

The ice-cream soda? It was born in Philadelphia in 1874, when a soda-fountain attendant absentmindedly plopped a scoop of ice cream into a glass of soda. His customer found the combination so delightful that the sprizzly soda was off and bubbling.

CARTOON Consider two cartoons, each depicting infantrymen hunched in muddy foxholes as shells burst overhead. The first caption reads: "Well if you knows of a better 'ole, go to it." The second caption: "Wisht I could stand up an' git some sleep." These classics, appearing nearly three decades apart, were the work of Bruce Bairnsfather, chronicler of the British Tommy of World War I, and of Bill Mauldin, whose Willie and Joe represented all U.S. dogfaces of World War II. Cartoonists in war—and peace—have always made it their business to dissect the horrors and madnesses, the pomposities and hypocrisies, the social foibles and fantasies of their times.

Unlike the gag cartoon, which is found mostly

"Believe It or Not"

Believe it or not, the last public appearance Le-Roy Ripley made was on a 1949 television program about the origin of "Taps." Ripley died of a stroke a few days later, but his syndicated cartoon strip survived. In its best years, it appeared in more than 300 newspapers in 38 countries and 17 languages, and reached 80 million readers.

Ripley's "Believe It or Not" cartoon feature was born in a moment of desperation and boredom. Ripley was a sports cartoonist for the New York *Globe*, where his employers had urged him to use "Bob" as his first name instead of LeRoy, which sounded unathletic to them. Stuck for an idea on a dull news day in December 1918, Ripley strung together a group of sports oddities in one cartoon feature. Included were two men who ran 100 yards in 11 seconds in a three-legged race, and an Australian who skipped a rope 11,810 times. Ripley thought about titling it "Champs and Chumps" but finally scrawled "Believe It or Not" on top. As reader response surged in, Ripley specialized first in sports oddities and, finally, weird facts of all kinds.

The cartoon item that brought Ripley national prominence was captioned "Lindbergh was the 67th man to make a nonstop flight over the Atlantic Ocean." Outraged Lindbergh fans fired off 200,000 letters and wires, failing to notice that Ripley had left out the word "alone" in his caption. Ripley was correct: 66 people had flown the Atlantic before Lindbergh—two in a plane, 31 in a British dirigible, and 33 in a German zeppelin.

The research for turning out a daily feature taxed Ripley severely, especially because he could read only English. In 1923 he hired a young Austrian clerk, Norbert Pearlroth, who knew 13 languages, and soon it was Ripley at the drawing board and Pearlroth at the public library. Pearlroth noticed in the late 1940's that American presidents who were elected every 20 years since 1840 had died in office. They ran the item with the headline "Who's Next?" and left blank the name of the president to be elected in 1960. He turned out to be John F. Kennedy.

Cartoons were first sketches for large works of art. This one is by Benozzo Gozzoli.

in magazines like *Punch* and *The New Yorker*, the editorial cartoon is at its best when bold and headline-fresh. One famous example appeared when Sen. Joseph McCarthy was at the height of his destructive powers; it came from the pen of the Washington *Post*'s Herbert Block. "Herblock," as he is known, sketched a hysterical McCarthy-esque figure scampering up a ladder with a bucket of water, to douse the Statue of Liberty's torch.

Yet the gag cartoon can strike with considerable social impact, too. A Peter Arno cartoon of the New Deal era presented a quartet of nattily dressed partygoers calling to a posh gathering: "Come along. We're going to the Trans-Lux to hiss Roosevelt." New York's Trans-Lux theaters may no longer show newsreels, but the cartoon lives on.

The cartoon, surprisingly enough, has been with us ever since skilled caricaturists decorated ancient Egyptian walls and Greek vases. Originally, the word, from the Italian *cartone* for "paper," was applied to artists' preliminary sketches for large works—paintings, frescoes, tapestries, and mosaics. The present sense of the word came into being in 1843, when *Punch* cleverly caricatured some of the ludicrous and overblown entries in a competition to select the designs for murals for London's new Houses of Parliament.

Modern concepts of cartooning, however, grew slowly out of caricature and social satire, beginning in the 16th century. In the early 18th century William Hogarth, in his series "A Rake's Progress," dug deeply at the dark side of the human condition. In 1832 Paris became the citadel

This is one World War II version of the political cartoon—a kind of satire born in 16th-century Europe.

of caricature with the founding of *Le Charivari*, a paper that played a crucial role in bringing down the "Citizen King," Louis Philippe. The pear-shaped monarch was an irresistible target for *Charivari*'s cartoonists. The paper's greatest contributor, Honoré Daumier, depicted the king as Gargantua—and won himself a six-month prison term. Eventually, *Le Charivari* inspired the creation of a number of papers: *Punch* in London; *Simplicissimus* in Munich; and *Judge*, *Puck*, and the original *Life* in the United States.

Benjamin Franklin designed America's first editorial cartoon in 1754. Calling for a united front against France, it depicted the colonies in the form of a snake sliced to pieces. "Join, or Die," the caption read. Paul Revere was another effective cartoon-propagandist. But true greatness in the art did not appear until 1869, when Thomas Nast began to assault New York City's corrupt Tammany Hall and, with his devilishly perceptive drawings, helped send its Boss Tweed to prison. "Them damn pictures," Tweed called them. In addition to his infamous Tammany tiger, Nast also designed the first Republican elephant and Democratic donkey. Watergate and the irrepressible editorial cartoonists of the 1970's were still 100 years away. Too strong, felt Adolph Ochs, founder of *The New York Times*, which has never run a political cartoon on its editorial page. "A cartoon," he is said to have explained, "cannot say 'on the other hand.'"

Humorous cartoons—gentler, funnier, and more concerned with bumbling husbands, castaways, and suburban living than with politics—came of age with the first issue of *The New Yorker* in 1925. Just as the English delighted in Ronald Searle's girls of St. Trinian's and Rowland Emett's zany railroaders, Americans chuckled at James Thurber's sad-eyed dogs and timid husbands, Helen Hokinson's stalwart clubwomen, and Charles Addams' cozy family of gentle monsters.

CASH REGISTER Strolling belowdecks on a transatlantic steamer in 1879, James Ritty, a Dayton, Ohio, saloonkeeper, chanced to notice a tachometer-like device in the ship's engine room. The instrument counted the revolutions of the propeller, and it occurred to Ritty that the same principle might be used to record customer transactions in his saloon. At that time his sales were not only pencil-kept and disorderly but also subject to the peculations of his bartenders.

Cutting short his vacation, Ritty returned home and with his brother soon created what became known as "Ritty's Incorruptible Cashier." This somewhat unwieldy machine combined a key-board, a large clockface that indicated in dollars and cents the keys being depressed, and a bell that signaled that cash was changing hands and, he hoped, not drifting into employee pockets. Unfortunately, Ritty's device did not go far enough, for it did not control the cash drawer or make a permanent record of transactions at the cashier's counter. Despite a number of improvements in the next few years, Ritty did not have the money to promote his invention, and he sold his business to a group of local businessmen who renamed the tiny firm The National Manufacturing Company. Soon the businessmen sold out to another Ohioan, John Henry Patterson. Patterson added an internal printing machine to the crude "thief catcher," which kept a permanent record of all transactions and also stamped out sales slips. Then with vision, energy, and determination, Patterson and his National Cash Register Company set out to sell the new machines—and revolutionized American marketing in the process.

CAT To protect its feathered friends, the birds, the Illinois legislature in 1949 passed a bill prohibiting cats from running free. The governor, Adlai E. Stevenson, justified his veto in this way: "The problem of cat versus bird is as old as time. If we attempt to resolve it by legislation who knows but what we may be called upon to take sides as well in the age old problems of dog versus cat, bird versus bird, even bird versus worm. [We] already have enough to do without trying to control feline delinquency."

Ailurophobes, or cat haters, have charged cats with delinquency, and worse, but cat lovers have gone so far as to deify the animal. In the ancient city of Bubastis, Egyptians venerated the cat-headed goddess Bastet, who represented pleasure, music, and the dance. Hers was the most elegant temple in all of Egypt, the scene of joyous festivals where wine flowed freely. Pilgrims brought mummies of their own cats there to be interred in sacred ground.

Egyptians worshiped the cat goddess Bastet.

If cats had a heyday, that was it, about 3000 B.C. The cats of Egypt, especially if they were black, led a rich, full, pampered life and, like their goddess, were said to possess nine lives. The law decreed that the bereaved household of a dead cat shave their eyebrows and enter a long period of

"Thief Catcher"

Whenever John Henry Patterson detected a note of complacency in the performance of his employees, he would chide them with the observation that "the business that is satisfied with itself is dead." Patterson, who made the cash register an essential tool of American retailing, was himself an energetic salesman who never took success for granted.

Born in 1844 to a prosperous family on a farm outside Dayton, Ohio, he served briefly in the Civil War, went on to college—a waste of valuable time he later decided—and eventually settled down to run a coal business in Coalton, Ohio, with a company store as a sideline. The coal business prospered, probably because he supervised every aspect of its operation, but the general store continually suffered losses. The reason, Patterson discovered, was that his clerks discounted prices to friends and even dipped into the cash drawer on their own behalf. Unable to keep an eye on everything, he decided to test a new machine he had heard about—the cash register. Eventually, Patterson bought the tiny company that made the machines and, with a selling genius unique in American history, turned it into a giant.

Most of all, Patterson believed in the "hard sell," and he bombarded each "P.P." (Probable Purchaser) with dozens of brochures, letters, and other promotional materials until some literally begged for mercy. His salesmen, eventually dubbed the "American Selling Force," were trained in special schools and groomed with as much care as troops being readied for battle. Their appearance, manners, speech, and sales techniques were finely tuned.

In return for high performance and absolute loyalty, he offered generous commissions and guaranteed territories to his salesmen, and a wide range of unheard-of benefits to his factory workers. The National Cash Register plant in Dayton featured good natural lighting, attractive landscaping, recreational facilities, subsidized hot lunches, medical care, inspirational lectures, and a training school. Frequently asked why he spent his money so recklessly, Patterson always gave the same answer: "It pays." And lest anyone ask about his seeming munificence, he kept a sign outside his office: "Omit all compliments about welfare work."

Patterson enjoyed the role of eccentric and frequently inflicted his latest passion on those around him. At various times employees endured forced horseback riding, vegetarianism, hot-water drinking, calisthenics, and "Fletcherizing," which required that every bite of food be chewed 32 times for better digestion and slimmer waists. Whether or not those activities were responsible, Patterson lived to be 77. He was on a business trip to Atlantic City when he died.

Cat tale: Puss in Boots claims new clothes for his shivering master in this engraving by Gustave Doré.

mourning. And killing a cat, accidentally or otherwise, was punishable by death.

Little is known about the cat prior to its domestication more than 5,000 years ago, some 45,000 years after the dog became somebody's Spot or Rover. The cat receives no biblical mention, though it has figured in the myths of the Orient. In ancient Burma and Siam, people believed that at death a holy man's soul entered the body of a cat and whiled away there until the tabby died, when the soul went straight to paradise.

The cat's good fortune continued for a time, as its species sailed the known world aboard Phoenician trading ships. The Romans hailed cats as defenders of the granaries against the evil rat. Indeed, the Roman goddess of grain and the harvest sometimes assumed the guise of a cat.

But in medieval Europe the cat began to fall from grace. Black cats in particular were thought to be the familiars of witches and warlocks. The black cat crossing one's path became a satanic omen. In Paris a midsummer custom was to burn a basket or sack full of live cats over a bonfire; the charred remains were grabbed up by the celebrants who believed them to be luck-bringers. In 1648 Louis XIV—otherwise reputed to be a cat fancier, treating his pets to the sumptuous luxury of Versailles—joined the festivities by kindling the fire and dancing by its flames. The bonfires glowed throughout France, England, and Flanders. The cat, which represented the devil, could not suffer enough, it was said.

After that, feline fortunes improved. Cat lovers, including such luminaries as Hugo, Balzac, the Brontë sisters, Gladstone, Darwin, Lincoln, and Mark Twain, were in the ascendancy once again. Samuel Johnson fed oysters to his cat, Hodge, at the fish stalls while cat hater Boswell shuddered. When Charles Dickens' cat, who was deaf but in attendance while the master wrote, reckoned it time to quit, he would snuff out the candle. Winston Churchill's marmalade cat, Nelson, was a conspicuous presence at wartime cabinet meetings.

According to one story, the smiling Cheshire cat of *Alice's Adventures in Wonderland* had its origins in the Cheshireman's pride in his political independence after the Norman Conquest—a pride that amused even his cats. So he shaped and sold his fine cheeses in the form of a cat, with a grin on its face.

Today, there are more than 30 million cats in North America, with one out of five U.S. households enjoying at least one puss-in-residence. In 1909 the Cat Fanciers' Association opened a studbook so that America's Longhairs and Shorthairs could be awarded the pedigrees they deserve (of which there are, officially, 36).

Cat lovers catch mood signals from the bend of the tail: carried high = proud and contented; extended straight back = stalking; curled against the body = scared or worried; and thrashing = angry. But it is unlikely that they know the number of bones in a cat's body—230 to a man's 206—or that the purring sound does not originate in the throat but in the cat's blood system, a vibration that arises from the wall of a major blood vessel in the chest area.

The cat's sense of hearing is sharp indeed, extending to such high frequencies that it catches the ultrasonic chattering of a small mouse about to venture abroad. The cat's eyes are keen, of

The Colosseum in Rome, where lions once roared, is now home to packs of cats living on mice and handouts.

course, gathering a great deal of light and allowing the cat to see quite clearly in the near-darkness. But it is almost color-blind, seeing only the changing light. If nothing is moving in its line of vision, then it sees nothing. To compensate, it moves its eyes slightly, making the scene itself move and thus become visible.

Life span? Many cats reach the ripe age of 17 or even more, upwards of 100 in a human equivalent. But that's only *one* life; there are still eight to go.

CERAMICS One modern-day soothsayer has suggested that if our civilization were dug up by archeologists thousands of years from now, the most obvious item to survive would be the toilet bowl. He may be right. Being ceramic, the toilet bowl is one of man's most indestructible creations, able to withstand the forces of decay and dissolution that eventually destroy most of our other products.

The oldest fire-hardened clay objects ever found were unearthed in Czechoslovakia. The pellets and small animal figures discovered in a crude kiln are thought to be about 25,000 years old, but pottery making has probably been around since the discovery of fire hundreds of thousands of years ago.

Though clay hardens in the air or in the sun, it will return to its malleable state when wet. When clay is heated, however, changes take place that prevent it from reverting to its natural state. Clay

Cats have always been good people-catchers, as shown here at Mrs. Goodman's cat hospital in New York City.

63

Even the walls were ceramic in the Porcelain Room of the Royal Villa at Portici near Naples.

duce semiprecious stones, came up with the combination of ingredients and firing technique. In 1710 Augustus the Strong of Saxony founded a royal factory at Meissen and hoped to keep the recipe secret, but by the end of the 18th century true porcelain was being manufactured all over Europe.

In colonial America most pottery was simple, crude redware made from common brick clay and glazed. (Frontier settlers had to make do with carved wooden "table furniture.") Porcelain was not widely available until the mid-1800's. Today the ceramics industry in the United States generates some $8–10 billion in annual sales.

Mass-production techniques were introduced in the early 1900's, and today clay is mixed in mammoth machines, designs are stamped on objects by a press, and firing is done while the pieces move through the kiln on a conveyor belt.

The industrial age spawned a new breed of ceramics. Mass-produced porcelain spark-plug insulators are harder than diamonds, and other ceramics are used to control the heat in atomic reactors. Because of their ability to withstand the rigors of extremely high temperatures, certain modern ceramics have even gone into space—as nose cones and rocket fins.

fired at about 900° F becomes earthenware; when fired at about 2200° F, the result is stoneware. When pure white clay, with powdered rock added, is fired, usually at a still higher temperature, the product becomes translucent and hard—porcelain.

The history of any great culture can be read in its ceramics. In many cases, pottery shards are the only surviving relics of the peoples that made them. Archeologists can read in these fragments the social habits and technical skills of the people as well as trace their trade routes, since pottery vessels were a popular item for barter in the ancient world. Some early potters probably smeared clay on the inside of woven baskets and put them in the fire, burning away the fibers and leaving an earthenware pot. Others made pots by shaping them with their hands, in molds, and by coiling a long clay "rope" to form the vessel's walls. Pots made on a potter's wheel, invented at least 5,500 years ago, are much more uniformly round. Ancient Greeks decorated pottery with clay paint instead of glaze, a style copied by Josiah Wedgwood in England centuries later.

The Chinese made the first porcelain about 800 A.D., and it later became the rage in Europe, where it was called chinaware or simply china. European ceramists tried for generations to make their own china but did not succeed until 1708, when a German alchemist, in an effort to repro-

CHAIR Since the day man tired of squatting on his haunches, the chair has been his alter ego, an extension of himself molded to his frame, its parts named after his—arms, legs, feet, back, and seat. The lowly of history slumped on stools; the well positioned had chairs with a back, with arms;

royalty sat on thrones; and the office of the pope is, appropriately, the Chair of St. Peter.

The golden throne found in Tutankhamen's tomb is, despite its ornateness, "basic" in design, as was the Egyptian folding stool, a handy, portable seat for traveling dignitaries in their day (and for campers in ours). The chairs in the Middle Ages were noble; in the Renaissance, elaborate; in the era of Louis XIV and Louis XV, luxuriously upholstered; in Classic revivals, chaste; in the Victorian Age, opulent; in the 20th century, experimental.

Eames chairs stacked up

New materials caused small revolutions in chair design, such as Samuel Pratt's method (in the early 1800's) for enclosing steel coil springs within the upholstery and, a century later, the coming of latex foam, bent plywood, and rubber webbing. In 1925 Marcel Breuer of the Bauhaus school was the first to use nickel-plated steel tubing. His inspiration, it has been said, came while admiring the handlebars of a new bicycle. And out of Milan in 1967 came the inflatable plastic lounge chair, packaged with foot pump and patch kit and weighing a mere 12 pounds.

CHEESE "How can you govern a country which produces 265 kinds of cheese?" The speaker was Charles de Gaulle and the country France. But where the general got his figures is anybody's guess because the varieties of French cheese, Frenchmen say proudly, are innumerable.

And when the rest of the world's cheeses are taken into account—going from such favorites as Emmentaler, which almost everybody calls "Swiss," to the Cheddars of either Somerset, England, or Wisconsin, U.S.A.—the cheese counter's mind boggles. The Nepalese, for example, have yak's milk cheese, the Lapps reindeer cheese, and to this day the Italians sometimes use milk of the water buffalo to create their beloved Mozzarella.

Made mostly from curds that have been concentrated and ripened, cheeses have been around since man started milking cows and goats and sheep. According to Greek mythology, the Olympian gods first blessed the world with the know-how of cheese making. But it was the monks in their 12th-century abbeys who produced Camembert; and the Trappists in 1816 who created Port Salut. Processed cheese appeared in Switzerland early in the 20th century, just before James L. Kraft, a Chicago cheese peddler, began experimenting with the pasteurizing of cheeses.

It may take scientific expertise to add special cultures to a cheese to develop a white mold on its rind or to inject molds to create blue-veining, but the end products—Camembert and Roquefort—are

customs

"Sit Ye, Rock and Think"
reads the headpiece of many an old rocking chair. This gentle offspring of the chair and the rocking cradle (circa the Middle Ages) was a Yankee notion of the mid-1700's, sometimes attributed to Benjamin Franklin. At the outset, furniture makers fixed curved runners—sharp and so narrow that they were called "carpet cutters"—onto the legs of an existing chair. The true rocker, which began to be produced about 1790, and was soon a fixture in every American home, outlived such bizarre variations as the English "digestive chair" devised by a Dr. Calvert. In the 1920's the rockers were banished to the attic, where most remained until January 1961, when John F. Kennedy brought his own to the White House.

---

at the same time delectable art. Reading the ripeness and quality of cheeses is an art, as well. The cheese expert taps a hard cheese with a mallet and knows that a hollow sound means "too many holes." He pinches the cheese for resilience and bores into it with a cheese trier or iron to check texture, color, and age. In the taster's jargon, cheeses may smell good or fresh or sweet or sour. But most of all they must carry the aroma of the milks they are made from, except for Japanese "blue cheese," which is made of soya flour and ripened by a special Oriental fungal mold.

CHEST OF DRAWERS The earliest ancestor of the chest of drawers was the trunk, an ancient storage container gouged from the trunk of a tree. These cumbersome dugouts were replaced by caskets and boxes, which as early as the 8th century

words

The French Had a Word For It

From the French *coucher* came the "couch," from the Arabic *soffah* the "sofa," and from the Turkish *divan* you-know-what.

But few people know one from another. Actually, the couch, a long, upholstered seat with a raised back and headrest, evolved from the "day bed," a 16th-century English design that also developed, in the France of Louis XIV, into the sofa. The sofa is for sitting rather than reclining on—Dagwood Bumstead notwithstanding—while the day bed is a couch-by-day and a bed-by-night. The daybed is itself a variation on the "settee." The settee gave us the *chaise longue* (French) and the "kangaroo sofa" (American), among others. In 19th-century England the "chesterfield" (overstuffed, buttoned, named for one of the earls of C.) appeared. No one seems to know just where the "davenport," a large sofa, came from. As for the divan, like those seats that ran along the walls of the Turkish council chamber, it is deeply cushioned.

in Europe became popular as strongboxes for safe-keeping jewels and relics. The chest was usually kept in an upper-story chamber, the most inaccessible room of the house. Over time the small chests gave way to larger chests, similar to the blanket chest and to a chest-with-drawers, a storage case with a single row of drawers on the bottom. Furniture makers began to see that drawers were a convenient way of compartmentalizing the space. An English inventory of 1596 lists a "cubborde with drawing boxes," perhaps the first recorded use of a stacked chest of drawers.

CHEWING GUM Most Texans and a good many other Americans know the name of Antonio López de Santa Anna as the Mexican general who led the devastating attack on San Antonio's Alamo in 1836. But Santa Anna also left the United States a happier legacy—chewing gum. In 1866 Santa Anna, the deposed dictator of Mexico, took refuge on Staten Island, New York. According to one tale, even as he prepared to flee his homeland, Santa Anna had the foresight to pack in his baggage a very large wad of chicle. (This gummy substance, made from the sap of the Yucatán's sapodilla tree, had been chewed in times of stress by Mexicans since the days of the ancient Mayas.) When Santa Anna thought it safe to return to Mexico some months later, he left behind his old chew, some say in a desk drawer.

Thomas Adams, an acquaintance on Staten Island and a sometime inventor, was intrigued by the stuff and thought he might find a way to vulcanize it into a new kind of rubber. Failing this, he tried to turn the chicle into an adhesive for false teeth, again without success. Finally, Adams boiled it, rolled it out with a rolling pin, and came up with an improved version of Santa Anna's original chewing gum.

Tested in a New Jersey candy store, the gum was a runaway success, and in 1871 Adams hurriedly developed and patented the first gum-making machine. The machine extruded what the manufacturer proudly called ribbons of "snapping and stretching gum," notched at regular intervals so that the retail shopkeeper could break off and sell penny lengths of the unpackaged product. Other manufacturers soon entered the field, offering appealing new flavors and eye-catching packaging. To keep ahead, Adams bought exclusive rights to a vending machine and placed hundreds of them in heavily trafficked public places such as railway stations. But the competition continued to nibble at the market until Charles R. Flint, one of the giants of finance at the turn of the century, induced Adams and five other companies to merge in 1899 into the American Chicle Company, the "chewing gum trust."

From that time on, chewing gum has built several fortunes, and reached virtually every segment of society. One manufacturer, William Wrigley, Jr., who chose to remain independent of the

Practice makes big bubbles: this creation is by Reinaldo Gutierrez, a Fleer worker in the Dominican Republic.

breeding that it was years before she would discuss it in print. But times changed, and Miss Post eventually conceded grudgingly that it would be all right "wherever formal standards of behavior are not in force." Presumably, if slugger Mickey Mantle chewed it to calm his nerves at bat, or if a discreet stick of gum helps the office worker pass his day with equanimity, even the arbiters of good manners must approve. But a few restrictions remain: "Certainly not in church, or during recitation periods in school," says the staunch Miss Post. "And certainly not when wearing formal clothes!"

chewing gum trust, put so much money into advertising that his gum at one time was the most advertised product in the world. Thanks to that sort of huckstering, per capita gum consumption has risen smartly over the years. In the late 19th century gum chewing was ranked as "mainly a female accomplishment; the few men who chew gum may be supposed to do so by reason of gallantry," burbled an 1890 issue of *Harper's*. But by 1914, when a formal survey was conducted, Americans of all ages and sexes were taken with the habit at the rate of 39 sticks per person per year; by 1925 the rate was 100 sticks. And in World War II servicemen reportedly chewed their way through more than 3,000 sticks per man annually, though they generously shared some of the sticky stuff with local folk they met: witness the Stone Age tribesmen in one of the Pacific islands who became adept at blowing bubble gum thanks to their G.I. mentors. Before gum chewing became popular around the world, it startled some newcomers to the United States. Sholom Aleichem viewed the habit through an immigrant's eyes: "People sit and keep chewing on something, like animals chewing their cud. Later I learned . . . it's a kind of candy made out of rubber. American people chew gum all their lives long without stopping."

There is also the story of Mission Gum Drop: the War Department, wanting to encourage Philippine citizens on Japanese-held islands, printed Gen. Douglas MacArthur's well-known promise "I shall return" on the outside of gum wrappers and dropped them on towns.

As for chewing-gum etiquette, social critics of the custom have been legion, and Emily Post, for one, thought it so far outside the pale of good

CHICKEN The domestic chicken has no privacy. Ever since its development from wild jungle fowl in Asia, probably 5,000 years ago, man has scrutinized and regulated its diet, weight, sex life, diseases, beauty—and fighting qualities. Cockfights were staged well before the birth of Christ, and it may be that the sport, rather than hunger, first focused man's attention on the chicken. Whatever the case, as early as 4,000 years ago, the Egyptians built brick incubators capable of housing 10,000 chicks at a time.

Because its meat is an inexpensive and often elegant source of protein, the chicken is probably the most common bird in the world. Farmers in the United States receive $6 billion per year for

Pugnacious roosters tangle during a cockfight in Costa Rica. The "sport" is one of the world's oldest.

eggs and broilers alone. Americans eat more than 40 pounds of chicken apiece each year, and 276 eggs, even though the industry has been hurt slightly by concern about the 250 milligrams of cholesterol found in each egg.

Typically, an egg farmer buys pullets at the time they are about to lay. They are already inoculated against disease, and are placed in laying houses and put on special diets. The champion egg-laying breed is the White Leghorn. A good hen produces nearly an egg a day, or about 300 a year. Farmers may use electric lights to create the length of day that is best for their breed. Eggs may be brown or white, with no difference in quality or nutritive value. Eggs and their embryos also are important in medical research; they make an excellent medium for culturing bacteria, testing drugs, and producing vaccines.

Most meat chickens are sold as broilers or fryers. These male and female chickens are usually 9 to 12 weeks old; scientifically fed, they can become 4-pounders in that time. Roasters are somewhat older, and usually male; many stewing chickens are female, well past their laying primes.

The modern U.S. poultry industry probably got its greatest boost from Daniel Webster. In 1849 he was an exhibitor at the first show devoted exclusively to poultry. It was held in the Boston Garden. Because of lively political interest in Webster, the press gave the show extensive coverage, and chicken farming became a respectable business, not just something for women and children to attend to "out back." For the chicken, the age of automation was just beginning.

Even a windup rooster might crow over the surrealist elegance of this lithograph, "Strolling," by Herbert Fox.

CHOCOLATE The Spanish explorer Hernán Cortés gave chocolate to the world. When he arrived at the Aztec court in Mexico in 1519, he found the cacao bean being used as money and was fascinated by *chocolatl*, a beverage served in gold goblets to royalty. Montezuma supposedly drank 50 cups a day. The Aztecs thought the cacao tree was a gift from their god Quetzalcoatl, who in their legend had been banished by the other gods for giving divine possessions to humans. Quetzalcoatl had promised to return, and in a mistake that would cost them their civilization, the Aztecs confused Cortés with their returning deity. They welcomed their conqueror with a golden cup of chocolate. The Spanish kept the cultivation and manufacture of chocolate a secret for a hundred years, but by the mid-1600's the

words

The Chicken and the Egg

The chicken, its products, and its habits infect our language like, well, chicken pox. "Don't count your chickens before they're hatched," is based on Aesop's sad fable about a woman who did. "Chicken-hearted" and "chicken-livered" suggest cowardliness. Yet such expressions slander the bird, which if not overly bright, is quite brave.

A "nest egg" is an egg, usually fake, placed in the nest to encourage a hen to produce more eggs. To "lay an egg," however, for humans at least, is to fail, a meaning derived from the early sports term "goose egg," for no score. In 1929 *Variety* headlined the crash:

"Wall Street Lays an Egg."

To "walk on eggs" is to be careful—extremely careful. "Chicken feed" is trivial, of course, except to chickens. "Running around like a chicken with its head cut off" is self-explanatory, at least to one who has seen a chicken in such a state.

"Egghead" is a pejorative term for an overly intellectual individual whose skull is perhaps high-domed and whose brains are on the soft side. Chicken Little may have been scrambled, but clearly the bustling, self-reliant Little Red Hen was not. The term "bad egg," meaning a bad person, first appeared in the mid-1800's.

About 50 years later, linguistic justice was done, and the term "good egg" also became 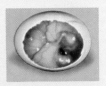 popular. The "Easter egg," most ubiquitous of egg symbols, originated in Persia. It was adopted by the Jews and later became a sign of the Resurrection for early Christians. With it arose the most profound of philosophical questions: "Which came first, the chicken or the egg?" The scientific explanation may be egg-headed and chicken-hearted, but it is correct: they evolved together.

beverage was served all over Europe.

Today, the leaders in cacao production are Ghana, Brazil, and Nigeria. The cacao bean grows in pods of 20 to 50 beans on the trunk and major limbs of carefully cultivated trees 15 to 25 feet high. The pods are split open and the beans scooped out, along with a pulpy whitish mass. Fermentation, at temperatures well over 100° F, separates the beans from the pulp, dries their hulls, and alters their original bitter, acid taste. Then the beans are dried further for shipping.

Within the beans are "nibs," dark brown particles of chocolate. When they are ground and heated, fats called cocoa butter are released. The remainder, called chocolate liquor, can then be pressed into bars and sold as baking chocolate. To get cocoa, manufacturers pulverize bars of chocolate liquor into powder. To get the kinds of chocolate we eat, they add cocoa butter and sugar and, for milk chocolate, powdered milk.

From the Aztecs on, people have had various beliefs about the powers of chocolate. The Aztecs, and later Casanova, thought it was an aphrodisiac. Some have felt that it inhibits dysentery. The truth is simpler. Because the cacao bean contains a mild stimulant called theobromine, plus caffeine, it picks one up somewhat, but not as much as a cup of coffee. And it tastes good. That is undoubtedly why the 18th-century Swedish naturalist Linnaeus formally named it *Theobroma cacao*, meaning that cacao was the food of the gods.

It's not the message but the medium: chocolate. In Barcelona, Spain a chocolatero *touches up his sculpture of Salvador Dalí at work on a chocolate canvas for entry in an annual springtime candymakers' contest.*

CHROMIUM The metal chromium helps put the rich red in a ruby and color the emerald green, and it is the base of a brilliant paint called chrome yellow. Princess Charlotte, daughter of King George IV of England, liked the color so well that she had her entire coach covered with it. That set an irresistible fashion for other coach owners, leading one scholar to speculate that the princess was the unwitting inventor of today's ubiquitous urban workhorse, the Yellow Cab.

Unlike many other indispensable metals, chromium was discovered relatively late. It was identified as a metallic element by Nicolas Vauquelin, a French chemist, in 1797. Because it is so active, chromium is never found in an isolated state. It appears most often as part of a mixture with oxygen and iron called chromite. A rare mineral, chromite is not evenly distributed around the world; the leading producers of the ore are the Soviet Union, South Africa, Turkey, the Philippines, and Rhodesia.

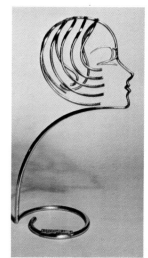

Precious metal: the Art Deco chrome hat stand sports a 1920's profile.

Because it can be polished to a bright finish and resists corrosion, chromium is often plated on other metals, thus producing the gleam on millions of bumpers and miles of trim. Mixed with other metals, it forms stainless steel (which is at least 11 percent chromium). Most importantly, it makes steel harder and stronger, a fact one 19th-century advertising circular elucidated with poignancy. Called *The Jail-Breaker's Catechism*, it told of a convict who repeatedly broke out of jail until he found himself behind bars made of chromium steel.

CIGAR Besides discovering America in 1492, Columbus also discovered the cigar. He and his crew were the first Europeans to see New World Indians smoking tobacco rolled in leaves. The word probably comes from *sik'ar*, the Mayan Indian term for smoking.

Rodrigo de Jerez was the first of Columbus' shipmates to try a cigar, on October 28 of the same year, in what is now the Dominican Republic. The Indians had already been puffing away happily for at least 500 years. The Aztecs perhaps puffed more happily than other tribes—they laced their cigars with hallucinogenics from such plants as mushrooms. This may be why one explorer noted, "The effect [of the smoke] is a certain drowsiness of the whole body accompanied by a certain species of intoxication. . . ." Tobacco alone seemed to be good enough for Europeans. In 1567 a French description of the effects of tobacco stated that smokers "say that their hunger and thirst are allayed, their strength is restored and their spirits are refreshed. . . ." Until the late 18th century, doctors prescribed smoking as an antidote for everything from bad breath to lockjaw.

Spain became the first European country to embrace cigar smoking. After the Napoleonic wars, however, which brought French and English troops to Spain, the practice spread to other European countries. Americans took up the habit about the mid-18th century and made their own at home. Cigars developed by Pennsylvania Dutch farmers in Conestoga, Pennsylvania, were favored by drivers of Conestoga wagons, and the smokes acquired the nickname "stogies." By the 1800's cigar factories were flourishing throughout the eastern United States. They turned out cigars in an amazing variety of sizes and shapes, eventually making them as small as the 1¼-inch delgado or as long as a 6-foot-2-inch model ordered by a maharajah. Most of the more popular shapes were less extreme: torpedo-shaped ideales, fat perfectos, thin cheroots, and long, straight panatelas.

Some of the world's best cigars, Havanas, are produced in Vuelta Abajo, a region in Cuba that is "a natural hothouse and a natural humidor" by

Back from America, Sir Walter Raleigh smokes England's first pipe while a servant rushes to save him.

virtue of its soil, wind, water, and sun. Curiously, when stored under proper conditions, Havanas all over the world ferment at the same time—which corresponds to the onset of the Cuban summer. The legend that these cigars are rolled by beautiful girls on their naked thighs is, alas, false.

Cigars have inspired a staunch devotion. The composer Franz Liszt obtained a dispensation to smoke cigars at the monastery where he spent the last years of his life. George Sand, one of the many prominent women who fancied cigars, wrote that they filled her solitary hours "with a million gracious images." (About one million American women are estimated to smoke cigars today.)

Ulysses S. Grant smoked about 25 cigars a day and gave more away—with explosive loads in them. The father of psychoanalysis, Sigmund Freud, once remarked, "A cigar may be a phallic symbol, but . . . it is also a cigar." Mark Twain, in his seventies, attributed his vigor to having never smoked—more than one cigar at a time. When Winston Churchill's tobacco store was hit by a bomb during World War II, the owner felt required to phone the prime minister at 2 o'clock in the morning to assure him that his supply of 8-inch Havanas had escaped unscathed. Love of cigars has assured at least one man a place in history. Woodrow Wilson's vice president, Thomas Marshall, dismayed at the poor quality of smokes made under government contract, allowed that "what this country needs is a really good five-cent cigar."

Tobacco seller's fantasy: passing of the leaf, and animals that smoke, in an 1860's ad by Lorillard company.

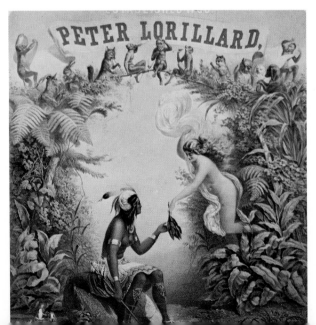

Pipe dream: a water pipe so long 10 girls must carry it.

The Artistry of Lighting Up

"**B**e nonchalant—light a Murad," an early cigarette ad implored, and since then the mannerisms smokers use to indulge their passion have been cultivated as personal trademarks. Smokers who wish to appear macho still hold a cigarette in a cupped hand, a style made famous by Humphrey Bogart. Bette Davis set the mode for a generation of women smokers when she puffed while looking meaningfully into the eyes of Paul Henreid (who lit cigarettes two at a time) in *Now, Voyager.* Authoritative cigar smokers still chomp their stogies while giving orders ("See!")—in the manner of Edward G. Robinson, whom grateful cigar importers once named "Mister Cigar." And what pipe smoker doesn't puff methodically and meditatively, *à la* Walter Pidgeon?

Cigar smokers are probably more rigid than most other smokers. Whole books have been written on how cigars should be lit and smoked. Examples: Use only a wooden match or wood shaving. (A gas lighter, never a fluid one, will do in a pinch.) Use a small flame and never let the flame actually touch the cigar.

In late 1800's bloomer-clad smokers puffed up a storm.

Pipe smokers have their own etiquette. The quick puffing of nervous cigarette smokers is definitely bad form. The pipe should be caressed in the smoker's hand, and some think the oils from the skin darken and individualize each pipe. The do's and don'ts of cleaning a pipe must be rigorously followed. Topping the list: Never clean the bowl with a knife.

Early tobacco users, the Indians of North America probably had the most rigid smoking customs of all. Tobacco smoke was an offering; if a celebrant mishandled a ceremonial pipe, the gods might withhold good fortune. Not to accept a proffered peace pipe indicated a willingness to participate in a bloodbath. In many European countries offering a cigarette still denotes hospitality.

The hardest-to-come-by skill is that of dyed-in-the-wool cigarette smokers—rolling your own. The practice goes deep into American lore. The Bull Durham tobacco tag dangling from a shirt pocket is practically the badge of the American cowboy, past and present (and tenderfoots pretending to be cowboys). It is said that an expert can roll a cigarette with one hand, in a windstorm, while on a horse at full gallop.

CIGARETTE The Spanish explorers who landed in Mexico in 1518 were probably the first to bum a cigarette. Their hosts were natives who smoked the earliest king-size version on record—hollow reeds nearly a foot long filled with crushed tobacco. The paper-wrapped cigarette was born much later, according to one account, in the thick of battle between the Egyptians and Turks in 1832. When an enemy cannonball smashed the communal clay pipe belonging to a group of Egyptian cannoneers, they stuffed their tobacco into the hollow paper torches used to touch off their guns.

Cigarette making as an industry was also a fortune of war. During the Crimean War (1853–56) English troops captured an entire train carrying Russian officers. The English traded their prisoners but kept the Russians' homemade cigarettes, which became such a hit in London that several tobacconists (including one named Philip Morris) began producing them for sale. Tobacco-shop owners in New York soon joined the competition.

Cigarette making was mechanized in 1880 when a Virginian, James Albert Bonsack, invented a machine that wrapped cut tobacco in a long paper tube and then cut the tube into cigarette-size lengths. Machine-made cigarettes lowered the price and put a pack within the reach of anyone who had a nickel. More than a billion cigarettes were manufactured in the United States in 1885 (more than that number are smoked daily in the United States now), but cigarettes did not become more popular than pipes, snuff, cigars, or chewing tobacco until 1921.

Almost everyone who smoked cigarettes became familiar with "smoker's cough," but no one did much about it until 1952 when the P. Lorillard Company, taking note of the growing trend toward filtered cigarettes in Europe, began making a cigarette with an efficient filter. Within six years, the filter market skyrocketed from a fraction of 1 percent of sales to 50 percent. Filter smoking shot up again after the U.S. Surgeon General's report in 1964 that "cigarette smoking is a health hazard." (Lung, throat, and mouth cancer, heart disease, emphysema, and facial wrinkling are all said to be caused by tobacco and its smoke.) Per capita cigarette consumption in the United States fell immediately after the report, but began to rise significantly again in 1971.

Why is a proven health hazard so popular? Behavioral scientists have suggested that smokers use cigarettes as a substitute for almost everything—from not having sex to not having been breast-fed as infants. One poll showed that cigarette smoking is so desperately important to some smokers that they fear they will lose control of their entire lives if they quit. (The millions of smokers who try to quit every year know how they feel.) Other experts believe that the need to smoke may be inherited. It should come as no surprise to anyone that recent scientific data indicates that nicotine is addictive. Whatever the appeal of cigarettes, it is so strong that many scientists believe that trying to persuade American smokers to kick the habit is futile. As Mark Twain put it: "To quit smoking is the easiest thing I ever did; I ought to know because I've done it hundreds of times."

CLOCK What is a day? Who decided it should have 24 hours? And 60 minutes per hour? Hieroglyphics show that to Egyptians an "instant" meant the time it took a hippopotamus to look up and check for danger. Hundreds of such nonstandard time units must have been used in the ancient world.

Italian astrolabe, 1582, for checking time, longitude, latitude.

But by roughly 1500 B.C. Egyptian astronomers had arrived at a system of 12-hour days and nights, or the 24-hour day. They marked the passage of the sunny hours by sundials and of the night hours by the rising of certain stars or by water dripping slowly out of a marked bowl. The Greek philosopher Plato is said to have devised a whistling water clock that called his students to study at 4 o'clock in the morning. Roman senators used a water clock to time their speeches, and some-times they muddied the waters to slow down the flow. In the north, where sunlight was scarce in winter, King Alfred of 9th-century England relied on his special 4-hour candles to measure time.

Finally, toward the end of the 13th century, the first "clock" (from the Latin *clocca* meaning "bell") struck in a monastery tower. A series of gears regulated the unwinding of a stone-weighted rope. When the stone reached a certain spot, an hour had passed, and a man climbed up

Compass-sundials like the one shown here (crafted in Augsburg, Germany, in 1566) were popular pocket items for centuries.

the tower to pull the bell and call the monks to prayer. By 1335 Milan had a public clock that automatically struck the hours. And by 1350 most European cities had tower clocks with faces and hour hands and a bell.

About 1500 a German locksmith replaced the rope-and-stone combination with a coiled-spring mechanism. A Dutchman built the first pendulum clock in 1656, and in 1675 an Englishman improved upon it, adding a pendulum to mark seconds.

During slower-moving eras standardization of time meant relatively little: no one was able to travel fast enough from one place to another for time differences to have an effect. By the end of the 19th century, however, when trains began to hurtle great distances in a short time, knowing

words

From Tweed to *Corde du Roi*

About 1830 a Scottish weaver shipped some wool cloth to a London merchant, billing him for so many yards of "tweel," a Scottish way of spelling twill, a fabric with a diagonal weave. Somehow the word was interpreted as "tweed" and it stuck.

The French had a fabric they called *serge de Nîmes*, after the mill town, and part of the expression stayed with us: denim. The names of many other kinds of cloth make it fairly simple to figure out their geographic origin: Madras, Kashmir, Tulle, Worsted, Jersey, Shantung. (The Dungri section of Bombay is responsible for "dungarees.")

Chenille, which is French for "caterpillar," is an apt name for this soft cloth with a fluffy pile. France also gave us *corde du roi* ("king's cord") and—for a wispy, transparent fabric—*chiffon*, or "wisp." The Persians used *shir o shakkar* ("milk and sugar") to describe the alternate stripes in seersucker, while the Hindi *chint* ("spotted cloth") and *goni* ("sack") evolved into chintz and the redundant gunnysack. And broadcloth? Easy. The English used to weave it two yards wide.

A corduroy bridge on Mt. Mansfield was named after the bumpy fabric.

what time it was—where—became crucial. In the United States, for instance, scheduling was nearly impossible, with each of four or five rail lines hewing to its own clock time—which inevitably differed from that in the towns they stopped at.

To make order out of such untimely chaos, the U.S. Congress in 1884 sponsored a conference in Washington, D.C., inviting representatives from many nations of the world. Because Britain was then a leading naval power and its observatory was extremely well equipped and already extensively used by shippers for navigation, the conferees agreed that the imaginary north-south (or longitudinal) line that passes

Galileo's pendulum clock.

through the naval observatory at Greenwich, England, was the starting point—or the prime meridian. As a result, it was agreed that an hour would be added to Greenwich Mean Time for every 15° of longitude east of the prime meridian, and an hour subtracted for every 15° zone to the west. (There are 24 of the 15°-wide time zones in all.) Where the zones finally meet on the other side of the world, a second demarcation was created: the International Date Line. There westbound travelers would lose a day and eastbounders would gain one. Eventually most of the nations in the world came to accept this time system. (Guyana, Liberia, and Saudi Arabia are still holdouts.)

Today's atomic clocks, their timing based on the very regular oscillations of the atoms of the element cesium, are the most accurate of all: the cesium clock loses only one second in 3,000 years. Such clocks have allowed scientists to quantify what they have long suspected: the earth's daily spin rate is not exactly 24 hours all the time. As a consequence, the atomic clock at the International Time Bureau in Paris, which coordinates accurate timekeeping at other observatories, is occasionally adjusted by adding a leap-second to a day to make up for the earth's occasional tenth-of-a-second dallying.

CLOTH The story of cloth has much to do with man's sense of comfort, beauty, and prosperity. Earliest man wore animal skins and crude garments made of twigs, grass, or bark. According to Genesis, Adam and Eve "sewed fig leaves together, and made themselves aprons." Prehistoric man learned to weave cloth, often copying various basketry techniques with which he was already familiar.

Butling-scutching-hackling (1783): preparing flax for linen was a cottage industry in County Down, Ireland.

Early civilizations depended on four basic natural fibers: linen, wool, silk, and cotton. Linen, woven from the inner fibers of the flax plant, probably dates from Neolithic times. The ancient Egyptians became known for producing fine linen, and invented just about every kind of weave known today.

For centuries woolens were the only fabrics worn in Europe and Asia. In medieval times the wool industry was the basis for the prosperity of Flanders and the great city-states of Italy, and later, for England's claim to commercial eminence. The softest, most luxurious woolens came from Angora and Kashmir goats, and the rarest and most expensive of all, from the vicuña of South America.

As for the beginnings of silk, one tale has it that a Chinese empress, about 2500 B.C., discovered how to unreel the cocoon of the silkworm, a painstaking process that can produce a filament 300 to 1,600 yards long. Before 100 B.C. bolts of Chinese silk were being transported westward, leaving by way of the Jade Gate on China's northwest border—the start of the Silk Road to Syria—and eventually ending up in Europe. The production of silk was a closely guarded Chinese secret until

Stained-glass windows in Semur-en-Auxois, France (1460), celebrate cloth workers: (left) a fuller tramples cloth in a vat; (right) a shearer trims the fabric.

552 A.D., when silkworm eggs were smuggled into Constantinople. From then on silkmaking became an international art. The women of the Greek island of Cos produced a diaphanous silk shift that shocked the good matrons of Athens. Centuries later, Japan's transformation to a modern nation was based on its silk industry.

In India the weaving of cotton goes back at least to 2000 B.C. But the heyday of the fabric that clothes the world came in the 16th century, when Sir Francis Drake waylaid a Portuguese merchantman in the India trade and made cottons the rage in Europe. From there it was only a step—through the rise and fall of economies, the emergence of the New World, the Industrial Revolution, and the birth of modern technology—to the Apollo astronauts who went off into space under layers of Teflon-coated yarn, fiberglass fabrics, nylons, and the "comfort layer" of cotton.

COAL Mankind has loved and hated coal. The people of Wales used it for funeral pyres to cremate their dead 3,000 to 4,000 years ago, and the Chinese were burning it more than a thousand years before the birth of Christianity. In the 12th and 13th centuries, poor people in England heated their huts with coal, but the nobles of the time were sure that its fumes were poisonous. In 1306 King Edward I of England forbade its use under penalty of death.

Coal was the fuel that fired America's Industrial Revolution. Late in the 1700's, as a result of the development of the steam engine, which demanded a long-burning, high-heat generating fuel, coal became an important raw material in the United States. About a century later one form of steam engine, the locomotive, made it possible to move vast quantities of coal to fuel-hungry manufacturers like the burgeoning steel producers in Pennsylvania and the Midwest. Many small fortunes—and at least one enormous family empire—were based on coal and coke. (Coke is made by baking coal to drive out the gases and tar.) Henry C. Frick anticipated the need for coke by steelmakers, and parlayed a $10,000 loan into one of America's great fortunes.

In 1871 Frick, a bookkeeper earning a few dollars a week, persuaded the Pittsburgh banker Thomas Mellon that if he could borrow enough to build 50 coking ovens in the bituminous coal region he could repay the loan in a short time. He was more than right, and soon had hundreds of coke production facilities. Just two years after his initial loan, he had enough leverage to borrow large sums in order to take advantage of a recession and buy a number of coal mines at panic-

An 1871 view of coal mine suggests that air pollution is not new.

selling prices. By 1882 he owned numerous mines and controlled 80 percent of the nation's coke production.

As the demand for cheaply produced coal grew in the late 1800's and early 1900's, so did the need for cheap labor. The first American miners were from the British Isles, and as George Korson, a coalfield journalist, put it: "In the eighties and nineties came the Slavs, Hungarians, and Italians in large waves to both the anthracite [mainly in eastern Pennsylvania] and bituminous [mainly in the Appalachians] regions. From the South, Negroes migrated to the western Pennsylvania mining counties. Some patches and coal camps stood out against the tides of immigration a long time, but ultimately none escaped. . . . The passage of time ultimately resolved differences. Slowly but steadily, conflicting groups began to understand John Mitchell's gospel, 'The coal you dig isn't Slavic or Polish or Irish coal; it's coal.' " In many cases the miners and their families lived in the small "company towns" that the

A late 19th-century family-owned coal mine near Pittsburgh: the youngest can play, but the others must work.

mine owners built—homes, stores, and all—and the laborers were constantly in debt to their employers. Since they rarely left the towns, and they shared the same hardships, joys, and communal occasions, cultural intermingling was inevitable—and so eventually was intermarriage. Coal thus became the fuel that heated up the melting pot.

Current tabulations show that the United States and Canada have nearly one-fifth of the world's coal supply underfoot. China and Russia claim three-fourths, while most of the scant remains are in western Europe. Based on these figures, there appears to be enough coal to provide energy for another 1,000 years at current levels of coal consumption. This wealth of fuel was formed between 250 and 400 million years ago. The giant plants and ferns that flourished in the earth's steamy atmosphere piled up in layers as they died, and new vegetation sprang up on top. Some of these layers of spongy, rotten wood, or peat, were more than 100 feet thick. As the earth's crust shifted and buckled, the peat beds were covered with water, earth, and sand, and placed under enormous pressure. Where the pressure was greatest, the peat changed first into bituminous (soft) coal and then into anthracite (hard) coal. The coal reserves of the world are composed mostly of extremely soft coal called lignite.

Getting coal out of the ground has always been a dirty process, but new machines have made it easier. There are surface mining shovels as high as a 20-story building, which can gouge in one sweep a hole big enough to swallow an elephant. Some deep mines have a "wall-slicer" that peels off the coal like an electric shearer fleecing sheep. Despite these and many other significant technological improvements, coal stands about where it always has in mankind's estimation. It is dangerous to mine, dirty to burn, but attractive because it is abundant and comparatively cheap.

COCKROACH The cockroach has roots, too. His kind have wandered the earth for 350 million years, surviving, multiplying, and changing very little. Roaches existed when the first seed ferns sprouted, and they were on hand at the birth and death of the dinosaur. They are the ancestors of every living insect.

It was only after the arrival of that relative latecomer, man, that the roach began to acquire its reputation as a bearer of disease and reveler in filth. And though most roaches do live in nasty surroundings, researchers have observed that when a roach encounters man, it hides and then carefully cleans its body.

There are some 3,500 species of cockroach. Most live outdoors, mainly in the tropics. Of the 53 species found in the United States, only a few have chosen to cohabit indoors with man. These include the German cockroach (called the Russian roach by the Germans) and the American, Oriental, Surinam, and Cuban. These names came into being because the insects were classified by their probable country of origin. The American cockroach most likely started life in Africa and arrived here on slave ships. American roaches are also called "waterbugs" and tend to be found in basements and sewers. The leading house and apartment dweller is the German roach. The adult is yellowish brown, about half an inch long, and has wings, although it ordinarily does not fly.

The business of a roach is the business of all living things: to eat, survive, and multiply. Roaches will eat almost anything organic, including all sorts of human food as well as toenail parings, bookbindings, clothing, orchid buds, paint, soap, and the insulation in television sets.

Nature has blessed the roach with several remarkable defense mechanisms. The insect is negatively phototropic, meaning that it is repelled by light and thus more active in the dark, when fewer predators are on the prowl. The roach also has a built-in alarm system, which consists of two long antennae and a pair of shorter projections, called *cerci*, at the tail. The cerci are covered with tiny hairs that can sense slight movements in the surrounding air. At first puff,

Of 3,500 species, a few, like this green tree-roach, are attractive.

nerve fibers in the roach's body transmit a message of peril, and before a twentieth of a second has passed, the roach is off and running. In addition, the roach's external skeleton can compress, letting it squeeze into the smallest of crevices. Curled up, the bug can even survive being stepped on. Some roaches have an added defense—the ability to spray enemies with debilitating chemicals. One such spray, called *quinone,* causes attacking beetles and ants to undergo seizures. A young roach, seized by the leg by a predator, can drop the leg and grow another. And if a roach does not expire from its first brush with an insecticide, it has the kind of memory that will help it avoid such danger in the future.

Roaches communicate in several ways by using chemicals called *pheromones.* One triggers the reproductive process. After fertilization the female German roach carries her egg pouch, containing 15 to 40 eggs, until the eggs are ready to hatch.

Other roach females release their egg cases, often making an effort to hide them out of harm's way.

Roaches also use pheromones to alert other roaches when they have discovered a rich food supply. This explains why large swarms of roaches seem to appear overnight, and it accounts as well for the unpleasant, musty odor that accompanies their congregation.

Researchers investigating nutrition, neurophysiology, genetics, metabolism, and even cancer find the roach a perfect lab specimen. It resists disease, needs little space and food, and is so hardy that it can survive radical surgery. For instance, a beheaded roach dies not from the loss of its head but from starvation.

The battle of man against roach is really a fight for control, not extermination—there are too many roaches for that. And often roaches develop resistance to lethal chemicals. The use of natural predators is less than promising, too, because the predators can be worse than the roaches. Among the roach's natural enemies are such unpleasant types as hedgehogs, tarantulas, centipedes, and red mites. And if the perfect roach-killer is found, roaches will undoubtedly do what they have been doing for thousands of centuries: hide in the dark, eat, breed—and adapt.

COFFEE "Black as the devil, hot as hell, pure as an angel, sweet as love." Such was Charles Maurice de Talleyrand's description of the perfect cup of coffee. In Turkey, where the drink was highly esteemed, the groom had to swear during the marriage ceremony always to provide it for his wife or wives. In France and England coffee was considered not only a drink but a panacea—useful for everything from sore throats to smallpox. In the Orient it was used for quite different purposes, often serving as the medium for dissolving deadly poisons. The expression "Well, here's your cup of poison" may be derived from such insidious Eastern practices.

Honored libation or valued commodity, bearer of good or bad tidings, coffee seems to have been used first as a stimulant in Ethiopia about 850 A.D. A goatherd named Kaldi, so the story goes, made the discovery while watching his animals kick up their heels after nibbling the red berries of a wild tree. Kaldi sampled the berries, was impressed, and passed on his information to a monk troubled by his inability to stay awake during prayers. Caffeine, the alkaloid in coffee that acts as both stimulant and diuretic, soon made its first convert.

Coffee drinking became popular in Arabia, perhaps about the 13th century. For a time the Ara-

bians exported coffee beans but doggedly refused to sell the seeds or seedlings that produced them. Nonetheless, visiting pilgrims spirited off seedlings to India, and in 1690 the Dutch pilfered a number of plants, installing them in botanical gardens in Holland and plantations in Java.

Louis XV was as much a coffee lover as Talleyrand, and during his reign a single fragile plant, housed in a glass box, traveled to Martinique—harbinger of coffee planting throughout the Caribbean. The journey was difficult, however, and along the way the seedling survived a kidnap attempt, an attack by Barbary pirates, a storm that shattered its case and doused it with seawater, and a water shortage that caused the ship's captain to cut off its supply. Fortunately, the plant's protector, a young French officer, De Clieu, shared his ration with his charge, and the plant arrived safely in Martinique.

The caffeine in coffee does stimulate the brain, and as the coffee tree flourished, a unique social

For some reason this 18th-century British coffee stall was designed to look like a tea kettle.

institution evolved in Europe to prove it: the coffeehouse. It was into such surroundings that Samuel Pepys ventured on the evening of February 3, 1663, because "Dryden, the poet I knew at Cambridge, and all the wits of the town were assembled."

Today, in the United States, coffee is drunk by more adults than any other beverage, and on a winter's day it is estimated that for every person 10 years old or older about two cups of coffee are consumed. The brewing of a good cup of coffee can be a fetish-ridden ritual for some, a tour de gadgetry for others, or simplicity itself—for those who use instant coffee. About one-third of all coffee prepared in the United States is now instant, an idea that began more than 140 years ago when Congress decided to substitute coffee for rum in soldiers' and sailors' rations.

Extracts were considered first; then in 1901 a Japanese chemist, Satori Kato, reportedly brewed the first pot of the instant mix in Chicago, some five years before an American chemist, G. Washington, produced a "refined soluble coffee." During World War I the War Department bought every ounce of instant coffee that was available; during World War II the government purchased 260 million pounds of it. Some 20 years later the process of "freeze drying" improved the flavor of instant and raised consumption to its present one-in-three ratio.

Do coffee lovers prefer to use a cup or a mug? Along with everything else, coffee manufacturers have researched this question, too. Thus far cups are in the lead away from home—66 percent to 13 percent—but the smaller, more delicate containers are losing ground in the kitchen, too. There, mugs trail by only 11 percent and seem to be gaining converts with each extra-large, devilishly angelic portion of coffee they offer.

Coin-operated vending machines go back to about the 1st century A.D., when the Greek mathematician Hero described an Egyptian holy-water dispenser like this.

COIN-OPERATED MACHINE About the 1st century A.D. worshipers in certain Greek temples could drop money into a mechanical device and receive a dollop of purifying water. Such was the pitch of the first coin-operated vending machine on record. In the years since, its descendants have been used to hawk everything from underwear to cigarettes, goldfish, flowers, postage stamps, perfume, and even worms.

For the seller a vending machine is a silent, vigilant, 24-hour salesman—one that is, also, acutely attuned to the difference between tolerable coins and intolerable slugs. For the buyer, the machine makes available familiar merchandise where and when it is needed. If all goes well, the transaction will be a speedy one. If, however,

a bent coin or mechanical failure intervenes—well, who has not known the embarrassment of shrieking at an inanimate hunk of metal, or felt the small bones of the hand or foot crunch on impact as rage transcends reason? This choleric approach led one early vending-machine inventor to issue the following lament: ". . . although the apparatus is perfectly successful when not designedly misused, articles such as paper, orange-peel and other rubbish have been maliciously placed in the slit

customs

It All Comes Out At The Wash

Americans seem to be finding companionship, and sometimes considerably more, in the public washing of their dirty linen. Call them laundromats, washerees, launderettes, or anything else, coin-operated washing machines bring people of diverse backgrounds together. And while their clothes spin, tumble, and dry, they often talk, just the way folks used to do in barbershops, beauty parlors, and general stores. The proprietor of one Miami washing-machine emporium even went so far as to introduce single men and women to each other. Using a matchmaking book to jot down notes on new single customers, she has a number of marriages to her credit.

Many coin laundries remain open at night to accommodate people who work during the day, thus creating a kind of nightclub ambiance against a backdrop of steam, bleach, and detergent. One Florida entrepreneur was so struck with the social possibilities of this situation that he added a bar, then brought in topless dancers. Other laundries are more sedate, providing such mundane if vital services as play facilities for children, coffee and cake, reading areas with TV, and even hair dryers.

provided for the admission of the coin. . . ."

Mostly vending machines work, selling almost anything, and coins clank into them at the rate of billions of dollars per year. At the turn of the century, for example, residents of Corinne, Utah, could buy ready-made, machine-dispensed divorce papers, with the name of a local law firm already imprinted on them. One had only to drop in $2.50 in coin, the instructions read, pull the handle, and take the papers to the attorney, who would see that the names were properly filled in and witnessed.

For a franc this machine provided Parisians with a gust of pine-scented oxygen.

Vending machines have sometimes been used to circumvent human problems. In 1822, when freedom of the press was not yet well understood in England, a bookseller named Richard Carlile built a machine to sell books—Thomas Paine's *The Age of Reason,* for example—that the government found objectionable. Carlile believed that if the buyer set the machine to release a particular book, the seller could not be held accountable. The courts of England were not amused, and one of Carlile's employees was sent to jail for selling blasphemous literature. A more successful device was the Electra-Bar, which was invented to replace unreliable bartenders. Electra-Bar, which went on the market in 1971 at a price of $9,960, could measure all but the most esoteric of drinks with great precision, keep track of the quantity dispensed, and record all sales, after collecting the coins. No drinks on the house or hands in the till with Electra-Bar on duty.

The craft of building efficient vending machines is now highly developed, but the machines of yesteryear were more fun. They were individualistic and often reflected the inventor's sense of humor. There was, for instance, a cast-iron bull's head, built to accept a coin through a slot in its forehead. When the customer complied and pulled the bull's horns downward, the creature snorted a blast of perfume into the buyer's handkerchief. And then there was the cigarette machine that sold only one cigarette at a time, but released it fully lit. Equally irresistible was the cast-iron hen that laid hard-boiled eggs when primed with coins.

The practicality of mass marketing transformed the vending industry in 1888, when Thomas Adams, founder of the Adams chewing gum company, began selling tutti-frutti gum in machines set on the elevated platforms of the New York subway system. His example was followed by vendors around the world. Some 10 years later, critics began worrying about machines that were selling not merchandise but the opportunity to gamble. Wrote one critic of such devices: ". . . a numerous family of this type has come into being, and has flourished and fattened on the public's purse, or, at least, the funds of that section of the public which needs considerable legal intervention and guidance to protect it from itself." The battle over coin-fed machines of chance is still raging, with the slot-machine industry arguing that it sells recreation rather than gambling.

Vending machines today touch almost every facet of our lives. They take our pictures and sell insurance, and provide us with change to put in other machines. Pinball machines entertain, as do electronic video games. Although no longer fully automatic, the coin-operated restaurant started by the Horn & Hardart Baking Company in Philadelphia in 1902 changed the way we eat. In its day the Automat, as it came to be called, was as American as apple pie. Unfortunately, so is another contrivance. In 1909, on a day that will live forever in infamy, the Nik-O-Lok Company installed the first coin-operated locks on the doors of public toilets.

COLLEGE The first colleges had few books and no buildings, but they were nonetheless symbols of success. The ancient Chinese may have been the first to experiment with colleges, more than 2,000 years before the birth of Christ. At that time, Chinese students labored at the study of literature to prepare for their civil service exams. About 500 years later, Indian scholars and their students gathered together to talk and contemplate in "forest universities," or ashrams. In medieval times, college was for the clergy, and later for those interested in politics, though many leaders rose to power without benefit of higher education. When the scholar Alcuin of York set up the palace school at Aix in 782, his first chore was to teach the emperor to read and write. The emperor was Charlemagne.

The first colleges were exceedingly simple in organization—and accoutrements—in comparison with today's massive multiversities. By the end of World War II, two universities in the United States had more than 20,000 students. Now more than 100 colleges surpass that figure. The University of California, the colossus of American education, employs as many as 56,000 people and offers 253 graduate degree programs at 9 campuses. In all, the university has 70 schools and colleges and 150 institutional centers and research stations. It has study centers also in 18 countries and delivers more than 10,000 babies per year in its hospitals.

In medieval times a book was a rarity; most books were rented from booksellers. Now more than 30 university libraries in the United States maintain collections of a million volumes or more. Harvard University's library, by far the largest in the United States, contains more than 9 million volumes.

Most people believe that college is a vital requirement for success, and statistics support this contention. One estimate suggests that a male college graduate earns at least $280,000 more during his lifetime than does a male high-school graduate. Other calculations place the figure even higher. Small wonder, then, that an increasing number of young people aspire to a college degree. In 1870 only about one out of 80 young people enrolled in college. A century later the figure had risen to two out of five. And Americans are not alone in their feelings: in Japan a college degree is of such importance that dozens of unsuccessful students commit suicide each spring when some 700,000 young people compete for less than half that number of openings in freshmen classes.

American women had a hard time too. In 1800 the idea that a woman might benefit from college was unthinkable, and during that century a number of otherwise sensible American educators delivered themselves of much foolishness on the subject. Charles W. Eliot, who took over the presidency of Harvard in 1869, stated: "The difficulties involved in a common residence of hundreds of young men and women of immature character and marriageable age are very grave. The necessary police regulations are exceedingly burdensome." A letter to the editor of *Godey's Lady's Book* appeared about the same time, written by John H. Raymond, president of Vassar. Though Raymond firmly believed in higher education for women, he nonetheless articulated the fears of many Americans: "Has she strength of brain enough to receive it? Has she sufficient moral earnestness and energy of purpose to carry her through? . . . Will it not destroy feminine grace and delicacy. Will it not break down her physical health?"

In 1885 a young male teacher with a Ph.D. joined the faculty at Bryn Mawr and expressed his misgivings this way: "I should, of course, prefer to teach young men, and if I find that teaching at Bryn Mawr stands in the way of my teaching afterward in some men's college, I shall, of course, withdraw." The young teacher was Woodrow Wilson, and he managed to survive the experience to become president of Princeton—and of the United States.

And one midwesterner, a farmer facing the perils of college for his daughters, who must have been very persistent, predicted spinsterhood for them and poverty for himself: "All the young men . . . who might have been agreeable acquaintances," he lamented, "and that would have made good matches for ordinary girls—why, they have nothing in common with a girl that's spent four years studying Latin and Greek and history. . . . The girls don't take any pleasure in their company, and the boys are afraid of them. . . . I guess I'll have a lot of college-educated old maids on my hands."

COMIC STRIP In 1975 a comic strip that had been needling the U.S. establishment on such issues as Vietnam, racial prejudice, Watergate, homosexuality, and women's liberation became the first strip to win the prestigious Pulitzer Prize for editorial cartooning. Garry Trudeau's "Doonesbury" was a far cry from its 1896 progenitor, Richard Outcault's "Yellow Kid," a panel cartoon that featured a bald, flap-eared boy in a yellow nightshirt.

At that time, William Randolph Hearst's New York *Journal* launched its Sunday supplement, *The American Humorist* (proclaiming it to be "eight pages of polychromatic effulgence that make the rainbow look like a lead pipe"), and lured Outcault and "The Yellow Kid" from Joseph Pulitzer's *World*. The Hearst-Pulitzer struggle over the feature led to the term "yellow journalism."

Hearst also saw the potential of the basic elements of the comics form: a running story with dialogue enclosed within each frame. Years before, he had brought back from Germany Wilhelm Busch's illustrations, *Max und Moritz,* and now he had his staff artist, Rudolph Dirks, create a strip based on those characters, dubbing them Hans and Fritz. On December 12, 1897, "The Katzenjammer Kids"—and comics as we know them today—were off and running.

The first successful comic to run daily came in 1907. "Mr. A. Mutt," its stringbean hero, one day

With a loving eye and gentle pen, artist Chic Young examines suburban life at sandwich-making time.

Spike-haired Mac or a career? In the hit comic strip, Tillie never could make up her mind.

visited a sanatorium where he met a diminutive inmate who fancied himself to be Jim Jeffries, the boxer. "Mutt and Jeff" went on together for generations, and in 1911 reprints of this strip became one of the first comic books.

Zap! Pow! Zowie! Our vocabularies gained color over the decades as the greatest comics artists, from "Krazy Kat's" George Herriman to "Pogo's" Walt Kelly, gave us exclamations like "heebie-jeebies," "baloney," and "good grief"; a generation of the Buster Brown hair style for small boys; such "gourmet" foods as the giant Dagwood sandwich and Wimpy's hamburger; and the statue of Popeye in Crystal City, Texas, "spinach capital of the world."

The comics inspired the early cartoon films (animated strips, really), casting them with the likes of Happy Hooligan and, years later, welcomed such screen personalities as Mickey Mouse and Donald Duck to the comic pages. Then, for better or worse, in the first issue of *Action Comics,* June 1938, the ultimate hero appeared, Superman.

By the time "Doonesbury" took the Pulitzer Prize, the daily comics were being read by more than 100 million Americans and an additional 200 million zealots elsewhere, in 42 languages and 102 countries. And the National Cartoonists Society was awarding an annual prize, the Reuben, celebrating the memory of Rube Goldberg, creator of "Boob McNutt" and countless zany inventions.

COMMON COLD The common cold is the most pervasive of all diseases. It strikes on the average half of all Americans every winter, and about one in five in the summer. Preschool children, the population group most vulnerable, average from 6 to 12 colds a year, and their parents suffer about 6. Other adults, if they are lucky, may get by with only two or three colds a year.

A cold is actually a cluster of symptoms that affect different people differently. The most common symptoms include runny nose or stopped-up nose, sore or dry throat, sneezing, a feeling of

Many Remedies, No Cures

Despite all his sneezing and suffering, man has been infinitely more inventive than successful in preventing and treating the common cold. Among his more popular remedies are:

Bed Rest. It isolates the victim and keeps his virus from infecting others. It also helps him to stay warm. But bed rest does not alter the course of a cold.

Alcohol. In old England cold sufferers reportedly hung their hats on the bedpost, drank gin until they saw two hats, then plunged into bed until the viral siege ended. Alcohol may indeed help one sleep—or see two hats—but it has no effect on colds.

Chicken Soup. Almost any hot drink can soothe a cough or ease the pain of a sore throat.

Vitamin C. In 1970 Nobel laureate Linus Pauling made popular the theory that massive doses of vitamin C could combat and even prevent colds. Careful studies conducted since then show no significant cold-combating benefits from it. But some vitamin C gluttons believe that the amount of time they feel too sick to work is reduced. Studies also show that smaller doses of the vitamin help as much as a massive intake, and most doctors caution against taking large amounts.

Drink Lots of Fluids. Fluids won't affect a cold, but they can make the patient feel better.

Antihistamines. Antihistamines fell out of favor when researchers showed that pink sugar pills worked just as well.

Nose Drops, Cough Syrups, Cough Drops, Cold Pills, and Potions. More than $750 million per year is spent on such concoctions. A few, notably those that contain aspirin, ease aches and pains. So will plain aspirin. Antibiotics don't help either. Hard candy soothes a cough as much as branded drops. Antiseptic gargles don't destroy viruses.

The greatest benefit of all these nonprescription drugs and treatments is probably psychological: the patient feels better because he has done something instead of just lying there.

A cure for catarrh—and everything else.

malaise, postnasal drip, headache, and coughing. Rarely is fever present, except in small children. The symptoms often appear about 24 hours after the invasion of the upper respiratory system by any one of more than 100 strains of viruses. The most common, called rhinoviruses, are small organisms, much tinier than bacteria, measuring about one 25,000-millionth of an inch. Their

British lithograph, 1883: surviving the common cold and its remedies.

size belies their hardiness: they have a kind of protective armor that lets them survive temperatures of -200° F and a force 100,000 times that of the pull of gravity.

Much is known about the common cold, but not about how to prevent or cure it. Colds seem to occur in three distinct waves each year. The first breaks in autumn shortly after schools have opened; the second appears in midwinter; and the last arrives with the flowers of spring. Despite the prevalence of colds in wintertime, however, it is not the frigidity itself that brings them on. Arctic explorers, researchers have noted, seem wonderfully free of colds—until they return to civilization.

Nor is there scientific evidence to support the claim that chills and wet feet can bring on a cold. The same is true for wind velocity and variations in humidity. Warm indoor temperatures during the winter, however, may dry the membranes of the nose and throat just enough to make them more vulnerable to viral invasion. But even that is not a certainty.

Scientists are sure that we have each other to thank for the transmission of colds. A robust sneeze can launch thousands of tiny, virus-bearing droplets at speeds up to 50 miles per hour. The droplets are then inhaled by someone else or carried to the nose, mouth, or eye by hand or on an article of clothing.

The viruses settle on the walls of the nose and throat, and enter the cells there. Their tough outer coating dissolves, and they begin to reproduce. Eventually the virus cells break down the walls of the host cell, which then dies. Such cell deaths occur hundreds of thousands of times in the course of a cold, and the body secretes fluids to wash away the debris. The result: a runny nose. In all, a cold can last from 2 to 10 days, and nobody really knows why it stops.

What's more, colds are expensive. Aside from the misery of a billion colds in the United States every year, there is the loss of an estimated 40 million workdays. The cost is more than $5 billion, including time lost from work, the price of treating colds, and loss of wages. Nonetheless, desperate sufferers, believing that doing something is better than doing nothing, spend more than $750 million a year fighting colds and trying to suppress their symptoms.

COMMUTER Of the 50 million or so workers who commute in the United States, the vast majority—roughly 48 million—drive. This is clearly the least efficient method (about 3,000 car riders can move along a 12-foot-wide strip of land in an hour, as compared with 40,000 on buses and 60,000 on trains), but it offers certain advantages. Despite traffic jams, breakdowns, and tolls, the car commuter can come and go, relatively speaking, as he pleases.

Grouped among those who do not drive are train, bus, ferry, and even bicycle commuters, who constitute a small but nonetheless growing segment of the shuttle work force. In Tempe, Arizona, for instance, where almost three-quarters of the population own and ride bicycles, road builders are required by law to parallel their highways with 8-foot-wide bikeways. In Davis, California, nearly 15 miles of bike lanes already exist.

Of all commuters, however, the train rider is the one who seems to suffer most. His stories of disaster are legendary and, when pushed to the breaking point by antiquated equipment and unreliable scheduling, he even fights back. Some years ago in Brazil, São Paulo commuters rioted after months of haphazard service; and in Osaka, Japan, a group of equally outraged commuters staged a sit-down strike on the rails, after hiking miles to meet a connecting train that did not exist.

In the United States commuter stories abound, though they may not always be strictly factual. According to one, a commuter was found lying on the rails, a loaf of bread in his arms. When asked what he

White-gloved and muscular, Tokyo's paid "pushers and packers" speed up the rush hour.

was doing, he replied that he had had enough waiting, and was going to end it all, but was afraid he would starve to death before a train came. At a hearing on the malfunctions of another line, a traveler complained that a particular train had simply stopped, miles from nowhere, and that there had even been a pregnant woman on board. But was she pregnant when the train left the station? a fellow commuter demanded. Habit, bordering on the unconscious, is a common defense mechanism among veteran commuters. One travel-weary warrior, having dozed off in church, reached instinctively for his commutation ticket when nudged by an usher with the collection plate. Comedian David Brenner tells of an encounter on an especially crowded train. His seatmate, noticing that Brenner was sitting on a copy of *The New York Times,* asked if he were reading it. "Yes," Brenner replied, rising, turning a page, then sitting down again, "I am."

In an attempt to determine what caused the most stress on commuter railroads, Swedish and American researchers examined travelers at various points on a number of lines. What they found was that the farther up the line or the earlier a commuter boarded a train, the less stressful his trip would be. The reason: early in a trip a commuter has a degree of control—he can choose where and with whom he will sit. Later on, as the train becomes more crowded, he has none.

COMPUTER The berserk computers of science fiction that threaten to take over the world are actually a bit late—the takeover occurred years ago. Few aspects of human endeavor are not now touched, or even controlled, by computers. These

Silicon chips are used in stoves, stereos, stoplights.

awesome electronic devices predict the weather worldwide, tell farmers how to produce the food we eat (and tell life insurance companies how long we will probably be around to eat it), set type, guard our national borders, check taxes, and even cook dinner, at least in homes that have push-button ranges. If all computers went on strike today, or were suddenly knocked out of commission, the result would be chaos, even in developing countries.

Technically speaking, a computer is any machine that can do calculations, but today the term is routinely applied to those electrically powered devices that store data, follow complex programs, and do infinitely difficult calculations at lightning speed. Nonetheless the abacus, which has been around for thousands of years, is a kind of computer, one that utilizes the principles of pebble counting in producing its remarkably fast and accurate computations. In ancient Rome shopkeepers actually used "little stones," or *calculi,* to keep their books. The terms "calculus" and "calculate" come from the singular form of the Latin word *calculus,* or "pebble."

The first calculating "machine" was built more than 300 years ago—in 1642—by the 19-year-old son of a French tax collector. The young man's name was Blaise Pascal, and his device could add and subtract, using a series of numbered wheels connected by ratchets. "It is unworthy of excellent men," Gottfried von Leibniz, a German mathematician, wrote a few decades later, echoing the lament of schoolchildren everywhere, "to lose hours like slaves in the labor of calculation. . . ."

people

Punch-Card Revolutionary

Herman Hollerith, father of the modern computer industry, showed little promise of great things as a child. In elementary school he hated spelling so much that he once jumped out of a window to avoid it. Later at Columbia University he did poorly in bookkeeping and mechanics, two of the basics of computer science. The turning point for Hollerith came in 1887 when he devised a way for the U.S. Census Office to catch up on its lagging tabulations: a punch-card infor-

mation-processing machine.

Called "statistical pianos" by some, Hollerith's revolutionary machines were accurate and fast. Actually there were two machines: one transferred information onto cards in the form of punched holes. A set of spring-loaded pins read and tabulated the data: where there was a hole, a pin popped through, completing an electrical circuit and causing a pointer on a dial to advance.

Processing the raw data from the 1890 census, the machines

showed a population of 63 million. People who believed that the country was larger complained. "Slipshod Work Has Spoiled the Census," the New York *Herald* reported, "Speed Everything, Accuracy Nothing!" But Hollerith's machines and tabulations proved accurate in both the 1890 and 1900 censuses, and he eventually made a fortune. His Tabulating Machine Company was one of three that formed the Computer-Tabulating Recording Company in 1911, later IBM.

He then devised the first machine that could multiply and divide.

Early in the 19th century an English mathematician, Charles Babbage, built a "Difference Engine," then designed a steam-powered "Analytical Engine," which contained many of the operating principles in use in today's computers—data storage, printout, even decision-making functions. Unfortunately, Babbage was never able to complete his master machine, mainly because metal technology could not meet his unique demands. His assistant in his labors was Augusta Ada Byron, daughter of the great romantic poet—and history's first computer programmer.

The first large-scale automatic digital computer was developed during World War II by a Harvard graduate student, Howard H. Aiken. His machine, named the Mark I, weighed 5 tons, contained 500 miles of wires and 3,304 electromechanical relay switches, and could perform 23-digit additions and subtractions in three-tenths of a second.

One of the biggest breakthroughs in computer design occurred in 1946, when engineers at the University of Pennsylvania developed a machine that used electronic pulses instead of mechanical switches for calculations. The final leap in computer technology came in the late 1940's and early 1950's, when computers were built that could store and retrieve operating instructions along with data. Since then significant advances have been achieved in miniaturization, programming, operational speed, and the creation of multiple terminals, so that people in different locations can use the same computer.

Modern computers can perform with incredible celerity. They can, for example, churn out 16 million additions in a second and multiply 14-digit numbers at the rate of more than 5 million a second. They can also produce 13,000 lines of type in a minute, store and retrieve hundreds of billions of pieces of information, and display answers to calculations on a screen, or even speak them. Some use microcircuits so small that if a 1,250-page Bible were printed by the same ultraviolet light process, it would occupy an area 1½ inches square.

Today most computers are either digital or analog. Digital computers perform calculations by counting. (A cash register is a mechanical digital computer: a hand-held calculator is a small ver-

The colors in this thermogram, or "heat map," of a human face are assigned by computer. Greens are cool, tans warm, and blacks hot.

sion of an electronic digital computer.) These machines can add, subtract, multiply, divide, and mix such functions in a continuous operation.

Analog computers do not count; they measure quantities, the way a speedometer measures speed by the distance the indicator moves on a scale. Most analog computers are used for calculations involving continuously changing measurements such as speed and temperature. The onboard computer that controls the flight path of an airplane or missile is an analog computer.

Can computers think? Although they were originally referred to by laymen as "mechanical brains," computers today have only about one ten-thousandth of the performance capacity of a human brain. Nonetheless, when matched against human competitors, they do surprisingly well. In chess games, computers often beat their human opponents, though in one match the computer was excused for eccentric play because it had recently been struck by lightning.

But are such machines thinking? This depends on how we define "think." Obviously, computers can solve problems, even when logic and hypothesis are required. They can also create computer art and write poetry. To do so, of course, computers use programs put into them by humans. Likewise, much of our own thinking involves information "programmed" into us at an early age by parents and teachers.

Even scientists are divided on the question, but many agree that what is known as the "Turing Test" might one day help provide an answer. Named after British mathematician Alan Turing, the test works like this: a human is seated at a computer keyboard with the freedom to ask any question, except those that are patently human—for example, what size hat do you wear? If after half an hour, the human cannot decide whether he has been conversing with a computer or another human, the machine, according to the somewhat subjective test, may be said to have intelligence.

In 1890 first data cards helped with the census.

CONCRETE A solar house built into a South Dakota hillside, the old Eddystone Lighthouse on the coast of England, a Thai fishing boat, Chicago's up-to-the-minute 74-story Water Tower Place, the ruined Temple of Fortune in Palestrina, Italy, dating from 20 years before the birth of Augustus, the latest innovation in railroad ties—what do these things have in common? They are made of concrete.

Concrete is one of the oldest building materials known to man. Emperor Augustus claimed that he transformed Rome from a city of brick into a city of marble. In truth, Augustus only added marble facades to existing buildings, which, unbeknownst to him, were solid concrete structures faced with brick. They have survived centuries of earthquakes, hordes of invading barbarians, and zealous urban renewers. The Romans had discovered that by combining their reddish volcanic earth with lime they were able to produce an extremely practical cement that set underwater and was fireproof.

Before there was concrete, however, there had to be cement. The recipe for concrete calls for gravel or crushed stone or sand (in earlier times, crumbled pottery and brick) and, most importantly, cement and water. The last two ingredients, when combined with the rest, bind the mixture together chemically and allow it to set as hard as natural stone.

Most areas that gave rise to early civilizations had deposits of natural cement—usually clay and limestone but also gypsum and volcanic ash. Natural cement is not of uniform quality, however, and until very recently no one really understood how it worked.

In 1824, perhaps 9,000 years after man had learned to use cement, Joseph Aspdin, an Englishman, took out a patent on a new synthetic cement. It consisted of a mixture of limestone and clay, heated to a high temperature and subsequently ground into a fine powder. With his formula Aspdin could produce cement of exactly the same quality each time. He called it portland cement, so that users would associate the concrete made from it with the popular gray building stone quarried on the British isle of Portland. Before the 1870's, when Americans built their own portland cement works in such areas of the country as southern Pennsylvania, San Antonio, Texas, and South Bend, Indiana, they imported cement by the barrelful—each weighing 376 pounds—from England. Although barrels have given away to sacks, the quantity of cement is still figured by the old standard; and a sack is one-fourth of a barrel.

Everyone is familiar with the ready-mix truck rumbling down the highway to deliver concrete for yet another house foundation or shopping mall, but what about the notion of building a concrete boat? Concrete plastered over an iron-mesh framework makes a boat that not only can float but is fireproof, leakproof, rotproof, creature proof, and hard to damage. One of the earliest concrete boats was built by a Frenchman in the mid-19th century. Concrete boats as big as 434 by 54 feet, and weighing 7,500 tons, plied the oceans during the 1920's. Today organized racing in concrete canoes has become the rage on many U.S. college campuses.

COOKBOOK "Sprinkle with pepper and serve" is the last step in a recipe for diced pork and apples from the world's oldest surviving cookbook, *De Re Coquinaria* ("On Cookery"), attributed to the 1st-century Roman gastronome Apicius. For the next 17 centuries men continued to write all the cookbooks, expert addressing expert, until English women took quill in hand. Prior to that time, favorite family recipes were handed down from mother to daughter, copied and recopied on pieces of paper or in ledgers by each succeeding generation of cooks. The basic cookbook written for the housewife rather than the trained chef with a staff of helpers was still to come. Probably the first was Eliza Acton's *Modern Cookery for Private Families,* published in London in 1845.

About that time, across the Atlantic, Eliza Leslie was hailed as the leading American cookbook writer. The ingredients in her recipes suggest that mid-19th-century America was a land of plenty. A "rich white soup" starts out with "a pair of large fat fowls" and two pounds of veal, and a "gipsy" soup calls for four pounds of venison, a hare, a brace of partridges, a woodcock, two celery heads, a dozen onions, and a half-dozen potatoes. The groaning board was piled high with foods that would seem exotic a century later: mussels, artichokes, turtles, and an orgy of oysters. Fresh oysters were delivered by express wagon from Chesapeake Bay to points west, and Abraham Lincoln, at his home in Springfield, Illinois,

Dressed to grill: 18th-century cuisinier wears the tools of his trade.

"The Mother of Level Measurement"

The august Boston publishers Little, Brown and Company took a dim view of issuing one more collection of recipes for the American housewife—particularly one that did not also tell how to do away with rats or mix face cream, though it did give tips on cleaning ivory piano keys. The writer—39, red-headed, and principal of a local cooking school—paid the printing costs, and 3,000 copies of her book rolled off the presses in 1896.

The woman was Fannie Merritt Farmer, and her book was *The Boston Cooking School Cook Book*. It soon outsold the firm's two blockbusters *Quo Vadis?* and *Little Women*, and by 1977, 10 revisions later, more than 4 million copies had been sold.

Fannie suffered a "paralytic stroke" in high school which left her with a limp and forced her to stay at home, where she helped cook for boarders. About that time, according to some accounts, Fannie, working as a "mother's helper," acted on a child's suggestion and developed a system of level measurements—an innovation later incorporated in her cookbook.

In 1887 Fannie, age 30, encouraged by family and friends, enrolled in the Boston Cooking School, primarily a teacher-training institution, and graduated two years later. She stayed on as assistant principal and eventually

Fannie Farmer made cooking schools popular and fashionable in the 1890's.

became the head of the school. With the publication of her book in 1896, Fannie Farmer became a household name. The art of home cooking was no longer a guessing game but a standardized procedure with reliable results every time. In 1902 she opened Miss Farmer's School of Cookery, teaching not only professionals but housewives and society women the art of plain cooking.

Her demonstration lectures on Wednesday mornings and evenings, which drew audiences of 150 to 200, were reported the next day in the Boston *Evening Transcript* and reprinted far and wide. As the famous and impatient Fannie limped vivaciously about the stage, assistants did the actual cooking. She often ate in the best restaurants, searching out new dishes. If baffled by a tasty

sauce, she would dab a bit of it on her calling card for later analysis.

From 1905 until her death 10 years later, she wrote a column for the *Woman's Home Companion* and lectured to women's clubs as far away as California. She also wrote six specialty cookbooks, including *Food and Cookery for the Sick and Convalescent* and trained hospital dieticians, her proudest achievements. As the result of a second stroke, she spent her last seven years in a wheelchair or on crutches. Her final lecture was delivered from the wheelchair 10 days before she died, in 1915, at age 58.

Postscript: A candy maker named Frank O'Connor, impressed with the grit of Fannie Farmer, named his chain of candy stores after her in 1910. Somehow "Fannie" became "Fanny."

was a frequent customer of the oyster seller.

Some cookbooks went beyond recipes to other concerns of the house. One advised: "Never give medicine to a very young child. Many have thus lost darling children. It will, if not murdered, be permanently injured. . . . If medicine must be given at all, give it to the nurse."

Few women had scales and weights in the kitchen, nor were there marked measuring cups and standard-size spoons. Most cookbooks did not specify precisely how much of what went into a dish. A handful of flour, a heaping spoonful of baking powder, and "nuts" of butter were common measurements. Cooking times were vague,

too, because of the unpredictability of an open fire. Leslie, in one of her books on cookery, was explicit in other ways, however. For example, to ripen cheeses "place [them] in the haystack, and keep them there among the hay for five or six weeks." Toward century's end, the Boston Cooking School turned the cookbook into a foolproof step-by-step cooking guide.

Over the decades *The Boston Cooking School Cook Book* (1896) and *The Settlement Cook Book* (1901), both still in print, two staples of the cook's corner, have been joined by such bestsellers as *Better Homes and Gardens New Cook Book* (nearly 19 million copies sold by 1975), *Betty*

Crocker's Cookbook (13 million copies), and Irma Rombauer and Marion Becker's *Joy of Cooking* (11 million copies).

The great U.S. cookbook boom rang out in the 1960's, when publishers began issuing 400 new titles a year, to join some 2,500 already in print. What touched off this American stampede to the kitchen? The answers are both gastronomic and social. Since the 1940's, Americans had become globe-trotters, returning home with more educated palates. The women's movement was nudging the male toward mixing bowl and stove, and he was finding his epicurean consciousness raised. Health fads, cooking schools, vegetable gardens, food processors, television cooking shows like Julia Child's ("The family that cooks together, stays together") made fancy cooking look easy.

Where apple pie had once been the *spécialité de la maison,* men and women were rolling Japanese sushi—raw fish and rice wrapped in squares of pressed seaweed. They had cookbooks on how to eat in high Gallic style while remaining slender *(cuisine minceur);* on food-processor cookery; on dishes from Pakistan and Sri Lanka; and, of course, on bread. "How can a nation be great if its bread tastes like Kleenex?" asked Julia Child.

CORK Cork has been carved into bottle stoppers, shoe soles, and buoys, ground up and pressed into boards and pipe coverings, used for insulation and soundproofing, and turned into an artist's paint known as Spanish black. While writing his great novel *Remembrance of Things Past,* Marcel Proust had the walls of his room lined with cork to guarantee peace. When he moved 13 years later, he sold the panels.

For centuries, from the 1600's until about 1920, cork was regarded as the perfect bottle stopper. It was more practical than bits of wood, braided grass, or wads of linen. It also was the only safe seal for carbonated soda water. Sweet-flavored sodas came to be called "pop" because the cork "popped" when it was drawn.

The secret of cork is its density. One cubic inch of it can contain 200 million cells, each one sheathed with a membrane of resin, and so closely packed that one cell touches as many as 14 others. Half the volume is air, which accounts for cork's lightness and ability to spring back into shape even after being heavily compressed.

The cork that pops from a champagne bottle seconds before midnight on New Year's Eve probably came from Portugal, Spain, or Algeria, the three largest cork producers in the world today. Although the cork tree, the evergreen oak, has been planted elsewhere—in California, for in-

The artist of Ferdinand the timid bull depicted corks growing the way children think they must.

stance—it seems to thrive only in the Mediterranean area.

After 20 or 25 years, the oak is ready for its first stripping. With long-handled hatchets the strippers make two lengthy vertical cuts and two short horizontal ones in the outer bark, then pry loose the rectangle, careful not to damage the inner layer of cork. The bark is then boiled and its gritty outer layer scraped off. The boiling drains away sap and tannic acid, further enhancing the cork's elasticity, and permits flattening of the slabs for shipment to manufacturers. In 8 or 10 years—and 8 or 10 new layers of cork—the tree will be ready for another harvest.

CORN The turkey and the deer may have seemed to be the most important foodstuffs served at the first Thanksgiving dinner, but in terms of its eventual importance to Americans the real guest of honor should have been corn. On that occasion, corn played a minor role, represented only as a gift. Quadequina, brother of the Iroquois chief Massasoit, brought to the gathering a deerskin bag stuffed with popcorn already popped.

More than a hundred years earlier Christopher Columbus' crewmen had found people in Cuba tending their corn plantings. They called the crop *maiz,* and that is still the best name for it. In Britain the word corn denotes any of several kinds of grain. But maize means corn as we think of it. The Plymouth colonists started calling the plant "Indian corn," probably to avoid such tongue-twisting words as *poketawes* or *hokotawes.*

From the Plymouth landing on, corn has been a remarkably pervasive force in American life. It saw the first settlers at Plymouth through their bitterest winters, after they learned from Indians how to cultivate the plant. When oak leaves are as big as mice ears, the Indians advised, plant the kernels of corn. Put a small fish in between them. During the Indians' planting seasons, their dogs quite literally led dogs' lives. Each hobbled about with a foreleg bound to its neck to keep it from digging up the small fish, probably menhaden, used as fertilizer. Later harvests were celebrated with husking bees. Girls who found red ears of corn during such get-togethers were entitled to kiss the men of their choice. In the South

Pop Goes The Corn Kernel

For all its modern ubiquity—in movie theaters and at circuses, on Christmas trees and in a bowl on the table in front of the TV set—popcorn is a grain of considerable historical significance. In all likelihood it was the first kind of corn that early man knew, and its explosive properties may even have been instrumental in getting him to eat it.

The oldest ears of corn, found by archeologists in west central New Mexico, are of popcorn nearly 5,500 years old. A 1,000-year-old popped kernel was found in a dry cave in southwest Utah. It had been fired by the forebears of the Pueblo Indians. On the east coast of Peru, 3,000 miles away, grains of popcorn were discovered in such perfect condition that after 1,000 years they still pop. French explorers, traveling through the Great Lakes region in the 17th century, found Indians popping corn in pottery vessels filled with hot sand, and the

Bang-up gift: in 1630 American Indians gave English colonists a deerskin bag filled with popped popcorn.

native Americans had even devised a recipe for popcorn soup.

In the 18th century a Spanish explorer saw, tried, and wrote of a special kind of Paraguayan popcorn with kernels on the tassel "that burst without becoming detached, and there results a superb bouquet fit to adorn a lady's hair at night without anyone knowing what it was. I have often eaten these burst grains

and found them very good."

The Indians believed that a tiny demon imprisoned inside each kernel made it pop. The demon, in fact, is water; each kernel of corn contains about 14 percent of it. When heated to 400° F, the water turns to steam and the grain to popcorn, a snowy puff 35 to 40 times the size of the seed that spawned it. Kernels that don't pop are known as "spinsters," and most manufacturers promise they will turn up only once in every hundred or so pops. White and yellow are the most popular kinds of popcorn. Yellow popcorn comes in two varieties: butterfly, irregularly flaked and thus best for buttering; and mushroom, which is compact and rounded and used in sugared preparations.

In all, more than 6 billion quarts of popcorn are eaten in the United States each year. Sales in movie theaters run well over $200 million a year.

Harvest home: thousands of bushels of corn are used each fall to decorate the Corn Palace in Mitchell, S.D.

corn was ground and served as hominy grits and hush puppies—bits of pan-fried batter used, so the story goes, to quiet dogs during fish fries. One bread recipe called for the inclusion of "a little Indian in your bread," meaning cornmeal. In 1835 an English visitor faced a common problem—corn on the cob—with this observation: "The greatest drawback is the way in which it is necessary to eat it. . . . It looks awkward enough, but what is to be done? Surrendering such a vegetable from considerations of grace is not to be thought of."

Most of the corn we eat today is not even visible, much less attached to the cob. It comes as part of the flesh of cows and hogs, which are fattened on it, and in milk, cheese, butter, and eggs. About 75 percent of the yearly corn harvest goes for fodder for livestock and poultry. And when other dietary uses of corn are considered, it is possible to say, conservatively, that each American consumes daily the end product of about three pounds of corn—or a pound per meal. Although that is obviously a substantial per capita consumption of the grain, this is only part of the corn we ingest, however it is refined, in our daily

Mexican god of maize was sculptured wearing a crown of corn.

lives. Corn also produces three mighty staples: starch, dextrin, and sugar.

It is hard to find an industry that does not use starch and dextrin. Because of their adhesive and binding properties, they are necessary in the manufacture, as well as the packaging, of everything from cotton clothing to wristwatch straps, cigarettes, charcoal briquettes, cosmetics, linoleum, adhesive tape, asbestos board, television cabinets, and even modern highways.

In addition to starch and dextrin, corn produces corn syrup and corn sugar. These are derived from starch by acid and enzyme conversion at a staggering rate: 2.5 billion pounds of syrup and a billion pounds of sugar (or dextrose) a year. The confectionery industry alone consumes some 800 million pounds of syrup and 50 million pounds of dextrose a year, churning out tons of hard candy, caramels, and nougats. And unless we restrict ourselves to fresh fish, fruits, and vegetables, we are purchasing corn's sweet by-products, which are included as an additive to almost every item we pluck from a supermarket shelf—including frozen fruits and vegetables, processed meats, pickles, yeast, and even the edible purple ink used to mark meats and cheeses.

Yet if man were not present to tend today's corn plants, the crop would die in about three growing seasons. This is because the corn plant has become so specialized that it cannot reproduce without the spaced planting only man can give it. Otherwise, its seeds fall too close to the parent hill.

And so, each spring about two weeks after the last killing frost, a fresh cycle of planting begins in every state in the union. The Midwestern corn belt produces the bulk of the crop, but corn is important elsewhere, too. In Georgia, for instance, it outstrips the state's annual peach harvest. In Vermont the corn harvest tops maple-sugar production.

Corn is all around us, touching our lives in ways beyond remembering. The next time someone pronounces something "corny," a good reply might well be, "What isn't?"

COSMETICS The U.S. government describes cosmetics as "articles intended to be rubbed, poured, sprinkled, or sprayed on, introduced into, or otherwise applied to the human body or any part thereof for cleansing, beautifying, promoting attractiveness, or altering the appearance. . . ."

Probably the most significant difference between today's products and those used by the Chinese and the Egyptians some 5,000 years ago is the staggering variety. Instead of gathering herbs and berries and even nuts and grinding them into various home concoctions, today's woman—or man— needs to go only as far as

1920: Vamp

the corner drugstore or supermarket for a dazzling selection of sticks and creams and powders and potions, in every imaginable color as well as some unimaginable ones, to cover, highlight, or alter any surface, crease, or hair on the body.

Not all cosmetics have been used for adornment. The hunters and shepherds of the Nile Valley about 7500 B.C. coated their skin with oil from the wild castor bean to protect it against the searing sun. Perfume was first used to scent the dead and in incense burned for the gods. The preparation of the scents took place in private chambers under the close supervision of priests, who kept the secret recipes. Early Egyptian adults and children applied a thick green paste to their eyelids to keep off the sun's burning

1930: Glamour girl

rays, although the fashionable also etched their eyes with a cream made from crushed ants' eggs.

Egyptians were probably the first to elevate the use of cosmetics to an art. Queen Nefertiti in the 14th century B.C. painted her fingernails and toenails a ruby red—the shade reserved exclusively for royalty. Women of lesser rank were obliged to tint their nails with a more subdued color, with a hue specified for each rung of the social ladder right down to the fringe nobility, who were limited to the palest shades. Historians have found that the most artful use of cosmetics was made by Cleopatra about 50 B.C. She rouged her cheeks with red ochre and applied henna to her palms to give them a youthful glow. She blackened her eyebrows and lined her eyelids with kohl, sometimes made of black galena, an ore found in lead; she painted her upper lids blue-black and the lower lids green. One of the sources of blue shadow was ground-up lapis lazuli, and the green came from malachite, the green ore of copper.

The Greeks reserved most of their body care for men. It was men—and courtesans—who bathed and oiled and perfumed their skin. Some Greek women might have dyed their brown or black hair blond, but that was the end of their self-indulgence. The courtesans, however, blackened their eyes, scented their breath with a special liquid, rouged with a Syrian root mashed in vinegar, and whitened their skin with the powder of lead, which ultimately ruined their complexions. One of the first skin-care products was a Greek invention attributed to Galen in the 2nd century A.D. He named it "cold cream," a combination of water, beeswax, and olive oil: the water evaporated and cooled the face. Today's cream of the same name does not differ much.

The Romans, however, did not bother with such things until they became the rich rulers of the world after defeating Phoenician Carthage in 146 B.C. Slaves of the Romans were often from more sophisticated societies than were their masters,

1940: Working girl

and, in imitation of them, the formerly ascetic Romans began to lighten their hair, whiten their skin with chalk, rub vermilion on their cheeks, stain their palms and soles with henna, shadow their eyes with gold from saffron, and blacken their eyelids with wood ash. Doomsayers pointed to the painted Roman faces as symbols of the empire's ever-growing corruption.

1960: Cleopatra look

The ideal beauty changed with each generation and from society to society, but the cosmetics revolution had its start in 15th-century England. New Italian cosmetics developed from scents and products brought back by the Crusaders, plus ravishing portraits of contemporary women and the new glass mirrors which the queen and some of her entourage had secured from the Continent—all contributed to the increased use of cosmetics.

For the first time, royal ladies saw themselves reflected neither in burnished metal nor in a pool of still water but in clear glass. It was a shock. Queen Elizabeth banned the new glass mirrors the minute she began to age. She continued to require her maids to dye her hair red, pluck her brows, and whiten her breasts and face, but she stopped looking at the re-

1970: Liberated woman

sult. (Her maids sometimes stuck a spiteful dot of vermilion on her nose.) Her contemporaries kept up by whitening their faces, too, often with the terrible Soliman's Water, made with mercury, which removed layers of skin, corroded flesh, and caused teeth to fall out.

Tudor chemists began to suspect what various whiteners were doing to skin, but few, if any, gave warning to their customers—who probably should have deduced the effect of the potions from their own observation, in any case. The Puritans, following their own beliefs, raged at what they considered to be feminine excess.

The 18th century produced the modern "powder room" for the application of England's ubiquitous powder: it went on wigs, faces, and hair. Women wore oiled forehead cloths and dogskin gloves to bed to fight wrinkles while they slept.

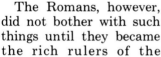

customs

Beauty Marks

Though the Bible warns against its use ("You shall not . . . tattoo any marks upon you") and various societies have employed it for everything from enslavement to sideshow entertainment, tattooing has a very real cosmetic history. In ancient Egypt, women of noble birth often displayed tattoos on the head, neck, and breasts, and in Iran, women wore beautifying tattoos well into the 20th century. The technique became a cosmetic must in certain upper-class circles in England in the World War I era. The leading tattooist, George Burchett, touted the marks as "Dainty Tints Imprinted on Society Ladies' Cheeks." Burchett also specialized in reddening pale lips, shading eyelids, coloring scars, whitening noses, and removing blemishes and tattoos. In 1920, when an Egyptian tomb was opened at Luxor, revealing a tattooed princess, Burchett's business boomed again. This time he specialized in tiny Egyptian-style insects, which he drew on the pale skin of fashion-conscious English women.

But in the next century the Victorian lady was to change all that; she one-upped fashion by saying no to, among other things, makeup. Her ideal was the naked face, a pink-and-white complexion, a small rosebud mouth, and large blue eyes—but obviously the only way she could achieve this look was to be born with it.

The story of America's cosmetics industry could very well start with David H. McConnell, who set out in 1886 to make a living selling books door to door. He got up a bottle of perfume to give out to buyers, and learned that his customers were far more interested in the scent than in Shakespeare. McConnell went into cosmetic production and sales, and astutely employed money-pressed housewives as his sales force. After 53 years in business, he changed his company's name from the California Perfume Company to Avon, after the river by which his beloved bard had lived.

In 1911 the first liquid cuticle remover appeared on the market, followed in 1916 by the first liquid nail polish. Both were instant successes as painted nails became the rage. Bright red lipsticks (still made from a castor base but colored with synthetic dyes) were packaged in metal cases and sold over the counter at a price anyone could afford. And the world primped for the greatest taste maker of them all: the motion picture.

Ancient Egyptian toilet cases containing cosmetics, eye brush, and pumice are much like today's.

After Helena Rubinstein made up Theda Bara with kohl, dark red lips, and white powder, the working girl rushed out of the theater to buy a new collection of cosmetics from the five-and-dime and transform her looks to match the ideal. She studied Clara Bow for details of brow and lip shape; when color films came, she studied Marilyn Monroe's highlighted hair and Elizabeth Taylor's eye makeup.

Every generation tries to keep up with changes of fashion, but some say that you can tell when a woman has stopped considering herself worth the effort by determining which era her style of makeup represents.

CRACKER Made of flour and water, baked and then dried, crackers filled the bill as an early convenience food—a portable bread that took up little space and resisted spoiling, sometimes up to 50 years. Pound for pound more nutritious than bread, crackers replaced bread as a standard military ration. The Roman soldiers ate biscuits on their marches, and when merchant sailors prepared to make ocean voyages of uncertain duration, the larder, of necessity, was simple: salt meat, dried peas, and crackers.

The shipboard crackers were called "pilot bread," "ship's biscuits," or "hardtack," and were

people

Sylvester Graham

When Aunt Polly "drowned" ailing Tom Sawyer in a cold shower, she was applying not only mankind's basic desire for cleanliness but also the very latest teachings of Sylvester Graham, a fiery pioneer in the field of personal health and hygiene. Graham was born in 1794, the 17th child of a Connecticut Yankee and not a healthy one at that. He studied for the ministry but took a job as an agent for the Pennsylvania Temperance Society in 1830. After a few months, Graham began wondering why moderation in food intake wasn't equally valuable. He had a point. The national stomach was bloated with an excess of meat and potatoes, and the national leg throbbed with gout. A farmer might work off such a diet, but more and more people were moving to cities and leading sedentary lives.

Verbose and puritanical but a rousing speaker, Graham stirred ire and admiration wherever he went among the unwashed, comfort-loving public. Much as Aunt Polly lectured Tom, Graham told reluctant Americans that they must brush their teeth, take cold baths at dawn, and warm sitdown baths at least once a week. He told them they must sleep on hard boards with thin mattresses, open the windows at night, chew food slowly, and eat green vegetables and fresh fruits. He warned them to abandon meat, alcohol, tobacco, coffee, tea, chocolate, pastry, and snacks. Thus purified, they were to space out their children, laugh at the table to aid digestion, eat their food cool, and, above all, eat only breads made from wheat grains with the germ and bran intact. None were available commercially, but Graham was so influential that bread and crackers were quickly produced—and named after him.

Graham made enemies of butchers and bakers, of tobacco and liquor producers, and of manufacturers of women's corsets. Women fainted as Graham's disciples lectured on the inner workings of the female body, but they rose as one to debone their corsets. Hotels set up Grahamite food tables. Graham's book, *Lectures on the Science of Human Life* (1839), transported his message where he could not go himself. Clearly a man ahead of his time, Graham and many of his ideas have now been widely accepted—and so have his crackers.

General store (1900): the cracker barrel is now a tin box and most goods are already packaged.

looked on as a source of variety in a monotonous diet. They could be made into gruel with the addition of water or used to soak up salt from meat—slightly improving the taste of both. After months at sea the crackers became rock hard, and only those infiltrated by weevils, which happened all too often, could be broken by hand.

On Columbus' fourth voyage food ran so low that his men had to scrape the bottom of the cracker barrel. According to one crew member, "Even the biscuit was so full of worms that, God help me, I saw many wait until nightfall to eat the porridge made of it so as not to see the worms."

In colonial America crackers were made by hand, each one individually shaped, and then baked in batches in oval-shaped tile ovens. The first cracker bakery opened its doors to business in 1794 in Newburyport, Massachusetts, using the centuries-old method. Almost 50 years later, in 1840, machines were introduced: they rolled out long strips of dough on conveyor belts, which passed under a mechanized shape stamper, and production immediately increased fivefold. The Gold Rush of 1849 greatly boosted demand for portable foods, and hard bread became a frontier staple. The cracker barrel became the centerpiece of the general store and has remained a symbol of a time when goods were sold in bulk. Nonetheless, by the 1890's ideas about advertising and packaging were changing America's buying habits, and by the end of the decade one company alone was selling 10 million packages of crackers per month.

CRAYON Crayons are as old as writing chalk, which dates from the Stone Age. When pigments were added to chalk, the colored sticks came to be known as pastels, a favorite artists' material. Edgar Degas, the French painter and sculptor of the 19th and 20th centuries, found the soft, delicate pastels the perfect medium for depicting ballet dancers embowered in gauze.

In America wax crayons were developed around the turn of the century by Binney & Smith. Called Crayolas (for crayon and oil), they arrived in stores in 1903 and sold for a nickel a box. To make crayons, liquid paraffin is heated and mixed with various pigments. The mixture is poured into a molding machine with over 2,000 holes in it, each the size and shape of a finished crayon. Excess wax is then scraped away, and the crayons are dumped into holding trays, encased in paper tubes, and boxed. To the simpler colors of simpler times, modern riches have been added: gold, copper, bronze, as well as peach, maize, and goldenrod—enough to fill a box with 64 different colors. There are even eight

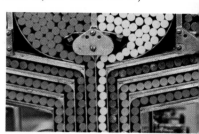

Getting them out may be child's play, but it takes intricate machines like this to box crayons.

fluorescent shades. In all about 2 billion crayons are sold each year—enough, if laid end to end, to encircle the globe with color nearly four full times.

CREDIT CARD The New York restaurateur Toots Shor surveyed his drinking establishment one day and offered this observation: "There was a time when you could see a flock of dollar bills on the bar. All you see now is pencils." Shor was referring to the ballooning use of credit cards, which now number about 300 million in the United States and finance some $80 billion of consumer spending annually. Scarcely a thing is left in the world that cannot be bought or borrowed on credit—from hand-carved folk art at a rural Nairobi market to "bunny"-driven limousines for touring the isle of Manhattan.

The idea of cash substitutes goes back to medieval times, when Germanic knights-errant used signet rings in place of their signatures to obtain credit. Appending a seal to validate a document originated with the Romans. (England's King John did not sign the Magna Carta, he merely sealed the document.) The knights used their rings, engraved with their coat of arms as proof of their financial standing. Traveling the wood-

Traveling German knights used seals as credit cards in the 13th century.

ed roadways with large amounts of cash was hazardous, so innkeepers kept a master list of seals and signet rings and billed the traveling knights later.

In the same way the pieces of plastic in our wallets symbolize our willingness and ability to pay later for what we buy now. Those who fail to pay—an estimated 40,000 persons each month—have their cards taken away, known in the trade as "plastic surgery." In days of old if a knight or prince was remiss in paying up, the creditor barred the castle gate until the nobleman sent out some cash.

The popularity of credit cards is basically a 20th-century phenomenon. The first ones were issued in the 1920's by oil companies and department stores. The term "credit card," was coined by Edward Bellamy in *Looking Backward, 2000–1887,* published in 1888. He predicted that citizens of the future would carry a single government card (or credit card) inscribed with each person's share of the "annual product of the nation." Purchases of nearly everything would be charged against the balance on the card, eliminating the need for cash or monthly bills.

Bellamy had vision, even if he erred in some of the details. In 1977 a number of banks were introducing a debit card, not a credit card. When a merchant forwards the charge slips to the bank, the amount of the bill is electronically deducted from the buyer's account and transferred to the seller's. Although there are still many kinds of plastic credit, Bellamy's idea of one comprehensive card may yet become a reality.

CROSSWORD PUZZLE For centuries, children have played a game called a "word square," where letters spell out the same words horizontally and vertically. The square was the ancestor of the crossword puzzle, which uses interlocking words across and down. A form of crossword puzzle appeared in England in the 19th century, but Americans made the puzzle a national passion.

The first puzzle was put together by Arthur Wynne and appeared in *Fun,* the Sunday supplement of the New York *World,* on December 21, 1913. Eleven years later, after various improvements in form, the young publishing partners Simon and Schuster asked the *World*'s trio of puzzle editors to prepare a book devoted to puzzles. The idea came from Simon's aunt. She wanted to please a puzzle-loving relative who found the wait between Sunday supplements intolerably long. This un-

When filled in with Bible verses, this puzzle tells a story about Jesus.

precedented volume, equipped with a pencil on a string, became a bestseller in three months. It heralded a 10-year puzzle craze. "Uncle Henry," a folksy philosopher for *Collier's,* disapproved: "Some people say it's good mental exercise and a wonderful way to increase the vocabulary. Did you ever in all your life see a time-killin', energy-wastin' game that didn't have such an alibi?"

The tools of the puzzle solver were Roget's *Thesaurus,* the dictionary, and the atlas, and sales of all three benefited from the fad. The Baltimore and Ohio Railroad ordered its main-line trains to carry dictionaries for the pleasure of puzzle fiends. It seems that everyone knew the Egyptian sun god was called Ra, the two-letter word for a printer's measure was em, and that Ireland was also Eire. Despite a decline the crossword has remained a daily feature in 90 percent of the world's newspapers. The exceptions are Oriental languages, which do not lend themselves to across-and-down manipulation.

Ultimate charge: even the ballooning costs of a wine-taster's tour of France can be paid for by credit card.

DESIGNS: *Lead into Gold*

From earliest times a few talented, often driven, beings have chosen to depict man's doings and his surroundings. Those artists have viewed the environment and rendered its stuff so as to make a statement about its substance. Most of us do not take in half of what meets the eye, but the painter looks, absorbs, and through his brush creates anew—superimposing his personality on what he sees.

The detail above, from "Daughters of Edward Boit" (1882) by the American John Singer Sargent, demonstrates how a painter can transform a commonplace scene into a thing of artistic wonder. Viewed from a distance the little girl with her doll seems to be portrayed in fine detail but a close look at the picture reveals that the figures and the surroundings are actually conveyed by masterful impressionist strokes of the brush. Like Sargent, the great visual interpreters of every era offer a unique and fascinating look at their world. We have but to examine their work carefully to enrich our appreciation of seemingly ordinary things.

The Social Scene

Sharing food or drink, chatting, laughing, dancing—that is to say, socializing—nothing is more everyday or more human, and many artists down the years have depicted the social scene and all its trappings. (In fact, as still lifes indicate, sometimes the paraphernalia of togetherness itself has an intrinsic visual value.) In times of intense religiosity, like the Middle Ages, most painters confined themselves to subjects from the Bible, but in later centuries, like those represented in the samples shown here, artists focused on secular good times. Whether they be of the mannered upper classes or of roistering peasants, the artists' views give us a feeling of how it must have been.

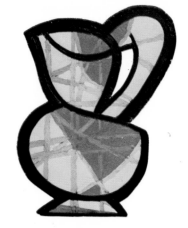

Detail from "Pitcher and Bowl of Fruit" (1931) by Pablo Picasso.

Detail from "Girl from Madrid" (c. 1925) by George Luks.

Detail from "A Cup of Tea" (c.1880) by Mary Cassatt.

"Le Moulin de la Galette" (1876) by Pierre Auguste Renoir.

Detail from "The Smokers" by Adriaen Brouwer (1605–38).

Detail from "The Wedding Dance" (1566)
by Pieter Brueghel the Elder.

Detail from "La Soupe" (1860–62)
by Honoré Daumier.

Detail from
"Conversation
Dans Un
Parc" by
Thomas
Gainsborough
(1727–88).

Detail from
"Pâté and
Basket of
Glasses" by
Sébastien
Stoskopff
(1597–1657).

Fabric of Life

During the second half of the 19th century, a debate raged in the art world about "art for art's sake"—meaning that only brushwork and color counted, not subject matter. Earlier painters were not bothered by such philosophical niceties, but they did know that a thoughtful rendering of textures, whether quickly stroked or carefully measured, could draw attention to more than just fabric itself. Hans Holbein the younger, who painted "The Merchant Gisze" (1532), below, reveals much about the subject by meticulously depicting the tools of the man's trade, his rich clothing, and the flowers set in a dainty vase, suggesting the merchant's appreciation of the finer things.

Detail from a portrait of Lord North by Nathaniel Dance (1735-1811).

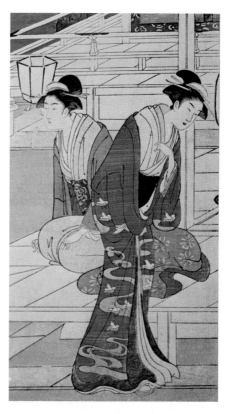

Detail from "The Madonna with Canon van der Paele" (1436) by Jan van Eyck.

Detail from "Portrait of Saskia" (c.1634) by Rembrandt.

Below, "Boots with Laces" (1886) by Vincent van Gogh. At bottom, detail from "The Washing of the Feet" (c.1317) by Duccio.

Detail from "Evening Under the Murmuring Pines" (c.1800) by Eishi.

Detail from "Woman with Chrysanthemums" (1865) by Edgar Degas.

Domestic Art

Anything can serve as a source of artistic inspiration—including the kitchen sink. Very little is left out of Grandma Moses' (Anna Mary Robertson Moses) ambitious "A Tramp on Christmas Day," below , painted in 1946. The whole family has gathered in the kitchen to share the spirit of the day, as the women calmly go about their preparations for the feast. Though one might wonder what the women who were performing the drudgery felt, the painters of these domestic scenes viewed them lovingly. Their pictures are infused with a feeling of quiet and gentleness, even when loneliness and pathos also have a place.

Detail from "The Dishwasher" by Giuseppe Maria Crespi (1665–1747).

Detail from "Women's Work"
(c.1911) by John Sloan.

Detail from "The Cook"
(c.1660) by Jan Vermeer.

Detail from "Woman
Ironing" (1904) by
Pablo Picasso.

Detail from "Girl at a
Sewing Machine" (c.1921)
by Edward Hopper.

Detail from "The Washer-
women" (c.1889) by Pierre
Auguste Renoir.

That's Art

After 1900 painters turned in many directions trying to liberate their imaginations and in the process, develop new techniques. The surrealists, for example, tried to transmit dream images to canvas, as in Salvador Dalí's "Persistence of Memory" (1931), bottom, right. More recently, artists have riveted their attention on seemingly trivial things, giving rise anew to the old question: "Is that supposed to be art?" According to one art historian, "a leap of the imagination" is true art's primary ingredient. However simple or distorted the views of modern artists seem, the works of many of them do represent an imaginative effort to reinterpret their world through their art.

Detail from "Floor with Laundry 1" (1970) by Sylvia Mangold.

"Woman Eating" (1971) by Duane Hanson.

"Campbell's Soup Can" (1964) by Andy Warhol.

"The Persistence of Memory" (1931) by Salvador Dalí.

"Fur-covered Cup, Saucer and Spoon" (1936) by Meret Oppenheim.

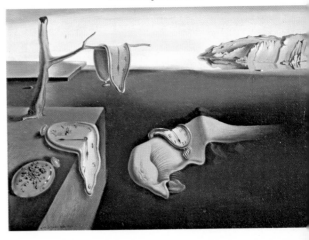

D *Wedge-shaped in Phoenician, D developed a bulging side in Greek and its present shape in Latin.*

DECIMAL SYSTEM The decimal system of positional notation (its full name) is probably the result of a biological accident—human beings happen to have 10 fingers. (The word comes from the Latin *decem*, meaning "ten.") Prehistoric peoples, it is thought, grew accustomed to thinking in units of ten, which they could easily visualize by looking at their own 10 digits. According to Ripley's "Believe It or Not," in the 1930's all the inhabitants of a village in Spain had 6- or 7-finger hands due to inbreeding; they used a number system based on 12, perhaps because of their biological deviation.

About 4,000 years ago the Egyptians devised pictographs based on the unit ten: the symbol for 100 was a rope, and that for a million was a man holding out his arms as if in amazement at so large a number. By about 600 A.D. the Hindus were using a base-10 system with simple, easy-to-write numbers whose values depended on their position in a sequence of numerals. Ten digits were used (0 through 9). The first digit was worth just itself. The second digit was worth 10 times itself; the third digit, 100 times itself, and so on. Thus each position in the sequence was worth 10 times more than the previous digit. It seems simple enough, but it took centuries to evolve and is one of the greatest accomplishments in the history of science.

The Hindu decimal system was not without its faults. It did not use a zero, but denoted an "empty" position in a numerical sequence with a period, which could be easily overlooked when the number was read. The zero is believed to have been used first in China sometime before 1000 A.D.

Arabian mathematicians popularized the Hindu system (which is why the numerals are termed "Arabic"), but their method did not replace the awkward system of Roman numerals in Europe for centuries. One reason was that the decimal had no way of expressing fractions until the decimal point was introduced in the 1600's. (Some European countries today use a comma for the decimal point.) Since then, the decimal system has been adopted almost universally—truly an international language for commerce and mathematics. But there are still some shortcomings. For example, there is no standard name for numbers with more places than 66. What comes after 999,999,999,999,999,999,999,999,999,999, 999,999,999,999,999,999,999,999,999,999—the first three 9's being vigintillions—is a mystery.

DELICATESSEN The common denominator of delicatessen food is its ethnic origin. Each group of immigrants brought its culinary heritage from the "old country." It helped make their strange new world a little more familiar. Most countries have fine food stores, featuring local delicacies and catering to the national taste. But there is something uniquely American about a delicatessen. One would expect to find all kinds of smoked fish and herrings in a Nordic *livsmedelsaffar* and a selection of sausages in a German *feinkostgeschaft*, but a well-stocked American deli will carry both sausages and herring as well as French and Italian cheeses, Greek olives, baklava and tabbouleh, to say nothing of bagels, corned beef, pastrami, and chopped liver.

The first delicatessen was located in colonial Philadelphia. Over the centuries the port of New York became the nation's delicatessen capital, with some 15,000 delis by 1959. Fewer than half are left—from tiny mom-and-pop enterprises, to Macy's food emporium, which offers 200 varieties of cheese and 50 kinds of bread to put it on. But the rest have not really disappeared. They have moved—lox, stock, and barrels—to Tulsa, Oklahoma; Savannah, Georgia; Denver, Colorado; and Lincolnwood, Illinois.

As Americans become better traveled and more sophisticated in their tastes, new items appear on delicatessen shelves: snow grouse from Norway, blueberries from Australia, string beans from Kenya, mushrooms from Romania, chocolates from Belgium, sole on ice from the English Channel, and, of course, the pellucid gray eggs of sturgeon from the Caspian Sea.

All these goodies seem to obey an inexorable law of economics: the farther from the consumer anything is grown, raised, or caught, the more expensive it will be. This law works impartially in both directions. Fauchon in Paris and Fortnum and Mason in London are two of the fanciest food stores in the world. At Fortnum and Mason the clerks wear frock coats and striped trousers. Both stores stock fresh truffles, quails, pheasants, the finest pâtés, and the rarest teas. Displayed there like so many jewels—and priced accordingly—are American peanut butter, ketchup, and popcorn.

DENTIST Modern dentistry is a triumph over more than 5,500 years of ignorance and anguish. Toothaches have always plagued man, but rational, lasting remedies to the problem have been known only about 200 years. Primitive man rarely worried about tooth decay and improper bite, but his teeth wore down because of his rough diet. The first dental surgery was probably as simple as

The Beat Goes On

There are at least two great truths about social dancing. One is that there is virtually nothing new under the sun as far as beat, steps, movements, or proximity of partners are concerned. The latest wiggle has almost certainly been performed before, somewhere. The second is that almost every new dance variation, with the possible exception of the minuet, has been seen by social conservatives as the onset of depravity, heralding a total breakdown in decency. Yet the pristine minuet did not last long. Why? Because too many people thought it a drag.

People have always been concerned about the moral effects of dancing. Homer was in favor of it, and so was Aristotle. Socrates thought that the best dancers probably made the best warriors as well. But Cicero saw no good in the practice. He wrote, "No man who is sober dances, unless he is out of his mind, either when alone or in any decent society; for dancing is the companion of wanton conviviality, dissoluteness and luxury."

With his rumble about wantonness, Cicero put his thumb on what has bothered arbiters of taste in every century: the suspicion that dancing is somehow linked to sexuality. Dryden called dancing "poetry of the feet," but he was only partly right. The truth is that dancing involves moving more than the feet: it brings two people together in some measure of closeness, and often their bodies touch. The issue of touching was what got the waltz in trouble in Germany in the late 1700's. Reported one observer: "The dancers held up the dresses of their partners very high so that they should not trail and be stepped on, wrapped them tightly in this shroud, bringing both bodies under one covering, as close together as possible, and thus the turning went on in the most indecent positions. . . ."

France takes the blame for introducing the idea of dancing in two's. In Provence about 1200, they did the farandole, which involved long lines, until they broke into partners, permitting couples to veer in all directions. That forced the gentry to "modernize" their houses by moving their fireplaces from the center of the room to one wall.

Before new dances are accepted they often go through a predictable cycle. Someone, usually unidentified, introduces a dance, and large numbers of followers take it up. Then social criticism begins, as it did with the polka, turkey trot, hootchy-kootchy, tango, rumba, conga, samba, foxtrot, lindy, jitterbug, and certainly the shaking that accompanied rock 'n' roll. While heads are wagging, more and more people find that the dance is fun, and it gains general acceptance. So it was with the twist, which looked raunchy to most people when it was introduced by rock 'n' roll singer "Chubby" Checker; but soon it became so common that First Lady Jacqueline Kennedy twisted at the White House with the secretary of defense.

Dancing allows the young of every generation the satisfaction of creating something that is both uniquely their own and shocking to their elders. With powerful incentives like these, it is no wonder that "new" dances spring up like crabgrass. It must have been a joy to Anna Slezakova, the peasant girl who was rumored to have spun the polka out of her own love of life, to watch thousands of others ignore the critic who labeled it "a kind of insane Tartar jig."

Whatever the new dance variation, there is one ironclad rule: it must not resemble the one that preceded it. Shortly after 1900, when the waltz had become something that decent people could do, it fell out of favor. The beat changed to syncopation, and in strolled the turkey trot and the bunny hug. And hug they did, as young women checked their corsets in the ladies' room and pressed close to their partners in what was called "button shining." Such closeness could not last forever, and the next fad was fast movement—without touching your partner. It was called the Charleston.

The human skeleton has not changed much over the centuries, and neither have the ways in which to frolic to music. The energetic cancan was a shocker in its day, and it made onetime Soviet Premier Nikita Khrushchev turn red when he saw it on a movie set. But he could have seen the same high kick in Egyptian relief carvings that are over 4,000 years old. And so the beat goes on.

Tudor bounce: Queen Elizabeth hops to it, dancing la volta *with Robert Dudley, Earl of Leicester, in this 1581 painting of court life.*

knocking out an aching tooth with a rock.

As early as 3700 B.C., there were dental specialists in Egypt, and Sumerian tablets dug up in the valley of the Euphrates give advice on dental treatment. Along with prescribing medicines and ways of treating teeth, the tablets suggest incantations and offer the theory that a burrowing worm was responsible for tooth decay. That theory was finally given up in Europe as late as the 18th century but persists to this day in some parts of the world. Anton van Leeuwenhoek, who invented the microscope, investigated the worm theory. After examining some worms supposedly smoked out of someone's teeth he wrote: "Let's imagine that the Patient . . . had eaten Cheese laden with young Worms . . . and that these Worms . . . insinuated themselves so far into the substance of the Teeth that they gnaw'd the sensible parts, and so occasioned great pain." In his day a standard treatment for an inflamed tooth was to drop oil of vitriol into the cavity. The modern name for that oil is sulfuric acid, and it stopped the pain—not because it slew the worms of decay but because it killed the nerve tissue in the tooth. Leeuwenhoek did observe, through his microscope, that the human mouth had large numbers of bacteria, and that was a beginning.

In the absence of a true understanding of what causes tooth decay, the earliest dentists spent most of their time pulling teeth and replacing lost ones. The Greek physician Hippocrates performed extractions, but only of loose, decayed teeth; for ailing teeth still firmly in place, he recommended cauterization. In the 2nd century A.D. the renowned Greek doctor Galen theorized that decay was caused by "disturbances" in the blood that inflamed the teeth. He also noted that pain caused by inflamed tooth pulp was different from that of diseases of the gums.

With the fall of the Roman Empire, in 476 A.D., Arab practitioners took the leadership in dentistry. Among other advances, they recommended the use of dentifrices and used a metal material to fill cavities. They identified dental tartar as harmful to teeth, and also described a method of transplanting teeth. Because of a religious prohibition against cutting flesh, the Arab specialists concentrated on pharmacology and cauterization.

In the 17th century, country dentists performed in public, drawing crowds with teeth.

Curb service: in China in the 1930's street dentists pulled teeth by the side of the road—and kept them.

In the Middle Ages in Europe, monks performed most of the dental work. When in the 12th and early 13th centuries church councils restricted the monks' medical activities, the work of dentistry fell to barber-surgeons. In England the Guild of Barber Surgeons was founded in 1308, and it lasted more than 400 years. Most physicians of the time regarded dentistry as demeaning.

The methods of dentists during England's Tudor Period (1485–1603) were colorful. They included bleeding the patient, a standard method of treating many ills. Humfre Lloyd, a London physician, based many of his prescriptions for toothache on the earlier work of Petrus Hyspanus, who became Pope John XXI in 1276. Lloyd offered a number of mouthwashes made from cucumbers, violets, henbane, thistle, and other plants. He also thought that putting various things in the patient's ear would relieve toothache, although there were grave debates about which ear should be selected. It depended in part on what material was used. Wild cucumber juice, for instance, belonged in the ear on the same side of the head as the aching tooth, whereas the juice of daffodils was assigned to the ear on the opposite side.

Modern dentistry was born in the 18th century in France. The leading practitioner was Pierre Fauchard, who published *The Surgeon Dentist* in 1728. Fauchard dealt with anatomy, decay, surgery, gum diseases, and medicines, and his book fostered much dental research. Fauchard himself invented the bandelette, an instrument for spreading crowded teeth. In England the dental turnkey was invented about 1840. It allowed the dentist to extract the most solidly positioned tooth, and it replaced the earlier pelican and straight levers. These two instruments depended for their pulling power on leverage from adjacent healthy teeth, and often did as much damage as good. All extractions were still done without effective anesthesia.

In the 19th century, world leadership in dentistry shifted from France to the United States. The X-ray machine was perfected for use in diagnosis, and bacteria were finally identified as the true cause of tooth decay. The first dental school in the world, the Baltimore College of Dental Surgery, opened in 1840. After an initial try with nitrous oxide (laughing gas), most dentists settled on ether as an anesthetic, and some of the pain went out of dentistry. Just after the turn of the century, American physician Albert Einhorn produced procaine (Novocain), which became the most popular painkiller. Fluorides came to be known as beneficial in the prevention of cavities.

Today there are about 110,000 dentists in the United States. They schedule over 335 million visits annually, and receive about $8.5 billion in fees. But because there are still not enough dentists to go around, the shift has been toward preventive dentistry as well as repair after the damage is done.

Dental specialties are now established. More than half of all dental specialists are orthodontists, who work at preventing or correcting misalignment of the teeth. Oral surgeons do extractions and other operations on the jaw and mouth. Pedodontists attend to children's teeth, and periodontists specialize in gum diseases. Prosthodontists make dentures, and endodontists do root-canal work.

Most dentists, however, are general practitioners, who are concerned with preventing damage to teeth as well as repairing them. In sight is a powerful tool to help them: the discovery that a particular bacterium, *streptococcus mutans*, is the chief cause of tooth decay, makes the development of a vaccine against decay more likely.

DENTURES The struggle of human beings to replace lost teeth, for vanity's sake and as an aid in chewing, began more than 2,500 years ago. The Etruscans were making partial dentures—designed to replace some teeth rather than all—about 700 B.C. They used gold for the base of the denture and added teeth from other human mouths or semiartificial replacements carved from ox teeth.

In the 16th century, dentists wired loose teeth with gold and constructed false teeth from hippopotamus or walrus ivory. Though used for several hundred years, ivory was never satisfactory. It was porous, changed color, and tended to make the denture wearer unpopular. One writer report-

people

He's A Dentist?

Dentists have become famous for inventions, literature, and varied activities that swamp their basic calling. Dr. G.W.A. Bonwill perfected the modern safety pin, and Dr. Thomas Welch originated Welch's grape juice. Sugar-coated chewing gum may harm the teeth, but a dentist, William F. Semple, added the sweetener, along with peppermint and vanilla, to chicle gum in 1869. In 1922 William Lowell, another dentist, invented the wooden golf tee, and 40 years later Dr. Cary Middlecoff became rich and famous for his ability to tee off.

When Marshal Wyatt Earp and his two brothers fought at the O.K. Corral in Tombstone, Arizona, a local dentist backed them

up and was wounded for his trouble. Doc Holliday had already taken down his dentist's shingle and earned fame as a man who favored firearms to settle arguments—for law and order, of course.

Perhaps the unluckiest dentist ever was Mahlon Loomis, who demonstrated wireless telegraphy 35 years before Marconi. Loomis got financial backing to develop his invention, but the "Black Friday" panic of 1869 broke his backers. About two years later another group that promised support lost all it had in the Great Fire in Chicago. Loomis died in obscurity, after predicting that others would perfect his idea and get the credit. He was right.

Paul Revere, though, was immortalized by Longfellow for his famous midnight ride. Known primarily as a goldsmith and silversmith, Revere also did dental work in hard times. In the first reliably recorded use of forensic dentistry in America, he identified the body of patriot Joseph Warren from dental work he had done on the man. Warren had fallen before British fire in the Battle of Bunker's Hill.

Afflicted with a mother who named him Pearl, but encouraged by a wife who urged him to write, Zane Grey, a practicing dentist, suffered through three bad-selling novels. Then he produced *Riders of the Purple Sage* and became a favorite author of Western tales.

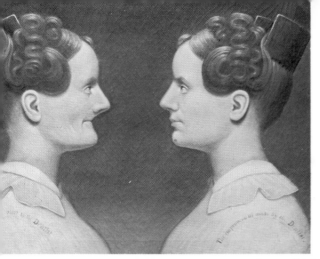

The virtues of false teeth are more than amply profiled in this 19th-century before-and-after advertisement.

ed in 1850: "Ivory gives to the air returned from the lungs an unsufferably offensive odor, which cannot be prevented or corrected. They [the dentures] may be washed half a dozen times a day and taken out and cleaned at night, but it will still be grossly perceptible."

On this unattractive property of ivory rests one of the most important legal decisions about freedom of the press. In 1733 or 1734, in his *New York Weekly Journal*, John Peter Zenger attacked the colonial governor, William Cosby. Among other things, Zenger said that Cosby had loathsome false teeth and an unclean mouth. The infuriated governor had Zenger jailed for seditious libel. At the trial Zenger's defense counsel admitted Zenger's authorship of the insults but claimed that they were not libelous unless the Crown could prove that Zenger was incorrect. The jury found Zenger not guilty, implicitly convicting the governor of bad breath. Truth, as a defense against libel, was firmly established.

Before about 1900, the lot of a denture wearer was often a miserable one. The lack of proper materials for building dentures, or the means to keep full or partial dentures firmly in place, made even great men like George Washington moody and irascible. Queen Elizabeth I, embarrassed by the loss of her front teeth, made public appearances with her mouth stuffed with fine cloth. Her concern that her face had sunk inward makes the point that early dentures were sometimes worn as a cosmetic measure and not always to aid in chewing. It was common for the wearer to remove his or her dentures at mealtime.

In the 1850's the introduction of colloid materials enabled dentists to take accurate impressions of the mouth. Charles Goodyear's discovery of vulcanized rubber, in 1839, produced a first-rate material for the base of dentures. Porcelain had already displaced ivory as material for false teeth.

After World War I various plastics and synthetic resins made dentures so natural looking and comfortable that the curse was lifted from one of mankind's oldest afflictions.

DEODORANT Each person sweats about a quart of liquid on an average day, mostly without noticing it. Conditioned by custom and advertising, he or she tries to assure that others do not notice it either. Most of the sweat emerges from the body's 2 to 5 million eccrine glands; its purpose is to regulate body temperature by evaporation and keep friction surfaces, such as the soles and palms, moist. It is colorless, odorless, and low in organic material. Another type of sweat flows from the less numerous apocrine glands, which become active only after puberty. These "scent glands" are stimulated by fear, sexual excitement, pain, or other emotional stresses and may have served some primitive social function. A third type, the sebaceous glands, buried deep in the skin, secrete an oily substance that lubricates the skin.

The culprit in body odor is not the sweat or the oil but the action of "resident" bacteria on these secretions after they form on the skin. Deodorant soaps and deodorants attempt to slow bacterial action. Antiperspirants, which are legally classified as drugs, inhibit the rate of perspiration. Deodorants and antiperspirants may vary in their helpfulness to particular people, and neither group of products is a substitute for a bath or shower. In some rare instances, people elect to undergo major neurosurgery to control, say, excessively sweaty palms.

Before sprays, roll-ons, and moistened pads, men and women depended on perfumes, talcum powder, and bicarbonate of soda to mask unavoidable body odor. Around the turn of the century, however, some women even believed that a faint body odor was attractive to men. They called it *bouquet de corsage*. In modern society it is generally considered repugnant—hence deodorants.

DEPARTMENT STORE When department-store magnate Marshall Field declared, in the 1880's, "The customer is always right," he was pointing out a fundamental change in consumer power. In rural, postcolonial America, the merchant had the upper hand. Farmers and frontiersmen spent their modest incomes on the necessities of life, and suppliers could take their time about getting goods to the only general store in town. There was no incentive to offer a wide variety of merchandise. Then came the Industrial Revolution, and an economy based on scarcity began to

GUM, the largest department store in Moscow, offers many vistas but little merchandise.

change to an economy of plenty. As incomes rose, so did the amount of money a person could spend on what he or she wanted rather than needed. The onset of mass production meant that manufacturers could make more of more products, and the spreading network of railroads could move everything faster and farther. Markets became national, not local, and the new freedom to buy or not to buy made it necessary for merchants to start promoting products.

The department store was a response to these 19th-century economic trends. In the mid-1800's sellers of dry goods and fashion items gradually added other lines of merchandise at separate locations, or departments, within the store. Today, the largest department stores attempt under one roof to satisfy almost every conceivable demand by customers.

The first department store in America is thought to have been the Marble Dry-Goods Palace, opened in 1848 in New York City by Alexander Turney Stewart. Like Macy, Gimbel, Bloomingdale, Hudson, and other merchant kings who were to follow, Stewart put a stop to the age-old practice of bargaining with the customer over price. His goods were for sale at announced, fixed prices. Other retailers, too, changed their traditional ways of doing business. They guaranteed customer satisfaction, and would take back faulty merchandise and refund the money. They bought and sold for cash—a new idea in those days and a novel one today. As competition grew fierce, irregular prices such as $3.99 began to appear.

Cash flow, 1900's: pneumatic tubes whisked money to the cashier in this Washington store.

The owners of large department stores had one thing in common: a profound aversion to anonymity. They knew that success depended on an unending parade of customers, and they sought publicity and advertised vigorously. Some sponsored entertainment, such as Christmastime Santas and Macy's lavish parade on Thanksgiving

Day. Others adopted distinctive wrapping paper, turning the shopper into a walking advertisement. In 1937 Selfridge's in London hired a Hollywood film producer and spent $150,000 just to decorate its facade in honor of George VI's coronation.

To keep the customers coming, the closeout sale was born, and so was the bargain basement. Some stores, like the fabled Nieman-Marcus in Dallas, found special niches in the marketplace. Overturning Marshall Field's adage about the customer being always right, Nieman-Marcus prefers to be a leader and has become a nationwide symbol of ostentatious elegance. What other store has ever offered "his and her" submarines as a possible Christmas present? In contrast, the galleries of GUM, Moscow's and perhaps the Soviet Union's leading store, offer very little variety and style in the limited selections of dry goods put up for sale.

In the mid-20th century the story of the department store closely paralleled the saga of the American city. When high-income populations began moving to the suburbs, department stores went along, opening branches though keeping the main store downtown. As downtown neighborhoods deteriorated, these "parent" stores usually suffered. Some merchants, however, learned to adapt to changes. In the 1940's Bloomingdale's in New York was thought of as the "poor man's Macy's." But the area around the store improved over the years as the pockets of slums were turned into fashionable apartment buildings and desirable places to live. Alert, the management turned the store into a modish, razzle-dazzle place, just as the chic and well-heeled moved into the neighborhood.

As the boom in suburban sales slackened, many department-store chains, seeking to stimulate sales, refurbished their downtown stores. As one industry dictum has it, "In this business, today's peacock is tomorrow's feather duster."

DETECTIVE STORY When the citizens of London went underground to escape the savagery of the German Blitz during World War II, they took along books to read. Their overwhelming first choice: the detective novel. Nor was this the public's first demonstration of its fascination with detective fiction. Ever since Edgar Allan Poe launched the genre, in 1841, with publication of *The Murders in the Rue Morgue*, the public has responded to detection with delectation. At the outbreak of World War II, one of every four new books of fiction in English was a detective novel, and it mattered little that some critics—and some writers—tossed them off as intellectual popcorn, scarcely worthy of being called fiction.

The most famous fictional detective of all time, Sherlock Holmes, had a human prototype: Dr. Joseph Bell, a surgeon and instructor in medicine at the Royal Infirmary in Edinburgh. Bell reportedly had the uncanny skill of looking at a stranger and deducing a remarkable amount of information about his life and habits. One of Bell's students, Arthur Conan Doyle, was impressed. Turning from medicine, he created a thin fictional detective who wore a deer-stalker hat and inverness cape, played the violin, had a cocaine habit, and smoked foul pipe tobacco. Doyle almost named his detective Sherrinford instead of Sherlock. There is speculation, but no proof, that Doyle purloined the last name from Oliver Wendell Holmes, whom he greatly admired, and the first name from a man he had whipped 30 straight times at bowling and thus was fond of.

Fictional detectives are often accompanied by sidekicks, whose role is to be helpful and inquisitory, thereby providing the infallible No. 1 with an opportunity to explain his thoughts to the befuddled reader. Dr. John Watson, Holmes' bumbling, good-natured chronicler, turned out to be such a good character that Doyle even wrote a play just about him—though it remains unpublished. Most other sidekicks just tagged helpfully along: Harry Vincent with Lamont Cranston, Bunter with Lord Peter Wimsey, Paul Drake with Perry Mason, a dog named Asta with Nick and Nora Charles, Archie Goodwin with Nero Wolfe,

Sherlock Holmes' point may be elementary, but the style of this Sidney Paget illustration is very sophisticated.

and Inspector Richard Queen with his remarkable son Ellery.

Sam Spade, Dashiell Hammett's hard-boiled hero, also had a partner, named Miles Archer. And though he died early in *The Maltese Falcon*, thus avoiding the discovery that Sam was having an affair with his wife, his memory lives on. (The movie version of the book starring Humphrey Bogart is generally regarded as the quintessential detective film.) Raymond Chandler's Philip Marlowe, however, traveled alone.

Private eyes, as they are called, got their name from the trademark of the Pinkerton agency, a wide-open eye with the slogan "We Never Sleep." Yet real detectives never achieved the fame of their fictional brothers. Hercule Poirot, who with Miss Marple helped Agatha Christie sell 350 million books, even received an obituary in *The New*

York Times when Christie decided to let him expire. He was the first fictional character to be so honored. Sherlock Holmes still has a considerable following, as indicated by the Baker Street Irregulars, and *The Encyclopaedia Sherlockiana*, which tells substantially more than most people would want to know about Holmes and his times.

Many writers have tried detective fiction, including Ernest Hemingway, John Steinbeck, Pearl S. Buck, George Bernard Shaw, and William Faulkner. Franklin Delano Roosevelt had a plot but could not complete it without the help of seven additional writers, Erle Stanley Gardner among them. Even Abraham Lincoln tried, publishing "The Trailor Murder Mystery" in the Quincy (Illinois) *Whig*. As prose, even detective prose, it did nothing to challenge the elegant simplicity of the Gettysburg Address.

The queen of detective fiction, Agatha Christie, never resolved her own, most personal mystery. It concerned her disappearance on the night of December 3, 1926. When her car was found abandoned some 15 miles from her home, it contained only her briefcase and personal papers. A hundred policemen were assigned to the case; for a time suicide was suspected. Bloodhounds were brought in, and airplanes skimmed the woods and hedges in a womanhunt that came ultimately to involve 15,000 people. Eleven days later, she was found, hundreds of miles away, in Yorkshire, and she seemed not to recognize her own husband, Col. Archibald Christie. Amnesia, it was reported officially, yet she had not forgotten everything. She had, in fact, registered at a small inn, using a name she had only recently learned—that of her husband's mistress. Christie never explained what had happened, or why.

DIAMOND A fine diamond is the hardest natural substance known to man (85 times harder than the corundum of which sapphires and rubies are made), and pound for pound it can bring a higher price than any other raw material on earth. But a diamond is really only a bit of crystallized carbon, one of the most abundant and widely distributed

people

The Prototype

François-Eugène Vidocq, the world's first professional detective, led a life only the most imaginative of mystery writers could have invented. By turns he was a soldier, jailbird, fugitive, spy, womanizer, and, finally, chief of the Sûreté, the French undercover police organization.

Vidocq lived to be almost 82 (he died in 1857), and in that time he dramatically changed the nature of police work. He was, for example, among the first to grasp the importance of fingerprints as a means of positively identifying a criminal, and was the first to introduce handwriting analysis in court proceedings. His voluminous records detailing the descriptions and methods of operation of criminals, plus his own prodigious memory, introduced science and administrative expertise to the existing erratic and often brutal system of law.

During his years as a forger, and later as an escaped convict determined to prove his innocence, Vidocq became an expert in the practices and poses of crooks. He perfected the art of disguise, though his first use of costume—at 15—was for quite a different purpose: he dressed as a woman to accompany an older woman on vacation without alerting her husband.

Vidocq managed to bargain with the Paris police and transform himself from fugitive to policeman. His personal belief in the usefulness of informers supports the suggestion that he launched his career as a stool pigeon. In any case, Vidocq had a highly pragmatic view of ethics and morality. As an old man, he admitted having accepted expensive presents from various important Parisians, but claimed that it was only to avoid being rude. He never took cash, he insisted. In fact, he may not have needed money, for he held patents on special papers and inks, all designed to make life miserable for forgers. And if he chanced to plug these products when testifying in court, was it not important to call such advances to the attention of criminals everywhere?

Vidocq's Sûreté eventually became a model for Scotland Yard and even the F.B.I., and the character of its founder was used over and over in fictional detection. Vidocq knew many of the best writers of his day, including Honoré de Balzac, who made him the prototype for his fictional Inspector Vautrin. Vidocq also helped inspire the character of Jean Valjean, Victor Hugo's monstrously wronged convict, and that of Inspector Javert, who relentlessly pursued Valjean. Alexandre Dumas used Vidocq's exploits in *The Count of Monte Cristo*, and Agatha Christie undoubtedly had him in mind when she created her immortal Belgian detective, Hercule Poirot.

After Vidocq's death, several young women appeared bearing wills alleged to be his. They had received them, it turned out, in the course of having affairs with Vidocq during his later life. A romantic to the last, Vidocq apparently enjoyed his seventies and early eighties as much as he had the rest of his life.

Cecil John Rhodes

In 1872 Cecil John Rhodes, a tall, gaunt 19-year-old Englishman, wrote out his last will and testament, bequeathing "all of which I might die possessed to the Secretary of State for the Colonies, in trust and to be used for the extension of the British Empire." At the time, the testator could only be judged eccentric if not downright daft, for his possessions added up to little more than a pickax, a change of rough clothing, and a land claim of 31 square feet in the newly opened Colesberg Kopje (now Kimberley) diamond fields of South Africa. But Rhodes was not one to concern himself about present realities: he saw clearly that for fast-moving and ambitious men tremendous wealth was to be made in diamonds. Furthermore he was driven by the desire to use that wealth to "paint the map red"—to extend British dominion in Africa from the Cape of Good Hope to Cairo.

Rhodes' route to the top began inauspiciously. A sickly boy, he was denied training in a profession and was instead shipped by his parents to the more healthful climate of Natal, on the southeast tip of Africa, where Herbert, his eldest brother, ran a cotton farm. But crop failures and dramatic tales of great diamond discoveries on Colesberg Kopje convinced the brothers to travel inland and stake a claim. Herbert became discouraged and soon

Cecil Rhodes "roughs it," albeit with mattress and pillows, in South Africa.

left, but Cecil persisted, certain that he would succeed. For eight years he split his time between England and southern Africa, managing to earn a degree in classics at Oxford, suffering major bouts of illness, and exploiting his claims in the diamond fields.

Gradually Rhodes succeeded, rising from digger (there were some 10,000 at Kimberley in 1871) to become a successful entrepreneur. In 1880, with capital of £200,000, he formed the De Beers Mining Company. Its unique purpose: to control and regulate the production and marketing of diamonds and so guarantee profits in a basically unstable business. In 1888 he bought out his only remaining rival, Barney Barnato, a Cockney street juggler turned diamond broker, for over £5 mil-

lion. By 1891 Rhodes controlled roughly 90 percent of the world's diamond production, as well as a portion of the Transvaal goldfields.

All the while, he remained deeply involved in schemes to extend British rule northward. He had entered politics in 1881 as a member of the Cape Parliament, a post he held for the rest of his life. Whenever there were territorial problems to be solved involving the Dutch, German, Portuguese, or Belgian colonials or the native Africans, it seemed Rhodes was there, looking for British gains. In 1890 he was named prime minister of the Cape Colony, "the only post big enough for him," but five years later he was forced to resign, having supported the disastrous raid to seize the government of the Transvaal.

His health declining, Rhodes spent the remainder of his life promoting the construction of railway and telegraph links across Africa and working for the economic development of Rhodesia, the territory he had secured for another of his interests, the British South Africa Company. In his truly last will and testament, the seventh he had written, he left most of his fortune not to the Secretary of State for the Colonies but to create scholarships for Rhodes Scholars—young men from the British Colonies and from the United States and Germany.

---

of all elements. For some 2,000 years virtually the only known source of diamonds was the streambeds of ancient India, where diamond "pebbles" were found occasionally in the alluvial wash. Though the gems were prized for their rarity and collected by royalty, no one knew how to cut them, and so they were far less spectacular in appearance than rubies or emeralds.

The first recorded instance of a diamond being given as a symbol of marital commitment was in 1477, when the future emperor Maximilian I sealed his vow to Mary of Burgundy by giving her a fine ring set with a diamond. Tradition had it

that a diamond imparted a kind of invulnerability to its possessor. Unfortunately, poor Mary died a short time later.

The discovery, about the 15th century, that diamonds could be used to cut other diamonds led to a new interest in the gem, and in the closing decades of the 17th century a Venetian lapidary, Vincenzo Peruzzi, developed what is known as the "brilliant cut." This manner of cutting the stone, which is an arrangement of 58 facets mathematically proportioned to obtain maximum "fire"—or refraction of light rays—gave the diamond a new and dazzling brilliance.

On weekdays Hasidic diamond merchants and craftsmen rule a block on Manhattan's West 47th Street.

"Diamond fever" originated in the late 1860's with the discovery of an incredible flawless diamond of 85.8 carats near Hopetown on the Orange River in South Africa. When the yellow-clay farmland around Hopetown was found to contain other diamonds, one family of South African farmers, the De Beer brothers, sold out immediately for what seemed a good price—£6,000—and disappeared, leaving nothing behind but their names. Today De Beers Consolidated Mines Ltd. is regarded as "the worldwide diamond-marketing monopoly." It not only produces 40 percent of the diamonds in the world, but it sets the prices through its Central Selling Organization in London.

Washing for diamonds: 18th-century Brazilian workers are watched.

As it developed, the diamonds that the first diggers mined on the surface of the De Beers farmland and the surrounding countryside were only a prelude to deep, underground deposits embedded in the hard rock called "blue ground," or kimberlite. Generally, kimberlite occurs in rock extrusions called "pipes," which are thought to be the necks of extinct volcanoes. Intense heat and pressure had forced these pipes nearer the surface. Once miners began digging into these deposits, operations were quickly consolidated, for only those rich enough to buy heavy machinery, pumps, and elevators could continue. By 1888 Cecil Rhodes had taken control, having "squared," as he liked to say, all of his rivals, and was on his way to becoming one of the richest and most powerful men in colonial Africa.

Only about 20 percent of the diamonds recovered are of gem quality; the rest are used for industrial purposes, mostly as abrasives. In any case, it may take about 250 tons of blue ground to yield one carat of rough diamond. In cutting, a diamond loses about half its weight. (The term "carat" is derived from the Greek name for the carob tree, *Ceratonia siliqua*, whose uniformly sized seeds were used to balance scales in Eastern bazaars; in the international system of weights and measures, 142 carats equal an ounce.)

The largest single diamond of gem quality found thus far is the Cullinan, discovered in 1905 in South Africa. In the rough it weighed an awesome 3,106 carats and measured 2 by 2½ by 4 inches. The stone was presented to King Edward VII on his 66th birthday by the Transvaal government, and after months of careful analysis was cut into nine large stones, including the Great Star of Africa (530.20 carats) and 96 smaller brilliants. The gems today are part of the British crown jewels.

In addition to carat weight, a diamond gemstone is evaluated by color, clarity, and style of cut. Diamonds are often thought of as being colorless. In fact, colorless, or white, diamonds are extremely rare and prohibitively expensive. Most gems have a tinge of color, and those of a strong cast are called "fancies." A famous "fancy" is the dark blue 44.50-carat Hope Diamond, now in the Smithsonian Institution. Clarity refers to the absence of imperfections, such as carbon spots or cracks, which might interfere with the free passage of light through the stone. A diamond is con-

In India diamonds are worn more often in the nose than on the finger.

sidered flawless only if no imperfections can be found in it with a 10-power magnifier. The cut, which refers to the arrangement and number of the facets, must be executed so exactly that each angle falls within a half-degree of each other angle; to miss is to lose a gem's full potential of "fire."

Gem-quality diamonds are one of the hottest investment items in the world. Though the value placed on them is almost entirely artificial, it is fair to assume that diamonds will continue to increase in price with each decade. As portable wealth, easily transported by people fleeing political upheaval, few things have greater value—and sparkle.

Tireless Diarist

Samuel Pepys, the most celebrated diarist in the English-speaking world, was a keen, shrewd, and tirelessly sociable observer. He not only lived through a fascinating period, but had the instinct to be in important places at important times. He was, for example, aboard the ship that brought Charles II back to England in 1660, and so became a visitor to the fun-loving Restoration court. He was also a classmate of John Dryden at Cambridge, president of the Royal Society, and friend of Sir Isaac Newton and "that miracle of a youth Christopher Wren."

As a diarist, Pepys wrote for no eyes but his own, using a code that was not deciphered until more than 122 years after his death, and with such absolute frankness that some passages of his diary remain unpublished.

The second son of a tailor and husband of the daughter of a French Huguenot exile, Samuel Pepys began his career as clerk to a distant cousin, the earl of Sandwich. At 25, he survived a gallstone operation and entered public service, where he rose to be secretary to the admiralty and a member of Parliament. His first entry in his diary, January 1, 1660, read, in part, "Dined at home in the garret, where my wife dressed the remains of a turkey, and in the doing of it she burned her hand." He closed his journal, because of failing

eyesight, on May 31, 1669.

The intervening 1.4 million words provide historians, scholars, and ordinary readers with an unmatched account of life in 17th-century England. The principal concerns of the day, not unlike our own, included money, power, and sex. People tended to eat and drink too much, and to worry overly about their appearance. Women flirted. Men took bribes and were filled with a sense of their own importance. The theater was the great diversion of the day. In the decade covered by his diary, Pepys himself attended some 300 plays. He proved to be a perceptive critic and, in the manner of the times, had an occasional fling with an actress. ("So I got into the coach where Mrs. Knipp was and got her upon my knee [the coach being full] and played with her. . . .")

Despite his own lapses, Pepys was inordinately jealous of his wife's diversions. Having agreed to let her take dancing lessons from a Mr. Pembleton, he became suspicious and returned home unannounced: ". . . Lord! How I listened and laid my ear to the door, and how I was troubled when I heard them stand still and not dance." Nonetheless, the marriage was, on balance, a happy one, as Pepys himself noted: "Anon comes home my wife from Brampton, not looked for till Saturday, which will hinder me of a little pleasure, but I am

The great diarist Samuel Pepys was berated at college for being "scandalously overserved with drink."

glad of her coming."

Pepys' account of the Great Fire and the Great Plague ring with immediacy. Recording the practice of locking survivors in their houses with dead victims, he wrote: ". . . the plague is making us cruel as doggs, one to another."

But the greater part of the *Diary*, as of Pepys' life, deals with matters in keeping with his philosophy: "The truth is, I do indulge myself a little more in pleasure . . . out of my observation that most men that do thrive in the world do forget to take pleasure during the time that they are getting their estate, but reserve that till they have got one, and then it is too late for them to enjoy it with any pleasure."

DIARY It was said about a much-married, much-divorced lady that, however full and busy her days, she would faithfully end each one by sitting down and writing: "Dear Diary and Gentlemen of the Jury. . . ."

The story, probably untrue, illustrates one approach to the keeping of a diary. Another, more rewarding to the reader, is simply to set down one's candid thoughts, as Queen Victoria, then 20 years old, did upon meeting her prospective husband: "Thursday, 10th October [1839]. It was with some emotion that I beheld Albert—who is *beautiful*."

Some of the most interesting diaries have been

"A horrid noise the flames made," Pepys wrote of the Great Fire of 1666, which razed most of London.

compiled by eminent writers: Rousseau, Swift, Tolstoy, Emerson, Sir Walter Scott, Katherine Mansfield, and André Gide. Others, perhaps not quite as candid, have been the work of politicians and public figures. When still a 22-year-old recently graduated naturalist, Charles Darwin took a number of blank diaries with him when he boarded the *Beagle* for its voyage to South America in 1831. Filled with the daily record of his observations, they became the basis for his theories on natural selection and evolution.

But one need not be famous to produce an extraordinary diary. One of the most unforgettable came from the hand of a young German-Dutch girl who spent the last two years of her life hiding from the Nazis in an Amsterdam attic. Her name was Anne Frank. Another was written by a 17th-century English civil servant named Pepys.

Pleasant as it may be for the reader, the keeping of a diary rewards the writer as well. James Boswell, the biographer of Samuel Johnson and no mean diarist himself, observed in 1762: "A journal will help to keep off the spleen." And today psychologists agree that the daily ritual of writing out one's frustrations and conflicts may be a good way to relieve them.

So why not look for that little red-leather-bound book with the tiny brass lock? It's probably in the attic, next to the carpet beater.

DICE Dice seem to have appeared in a number of different societies, none of which had any known contact with one another. They evolved in many forms, but eventually they took the shape of

Late 18th century: men emote at London's bustling gaming tables.

cubes with from one to six small dots on each face. Dice are one of the oldest gaming instruments known to man. Innumerable games are played with them. Craps, the most popular gambling game in America, is played with two dice; chuck-a-luck is played with three; in the favorite tavern games of poker and liar's dice, five dice are used. In such classics as backgammon, as well as in hundreds of other track games, two or more dice are cast.

It is not known who invented dice or even if they were "invented." Legends say that a Greek named Palamedes created them during the siege of Troy. Another story is that they were made up by the ancient Lydians. All of this is refuted, however, by the fact that dice with markings practically the same as on modern dice have been found in Egyptian tombs dating from before 2000 B.C. and in Chinese excavations dating as early as 600 B.C. Dice are also mentioned in the Rig-Veda, the oldest and most important Hindu sacred work.

Some scholars attach religious significance to the markings on some early Korean and Chinese dice. Despite lack of hard evidence, most agree that those societies certainly used them for lotteries and gambling. In ancient times dice were usually cast from dice cups. The Greeks had cone-shaped beakers, while the Romans had cylindrical vessels similar to those in use today. The American Indians wove special baskets, usually about 10 inches in diameter, in which they tossed their dicesticks.

Many ancient dice were not cube-shaped. In fact, some of the earliest were four-sided and made from the knucklebones of sheep. Pyramidal, pentahedral, and octahedral dice have also been found, but most of the dice throughout history were just like the six-sided ones that are used today.

Medieval German die is carved as a human figure.

Juvenile crime, 1880's: on the way home from school, children in New York stop to pitch dice for candy.

DICTIONARY Editing a dictionary is not a job for people with short attention spans—or short lives. The first great French dictionary, that of the Académie Française, took 56 years to complete, and the *Oxford English Dictionary* 71 years. The basic German dictionary was published in

Architect of Words

The man who almost single-handedly put together the *Oxford English Dictionary* never went past the eighth grade in school. However, James Augustus Henry Murray, son of a village tailor in Scotland, showed an early aptitude for words. He could name the letters of the alphabet when he was 18 months old, and at seven amused himself by deciphering passages from the Bible in Chinese. At 20 he became the headmaster and one-man faculty of a small country school, but still found time to teach himself some 25 languages and pursue his fascination for early English dialects.

This interest, and his scholarly publications, prompted England's Philological Society to offer him the job of editing a new English dictionary, a project that had been started 22 years before, in 1857, and then abandoned. Murray accepted, estimating that the job would take him about 10 years. His first shock came when the material already collected arrived: many of the 2.5 million slips of paper, dotted with references and citations, were nearly illegible. To house them, and the millions of others he would collect himself, Murray built in his garden a 30-foot corrugated metal shed. He christened it the "Scriptorium" and made the odd structure his office.

Despite an exhausting succession of 80-hour weeks and the clerical help of his 11 children (he paid them a few pennies an hour for their labors), Murray took five years to complete volume one. Even then, in all its 352 pages, it advanced the project only from "A" to "Ant." In a later volume the single word "do" required six months to complete.

In 1901 the F–G volume appeared. By that time, however, the fame of the project had spread around the world to the extent that a school in Singapore offered to teach English "up to the letter G."

When Murray died in 1915 at 78 years of age, he had earned a knighthood, many honorary degrees, and had reached the letter "T." The completed dictionary, containing 414,825 words, finally appeared in 1928. It had missed its deadline by 39 years and had run over its budget by £291,000.

For 36 years James Murray (right) battled to complete the Oxford English Dictionary. *The final volume appeared in 1928, 13 years after his death.*

1960, 106 years after it had been launched by the Grimm brothers, who relieved tedium along the way by collecting fairy tales. The standard Italian dictionary, begun in 1863, is still unfinished.

Nonetheless, dictionaries have been published in almost every living language, from Afrikaans to Zulu, as well as some dead ones, such as Babylonian and Egyptian (defining hieroglyphics). The first bilingual dictionary (English-French), for travelers to France, was compiled in 1480 by William Caxton, who is better remembered for having introduced printing to England.

Dictionaries generally give the spelling, pronunciation, and meaning of words, but the Oxford set itself the additional task of tracing the derivation of every English word known since 1150 and illustrating its usage with examples. The immensity of this task is indicated, for instance, by the fact that the word *good* has had some 20 different spellings over the past 800 years.

Lexicographers have never really agreed on whether a dictionary should be "descriptive" and report what people say, or "prescriptive" and tell them what they should say. Noah Webster, whose first major work was the *Compendious Dictionary of the English Language* (1806), stated that his concern was for "what the English language *is*, and not, how it *might have been made*." Samuel Johnson, whose 1755 dictionary was a remarkable one-man creation, proclaimed it a work "by which the pronunciation of our language may be fixed . . . and its purity preserved."

The publication, in 1961, of Webster's *Third New International Dictionary*, which adhered to the precepts of its namesake and included the expression *ain't*, renewed the controversy. One critic, using but a few of the 100,000 new words included in the tome, noted: "A passel of double-domes at the G. & C. Merriam Company joint . . . have been confabbing and yakking for 27 years . . .

and now they have finalized . . . [a] swell and esteemed book." Other critics objected to the inclusion of a special sense of *dig* (as in "I don't dig British money"), which quoted Jimmy Durante as the authority. Critics also were dismayed by some of the other authorities cited. And Webster's *Third* entered for the first time such words as *booboo*, *drip-dry*, *hipster*, *countdown*, and *sit-in*, which for better or worse are part of the language.

Another perennial controversy has centered around the exclusion by most lexicographers of certain short words, usually of four letters, which almost everyone knows and many use without inhibition. On this subject, Dr. Johnson had one of the earliest and probably still the most telling comments. When commended by two ladies for his omission of such words, he replied, "My dears! Then you have been looking for them?"

DIESEL ENGINE On February 17, 1894, Rudolf Diesel, a 35-year-old German engineer, approached a monstrously heavy contraption that consisted of a 10-foot-tall iron cylinder surrounded by rods, gauges, and a flywheel. He had had the machine assembled in a workshop in Augsburg, and now he gingerly pushed the starting lever—gingerly because the previous model, completed a year earlier, had exploded and nearly blown his head off.

This time, the machine produced a mighty noise and ran for a full minute before shuddering to a halt. Clearly, there was still work to be done, but the occasion called for celebration because it had vindicated a notion that had preoccupied Diesel, sometimes for 20 hours a day, during the course of the previous 16 years.

The notion, based on the long-known principle that the compression of a gas causes an increase in its temperature, was that an efficient internal-combustion engine could be built. Such an engine had already been invented by a man named Nikolaus Otto in 1878, but it was a puny, unreliable gadget whose principal function was to propel "horseless carriages," which at the time were little more than rich men's playthings. Diesel's target was to improve upon the steam engine, the mighty brute that had borne the Industrial Revolution on its broad but inefficient shoulders.

Even the best steam engine available in 1894 was little more than an oversize teapot, converting only some 7 percent of its heat energy into useful work. Diesel believed that he could improve that ratio tenfold. Furthermore, the engine he envisaged would be able to use virtually any combustible material for fuel—coal dust, whale oil, or even a fairly new substance called petroleum, which the

Americans were discovering in great quantity.

Diesel was on the right track. After some further refinement, his invention caught the eye of a visiting American named Adolphus Busch, whose first love was his thriving brewery in St. Louis but who had an eye for promising ideas. Busch bought the North American rights to Diesel's engine and thereby helped speed its introduction. But one wonders whether either man had really foreseen to what extent it would supplant other sources of power. In a speech before the American Society of Mechanical Engineers in New York in 1912, Diesel was able to report that 365 ships—140 of them submarines—then in service were diesel-powered. Today, nearly every kind of seagoing craft is routinely fitted with diesels. In that same speech, Diesel told his listeners that he had only weeks earlier completed the design for the first diesel-powered locomotive. Two decades later, another diesel locomotive was hauling passenger trains from Chicago to Denver in a nonstop 12-hour run averaging 83.69 miles per hour. Furthermore, the first locomotive to make that run was still in service after 25 years and more than 3 million miles. Today, to the regret of railroad buffs, there is not a single steam locomotive in regular service anywhere in the United States, and precious few anywhere else in the world.

Because they are more efficient than gasoline engines, and can develop many times the power, diesel engines are used in long-haul trucks, in passenger buses, and in fire-fighting equipment. The dirigibles *Hindenburg* and *Graf Zeppelin* were

Power play: construction of the Alaskan pipeline, shown zigzagging across the Brooks Range south of Prudhoe Bay, relied heavily on diesel engines.

The Flawed Model

If one were to compose a biography suitable for a successful inventor, it might read something like this: Born of hardworking parents, he early showed a fascination for mechanical objects and spent endless boyhood days haunting museums of science. In school, where his talents were soon recognized, he was taken under the tutelage of important scientists whose work he was eventually able to improve upon. Through some luck, but mostly long and hard work, he justified his promise and saw his ideas bear fruit. In the process, he amassed several fortunes and cheerfully lost them in visionary investments. But in the end, he lived to gain the esteem of his colleagues and the gratitude of the public, whose burdens he had helped to lighten.

Rudolf Diesel, born in 1858, the only son of an immigrant Bavarian leather craftsman living in Paris, passed much of his boyhood in the vast display galleries of the *Conservatoire des Arts et Mètiers*. He gained entry, at the age of 12, to the finest high school

Dr. Rudolf Diesel

in Paris. He won a scholarship to a special technical school in Munich, where he became the protégé of Professor Carl von Linde, its most renowned teacher and a pioneer in the development of refrigeration. During one of von Linde's lectures, Diesel noted in the margin of a book: "Study the possibility of practical development of the isotherm"—the key to an efficient internal-combustion engine.

This study eventually led to the first successful model of the engine that still bears his name. And he made a fortune—the sale of international rights to his invention brought him over 3 million marks in cash and stocks, which he spent on a lavish house and on real estate speculations and schemes such as the construction of an electric auto-

mobile. A social philosopher as well as a scientist, he believed that machines, unwisely used, threatened to crush the dignity of man, and devised a noble but impractical scheme whereby workmen could, penny by penny, purchase control of the enterprises that employed them.

In only one detail did the life of Rudolf Diesel depart from the model biography. In 1913, at the age of 55, he was invited to England to preside at the ground-breaking of a new diesel-engine plant after addressing a meeting of the Royal Automobile Club. While crossing the English Channel aboard the steamer *Dresden*, he dined on the evening of September 29 with two of his oldest friends and agreed to meet them at breakfast.

He failed to show up. A visit to his cabin showed that his berth had not been slept in, and a search of the ship revealed his hat and coat, neatly folded, near the rail of the afterdeck. Why he had jumped overboard, as he almost certainly did, no one has ever been able to ascertain.

---

powered by diesel engines. So are dredges, conveyors, rock crushers, bulldozers, and graders. Diesels pull plows, harrows, harvesters, sprayers, threshers, and balers. They are used in flour mills, ice plants, canneries, sawmills, breweries, laundries, grain elevators, coal mines, and stone quarries. They serve also as a means of generating electricity. Though too heavy to hurtle through space, they provide the power for the parabolic antennas of tracking stations.

Current interest in the diesel engine centers on its use in passenger cars, where it can provide drivers with the double benefit of greater durability and superior fuel economy. It can even run on heating oil. Manufacturers do not recommend using this kind of fuel, but it would work—and have the additional advantage of short-circuiting a lot of federal and local taxes. As far as economy is concerned, it is not likely that any of the current car models will set new records.

In the 1930's a diesel-powered car was driven from New York to Los Angeles at a total fuel cost of $11.22. And a diesel Duesenberg competed in the 1932 Indianapolis 500 and completed the race at an average speed of 86 miles per hour, without making any refueling stops.

DISCOUNT STORE "Discounting," said the head of a large retailing chain, "is nothing more than selling inferior merchandise on Sunday." Although he was being facetious, he gave voice to a common misconception about discount stores. Because their prices are lower than those elsewhere, and lower than those suggested by manufacturers, some consumers assume that the merchandise is not as good.

Discount houses, or "mass merchandisers," as many now prefer to be called, exploded on the American retailing scene after World War II, even though the practice of selling at less than full price had been around since 1910. The discounters knew a fundamental secret about shoppers: they love to save money by paying less than they ex-

Little but the prices change on New York's Lower East Side, perhaps the original discount center.

1959: Shoppers in the fish market in Hamburg, Germany, are offered a deal in stuffed aquatic animals.

pected to, and they are likely to spend the savings on something else.

New England is sometimes called "the cradle of discounting," because it was there that "mill outlets" sprang up in abandoned factories and warehouses. These stores were rough and ready, in unfashionable locations, displaying clothing on plain pipe racks and accepting only cash-and-carry trade. One of the first was born in 1936, when Anderson Little, a manufacturer of men's clothing, was stuck with a large canceled order. To get rid of the surplus, Little sold the clothes directly from his factory in Fall River, Massachusetts.

Throughout the time the discount houses have been revolutionizing retailing, no one has liked them but the customers. For the savings, consumers will give up personal service from clerks and shop happily in stores that pay no attention to decor. Traditional department-store owners, however, saw discounting as prejudicial to sound

The oil embargo of 1973 reduced Japan's exports, leaving discounters with surplus homemade goods.

pricing. It was that attitude that gave the Two Guys chain its name. When Herbert and Sidney Hubschman opened a small store in Harrison, New Jersey, and began by selling appliances for $5 or $10 above cost, with customers writing out their own sales slips, it enraged a nearby competitor. He made a public remark about "those two bastards from Harrison." The Hubschmans laundered his statement and named their store Two Guys From Harrison—since abbreviated.

Traditionally, discounters have had trouble with manufacturers, many of whom refuse to sell to them. What helped to change the manufacturers' minds was the giant volume of business the discounters generated. Between 1960 and 1970, for example, traditional department stores increased their sales 78 percent, chain retailers went up 157 percent, and discounters jumped their sales 529 percent. Riveting figures like these made discount stores a fact of American life, and the manufacturers capitulated in the grand tradition of "If you can't lick 'em, join 'em."

DISHWASHER In the wake of every feast or routine meal comes the inevitable: cleaning up. In a lifetime a human dishwasher can expect to wash about 2.5 million dishes, glasses, pots, and pans. Yet despite this messy fact, the electric dishwasher was a long time coming, and even now most Americans do not have one.

The belief that there had to be something better than soapy water, elbow grease, and red knuckles first arrived at the U.S. Patent Office in 1850, when a man named Houghton, from Ogden, New York, received a patent on a wooden contraption that splashed water on dishes. In 1886 Mrs. Josephine Cochrane built a dishwasher in

"I Divorce Thee"

Since the emergence of marriage as a social institution, men and women have been almost as adept at putting it asunder—in both elaborate and simple ways—as in honoring it. An Arab Muslim man, for example, who wants to divorce his wife merely assembles two witnesses and his wife and tells her, "I divorce thee." He then keeps the children, because he owns them, and can remarry almost as soon as he has uttered those fateful three words. His wife, however, has to wait three months to verify that she is not pregnant. If she is, she is not free to remarry until she has borne and reared the child.

All this would seem enormously unfair to traditional Eskimos. When an Eskimo husband and wife are tired of marriage, especially if they have no children, they simply live apart, most often with someone else. An Australian aborigine woman, on the other hand, who might be one of 20 or more wives, can only start divorce proceedings by eloping with someone else. Otherwise, she must persuade her husband to give her away or divorce her.

The ancient Chinese had layer upon layer of rules and rituals governing marital partings. A marriage might end because of incompatibility, but only if the woman's family agreed to take her back. A husband had a good deal more choice if he wished a divorce. Among the choices most often used were adultery—or conduct his parents did not approve of. His parents' disapproval, however, counted for naught if they died and his wife mourned for them. In ancient Athens, as among the Eskimos, an unhappy husband or wife simply moved out, no explanations required.

Annulment—a legal ruling that a marriage never existed—sometimes replaces divorce, particularly in countries where a religion forbids it and there are no divorce laws. Throughout history the rich and powerful have had an easier time getting ecclesiastical authorities to announce an annulment. For King Henry VIII of England, however, who wished to have his marriage to Catherine of Aragón annulled, the task proved to be especially difficult. The problem was that Henry had received a special dispensation to marry Catherine in the first place, because she had been his brother's widow, and, according to Leviticus 20:21, that is impure. Henry wanted to marry another woman, Anne Boleyn, who resisted all advances until Henry did the honorable thing and put a

The angel of divorce sunders a bad marriage. Interestingly, this pro-divorce "Rescue" was engraved in 1905.

ring on her finger. Considerably frustrated, Henry argued that church authorities should never have given him his first dispensation. When the church failed to concede his point, Henry severed ties with it. He then divorced Catherine, married Anne, and went on to found the Church of England, with himself as spiritual leader. Later he reversed himself and annulled his marriage to Anne in exceedingly permanent terms: he had her head cut off for allegedly committing adultery.

Henry VIII was not the only ruler to use annulment to escape a marriage. In 1809 Napoleon Bonaparte used this device to divorce Josephine, offering as grounds that she was sterile. Since Josephine had two children by a previous marriage, Napoleon made it clear that he was an emperor first and a biologist only when it suited his needs.

In all, Henry VIII was married six times, which may be something of a record for royalty. Nonetheless, his performance seems modest in comparison with that of Mrs. Beverly Nina Avery. As of late 1957, she had been married and divorced a total of 16 times. Along the way, she had even married—and divorced—two different men twice. Equally as forgiving—or foolish—was James Williams of Cedar Rapids, Iowa, who married one woman four times on the way to entering the holy state of matrimony a total of 16 times.

The records do not show what the divorce settlements were for these 32 marriages, but they almost certainly did not match the payment Edward J. Hudson made in 1963 to Mrs. Cecil Amelia Blaffer Hudson. He paid a total of $9.5 million for his freedom, at a time when Mrs. Hudson was reportedly scraping along on $14 million of her own. This settlement eclipsed the more widely publicized award of $6,393,000 conferred on Barbara "Bobo" Rockefeller by her departing husband, Winthrop Rockefeller.

Yet all divorce settlements do not involve only cash. After a considerable struggle in 1977, Marcia Borders of Hutchinson, Kansas, won permanent custody of a Persian cat named Bear. The judge, however, being a fair man, awarded visiting rights to the former husband. In another case that same year, a man was ordered to pay $250 per month to provide support for his daughter's show horse. The horse's name: Monkey Business.

In the 1930's the dishwasher was a functional if not aesthetic triumph.

her home; her model led to the founding of a company that sold kitchen equipment. These early models, however, suffered from a common failing: they substituted one kind of manual labor for another. Instead of washing dishes by hand, the homemaker had to use muscle to heave the crank that powered the machine. It was not until 1911 that a motor-powered dishwasher finally appeared. Dishwashers with automatic controls arrived in 1940.

Dishwashers were not an instant success, for a number of reasons. First was the expense of installing plumbing. Second was the problem of pre-rinsing and scraping dishes before loading them into the machine and the general lack of good detergents. Finally, many of the machines were bulky, ugly, and noisy. Consequently, it took nearly 50 years for factory shipments of dishwashers to reach the million mark. By that time, "power" cycles were blasting dirt from dishes, detergents worked, and most machines were smaller and quieter than earlier models. Many families, in fact, were coming to enjoy the savings in time, estimated to be as much as 30 eight-hour days a year for a family of four.

Aside from saving time and replacing humans in a boring job, automatic dishwashers really do get dishes cleaner. Spraying water too hot to handle (140°–160° F, ideally), they also eliminate the need for hand-drying with towels, which may contain bacteria. The new generation of dishwashers even promise to use less water and no detergents, thus avoiding pollution problems. They will feature ultrasonic cleaning, in which high-frequency sound waves will pry dirt from cup and plate.

DOCTOR For the most part, the doctor-patient relationship throughout history has reflected the gratitude of the patient for the dedication, wisdom, and unselfishness of the doctor. There have been exceptions, however, some of a mercenary nature, others a good deal more serious. During the 5th century, for example, in the Visigoth kingdom in southern France and in Spain, doctors were required to leave a cash deposit with the family of each of their patients. If the treatment—and patient—failed, the family did not have to pay the bill and the doctor lost his deposit.

The Merovingians to the north applied considerably more pressure: their penalty for "medical neglect" was death. Thus, in the year 580, when Queen Austrichildia came down with dysentery, her husband, Guntram, urged his physicians to do their very best. Unfortunately, she died and not long thereafter so did her doctors.

In 1348, with the Black Death sweeping Europe, four physicians were treated even more harshly: they were tortured at the Castle of Chillon, on Lake Geneva, until they confessed to having spread the disease—on purpose—and were then put to death. Three centuries later, when plague swept London, killing as many as 12,000 people in a single week, doctors, perhaps not unwisely, took heed. So many fled the city that pharmacists had to care for the sick and dying.

In New York, in 1788, a medical student named John Hicks, Jr., waved the arm of a corpse at a group of children and touched off three days of rioting, which became known as "The Doctors' Mob." Eight people were killed and a score injured. John Jay, soon to become the nation's first Chief Justice, was knocked unconscious by a rock, and an innocent bystander named Sir John Temple saw his house looted. The mob had mistaken "Sir John" for "surgeon."

Part of the public hostility toward doctors was undoubtedly due to the imperfect state of the medical arts. Still, perhaps it was better to have a doctor than have no help at all. Of the 100 settlers who established themselves in Jamestown in May 1607, only 40 were alive by autumn, and nearly half of the passengers aboard the *Mayflower* died within three months of their landing. Conditions were harsh and unsanitary in the New World; perhaps if the groups had included a physician they might have fared better.

Quack attack: metal bars known as tractors were used by 19th-century charlatans to treat almost everything, as shown in this satiric print by artist James Gillray.

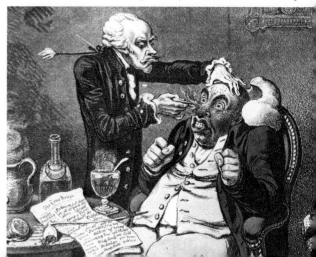

Because of the chronic shortage of doctors in the colonies, anyone with formal education was expected to lend a hand. One of the most successful was John Winthrop, who arrived in 1631 and became governor of Connecticut. Though trained as a lawyer, Winthrop soon developed a very large medical practice. Those he could not see personally, he treated by mail, including Roger Williams, who had founded his own settlement in Rhode Island.

Cotton Mather, best known as a fiery preacher and writer, not only practiced medicine but initiated in 1721 the first mass inoculation against smallpox. Unfortunately, he was years ahead of his time—Edward Jenner had not yet demonstrated the efficacy of his vaccines—and he killed as many people as he protected. For his pains, he was attacked in the newspapers and told to remain in his pulpit. One of his associates, a midwife, Margaret Jones, was tried, convicted, and hanged as a witch—the first to be so executed in Massachusetts.

Though sometimes untutored, 19th-century horse-and-buggy doctors had the virtue of making house calls.

Though medical progress in America generally paralleled that in Europe, the very nature of frontier life created certain unique problems—and opportunities. An army surgeon, J.H. Bill, for instance, devised a special instrument for extracting arrows. Another army surgeon, William Beaumont, treated a young man whose abdomen had been blown open by a shotgun blast. The patient survived, but was left with a wound of such size that it would not heal, thus giving Beaumont the chance to observe the workings of his stomach. Over a 10-year period, in a series of classic experiments, he kept on observing, even inserting bits of food on lengths of string into the cavity in order to check rates of gastric absorption.

Quackery has always been part of medicine, and one of its earliest American practitioners was Elisha Perkins, who had studied at Yale. In 1795 he brought out Perkins' Patent Tractors, which consisted of a pair of small metal bars. According to Perkins the bars could cure everything from gout to an aching head, if used to massage the afflicted area. Eventually Perkins was exposed, though not before he had amassed a small fortune, and even sold a pair of "tractors" to George Washington.

The most successful American quack of all time was John Romulus Brinkley, who in 1915 received a doctor's diploma from a shadowy institution known as the Eclectic Medical University of Kansas City. Over the next 27 years Brinkley collected an estimated $12 million by promoting the use of goat testicle extracts and sections as a cure for sexual impotency and a rejuvenator of aging pa-

people

Hippocrates

According to Greek mythology, Aesculapius, the god of medicine, was slain by Zeus because the ruler of the gods feared that Aesculapius might make all men immortal. Judging by the state of the art before Hippocrates, Zeus could safely have held his fire.

Virtually nothing is known about Hippocrates' life except that, like many of his modern disciples, he was born (circa 460 B.C.) into a medical family. History records that he taught and traveled widely, and that he lived to be over 80 years old.

His fame rests on the collection of some 70 treatises attributed to him. In them, he proposed and demonstrated the revolutionary theory that illness was due to bodily malfunction rather than the workings of malevolent spirits or angry gods. From this it followed that doctors might well observe patients closely, prescribe a good diet, use gentle massage, and try to encourage the body's natural healing processes. Hippocrates' writings demonstrate that his powers of observation were acute:

"Persons who are very fat are apt to die earlier than those who are slender," he wrote, and, "When sleep puts an end to delirium, it is a good symptom."

Hippocrates' second major contribution to medicine is the oath, based on his teachings, that bears his name. As recognition of the ethical responsibilities of all physicians—to pass on knowledge, to do their patients no harm, to respect patients' confidences—the Hippocratic Oath is still sworn today by medical-school graduates all over the world.

tients. In Europe Serge Voronoff, operating on a slightly more sophisticated level, performed the same sort of quackery—for the same sort of rewards.

One of the most explosive issues in doctor-patient relations involves house calls—does he or doesn't he? The story is told. for instance, of a doctor who telephoned a plumber late one night to report a flooding toilet. "Don't worry, Doc," the plumber told him cheerfully, "just toss in two aspirins. If it's still flooding in the morning, let me know." Yet the house-call problem is hardly new. A treatise by Susruta, an ancient Hindu physician, urged medical students to question closely the messenger sent to bring the physician. In the 13th century the citizens of Padua were critical of doctors who refused to make house calls. Surgeons in Tudor England, on the other hand, were expected to live in a patient's house until he or she had recovered. In upstate New York in the early 1800's, the Clinton County Medical Society tried to reach a compromise, setting fixed fees for particular sorts of visits. Their list specified 25 cents for a day visit, 38 cents for a night call, 20 cents per mile ridden, and one dollar for consultations.

Fortunately, or perhaps unfortunately, the

Fighting Chinese Shar-Peis offer foes little but a mouthful of fur.

whole question may soon become computerized. In an experiment at the prestigious Mayo Clinic in Rochester, Minnesota, 154 patients were asked to describe their symptoms in response to questions put to them by a computer. The results: computer questioning produced 96 percent of the information later obtained by physicians. In another experiment, a computer was programmed to make delicate differential diagnoses in cases of congenital heart disease. The computer performed as well as one examining physician and better than another—but not in the patient's house.

DOG Oldest of all domesticated animals, dogs are probably descended from an ancient wolflike creature, *Tomarctus*, that lived about 15 million years ago. No one knows definitely when the first wild dog crept close to the fires of men, but it seems that dogs worked as trackers of game for Stone

words

It's a Dog's Life

Dogs have been with us so long that no one really knows where the word "dog" comes from. But the animals themselves, and the things they do, have become part of virtually all human languages. When Winston Churchill, a master of English style, wanted to describe the depths of the depressions that periodically gripped him, he spoke of the "black dog." Often enough, dogs are used to describe something servile or humble, treacherous or unworthy. But not always, for every dog has his day, as in "Love me, love my dog," which expresses the feeling of owners who are one with their pets.

"You can't teach an old dog new tricks" suggests that dogs, like humans, become set in their ways. In Estonia old dogs are treated a bit more reverently, as in "If the old dog barks, he gives counsel." The Yugoslavs express the same sentiment in slightly

different terms: "If the old dog barks, look for the reason." "Dog eat dog," which describes a desperate struggle for survival, is really rather unfair to the animals. As the Hausa people of Africa put it, "Does dog eat dog?" the implied answer being no. The Greeks and Romans were more definite: "Dog won't eat dog."

Dogs, however, also play a part in sayings that are not flattering to them. Aesop helped launch this trend with his story about the "dog in the manger," a snapping, snarling beast who refused to let others eat what he himself did not want. Other expressions:

"Put on the dog"—to make a flashy or pretentious display.

"Call off the dogs"—to stop doing something disagreeable or unrewarding. Hunters call dogs off unpromising trails.

"Go to the dogs"—to take a final, destructive course of action. (Medieval princes used to pitch

scraps to their dogs; sometimes humans got the same treatment.)

"Dog days" are those sultry summer days when no air stirs and even breathing is punishment. The expression comes from the Romans, who theorized that in certain seasons the Dog Star (Sirius) added its heat to that of the sun and thereby intensified the afflictions suffered by those below.

A "gay dog" is not simply a charmer, he is a philanderer who roams dangerously far from his own hearth. Gay dogs often end up "in the doghouse."

"Dog tags" are worn by soldiers, who are as regimented as dogs in a pound. During World War II, front-line journalist Ernie Pyle labeled all soldiers "dogfaces" because of their dog tags. And when dogfaces had too much to drink, they followed ancient advice and took a bit of the "hair of the dog."

Age men in Europe 10,000 to 20,000 years ago.

The ancient Egyptians probably developed the first true breed, the saluki, and since then man has bred and used dogs as everything from pets to guards, police aides, shepherds, rescuers, soldiers, medical assistants, and even thieves and smugglers. Dogs and their habits and history are deeply ingrained in all human cultures, though in varying terms. For some, dogs are symbols of loyalty, yet almost all biblical references to dogs are derogatory. The name Fido, once common for dogs, is from the Latin word for "trusting," and legends of canine loyalty are numberless.

Some people love dogs so much that they lose all sense of distinction between man and animal. Virginia Woolf, normally a most serious writer, found herself in such a position and wound up doing a biography of a cocker spaniel that had belonged to poet Elizabeth Barrett Browning. For reasons that are not clear, the dog's name was Flush, which was affectionately expanded to "Flushie." Moreover, Woolf freely assigned human thoughts and emotions to the dog, as in this passage: "Flush knew before the summer had passed that there is no equality among dogs: there are high dogs and low dogs."

Flush was just one in a long line of pampered dogs. Some are even pampered after death. Chinese emperors, for example, buried their dogs beneath tombstones of marble, ivory, silver, and gold. Today, roughly 75 percent of the occupants of all pet cemeteries in the U.S. are dogs. Nor are these cemeteries anything less than serious: they feature benches for reminiscing, burial and cremation certificates, and caskets in a variety of sizes and colors. Thus reports the brochure of Paw Print Gardens: "The Chapel in Paw Print Gardens is dedicated to 'God's Little Ones.' . . . From the steeple of the Chapel melodious music flows to all corners of the gardens. . . . Funeral services and private viewing are held in the Slumber Room of the Chapel."

Dogs have an illustrious history as servants to men. In folklore, a dog's nose is cold because Noah used one to plug a leak in the ark. The word "cynotherapy" denotes the practice of healing by

Down, boy! One of the thousands of canines trained during World War II, this paradog hits the silk at 1,500 feet up.

means of dogs, which can involve the use of parts of dead dogs, as in folk medicine, or simply allowing a dog to lick an injury. In medieval England the cure for a cough was thought to be a hair from the cougher's head fed to a dog in a bread-and-butter sandwich. Aztec priests, on the other hand, used chihuahuas as living hot-water bottles. In the Middle Ages the "Spaniell gentle" was thought useful when held to the abdomen "to succour and strengthen quailing and quamming stomackes." Today, man also ministers to dog. There are more than 30,000 veterinarians in the United States, and thousands of small-animal hospitals.

The stories of humans plucked from icy death by St. Bernards are, also, true. These great dogs, originally bred by the monks of St. Bernard Pass hospice, were first used as watchdogs and pack animals. Then in the 1750's they were trained for rescue missions in the snows of Great St. Bernard Pass, which connects Italy and Switzerland. In the years since, the dogs reportedly have saved more than 2,500 lives, so no one really cares that they consume five pounds of food a day and never tote kegs of liquor around their necks while doing rescue work.

Dogs sometimes have been trained for lives of crime by unscrupulous masters. Le Diable was a smuggler of lace. His owner dyed him different colors for different missions, and packed contraband lace under a false skin, so that the dog could slip across the French border. Before he was shot by a customs official, Le Diable reportedly transported lace worth more than 50,000 francs. In New Zealand a sheep rustler taught his dog to steal by opening gates and driving flocks of sheep through isolated mountain passes. The dog was eventually caught, brought to trial, and, so the story goes, hanged.

Fortunately, dogs more often work on the side of law and order. Some are employed to sniff out hidden narcotics, others to patrol. Macy's, the New York department store, has been using patrols of Doberman pinschers for years. The dogs prowl the store at night, discouraging thieves from hiding out at closing time and walking off with goods when the store opens in the morning.

Closely associated with guard dogs are those that serve as soldiers. As early as 700 B.C. dogs were used against foot soldiers, and the Gauls went so far as to develop armor for their fighting dogs. Attila, the rapacious Hun, used packs of dogs to guard his camps. During the Crusades the Christians' dogs were said to be able to smell the difference between a Christian and infidel, and so attack appropriately. Nearly two centuries after Benjamin Franklin recommended the use of dogs for the military, the U.S. Armed Forces K-9 Corps became a reality—in 1942. More than 19,000 dogs were shipped to training centers, though nearly half were rejected. The rest performed remarkably well as sentries, scouts, messengers, mine detectors, and sledge and pack animals. More than 500 dogs were used during the Korean War, and others took the field in Vietnam.

Through such organizations as The Seeing Eye, Guide Dogs for the Blind, and Leader Dogs For the Blind, blind people have become more independent. Guide dogs are usually German shepherds, but some programs use golden and Labrador retrievers, collies, and boxers. An even newer idea is that featured by the American Humane Hearing Dog program, which trains dogs to recognize sounds and alert deaf people to them. Such dogs can be taught to distinguish among the cry of a baby, the sound of a smoke alarm, or the ringing of a doorbell.

In return for their efforts, all that most dogs require is kindness and food, so it seems only fair that American dog lovers spoon out some 5 billion pounds of dog food every year, at a cost of $1.5 billion. Surely, the affectionate, helpful animals are worth the expense. As Mark Twain put it, "If you pick up a starving dog and make him prosperous, he will not bite you. This is the principal difference between a dog and a man."

DOLL As every mother knows, a child can make a doll out of almost anything if she (or he) has a mind to. A forked stick, a handful of straw, or a shapely stone, combined with a willing imagination, can transport its young mistress or master into the realm of child's play for hours at a time. At the dawn of civilization, and in many remote cultures even today, most children's dolls were made in that way. But in ancient times dolls (or more likely "idols") also played significant roles in adult life, serving as fertility figures, as representations of the dead, as protectors against evil, and as

To avoid actual physical examination, Chinese women marked their afflictions on "doctor ladies" and gave the dolls to physicians for diagnosis of their ills.

A Mansion in Miniature

Grownups, no less than children, have been enchanted by the miniature world of dollhouses and dolls. But probably none realized that fantasy world more magnificently than Queen Mary, consort of George V of England. For in 1924 the people of England presented their beloved 57-year-old queen with a truly regal dollhouse, designed by noted British architect Sir Edwin Lutyens, and constructed and furnished over a four-year period by a multitude of artists and craftsmen—at a cost of a million dollars.

This handsome Georgian-style toy, is 100 inches long, 62 inches deep, and three stories high. It stands atop a substantial base containing pullout drawers packed with machinery to run the house. A formal garden, perfectly laid out in a drawer, pops into verdant bloom when pulled out. At the flick of a switch, the house's four facades reveal a wonderland of rooms and furnishings impeccably fit for a queen.

In this tiny but working world, hot and cold water flows out of silver taps into alabaster bathtubs, then drains into basement reservoirs; a tiny gramophone plays "God Save the King" in the nursery; pastry ovens, fired by tiny pellets of coal, bake crumpets in the kitchens; and elevators transport imaginary riders.

Royal cultural life is also well served—in miniature. Queen Mary's library contains hundreds of tiny, mostly original, handwritten books, bound in leather, by noted British authors of the day, including G.K. Chesterton, A.E. Housman, and Somerset Maugham. Postage-stamp–size watercolors and engravings by famous artists pack the drawers.

Her Majesty's wine cellar is no less handsomely stocked, with miniature bottles of champagne and Madeira and Bordeaux. These and all the other marvelous minutiae in Queen Mary's dollhouse remain at Windsor Castle, a Lilliputian record of the royal comforts of the 1920's, now preserved for posterity.

Italian walnut shelves line Queen Mary's finely furnished mini-library.

participants in mystical and magical events.

The earliest-known ritual dolls have been found in Europe from France to the Soviet Union. They are artifacts of the Aurignacian culture that existed there some 40,000 years ago. Of many examples unearthed, the Willendorf Venus, discovered in Austria near the Danube River, is probably the finest. Carved in limestone, about 4 inches high, still showing traces of its original red paint, it is very much a female figure, with exaggerated breasts and hips.

Peddler dolls, complete with trays of notions, were popular in England in the late 19th century.

Ancient fertility idols have also been found in excavations at Mohenjo-Daro in Pakistan, on the island of Naxos in the Aegean Sea, at Hissarlik in northwest Turkey, in the ruins of some southwestern American Indian settlements, and in many other widely scattered early communities. In some early civilizations, like those of Egypt and China, dolls came to be used as substitutes for the human sacrifices that formerly were buried with important persons.

Clay dolls made by adults for children began to appear at least as early as the Greek and Roman civilizations. A girl would keep her dolls until she was ready for marriage, making a ritual visit to the altar of Artemis (the goddess of unmarried girls) if she were Greek, to the altar of Diana if Roman, to put them aside. In Syrian villages today a girl still uses doll symbols, hung in her window, to announce that she has come of marriageable age.

By medieval times wooden dolls, some fitted with movable limbs, were a regular feature of childhood for both boys and girls in wealthy families. Often the figures represented virtuous adults—chivalrous knights, the Holy Family, and kings and queens. The children of poorer families, then as now, had homemade dolls made of whatever was at hand—straw, rags, stockings, old spools, corn husks, or even bread dough.

Modern dolls, with neatly crafted faces and bodies and suitable attire, date from the 14th century. Not surprisingly, they were a French idea and were used as mannequins to display dress fashions and hair styles. The first "fashion dolls," life-size figures, are on record as a gift in 1396 to the eight-year-old French bride of Richard II of England. Robert de Varennes, court tailor to Charles VI, was paid the then-substantial fee of 459 francs to create an entire wardrobe for the dolls, made to the girl's own measurements, which was shipped to the tiny queen. A hundred years later Anne of Brittany bestowed a life-size doll and a French-made wardrobe upon Queen Isabella of Spain.

In time, enterprising French stylists were sending "fashion babies," as they were sometimes called, to wealthy customers in and out of courts throughout Europe, and eventually to the American colonies, too. These dolls were so highly valued as fashion guides that they were protected by diplomatic courtesies, even during hostilities between France and England. In 1704 the Abbé Prévost wrote of this phenomenon: "By an act of gallantry which is worthy of being noted in the chronicles of history, for the benefit of the ladies the ministers of both Courts granted a special pass to the mannequin; that pass was always respected, and during the times of greatest enmity . . . the mannequin was the one object which remained unmolested."

Meanwhile, the craft of making toy dolls was growing in importance. As early as the 15th century, Germany became the leader in producing clay dolls, the majority of which were assembled in Nuremberg. Wood soon replaced clay. Dolls of wood, though cruder than those of modeled clay, could be constructed to provide for articulated arms and legs. Soon the Dutch and Austrians developed local industries, and wooden dolls were exported to other countries on the continent. Sir Walter Raleigh included a few of these "puppets and babes" in the inventory of gifts he took to the Indians of the New World.

In the 19th century professional dollmakers began to specialize even within their craft. Body casings, once made of stiff leather, were constructed of soft sheepskin or kidskin and, after 1850, of gutta-percha. Stuffings, formerly of coarse bran, were fashioned of horsehair, dried seaweed, or sawdust. Arms, hands, and feet made of porcelain became more realistic looking, and the introduction of ball joints gave the assembled doll greater flexibility. Doll heads were made with better attention to eye, nose, and mouth detail. Dresden dolls (with glazed porcelain heads) and French bisque dolls (with unglazed ceramic heads), often embellished with wigs of human hair, came into prominence about 1820.

In the 19th century, fascination with machinery also had an effect on doll design. In the 1820's a "sleeping eyes" doll, whose eyes opened and shut by means of counterweights, was created, as well as an automaton-like doll that actually walked. In 1827 Johann Nepomuk Maelzel, a friend of Beethoven's and developer of the metronome, patented a voice-box mechanism that enabled a doll to say "Papa" and "Mama" when squeezed. (Many decades later Thomas Edison tried, unsuccessfully, to market a similar mechanism.) Before the 19th century, professionally made dolls most often were designed to look like elegantly dressed women, but in that century doll figures became much more varied; they included infant dolls wearing simple nightgowns, peddler dolls with baskets of wares, little-boy dolls in sailor suits, rag dolls, and peasant dolls.

customs

"Klappers" and "Knockers"

Direct selling is the most personal form of retailing. It is the art of moving merchandise to the buyer, and so is different from other kinds of retailing, where the merchant's goal is to get the customer to come to the merchandise. Whether the principle is applied to the medieval peddler hawking religious artifacts from castle to castle, or the modern Fuller Brush salesman, it remains the same: the seller must meet the consumer on home ground, face to face, and close the sale by personal persuasion. Throughout history, door-to-door selling has had a meaningful economic impact in many societies. It has meant opportunity for those too poor to set up stores or factories; it has provided valuable part-time employment for many who need it; the demands of early American peddlers helped create new road systems; and traveling salesmen have certainly starred in many a joke.

Peddlers, as they used to be called, played an important part in the building of America. They were there with the pioneers. They traveled on foot or on horseback before roads made wagons possible, and they carried more than tinware, clocks, buttons, shoelaces, knives, woodenware, and anything else they thought would entice customers: they also carried the news. In a time when communication was anything but instantaneous, peddlers traded in gossip and impor-

In cap and overcoat, peddlers roamed the breadth of 19th-century Russia.

tant national news. In revolutionary Boston, Samuel Adams distributed political broadsides by passing them out through peddlers, thus reaching, for example, citizens who had not heard of the Boston Massacre. Sometimes peddlers also offered special services such as blacksmithing, carpentry, cobbling, and gunsmithing. The last was particularly important in frontier days. As firearms grew more complex, the average owner was less able to repair those vital tools. If a peddler who specialized in guns could not fix a damaged weapon, he could always sell the needy householder a new one, "lock (trigger mechanism), stock and barrel."

Some of the early peddlers even managed to get along with the Indians. The Cherokee called the peddler *Jew-wedge-du-gish,* "the egg-eater," which they derived from their observation of the habit of orthodox Jewish peddlers of carrying hard-boiled eggs (which they did, of course, to ensure a kosher diet). The peddlers sometimes called themselves "klappers" or "knockers" because of their door-to-door travels.

The role of peddler in America's early days typically fell to those latest arrived in the country. The first were New England Protestants, commonly known as "Connecticut Yankees," and upon them fell the first frowns of more settled Southerners who were sure that peddlers were, by definition, crooked. They were the first to hear "Damnyankee" as one word. The hard evidence that peddlers were particularly scurrilous is difficult to find.

Benedict Arnold began his career peddling woolen goods, and only really got into trouble after he joined the army. Jim Fisk, a famous railroad tycoon of slippery morality, started as a tinware peddler. Fisk noticed early on that the better known a salesman was, the more comfortable

Dolls in the 20th century continued to evolve both in design and social relevance. Thanks to television, dollmakers have churned out millions of celebrity dolls—sports figures, TV personalities, and film stars. Sonny and Cher dolls, as well as Evel Knievel and Muhammad Ali dolls, enjoyed enormous popularity, only to be supplanted by a new generation of equally transient "heroes."

Dolls featuring the "capability" to perform natural functions—crying, wetting, eating, burping, even developing breasts—were also highly successful. In the process, and in keeping with the less inhibited times, dollmakers also began creating dolls with distinct male and female organs. In a sense, the world has come full circle—back to the fertility dolls of ancient times.

DOOR Intended to provide privacy, the earliest doors were probably made of animal hides, pieces of cloth, even twigs. When doors acquired the additional purposes they still serve—to impress those who pass through them and protect the people

people felt buying from him. He used circus-type posters to advertise his arrival, and draped his wagon with flags and bunting. Clearly, these two men are not enough to label the whole group of peddlers as unscrupulous. Perhaps the designation arose from a natural distrust of outsiders. Abraham Lincoln's father was a part-time peddler, and so was Richard Sears, who sold watches. When he found he needed a watch repairman to help his trade, he hired Alvah Roebuck. Together, the two of them did quite well in retailing.

Although the Fuller Brush Company is not the oldest or largest direct-selling organization, it is probably the most ingrained in American culture. Saddled with the reputation of the peddlers of an earlier day, Alfred C. Fuller nonetheless built a huge business on personal selling. He learned to say, "I'll step in," instead of "May I come in?" In one act of diplomacy, he made up for a thousand traveling salesman jokes. When "a red-haired woman," as he called her, seemed more interested in him than his brushes, he stoically went on with his sales pitch. She said, with double meaning, "Do not lead me into temptation." Fuller replied, "Madame, I am not leading you into temptation, but delivering you from evil." She

bought three brushes. Fuller also valued rain as a powerful means of keeping the housewife at home. As one of his employees later put it, "Give me a rainy year and I'll buy a Cadillac." Chased by dogs and resisted by strong-willed housewives, the men of Fuller Brush have built a legend.

Door-to-door selling is the older of the two basic direct-sales techniques. The other is the "hostess party," as employed for example by Stanley Home Products and by Tupperware. According to one account, which may be apocryphal, the idea of the hostess party originated with a young Stanley Home Products salesman. While selling door to door in the time-honored way, he chanced across a group of women having coffee together. The hostess let him give his sales pitch anyway, and he sold a lot of products. He gave the hostess a small gift and began setting up other parties so he could talk to several customers at once. His sales shot up sharply, and he was able to spend more time where he was happiest—in a local pool hall.

From those first backpacks, pushcarts, and wagons, some 3 million Americans have come to devote their time to trying to enter the minds of the customers they talk with. It is a $6 billion business every year. Like the peddlers of old, modern direct-sales employees often switch to other occupations. But along the way, they have had the opportunity to work at a business that is easy to enter and highly responsive to individual initiative.

Perils of peddling, 1880: bitten more than 40 times, Michigan peddler Norman Freeman fought back and survived this terrifying attack by dogs.

and things behind them—builders turned to sturdier materials that they could ornament. Syrians used stone or marble for the doors of palaces, temples, and tombs. Where wood was plentiful, doors were made of heavy planks bound in decorated metal sheaths—not unlike those in King

Perfect portal for those on the wrong side of a jail door: it leads to freedom and you can walk around it.

Solomon's Temple, which according to the Bible were "of olive tree," carved with cherubim and palm trees, and overlaid with gold.

Even more elaborate and durable were the bronze doors of the Pantheon in Rome, which are still in place after 1,800 years. Probably the most beautiful doors are those at the eastern entrance of the Baptistery of the Piazza del Duomo in Florence, Italy. Lorenzo Ghiberti lavished 27 years on decorating them with 10 bas-relief biblical scenes so striking that Michelangelo is reputed to have called the entranceway "the doors of Paradise." More significant in history, perhaps, were the wooden doors of the Church of All Saints in Wittenberg, to which Martin Luther nailed his Theses on October 31, 1517. They were destroyed in a fire in 1760.

Other doors have contributed to the making of history. A low door in a passageway at the château of Amboise caused the death of King Charles VIII in 1498 when, rushing out to a game of tennis, he struck his head against its lintel. A gate in the grand vizier's palace in Constantinople provided the name—the Sublime Porte—by which the Ottoman Empire was for centuries known to Europeans. And Governor George Wallace, by publicly "standing in the schoolhouse door" of the University of Alabama, defied the federal government and propelled himself into political prominence.

The largest doors are in the Vehicle Assembly Building of the Kennedy Space Center in Florida. They are 456 feet high—tall enough to wheel St. Peter's Basilica through—and they take 45 minutes to open. The most foreboding doorway is in Dante's Inferno. "All hope abandon, ye who enter here," it warns.

Over the years, man's ingenuity has prompted him to slice doors in half horizontally, so that he could open just the top, and to chop them at the top and bottom, presumably so that they could provide a "visual barrier" for people who congregate in certain kinds of public places, like saloons. The French invented a door paned with glass. Americans popularized doors with louvers or screens. Sliding doors originated in Japan. Folding doors, a seemingly modern idea, were already in use in Pompeii in the 1st century A.D.

Recognition is due to Theophilus Van Kannel of Philadelphia, who, on August 7, 1888, received a patent for a "storm door structure," now better known as the revolving door. It was, as its inventor claimed, "an entrance for all seasons." It kept wind, snow, rain, and dust out, and warmth in. Furthermore, no one could slam it. Its only defect is that someone might get stuck inside one. Even this marginal hazard has been eliminated by still another invention: the air door, which consists of nothing more than a circulating column of air acting as an insulating barrier.

Air doors have been installed in such high-traffic areas as the entrances to department stores, and may find use elsewhere. They do, however, fall a little short in providing privacy. And one wonders what Martin Luther would have done with an air door in 1517.

DOUGHNUT The genesis of the fried cake called the doughnut is as mysterious as the cake is delicious. Archeologists digging in the southwestern United States, for example, have unearthed petrified fried cakes with holes in them, thus making the doughnut the handiwork of prehistoric Indians. Other scholars, however, see the doughnut as naught but a modern mutation of *okykoeck*, the fried bread brought to the New World by early Dutch settlers. Since contact between those settlers and prehistoric southwestern Indians seems highly unlikely, the best that can be said about the doughnut is probably this: it was an idea whose moment rolled around several times.

The hole in the doughnut is also subject to speculation. One story has it that Hanson Gregory, a sea captain, added—or subtracted—the hole in 1847 as an aid to more thorough cooking and better digestibility. Another story suggests that Captain Gregory put the hole in the doughnut so that he might hook a cake or two over the spokes of his ship's steering wheel. No matter, the doughnut was born again during World War I, when two Salvation Army workers fried bread to leaven the spirits of soldiers stationed in France. The creation won a name from the fact that "doughboys" were "nuts" about—doughnuts.

DRINKING VESSEL

Prehistoric people drank from just about anything that was hollow and would hold liquid—gourds, animal horns, coconut and egg shells, even human skulls.

By the 3rd century the manufacture of glass household articles and glasses was common in Rome and parts of the empire, but a century later it had died out in most of Europe. Glass

Grim dipper: hazards of the public tin cup were portrayed in this ad.

became a luxury item, and for centuries Venice enjoyed a virtual monopoly of the glass trade. By the 16th century, artisans in France, the Lowlands, and England began to produce glass.

Glasses became common in England in the 1600's, but few were exported to America because they broke so easily. "Puzzle jugs" of the same period were a challenge to drinkers; the jugs had several spouts, but only one worked. Other drinking vessels were made with two or more handles so they could be passed easily from person to person.

In colonial America, guests at an inn usually drank from a communal bowl passed round the table, even when the revelers were total strangers. In the late 17th century, Americans used leather drinking cups,

"Fuddling cup," actually three cups in one, could easily addle the unwary.

which were stitched and waxed and fitted with a silver rim. Wooden and pewter tankards and earthenware vessels were popular until the early 19th century, when glassmaking began to be mechanized. Nonetheless, the communal drinking cup, usually made of tin, was common in public places such as schools, offices, and railroad cars, until the early 1900's. It died a lingering death after doctors began crusading for better health through better sanitation—a crusade that popularized the individual paper cup, invented in 1908. These throwaway cups were first used in large white porcelain vending machines which dispensed (if you were lucky) a cup of ice water for a penny. The new device was enthusiastically endorsed by members of the Anti-Saloon League, who believed that men were enticed into saloons to get a drink of water. Modern cups and glasses have to be stronger than ever before—not because they are dropped more often but because they must withstand the rigors of going through a dishwasher.

DRINKING WATER It is possible that the water you sprinkled on the geraniums this morning contains some of the same molecules that were in the bath water of Adolf Hitler. Because very little water is lost and very little is created in nature, the earth's supply of water is about the same now as it was when man began to record history. It varies in distribution and form, evaporating into the atmosphere and falling again as rain or snow, or penetrating the soil to rise again in plants, and seeping into ponds, lakes, and oceans.

The ancient Romans were quite knowledgeable about the human need for clean water, and the systems they built to carry it are engineering marvels. Awed by the network of aqueducts, Sextus Julius Frontinus, the water commissioner of Rome at the end of the 1st century A.D., con-

During the Middle Ages water peddlers often drew and sold water from public wells.

gratulated Roman genius: "With such an array of indispensable structures carrying so many waters, compare the idle Pyramids, or the useless, though famous, works of the Greeks."

When the Roman Empire fell, so did standards of water quality. The aqueducts were neglected, for want of a central authority and the public funds to keep the water system going.

The worst times for purity of drinking water were the Middle Ages. The archbishops of Salzburg had their water delivered by messenger, while ordinary citizens dipped their buckets in wells or the town fountains. But the streets of Europe grew filthy, as did the wells, and epidemics like the Black Death of the mid-14th century killed hundreds of thousands of people. Chief among the medieval water polluters were the tanneries and slaughterhouses located along riverbanks of cities. In 1366 a French parliamentary decree stated that all slaughtering of animals must be done outside Paris. The municipal records of Paris show that in a single year 269,256 animals—sheep, oxen, calves, and pigs—were killed and butchered. In 1425, in Essex, England, the ale makers found that tainted water was making their product unpalatable. They complained bitterly about the tanners who despoiled the local stream, and accused them of "impayring and corrupcion of the said water."

The 1892 cholera epidemic in Hamburg, Germany, dramatized the need to filter water to remove germs. While a substantial number of the citizens of Hamburg fell victim to the disease, the inhabitants of Altona, across the Elbe River, did not. The difference was that the Altonians were drinking filtered water.

The Greeks and the Romans believed that certain kinds of water had therapeutic or curative properties, and some of the spas built by the Romans throughout their empire are still in existence—Bath, England; Baden, Switzerland; and Tiberias, Israel. The word *spa* comes from the commune of Spa, in Belgium, the favorite mineral springs of such nobles as Peter the Great and Kaiser Wilhelm II. Mineral waters are prescribed for various physical disorders—alkaline waters for ulcers and magnesium waters for liver problems. Apart from its supposed health benefits, the spa is a place to socialize and relax.

Without water, the simple combination of hydrogen and oxygen, there is no life. Jericho, the city made famous by Joshua, sits nearly a 1,000 feet below sea level in a burning desert north of the Dead Sea. A spring at Jericho, which gushes up 1,000 gallons per minute, has been refreshing visitors since 9,500 years before the birth of Christ.

DRUGSTORE Although the world's first drugstore opened for business in 754 A.D., more than 1,000 years of trial and error were required to perfect the four cornerstones upon which the modern practice of pharmacy was eventually to be built: the premeasured pill, the compressed tablet, the gelatine-coated capsule—and the soda fountain.

Nonetheless, that first drugstore, which was located in downtown Baghdad, offered a wide range

of medicaments such as camphor, cassia, aconite, cubeb, cloves, senna, cannabis, tamarind, sandalwood, alcoholic preparations, and fruit syrups—radical and probably welcome departures from prescriptions used in other areas of the world at that time, which relied heavily on lizard blood, frog toes, and antelope droppings.

One of the earliest references to the existence of drugstores in Europe occurs in an edict issued by Frederick II, Holy Roman emperor, in 1240. It fixed the price of drugs and prohibited pharmacists from entering into secret partnership with physicians. Other regulations in other places and times provide insight into the trade practices of the fledgling profession. For example, in the 15th century the city of Dijon, in France, ordered that no pharmacist could receive a legacy from a former client, and 16th-century French pharmacists had to swear that they would not slander their teachers or masters, and to promise "never to examine women privately, unless by great necessity."

Even reigning monarchs dabbled at compounding new drugs. Henry VIII was the originator of "The King's Majesty's Own Plaster," a paste of powdered pearls and guaiacum resin. The king's interest is understandable because guaiacum, an import from the Americas, had the reputation, regrettably unfounded, of curing venereal disease.

A substance made of the bark of a New World tree and named cinchona—after the Countess Chinchón, the wife of the Spanish viceroy of Peru whose stubborn fever it had cured—made its appearance in Europe about 1638. Its active ingredient, quinine, for centuries was used in the treatment of malaria. Only recently have more effective drugs been developed. The *pil perpetuae*, on the other hand, did not stay very long in the pharmacopoeia; it was a purgative, in use in the 17th century, which consisted of a pellet of solid antimony. Its initial cost was high, but it could be used over and over again, serving the needs of an entire family for posterity.

Schwab's Pharmacy, Hollywood, 1949, where Lana Turner was supposedly discovered.

Despite some specific successes, the lack of effective remedies for many of mankind's ills probably prompted the appearance of nostrums, elixirs, and patent medicines whose labels read like the table of contents of a medical textbook. Their proliferation, due in large part to the generous amounts of alcohol they contained, led to public demand for control and, eventually, the first federal legislation in the United States aimed at the drug industry. Enacted in 1848, it prohibited the importation of substituted, adulterated, or substandard drugs. If Americans were going to poison themselves, they would thenceforth do it with homemade concoctions. Finally, 90 years later, the federal Food, Drug and Cosmetic Act addressed the real problem by prohibiting false advertising and requiring informative labeling of products.

Well into the 19th century, drugstores were dark, forbidding places, lined with jars bearing Latin labels and glass cases full of shriveled animal parts and spatulas, scales, retorts, and other chemical apparatus intended to invoke the lost powers of the alchemists. The installation of one of the first soda fountains in an American pharmacy, by Elias Durand of Philadelphia about 1825, was not so much an innovation as a long-overlooked source of additional income—the Baghdad drugstore had sold syrups and confections of sugarcane. Nonetheless, the soda fountain

revolutionized the American drugstore and turned it into a unique institution that combined the social and economic functions of a French café, an English club, an Arab bazaar, and, despite the druggist's best efforts, it became something of a day-care center for teenagers.

Prohibition, which sharply curtailed the number of public gathering places, was probably the major reason why, by 1929, 60 percent of America's 58,258 drugstores had installed a soda fountain. The decline of this number to less than one-third by the 1970's was due to several factors: competition from other sources like ice-cream parlors and drive-ins, the scarcity of personable young men willing to work for a low hourly wage plus all the ice cream they could eat, and more profitable utilization of floor space for items like cosmetics. (It was logical that drugstores should carry cosmetics. The description of the Sage Durban's apothecary shop in the *Arabian Nights* lists "balms, salves, powders, and pomades" among its wares.)

Other changes have affected U.S. pharmacies. Of the more than 1.5 billion prescriptions dispensed in a typical year, perhaps half are filled by independent drugstores. The rest are handled by chain and department-store pharmacies, hospital dispensaries, supermarkets, and discount houses.

The nature of prescriptions, too, has changed. Although most drugstores still keep a mortar and pestle lying around somewhere, as well as a pair of scales, more than 98 percent of prescriptions require the pharmacist to do no more than take some capsules or tablets out of one bottle, put them in another bottle, and type up a label for it. What he does with the rest of the 20 minutes you have to wait remains one of life's dark mysteries.

Trusting patients in a Swiss village watch calmly as their druggist prepares their medicine, in 1879 scene.

DRY CLEANING "Take cold lye and warm it a little with wine lees and stir well, but take care that it should not be applied in too warm condition." A *hausfrau* who followed this helpful cleaning hint, which appeared in a booklet published in Nuremberg in 1532, would probably have gotten all but the most stubborn stains out of her husband's doublet. In the process, however, it might also have shrunk beyond recognition.

The beginning of modern dry cleaning—so called because it used an organic solvent instead of water—is legendarily credited to a Frenchman,

In the summer this 1920's presser must have wondered if he wanted a "white-collar" job.

Jean-Baptiste Jolly. The story relates that one day in 1825 a maid in Jolly's household accidentally upset a lamp, spilling camphene (distilled turpentine) on a tablecloth. Desperately, she tried to wipe up the proof of her clumsiness, but the more she rubbed the brighter and cleaner the area became. A dyer by trade, Jolly may not have known what an organic solvent was, but he recognized a good thing when he saw it. In short order, his process became known throughout France and made its way across the Channel to Britain. The English must have been awaiting it because in London, by 1854, according to one observer, there were more than "three thousand master dyers and scourers [cleaners] within a radius of ten miles of St. Paul's."

Although camphene cleaned clothes as effectively as it had Jolly's tablecloth, it had two serious drawbacks: it was highly flammable, and it left an odor. Other solvents, such as naphtha, benzene, and later on a new kerosene by-product called gasoline, had the same disadvantages. Eventually, chemists turned to a family of chemicals known as chlorinated hydrocarbons. These included the familiar carbon tetrachloride, which proved to be dangerously toxic, and perchloroethylene, now the most commonly used cleaning fluid in the world.

Over the years, unusual and delicate items, such as rare laces, ostrich plumes, and elaborate costumes, have been brought in for dry cleaning. A Massachusetts concern was asked to clean a live elephant that, as part of a publicity stunt, had been dyed a glorious pink. Records do not indicate how much cleaning fluid was required, but the job was accomplished successfully, and the pachyderm was restored to its original dull gray color. And it did not shrink.

DUPLICATING Some 3,000 years ago, multiple copies were made by rolling an inscribed tube over wet clay tablets. Despite some early attempts at creating duplicating devices, a businessman in the 1800's who wanted copies of a letter or invoice still had to have a clerk copy it by hand. (Duplicating is usually considered the making of quick and inexpensive copies on office machines and does not include printing or the use of carbon paper.)

Today, most duplicates are made by one of four processes. One of the oldest is the stencil duplicator, or mimeograph, perfected in the late 1800's. A special emulsion allows ink to pass through the typed "stencil" when the sheet is placed on an ink-filled printing cylinder. A mimeograph will make up to about 5,000 copies. In an offset duplicator, the master, with a grease-base image, is put on a drum. As it turns, the image picks up a grease-base ink and transfers it to a rubber roller (the offset), which immediately transfers the image to the paper. Offset can produce thousands of copies.

The spirit duplicator, sometimes called the ditto, got its name from the alcohol in the fluid used to dissolve a portion of a dye-impregnated master image and transfer it to the paper. The master, made by typing on a sheet backed by a waxy paper containing the dye, will make up to about 300 copies.

Xerography (from the Greek words meaning "dry writing"), the most common duplicating process, reproduces images with charges of static electricity. The image of the original is projected through a lens onto a light-sensitive drum, which maintains an electrostatic charge in the dark areas (corresponding to the type or lines on the original). These charged areas then pick up a black powder, somewhat like the way a comb charged by combing hair will pick up bits of lint. The drum next applies the powder to ordinary paper, which is heated briefly to bond the powder. Xerography will produce thousands of copies.

Deadly duplication: in this Rossetti painting, a young man and woman meet their doubles, meaning death is near.

Xerography was born in a rented room behind a beauty parlor in Astoria, Queens, New York, on October 22, 1938, when a penurious young inventor and patent lawyer, Chester F. Carlson, inked "10-22-38 Astoria" on a piece of glass. Working in a darkened

room, he and his assistant charged a sulfur-coated metal plate, exposed the glass and plate to light, sprinkled the plate with a dye, and pressed a sheet of paper to the metal. When they removed the sheet, it bore a perfect copy of Carlson's written legend.

At that time most duplicating machines required a trained operator and took about 30 minutes to make a single copy, but no one jumped at the chance to use Carlson's streamlined process, which could produce a copy in a few minutes. He was turned down by some 30 companies, including International Business Machines. Eventually, in the late 1940's, the Haloid Company in Rochester, New York, began dickering for production rights. Now the Xerox Corporation, it sold its first copier in 1950 and today sells and leases more copiers than any other manufacturer. The invention made Carlson a millionaire many times over.

In the late 1970's more than 2 million xerographic machines, produced by many companies, spewed out some 80 billion copies a year—enough, if laid end to end, to girdle the equator more than 500 times. The newest machines can reproduce in color, turn microfilm into full-size copy, enlarge or reduce the original size, send and receive copies over the telephone, copy on both sides of the paper, and, finally, sort, collate, and staple.

Some of the advances have been mixed blessings. Government agencies and financial institutions are worried that color duplicators will be used to illegally reproduce negotiable documents, including paper currency. Many leaks of secret government information, including documents in the Watergate scandal, were made via duplicated copies. Librarians and teachers argue that students need the freedom to copy, while authors and publishers want more copyright laws to protect their works from being pirated.

Aside from its technical revolution, duplicating has wrought great social changes. As social historian Marshall McLuhan put it, "Whereas Caxton and Gutenberg enabled all men to become readers, Xerox has enabled all men to become publishers."

Xerography, as well as the other duplicating processes, is used to reproduce everything from jokes and love letters to three-dimensional objects, including "Xerox portraits" of faces pressed against the scanning glass. The almost universal urge to duplicate has even caused the coining of a new word—"xeromania."

DUST We all bite the dust, every day. In a busy house, as many as 100,000 dust particles dance in a cubic centimeter of air. Some are mineral flecks blown in by the wind; others may be bits of cot-

Driven by a dust storm, hundreds of jack rabbits jam the main street of a Kansas town in this photograph.

ton, wool, wood, and hair. The nuclear fallout we fear (though there is actually very little of it) comes attached to dust roiled up in the atmosphere by atomic explosions. But dust provides beauty and utility as well. The rich reds and oranges of a sunset come from the scattering of light by dust particles. Because blue light scatters more than red does, the reddish tones remain longer.

Dust also forms the nucleus of raindrops and snowflakes. Without it, much less rain and snow would fall because it would be harder for droplets and snow crystals to form. Dust is relatively scarce in desert areas and over the oceans, suggesting that those suffering from the hives, asthma, or allergies that dust can provoke might be most comfortable in a state like Arizona—or at sea.

DYE Because their remains are formed largely of stone and marble, we may think of the Middle Ages and even antiquity as drab, gray historical periods. Far from it, they were eras of brilliant color: banners and hangings and tapestries, dazzlingly bright costumes and superb trimmings for temples, churches, public buildings, private houses, vehicles, and animals. As a result, the finding, processing, and use of dyes was an important, highly profitable business but fraught with deceit, fakery, and even piracy.

Purple, for instance, the rarest color of all, was produced in ancient times. It was obtained from the mucous gland of a Mediterranean shellfish. The demand for it, at the present-day equivalent of $7,000 an ounce, was one of the bases of Phoenicia's great wealth. It became the imperial color, and under the Romans production of the dye was regulated by a monopoly. In England purple, also extracted from shellfish, was used to dye the rich robes of church officials.

Yellows and oranges came from a variety of plants: saffron, fustic, turmeric, weld, henna, and safflower, which has been identified as a coloring agent in Egyptian funerary garments.

Saffron, which produced a particularly intense color, was smuggled into Europe, in one instance by a pilgrim returning from Tripoli who hid a few bulbs in a hollowed-out staff. "Had he been apprehended," wrote Richard Hakluyt, who chronicled the story, "he had died of the fact."

Deep, vibrant blue came from two plants: indigo, which was native to India, and woad, which grew profusely in Europe. However, by the 16th century the Dutch trading companies were dealing in indigo. To protect local production, woad growers in France persuaded Henry IV (1589–1610) to decree that anyone using indigo should be put to death. In England, indigo was denounced as "harmful, balefully devouring, pernicious, deceitful, eating, and corrosive." In Nu-

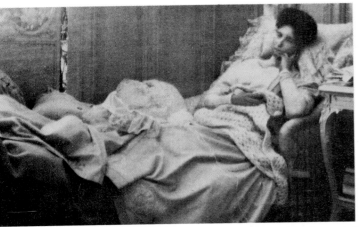

Study in mauve: Alexandra's boudoir at the imperial palace was the most famous in all of Russia.

remberg, dyers were required to swear that they would never use the substance. Its advantage was that an indigo plant gave out about 30 times as much dye as a woad plant of similar size, and the European demand for indigo increased. Also, woad production fouled the air with an incredibly noxious odor. Its stench was so revolting that Queen Elizabeth forbade the establishment of any woad mill within five miles of her country residences. In addition, the profit to be made from indigo was so great that not even rumor that the harvesting or handling of indigo plants caused sexual impotence could discourage producers.

The brightest, most desirable red was obtained from the desiccated bodies of the small cochineal insect called *Dactylopius coccus*, which is native to Mexico. About 100,000 of these creatures were required to produce a pound of dye, and only females sufficed. The insect thrives on the prickly pear cactus, and in the early 19th century special plantations were established in Spain, mostly in the Canary Islands. In hopes of profiting from the growing demand among Europeans for cochineal, the Dutch bribed a Spanish official, inducing him to steal breeding stock and, under armed guard, convoy it to Java. The scheme did not succeed because the insects failed to reproduce in their new home. But production in the Canary Islands reached some 1.5 million pounds in 1869.

One of the more astonishing aspects of the history of dyes is that, until 1856, the civilized world continued to rely on the same dozen-odd natural substances for color. And it might have for some time, if not for the sloppy laboratory technique of William Henry Perkin, who was a student at the Royal College of Chemistry in London. Perkin, then 18 years old, took advantage of his Easter vacation to try to synthesize quinine. He succeeded only in producing an ugly black sludge. Curious about what it might be, he dissolved some in alcohol and found it made a brilliant purple liquid. Strips of silk dipped in the liquid not only sopped up the color but retained it after repeated washings. Perkin subsequently sent samples to Britain's leading dyeing firm, Pullars of Perth, and received this optimistic reply: "If [the ladies] once take a mania for [your colour] and you can supply the demand, your fame and fortune are secure."

Fortunately for Perkin, the most important lady in the English-speaking world, Queen Victoria, fell in love with the color, which Perkin had named mauve. The queen wore a mauve dress when she officially opened the Great Exhibition of 1862. The color became so popular that *Punch*, the humor magazine, reported that London bobbies were directing loiterers to "get a mauve on," while the painter James Whistler harrumphed that "mauve is just pink trying to be purple." Victoria's granddaughter Alexandra, who married Czar Nicholas II, was so taken by the color that she had her boudoir at Tsarskoye Selo, the imperial palace near St. Petersburg, done over entirely in mauve—carpet, walls, pillows, curtains, and furniture. Because the chamber so perfectly symbolized the capriciousness and extravagance of the last Romanovs, it became, according to her biographer, the most famous room in Russia.

Perkin had been trying to synthesize a drug when he stumbled on his discovery. In 1932 another scientist made a similar sort of discovery—in reverse. Dr. Gerhard Domagk, while studying the properties of a new dye for leather called Prontosil red, observed that it was also a surprisingly effective microbe killer. With additional clinical work Prontosil red became known around the world as sulfonamide—man's first specific antibiotic drug.

ELEVATOR Elevators are the world's safest way to travel. In a typical year the 345,000 elevators in the United States lift and lower some 43 billion passengers a distance of 1.5 billion miles—with only 15 fatalities. Walking up and down stairs, according to one insurance company, is at least five times more hazardous than riding in an elevator.

It was not ever thus. The modern elevator was born in 1854, the year of the Crystal Palace Exposition in New York. At the exposition, Elisha Graves Otis had himself and some freight hauled up on his "safety elevator" and, to prove his point,

In 1854 Elisha Otis demonstrated the reliability of his new hoist.

ordered a workman to sever the lift rope with an ax. A stunned crowd watched in horror until they realized that Otis and his elevator were safely motionless.

Otis' elevator was not the first device men had used to hoist objects and people. From the builders of antiquity to Louis XV, who had a "flying chair" installed outside his room in Versailles in order to travel up to his mistress' quarters, a variety of techniques had been devised and refined. Still the state of the art in 1854 was such that the New York *Tribune*, in describing Otis' feat, used the words "daring" and "sensational."

Despite this excellent publicity, it took Otis three years to sell his first passenger elevator—to E.V. Haughwout's five-story china and glass emporium on Broadway in New York. Making use of a system of steam-driven belts, it whisked passengers along at a speed of 40 feet per minute. (At this pace, it would take 35 minutes to reach the top of the world's tallest building, the Sears Tower in Chicago, a trip the building's express elevators make in exactly one minute.)

Department stores and hotels were among Otis' earliest customers, but doubts remained. Thus the Fifth Avenue Hotel in 1866 cautiously announced its first passenger elevator in known terms: "a perpendicular railway—intersecting each story . . . independent of the ordinary and usual approaches from floor to floor."

Fortunately, the safety device on which Elisha Otis risked his reputation, if not his life, was simple and it worked: it consisted of a wagon spring attached to the top of the elevator and compressed by the pull of the lift rope. If the rope parted or was cut, the spring snapped out, driving metal jaws into cogs in the elevator's guide rails and securing the platform. Much improved and backed by other devices, the same basic system is in use today.

In this vertical airport of the future, multiform elevators provide the lift.

The next problem, especially as buildings became taller, was to increase speed. One scheme, actually installed in a 10-story building in 1873, consisted of placing an elevator at one end of a rope and an empty iron bucket at the other. When the bucket was filled with water, the elevator went up. When the bucket was emptied, the elevator started down—until stopped by a hand brake.

Other systems, more conducive to passenger placidity, used hydraulic pistons. Their basic flaw, however, was that a deep hole was required beneath each building to house them. Ultimately, electricity and steel cables were utilized to solve the problem.

Greater speeds required better reflexes on the part of elevator operators, who had been able to watch for waiting passengers through open grills. Soon call signals were introduced and, in 1924, automatic signal-control systems. Operators then had little to do except punch buttons and pass the time until retirement.

Progress, however, is not without cost. Otis' first passenger elevator sold for $300; today, a single express elevator can cost more than $150,000. Custom-designed cars are built in a variety of sizes and shapes—round, triangular, and octagonal—and signals have been modified, too. At Pepsico's former headquarters in New York, up and down indicators were red and blue, in honor of the company's distinctive logo. The elevator cars at 111 East 59th Street have braille markings beside the floor buttons, because the building's occupant is the New York Association for the Blind.

As buildings grew still taller, and elevators had to move more and more people, a problem became evident. Banks of elevators take up rentable space not only on the street floor but on every floor. Many solutions were suggested. Yet the most aesthetically pleasing might have been figured out by a bright child: take the elevator out of the lobby altogether and slap it on the outside of the building. John Portman and other architects did precisely this for hotels in Atlanta, San Francisco, and other cities. The result is an unforgettable ride for passengers and a delight for spectators, especially at night when the elevator cars look like giant illuminated yo-yos spinning up and down the side of a building.

customs

Social Blue Books

Etiquette has been defined as "the power of littles," "the oil of civility," and "the beautiful frame which is placed around a valuable picture to prevent its being marred." In simpler terms, it is the system of behavior that a particular society deems to be polite. Throughout history, following etiquette in all its forms has been a necessary bit of personal equipment to those who wish to rise in society and remain comfortably at the top.

Good manners and etiquette probably were born when the first puny caveman stepped out of the way of a stronger caveman. Indeed, many of the gestures we now recognize as "mannerly" are thought to have originated as signs of submission. The kiss on the hand, for example, bestowed by a subject on his lord or a gentleman on his lady, began, very possibly, with the kiss of submission—when the chastised "thanked" his punisher for having corrected his errant ways. One explanation of the handshake traces it to a time when most men carried weapons: the thrust of an open right hand (the weapon hand) showed that its owner had friendly intentions.

Kneeling, bowing, curtsying, prostrating oneself before a superior—all were gestures of submission. Even the relatively modern custom of tipping the hat as a greeting may be related to medieval codes of chivalry: a knight in full armor might have raised his visor to show his face, signifying that he meant no harm.

Evolved over many centuries in many parts of the world, the rules of etiquette often developed in contradictory ways. Partly for outsiders, but mostly for those within a society, etiquette books were published in great numbers, especially in the 19th century and in countries undergoing social upheaval as a result of the Industrial Revolution. In no country were such books more avidly collected than in the United States, where showing "good breeding" became something of a national obsession.

Virtually every social situation had its rule. *Ladies and Gentlemen's American Etiquette*, for example, written by "An American" about 1820, specified: "It is in bad taste for a lady to draw on her gloves when visitors enter, for it seems to say that their presence prevents her employing her hands." On the subject of dining it recommended, among its many cautions: "Never use your *knife* to convey your food to your mouth, under any circumstances; it is unnecessary and glaringly vulgar. . . . Bread should never be cut less than an inch and a half thick. There is nothing more plebeian than thin bread at dinner."

On the matter of social singing, the authority urged a gentleman to learn one or two songs just in case he should be called upon to perform, but to "avoid those songs which the music and words point out as especially composed for the softer sex. Imagine, for instance, the sweet sounds of 'I dreamed I dwelt in marble halls' issuing from a mouth surrounded with black whiskers and buried in moustaches."

Introductions called for great and careful consideration. "If, while walking with one friend you meet another, never introduce them without having previously ascertained that it would be agreeable to both. . . . In making introductions be careful to introduce the lower to the person in the higher rank. When rank and station are equal, *age* will be the best guide. . . . If you are a gentleman and meet a lady of your acquaintance in the street, it is *her part* to notice *you first*, unless you are very intimate. . . . On the continent of Europe, the fashion in this instance, as in many others, is exactly the reverse."

One of the most complex and troublesome sets of rules had to do with what one author called "paste-board politenesses," the exchange of calling cards as part of ceremonial visits. In the latter half of the 19th century most etiquette books devoted at least a section to the subject. The size of the card, the style of its engraving, and its wording, but most of all the manner of its delivery, were subtle points to master.

In *Our Deportment*, published in 1882, the authoritative John H. Young explained: "A person may make a card serve the purpose of a call, and it may either be sent in an envelope, by messenger or left in person. If left in person, one corner should be turned down. To indicate that a call is made on all or several members of the family, the card for the lady of the house is folded in the middle. If guests are visiting at

ENVELOPE When, or for what reason, man was first impelled to put something down in writing is not known. More than likely, however, it was not long before someone else came along and sneaked a look at what he had written.

Envelopes originally were intended to protect important documents and shield them from prying eyes. Like writing materials, they were made of cloth, animal skins, or vegetable reeds. The Babylonians used a thin sheet of clay that was wrapped around a message, crimped together, and baked—a cumbersome procedure but still easier

Bad manners: 1. tipping back; 2. mouth too full; 3. feeding dog; 4. knife wrong; 5. arguing; 6. lounging; 7. child on table; 8. drinking from saucer; 9. shirt sleeves; 10. finger in mouth; 11. scratching and often leaving table.

the house, a card is left for each guest. To return a call made in person with a card inclosed in an envelope, is an intimation that visiting between the parties is ended. Those who leave or send their cards with no such intention, should not inclose them in an envelope. A card left at a farewell visit, before a long protracted absence, has 'P.P.C.' [French for "To Take Leave"] written in one corner. . . . P.P.C. cards are not left when the absence from home is only for a few months, nor by persons starting in midsummer for a foreign country, as residents are then supposed to be out of town."

As Americans moved into the modern era, authorities became bolder, endorsing social exclusiveness as an appropriate objective of etiquette. Annie Randall White, writing in *Twentieth Century Etiquette* (1900), chirped: "Etiquette throws a protection around the well-bred, keeping the coarse and disagreeable at a distance, and punishing those who violate her dictates, with banishment from the social circle."

Mrs. White confronted many new social situations and provided for each. On using the telephone, she advised: "Stand near the telephone, place the receiver to your ear, after having rung the bell, hold your lips close to the transmitter, and, after the person whom you desire to hear from has made himself known, talk in a low, even tone of voice. Many make the mistake of shouting."

Twenty years after Mrs. White issued her dictums, Mrs. Emily Post wrote *Etiquette, the Blue Book of Social Usage*. Within a few months after publication, it became the bestselling nonfiction book in the country. Mrs. Post's modernized recommendations reflected, somewhat ruefully, the enormous changes that had taken place since World War I.

On the subject of theater behavior, for example, she sputtered: "It might be tentatively remarked that prinking and 'making up' in public are all part of an age which cannot see fun in a farce without bedroom scenes and actors in pajamas, and actresses running about in negligés with their hair down. . . . In other days it was always thought that so much as to adjust a hat-pin or glance in a glass was lack of breeding. . . . But to-day young women . . . are continually studying their reflection in little mirrors and patting their hair and powdering their noses . . . in a way that in Mrs. Oldname's girlhood would have absolutely barred them from good society."

In some ways Emily Post's death in 1960 marked the end of polite society's influence on American mores. In the 1960's etiquette and etiquette books were not just unimportant, they were consciously flouted, and bad manners and boorishness were often celebrated for their shock value. Mrs. Oldname's daughter was now using four-letter words—in public—and the President of the United States was lifting his shirt to show his surgical scars.

Whether formal behavior will ever regain its primacy—and who shall set the new rules if it does—is anyone's guess.

than trying to fold or roll a clay cuneiform tablet.

With the advent of postal service, envelopes acquired yet another purpose. An enterprising Frenchman named De Valayer in 1653 obtained permission from King Louis XIV to establish a postal system in Paris. He set up boxes at strategic corners and announced that he was prepared to deliver any letters placed in them if they were enclosed in envelopes that he alone sold. The scheme failed, but only because an enemy of De Valayer's began posting live mice in his boxes.

Early in the 19th century, postal authorities in England faced another problem. Because the recipient of a letter paid the postage, correspondents learned to transmit brief messages ("Arrived safely. Returning Thursday.") by means of prearranged envelope markings. The addressee would decipher the code, hand the letter back to the postman, and refuse to pay. Postage stamps were designed to put an end to this game.

In a modest way, envelopes have experienced their share of technological refinement. First came the gummed flap, then the see-through window, then the tamper-proof closure and pressure-sensitive seal. Most recently, a chemical company introduced envelopes made of "spunbonded olefin." The substance looks like paper, and can be written on like paper, but it is lighter than paper, insensitive to water and chemicals, and virtually impossible to tear.

ERASER In 1858 Hyman L. Lipman, an American, put an eraser on one end of a pencil. By creating a better way of rubbing out human error, he earned $100,000. This undoubtedly was more than the pay of the Babylonian who used his thumb to smudge out an error in cuneiform on a wet clay tablet. Even Egyptian hieroglyphics, set down in ink on papyrus, could be corrected—with a damp cloth—because Egyptian inks were soluble in water. And if the ink had already dried, it could be scraped off with a metal blade. In theory (there is no real proof), hieroglyphics carved in stone could be corrected, too, by chipping out the mistake, filling in the hole with plaster, and chiseling a new symbol.

As civilizations rose and fell, however, man's need to communicate outstripped his ability to avoid errors. And with the marketing of the typewriter, in the 1870's, the problem became acute. Joseph Priestley, the English discoverer of oxygen, had already discerned the property of rubber as an eraser. In 1770 he announced that bread crumbs, commonly used for rubbing out mistakes, were passé and that rubber was in. Nonetheless, it took the discovery of vulcanized rubber, in 1839, to

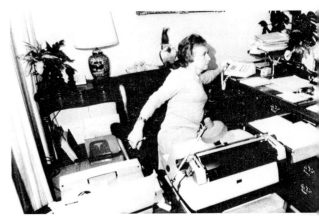

Gummed erasure: Rose Mary Woods shows how she might have caused history's most famous deletion.

make rubber erasers practicable.

By 1888 some 100,000 typists were at work in the United States, all inevitably making typing errors. Erasures by means of rubber were now possible, but could be blotchy, and many typists preferred to type their work over and over until it was letter-perfect. They suffered on, as did their bosses, until the 1960's, when two new techniques for erasing appeared. One was correction paper, which consisted of thin paper strips coated with a chalklike substance. It worked well enough on white paper, but it left outlines around corrections on different colored papers.

About that time Bette Nesmith Graham, a Texas secretary, saw her idea for a better eraser hit the market. She was also an artist, and in 1951 had conceived of a liquid for painting out errors. Her idea, eventually marketed by the Liquid Paper Corporation, soon became a reality. Since then, even typewriters have been equipped with devices to mask mistakes. The business of correcting mistakes should continue to be lucrative, because technological perfectibility seems to run considerably ahead of human perfectibility.

EYEGLASSES A Franciscan friar, William de Rubruk, traveling in Mongolia in the 1250's, may have seen some of the local folk wearing pieces of convex quartz in frames of tortoiseshell (a lucky substance to them). When he returned he had some long talks with fellow Franciscan Roger Bacon, who then included drawings of convex lenses in his *Opus Majus*, published in 1268. The first true eyeglasses appeared in Europe in that century. They did not have a bridge (sometimes the two eyepieces were riveted together), and it was most difficult to keep them balanced on the nose. Nevertheless, by 1300, Venice, the glassmaking center of the world, began to export eyeglasses with convex lenses. Shaky or not, they improved the vision of those who had trouble seeing up close. That problem stems from two different sources: hyperopia, or farsightedness, in which the axis of the eye is too short for near focusing; and presbyopia, the too-familiar condition of middle and old age, which arises when the lens of the eye, losing flexibility, can no longer become thick enough to make things nearby look clear.

After the invention of the printing press in the mid-15th century, and the spread of reading, more and more older people discovered they needed glasses to see the print. Lenses were made in rough grades of intensity and sold in shops or by peddlers on the street: a customer usually tried on glasses until he found the right correction.

Centuries earlier, Nero had held a faceted jewel to one eye in order to make out the details of the games in the arena far below. Not until the late 15th or early 16th century, however, did craftsmen grind concave lenses that finally let the nearsighted (myopic) see. Thousands must have experienced the excitement that writer Jane Howard describes. Putting on her first glasses at the age of eight, she exclaimed: "Mommy, Mommy, there are leaves on the trees!"

Why did these 1874 glasses feature blinders?

Concave lenses came to be ground in gross thicknesses for those so myopic that they could hardly see any distance at all. A London shop in 1852 received a request from the secretary of an English lord for "a pair of spectacles such as he thinks will suit a youth of 16 years of age, who has never worn any, but is so shortsighted as to be obliged to hold his face close to his plate when he takes his meals."

Benjamin Franklin had both vision problems: he was nearsighted, but when he got older he could not read easily either. So he got two pairs of glasses and switched back and forth. Tiring of this, he ordered the top halves of the distance glasses to be sawed off and had them cemented to the bottom halves of the reading glasses, and so invented the first bifocals.

From the time when judges in ancient China wore spectacles of smoky-colored quartz to mask their expressions when they heard legal evidence, there have been eras in which glasses were considered to be status symbols. Often people wore empty frames for adornment and as a way to improve their social standing. Nearsighted Pope Leo X in 1517 posed wearing a pair of stern-looking eyeglasses for a portrait by Raphael.

In the 17th century glasses became a fad in the Spanish court. A countess who visited Madrid in 1679 reported: "I was surprised to see many young ladies with great spectacles on their noses and fastened to their ears. But what seemed strangest to me was that they made no use of them . . . only discoursed while they had them on. I was told that it was done to make them look serious. . . ." She noted that men were equally given to wearing glasses: "It is so common a thing to wear them that I understand there are different spectacles according to rank. As a man increases the size of his fortune, he increases the size of his lenses."

Today people use eyeglasses as sun shades. (The Eskimos, who needed such protection, used slitted wood for that purpose.) Sometimes wearers use the "shades" to lend themselves a little glamour and mystery. Plain old vision-correcting glasses occupy a more ambivalent position. Many politicians, actors, and sports heroes, as well as ordinary people, not only wear glasses but flaunt them by choosing unusual styles and colors for frames and lenses. Others hide their poor vision behind a pair of contact lenses. For many people, contacts provide a better visual image than do glasses, but for many others they provide a better self-image.

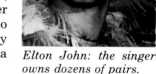

Elton John: the singer owns dozens of pairs.

Glass contact lenses were tried in the 1880's, although the indefatigable Leonardo da Vinci had conceived the principle of them much earlier. The first contact lens covered the whole white of the eye (the sclera). It was made for someone who had had an eyelid amputated, and the person wore it for 20 years. The uncomfortable glass scleral lenses were not well received. Plastic lenses in the 1930's helped, but not until the advent of smaller corneal lenses in the 1940's and 1950's did many people turn to contacts. The soft plastic used in heart-valve implants is the basis of today's soft lenses.

Today, one of every two Americans wears glasses or contact lenses—mostly for presbyopia or myopia, less for farsightedness, astigmatism, and other problems. But few wearers realize that accurate vision correction is really a recent blessing.

FAD According to one observer of the social scene, fads are "trivial fancies pursued for a time with irrational zeal." Fads are generally silly—in retrospect, at least—and usually unpredictable.

Who would have imagined, for instance, that in the mid-20th century men and women would sit around a game board for hours at a time, making interlocking words out of letters stamped on little wooden squares? Or risk injury to their spines by attempting to spin a Hula-Hoop around their hips? Or stretch out to sleep, or whatever, on a mattress filled with water?

The Incroyables *were 18th-century French dandies.*

"Irrational zeal" of a different but equally unpredictable nature gripped the sensible burghers of Holland in 1634. Tulips had been introduced there about 70 years earlier and cultivated, then as now, in neat, colorful rows. Unusual flowers had always fetched a slight premium, but one fancier apparently made the mistake of paying too well for a particularly spectacular specimen. Word of this windfall spread quickly, and within weeks nearly everyone in Holland—merchants, nobles, carpenters, chimney sweeps—was trading in tulips. Special markets sprang up just for buying and selling bulbs. Supported by the expectation that there was always someone willing to pay more, prices skyrocketed to the point where single bulbs sold for 2,500 or 3,000 florins—enough to feed a dozen families for a year. Then, three years after the wild speculation had begun, the tulip market crashed overnight, leaving a trail of bulbs and bankruptcies.

Another get-rich fad, contrived by a Neapolitan banker, Lorenzo Tonti, captured the imagination of Frenchmen in the 17th century. The basic idea was this: participants contributed a certain amount of money to a fund, which provided the members with an annuity for life. When a member died, his share would be divided among the survivors. Some survivors fared extremely well. A woman who lived to be 96 was collecting 73,000 livres a year for her investment of 300 livres. Although the "tontines" were designed to reap handsome profits for the sponsor, there was nothing dishonest about them. (Tontines were even used by European governments to raise money.)

Clothing, too, has been a mine of material for fads. Miniskirts, crinolines, zoot suits, Nehru jackets, Davy Crockett raccoon skin caps—all seem a little silly now but not nearly as much as the ribboned and tasseled costumes and plumed hats affected by 18th-century English dandies. Known as "macaronis," because their style of dress originated in Italy, they were immortalized in the verse that tells how Yankee Doodle "stuck a feather in his hat and called it macaroni."

Food and how to eat it has been another popular subject for fads—from Horace Fletcher, who urged his disciples to chew vigorously ("Nature will castigate those who don't masticate") to grapefruit diets, macrobiotics, and the recent liquid protein diets.

Mah-Jongg, marathon dances, Couéism ("Day by day, in every way I am getting better and better"), flagpole sitting, 3-D, panty raids—just the mention of these fads may kindle a spark of nostalgia in the eye of someone who is the right age. And for those who are too young to have participated in any of these, nostalgia itself is a thriving fad.

Even though fads are reflections of their time, they have a way of returning for an encore. Commenting on the wide public interest in the traveling exhibit of treasures from the tomb of Tutankhamen, a newspaper headline noted: "Museum Show Inspires Tutmania." Other stories described the glut of Tut-inspired merchandise: eye makeup *à la* Cleopatra, scarab rings, Egyptian motif towel and pillow sets, and even a disco dance called the King Tut Strut. Much of

Media-inspired fads: boy at left nose-balanced a teaspoon for a record 41 minutes; coonskin cap haircut at right dates from the Davy Crockett craze of the 1950's.

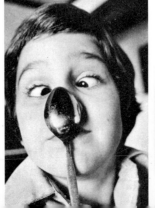
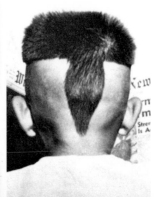

this happened once before, when Tut's tomb was discovered in 1922. The Egyptianism craze began with women's fashions and ended in what became known as Art Deco style.

Nothing, it would seem, expresses the malaise of our time more loudly than unisex fashions. Scholarly articles suggest that unisex is a symptom of young people's depersonalization, alienation, and loss of ego identity. Possibly. The phenomenon was described in the London *Times* in a bit of doggerel: "For such the fashion of the day,/ They make it difficult to say,/ Whether the *pretty things* we meet,/ Parading through their fav'rite street,/ A Male or Female we may call,/ Their shapes are so equivocal." Date: January 7, 1796.

Open and slosh in a helmet: even the enemy might have hesitated before invading this World War II repast.

FAST FOOD In 1954 Ray Kroc, a salesman of electric milk-shake mixers, delivered a big order to a drive-in restaurant in San Bernardino, California. He saw a place crowded with people waiting to be served milk shakes and hamburgers. Kroc was so impressed that he persuaded the owners of the drive-in, two brothers named Richard and Maurice McDonald, to let him franchise the restaurants nationally. Then, in the 1960's, Kroc bought the chain outright. A little more than a decade later, 5,000 McDonalds were doing business around the world—including a half dozen in Paris—and small children were learning to say "Big Mac" right along with "Mama." In the process Ray Kroc had amassed a fortune estimated at $500 million.

After a killing first bite, this South Sea islander ate his fish raw.

Despite the current popularity of fast-food restaurants, it is not correct to assume that they are a 20th-century phenomenon. The ancient Romans, on their way home from work, for example, would stop for a bowl of stew or a plate of vegetables at street stalls. If a birth date for modern fast foods were to be chosen, it might well be June 9, 1902, for on that day Frank Hardart, a footsore onetime waiter, decided to make customers serve their own food. With a partner, Joe Horn, he opened a new sort of restaurant, in which foods were displayed in compartments behind glass windows. To get the food they wanted, customers had only to drop the right number of nickels into the proper slot. They ate the idea up—and the Automat was born.

An earlier contribution to quick service at reasonable prices was made by an Englishman, Fred Harvey, who opened a restaurant in Topeka, Kansas, in 1876. And when he decided to hire pretty young waitresses and advertise them as "young women of good character, attractive and intelligent," business definitely picked up. By 1912 Harvey was operating a chain of 77 restaurants and 60 railway dining cars, and the Harvey girl had become part of American folklore. Another food-chain operator was Howard Deering Johnson. In the late 1920's young Johnson was selling homemade ice cream in his Wollaston, Mass., patent-medicine store. Then he began selling his ice cream at Massachusetts beaches, an idea he expanded to include roadside restaurants. His main contribution to "convenience food" was a "commissary" system of preparation: all food was cooked and processed centrally, thus assuring uniform quality and lower costs. Today, for example, the french-fried potatoes served at McDonald's are peeled, sliced, and cooked, though only partially, at a number of factories in Idaho.

All the ingredients for a fast-food boom—self-service, high volume, pleasant surroundings, and minimal preparation—were available by the 1930's. What was needed to trigger the explosion was a different sort of American life-style. After World War II, it appeared: Americans rode everywhere in their cars, and more married women were working than before the war. But traditional "white-tablecloth" restaurants had become increasingly expensive, so eager eater-outers were on the lookout for a cheaper and faster way to dine away from home.

The perfect fast food, it has been said, is something that a customer can munch in the time it takes him to walk from the cash register to the door. Hamburgers come closest to this definition and are, not surprisingly, the cornerstone of the fast-food industry, selected by nearly 90 percent of all customers. What is surprising is that the hot dog, traditionally a crowd pleaser, at least at baseball games, is an also-ran; it accounts for but 2 percent of sales, about the same as such ethnic entrees as tacos.

Fast foods are cheap. But are they food? Of course they are, but Harvard nutritionist Jean Mayer points out that a steady diet of them could give a customer scurvy. Mayer also says, "There is nothing at the burger places that makes it necessary to have teeth." What most fast foods will do is build a bulge on your waistline. A super burger, a chocolate shake, and a small order of fries add up to 1,089 calories, nearly half of an adult male's daily requirement. Why then do people line up at fast-food emporiums? Sociologist David Riesman offers this explanation: "Americans have had a lot of experience being cheated and exploited when they eat out, and they feel unsure of themselves." At most fast-food places, they don't have to worry about picking up the wrong fork—it is not necessary to pick up any utensil at all. In fairness, most of America's 50,000 or so fast-food outlets are clean, relatively friendly places. And Americans respond: of the nearly $200 billion spent annually on food, an amazing 27 cents of every dollar goes to pay for meals eaten away from home. And of the 27 cents, all but 2 cents is spent on fast foods.

In 1939, when he was not even a second lieutenant, Harland Sanders discovered that it was possible to cook chicken in seven minutes using a pressure cooker. Now, 2.3 billion pieces of Kentucky Fried Chicken are served annually. Placed end to end, they would gird the earth nearly 75 times. A final tidbit: during the time it has taken you to read this article, some 40,000 McDonald's hamburgers have been sold—and eaten.

FIRE FIGHTING Emperor Augustus organized what was probably the world's first fire department about 2,000 years ago in Rome. His firemen fought the blazes with blankets soaked in vinegar for smothering the flames, catapults for knocking down walls, and crude water pumps. Other fire fighters in Rome's 20 or more fire companies specialized in handling mattresses, presumably for catching citizens leaping from burning buildings.

After the fall of Rome, the fire pump was forgotten; the Dark and Middle Ages were bright with conflagrations, which nearly wiped out many cities. St. Petersburg, Copenhagen, Munich, Cairo, and London were all hit, and Constantinople lay in smoking ruins more than a dozen times.

The general indifference to fire fighting changed after the Great Fire of London, which started at 1 A.M. on Sunday, September 2, 1666, and burned

Vase brigade: maidens help damp a fire in ancient Troy, in a detail from a 16th-century fresco by Raphael.

out of control for five days, laying waste to more than 13,000 homes. The fire-fighting equipment of London, the largest city in the world at the time, consisted chiefly of buckets and hand squirters that held two quarts of water. Virtually before the ashes were cool, London fire fighters began trying to improve their skills and equipment. Within a year, the first fire-insurance policy had been written.

A severe fire in Boston in 1711 prompted similar improvements. The city became one of the first in the colonies to buy fire engines and create engine companies made up of volunteers. They were authorized to pull down or blow up any house to stop the spread of a fire. Citizens groups were formed to assist the firemen and help rescue the possessions of fellow members. Along with their other tools, the volunteers carried bed keys to take apart beds (usually a family's most valuable possessions) and carry them to safety.

The early fire companies, which numbered George Washington and Benjamin Franklin among their members, used fire engines that were pulled by men, were supplied by buckets, and were pumped by hand. Some of the volunteer fire companies were enthusiastic to a fault. The great prestige, and sometimes a monetary prize, which went to the first company to arrive on the scene of a fire, produced a fierce rivalry in many cities. Companies raced each other to the flames, hitting and injuring pedestrians on the way. Some companies sent men ahead of the engine to hide the fire hydrant under a barrel until their particular company arrived. Many firemen were recruited simply for their cunning as street fighters.

After a particularly violent street brawl in Cincinnati (during which a building burned to the ground—not an uncommon occurrence), the city fathers voted to select firemen for reasons other than their bellicosity and to pay them. Volunteer firemen invaded the city council's meeting room in protest. The councilmen explained that the city had bought a new steam-powered pumper that could not be entrusted to untrained ruffians. Wisely, the city hired one of the volunteers' mightiest brawlers as the new fire chief. Both the steamer and the professional firemen were a success. In 1854 a Cincinnati fire department official reported: "Engine Houses are no longer nurseries where the youth of the city are trained in vice, vulgarity, and debauchery. . . ."

By 1870 most of the heavy steamers were pulled by horses. At the sound of the alarm, some of the steeds would trot to their assigned places under harnesses hanging from the ceiling. Fire dogs, usually Dalmatians, ran in front of the horses to clear the way. They also came in handy for guard duty at the station house. One New York company had a cat that learned to slide down the brass pole from the dormitory to the fire engine.

Despite better equipment and personnel, once a fire got cracking, it was generally out of control. One October evening in 1871, after weeks of drought in Chicago, a fire-tower watcher misdirected crews, allowing the fire that started in the O'Learys' barn to become a holocaust. Whipped by Chicago's fierce winds, the blaze killed some 250 persons, and 18,000 structures lay in ruins. But Mrs. O'Leary's cow should not be held responsible. Michael Ahern, a local reporter, admitted years later that he had added the beef fat to the fire to enrich his story—as if the fire itself had not generated enough human interest.

Firemen fought flames then much as they do now. At the site of the fire, the men plan their line of attack. Their order of priorities: to rescue any endangered occupants; to locate the fire in the building; to "ventilate" the fire by cutting through the building above the flames to allow potentially explosive gases to escape; to place the hose lines and "knock down" the flames with water; after the main fire is out, to "overhaul" the site to discover small hidden fires; and finally, to clean up.

Firemen still use the same basic equipment, but pumpers and ladders have had to grow to keep up with ever-taller buildings in most cities. One of the world's mightiest fire engines is the super pumper used by New York City firemen—a 34-ton, 43-foot "18-wheeler" tractor-trailer equipped with a pump powered by a 2,400-horsepower diesel engine.

The 7-ton, stainless-steel centrifugal pump can deliver 8,800 gallons of water a minute. The pump's six impellers (which "blow" the water through the hoses like a fan) produce a hose pressure of 350 pounds per square inch (ordinary pumpers produce 175 p.s.i.). Throwing a valve lets the impellers work in series, doubling hose pressure and providing enough force to rip apart a burning building, if necessary, to contain a fire.

The pumper only pumps. A super tender and three satellite hose tenders with turret-mounted water cannons are required to handle the output of water. So great is the reactive force of the water leaving the cannon nozzle that the super tender uses hydraulic outrigger steel arms to prevent the cannon from being ripped from its mounts. The first time the super units battled a blaze, firemen expected to be overwhelmed but were unprepared for one surprise. "We were awed by the splashing noise," a chief recalled. "It sounded like Niagara Falls."

But more than super engines are needed to prevent modern skyscrapers from becoming blazing infernos. The most up-to-date ladders cannot reach above seven stories, so firemen must go into the buildings dressed in "space suits" designed to supply oxygen and reflect heat. In the development stage are "flying fire engines," which will hang on cables beneath giant helicopters and carry as many as 16 fire fighters and their equipment to any level of a high-rise building.

Comical or not, this early 1900's German fire truck had elements of modern engines: a motor (rear of cycle), bandages (wagon seat), and a hose, ladder, and bell.

FISHING A line with a worm on one end and a fool on the other. That definition seems as good as any. The bait may vary, but at the other end of the line nothing is altered. In the springtime each year, eager anglers pour down to lakeshores and riverbanks in search of freshwater fish. And each year, despite millions of dollars spent on equipment, despite the cleverest lures in history, the fisher folk are doomed to interminable hours of unsuccessful casts, tangled lines, spurned bait, and impaled thumbs. Theoretically, this somnolent sport should appeal to no one over the mental age of 12. Instead, fishing continues to attract business leaders, politicians, intellectuals, and writers to an extraordinary degree. What has hooked them?

In part, of course, it is the season. Fishing automatically summons thoughts of lyrical spring days, when minutes, like dragonflies, hover motionless over water. Perhaps more important are the benefits derived from angling's lack of speed. Unlike any other outdoor sport, it allows the mind to unreel and stretch itself. With luck and time and endurance, the angler gets the long-awaited result. Out of dark water, the fish flashes to the surface like a new idea—and in that instant the sport justifies its glorious history.

History's most prominent fisherman was, of course, St. Peter, who later turned to netting souls. In the years A.D., angling was seen as something more than the mere coaxing of cold-blooded vertebrates from water. Consider, for example, Shakespeare's metaphor: "Your bait of falsehood takes this carp of truth, and thus do we . . . by indirections find directions out."

With such distinguished observers and enthusiasts, it was only a question of time before the sport acquired its own philosopher. Izaak Walton, a draper by trade, was a biographer by avocation, but his chronicles have been forgotten. Only the discursive jottings on his favorite hobby have endured. *The Compleat Angler*, published in 1653, remains as fresh today as it was in Oliver Cromwell's time.

Through Walton, millions have learned to put as much lead "as will sink the bait to the bottom and keep it still in motion, and not more." Through Walton's American disciple Washington Irving, millions more have been apprised of the fact that "there is certainly something in angling . . . that tends to produce a gentleness of spirit, and a pure serenity of mind."

That "something" persists today, and it remains one of angling's surest lures. Its name is failure. No matter how fine his equipment, no matter how limitless his patience, it is the angler who is cast most often as the poor fish. The odds, as always, still favor the quarry; yet to the true fisherman that very failure is a kind of triumph. His sport lacks the compulsive pursuit of hunting or the dizzying zest of mountain climbing. But it grants something else—a philosophy, an acceptance of and ultimately a grudging admiration for unyielding nature. It is that philosophy that lured such beleaguered politicians as Franklin Roosevelt, Hoover, Eisenhower, and Kennedy. It is that philosophy that prompted Henry David Thoreau to describe time itself as "the stream I go a-fishing in." And it is that philosophy that underlies great American novels as diverse as *Moby-Dick*, *Huckleberry Finn*, and *The Old Man and the Sea*, in which an angler's prize catch is finally reclaimed by nature.

The Old Man and the Sea has a very contemporary resonance. For too long, fishermen have been journeying down to their favorite spots, only to find them defiled. In many parts of the United States, in fact, nature has begun to reclaim its property—with a necessary assist from concerned people and governments, and at an enormous price. The reclamation is often underwritten by America's more than 30 million anglers; the $140 million they pay in license and permit fees is used to support conservation programs.

Yet even if the streams revive, even if trout, muskellunge, and bass thrive tomorrow as they did in Walton's day, a fisherman's luck will remain random and

Stake out: natives in Sri Lanka perch precariously on slender poles as they spear fish in tidal waters below.

In the ooze beneath a dried rice paddy in Thailand, children find—and catch—small fish with their toes.

capricious. For most anglers, that will be all right. In the end, they do not gear up for the sole purpose of bringing back a haul of walleyed pike or edible perch. They also go out in the spirit of adventure novelist John Buchan (*The Thirty-Nine Steps*), who once peered beneath the surface of the water and caught the essence of the sport: "The charm of fishing is that it is the pursuit of what is elusive but attainable, a perpetual series of occasions for hope." Hope remains the best bait of the angler, and of the nonparticipant as well. In the end they are all in the same boat.

FLAG Among ancient peoples it was customary for the leader of a procession to carry a long pole topped with a magical symbol and decorated with streamers. Such a symbol, often an animal effigy, was thought to ward off evil. The earliest flags probably developed from this practice.

Flags called *vexilla* were carried by Roman legionnaires about the year 100 B.C. A *vexillum* was a square of fringed cloth, usually purple, red, or blue, hung from a crossbar and carried atop a lance. (The study of flags is still known as vexillology.) Roman soldiers also used a dragon flag—a long piece of cloth attached to a pole so that wind blowing in the "jaws" made the "dragon" writhe—to scare the enemy. The dragon flag is believed to have originated with the Chinese, who flew silk flags as early as the 5th century B.C.

The Bayeux Tapestry, made not long after the Battle of Hastings (1066), shows that by that time flags were in common use. Many early flags represented the king or commander in a war and were at his side through the thick of battle. The royal standard, however, was usually kept at the center of the fighting force, away from the front lines, and was guarded by handpicked knights, who could not leave the battlefield so long as the flag was still flying. At Hastings the Normans first struck down the opposing commander, King Harold, and his flag and then the royal banner.

These flags gradually gave way to national flags with symbols that were meaningful to everyone.

One of the first flags was that of the city-state of Genoa in the 12th century; it adopted as its national symbol the cross of St. George. The origins of most of the national flags are associated with patriotic legends. For example, one of the oldest still flying, the Danish Dannebrog (meaning "Danish cloth") is said to have originated in 1219 when battle-bound King Waldemar saw a white cross in the blood-red sky. The flag of Austria, the story goes, was born when an Austrian duke raised his tunic in place of the flag lost on the battlefield. The tunic was stained red with blood except for a white stripe where the duke's belt had been.

Some flags display national symbols—the Soviet flag has the hammer of the industrial worker and the sickle of the farmer; Portugal's flag carries navigation instruments, representing the nation's explorers; and the flags of many Arab countries have the star and crescent of Islam. According to one story, the crescent moon symbol originated when Philip of Macedon, father of Alexander the Great, laid siege to Byzantium in 339 B.C. Philip's army, about to undermine the walls of the city, was discovered by the light of a bright crescent moon. The Byzantines adopted the crescent as the badge of the city, a practice continued by the conquering Romans. It later became the symbol of the Islamic armies, who captured Constantinople in 1453.

Pledge allegiance: flags have long symbolized state; saluting changes.

The story of Betsy Ross and the first Stars and Stripes is now believed to be erroneous. Although the famous Philadelphian was a flagmaker, it seems unlikely that she would have been asked to make a flag symbolic of independence in June 1776, as legend maintains, before the Declaration of Independence (adopted by Congress on July 4).

Flags the world over are displayed according to complex rules of etiquette. In many countries, including the United States, flag etiquette is enforced by law. (Britain, which has no flag code at all, is an exception.) In the U.S. to "publicly . . . cast contempt upon" the American flag is a crime. Such cases still come to trial, even though the definition of "contempt" is a complicated matter. No charges were made some years ago when a manufacturer brought out a girdle decorated with stars and stripes, but the public outcry was so great that the company withdrew the item.

FOOD PROCESSOR In the course of looking for a better way to concoct his favorite drink, Stephen J. Poplawski, an inventor by profession, built and in 1923 patented a device with "an agitating element mounted in the bottom of a cup and a driving motor mounted in a base." The machine turned out milk shakes (which the inventor loved) of such perfection that, as Poplawski later conceded ruefully: "I did not think then of using the mixer . . . for the maceration of fruits and vegetables." Unhappily for him, another man did, one who had the financial backing of Fred Waring.

Early blenders, with their utilitarian appearance and simple on-off switches, created only a mild stir. But today, with the addition of ticking timers, flashing lights, and push buttons for as many as 20 speeds, they are as obedient as they are sophisticated—whipping, mashing, creaming, and beating almost anything pitched into their humming steel jaws. One manufacturer even promoted a new technique, "Spin-cookery," which makes the need to chew all but obsolete.

The first food processor, and in some ways still the best, was the human hand. The second was probably a knife or a scraper. The third was the mortar and pestle, used 4,000 years ago much as it is today: to grind spices and grains. Other devices appeared as the centuries passed. Perforated bronze bowls, for example, perfect sieves or colanders, have been discovered in the ruins at Pompeii. In fact, in the list of "articles required for the kitchen of a family in the middle class of life," which appeared in Mrs. Isabella Beeton's *The Book of Household Management* in 1861, there is little that would have confused or astonished a Roman chef.

The first breakthrough in modern food processors was achieved even before Poplawski by two young men, L.H. Hamilton and Chester A. Beach. Their creation, which they perfected in 1912, was a high-speed, lightweight, universal electric motor. At first their intention was to sell it for use on home sewing machines. Then, to make the motor more attractive, they decided to provide attachments—for sharpening knives, polishing silver and brass, and mixing cake batter.

The latest descendants of that versatile motor, as well as of the mortar and pestle, are today's high-powered processors. Nothing since sliced truffles, for which some mixers have a special blade, has so captivated food experts. "As necessary as a good stove," said one authority. Another declared with considerable wisdom that the "invention, in the minds of serious cooks, ranks with that of the printing press, cotton gin, steamboat, paper clips, Kleenex, wastebaskets, contour sheets, and disposable diapers."

FOOTWEAR Considering the delicate construction of feet (26 bones, 19 muscles, and 107 ligaments per foot) and the mileage expected of them (65,000 in an average lifetime), people for centuries have been treating their feet miserably.

From the mid-14th to the mid-15th centuries, Europeans were mad about narrow shoes that measured up to three feet in length and ended in a needlelike point. Called *poulaines* or *cracowes*, because they were reputed to have originated in Poland, where they supposedly kept the witches away, they were so cumbersome that the wearer had to anchor the tip to a chain worn around his shin. Toe length was regulated by law, and only the rich were permitted extremely elongated tips. At the turn of the 15th century, however, the accent switched to width, with shoes measuring well over 12 inches across. Sensible Mary Tudor decreed that they had to be reduced to a mere 6 inches. Next came the *chopine*, a platform shoe with a wooden sole that sometimes reached heights of 20 or so inches. Its purpose was to make a woman look stately (as Shakespeare's Hamlet observed, "Your ladyship is nearer to heaven than when I saw you last, by the altitude of a chopine"), but it prevented her from budging without the support of two servants. The Venetians, who had created the style, eventually banned it because it proved hazardous to pregnant women, who could fall and miscarry.

In the 17th century King Louis XIV, who wished to appear taller than he really was, elevated himself on high heels, and his courtiers hastened to copy the new style. Women began wearing high heels too, higher than men's heels, which put tremendous pressure on the ball of the foot and thus assured steady employment for generations of podiatrists. In the Napoleonic era, ladies were expected to be fragile and dainty, to be admired, and so were shoes. Empress Josephine is said to have returned a pair of evening slippers to her shoemaker for repairs after having worn them just once. "Ah, I see what it is," he replied after examining them. "Madame, you have walked in them."

Some people, however, were more sensible than

This daring view of a 16th-century courtesan revealed the height of fashion: chopines.

others about footwear. The Hittites, for example, who lived in rocky, mountainous regions, wore high shoes with curled-up toes; the Egyptians, Babylonians, and Athenians wore open sandals. An even more practical solution perhaps was to wear shoes outdoors but go barefoot indoors. Both the Greeks and the Cretans shed their shoes upon entering the house.

The Romans got off on the right foot by designing a wide selection of footwear. There were special sandals for senators and others just for the emperor. Legionnaires were issued sturdy hobnailed boots. For dress-up occasions, patricians usually wore the *mulleus*, a sort of high open-toed slipper. (Women still wear them and call them "mules.") For sport and play, there were wooden-soled sandals articulated with bronze hinges. Women's shoes were ornamented with embroidery, beads, and baubles, and came in a variety of colors—red, yellow, white, and green as well as basic black.

All these, of course, were for the rich. Peasants usually went barefoot or made do with whatever materials were easily available. In Spain, for instance, poor farmers learned to plait shoe soles from fibrous esparto grass, and named the footwear *espadrillas*. In Germany a simple square piece of leather perforated around the edges and laced together, the *Bundschuh*, was so common a form of footwear that it became the emblem of the peasant revolts that swept the countryside in the late Middle Ages. According to a popular story, another humble article of footwear became an instrument of protest when French workmen, threatened with unemployment, discovered that a well-thrown *sabot*—the carved wooden shoe they had traditionally worn—could effectively put a whole machine out of commission. Hence, *sabotage*.

The moccasin, soft and foot-fitting, is often considered an American contribution, but archeologists have discovered that moccasin-like shoes

customs

Little Old Ladies, Look Out

What has rubber bottoms, comes in twos, is red or pink or chartreuse or lavender, and costs as much as $60? If you answered "sneakers," you are not only wrong but hopelessly out of date. Sneakers, a vanishing breed, are canvas-top shoes which come in white and black and sometimes blue and, after a few wearings and washings, turn to a shade borrowing a little from all three. They once cost around $2.98 and, according to mothers everywhere, ruined your feet if you wore them all day long.

Those other things are "athletic footwear." It is a somewhat elastic term because the shoes are donned not only by super athletes such as Julius Erving, Billie Jean King, and Fran Tarkenton, but also by other enthusiasts— Woody Allen to an opening night of the Martha Graham's Dance Company, Mick Jagger to his wedding, and Jacqueline Onassis while striding along New York's Fifth Avenue.

Sneakers originated with Brazilian Indians, who, the story goes, stuck their bare feet into liquid latex from the rubber tree

Big Sneak: mounted on a giant roller skate, this 7-foot racer is the creation of California artist Louis Mueller.

and then let it harden. In America and Britain sneakers first achieved genteel popularity, about the turn of the century, among devotees of croquet and, later, among tennis players. The same good traction and fast starts that commended them for tennis also led to their use in other outdoor pursuits. By the 1960's so many purse snatchers and muggers had taken to wearing sneakers in their work that they came to be known as "perpetrator boots" or "felonies."

Fancy athletic footwear first came to public attention during the 1968 summer Olympics in Mexico City, when two of the manufacturers persuaded competitors to wear their attention-getting products. Their subsequent popularity has been ascribed to various factors: the youth culture, the trend toward casual dress, the cult of physical fitness started by President Kennedy. Whatever the reason, more than 220 million pairs of athletic footwear are sold annually in the United States.

A good many of them come from the tiny Bavarian town of Herzogenaurach, where, toe to toe, are located the factories that produce Adidas and Pumas, two of the bestsellers. Adidas sounds vaguely Italian, but in reality is the acronym for the name of the company's founder, Adolf "Adi" Dassler; Puma was started by his brother and archrival, Rudolf.

Pardon me but your wheels are slowing. In the 1870's the pedespeed challenged the roller skate—and lost.

were worn in northern Europe during the Bronze Age. Two distinctive kinds of footwear, however, do owe their origins to the New World: sneakers and cowboy boots.

More recently, a new type of footwear, negative-heel shoes, have appeared on the market. They were created by a young Danish student of yoga, who discovered that if she raised the front of her foot but kept the heel close to the ground she could achieve the yoga standing lotus posture. Shortly after, she noticed that Brazilian Indians, models of fine posture, left footprints in the sand where the heel was deeper than the rest of the foot. That was all the proof she needed to go ahead with her design. Predictably, negative-heel shoes are meant to exert a downward pull on the back of the leg, straighten the calf and thigh muscles, keep the pelvis level, and permit the diaphragm to move freely. Whether they accomplish all this and are also beneficial for feet is a matter of debate among orthopedic surgeons.

But proponents of the shoes-should-be-fun school have not given up despite contrary orthopedic advice. One of the latest entries is a clear lucite disco shoe featuring a flashing light bulb.

FROZEN FOOD It was World War II that put frozen foods in the American kitchen. After Japan conquered Southeast Asia, America's major source of tin was cut off. Because of the scarcity of tin, most canned goods were limited to military use, and the frozen-food industry, until then a supplier of "luxury" foods, expanded rapidly to fill the civilian void. Production of frozen vegetables alone jumped nearly 300 percent from 1942 to 1946.

Frozen foods, however, had gained public accep-

tance slowly. Companies that canned foods or packed them in other ways made critical statements about the nutritional value of frozen foods. One well-known restaurant chain even wrote on its menu: "No frozen food deception here. Your doctor will tell you frozen foods can't give you all the fresh food vitamins." Nevertheless, the American Medical Association issued a statement giving its approval to frozen fruits and vegetables. Even today some frozen-food manufacturers admit that their products can be less than nourishing if improperly handled by distributors and consumers. And often enough they are. One estimate is that a frozen product is likely to go through three to five freeze-thaw cycles before it is finally used, damaging both texture and nutritional value along the way. Even a consumer's refrigerator can be harmful: if the freezer compartment does not remain between 0°F and 8°F, frozen-food packages may partially thaw, causing the product to lose a portion of its vitamins. Because of their convenience and price, however, frozen foods generate hundreds of millions of dollars in sales each year. As a result, the more than 3,000 separate items now frozen seem likely to remain standard groceries for some time to come.

Horror d'oeuvre: morsels of mammoth, frozen for 250,000 years, appeared on the Explorers Club menu in 1951. The animals might have died by falling through thin ice, as shown in sketch by a Russian scientist.

FURNACE The first people to have central heating were probably the ancient Greeks, who, about 2,300 years ago, built their rooms over flues warmed by outside furnaces. The Romans later improved this system by building the floors of their rooms on pedestals, so that the heat from their furnaces could circulate more freely. (Several of these heating systems were discovered beneath the rubble of bombed-out buildings in

Bird's Eye

Clarence Birdseye held patents on harpoon guns and heat lamps.

Clarence "Bob" Birdseye, whose name became synonymous with frozen foods, never really claimed to have invented the process. Instead, he gave credit to the Eskimos, who had been freezing meat for centuries. Another investigator, Sir Francis Bacon, actually died as a result of experimenting with keeping meat fresh by packing it with snow. One bone-chilling day in England in 1626, he interrupted a journey to test one of his ideas. He bought a fowl, killed and dressed it, then stuffed it with snow. Bacon lived to pronounce his experiment a success, but expired soon thereafter—of bronchitis brought on by exposure.

Despite Birdseye's modesty, he was the person who made quick-freezing possible on a commercial scale. Inventor, self-trained scientist, explorer, trapper, and adventurer, he was also a great storyteller. Consider his yarn about the origin of his name. It seems that one of his ancestors worked as a page for an English queen in the days when people were given names for their work, appearance, deeds, or behavior. During a hunting trip, the story goes, a hawk threatened the queen. The page put an arrow through its eye. Forthwith the queen named him "Bird's eye."

Even the better-documented parts of Birdseye's life seem slightly apocryphal. For example: he helped pay his way through college by trapping and selling black rats to a geneticist and frogs to the Bronx Zoo. During World War I, Birdseye and his wife lived in Labrador, where he trapped animals and traded furs. He noticed that food frozen in midwinter tended to taste better than similar foods frozen at slightly warmer times. It was the speed with which something was frozen, he concluded, that made the difference: the faster the freeze, the less chance that ice crystals would tear apart cell walls and release natural juices. Soon the Birdseyes were having fresh-frozen cabbage with their meals. Birdseye packed the cabbages in a barrel, then froze each layer in salt water. When he wanted cabbage, he simply chopped a layer out with a hatchet. After World War I, Birdseye went into business as a fish wholesaler, eventually putting quick-frozen fish on the market. He ran out of money, then found backing, and in 1929, an excellent year to sell anything, sold his company to the future General Foods Corporation—for $22 million. Birdseye himself earned nearly $1 million on the sale.

London after World War II.) The Greeks and Romans also used bronze braziers, small portable fireboxes, and stoves with flues. In general, a stove is intended to heat a single room, whereas a furnace is designed for a central heating system for a structure.

Almost 1,500 years elapsed before central heating was rediscovered by modern civilizations. Europe's Dark Ages and Middle Ages were dark indeed, often because of smoke. Fires were built anywhere in a dwelling; a dank hallway might be heated with a roaring log fire. And no provision was made to get rid of smoke: it simply found its way to the nearest window or doorway. Fireplaces were an improvement, but they let about 80 percent of the heat escape up the chimney.

Stoves were more efficient and, once knowledge of their advantages was widespread, became the center of family life in many homes throughout Europe. Their design was improved by Benjamin Franklin in 1744. The "Pennsylvania fireplace," as Franklin referred to his invention, was more than a stove. It drew in fresh, cold air through special ducts, then heated the air in a closed chamber, and discharged it into the room. The same basic principles are used in today's modern hot-air furnaces.

The Franklin stove was so successful that peddlers took to the highways with as many as 25 loaded on a single wagon. Often their sales pitch was delivered during a demonstration on a cold day in a saloon or general store. The stoves sold rapidly, but detractors warned that the newfangled devices were without biblical sanction and poisoned the air as well.

Steam, a new source of power in factories during the 18th and early 19th centuries, was also a source of heat for homes and other buildings. In 1826 the frugal and celibate commune of Rappites in Economy, Pennsylvania, warmed their workshops with pipes extending from their steam boiler. At about that time, central steam heating was installed in the British Parliament buildings. Eventually furnaces were used to heat hot water or air, which was then circulated by pipe or duct through various structures.

In spite of its advantages, many people disapproved of central heating. One critic said that such systems might produce "a mild state of moral insanity." Nevertheless, most homes in North America today are heated by hot-air furnaces; most in Great Britain and Europe, by hot-water systems. Heavy worldwide use of fossil fuels—petroleum, gas, and coal—may one day make today's furnaces as antiquated as the Franklin stove. In various parts of the world, a new and more basic kind of heating is being used already: solar heating.

Funeral and Burial Rites: Death Is an Occasion of Significance

George Bernard Shaw, the noted British dramatist and writer, was sure that death was no time for weeping. "The instinct that makes people send flowers is a right instinct," he wrote, "and the inculcated notion that they should wear black and pull long faces is a monstrosity. If we cannot rejoice in the memory of the dead we had better let them alone. . . ."

Shaw demanded too much of mankind. Since well before recorded history, people have done just about everything except leave their dead alone. Every society has developed rules and rituals to cope with the dread mystery of death and with the physical presence of the corpse.

Religion normally plays an important role in these rituals, but even in societies that did not believe in an afterlife, such as ancient Rome, death was an occasion of significance.

Corpses deteriorate, so every society has had to decide whether to fight the process or help it along. The decision often turns on belief: will the departed need his or her body in the future? The Indian Parsis, a wealthy sect, believe that mortal flesh defiles the earth and the fire that might otherwise be used to consume it. Thus they place their dead on *dokhmas*, or "towers of silence," so that carrion-eating birds can pick the bones clean. This is considered an act of true purification. Unfortunately, for reasons no one can explain, an important species of vulture recently has refused to touch the Parsi dead. The Parsis reportedly are considering some form of flameless, electric cremation as an alternative.

Some Australian aborigines placed their dead in trees to rot, while other groups believed that the flesh should be eaten by relatives, who would thereby acquire the finer qualities of the departed. In Melanesia the Trobriand Islanders first buried their dead, then dug up the bones and fashioned them into spoons and other utensils. For them, this was an act of piety. Eventually, the utensils were placed in caves overlooking the sea. What links these practices is the idea of a second burial for the more permanent parts of a body.

Believing that the departed soul would eventually return to its body, the Egyptians developed the art and artifice of mummification. The practice was not at all democratic but was based on the ability of the deceased or his family to pay. After extracting the brain and entrails of a corpse, Egyptian artisans packed the body with aromatic spices and placed it in a salt bath for 70 days. Then they wrapped the corpse in gummed cloth and laid it in a case.

Modern authorities believe that the remarkable state of preservation of the Egyptian dead is due mostly to the bacteria-free dry air and sand of Egypt. As evidence, they note that common people, who were merely salted away, are as well preserved as mummified royalty.

The kings of Thebes started work on their tombs as soon as they came to power. The tombs were not pyramids but caverns hacked out of solid rock. Since work on the tomb continued for the life of a king, the size of the cavern is an indication of the duration of his reign.

Embalming, though the most commonplace method, is not man's only technique for preserving a body. In Africa the Loango people smoked corpses. Another belief in parts of Africa is that the corpse of a person preserved in this way should be placed where he died. Thus if someone dies while visiting a friend, the smoked corpse must be displayed, standing up, in the friend's hut. Alexander the Great reportedly was preserved in wax and honey, and after Lord Nelson's victory at Trafalgar, his body was returned to England stashed in a cask of brandy.

Cremation began with the belief that evil resides in a corpse. The ancient Greeks, thinking a bit more positively, believed that burning a body set its soul free, so they cremated every corpse, except those of people struck by lightning, suicide victims, and children too young to have grown teeth. To be deprived of cremation was to be made an outcast, albeit a dead one.

Western society, largely Christian, has had difficulty accepting cremation. Those who argue against it say that it makes no provision for an afterlife. Strict Bible readers, believing in the resurrection of the body, feel that the body must be intact to be reborn. Because such feelings run deep in Western culture, people who have elected to be cremated have worked hard to ensure that their relatives would carry out their wishes. One man was determined to be cremated, but his surviving daughter resisted. Learning that her father's considerable estate would go to a cremation society rather than to her if he were buried, she found merit in cremation.

Richard Hull, a 17th-century

Pennsylvania, early 1970's: life goes on—and so does the restaurant business.

Englishman, was convinced that on Judgment Day the dead would rise from their graves, and the world would be "reversed." To be prepared, he ordered that he be buried upside down, astride a horse. Dutch settlers in colonial America took pains to ensure that a pipe of wine—126 gallons—would be available should their mourners become thirsty. Irish wakes float similarly on a flood of strong drink, but the convivial glow of the occasion masks an older Irish belief—that the soul of the dead might otherwise prowl the houses of those surviving. The practice of staying "awake" is designed to inhibit such meanderings.

The gravestones we raise today have their origins in similar fears of death. Primitive peoples used them to hold down the evil spirits of the dead, and to mark the grave so that it might be avoided. In the same way, the heavy coffins used by the ancients were constructed as much to keep the dead from confronting the living as to protect the bodies.

Many societies have believed that if a man must die, he should not be alone. In India, China, and the Fiji Islands, there used to be great social pressure on the widow to "depart" with her husband. A *sati*, or "good woman," in India would hurl herself onto her husband's pyre. In Fiji the first Christian missionaries were astounded by similar practices. But their efforts to keep widows from immolation met with little success. The Dayaks of Borneo felt it necessary to cut off heads in bat-

In Bali, where mass funerals are common, bodies are carefully placed in sacred towers for cremation.

Ritual parting: in West Africa members of the Senufo tribe express their sorrow in a funeral dance.

tle to provide company for their own deceased tribesman.

Such savagery shocks us today, when our own funeral customs seem to make eminent sense. Most people would not wear bright colors to a funeral, and black remains the preferred shade for mourning. Few people realize that black became a mourning color because our forefathers were afraid of ghosts and tried to hide their white skins by painting them black. African blacks developed a similar custom, but they chose white as the appropriate color. From painted skins to colored clothing was but a short step. Flowers, still a proper tribute at many funerals, first came into use on the biers of virgins. In ancient times, flowers meant purity, but now they are fit for all.

"Bathing, wine, and love-affairs—these hurt our bodies, but they make life worth living." So

reads the inscription on a Roman tomb. It continues: "I've lived my days. I revelled, and I drank all that I desired. Once I was not; then I was; now I am not again— but I don't care!" The Roman did care, of course, or he would not have bothered carving his message. So did the loving widow who erected a stone for her husband that read: "Rest in peace— until we meet again."

The planned sentiments inscribed on tombstones, however, lack the originality that certain notables have revealed. Sir Walter Raleigh knew ahead of time that he was to be beheaded, but how many of us would have said: "This is a sharp medicine, but a sure remedy for all evils." Queen Elizabeth was remarkably truthful: "All my possessions for one moment of time!"

Both George Washington and Louis XIV were calm and brave at the end. Washington said to his secretary: "I am just going. Have me decently buried, but do not let my body be put into the vault in less than two days after I am dead. Do you understand? It is well." Louis XIV encouraged his weeping survivors with these words: "Why weep ye? Did you think I should live for ever? I thought dying had been harder."

All in white, the color of mourning in the Far East, a woman tends a grave.

GADGET The inventors of the world's countless gadgets seem to be in a conspiracy to disprove the maxim "Necessity is the mother of invention." Who really needs a parakeet diaper, a swallowable tapeworm trap, or a portable beer warmer? But being unnecessary is what the gadget is all about. The word may derive from the French *gâchette*, referring to the catch of a lock; but one dictionary defines gadget as "any small, especially mechanical, contrivance or device" or "any interesting but relatively useless or unnecessary object." Perhaps this latter definition is epitomized by the gadget that was a hot little item some years ago: a small box with a toggle switch on top. When the switch was turned on, the box lid opened; then a mechanical arm emerged, turned the switch off, and the box closed.

Uphill all the way: this 1912 vacuum used foot-bellows to create suction.

Gadgets probably have been around as long as humans. Early inventors, Leonardo da Vinci among them, were full of ideas that might have become gadgets, but few left the drawing board because the means to manufacture them were lacking. This situation was changed by the Industrial Revolution. Useless whatchamacallits and thingamabobs proliferated at a surprising rate during the 18th and 19th centuries—yokes for hitching turkeys to wagons, cast-iron knee warmers, spring chair legs, and some doodads no one can now imagine a use for.

Gadgetry became a multimillion-dollar industry soon after World War II, when war-weary Americans longed to try new things and had the money to pay for them. One of the most successful whatsis was essentially a sheet of glass that got hot when plugged into a wall socket. Who would think that anyone with a working stove would need a gizmo to keep the food warm after it was cooked? Since the Hotray was brought out in 1948, however, more than 12 million eager buyers (now some 500,000 a year) have wondered how they ever got along without one.

No one has satirized the American weakness for gadgetry better than Rube Goldberg, the cartoonist who published his first barbs more than 70 years ago. His unlikely inventions became so much a part of the American fabric that today "Rube Goldberg" is defined by Webster's as an adjective meaning "accomplishing by extremely complex roundabout means what actually or seemingly could be done simply." More than one idea for a thingamajig that first appeared in a Goldberg cartoon has actually been marketed. For example, few businesses or post offices are without at least one device to automatically moisten gummed labels or stamps. Goldberg's inventor, Professor Lucifer Gorgonzola Butts, proposed the idea years ago, albeit in a somewhat more complicated form: a dwarf robot overturned a can of ants on the gummed side of a page of postage stamps, which were then licked by an anteater that had been starved for three days.

One reason that gadgets keep rolling off the assembly lines is that once you let one gadget into your home, another is usually required to take care of it. Thomas Jefferson in the late 1700's invented a clock that told the day of the week as well as the time of day, but then he had to invent a folding stepladder to reach the clock for winding. Similarly, the invention of the unprotruding cork required the invention of the corkscrew; the tin can, a can opener; the coffee pot, a coffee mill.

Gadgets tend to produce revolutionary "advances" with each new generation. For a time

Workable or not, Rube Goldberg's tours de farce captivated three generations of gadget-conscious Americans.

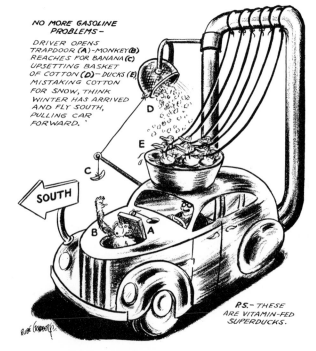

NO MORE GASOLINE PROBLEMS—

DRIVER OPENS TRAPDOOR (A)—MONKEY (B) REACHES FOR BANANA (C) UPSETTING BASKET OF COTTON (D)—DUCKS (E) MISTAKING COTTON FOR SNOW, THINK WINTER HAS ARRIVED AND FLY SOUTH, PULLING CAR FORWARD.

SOUTH

P.S.—THESE ARE VITAMIN-FED SUPERDUCKS.

Crankpot: according to its creator, a swimmer with this machine could cruise at speeds up to 6 m.p.h.

after coffee was first drunk in Europe and the United States in the 17th century, people were satisfied with boiling the grounds in water. Then in 1800 a Frenchman invented the first percolator, called the "big gin," and coffee connoisseurs soon refused to make coffee without one. The electric percolator arrived in 1908, the automated electric percolator in 1931, and now there are automatic brewing machines. Today myriad types of coffee makers that drip, perc, foam, hiss, and bubble are annually among the bestselling of all gadgets. If it is any consolation, consumers are not the only ones who spend big money on gadgets; manufacturers do too. A little thing like the drip guard on an ice-cube tray cost Frigidaire nearly $2 million to develop.

Why do people spend so much on gimcracks they don't need or, at least, could do without? Ralph Waldo Emerson believed the reason is the eternal human striving for improvement: "If a man make a better mousetrap, the world will beat a path to his door." Chaytor Mason, a psychology professor at the University of Southern California, said that three stimuli keep Americans inventing gadgets: our political freedom, our competitive society, and the fact that "this country just seems to spawn a little craziness." Dominic Tampone, president of New York's Hammacher Schlemmer specialty store and organizer of a gadget company, believes that, "gadgets satisfy the toy-desires of the individual. They may, in fact, be practical too, but basically they represent an emotional reaction to wanting something else to play with."

Whatever the reason, nothing indicates that the gadget boom will bust. Gadgets of the future are already springing from the minds of inventors: self-stirring sauce pans, faucets that turn on and off as one's hands get near them, lifts that automatically raise kitchen appliances to eye level, and watches that will tell the hour on any planet in the solar system. The time may even be near

when the U.S. Patent Office enacts a rule foretold by Aldous Huxley in his 1932 novel *Brave New World*: no gadget would be approved unless it requires at least as much apparatus as, if not more than, the most complicated model in existence at the time of application.

GARBAGE Through most of human history, refuse has been a symbol of progress—the man-made chaff of a world become more and more greedy for the fine grain of life. It has also been a sensitive index to the degree of industrialization of a people: in 50 years, for example, Americans have gone from producing roughly 2.8 pounds of refuse daily to nearly 8 pounds, and that does not account for all the industrial wastes generated in supporting our consumer habits.

Not long ago true "garbage," that is, the by-product of food preparation and consumption, accounted for most refuse, and it had a convenient way of decomposing if left out in the open air long enough. With plenty of space around most settlements, people tossed out leftovers and gave little more thought to the matter. As communities grew, pigs and other animals with insensitive appetites helped nature along by digesting a certain amount of garbage, too, although they caused problems of an equally unsanitary sort. As late as 1914 Chicago's cows, mules, and horses left an estimated 600,000 tons of manure in the city streets each year.

Ben Franklin is credited with being the first American to instigate a municipal drive against garbage. His solution, deemed very expeditious in its day, was to hire workers to dump refuse in the Delaware River. It was not for another hundred years, however, that most U.S. cities launched full-scale collection services. Municipal incinerators, usually in the densest part of a city, burned the refuse to the general discomfort of everyone around. Naming them "crematories," as a few communities did, gave them a little more class but did nothing to improve the foul air or the status of the menials who collected for them.

Other communities carted refuse to dumping grounds, where it attracted rats and vultures. (In some cities, carrion-eating birds were protected by law.) Garbage and its associated evils were ripe for social reform. One of the first new thinkers to come along was Col. George E. Waring, who was appointed commissioner of street cleaning for New York in 1895. Waring sweetened the lot of garbage men by dressing them up in handsome white uniforms and giving them quasi-military job ranks. He proposed also that the citizenry sort their garbage for more efficient disposal at its final destination and to make it possible for the sanitation department to recover some resalable articles.

Well intentioned as these efforts were, Waring and his modernist successors could not keep pace with the growing production of solid wastes. By the 1970's the United States was generating nearly 300 million tons per year (excluding wastes from agriculture, mining, and fossil fuels) at an annual disposal cost of over $5 billion. Finding places to put wastes was getting harder and harder. And the long-term effects of vast amounts of decomposed material leaching into the soil, in addition to clouds of chemicals produced by burning, were genuine causes for alarm. Some scientists even suggested, in 1977, that gases generated by the dumping of wastes into the oceans were producing sharp booms along the Atlantic coast.

Just when the problem of waste removal seemed to be on the verge of getting totally out of control, along came the energy crisis, which demonstrated once again that it is an ill wind that blows nobody good. The notion of resource recovery, previously discarded as too expensive or "un-American," has gained a new lease on life. Government, industry, and groups interested in ecology are looking for practical ways to recycle refuse. Technology is under way for making solid waste into a variety of novel fuels—from burnables pressed into high-energy combustible bricks to chicken droppings transformed into methane gas. Worn automobile tires are being tried as artificial reefs where fish can lodge in comfort. And earthworms have been mobilized to gobble garbage, with high-quality fertilizer a second-stage benefit.

Meanwhile, garbage has gained an assortment of other fans. Henry Kissinger, when he was secretary of state, discovered to his anguish that his household garbage had been picked over by an enterprising reporter in search of a political scoop. Adoring fans in pursuit of their favorite performers collect discarded gum wrappers and soda bottles as cherished souvenirs. Social scientists delving into our behavior have spent years solemnly sorting through garbage pails to come up with reports on the likes, dislikes, and nutritional habits of different economic groups. All in all, garbage is beginning to have an odor of respectability.

GARDEN The first garden may have gotten started thousands of years ago when a caveman—or, more likely, woman—threw out some seeds from something she was preparing for a meal. When plants sprouted outside and produced a crop, she learned to save the seeds and sow them

The Gold Pavilion in Kyoto, Japan, gleams in its

in a small plot of ground that had been broken up with a stick. Since then few places of human habitation have been without at least a small plot of vegetables—or flowers.

A fabled garden of antiquity, the Hanging Gardens of Babylon, one of the Seven Wonders of the World, probably did not actually hang but was set on a series of ascending terraces planted with flowers, trees, and shrubs. The terraces were connected by palatial marble stairways and were watered by bubbling fountains fed from cisterns on the uppermost terrace. Another royal Babylonian garden contained some 70 varieties of aromatic herbs.

Roman courtyard gardens, which were covered over by the eruption of Mt. Vesuvius in the 1st century A.D., have been excavated at Pompeii. Landscapes had been painted on the surrounding walls to create for the gardens a pastoral setting. (A similar ancient villa garden was the model for the garden commissioned by the oil multibillionaire J. Paul Getty in southern California.) The emperor Nero took even more pains to provide the proper backdrop for his garden in the center of Rome: he cleared some 300 acres and had the landscape carefully transformed into picture-book croplands, pastures, and woods, and he even included an artificial lake.

But the opulent Roman gardens were outdone by the more extravagant Byzantine gardens. Along with flowers and shrubs, some of these gardens featured silver and gold trees and

This miniature depicts Indian royalty taking their ease in the gentle breezes that waft through a gazebo.

winter-garden setting.

mechanical birds that flapped their wings and sang, set among fountains that spouted wine or perfume. Arabian gardens of the period used only water in their fountains, but dramatically exploited the optical and musical qualities of the leaping water, transforming the whole into a cool, relaxing oasis.

The garden at Versailles, designed in the 1660's by Louis XIV's landscape architect André Le Nôtre, survives largely unchanged to this day. He planted and rearranged 15,000 acres to provide a panorama of fountains, reflecting pools, terraces, hedges, flower beds, and woods in perfect geometric precision. The Versailles garden was so overwhelming that it became the standard of design in most of Europe well into the 1700's. In many of the Dutch versions, fewer fountains were used (water is no novelty in a land of canals), and the hedges were trimmed and worked into ornate sculptured shapes. Botanical gardens of the period were more functional; they were "museums" of exotic and medicinal plants brought back by explorers from all parts of the world.

In the 1730's, however, a revolt began in England against formal gardens. The leader of the new wave, William Kent, built a garden in which the streams and paths, theretofore arranged in regular patterns, meandered aimlessly. In later English gardens the trees and shrubs were allowed to assume their natural shapes rather than being pruned. The principle governing the new gardens, as Horace Walpole wrote, was that "nature abhors a straight line."

Most large gardens today are functional in design: the trees, shrubbery, flowers, ponds, and paths are intended as a harmonious backdrop and peaceful retreat from nearby office buildings, residences, and thoroughfares. By contrast, small private gardens seem to have returned to archaic styles. Indoor, apartment, and suburban gardening has attained unprecedented popularity, turning many homes and apartments into virtual farms of windowsill boxes and flowerpots (originated by apartment gardeners in ancient Rome). Apartment terraces and patios have become mod-

Fit for a King

Once, as André Le Nôtre was showing the plans for the gardens at Versailles to Louis XIV, the king bestowed a lavish gift on his landscape architect. After the third such gift, the story goes, Le Nôtre covered his drawings and told the king, "Sire, you will not see anymore for otherwise I should ruin you."

Le Nôtre was born to his profession. His father and grandfather were gardeners for French royalty. However, young Le Nôtre showed such promise for drawing that he left the family profession for a time to study painting. He later decided to become an artist: his paints were to be flowers and trees and his canvases, landscapes.

Succeeding his father as chief gardener at the Tuileries in 1637, he redesigned the gardens and the main avenue, now known as the Champs-Elysées. Early work revealed his genius for symmetrical design and breathtaking vistas, and upon completion of a château garden in 1661, Le Nôtre was asked by Louis XIV to design the grounds at Versailles. Both he and the king conceived of the palace gardens in heroic terms, and at one time hundreds of artists, craftsmen, soldiers, and laborers worked on the project around the clock. According to a contemporary account, many men died of malaria while transforming the swamp into a paradise; their bodies were carried away at night so as not to alarm the workers. The creation of such

A peasant plucks fruit at Versailles.

extravagances and others, including rerouting rivers from farmlands to supply the gardens' monumental fountains, added much to the growing resentment of the crown.

The garden was inaugurated in stages, beginning in 1664, and was copied throughout Europe. At the same time Le Nôtre was involved in other great projects, including gardens at Chantilly and Saint-Cloud. His style greatly influenced Pierre-Charles L'Enfant's 1791 plan for Washington, D.C.

Le Nôtre died in September 1700 at the age of 87. History remembers him as one of the greatest landscape artists ever. But Le Nôtre did not rest in peace. Some believed that his extravagant gardens, particularly at Versailles, helped bring on the French Revolution. Nearly a hundred years after his death, French citizens dug up Le Nôtre's bones and scattered them on the ground.

ern hanging gardens festooned with vegetables, herbs, and flowers.

One New Yorker transformed the tar-paper roof around his little penthouse office into a flowering jungle, commanding an exciting view of the South Street Seaport over a foreground of grass dotted with more than a hundred varieties of plants—considered enough for a two-acre area. Seed companies have developed small, hardy varieties specifically for urban gardeners, and it is not unusual to find tomatoes, mini-carrots, lemon-size eggplants, small ears of corn, and baby watermelons vying for their place in the sun on a little patch of city terrace. Members of one brownstone-rooftop farm co-op can offer their guests what must be the last word in unique chic—an opportunity to pick their own strawberries for their daiquiris.

GENEALOGY The study of family pedigrees began, if we go back to the Old Testament, when the sons of Adam and Eve thought to tell their children where they came from.

For most folks, tracing back two or three generations is the limit of knowable family history. (Everyone must, for example, trace through 30 forebears before arriving at the names of one's 32 great, great, great grandparents.) But for families who by custom or law have been entitled to certain high privileges, keeping genealogical records and lording them over others have always been serious business.

In early times tribal or clan leaders often based their right to rule on descent from a god, a legendary hero, or an animal of supernatural powers. Later, the kings and petty princes of Europe similarly claimed rights to power and wealth on the basis of birth and took care to see that all their children made suitably royal marriages to preserve the blue-blooded quality of the line. (The term "blue blood" originated in Spain, where it meant a noble of pure Spanish descent whose blood, in the veins showing through the fair skin, appeared more blue than the blood of a swarthy Moor.) As society became more literate and formal written records could be kept, the histories of royal and noble families that once had been committed to memory by bards and minstrels were set down in writing by monks and court scribes. (The term "pedigree" derives from the Latin words for "foot" and "crane" and refers to the characteristic diagrams suggestive of birds' tracks that early and subsequent genealogists have made to illustrate lines of descent.)

John Burke, an Irishman of modest antecedents, was one of the first to begin to make geneal-

Complicated medieval consanguinity tables indicated which relatives were forbidden to marry each other.

ogy something of a scholarly science. In 1820 Burke issued the first *Genealogical and Heraldic Dictionary of the Peerage and Baronetage of the United Kingdom,* commonly known as *Burke's Peerage* and considered by some a dictionary of snobbery. A thoroughly fastidious researcher, Burke went on to produce such genealogical works as *The Commoners of Great Britain and Ireland* (he renamed it *A Dictionary of the Landed Gentry* in later editions, possibly to improve circulation) and *The Portrait Gallery of Distinguished Females.* Other volumes compiled by Burke and his son covered such gilt-edged groups as *The Knightage of Great Britain and Ireland;*

people

One Big Family

The Church of Jesus Christ of Latter-day Saints, popularly known as the Mormon Church, holds that God can make salvation possible for non-Mormon forebears if their descendants identify them and dedicate prayers in their behalf. Accordingly, the Mormons maintain the most extensive data bank on genealogy in the world.

The library contains more than a million rolls of electronically indexed microfilm bearing family histories of 60 million Mormons and non-Mormons. (Vaults burrowed into the granite of nearby mountains guard copies of each roll.) This compilation, were it in books, would make 4.5 million volumes. The library also shelves 200,000 relevant historical works of both American and international scope. The Mormons' ultimate goal is to record the pedigrees of the entire family of man.

Extinct and Dormant Baronetcies of England; The Royal Families of England, Scotland, and Wales.

Although Burke stopped short of detailing all generations, he frequently passed on such tidbits as the Countess of Roden was descended on her father's side from the Steward to William the Conqueror, and in 1813 she was married to a Joscelyn, who could also trace his ancestry all the way back to the Norman Conquest.

Twenty-three generations would involve 16,777,216 direct ancestors and 25 generations would involve over 67 million. Geneticist Theodosius Dobzhansky points out that 33 generations amounts to billions of forebears for each individual, much more than the population of the world. This indicates that the lines of ancestry of each of us intersect time after time with a huge number of other people's. In this sense all of us are related, albeit distantly in most cases.

Doubtless, the most fascinating of Burke's ongoing volumes to American readers is *Presidential Families of the United States of America*, published in 1975. Burke's genealogists found traces of royal blood in 12 presidents: George Washington, Thomas Jefferson, James Monroe, John Quincy Adams, William Henry Harrison, Benjamin Harrison, James Buchanan, Abraham Lincoln, Ulysses S. Grant, James Garfield, Theodore Roosevelt, and William Howard Taft. Another president, Richard M. Nixon, is supposed to be a direct descendant of King Edward III of England.

Nowadays, however, pride of ancestry belongs not just to the few but to the many. Almost everyone seems to want to find his or her roots, and far from worrying about the skeletons that may turn up in the closet, many take a certain lusty pleasure in discovering a horse thief or a colorful eccentric in the mix. And, of course, practical benefits may derive from tracking down one's ancestors. Medical mysteries, such as the genetic disposition of some families to certain diseases, are beginning to be unraveled thanks to the growing body of records on family history.

GLASS Atop Mt. Palomar in California is one of the largest pieces of glass ever made. It is the 200-inch mirror cast in 1934 for the Hale telescope. The purpose of this 14.5-ton disk is to aid astronomers in exploring the heavens. It has been superseded only recently by the 236-inch telescope built by the Russians. Still another huge piece of glass, found at Beth She'arim, near Haifa, in Israel, weighs nearly 9 tons and measures 11 feet by 6.5 feet; it was probably cast as one piece sometime between the 4th and 7th centuries, but no one knows what it was for.

The history of glass is full of mysteries and questions; common as glass is today, its story is rich in royalty, luxury, and secrecy. The discovery of glassmaking was very probably by chance. The Egyptians were one of the first people to make glass on a large scale. Their rulers were partial to solid glass beads, blue ones in particular. Some have been found that date from before 2000 B.C. They also made small jars and bottles and tiny glass containers, small enough to be hidden in the hand, which were used to catch the tears of mourners and were then buried in the tombs. Because Egyptian rulers believed that they would live in the next world in much the same way they had in this one, their wealth was buried with them. Using methods probably derived from metal casting, they had glass mummiform figurines molded to represent the servants who would attend them in the future life.

Only royalty could afford hollow glass objects made by another time-consuming method. Different shaped sand "cores" were dropped into molten glass. When the glass had cooled and hardened, the core was removed. Glassblowing was the greatest technological advance in glassmaking. Probably in the 1st century B.C. a workman chanced to blow a puff of air through the pipe he was using to stir molten glass. The resultant bubble meant that the difficult core method could be replaced, at least for certain kinds of containers.

New York's original Penn Station was a triumph of glass and steel.

For some, glassblowing proved a hazardous profession. According to Petronius, a satirist of the 1st century A.D., a workman approached Tiberius, the Roman emperor, with a gift. It was a glass goblet. After Tiberius had examined the goblet, the workman dashed it to the ground. Instead of shattering, the goblet bounced and sustained only a dent, which the workman quickly fixed with a small hammer. Tiberius asked if anyone else knew this secret of making unbreakable glass. Blown up with pride, the workman replied that he alone understood the process. Tiberius had

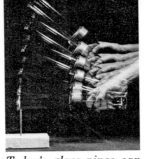

Today's glass pipes can even be used to drive nails into a board.

him beheaded. The making of unbreakable glass, he reasoned, would mean that gold and silver would lose their value, and that he would not permit—that would be economically disasterous.

A similar concern for the exclusiveness of glass-making techniques showed up in Venice in the 15th century. Venetian craftsmen were the best in the world. They worked on the island of Murano but were forbidden to leave Venice or to teach their trade to others, with severe penalties for any violation.

Glassmaking was the first industry established in America. In the Jamestown colony, Capt. John Smith and his followers set up a crude glassworks where most of the work was done by hand. Today, by contrast, a single machine can spin out some 2,000 light bulbs per minute.

The greatest disappointment in the story of

customs

The Hand You Glove to Touch

Now reduced to little more than simple utility, the glove at various periods of history has served as a pledge of friendship and love, a symbol of hatred and defiance, a token of loyalty, a mark of honor, and a guarantee of safety.

One of the earliest references to the wearing of gloves was made by Xenophon, the Greek historian, in ridiculing the effete manners of the Persians: "It is not sufficient for them to clothe their heads, and their bodies, and their feet, but they have coverings made of hair for their hands and fingers." Musonius, an early Christian moralist, also complained: "It is shameful that persons in perfect health should clothe their hands . . . with soft and hairy coverings."

Nonetheless, as early as 960 A.D., gloves became part of the ceremonial attire for bishops. (They are now considered optional.) Gloves, embroidered with gold and encrusted with precious stones, were also early emblems of royalty. It is said that Richard the Lion-Hearted, obliged to disguise himself on his way home from the Crusades, was recognized and taken prisoner because he had not been able to part with his costly gloves.

As the symbolic extension of the hand, gloves often were used to denote royal protection or favor. In medieval Germany, for example, the king's glove was displayed on market days to warn off robbers. Until 1820 throwing down a glove, or gauntlet, was part of the coronation ceremony of English monarchs, an invitation to anyone who dared dispute the king's right to rule.

Women did not begin wearing gloves until the 10th or 11th centuries. Once they did, however, it was not long before a lady's glove became a token for favors not yet bestowed. Noble knights carried ladies' gloves into tournaments and battles. One of them, at the court of a king of Castile, was put to a stern test when his lady fair daintily dropped her glove into a pit of lions. Unhesitatingly, the knight jumped in after it, plucked the glove out, and, according to Robert Browning's version of the story, heaved it in the lady's face.

During the 16th century perfumed gloves, which were reputed to protect the wearer against pestilence, became the rage in Europe. And if they did not actually ward off plague, at least they helped compensate for the extremely low level of personal cleanliness prevalent at that time. Both sexes also affected the wearing of special gloves at night to soften and whiten the hands. The very best and most effective gloves were made of chicken skin. Gloves, it is believed, were even used as murder weapons. During the 16th century Jeanne d'Albret,

mother of the future King Henry IV and a fervent Huguenot, bought a pair of scented gloves from Catherine de Medici's perfumer, whom the queen had summoned to Paris from his shop in Milan. Since Catherine hated Protestants, it was rumored that she had her perfumer mix in a deadly dose of poison with the perfume. In any case, four hundred years later Jeanne d'Albret's death remains a mystery.

Many portraits of illustrious Renaissance figures show them displaying a pair of gloves, or wearing one and showing the other. This practice may have had artistic significance, but a simpler explanation is that the gloves did not fit very well. The thumbs on a pair made for Queen Elizabeth were at least 5 inches long.

Except for the use of rough coverings for protection, common people did not wear gloves until well into the 19th century. The honor of becoming the Henry Ford of the glove belongs to a Frenchman named Xavier Jouvin. A native of Grenoble, the French glove capital since the 14th century, Jouvin made detailed studies of hands in a dissecting room. Armed with his findings, he perfected in 1834 a series of sharp-edged iron forms capable of cutting out a half-dozen gloves at a time thus "mass-producing" gloves of standard shape and size.

glass has to do with Cinderella's glass slipper. The author of the children's story, who wrote in French, intended that the lost slipper be made of fur. So he wrote *pantoufle en vair* ("slipper of fur"), which the translator read as *en verre*, which is the French way of saying "of glass."

GLUE If you recently bought a new car, you got for your money a quantity of steel, glass, chrome, and vinyl—and 25 pounds of glue. Glue put the crackle in the paper money you used to make a down payment. Surprisingly, glue is part of many common items, such as clothes and writing paper, and yet no one is precisely sure how it works. Some 3,000 years before Christ the Egyptians already knew how to make glue. They boiled animal skin, bone, and sinew and were left with a thick material that made things stick together.

The key ingredient in glue is a protein called collagen. Strictly speaking, only products made of animal parts should be called "glue." The powerful synthetic glues developed in the 1930's are properly called "adhesives." By whatever name, these chemical glues are startlingly strong. In a dramatic demonstration in 1957, a crane hoisted an automobile and four passengers several feet off the ground with a harness that was attached with a single drop of adhesive.

Adhesives work for at least two reasons. They form a physical bond between the materials being joined. In many cases they create a chemical bond as well, the molecules of the adhesive attracting the molecules of the material being joined. As a result, adhesives can be used in place of rivets in the construction of some jet airplanes, and there may be as much as a half-ton of glue per plane. Medicine, too, has benefited. A new type of adhesive bandage can stick to the gums and helps stop bleeding after dental surgery. It then gradually dissolves and is harmlessly absorbed by the body. The term "fast-drying" understates the power of some surgical adhesives, such as those used to set broken bones. They bond in an instant, leaving the doctor no room for error. And one man, using a super-strong adhesive to repair a shattered ceramic angel, found the skin of his hand frozen to the figurine within 30 seconds. It took a surgeon to separate man and statue, leaving a thin slice of skin forever attached to the figurine.

GOLD Gold is what we make it—valuable. And for thousands of years most of humankind has accepted the belief that this bright, heavy, soft, yellow metal does have a value all its own. As a result, medieval alchemists struggled to find a for-

mula that would turn baser substances into gold. In 1450 Bernard of Treves thought he had an answer: to equal parts of olive oil and vitriol, he added the yolks of 2,000 eggs and cooked the goo for two weeks. He was disappointed, of course, and so were other royal seekers, such as Heraclius I of Byzantium, James IV of Scotland, and Holy Roman Emperor Rudolf II. Beneath his bedroom, Charles II of England had an alchemist's laboratory accessible only by private stairway, but privacy was no help in making the conversion either.

Although originally perfected in 1717 by Sir Isaac Newton, master of the British mint, the gold standard—paper money redeemable in gold—was not widely adopted until the 19th century when the "Age of Gold" was ushered in with the gold strikes in California, Australia, and South Africa. By 1873 there were nine countries on the gold standard; by 1912, because of the increased supply of the precious metal, 49 countries used notes redeemable in gold.

The enormous indebtedness brought about by World War I disrupted the worldwide gold standard. Many countries returned to that monetary system in theory, but war-caused inflation result-

During the 17th century, Japanese miners scratched for gold in torch-lit caves, as in this wood-block print.

ed in a continued inability to bridge the gap between actual gold held and the face amount of paper notes issued. Finally, in 1931, Great Britain abandoned the gold standard; the United States followed in 1933.

The fact that today gold has been divorced from most currency systems has not changed its allure. Many people believe that even if their national currency should depreciate, the gold they possess will retain its value and perhaps even appreciate. In 1975, however, Americans proved relatively immune to the gold bug. For the first time in years, they were offered the chance to buy and own gold bullion—legally. And for the most part, they ignored the opportunity. But a year later the public awakened to the possibilities of profit, and gold prices have been doing a dance ever since.

Monetary concerns apart, gold does have its uses. It is almost indestructible and never tarnishes. It also conducts electricity well, and thus is vital in certain costly electrical circuits. Because it is soft, gold can be hammered wafer thin and used in various kinds of plating. One ounce can produce a sheet nearly 100 square feet. The plating of public restrooms was one of Lenin's ideas for gold, though he did not follow through with it. The first American to walk in space was connected to his Gemini vehicle by a golden umbilical cord, designed to stop radiation.

Chances are slim that humans will lose their

Fool's goal? In medieval days attempts by alchemists to make gold out of baser metals were considered logical.

fascination for gold, for it remains a symbol of power, prestige, and permanence. Ancient Greek legends recounted that gold was created by Zeus, and the proper metal to adorn temples and appease the gods. This view has been slightly refined at a hotel in Japan's Izu peninsula, where a visitor can pay about $8 to sit in a golden tub for two minutes, believing that he or she will gain at least three years of life.

GOLF Probably no other game devised by man inspires a more bizarre mix of devotion and loathing in its devotees than golf. One authority defines golf as "a game of discipline, hope, and despair." Few serious golfers have not shared, at least briefly, the feelings of comedian and golfer Buddy Hackett, who said, "I'd like to take my swing back far as I can and hit myself in the head. . . . Why did I begin?"

No historian knows why, or when, the first man took up golf clubs. Traditionally, the Scots have been credited—or blamed—for inventing the game, which was a popular pastime by the early 15th century at St. Andrews, about 55 miles northeast of Edinburgh. However, some experts believe that the sport may have been started even earlier by the Dutch; the name itself is thought to derive from a Dutch word meaning "club." Other authorities assert that the first clubs were actually the crooked staffs of shepherds, who used them to wallop pebbles while their sheep grazed.

Some of the first references to golf are contained in royal edicts outlawing it. In 1457, during the reign of King James II, the Scottish Parliament decreed that "Futeball and Golfe be utterly cryed downe and not be used. . . ." Although King James IV (1488–1513) played the game himself, he said golf was an "unprofitable" sport and should not be permitted to take time from important duties. In general, kings were concerned that their citizenry would waste time on the links when they ought to be practicing archery, the better to defend their nation. As might be expected, golfers ignored most royal entreaties to abandon their "forbidden, disgraceful recreation."

By the 1600's the bow had become less important to national defense, and golfers felt freer to tramp the links. Mary, Queen of Scots, in the mid-16th century, became the first-known woman golfer. Educated in France, she called the boys who retrieved the balls "cadets" (pronounced "cad-day"), thus giving caddies their name.

It is possible that golf was played in the United States before the American Revolution, but the first permanent golf club with its own links was not officially established until 1887, at Foxburg,

Lady of the Links

In 1932 Grantland Rice, the sports columnist, took an 18-year-old track star and Olympic gold-medal winner to Los Angeles' Brentwood Country Club to see what she could do with a golf club. She was a natural athlete (setting a world record the first time she hurled the javelin) and an excellent softball player, diver, swimmer, marksman, cyclist, and skater. Although she had never swung a golf club, her first shot sailed 200 yards straight down the fairway.

The girl, Babe Didrikson, daughter of a Norwegian sailor who had retired to Port Arthur, Texas, began practicing—12 hours a day. Three years later she won her first tournament and shortly thereafter went on tour, delighting galleries with her 250-yard drives and trick shots. Often she would saunter up to the tee and wallop the ball without breaking stride. In 1938, in an exhibition match in Los Angeles, she was paired with a 250-pound wrestler, George Zaharias. Walking down the fairway on the sixth or seventh hole, Babe glanced over her

For more than a decade, athlete Babe Didrikson ruled women's golf.

shoulder and asked her partner what he was looking at. "I'm looking at you," he said. "You're my kind of girl." Said she, "You're my kind of guy." And a year later the "Crying Greek from Cripple Creek" and "The Babe" were married. For the next 18 years they were inseparable.

Under George's guidance Babe turned professional in 1947 and a few years later, in the Tampa

Open, shot 288 for 72 holes—the first score by a woman that could compare with the best that male golfers could do. With George's help, Babe went on to put women's professional golf on a paying basis. For four years in a row, she was the leading money winner on the women's tour.

Then, in April 1953, Babe learned she had cancer. "We'll fight it together," George told her and shortly thereafter Babe underwent surgery. Two months later, she walked out of the hospital and resumed playing one or two holes of golf a day. In 1954, only 15 months after her operation, she won the U.S. National Women's Open, and later the Tam O'Shanter. She was hospitalized again the next year, however, and died in 1956, her golf clubs tipped in a corner of her room where she could see them. She was, as she said, "the first woman to play the game the way men play it—to hit the ball instead of swinging at it." Most experts still refer to her as the greatest woman athlete who has come along to date.

Pennsylvania. In 1888, when a group of enthusiasts laid out a 6-hole course near Yonkers, New York, and played on Sundays (as well as weekdays), they were belabored by preachers and ridiculed by passersby who regarded the game as "ridiculous folly." Nevertheless, the group persisted and founded the St. Andrews Golf Club of Yonkers, the country's second golf club. Although many other Americans agreed that golf was inane (Mark Twain called it "a good walk spoiled"), the sport gained converts rapidly, mostly among the wealthy and leisured. In 1895 the newly formed United States Golf Association (USGA) held its first national amateur tournament.

After Francis Ouimet, a 20-year-old ex-caddie from Boston, beat two favored British professionals in the U.S. Open in 1913, golf became a public obsession. According to Will Rogers, golf has made liars out of more Americans than anything except the income tax. By 1914 it had more than 750,000 devotees, and USGA membership rolls listed more than 200 clubs. Today the United

States has some 12,500 public and private golf courses, which are used by nearly 16 million golfers. In all they invest more than $350 million in equipment each year.

A 1668 canvas by Adriaen van de Velde, shows golf on ice in Holland, where the game may have originated.

GRAFFITI Graffiti, plural of Italian *graffito* ("scratching"), have served archeologists in dating and identifying cultures and particularly in the study of ancient languages. Graffiti in the Agora, ancient Athens' marketplace and forum, provided archeologists with landmarks in writing history.

Greek mercenaries and Roman legionnaires hacked out their names on Egyptian monuments. Not even the Great Pyramid at Giza was safe from the stylus in the hand of a Greek tourist from Pamphylia, whose prealphabetic, syllabic inscription was a rich mine to linguistic scholars.

To stop Romans from scrawling in the public latrines, officials painted pictures and symbols of the gods on the walls, making their defacement not merely a civil but a religious offense punishable by death. A Roman householder's graffito, still extant, begged passersby not to scribble (*scarifare*) on his wall.

Medieval graffiti began to appear in the 12th century, mainly in churches. Still to be seen on pillars and walls are masons' plans, knightly crests, pictures in the style of manuscript illuminations, and, in beautiful script, epitaphs in medieval Latin, Norman French, or Middle English, often with drawings of Death with his scythe and a comment, such as "Death is like a shadow that always follows the body."

The Tower of London's graffiti record faith and fortitude through a ruthless era, scratched with a nail or written sometimes in a prisoner's blood. The nobility mostly did not (perhaps could not) write, but some drew their family coats of arms on the cell walls. Most eloquent, as well as most literate, were religious prisoners. Thomas Abell, chaplain to Catherine of Aragon, the first wife of Henry VIII, and one of many clergymen condemned by the king, drew a rebus of his name— the letter "A" inscribed on a bell.

In 18th-century England graffiti took a poetic turn on tavern walls, doors, windows, and

Even these cacti bear signs of man's compulsion to make his mark.

complaisant ladies' dwellings, boasting of conquests and complaining of the consequences. After taking his pleasure, one reveler wrote this on a window in Chancery Lane, London: "Here did I lay my Celia down; I got the pox and she got half a crown." Among many inscribed with a diamond on window glass was this lover's plaint: "This Glass my Fair's the Emblem of your Mind, Which brittle, slipp'ry, pois'nous oft we find," and her tart retort: "I must confess, kind Sir, that though this Glass/Can't prove me brittle it proves you an Ass."

Whether because of its privacy or its function, the public convenience in all lands and eras has evoked the greatest number of graffiti, the most uninhibited, and in subject matter the most consistently devoted to sex and excretion. Noted by earlier graffitologists and repeated by Alfred Kinsey in his studies of sexual behavior was that while men scrawled obscenities and four-letter words on privy walls, women preferred romantic fantasies, such as initials enclosed in pierced hearts or mouths drawn with lipstick. But collections from campus washrooms in the 1970's revealed that women now have as bold a graffiti repertoire as men and as little inhibition in using it. Like the men, they boast of their conquests, complain of the anatomic inadequacy of the opposite sex, and make Freudian interpretations ("War is just menstruation envy"). Regarding academic *latrinalia* (a term coined by anthropologist Alan Dundes), men revealed no difference from the traditional pornographic spontaneity, but the disciplines displayed themselves in learned "one-upmanship." From the humanities department at Harvard came these: "Luther eats Worms," "Shakespeare eats Bacon." From the physics department "Planck is inconstant," "Niels is Bohring."

Cultural investigators see the wall writings as a "people's press," a medium of expression for those who have no access to the established media. Social scientists regard them as a safety valve for popular discontents. Psychologists speak of subconscious motivations, such as sexual frustration, regression to infantile play with dirt, or simply the need to assert one's identity in the anonymous crowd. Still others interpret the phenomenon as

Ageless urge: the three-word graffito below is common— and modern; the cross at right was cut by Christian Copts to deface Egyptian wall carvings of pagan gods.

"Write It, Don't Say It"

By all accounts, the first greeting cards were used to commemorate a most important day: the first day of the new year. An Egyptian custom was to send presents on that day, along with some sort of written message. The Romans also believed that January 1 was a time for gifts and greetings. An especially popular gift was a lucky penny, made of copper and bearing the likeness of Janus, the Roman god with two faces, so that he might keep an eye on the past and future. Later, such symbols were depicted on terra cotta tablets.

If there is no doubt about the first greeting-card holiday, there is also no doubt about which holiday has given rise to the most confusion: Valentine's Day. For the loving messages we transmit on February 14 may—or may not—have their origins in the martyrdom of a bishop named Valentine.

Some authorities suggest that St. Valentine's Day grew out of the Roman pagan feast of Lupercalia, celebrated in mid-February, when birds supposedly mated. Among the ceremonies of that day was one in which Roman maidens would write their names on slips of paper and drop them into a container set up in a public place. Bachelors might draw a name and thus acquire a female companion for the coming year.

Sources differ on whether these young women were blind dates—or mistresses—though it may suffice to say that the Christian Church regarded these "love lotteries" as squalid. For centuries the church fought the rites, even substituting at one point the names of saints for the names of maidens. The promise of spiritual fulfillment by a particular saint seemed less than fetching, however, to Roman bachelors and to their confreres in other European countries, and so the love lotteries continued.

Be Good and enjoy a Merry Merry Christmas.

In the 1920's Santa used the telephone to deliver greetings in person.

Peace and happiness be yours to day.

A wise and ennobling message, especially from a girl wearing a daisy.

St. Valentine himself was supposed to have been martyred by the Roman emperor Claudius II about 270 A.D., though the nature of his crime is not clear. One legend advises that Bishop Valentine was especially noted for his love and charity, and so people selected the anniversary of his death as a time to dispatch tender messages. Although the Catholic Church has dropped St. Valentine from its official liturgical calendar, along with many other saints, his existence has not yet, at least, been disproved.

Valentine's Day is not taken seriously today, but in 19th-century America a Valentine had to be handmade and handwrit-

Good news from across the sea: this New Year's card shows a Jewish family in a shtetl *cottage receiving money sent to them by relatives in America.*

ten—in Spencerian script. Furthermore, its verses had to be original, and so such aids to amorous verse as *The Young Man's Valentine Writer* and *The Quiver of Love* appeared.

Christmas cards have a less complicated if no less emotional history. Sir Henry Cole, new director of the Victoria and Albert Museum in London, launched the genre in 1843 because he had no time to write Christmas letters. Instead he commissioned artist John Horsley to create a painting depicting both merry and charitable Christmas scenes and had it reproduced on cards. Cole's first card was a success. About three decades later, after the installation of free mail delivery, a German immigrant, Louis Prang, founded the American Christmas card industry. He employed a lavish printing process that used limestone quarried in Bavaria, and with it he was capable of reproducing 17 colors in a single picture. Because Christmas is one of the most sentimental of holidays, humor and double-entendre cards do not sell well. Santa Claus does, though he has put on weight over the years.

Fowl play: only a monster could have eaten turkey after opening this card.

The birthday card goes back a way, as this unctuous 1900's card shows.

Mother's Day and Father's Day are relatively recent creations. Mother came first, in 1907, and Father's Day followed in 1924, after presidential endorsement by Calvin Coolidge. Initially it was suggested that the dandelion be made the official Father's Day flower ("the more it is trampled on, the more it grows"), but more sensible and sentimental heads prevailed, and the rose, thorns and all, was selected.

It is clear that wit and bawdiness have become partners with sentiment in the greeting-card, or social-expression, industry as it is sometimes known. Foreshadowed by the anonymous "vinegar valentines," masterpieces of insult that sprang up in the 1850's, "studio cards" supply humor and insult for every occasion. Hallmark Cards, the industry's largest producer, was once challenged to create a card for one of our more obscure celebratory days. Undaunted, they reached into their inventory, and found that it was there: "Thinking of you on Ground Hog Day."

Male chauvinist dig: few valentines have been more pointed than this.

THE FLAPPER.
What a pity that you weren't born a boy,
For all the boys rough ways you love to employ.
You bob your hair and you rouge your cheeks,
And smoke cigarettes till your breath fairly reeks,
You play boys' wild games, and when you ride,
In masculine breeches the horse you stride,
You roll your stockings and show your poor knees,
Pray act more maidenly, if you please.

Bow at the ready, Cupid coaches an eager-looking bench-warmer.

one form of aggression against authority.

Students of modern graffiti protest that no single interpretation can explain the multiplicity of forms that the wall writings assume. They contrast the confessional aspect of toilet walls with the philosophical or polemic exuberances of more open spaces. They cite the inventiveness of the graffitists in converting conventional literary and rhetorical devices to unconventional uses. Some examples: Pun: "Does the name Pavlov ring a bell?" Rhyme: "Nietzsche is pietzsche." Proverb: "Chaste makes waste." Metaphor: "Life is a bowl of pits; someone else got the cherries." Irony: "Ban the bomb, save the world for conventional warfare." Parody: "Have patience, radicals, Rome wasn't burned in a day." Epigram: "Today's tomorrows are yesterday's todays."

Graffitologist Frank J. D'Angelo observes in the *Journal of Popular Culture* that although specific psychological motivations may lie behind specific categories of graffiti, no subconscious drives are needed to explain the phenomenon itself—its playfulness, creativeness, and linguistic ingenuity. It is a virtuoso performance, paradoxically anonymous, with the transparent purpose of eliciting shock, outrage, or laughter.

GUITAR The first guitar was undoubtedly a hunting bow. One myth has it that Hermes stole valuable cattle from Apollo, and, when caught, escaped the god's wrath by playing a lyre and wailing flattering songs. Hermes' lyre was fashioned from a hunting bow with three cow-gut strings stretched across an empty turtle shell. Apollo apparently was so impressed by the instrument that he traded all his cattle for it.

The guitar, a direct descendant of the lyre, was invented and reinvented, and changed and shaped, in many cultures and ages. The earliest instrument that has most of the characteristics of a modern guitar appeared in a Hittite bas-relief, dating from before 1000 B.C. In virtually every language that assigns gender to inanimate objects, the guitar is feminine. And there is little doubt that its modern shape most graciously reflects the gentle curves of a woman's body. This is probably not the reason that the vast majority of great guitar players are men. The answer more likely involves a simpler physiological truth: men are stronger, and holding and strumming take muscle.

Guitars seem to evoke political feelings in some cultures. In the 1920's the guitar was temporarily forbidden to the students at a university in Sverdlovsk, Russia. Soviet authorities contended that the guitar was a middle-class instrument, unworthy of workers. Ten years later, in the United States, some critics held that strumming a guitar had obvious Marxist overtones. And when Elvis Presley burst upon the American scene with his guitar, he became a symbol of license and rebellion, horrifying parents even as he delighted their children.

The guitar is now the second most popular instrument in the United States, and the only close rival of the piano. In addition, it is relatively inexpensive and fairly easy to play—badly. To reach the heights scaled by the likes of Andrés Segovia, for decades the world's leading classic guitarist, is quite another matter.

Beethoven called the guitar "a miniature orchestra." And Stradivarius, better known for his violins, made many guitars. Schubert, too poor to afford a piano, composed some of his music on a guitar, and Benjamin Franklin earned pocket money by giving guitar lessons to young women.

Today the manufacturing of guitars is big business, so much so that the Columbia Broadcasting System paid more in 1965 to acquire a guitar-making company than it had for a controlling interest in the New York Yankees. Perhaps because, as Carl Sandburg said, to so many people the guitar is "a portable companion—a small friend weighing less than a freshborn infant."

For nearly 1,000 years the guitar in various incarnations has made music for creatures as diverse as angelic Renaissance madrigal singers (guitar as lute) and devilish stars like Ace Frehey of the rock group Kiss.

In the early Greek alphabet the letter "H" was shaped like two small window panes, one atop the other.

HAIRSTYLES Sometimes it seems as if hair grows on human heads mainly to be fussed with. In the name of fashion, countless modes of frizzing, bleaching, chopping, and faking it have been devised. Africans who stiffened their hair with dung or the courtly Japanese geishas who coated theirs with lacquer were no less style conscious than today's jet-setter off to Kenneth for the

From medieval bun to ballpark Afro, hairstyles have always had a lot in common: their differences.

newest fashionable cut. In imperial Rome, styles changed so swiftly that one statue of a noble matron was constructed so that its coiffure could be regularly brought up to date.

History suggests that curly styles have been favored more than straight. The noble Assyrian warrior sat patiently while slaves applied a heated device resembling a carpenter's plane to his hair and square-cut beard, giving him the overall crimped look that was considered the mark of nobility. Greek ladies were curled with round irons and terra-cotta rollers, and Roman matrons got their hair twisted into ringlets around hollow tubes heated with rods. They ornamented their high-piled curls with precious combs, jeweled diadems, and golden nets. The wealthiest had their coiffures powdered daily with pure gold dust.

Wigs have seemed a good alternative to hours of hairdressing since Babylonian times. King Louis XIV of France wore one because his hair was thinning, and all his courtiers followed suit. To

the stern English Puritans, however, falseness of any kind was an abomination. During the reign of Elizabeth I, they issued a warning that any woman who got her man by misleading him with "false hair, Spanish hair pads . . . [or] high-heeled shoes" would be punished as a witch. The edict had little effect on the vain queen herself: Elizabeth was reputed to own some 80 wigs.

Whether it was the "Greek revival" look worn by Napoleon's Josephine or the severe forehead made popular by Queen Victoria, hairstyles have usually been dictated by the noble or the rich. The court of Louis XV saw slim-necked ladies staggering under three-foot upsweeps, some adorned with the model of a full-rigged ship or a real bird in a cage. Unfortunately, the style attracted vermin as well as admiration.

The right hairstyle has sometimes been a matter of politics, religion, or profession. The 17th-century English Royalist Cavaliers, in opposition to the parliamentarian "Roundhead Puritans," wore long, flowing curls. In the 1960's youths flaunted long unfettered locks to protest many forms of institutionalized restriction. The shaved heads of Buddhist and Christian monks signify renunciation, whereas the single long lock of a Muslim man offers Allah a handle by which to pull him up to heaven. The gray wig of the British barrister and the carefully sectioned plaits of the Masai warrior symbolize their high callings.

The dark-haired Mediterranean people were the first to embrace the myth that blondes have more fun. Athenian ladies cultivated a look of golden innocence with a pomade of potassium and flower petals, and Romans scoured their hair with a yellow soap called "Batavian caustic." Most coveted of all was a blond wig made from the hair of northern barbarians—though for a time blond hair was the sign of the Roman prostitute. The secret of the fair-haired Italian beauties of the Renaissance was saffron and onionskin dye. Until fairly recently, most hair colorings produced tones ranging from shoe-polish black to strangulation blue to orange. Perhaps the lack of subtlety was one reason that bleached blondes were considered hussies in the 1930's. Contemporary hair dyes offering a rainbow of realistic hair shades are based on coaltar derivatives (some of which are being studied as possible allergens and carcinogens).

Throughout most of history, hairdressing was done by slaves, an occasional barber (who also acted as surgeon), or by ladies' maids. When the marcel wave, a cascade of soft undulating waves beginning at the scalp, became popular in the 1870's, women flocked to the "hairdressing stores." The new waving iron, the invention of M. Marcel Grateau, had made it all possible. The marcel won instant popularity in the United States. It was the beginning of the American beauty parlor industry, and the age when stage and movie stars would become the arbiters of taste was soon to arrive.

German-born Charles Nestle (originally Nessler) was determined to perfect a wave that could be properly called permanent. In his first experiment, he baked off all but one lock of a woman's head. But Nestle was jubilant—the one lock curled, permanently. His perfected process used a chemical solution and took six hours. Hairdressers feared its success would ruin business forever. Instead, the "perm" became the very foundation of the hairdressing business, which puts up-to-date styles within reach of every woman and man.

Call it what you will—dry look, beehive, Afro, or wedge—hairstyles change today as swiftly as hemlines. In the 1960's a whole generation of young men copied the changing hairstyles of the Beatles. In the movie *A Hard Day's Night*, when someone asked George Harrison what he called his hairdo, Harrison quipped, "I call it Arthur."

HAMBURGER Although hamburger is generally considered an American food, it originated neither in the United States nor in Hamburg, Germany, as many think. Meat is believed to have been ground in medieval times by Tartar nomads who lived on the steppes of Asia. These rugged horsemen often ate meat raw, and sometimes "tenderized" it by leaving a slab under the saddle during a hard day's ride. They then scraped away the loosened morsels of meat, seasoned the mush with salt, pepper, and onion juice, and ate it raw—the original Tartar steak.

As the story goes, Hamburg merchants trading in Asia took the recipe back to Germany and spread the fame of "Hamburg steaks" far and wide. Later some Hamburg cooks—no one can say when—decided to broil the meat. In 1888 an English physician, Dr. James H. Salisbury, recommended that his patients eat well-done hamburger meat three times a day to relieve a host of diseases, including anemia, rheumatism, and gout.

About the turn of the century, people began referring to cooked Tartar steak as "hamburger."

---

customs

Only the Hairdresser Knows for Sure

The commercial beauty shop has been a part of American life for about a hundred years. Before that, ladies in big cities relied on dolls imported from Europe, dressed and coiffed in the latest fashion, to show them or their maids what to aim for in the privacy of their own homes. Late 19th-century "fashion plates," or pictures, issued by the Hair Dealers' Association in New York, were reproduced in contemporary fashion magazines. As the traditional Puritan outlook gave way to an easier acceptance of things physical, more women, and men too, repaired to the beauty parlor for what they hoped would be a visible transformation.

When your haircut or facial does not fulfill the dream of instant beauty, the experience can be traumatic, despite the mental lift that comes from having someone fuss over you. Many people use their hairdressers and cosmeticians as therapists—a role bartenders would easily recognize. In Florida some hairdressers can even take courses that teach them where to direct customers who complain of depression, alcoholism, or the problems of single parenthood. Consequently, hairdressers have to sustain the stress of being an impersonal sounding board for a constant flow of customer fury, loneliness, or frustration. Many go home and take it out on their spouses, which may explain the high divorce rate among cosmeticians.

In ultra expensive, sleek "sa-

Permanent weave? This 1930's device did a lasting job of curling hair.

lons," however, the pressure sometimes switches to the customer. One New Yorker reports that if she behaves well (that is, according to the values of the shop), she departs with an added emotional bonus: at Vidal Sassoon, she feels sexy and powerful if she has managed to click with the washer, colorist, and stylist; at Elizabeth Arden she exits a lady if she knew just what to tip without fluster; at Richard Stein she rewards herself with a "psychically okay" stamp, providing she did not slump in her chair or lapse into the gaucherie of engaging the beautician in shoptalk.

And how self-confident is a woman who woos her hairdresser's continuing attention with a $4,000 Christmas gift or a two-month loan of her Spanish villa (travel expenses paid) or who herself cooks and caters a lavish dinner in his home for 20 of his personal friends? Gifts like these were reported to have been bestowed on beauticians operating in the affluent society.

Although the term "Salisbury steak" is still used, it is generally considered simply a fancy name for the same thing. During World War I, in an effort to "cleanse" the English language of German words, the term Salisbury steak enjoyed a brief popularity. Now "hamburger" is commonly shortened to "burger" and often coupled with almost any prefix to denote a special type of dish—cheeseburger, Mexiburger, a guacamoleburger, even the incongruous vegetarianburger.

The history of the hamburger in the United States has many versions. Some say hamburger meat was introduced to Cincinnati by German immigrants. As for the hamburger patty in a bun, some claim that it was first served at the St. Louis World's Fair in 1904. Kenneth Lassen, owner of Louis Lunch in New Haven, Connecticut, believes that his grandfather, Louis Lassen, was the first to serve hamburgers on these shores, at Louis Lunch, in 1904. The New Haven Preservation Trust designated the 14-stool diner a city landmark in 1967. Americans eat more than 53 billion hamburgers a year—some 30 pounds of hamburger for every man, woman, and child. But they have not captured at least one hamburger record, according to the *Guinness Book of World Records*. In 1975 an Australian cooked the world's largest hamburger, weighing 2,859 pounds and measuring 27½ feet around.

Amber waves of buns. This field of McDonald's rolls salutes the king of American fast foods: the hamburger.

Handkerchief: Status Symbol

Understanding the handkerchief is not as simple as blowing one's nose. This square of cloth has had its social ups and downs through the ages, and many uses. In Rome, two centuries before the birth of Christ, only the wealthy could afford a white linen *sudarium* (from *sudor*, meaning "perspiration"). This piece of cloth was mainly used for mopping the brow.

In later Roman times, waving a handkerchief was a way of voting on whether a defeated gladiator was to be pardoned or put to the sword. Handkerchiefs were also used to greet a person of rank or to "applaud" actors in the theater. Although an influx of foreign flax made these cloths cheaper, so that ordinary Romans could afford them, the rise of pomp in the Christian Church turned handkerchiefs back into status symbols. Eventually, they became a required part of clerical attire.

In the Middle Ages *sudaria* and *oraria* (from the Latin *os*, meaning "mouth") were visible in church and coronation rituals. Some priests apparently were still confused, because church authorities specifically warned against blowing the priestly nose on the surplice and chasuble.

An Ozark girl looks for dried-dew initials of a husband-to-be on handkerchief she hung on bush.

During the Renaissance handkerchiefs were items of fashion among the wealthy. Personal cleanliness was only one motive. More than that, handkerchiefs had to be beautiful so they could be carried in the hand for show. Ladies had their portraits painted with a handkerchief held gracefully to attract attention to the beauty of their hands. In the 16th century personal cleanliness was not a social imperative in the French court, so ladies carried little squares of cloth soaked in perfume. Henry III, king at the time, was fond of handkerchiefs, but his male subjects blew their noses through their fingers.

Handkerchiefs have long been linked with love and courtship. In 17th-century England ladies gave their handkerchiefs, adorned with buttons, to their suitors. When King Charles II prohibited the importation of expensive, frivolous buttons, the result was widespread button smuggling. But it was snuff, not love, that made handkerchiefs commonplace. Snuff takers used them to keep tobacco from spotting their clothes. Having lost its ornamental value, the handkerchief was packed away in the pocket, where it remains today.

"Put It There"

Because they are so uniquely human, hands are especially eloquent instruments of communication. They beckon, point, reject, threaten, reassure, punch, and even convey unconscious feelings. A behavioral scientist has suggested, for instance, that touching the mouth at moments of tension is really an attempt to recapture the security and comfort experienced at the mother's breast.

Student shake: beer and dueling were staples of German student life.

The custom of shaking hands also has unconscious meanings. Many consider it a disclaimer of aggressive intention, as in this explanation by writer Edwin Radford: "When two persons took the right hand of each on meeting, and particularly on parting, it was a very effective preventative of either of them getting to his sword!"

But the shaking of hands predates the introduction of the sword. Even in primitive times if a man extended his bare right hand, that is, his weapon hand, it meant he was coming in peace.

The offer of a hand is not the symbol of friendliness in all societies, however. In China the custom was to join one's own hands in greeting; in India and Southeast Asia, the hands traditionally are placed palm to palm and held in front of the face.

Handshaking has seemed to satisfy two needs. One is to punctuate with some ritual the acts of greeting and parting—a need that impels us to begin a letter with "Dear Mr. Jones" and end it "Yours faithfully," even though we may despise Mr. Jones heartily and hold him in no allegiance whatsoever. The other is to express a sense of equality. People do not shake hands with their butlers except possibly when they retire after a lifetime of service, or with royalty save at its express invitation.

Different societies have their accepted rules about who shakes hands with whom, but the French not long ago added a caveat of their own. Toward the end of President Charles de Gaulle's public life, guests at formal receptions in the Elysée palace received one of two kinds of invitations: with or without a small blue triangle in the top left-hand corner. The purpose of the mark was to indicate who would—and who would not—be expected to join the receiving line. Those with triangles were not accorded a prestigious press of the president's 76-year-old hand.

HAND Look at the skeleton of any quadruped: the backbone is an arch sturdily supported by the legs, and in turn supporting the rib cage and the internal organs of the body—a neat bit of engineering. Try setting the animal on its rear limbs, however, and disaster will soon follow.

Yet this unnatural, upright position does offer an advantage: it raises the forward limbs. And in the case of mankind this bit of skeletal realignment has led to the creation of the most extraordinary instrument ever assembled: the human hand. For a brain, however developed, is restricted without a hand to carry out its commands. And hands—working, seeking, touching, and solving—have played a crucial role in stimulating the development of the brain. What other parcels of skin and bone can both peel a grape and crush a walnut, can dial a telephone and tickle a baby, can sign a check and perform open-heart surgery? Hands can even "see" in the dark by touch, read braille, paint pictures like the *Mona Lisa*, and type 120 words per minute.

Hands contain one-third of all the sensory receptors in the human body, 27 bones, and a preponderance of the body's sweat glands—a useless, occasionally annoying reminder of the days when moist palms gave apes a surer grip on tree branches. Hands also reveal a great deal about our occupations and our health, although any study of cadavers will show that they are unreliable indicators of longevity.

For reasons that are still unclear, left-handedness has historically been maligned. *Sinister* is the Latin word for "left," as *gauche* is in French—or, as an Englishman might pronounce it, "gawky." On the other hand, we have *dexter* and *droit*, as in "dexterous" and "adroit," in support of right-handed superiority. To be sure, Jack the Ripper was left-handed, but so were Leonardo da Vinci, Charlemagne, Cole Porter, Harry Truman, and Babe Ruth.

Symbols on Moroccan women's hands before a special ceremony assure luck in family matters.

Another unexplained thing, possibly the tip of some evolutionary iceberg: over the past few decades the average glove size for men has declined from 10 to 9, while that for women has increased from 6 to 7.

Hard Liquor License

At the same time that hard liquor has warmed hearts, it has oiled our language. Some words and phrases now in common parlance refer directly to drinking and its effects and consequences. But there are other terms in American English that seem to have no immediate connection with drinking, yet owe their existence to the drinking and making of hard liquor.

One such word is "gibberish," which seems like the noises made by a drunk. The word probably originates from Geber, the Latinized name of the famous 8th-century Arab alchemist Jābir ibn Hayyān. In 14th-century Spain another Geber also wrote on alchemy, hoping that this name would impart greater credibility to his theories. One Geber described distillation in such puzzling language that Samuel Johnson's dictionary credited him with "gibberish."

"Brand name," now in general use to mean the label of any kind of product, also owes its origin to the liquor industry. When early American distillers shipped a barrel of whiskey, they branded their sign on one end of the keg. About the same time, the phrase "at loggerheads" was born. To make a bracing drink called a flip, one mixed strong beer, a sweetener such as sugar or molasses, and rum. The fluid was then stirred with a loggerhead, or red-hot poker. When a lively political argument sprang up in the tavern—sometimes because of too many flips—the disputants were likely to reach beyond words for a loggerhead to swing.

The risky practice can be blamed in part on "Dutch courage," the 17th-century phrase that, falsely or not, presumed that the Dutch were particularly heavy drinkers and boastful in their cups. Or perhaps they were thought to be "cocksure," another general term that springs from drinking practices, and not poultry. It refers to the reliable

An intoxicated strong man

way that a cock, or tap, prevented too much liquor from flowing from its container. No use wasting "grog," a term for firewater that is sometimes used to denote any hard liquor. Originally, grog was a stiff jolt of rum and water. It got its name from Adm. Edward Vernon, a British officer whose men nicknamed him "Old Grog" because he chose to wear a coarse coat made from grogram, a mixture of wool and silk. Vernon was convinced that a daily dose of rum and water would keep his sailors from contracting scurvy.

Luckily for Vernon, his place in history does not rest entirely on watery rum. He is also the namesake of George Washington's beautiful estate in Virginia. By all accounts, Vernon's issue of grog was entirely legal, which means he was not a "bootlegger."

A tipsy prince supported by two concubines is the subject of this Mogul miniature from 18th-century India.

This term may have originated earlier, but really embedded itself in the language during Prohibition. It referred, originally, to the tax evasion practiced by whiskey sellers. They would carefully peel the government's tax stamps from a legal bottle of whiskey, concealing the stamps in their boots until they could be affixed to an illegal bottle—hence, "bootleg." "Bootlegger" came to mean anyone who sells illegal whiskey.

His cousin, usually Southern, is the "moonshiner," who makes a number of different potions, usually at night. Moonshine has no standard but that it be powerful. Here is Irvin S. Cobb's description: "It smells like gangrene starting in a mildewed silo; it tastes like the Wrath to Come; and when you absorb a deep swig of it you have all the sensations of having swallowed a lighted kerosene lamp." It tastes, in short, quite a bit like "hooch" or "booze," both of which were terms for liquor of poor quality and head-cracking potential.

The word "hooch" is attributed, probably unfairly, to the Hoochinoo, which was the name of a Tlingit Indian tribe in Alaska. There seems to be no doubt that in the late 1800's American soldiers stationed near the Indian settlement made a powerful whiskey, but the Indians got blamed for the potion. "Booze" comes from the 14th-century words "bouze," "bouse," and "bowse," which were derived from a Dutch word meaning "to guzzle liquor." All have to do with drinking heavily, so the American distiller E.C. Booz, who put his name on his whiskey, was benefiting from a term centuries old.

Booze, or anything else alcoholic, exacts a price for overuse. This is the "hangover," as in "hung over like a willow tree." In Germany, they say *Katzenjammer*, which means "wailing of cats," and in France overindulgence results in *queule de bois*, or "wooden mouth." How very elegant.

HIGHWAY Bronze Age traders traveled routes across Europe to transport amber from the shores of the Baltic to the Mediterranean and the Adriatic. Two thousand years ago, caravans bearing their precious cargo of silk—also jade, ivory, and furs—plied the elaborate, well-maintained systems of roads between the heart of China and Antioch, in Syria. Centuries before the birth of Christ, the Royal Road of Persia, connecting the Aegean Sea and the city of Susa near the Persian Gulf, served as the backbone of the Persian Empire. Describing the mounted couriers who used this highway, Herodotus noted admiringly that "neither snow, nor rain, nor heat, nor darkness of the night" could stand in their way.

Later, but most remarkable of all, were the two great parallel roads that the Spaniards found on their conquest of the Inca Empire. One, 24 feet wide, ran for 2,250 miles along the coast. The other scaled the heights of the Andes, sometimes in grades too steep for Spanish mules. Because the Incas had no knowledge of the wheel, the road had been designed for surefooted llamas and for seemingly indefatigable human runners who, in

"When the road is a ribbon of moonlight over the purple moor," a poet wrote, "a highwayman comes riding. . . ."

relays, could cover the 1,200 miles from Quito to Cuzco in five to seven days.

The Romans, generally credited with creating the first modern highways, contributed superb engineering and single-minded thoroughness to their construction. With 53,000 miles of main highways

---

customs

Headger

Hats often reveal something about the social status and values of their wearers. Thorstein Veblen, in his *Theory of the Leisure Class* (1899), suggested that elegant gentlemen wore lustrous cylindrical hats to proclaim that "the wearer cannot when so attired bear a hand in any employment that is directly and immediately of any human use."

In almost every culture, headgear has served as a sign of rank. One reason may be its close association with the human brain, which most distinguishes us from other animals. Another is that it is readily visible and enhances the wearer's height. The placement of a royal crown, whether celebrated in a cathedral or a remote African village, symbolizes the marriage between a sovereign and the body politic he will rule. The removal of the hat as a greeting or as a sign of respect may well be related, in a precautionary sense, to the primitive custom of removing articles of

Japanese street flutists wear baskets to hide their faces when passing around the cup after a performance.

clothing as a sign of submission.

Psychiatrists—and purveyors of toupees—have observed that a head of luxuriant hair is frequently thought of as a badge of manliness. This may explain the wide-ranging variety of male headgear that is intended to simulate hair: the war bonnets of the American Indians, the bearskins of the British Brigade of Guards, the round plumed hats of the Italian Bersaglieri, and the red plumes of the French Garde Républicaine.

Large male headgear has been characteristic of patriarchal societies: the conical, towerlike hat of the Assyrians, the familiar broad-brimmed black hat of the Pilgrims, the papal triple tiara. Because women have had fewer occasions to proclaim their rank, headdress has had an entirely different significance for them. In Talmudic times Jewish female headdress was dictated by men and primarily intended as a mark of modesty. A young girl who had not yet attracted a man was permitted a certain amount of self-advertisement, but a married woman was expected to wear a head covering outside the house.

Modesty has long since surrendered to the dictates of fashion, and now hats for both men and women are used more as protection against extremes of climate than as signals about status. Hats are downright necessary for some, especially those in hazardous activities, as miners, football players, bee-keepers, and deep-sea divers will testify.

and another 100,000 miles of secondary roads, the Roman system had more improved roadway than existed in the United States in 1904. A traveler could journey the length of the empire, from Hadrian's Wall in northern Britain to the frontier of Ethiopia, on comfortable roads.

He could also do it in relative safety. By the time travel resumed after the long sleep of the Dark Ages, highwaymen posed such a hazard that King Edward I of England ordered all roads in his realm cleared of trees for a distance of 200 feet on each side. The *Guide des Chemins de France*, published in 1553, included among other useful information for travelers a list of places where brigands were likely to lurk. Nonetheless, in a period of 12 years, no less than 250 highwaymen were hanged at the public gibbet in Tyburn alone.

Through the centuries other hazards persisted

Trade center of Bavay in France enjoyed prosperity thanks to the good cobbled roads leading to it.

as well. When Maria Leszczynska, daughter of the king of Poland, set out for Paris in 1725 to marry Louis XV, thousands of peasants were conscripted to repair the roads over which she would travel. The roads, however, wrote a member of her escort, were so bad that "the Queen was frequently terrified of simply sinking into the morass, and . . . members of her entourage had to remove her by the arms from the coach which had become firmly bogged down."

Bogging down, a problem that had always vexed road builders, was solved by two Scotsmen, Thomas Telford and John Loudon McAdam, during the first quarter of the 19th century. Telford, who almost single-handedly established the practice of civil engineering, earned the nickname "Colossus of Roads." McAdam, a successful administrator as well as an engineer, campaigned to make the

words

Keep It Under Your Hat

As head covering, receptacle, and status symbol, the hat (almost always a man's hat for some reason) has found many niches in colloquial language.

"Old hat," "hats off," and "keep this under your hat," are self-explanatory, but "a feather in one's cap" has several origins. Among American Indians and Lycians it was customary for a warrior to mark the killing of an enemy by adding another feather to his headdress. In Hungary, only one who had slain a Turkish enemy had the honor of adorning his hat with a plume.

"Tossing one's hat into the ring," meaning entering a political race, is attributed to Teddy Roosevelt's announcement of his candidacy in the 1912 presidential campaign. A more elaborate speculation about the origin of that phrase also sheds light on the phrase "at the drop of a hat," which suggests the hair-trigger nature of a true brawler.

At one time tossing one's hat into a ring was the only way to accept a challenge. In the early 18th century, before boxing had formal rules, the local champion set up a makeshift ring at a town or county fair. Any man who wished to challenge him for the championship tossed his hat into the ring. The two combatants chose seconds, and the gory spectacle began. Men fought barefisted, and both fighters were soon covered with blood. Seconds used sponges to wipe off the sweat and blood. Combatants fought until one was knocked out or too exhausted to continue. At that point, the second threw the sponge into the ring to indicate that his man had had enough.

"Doff" and "don" are North English colloquialisms for "do off" and "do on." "Talking through one's hat" is probably what someone does when he gives you an opinion off the top of his head. "Eating one's hat" was first found in Charles Dickens' *Pickwick Papers*: "If I knew as little of life as that, I'd eat my hat and swallow the buckle whole."

In cricket, a bowler who took three wickets on successive balls was entitled to a new hat at the expense of the club. By extension, a "hat trick" in hockey describes the scoring of three goals by a player in one game. And the paid-in-full pension benefits that sometimes go with high executive position are occasionally referred to in England as "top hat arrangements."

construction and repair of roads a full-time government responsibility. For a good roadbed, he recommended using a layer of large rocks followed by a layer of small stones, with gravel or slag as a binding material. He did not, however, consider using bitumen—natural asphalt—as a surface for roads. That idea was first tried in 1854, 18 years after his death, by an anonymous engineer, and is what most people think of when they hear the words "macadam road."

In America the first roads were simply superimposed on old Indian trails, like the Connecticut Path, which led from Boston to Springfield and Hartford. The Post Road, linking Boston and New York, was opened in 1673 and was eventually used to carry mail. By 1729 a letter posted in Boston would reach Williamsburg, Virginia, in four weeks.

One reason for the lack of interest in road building may well have been that as late as 1760 there were only 38 privately owned wheeled vehicles in Philadelphia, and just 22 in Boston in 1768. This changed with the opening of the wilderness. To accommodate westbound settlers, enterprising Yankees imported a recent British invention: the turnpike. The first such road charged travelers the exorbitant amount of $3.10 to cover the 62 miles between Philadelphia and Lancaster. Nonetheless, it proved so profitable that, by the 1830's, 278 private companies were operating turnpikes in New York State alone.

The notion that highways should be freely available to all travelers, as they had been under the Romans, finally occurred to Congress in 1802. Work on the National Road, which followed closely the present U.S. 40, was begun in 1811 and finally reached Illinois in 1838. By then, however, the steam locomotive had come on the scene, convincing many that all other forms of transportation would become obsolete. And so the last sections of the National Road were left unsurfaced.

They might well have remained that way were it not for the bicycle. Introduced to America at the Centennial Exposition in Philadelphia, the new device became so popular that bicycling clubs sprang up all over the country and soon banded together into the League of American Wheelmen. Its purpose was "to ascertain, defend, and protect the rights of wheelmen, to encourage and facilitate touring." The indispensable requirement of touring was roads to tour on. Politicians, influenced by railroad interests, had ignored with impunity the demands of the owners of the 8,000 automobiles registered in the United States in 1900. But when 4 million bicycle owners spoke up, they were wise enough to listen.

words

Hellos

"Hello" is probably the most common form of greeting in the English-speaking world. Of uncertain origin, the word is believed to be essentially onomatopoeic—an imitation of instinctive human sounds that people have made since ancient times in calling to one another. The "hello" we know first came into general use in the second half of the 19th century, although English hunters have been "hallooing" to their dogs across field and forest as far back as anyone can trace, and Frenchmen have been shouting "holà" to flag down coach and ferrymen for centuries. As a quick friendly greeting, Englishmen in Chaucer's time were likely to say "hallow," with the accent on the *ow*, and Shakespeare's characters added "hillo," "hollo," "holloa," and "hilloa."

In 19th-century America "hullo" was a popular country greeting. The telephone eventually gave the word new importance. When the first switchboard was set up in the salty town of New Haven, Connecticut, someone decreed that phones should be answered with a brisk "Ahoy, ahoy." But good sense and the practical genius of Thomas A. Edison prevailed. Edison is supposed to have been the first man to say "hello" into the speaker. Almost overnight, telephone operators became known as "hello girls," and in 1901 Charles K. Harris, the ballad maker, penned the immortal song "Hello, Central, Give Me Heaven," about a young girl trying to reach her mother in heaven.

"Hello" lost some of its bright-penny shine in the 1920's when Texas Guinan took to greeting customers at her speakeasy with "Hello, sucker!" Not long after, Emily Post pronounced "hello" as vulgar, though she thought a pleasant tone of voice might ameliorate its effect. Under no circumstances, however, was it to be used in church or even on church grounds after services, because it was at best "too familiar."

Telephone operators were called "hello girls" in 1882 when this photograph was taken in Richmond, Virginia.

HOSIERY In 1560 Queen Elizabeth's silk-woman presented Her Majesty with a pair of black knit silk stockings for a New Year's gift. "And from that time unto her death, the Queen never wore anymore cloth hose," reported John Stow, a contemporary chronicler. Because gowns were floor length, this switch in the queen's wardrobe was noticed only by a favored few. Fewer still were aware that Queen Mary, the redoubtable grandmother of the present Elizabeth, sometimes wore stockings with a colorful band of Union Jacks around their tops.

Unusual hosiery—putteed landing gear—on "Plane" by Tyler Hoare.

Originally full-length, leg-hugging hose in colors and patterns were for men only, while women wore plainer styles. Mary Queen of Scots put on her finest for the executioner, including blue stockings with modest silver decorations at the ankle. By the 1700's, however, when ladies' ankles were permitted to peep out below the hemline, embroidered designs became fashionable—largely to hide the stockings' side seams. Called clocks, they are still on men's hosiery, the vestigial remains of this practice. Flesh-colored stockings became prized during the Directoire period in France (1795–99), when clinging, transparent fabrics required the illusion of nudity underneath.

Sheer silk stockings did not become popular until the 1920's, but they were costly and manufacturers began a search for substitute fibers. The hosiery makers' red-letter day is October 27, 1938, the day on which the Du Pont company announced that it had received a patent for what one newspaper had described as a "new silk made on a chemical base." They called it nylon. When stockings made of this miracle yarn went on test sale a year later in Wilmington, Delaware, stores announced that they would honor delivery only on local orders, so that market researchers could more easily compile data on customers' reactions. To their surprise they discovered that women from New York, Baltimore, and Philadelphia had rented hotel rooms or apartments just so they could qualify to buy them.

Good as it was, nylon has not lived up to all its expectations: "New hosiery held 'strong as steel'," promised a newspaper headline in 1938, but it never happened. Indeed, one of the banes of hosiery manufacturers is the recurrent rumor that locked away in a secure vault is a formula for a runproof stocking. In reply, they could well point to the sheer technological feat of producing hosiery in the first place. A pair of panty hose consists of 4 miles of yarn, half as thick as human hair and knitted into 3 million individual loops.

HOSPITAL The moral concept that man had a responsibility to care for the afflicted was well established centuries before the Christian parable of the good Samaritan. It is known that hospitals existed in Ceylon in 437 B.C., and a memorial stone put up by King Ashoka of India in the 3rd century B.C. recalls that "everywhere the King Priyadarschin, beloved of God, erected two kinds of hospitals, for men and for animals. Wherever there were no healing herbs . . . he commanded that they be brought and planted."

Wars created a large-scale need for hospitals. As their empire grew and soldiers no longer could be sent home for treatment, the Romans established a chain of military hospitals. One of the hospitals, excavated near modern-day Düsseldorf, Germany, was said to be "much in advance of any military hospital until quite modern times." Although Jerusalem already had a Christian hospital, built to care for pilgrims to the Holy Land, the Crusades occasioned the founding of several knightly orders devoted to the care of the sick. One, the Order of St. John, survives as the Sovereign Order of Malta. This order still operates hospitals and cares for the sick in many parts of the world.

If one had the misfortune to fall sick in 1284, the most comfortable (and safest) place to be was in Cairo, site of the al-Mansur hospital. There, patients were cared for in airy, spacious wards cooled by murmuring fountains. Musicians and

A medieval hospital with outpatient service is shown in this illuminated manuscript from 15th-century Florence.

storytellers lulled the sleepless, and 50 readers recited the Koran. Upon discharge, convalescents were given the equivalent of $12 so that they would not have to return to work immediately.

Cairo's fine facility was one of the few exceptions, however. In most of the world, ignorance, rather than callousness and cruelty, produced abominable conditions in would-be houses of healing. More than a thousand years after it was founded in the mid-7th century, inmates at the Hôtel-Dieu hospital in Paris were packed three to six in one bed, regardless of their sex or state of health. Food was miserable and doled out preferentially to those who were most zealous about reciting their rosaries. The air in the unlighted halls was so fetid that attendants would not enter without a vinegar-soaked sponge pressed to their faces. Recovery from surgery was rare, and the death rate for all patients was about 20 percent. Indeed, London's St. Bartholomew's hospital, founded in 1123, required patients to pay a burial deposit upon admittance (a practice that remained in effect until 1836).

Dirty, overcrowded hospitals were always a problem: here corpse and patient share, in print by Daumier.

The lying-in hospitals of Europe, established to assist indigent mothers to give birth and recover their strength, became from the mid-1600's to the late 1800's chronic purveyors of childbed, or puerperal, fever (a streptococcal infection). During much of that period the disease killed 10 to 20 percent of all who entered—and most poor women had nowhere else to go. The epicenter of one epidemic that stormed across Europe from 1773 to 1776 seemed to be Lombardy, Italy, where the fever supposedly claimed the life of every hospitalized new mother for an entire year. The causes of the disease were variously attributed to the weather, or as Dr. Oliver Wendell Holmes conjectured, "within the walls of lying-in hospitals there is often generated a miasma . . . which has killed women in an Old World hospital so fast that they were buried two in a coffin to conceal its horrors."

Conditions in those charity hospitals were uniformly wretched, whether the women occupied filthy, unventilated individual stalls, as in La Maternité in Paris, or shared floorspace covered with straw and dirty linen, as in Budapest. Deplorable conditions persisted even after enlightened physicians understood the need for cleanliness. One doctor described a situation at the hospital in Graz, Austria, in 1858. While waiting for their next delivery in the dissection room, the students would "often devote their attention to dissecting [unembalmed cadavers of recent victims of disease]. When they are summoned to the lying-in hospital . . . they do not make any pretense at disinfection. . . . The students cross the street with hands wet and bloody from dissecting; they dry their hands in the air, and stick them a few times into their pockets, and at once proceed to make examinations."

Fortunately for patients in future generations, those centuries of ignorance and filth were drawing to a close. By the turn of the century asepsis was the rule rather than the exception, and hospitals became genuine houses of healing—well equipped and staffed with trained personnel.

The revolution in medical care that has occurred in the past few decades has largely centered on the hospital. Virtually the only piece of equipment that is not totally new is the bed, though even that has been improved—at a price. A bed, with an "air-fluidized" mattress, intended to soothe burn victims, paralytics, and chronic insomniacs with a flow of humidified air, costs about $8,000.

Other modern equipment—kidney dialysis machines, automated blood-gas analyzers, ultrasonic probes, linear accelerators for radiation treatment—is even more expensive. A single computerized axial tomography scanner can cost in the neighborhood of $1,000,000. Whether such devices, which can serve only a relatively few individuals and are idle at other times, are worth the money, or help mainly to increase hospital costs and therefore the costs to society, is a subject for ethical debate. What virtually everyone seems to agree on is that, technology aside, hospitals could be doing a better and more humane job of caring for patients' well-being. In the U.S. 10,000 nurses were asked, among other questions, whether they would willingly choose to be a patient in their own place of employment. More than 38 percent replied, "No."

There is progress. A New York architect has proposed that in hospitals of the future the conventional rooms be replaced by plastic capsules that would enclose the patient in a germ-free environment. The capsules would travel on an overhead electric monorail system, whisking the patient to X-ray, treatment, recovery, or visiting areas. Holding tanks and a self-contained incineration system, with access through a trapdoor in the mattress, would eliminate bedpans.

And a little buzzer system could be built into the capsule, so that nurses could wake up patients in order to give them their sleeping pills.

HOT DOG Americans delight in devouring hot dogs, and do so at the rate of 80 per person per year—enough to reach to the moon and back two and a half times. In fact, hot dogs already have been there, as finger food for the moon-bound Apollo astronauts. Strictly speaking, however, a hot dog takes on its true identity only when a frankfurter is added to a roll. According to one source, it was in St. Louis in 1883 that this union was first slapped together by a sausage peddler named Feuchtwanger.

The frankfurter itself has an older pedigree, dating from 1852, when members of the butchers' guild in Frankfurt, Germany, created and named it. According to legend, one of the butchers owned a dachshund, and so the sausage was drawn and shaped to match the dog's long body. Shipped to America, "dachshund sausages" became instantly popular but were rechristened "hot dogs," according to another story, because a New York newspaper cartoonist had trouble spelling "dachshund."

Today hot dogs are most closely linked to baseball—and to thrift. Though they may not seem so, they are relatively inexpensive and only the most inept cook can ruin them. In addition, they permit meat companies to use more of an animal than the public might otherwise accept. Over the years,

such inelegant parts as snouts, ears, stomachs, spleens, lips, lungs, and even salivary glands have found their way into the grinder and thence to frankfurter casings.

The need for a truly inexpensive hot dog led to the founding of Nathan's, the world's most famous hot-dog emporium, at Coney Island, New York, in 1916. Nathan Handwerker, an employee at a restaurant that sold hot dogs for a dime, launched the boardwalk establishment, cutting his price to a nickel. He reportedly did so on the advice of a singing waiter and his piano accompanist: Eddie Cantor and Jimmy Durante.

Hot dogs became a part of baseball in 1893, when peddlers first hawked them at St. Louis Browns games. Babe Ruth so loved hot dogs that he once devoured a dozen, along with eight bottles of soda, during a game. Shortly thereafter the Babe was rushed to a nearby hospital to have his stomach pumped out. Prodigious though it may have seemed, Ruth's repast was but a snack in the lexicon of hot-dog munching. The world's record stands at 21, only nine more than Ruth's total, but they were consumed in 4 minutes and 15 seconds, or one every 12 seconds.

HOTEL By and large, the most serious hazard facing the modern traveler who stops at an unfamiliar hotel is that he will receive a bill that is well padded and a mattress that is not. In 1315, however, the practice of murdering travelers in order to steal their luggage was so firmly established on the European continent that the king of France ordered innkeepers to pay a heavy fine if any of their guests should meet an untimely death while under their roofs.

Hotels and inns are as ancient as travel. The Bible mentions, of course, the crowded inn in Bethlehem and an earlier one at which the sons of Jacob stopped on their return from Egypt. Romans maintained overnight accommodations along their highway network, and Marco Polo stayed at relay houses during his long journey through China.

In 1577 the author of *Description of England* wrote glowingly of "sumptuous innes . . . very well furnished with naperie" where "each commer is due to lie in cleane sheets wherein no man hath beene lodged since they came from the laundresse." There were, in fact, some 6,000 inns in England at that time.

In colonial America, however, travelers were not so lucky. They were fortunate to find any kind of sheets on the beds or, indeed, any unoccupied bed. Most inns had only two sleeping rooms, one for men and one for women—though

Skiers "hotdogging," or showing off fancy maneuvers: the idiom comes from the exclamation "Hot dog!"

even this distinction was not stringently enforced. The first five or six guests to arrive took the bed; the later arrivals were relegated to the floor. The custom of "no privacy" was so well established that in 1794, when the first modern hotel in the United States, the City Hotel in New York, opened, it could boast of having 73 rooms but none of them with locks.

This, together with the practice of hotel keeping, changed on October 16, 1829, with the opening of Boston's Tremont House. Designed by a Yankee, Isaiah Rogers, to be a "palace for the people," the Tremont occupied a square block and was America's largest building at that time. It contained richly carpeted drawing rooms and public parlors, and a dining room that could seat 200 guests. Its reading room was stocked not only with books but also with the latest American and foreign newspapers—at a time when Boston did not have a single public library. The Tremont House also had 170 single and double rooms, all with keys. Among its other innovations were desk clerks, bellboys, and indoor plumbing ("eight water closets and eight bathing rooms" located in the basement). For the use of these facilities, guests were charged the uniform rate of $2 a day, including four meals. Overnight, the Tremont House set a new standard for hotels.

In 1888 the little-known Victoria Hotel in Kansas City, Missouri, became the first to boast a bath for every room. Ten years later the Bristol, which next to the newly opened Ritz was the most elegant hotel in Paris, still had only one bathroom per floor. Guests wishing to take a private bath could order one from the Bath-at-Home-Service, which would deliver an empty tub and tanks of water to their rooms.

The best hotel rooms have a personality of their own: this one in California comes equipped with a water mill.

Puttin' On The Ritz

Ritz, by Madame Ritz

A good number of men and women, from Amelia Bloomer and Captain Charles Boycott to the Earl of Sandwich and the Reverend William Spooner, are remembered as nouns in the language. Far fewer individuals have made a contribution so unusual or distinctive that they have been immortalized as adjectives.

One of them, César Ritz, was born in the Swiss village of Niederwald in 1850. The 13th child of a farming couple, he tended the family's cows until his father insisted that he become an apprentice wine waiter at a nearby hotel. After a year he was not only fired but told, "You'll never make anything of yourself in the hotel business. It takes a special gift, and you haven't got it." He tried again, was fired again, moved to Paris and was fired a third time—for breaking dishes.

A lesser man would have called it a career, but Ritz persevered and gradually rose through the ranks of restaurants and hotels in Nice, Monte Carlo, Lucerne, Baden-Baden, and other watering spots of the rich and titled. By 1888 he had made enough of a name for himself that a former client, Rupert D'Oyly Carte, invited him to manage a new luxury hotel being built in London. The hotel—the Savoy—became a sensation, largely because of its elegance, perfect service, and the fact that Ritz had brought with him a chef named Auguste Escoffier.

In 1896 Ritz was persuaded to open a hotel in Paris that would bear his name. He took two years to find a suitable building—a mansion on the elegant Place Vendôme—and assemble the right furnishings. Ever assiduous, he ordered apricot-colored lampshades, believing that their muted light was more flattering to women.

There are now Ritz hotels in a half-dozen cities, some better and some ritzier than others. There are also dozens of enterprises in London and New York alone, from shirt-makers to a fish-and-chips shop that bear the august name. "The Ritz is *not* ritzy," César's son said when told that his father's hotels might be too fancy for some. What it is, its celebrated guests agree, is the sort of place that makes its wealthiest clients feel as if they have not left home, or at least that they have all the conveniences and thoughtful attention they might receive while visiting a hospitable friend. The hotel's secret of success lay in Ritz's daily reminder to his staff: "People like to be served, but invisibly." Perhaps he was inspired by the memory of his own bumbling forays as a waiter.

Competition prompted hotels to offer an impressive number of innovations, including the first innerspring mattress, invented in 1831 by a manufacturer of women's bustles, the first bathtub, as well as hot running water and steam heat. The Tremont House, which had started it all, also pioneered the use of four-tined forks, which patrons took to calling divided spoons. Hotels popularized the use of telephones, gas jets—later, electric lights—safe-deposit boxes, and elevators. One "first," however, proved premature. When it opened in 1870, the Palmer House advertised itself as the first fireproof building in Chicago, a claim that went up in smoke during the Great Fire the following year.

In addition to serving the needs of travelers, hotels have been freely used by novelists, playwrights, and filmmakers. *Grand Hotel*, which starred Greta Garbo, Joan Crawford, and two Barrymores, was supposedly set in Berlin's palatial Adlon Hotel. *Separate Tables, Weekend at the Waldorf, Room Service, Hotel Sahara, The Horn Blows at Midnight, Stage Door, The Best Man*, and *Plaza Suite* are only a few of the dozens of plays and movies that have used the compartmentalized world of the hotel as a setting.

Hotel rooms have also served as settings for real-life drama. One of the most famous—the original "smoke-filled room"—was Suite 408–10 at the Blackstone in Chicago where, after long hours of haggling on June 11, 1920, a group of Republican leaders at the party's national convention broke the deadlock and nominated as presidential candidate a well-meaning senator from Ohio named Warren Gamaliel Harding.

In the early 1900's one town in Illinois suspected that many epidemics were fly-borne and provided a fly trap for every family. These boys received theirs at school.

HOUSEFLY Flies have lived more comfortably with man than man has with flies. Since the beginnings of communal life, these pesky creatures have attended his migrations, crazed his beasts, and invaded his food. In the Old Testament, God considered flies annoying and pestilential enough to inflict as a plague upon Egypt, and, as the Bible tells it, "there came great swarms of flies into the house of Pharoah and into his servants' houses, and in all the land of Egypt the land was ruined by reason of the flies." The homes of Moses and his people, however, remained unmolested.

The common housefly (*Musca domestica*) flourishes only in close association with human society, breeding rapidly in animal and human wastes and in rotting vegetable matter. The insect speeds from egg to maturity in about two weeks. It is the most widely distributed insect in the world, surviving from subpolar regions to the tropics by being adaptable, omnivorous, explorative, and prolific.

"Kill a fly in May, you've kept thousands away," goes an old English rhyme. The observation is borne out by research, which posits that a single female, laying her first 120 eggs in the spring, commonly in April, could number by September some 325,923,200,000,000 descendants. In a laboratory in India, a chunk of manure about 6 inches square was observed to hatch 4,042 flies. Luckily, nature prevents the survival of all these offspring.

Though some find the housefly charming, admiring its catlike habit of washing itself, others have long suspected it of spreading disease. In 1498 Bishop Knud of Denmark noted that the approach of plague was often heralded by an increase in flies. It was only after the science of bacteriology became established that the housefly's unhealthy habit of flitting from sewage to sauce fell under scientific scrutiny. Today the housefly is accused of carrying many diseases, including dysentery, typhoid, cholera, salmonellosis, tuberculosis, and leprosy.

Surprisingly, however, the fly has also been a healer of disease. World War I doctors noticed that "flyblown" wounds often healed quickly, and some particularly resistant infections came to be treated successfully with sterile housefly maggots. This crawly cure became unnecessary when medical researchers extracted the healing substances, allantoin and urea, which the maggots excrete.

Through the ages, man has tried to swat, squash, fry, trap, and poison flies, but to small avail. The species has withstood even such toxic insecticides as DDT, evolving resistant strains with amazing rapidity. To date, the most effective widespread control of the housefly has been won by modern sanitation and by the automobile, which evicted the horse (and what is important about that fact—horse manure) from urban life. But wherever man lives primitively or keeps animals, the persistent fly will go on buzzing in his ear and dropping in his soup.

HOUSEPLANT The ancient Greeks were among the first people on record to take up the hobby of growing plants indoors. About 2,500 years ago they kept small exotic plants, probably imported from Persia and India, in bell-shaped jars, or terrariums. For the wealthy, these "gardens of Apollo" were but a vicarious delight, particularly since the potting and care of the plants was delegated to household servants. Later, the Romans built large glass-enclosed greenhouses for cultivating full-size fruit trees, grape vines, vegetables, and flowers. One of these plant-forcing houses, excavated in the ruins of Pompeii, was apparently heated and humidified by steam, conveyed by terra-cotta pipes from outside boilers.

During the Middle Ages, when much of the Western world was involved in wars and political upheaval, the raising of herbs and medicinal plants survived only in the relative calm of monasteries. The monks wrote some of the earliest treatises on the care of houseplants and made careful drawings of some of the specimens of their time. Many of the Latin and Greek names given to the plants by those early horticulturists are

The top of a stand made in China for a picture scroll depicts different kinds of indoor plants in magnificent vases as dominant household adornments.

still used by modern-day indoor gardeners.

During the Renaissance, European horticulturists kept citrus trees in rustic buildings (called orangeries) during the summer and put them in heated cellars during the winter. One orangery built in 1619 in Heidelberg, Germany, held 400 trees.

Perhaps the biggest boon to indoor gardening came in 1687 when a Frenchman invented a method of making clear, flat glass. Louis XIV had the new glass installed in expansive windows in the palace at Versailles, and soon court ladies had potted plants growing on the windowsills of nearly every boudoir and salon in the palace. The king himself at one time had a glass-enclosed orangery containing 1,500 plants.

"Parlor gardening" flourished in England in the late 1800's and was quickly adopted in the United States. In 1884 a book written by Miss Cornelia J. Randolph (a granddaughter of Thomas Jefferson) helped to popularize houseplants in America. The author advised that the choice of houseplants should be "governed by the style of the parlor to be beautified" and warned that ageratum, with tiny white or blue flowers, was "well down the social ladder" compared with the showy gladiolus and oxalis.

The current rage for houseplants began in the 1940's as a way to soften the spare and stark interiors of "modern" houses. But as early as 1905 architect Frank Lloyd Wright had begun designing houses that were to be a "wedding" of nature with the indoors and included indoor gardens. Today no interior, whether it be a corporate office, hospital, truck stop, bowling alley, or an office in the executive wing of the White House, is complete without a display of ivy, rubber trees, or hanging ferns.

Although it may not fit most people's first definition of "houseplant," the ivy engulfing this cottage built in 1615 near Ash, England, adds new dimensions to the word.

A table-size bonsai maple tree looks as if it belongs in a fall landscape.

Americans spend some $2 billion a year buying houseplants, some of it at plant parties where the salesperson extols the beauties and joys of plant ownership. Those dollars are seeding the pot for many auxiliary businesses. There are roomscape planners for office and home, indoor plant maintenance people, and those who do not want to get too emotionally involved or tied down can rent-a-plant. At least one record company offers a recording of music that is purported to soothe plants. (Some experts believe that plants respond to speech, thoughts, and prayers.) "Plant doctors," a new group of healers, are available to care for ailing plants. And they make house calls.

HYPODERMIC Sir Christopher Wren, the English architect who designed St. Paul's Cathedral in London, was probably the first to inject a drug into a living organism. Wren made his device from an animal bladder and a hollow quill. In 1656 he began using this instrument and, by squeezing the bladder, injected opium and another drug into the veins of dogs. The pooches survived the experiments little the worse for wear. A year later he made what was probably the first attempt to inject a human being. According to one story, the subject was a misbehaving servant at the Court of St. James's. Before the injection could be administered, however, the fellow fainted (or shrewdly pretended to lose consciousness) and spared himself further discomfort.

Although Wren's methods were crude, his contribution was one of the most important in medical history. For the first time drugs could be introduced into the bloodstream so that their effect is almost immediate. However, some of the early experiments had discouraging results, and the practice was used only intermittently.

In 1853 a Scottish doctor, Alexander Wood, gave injections with a glass syringe and plunger fitted with a needle, forerunner of our modern hypodermic (a word derived from the Greek, meaning "under the skin"). Wood called his device an "elegant little syringe." His patient was an elderly spinster whose neuralgia kept her from sleeping. Like other doctors of his time, Wood was unaware of the dangers of morphine, so he loaded his hypodermic with a heroic dose (two-fifths of a grain) of the narcotic in a sherry solution and gave her a shot. The patient slept so soundly that the doctor had difficulty arousing her when he visited the next morning.

In the same year a French doctor, Charles Gabriel Pravaz, injected horses experimentally with a metal hypodermic. Pravaz's "hypo" did not have a plunger; the solution was forced through the needle by screwing a piston into the syringe. Although Dr. Wood is generally given credit for being the first to use hypodermic therapy, Dr. Pravaz is called the "father of the hypodermic method" in many standard medical histories.

Since the time of Wood and Pravaz, hypodermics have been improved vastly; most noticeably, their smaller size eases the sting of the needle, but they still hurt. Through modern metallurgy, needles in outside diameters of sixteen-hundredths of an inch can be produced. Syringes are usually of tempered glass, which can withstand rapid temperature changes from freezing to boiling. One of the most effective developments is the disposable, sterile syringe prefilled with medication in standard dosages. It permits medical and emergency personnel to administer lifesaving drugs within seconds. Mass inoculations, like those at military induction centers, are sometimes made with a needle-less hypodermic gun, which shoots the vaccine through the skin in a high-pressure jet, usually with less pain than with a needle. However, the best way to avoid the ouch, according to doctors, is to relax and think of something pleasant.

The formidable hypodermic needle actually delivers—sometimes lifesaving—serums with little pain.

IMAGES: *New Perceptions*

Vitamins that look like magic carpets (above), mites of monstrous proportion, skulls in rainbow hues. From beyond the range of the senses they come—new images of everyday things. Created by energies the eye cannot normally perceive and technologies it cannot match, these late 20th-century probes into the depths of the commonplace are often beautiful, sometimes bizarre, and almost always informative. Vitamin C crystals, for example, when heated, magnified 80 times, and illuminated by polarized light, produce the exquisite kaleidoscopic portrait shown above. On the pages that follow, dozens of equally astonishing and often scientifically important pictures of ordinary things appear, almost all transcribed by segments of the radiant spectrum we never see—X-rays, beams of electrons, infrared and laser light. The result is a remarkable gallery of scenes from beyond the limits of visible light, images that reexamine ordinary things and reveal new continents within the old.

Animal

Without cues, the human eye reads the unknown in familiar terms: the picture below might be of a tropical plant; that at the right, of an Arctic ravine. Both, in fact, show minuscule portions of the most pedestrian of everyday things—a feather and an egg. These unique views of the animal world beguile the untrained eye, and for excellent reasons: they are highly magnified and project an intense, almost three-dimensional feeling. Both images are the work of a remarkable device, a scanning electron microscope, that uses a beam of electrons to create on a cathode-ray tube pictures of the microworld we would otherwise never see. An impossible accomplishment? Not these days, and certainly not as difficult as threading a bee's stinger through the eye of a needle (far right, bottom).

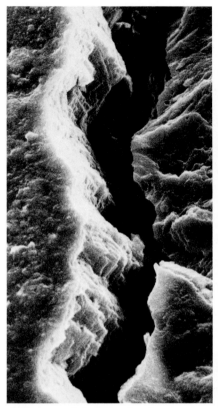

A tiny crack in an unbroken egg shell becomes a yawning canyon when magnified 7,000 times by a scanning electron microscope.

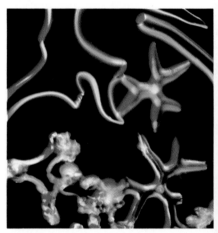

Even sponges have bones, or spicules, but when exposed to polarized light they might be bits of rainbow.

Palm frond or prehistoric plant? The scanning scene at left shows a pheasant feather magnified 200 times.

A dust mite, enlarged nearly 1,000 times in this scanning micrograph, looks like a man-eater.

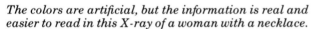

The colors are artificial, but the information is real and easier to read in this X-ray of a woman with a necklace.

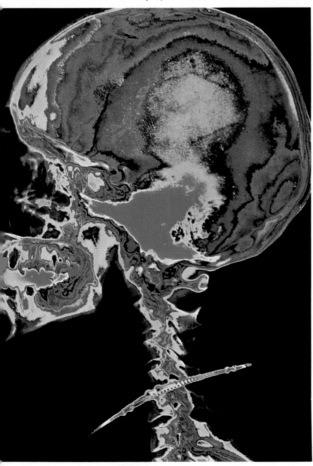

Magnified 6,500 times, this tinted scanning scene shows a single skirmish in the body's war on disease: a white cell eats up an invader.

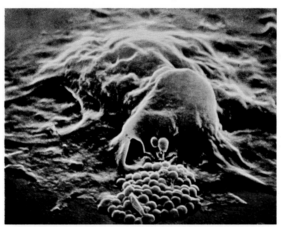

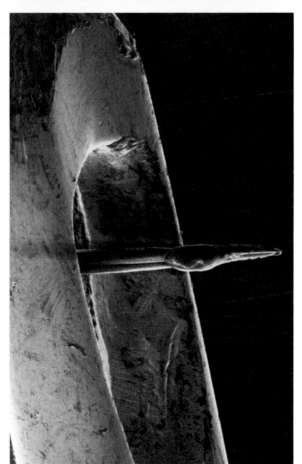

In a magnified comparison with a bee's stinger, the eye of a needle seems crude at best.

Vegetable

The human eye scans the everyday world through a tiny crack in the radiation universe—the world of visible light. Yet over this narrow band of energy, man exerts a degree of influence that he cannot match with any other form of radiation. The shimmering beauty of flowers reflected in dewdrops and the delicacy of bread molds in a light microscope are two examples from the plant world of man's light-taming skills. But it is in the development of a new sort of light—laser light—that researchers have most dramatically altered the way we record everyday things. Laser beams are capable of creating unique patterns on film known as holograms (far right, bottom). When illuminated, holograms produce three-dimensional images, pictures the eye can "look" into and in which, by moving from side to side, the eye can pick out objects located to the side and even behind other elements perceived in the frontal view.

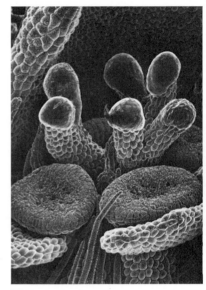

The spurge flower is easy to miss in sidewalk cracks, where it grows, but not when magnified 320 times.

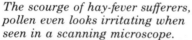

The scourge of hay-fever sufferers, pollen even looks irritating when seen in a scanning microscope.

Kirlian photography created the picture below—after the leaf was removed. Proponents of the method, which uses electricity and film, say it reveals a kind of organic energy.

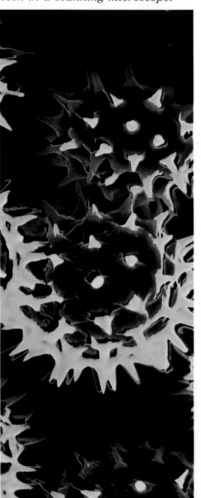

Magnified by an electron microscope, the fibers in a facial tissue look like jungle vines.

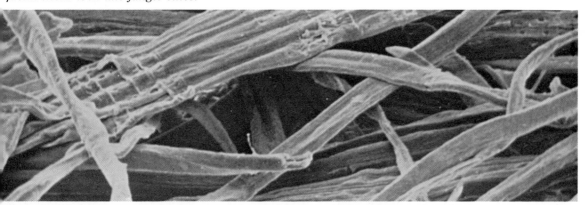

Acting like lenses, dewdrops create a cascade of flowers. Picture was taken with a standard camera and magnified 5 times.

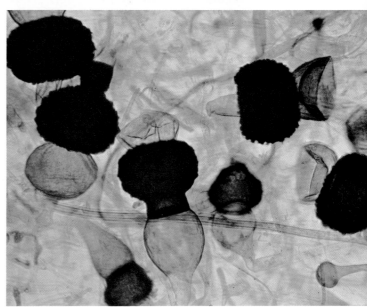

Magnified 40 times in a light microscope, bread molds are fragile and translucent.

Created on film by laser beams, holograms are light-controlling patterns and not pictures. When lit (a red laser was used below), they produce three-dimensional images.

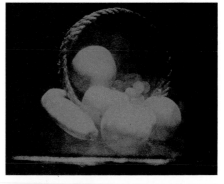

Mineral

"The whole of science," Albert Einstein once wrote, "is nothing more than a refinement of everyday thinking." And a reexamination of everyday things, he might have added, as these remarkable images from the mineral world indicate with such spectral beauty. For each reveals, because of the way it was made or enhanced, something unique about its subject matter. Taken with a combination of techniques, the picture at far right (top) shows shock waves bending in front of a speeding bullet, while the X-ray to its left reveals the shadowy substance of a seashell. Both echo in visual terms another of Einstein's thoughts: "The most beautiful thing we can experience is the mysterious. It is the source of all true art and science."

This snowflake was trapped and photographed on a cold glass plate.

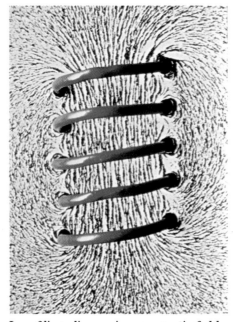

Iron filings line up in a magnetic field.

Giant cable or barbed wire? This scanning micrograph shows a single stitch in a nylon stocking. More than 700 are required to produce a square inch of fabric.

Color-coded for clarity, an X-ray of a jeep becomes a portrait of a candy-coated car.

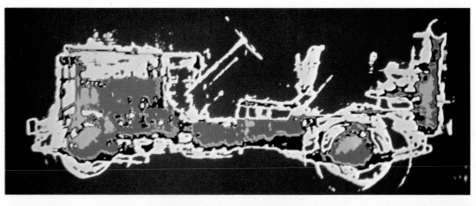

X-ray at the left reveals the symmetry of a
spindle shell from the Philippines.

In less than a thousandth of a second, a bullet
and its shock waves zip over a flame.

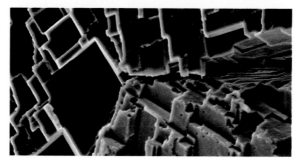

Magnified 2,800 times, cast aluminum reveals a
structure as angular as an urban map.

Dimension

Like high magnification, great distance, if tamed by new technologies, can create extraordinary pictures of hidden worlds we might otherwise never explore. The exquisitely honed tolerances of a 200-inch telescope in California, for example, drew from deep space the ghostly portrait of Orion's Great Nebula shown at right. Captured by the technological might of the Apollo space program, the picture at bottom reveals the cool daintiness of planet Earth as it could never be seen without space travel. Even heat radiation and laser light can narrow the breadth of space, be it as great as that above a roaring Caribbean hurricane (far right, top) or as intimate as the few inches in a three-dimensional holographic study of a man (far right, bottom).

Photographed at high speed in a tube, light waves appear as concentric circles.

On their way to the moon, the men of Apollo 16 looked back and made this picture of home.

More than 1,600 light-years out in space, the Great Nebula of Orion glows with spectral energy.

186

High above the Gulf of Mexico, an infrared sensor on board a Nimbus satellite record-ed this view of Hurricane Camille. Color was added to identify cold cloud patterns (white and blue).

These images of Andy Warhol, in which he is seen opening and closing a paper, were made from a single curved hologram. Known as an integram, because it blends in holographic form the frames of a movie, such a hologram actually shows motion in three dimensions.

ICE CREAM The first dish of ice cream, according to one authority, probably was made thousands of years ago when someone accidentally left a bowl of milk outside on a cold night. Another expert theorized that perhaps the "milk and honey" referred to in the Bible was actually an early ice cream. The Chinese definitely were mixing snow and fruit juices 3,000 years ago to make desserts, and Alexander the Great in the 4th century B.C. enjoyed ice cream made from honey, fruit juice, and milk, which was frozen with snow carried down from the mountains by relays of slaves. The first written recipe for ice cream is believed to have been set down by a Roman general, Quintus Maximus, who was nicknamed *Gurgeo* ("the Glutton").

Ice-cream making seems to have been forgotten in Europe until 1295, when Marco Polo brought recipes for water and milk ices to Venice from Peking. When Catherine de Medici married the French Duc d'Orléans (later Henry II) in 1533, she brought *gelatieri* (ice-cream makers) to France as part of her retinue. When the daughter of Henry IV married Charles I of England in 1685, ice cream crossed the English Channel. Charles was so taken with the delicacy that he is reported to have paid the ice-cream chef handsomely to keep his favorite recipe a secret from the commoners.

By 1700 the treat had become popular among the well-to-do in the American colonies. In a single hot summer, in 1790, George Washington ran up a tab for $200 with a New York ice-cream merchant. Two decades later Dolley Madison served ice cream at a state dinner in the White House (probably strawberry, since it was described by one of the guests as "a large, shining dome of pink").

Americans took to ice cream with a passion. An American woman, Nancy Johnson, invented the hand-cranked freezer in 1846, and a few years later an enterprising resident of Baltimore built the first ice-cream factory. In 1859, the first year the United States began keeping statistics on ice-cream eating, the country consumed about 4,000 gallons.

By the end of the century, consumption had increased more than a thousandfold—to over 5 million gallons. Today Americans consume more than a billion gallons of ice cream and related frozen confections a year—in excess of 20 quarts for every man, woman, and child—which is well above the total for any other nation.

With typical American inventiveness, ice-cream entrepreneurs devised variations on the basic theme. In the fall of 1874 a soft-drink concessionaire in Philadelphia added ice cream to his carbonated beverages, and the ice-cream soda was born. The concoction was so good that many ministers considered it too sinfully enjoyable for the Sabbath and preached against it. One proprietor of an ice-cream parlor in Evanston, Illinois (and perhaps others), where the town fathers had legislated against the "Sunday Soda Menace," thought of circumventing the law by omitting the carbonated water—just ice cream and syrup. The delight was first called a "Sunday" and later the more elegant "sundae."

At the St. Louis fair in 1904, or so the story goes, an ice-cream vendor ran short of dishes. Next door, a maker of thin Persian waffles rolled one of his confections into a cornucopia, and the ice-cream cone was introduced.

In 1919 a boy in an Iowa sweet shop faced a terrible quandary: he wanted candy *and* ice cream but only had a nickel. He finally chose the ice cream, but the owner, inspired by the awful decision, invented the chocolate-and-ice-cream Eskimo Pie. An Ohio confectioner imported the Iowan's idea, but his fastidious daugh-

Nearly 150 years ago, Boston's Washington Street rejoiced in Lee's Saloon, where the band played "The Ice-Cream Quick Step" as patrons were served giant scoops.

Idiom or Idiocy?

If someone is "cut out" to "cut up," shouldn't he or she really "cut it out?"

If a "yellow-dog contract" is nothing but "a pig in a poke," one that promises "pie in the sky," can a "wildcat strike" be called?

When a young mother "puts" her children "down," is she tucking them into bed or is she criticizing them?

How does one explain such weird and wonderful expressions in a language as rich as English, especially to a foreigner? One does not—at least not very easily—and that, according to the guardians of our language, is "part and parcel" of the definition of an idiom.

Nonetheless, most grammarians and linguists do agree that idioms are (1) peculiar, (2) pervasive, (3) approved by usage only, and (4) do not mean what they say. For a "wallflower" is certainly not found on wallpaper, not any more than "hot dogs" stick their tongues out and pant. And a "wet blanket" at a beach party is certainly not a kind of bed covering left too long at the tideline, or a "red herring" a colorful, gustatory delight, or "red tape" sticky, useful, and stored on spools.

Don't care what others think? You are as "independent as a hog on ice."

How illogical they all are, and yet how drab speech would be without its sprinkling of idioms. For they are the shooting stars of language, its archeological shards, its penny poetry chants.

Many idioms, of course, are now clichés, and so some purists try to weed them out. Others prefer to pull them up and examine their roots, a task at once instructive and delightful. Take, for instance, idioms that come in pairs, like "kith and kin." Kith comes from Old English and refers to people you know; kin, as in kindred, are relatives. "Bag and baggage" is army talk: baggage

referred to army property; a bag contained a soldier's personal gear. In maneuvers or war they were moved out together—including guns, which used to be composed of "locks, stocks, and barrels." The expression "down and out," first applied to unconscious boxers, is used to describe unfortunates like the alcoholic inhabitants of "skid row."

The seafaring British have provided us with many salty if hard-to-fathom idioms. When, for example, a situation is "touch and go," it is like the keel of a boat that is almost, but not quite, aground. "High and dry" is aground—with the tide out. When "taken aback," one is like a back-winded sail, a nautical tactic used to stop a boat in the water. Giving a "wide berth" to someone or something refers to the necessary practice of leaving anchor room around ships so that they may swing without striking each other.

Argument has its own sharp-edged armamentarium of idioms. The phrase "a bone of contention" suggests dogs squabbling over a bone; but when peace is made the contenders "bury the hatchet," a ritual practiced by

Artist's Soap Box Derby entry: a way of "going in style."

This couple demonstrates the art of "looking daggers."

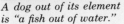

A dog out of its element is "a fish out of water." *A body is "taken aback" by such a thing.* *It could be "over his head" but maybe not.*

by popularizing to "shred," or destroy, evidence.

The trickiest idioms for newcomers to learn involve prepositions. Why should we put by money for the future, yet put up with boring visitors? Confusing, to say the least, especially when we also put up guests and put up peaches. And then, too, girls are likely not only to make up their faces but to make up tests at school after having made up excuses for missing the tests in the first place. After a fight, of course, they are free to kiss—and make up.

Some meanings can only be deduced from context, a situation that gets "down-to-earth" people "down at the mouth" about English.

It is impossible, though, not to cherish a language that is as rich in invective as English. Though we no longer hurl insults with the gusto of the Elizabethans, it is still possible to call someone a bonehead, fathead, hothead, egghead, skinflint, spoilsport, turncoat, diehard, dropout, upstart, or copycat. Later, of course, one can do the obvious and "curry favor," "apple polish," and "make up."

American Indians. If something is humiliating, it may involve "eating crow," which comes from ancient associations of the crow with unpleasantness and strife. No doubt crows are awful to eat, and so eating "humble pie" would certainly be an improvement.

Equally old is the idea of playing "devil's advocate." When ecclesiastical assemblies met to vote on the canonization of new saints, a person, the "devil's advocate," was selected to bring out whatever wickedness he could find in the candidate. Such findings, however, often turned out to be "moot points." The "moot" was an Anglo-Saxon assembly in which argument was as rampant as it was raucous.

Some of our most overworked idioms are also the most current, teetering in a kind of verbal no-man's-land between ephemeral slang and permanent cliché. To "do a number" probably came from vaudeville parlance, but we now go a step further and "do a

number *on*" someone, meaning to deceive (by an action or something else). The Watergate period made its own idiomatic history by reviving the expression to "deep six," meaning to drown something six fathoms deep, and

This scene from an old serial film shows how the "cliff-hanger" got its name.

From the hoi polloi to the crème de la crème, they cry, "I scream, you scream, we all scream for ice cream!"

ter suggested that he put the messy concoction on a stick, thus donating to a grateful world the "Good Humor Ice Cream Sucker."

With the forms of ice-cream confection virtually settled, American pioneers turned to concocting new flavors. In 1925 Howard Johnson opened his first store, a patent medicine shop, in Wollaston, Massachusetts, where he also sold three flavors of ice cream. By 1928 he had developed the famous 28 flavors. In the early 1950's a California advertising agency came up with an idea for Burton Baskin and Irvine Robbins, two California ice-cream makers: a different flavor for every day in the month—31.

Since then the company laboratories in Burbank have come up with more than 500 flavors—beginning with Apricot Brandy and ending with Watermelon Ice. A few flavors have been rejected because they did not catch on with the consumers, including Fig Newton and Prune Whip. Research departments of prestigious universities, notably Ohio State, have joined the search for new flavors, occasionally with disappointing results, such as Sauerkraut Sherbet, Squash, and Mustard.

Despite the hundreds of fanciful new flavors, America's favorites remain the old standbys—vanilla, chocolate, and strawberry in that order.

INFLUENZA Influenza (from the Italian for "influence"—influence of stars, it was thought) is an old disease. Hippocrates described it. At least 10 pandemics (worldwide epidemics) of influenza have occurred at irregular intervals over the last 250 years—in 1732, 1781, 1802, 1830, 1847, 1857, 1889, the famous "Spanish flu" in 1918, the Asian flu in 1957, and the Hong Kong flu in 1968. Although modern medicine can control the disease in normally healthy children and adults, influenza was a scourge for many centuries.

The death-dealing Spanish flu entered homes throughout the world. In its most severe form the disease ran an all too recognizable course. Fluid would suddenly fill previously healthy lungs, causing difficulty in breathing. The victim turned feverish, became purple in the face, and within a day or two died of suffocation or hemorrhage. Whole families were often afflicted, leaving no one to provide nursing care. Worldwide, the flu killed over 20 million people. In 1918 one out of four Americans caught this contagious, virulent illness, which spread as far and as fast as the common cold. It probably took hold in crowded Fort Riley, Kansas, when farm recruits brought this pig-transmitted virus into camp. (Hogs in the Middle West died of the 1918 flu as fast as people.) Nearly 550,000 Americans died, which was 10 times more than the number of U.S. soldiers killed in battle in World War I.

Flu was first studied as an epidemic in 1510, but it is still not completely understood, although scientists are getting close. Much research in the early 20th century concentrated, unsuccessfully, on the respiratory tracts of animals and humans until an accidental discovery in 1974. American scientists, seeking to detect another virus in the feces of imported Oriental pet birds, found 15 strains of the 1918 A-type flu virus. (There is also a B virus that produces less serious epidemics which turn up every four to six years.) Since 1974 hundreds of strains of flu viruses have been found in birds, especially in migrating ducks. These may be passed to man by domestic animals that come in contact with water infected by the bird droppings. When new, virulent strains occur, some researchers speculate that they may be caused either by a major mutation of the virus or by the transmission of new influenza viruses by animals such as birds.

At the height of the influenza epidemic of 1918, many wore masks.

INSURANCE Since ancient times, people have exchanged some of the risks and uncertainties of life for the price and relative security of insurance. Nearly 6,000 years ago, for instance, sea traders in Babylon entered into what were known as bottomry contracts. According to such an agreement, the trader received a loan to buy goods, and for an extra fee the lender agreed to waive repayment of the entire loan if the goods were lost at sea. Such insurance was desperately needed because the traders pledged their property as well as their lives and those of their families as slaves as security for the loans. The Babylonians also devised contracts to protect merchants against the theft of food. The Code of King Hammurabi, set down nearly 4,000 years ago, legalized this arrangement.

About 600 B.C. Greek and Roman "burial societies" developed a kind of group insurance. The members of the societies paid dues, and when a subscriber died money was taken from the treasury to pay for the funeral. Thus the individual cost was shared by the group, the basis of many types of insurance today.

As urbanization and industrialization made life increasingly complex and dangerous, new types of insurance were written. Fire insurance, for example, became common in England after the Great Fire of 1666, and, at about the same time, Lloyd's coffeehouse in London became the gathering place of marine insurers.

In the early 1700's fraudulent "bubble" insurance companies proliferated in England and offered all kinds of overinflated schemes promising to insure virtually anything. One company even wrote policies on "The Assurance of Female Chastity." During the second half of the 19th century, policies were written to protect against plate-glass breakage and steam-boiler explosions, and to provide employer's liability. Automobile insurance

was offered for a British electric cab in 1895. On May 6, 1919, President Woodrow Wilson became the first airplane passenger to be insured against accident.

Many of the early insurance policies were based on gamblers' odds, and many companies went bankrupt when their luck faltered. As insurance coverage became more widespread and the terms of policies more complex, insurance administrators began using scientific techniques to establish just what their risk was.

In general, the larger the group insured, the more accurately experts can predetermine losses. Using computers and unbelievably intricate mathematical formulas, today's actuaries can even determine, for example, how many insured automobiles of a certain kind will be involved in a particular type of accident over a period of time. With this information, they can also determine what the company will have to charge for its policies to generate a profit margin by reinvesting the premiums.

Despite their mathematical expertise, insurance companies often fail to recognize and predict the unpredictable. An especially costly part of their overhead is the payment of claims to dishonest policyholders. One ring of insurance thieves in Detroit, for example, was accused of staging phony automobile accidents and, with the help of unscrupulous doctors, lawyers, and policemen, bilking insurers of more than $1 million. There is also a small town in Florida that insurance agents refer to as "Nub City," because it has been the source of more than 50 accident claims for loss of toes, fingers, and other nonvital portions of the body. So widespread are such deceptive practices that insurance authorities believe that somewhere in the neighborhood of 20 cents of every insurance dollar goes to pay fraudulent claims.

Victims of death-bed insurance racket in Pennyslvania burn $250,000 worth of policies on Christmas Eve, 1881.

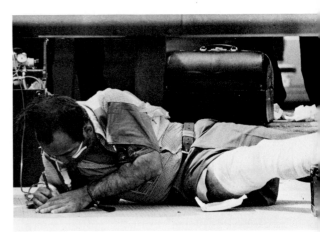

What is the injured man doing after being treated and waiting for the ambulance? Filling out insurance forms.

Lloyd's of London

Lloyd's insured Dietrich's gams: $500,000.

No one knows where he came from, exactly what he did, or whatever became of him. Yet it is known that Edward Lloyd gave his name to the world's best-known association of insurance underwriters. The first mention of him appeared in an advertisement for his coffeehouse in the *London Gazette* in 1688. Even then his establishment was a gathering place for sailors and ships' captains, who met to transact their business and hear the shipping news. In 1691 Lloyd moved to London's busy Lombard Street, and his clientele followed. He served coffee, tea, sherbet, meals, spirits, and news to his patrons. Gradually he established a network of correspondents in other English ports and on the continent. Occasionally, when the hubbub became too loud in his quarters, he or a waiter would ascend a pulpit and read the news aloud to his "regulars," who sat before small tables in booths. Possibly, Lloyd was involved in some unsavory deals as well, such as the slave trade in the British colony of Barbados.

Many of Lloyd's customers put up money to insure the safe arrival of various ships at their ports of call. In fact, the use of the term "underwriter" may have been launched by Lloyd's insurers, who often wrote their names on brokers' slips under the amounts they were willing to cover in case of loss.

Located on London's Lime Street, Lloyd's is an association of underwriters, not an insurance company. Individual underwriters, grouped in syndicates, put up money to insure various properties or undertakings. Each syndicate has one active underwriter, functioning on behalf of his fellow members, who sits in "The Room" on a pewlike bench and says "no" or "yes" to requests for insurance by brokers. Each member is liable for the syndicate's share in the risk. A bell from a ship that foundered in 1799 is occasionally rung to announce important news—one ring for bad news, two for good—but mostly it serves a ceremonial function.

As everyone knows, Lloyd's has insured almost anything, from happiness to hurricanes, but there is one thing they will not insure—human lives. As one underwriter once remarked, "Everybody dies, so what's the fun of writing life insurance?"

INTELLIGENCE TEST The intelligence quotient test is not administered every day, of course, but "The Number" sticks for all time in the mind of anyone who has ever heard his score. It helps mold one's self-image, often deleteriously. Luckily for low scorers, school and college dependence on IQ test results is going out of style. The tests have been attacked as biased in favor of middle-class whites because they tend to measure information rather than intelligence and because they do not probe for "creativity quotients" or determine the extent of the drive and persistence so important to achievement. Moreover, children have been shown to swing as much as 20 points from one testing to another.

Another negative aspect of intelligence rating is that children can be hopelessly stereotyped because IQ scores often determine placement in ability groups. Consider the Florida teacher who noticed numbers between 130 and 160 next to her students' names and immediately upgraded her curriculum only to discover later that the numbers designated the kids' lockers.

The first IQ ratings were published in France by psychologist Alfred Binet and his young colleague

A forerunner of IQ testing judged attributes by facial types. These show (left to right) kingliness, dullness, stupidity, retentive memory.

Théodore Simon. Binet had been working some 15 years on related projects, always preoccupied with what intelligence is and how it could be measured and developed. Having tried head, hand, and memory measurements, he gave up on ever finding the short, reliable indicator he sought. But when the French government asked him for a way to distinguish normal from feebleminded children, he and Simon put together 30 task-related problems involving repeating digits, word definition, comparison of line lengths, and naming objects. With these, Binet could distinguish among idiots (those having the learning level of a two-year-old), imbeciles (of a five-year-old), and morons (of a nine-year-old). In America the imported tests originally were used to isolate mentally deficient people in the naive hope that to do so would eliminate crime and poverty.

In the 1908 revision of their examination, Binet and Simon divided the "mental age" of test takers by their chronological age, coming up with an Intelligence Quotient of 100 as average for any given age.

Today's testers follow a bell curve: about 68% score between 85 and 115, and fewer than 3% score below 70 or above 130 points. Most of the 200 kinds of intelligence tests available today question verbal, numerical, spatial, and reasoning skills, and increasingly give separate scores in each category rather than computing "The Number."

IRON Against the timeless inevitability of wrinkles—in togas, trousers, and even flapper flounces—women for centuries have taken up their irons. Even the rude Vikings ironed, using mush-

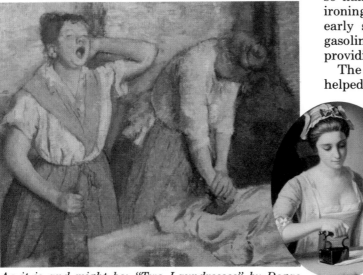

As it is and might be: "Two Laundresses" by Degas and "A Laundry Maid Ironing" by H. R. Morland.

room-shaped glass objects, called "slickenstones," to press away creases. With the help of "goffering" irons, noble Athenians went crisply pleated to the marketplace. And in progressive households in the mid-19th century, a vast armory of devices—mangles, crimpers, and bosom boards—went into operation on ironing day. A shiny finish was produced by polishing a garment with a "mangle bat," which resembled a cricket bat. The British Royal Navy got a good shine on its pants by pressing glossy magazine pages together with the trousers, thereby transferring the shine to the fabric.

Heat, of course, has always helped tame errant fabrics. But irons heated in a fireplace can add soot as well as smoothness. With the appearance of stoves, cleaner flatirons or "sadirons" arrived, so named not because of the inherent misery of ironing but because "sad" also meant solid. The early self-heating irons, which operated on gas, gasoline, or alcohol, sometimes exploded, thus providing occasional, if dangerous, relief.

The arrival of electricity on a full-time basis helped liberate the ironer on laundry day. Electric home irons, in fact, were available as early as 1896, but electricity was not, because early utilities sometimes provided power only at night, or, in one case, only on Tuesdays.

Can the ability to iron a future husband's shirts make marriage possible? Yes, early advocates of electric irons avowed, pointing out that couples unable to afford servants could marry anyway, now that grooms could provide their brides with electric irons.

The upper and lower case "J," which grew out of "I," were not fully developed until the 17th century.

JACKET Modern man need only examine his suit jacket to be reminded of a time when men dressed—and lived—more flamboyantly than they do today. For contemporary styling owes a considerable debt to the sword, the horse, and the masculine elegance of earlier, more romantic, times. A single back vent in a modern jacket, for instance, reflects a deeper cut in longer 17th-century jackets, which, when a gentleman leaped to horse, enabled the garment to part and fall easily on either side of the saddle. The swallow-tailed morning jacket, now used only for the most for-

mal occasions, derives from that period, its origins forgotten. To permit quick access to the sword handle, and to keep swords from getting tangled, other jackets added a pair of side vents, a style that survives in today's double-vented suits and jackets.

Legend has it that Frederick the Great of Prussia (reigned 1740–86) ordered rows of buttons sewn on his soldiers' jackets to break them of wiping their sweaty faces and runny noses on their sleeves. But the small row of ornamental buttons on today's jackets actually dates from the reign of Charles I in the 17th century, when sleeves were cut long and deliberately flopped back six inches to expose a contrasting lining. The huge cuffs were held in place by rows of buttons.

The word "lapel" is derived from the verb "to

lap," or fold back. When stylish collars stood up stiffly in back, the front of the jacket could be lapped over to button in front. This required that collar and lapel be separated by a deep cut, which survives as the traditional nick (and fake buttonhole) on modern lapels. Even the body of the jacket has ancestors, including the corset-like Renaissance doublet, to which sleeves could be added or not, and the simple collarless jacket that common folk wore throughout the Middle Ages.

The word "jacket" comes from the French *jaque*, or its diminutive, *jacquette*, a sleeveless leather coat normally worn over chain mail. In England such a coat was called a "jerkin."

Jacket-style "evacuation gown": babies fit in "kangaroo" pockets.

Why do men's jackets button on the left and women's on the right? Some historians suggest a practical answer. Because women most often carried babies on their left hip, and men reached for their swords with their right hand, the lesser task of buttoning was left to the unoccupied hand.

JEANS "A righteous garment" is how an anti-establishment youth of the 1960's described blue jeans. Movie star Lana Turner wore them studded with diamonds. But Henry Kissinger wore them too. In Russia they sold for as much as $140 a pair on the black market. They won a Special Coty Award, and several pairs are ensconced in the permanent collection of the Smithsonian Institution. Basically jeans are work pants.

In San Francisco in the 1850's, Levi Strauss' "waist overalls" were priced at 22 cents. To make them fit, one sat in a watering trough until they shrank to suit the wearer. "Those pants of Levi's" were just what the West needed—in the gold mines of California and the silver mines of Virginia City, Nevada, on the range, and on the new roadbed of the Central and Union Pacific railroads. They were so tough, legend goes, that when the coupling broke between two train cars, the trainman whipped off his Levi's and tied the cars together with his pants.

Jargon

"The Lord is my external-internal integrative mechanism. I shall not be deprived of gratifications for my viscerogenic hungers or my need-dispositions. He motivates me . . . toward a nonsocial object with effective significance." This, a Vassar College president suggested, is how jargonists might rewrite the opening of the 23rd Psalm ("The Lord is my shepherd; I shall not want. He maketh me to lie down in green pastures. . . .").

Traditionally, jargon has been associated with professions, and indeed every trade and profession does have a technical language that is clear to those who use it. Too often, trade talk is overblown and overused even among the cognoscenti. And when it overflows onto innocent laymen, it becomes a kind of double-talk that attempts to make things appear bigger and more impressive than they really are. Doctors and lawyers are severe offenders. As far back as 1699, poet Samuel Garth used these words to describe a physician: "The patient's ears remorselessly he assails/ Murders with jargon where his medicine fails."

Most recently, however, every class or group worth its titles and power structure has seen fit to insulate itself behind its own vocabulary. As a result, a spade is no longer a spade but, according to one Pentagon memo writer, a "combat emplacement evacuator." Art Carney as a sewer cleaner in the long-running television series *The Honeymooners* calls himself an underground sanitary engineer. And the kindly, helpful woman who once directed one to the right reference book is no longer a librarian but a "learning resource center person."

Bureaucratic jargon, designed to say as little as possible in the most impressive manner, is for people who want to score bold thrusts and not rock the boat. It also serves to sugar-coat unpleasant truths. Somehow, "culturally deprived environment" sounds better than "slum," and "effective ordnance delivery" seems less harsh than "target demolished." Understandably, new ideas require new jargon formulations. Thus the feminist movement has provided "consciousness raising," "male chauvinist pig," and such unisex constructions as "chairperson" and "spokesperson."

More often, perhaps, jargon helps fill a void. Those art critics who understand what "minimal sensibility" means, have managed to keep the knowledge to themselves. Yet some jargon enriches the language. To truckers and their CB radios, we owe not only "smokey" for a state policeman but also "county mounty" for a local officer, and "motion-lotion" for gasoline. And advertising men have contributed not only "Let's run it up the flagpole and see if it waves" but also the less familiar "Let's get down on all fours and look at it from the client's point of view."

Young Levi Strauss made his first pair for a miner out of brown canvas he had intended to sell for tents and wagon tops. Later he switched to denim, a fabric loomed since the Middle Ages in Nîmes, France. (*Gênes*, the French name for Genoa, was given to the sturdy pants worn by Genoese sailors.)

Levi's pants, despite rough competition from other companies, have remained essentially unchanged for almost 130 years. What changed was America. In the 1960's cheap, practical, and unpretentious jeans expressed the affluent generation's rejection of the gray-flannel capitalism they blamed for all of society's ills. The grubby look, to the horror of parents and educators, became the hallmark of a generation seeking peace, equality, and ecological sanity. In the Levi Strauss museum in San Francisco hangs a pair of patched blue jeans, worn by one woman every day for 17 years.

Ironically, the symbol of the protest suddenly became chic. In the early 1970's American mills were turning out enough denim to gird the earth nine times at the equator. Bibles were covered in it, cars upholstered in it. Second-hand jeans went for fabulous prices on New York's Fifth Avenue and were shipped abroad to Europeans.

Marlon Brando wore them to black-tie affairs. In the suburbs middle-aged chairmen of the board wore them. And social historians had a heyday unraveling the symbolism. "Civilized man's last gasp for freedom," one observer called it. The jeaning of America had become the jeaning of the world. In Italy a huge billboard depicted Michelangelo's fresco of God stretching forth his hand to Adam—as God offering a naked Adam a pair of jeans. Levi Strauss would not have been surprised. He believed that a good pair of pants was what the people wanted.

people

Gold in Them Thar Jeans

When Levi Strauss sold his first pair of jeans, they were not blue and they were not denim. He was 21, a recent immigrant from Bavaria, when he landed in San Francisco in 1850 with gold on his mind. His brothers back East had grubstaked him to some dry goods and bolts of canvas, which young Levi intended to sell as tents and wagon tops to raise cash to buy himself a claim. Legend has it that a single encounter with a disgruntled miner changed his career. Eyeing the goods, the miner allowed as how Levi should have brought pants. "Pants," he said, "don't wear worth a hoot up in the diggin's."

In short order that miner had the toughest pair of brown canvas pants in the West. Soon other prospectors came around looking for "those pants of Levi's," and he had a name for his product. Within a few years he switched from canvas to French denim, reputed to be the strongest fabric in the world, and later added the indigo dye that puts the blue in blue jeans.

Meanwhile, Jacob Davis, a tailor in Carson City, Nevada, came up with the idea of copper-riveted pockets. Miners kept chunking ore into their pockets and ripping them out. One day, after having repaired the same miner's pockets several times, the tailor sneaked off to the harness shop and reinforced the seams with rivets. Davis knew he had a good thing, so he went down to see Strauss in San Francisco: the two men took out a patent on riveted pockets.

Strauss developed the first and largest garment-making business west of the Mississippi River, and his reputation for probity and public spiritedness became a San Francisco legend. "You can buy Levi's for a dollar, but you can't buy Levi Strauss for a million dollars," it was said. As a philanthropist, Strauss established 28 scholarships at the University of

Denim apparel is America's most important contribution to fashion.

California, and privately helped many young people on their way. An astute businessman dedicated to the development of his city, he was director and board member of many companies and encouraged the building of railroads.

Strauss remained true to his Jewish religion. Though he never married, he lived surrounded by his nephews and their families. Upon his death in 1902 the nephews inherited the company. Today Levi Strauss & Company is the largest apparel manufacturer in the world.

In recent times, Levi's have been regarded as everything from a symbol of protest to *haute couture*. But Strauss intended them as work pants, tough enough for the cowboys, miners, and railroad men who were helping to build a nation. The pants are still tough today. One modern construction worker, perched atop a tall building in Fort Worth, Texas, got hooked in a pocket of his Levi's by a crane that swung him out over eternity. "I thought I was gone, but the hook had me caught so that the Levi's didn't rip until another man . . . got me to safety," he wrote in gratitude to the company.

JEWELRY Between the bone necklace of Stone Age man and actress Elizabeth Taylor's million-dollar diamond purchased from Cartier in 1969, there is not, humanly speaking, a very great gap. Ornamenting the body with beautiful or rare objects is an ancient practice. The very earliest items of jewelry known are periwinkle-shell necklaces dating from the Old Stone Age, and in contemporary stone-age cultures, like that of the Australian aborigines, jewelry is fancied even though clothing is not.

To protect himself in a world of mysterious forces, ancient man often wore charms and amulets that he thought were endowed with magical powers. Brilliant gemstones, rare gifts of the earth, held a magic of their own. The Babylonians, who were interested in astrology, assigned planetary influence to gems by color. Eventually the 12 tribes of Israel, the 12 apostles, the 12 orders of devils, and the 12 of angels each had its mystical stone, a zodiac-inspired tradition that survives today in the 12 birthstones, a special one for each month.

If gems could ward off evil, they could also cure sickness, thought the ancient Greeks. A dose of powdered lapis lazuli was considered good for snakebite, coral was prescribed for sore eyes and blood spitting, and amethyst for hangovers. Stones too hard to be pulverized could be worn around the neck to do their work—those charms were ancestors of the locket. People in the Middle Ages believed that rings and pendants set with fossilized shark's teeth or a bit of "unicorn's horn" could ward off dropsy or poisoning.

Many of the styles of jewelry we prize today were already popular in the ancient world. Bronze Age man held his garments together with studs very much like those used today. Jewelry revealing highly sophisticated techniques of goldworking were found in the Sumerian tombs of Ur, dating from about 2500 B.C. And to the dry climate and sumptuous tombs of the ancient Egyptians, we owe an unmatched treasure in earrings, bracelets, necklaces, and pendants, a tribute to nameless artisans whose styles are copied even today.

Pearls were the favorite ornament of the ancients, who imagined them to be solidified dewdrops or tears. In Roman times the passion for pearls was so great that the Caesars issued sumptuary edicts forbidding unmarried or childless women and women under 55 to wear them. But luxury triumphed for royalty: Constantine's crown and helmet, Nero's scepter, and the boots of the mad Caligula were all encrusted with pearls. Cleopatra, in a famous flamboyant gesture, once dropped a pearl earring in wine and quaffed it. The legendary survivor of that pair was mounted by Cartier as a pendant.

This snake-ring bracelet was created for actress Sarah Bernhardt: 1906.

Rings probably were invented by the Egyptians as an easy way to display a signet, or stamp, of authority. The Bible reveals that the pharaoh gave his own ring to Joseph, and there is reason to believe that that very ring was discovered in a mummy case said to contain Joseph's body. When a ring marked with the initials W.S. turned up in a field in Stratford-upon-Avon, England, the supposition that it was the one Anne Hathaway gave to Shakespeare was irresistible.

The engagement ring may have originated in the custom of breaking a coin to celebrate the betrothal of a couple and giving half to each. The practical Roman bride, however, received a signet ring sometimes accompanied by a small key, which gave her rights to the household property. The sentimental Victorians continued the 16th-century custom of giving each other delightful acrostic rings with stones set in this order: ruby, emerald, garnet, amethyst, ruby, and diamond. The expensive message, decoded from the first letter of each gem, spelled REGARD.

Portable and precious, jewelry has been used as a form of exchange in place of money. In an unstable economy, gems and jewelry are probably better than money for hoarding, pawning, or sewing into a hatband or draping on one's person if it becomes

"Electrical jewels" for stage artists were introduced in 1884; this dancer carried batteries weighing 2 pounds.

expedient—or necessary—to flee the country.

In the greatest jewel robbery on record, some $6 million worth of rare stones and jewelry of precious metals was stolen from a safe-deposit box in a Palm Beach, Florida, hotel. Imitation jewels, in use since Egyptian times, still confuse the unwary, including thieves. Cubic zirconia, for example, a product of the laser industry, looks just like a diamond, except to experts.

For all their practical value, precious gems retain their magic for good or ill, their luster of immortality. Most cursed of all gems, the famous Hope Diamond left a trail of bizarre deaths as it passed from the hands of Louis XIV of France to a series of owners who committed suicide, were murdered, or who were killed accidently. For the moment, it resides under guard in the Smithsonian Institution, a reminder of the powers attributed to the rare stuff of the earth.

JIGSAW PUZZLE Not long ago, manufacturers of jigsaw puzzles, ever on the lookout for new and intriguing subjects, decided to try maps of subterranean installations like the New York City subway system, the London Underground, and the Paris Métro. Addicts dutifully bought them, but few realized as they struggled to master the intricacies of the Bakerloo Line or the East Side IRT that their pastime had turned full circle.

For the world's first jigsaw puzzles, which appeared in the 1760's under the somewhat unappetizing name of "dissected maps," were just that—chopped-up maps. The brainchild of an English printshop owner, John Spilsbury, the puzzles were intended to help children learn geography. As the idea caught on, other subjects were introduced, including such weighty titles as "Chronological Tables of English History for the Instruction of Youth" and "Bowles' Moral Pictures. . . . Being Lessons for the Young and the Old, on Industry, Temperance, Frugality, etc. . . ."

These early puzzles were made of wood and cut one at a time, which made them expensive. Some of Spilsbury's sinuous creations cost the equivalent of $5, a large sum of money at the time. In the 1890's the invention of the die press made it possible to stamp out dozens of cardboard puzzles at a single blow, and thus satisfy the demand of puzzle fiends around the world, a group that ultimately came to include King Edward VII, Teddy Roosevelt, and Czar Nicholas II.

As might be expected, the Depression caused a surge in the popularity of time-consuming jigsaws. But even as thousands of families hunched over kitchen tables laboriously assembling "Kittens at Play" or "Sunrise at Grand Canyon," the more affluent enthusiasts were grappling with the maddening creations of two New York puzzle makers, Frank Ware and John Henriques. Together they revived the original one-of-a-kind, hand-cut, wooden puzzle—with a vengeance. Known as Par Puzzles, because each was assigned an estimated time of completion, they were designed to be as mind-numbing as possible and did not even provide a picture for guidance. In addition, their pieces were often bizarrely shaped, and the puzzles themselves sometimes contained open spaces. Un-

A big jigsaw puzzle (30' x 34') was set up in London's Trafalgar Square.

justly, some puzzles had irregular edges, and others had no right-angle corner pieces. The price of such puzzles was high: from $75 to more than $2,000 for a 10,000-piece nightmare. Because most people do not like to do a puzzle more than once and in order to compete with mass-produced products, the partners set up a puzzle lending library.

For years, some puzzle lovers indulged their interests behind closed doors, believing that puzzle addiction, if not downright sinful, was certainly nothing to brag about. However, a survey by a puzzle manufacturer has shown that puzzle aficionados tend to be well educated, upper middle class, and avid book readers. They are also systematic thinkers, goal oriented, and ready to accept new challenges. To satisfy such demanding customers, producers have jigged and sawed some extraordinarily difficult subjects. One of them is a reproduction of Jackson Pollock's painting "Convergence," a dizzying mix of smudges, blobs, and drippings cut into 340 pieces that at first—and second—glance look the same. To be helpful, the manufacturers suggest that the puzzle be confronted as a group project. "It would probably take one man 28 hours," they advise, "and he would be a raving maniac." Other studies in puzzle terror include "Little Red Riding Hood's Hood," which consists of 506 red pieces. And for those allergic to red there are, in the same monochromatic vein, "Snow White Without the Seven Dwarfs" and "Closeup of the Three Bears."

Yet even these novelties are not new. For years, puzzlers who found conventional seascapes or woodland panoramas a bore simply flipped all the pieces over and went to work on the blank side.

198

JUKE BOX One would hardly suspect, when walking into the local diner, pizza parlor, or tavern, that the juke box is an endangered species. The ponderous magnificence still sits there in the corner, its maw swallowing coins (a nickel a play has long since passed into history), its bright strips of colors oozing into one another, its big belly rumbling out the latest cacophonic entry in the pop music field. But the music maker may no longer be a fixture at its familiar haunts in a decade or so, for the times are increasingly out of joint for the juke.

Just about every kid who once eagerly forked over his allowance to hear the top 10 on the Hit Parade can now record them, free for the taking, right off the airwaves on his little cassette record-

In the 1940's the sound of a Wurlitzer was "what America's all about." Today, jukeboxes are camp.

er. Even if he were willing to feed the beast for old times' sake, he might soon have trouble finding a juke at a suitable location. For the local hangouts are slowly yielding to the fast-food chains, where quick turnover spells profits, and in that environment there is no place for the juke.

The juke box has had a long and colorful, if somewhat disreputable, history. Its name may come from an African word meaning "misconduct" or "disorderliness." In the Gullah dialect a juke house is a brothel where, presumably, raucous music was played. The immediate predecessor of the juke box was the coin-operated piano, a ubiquitous furnishing in bars and restaurants from coast to coast in the early 20th century. The juke also boasts other mechanical music machines as ancestors: a violin-playing mechanism, coin-activated music boxes, and a crank-operated device that played Mr. Edison's talking cylinders through a speaker horn. At the turn of the century, potential customers were advised: "Drop a

Nickel in the slot,/ Turn crank gently till it stops."

The familiar multiplay monster of modern times, offering scores of selections, did not become a fixture of American life until the 1930's with the repeal of Prohibition and the perfection of high-volume, electrically reproduced sound. It changed America's music listening habits as kids—and grownups too—threw millions of nickels into the jukes to revive a recording industry hard hit by the advent of radio. Who can tell how many superstars, from "Der Bingle" to Elvis Presley, owed their success to the jukes? Others profited, too, including organized crime, which muscled into the distribution end of the industry in the 1940's.

Many besides the mob may mourn the disappearance of the box. Already the picture grows a little dim—that image of a bunch of teenagers sitting in a booth at the soda parlor. A kid rises, puts a nickel in the juke box, presses G–7, and suddenly the Andrews Sisters are belting out "Don't Sit Under the Apple Tree." Everybody dances.

JURY Trial by jury, though one of the chief glories of Anglo-American jurisprudence, has also been the frequent target of wits, poets, and philosophers who have found it difficult to believe that

A jury of great nobles, presided over by the king, sat at the treason trial of the duke of Alençon in 1458.

12 ordinary people could put aside popular prejudice in the interests of justice. Mark Twain concluded: "The jury system puts a ban upon intelligence and honesty, and a premium upon ignorance, stupidity, and perjury."

In one of the earliest jury trials on record, the people of Athens, in 399 B.C., brought the great philosopher Socrates before the bar of justice. His alleged offenses included denying the gods and corrupting the city's youth. To judge his guilt or innocence, 501 freemen of Athens sat as the jury and heard the charges. Using wit and logic, Socrates faced his accusers and made a brilliant "defense," or so the record by Plato reveals. As soon as the testimony ended, however, the jury voted to convict the aged seer by a majority of 281 to 220. When Socrates refused to plead for mercy, the jurymen were so enraged that they condemned him to death by an even larger majority.

In postclassical times the jury system was nearly forgotten. Other means, including trial by ordeal, came to be preferred. The basis of this form was the notion that only God could judge the hearts of men, and He would reveal His verdict by means of a sign. Thus a presumed malefactor might be required to plunge his arm into a kettle of boiling water, and if after three days or so the limb appeared injured, it was a sure sign of the Almighty's wrath. Under this system the accused was twice punished: when his arm was burned and when the sentence was carried out.

Another form of medieval justice was the "wager of battle." If one baron accused another of stealing a pig, the two would meet in public combat, with Heaven presumably blessing the arms of the innocent. A contestant could hire a champion to fight in his stead. So when a blow fell or a sword struck home, the injury sustained by the employer was merely symbolic while someone of lesser stature suffered the wounds.

However, there was one form of medieval justice that presaged the jury system. This was trial by compurgation. In certain circumstances the acquaintances of the accused were called upon to state under oath whether they believed or disbelieved his protestations of innocence. This was, in fact, a popularity contest. The generous village barman charged with a heinous crime might find ample support among the locals, while the tax collector, innocent of all wrongdoing, could well be condemned on the flimsiest of charges. But by the 14th century in England, the role of the compurgators was undergoing a change: these onetime character witnesses were being impaneled to weigh the evidence. They had become a jury. It was not until the 17th century, however, that jurymen became judges of fact.

Juries varied in size for some time before the number of jurors became set at 12. Why 12? No one knows, although one author speculates that inherent in its choice is an Anglo-Saxon "abhorrence of the decimal system." Juries in themselves hardly guaranteed fair trials. But certainly it was conscience that led 12 London jurymen in 1670 to acquit the not-so-gentle Quaker William Penn of charges of inciting to riot. Penn's crime had been the public preaching of his Quaker faith, and when the jurymen refused to consider this an incitement, they were duly hauled off to the royal dungeons to ponder their folly. But in a landmark decision, the Lord Chief Justice ordered the jurymen released, thus establishing the independence of juries. There were other means of pressuring juries. By common practice, jurymen were denied seats, food, and water during a trial, a custom that 18th-century poet Alexander Pope satirized: "The hungry judges soon the sentence sign, And wretches hang that jurymen may dine."

The tradition of jury trial was carried to the New World by the Pilgrims in 1620. Despite its flaws, in the centuries since trial by jury has become a bulwark of freedom.

The letter "K" came from the Phoenicians via Greeks, Etruscans, and the Romans, who used it very little.

KETCHUP Mash the meat of a three-pound lobster, add some cayenne, stir in a bottle of sherry, and according to Eliza Leslie's *The Domestic Cookery Book* (1837), you have ketchup—lobster ketchup. In all, American cookery in the 19th century boasted some eight varieties of ketchup, including walnut, oyster, mushroom (England's favorite), lemon, anchovy, and even tomato. These tasty sauces, often mixed with butter and poured on meat, had in common a base made from the juices of fruit, shellfish, or vegetables, which was complemented with spices or spirits.

English sailors in the 17th century probably launched the genre when they brought back from Malay a pungent sauce called *kĕchap*, a word that may be derived from the Amoy Chinese *kétsiap*, for the brine of pickled fish. In 1748 Mrs. Harrison's *Housekeeper's Handbook* cautioned: "I therefore advise you to lay in a store of spices . . . neither ought you to be without . . . kitchup."

Until well into the 19th century, few people in

Peck and Peck

It may be, as at least one chemist supposes, that the custom of kissing had its origins among cavemen who licked each other's cheeks for the salt. Another view points out that apparently amorous snails touch their antennae together, while birds peck bills, and cats lick one another. All of these habits might be conceived of as a kind of biological imperative that has worked its way up the evolutionary scale, culminating in the exchange of kisses among human beings. But if that is so, then why did kissing evolve as an almost purely Western custom? Though Eskimos, Polynesians, and Laplanders do rub noses as a form of greeting, many non-Westerners have viewed the kiss as European decadence.

Decadent or not, kissing in all its many forms is obviously here to stay. It was Lorelei Lee, Anita Loos' fictional personification of the 1920's flapper, who sang: "A kiss on the hand may be quite Continental, But diamonds are a girl's best friend." If Lorelei were still in circulation at her old European haunts, she might just have to settle for the gallant gesture rather than the rocks.

Hand kissing had a European renaissance in the 1960's, but it still awaits acceptance in North America. Not that kissing itself is in disrepute on this side of the Atlantic. On the contrary, the last few decades have seen a veritable epidemic of public nuzzling, bussing, smacking, and smooching, or, as the scientifically inclined call it, osculating. Where once, in a more discreet time, a gentleman might bow to a female acquaintance, chances are that now he will buss her cheek by way of a cheery good-bye or hello. And where once a goodnight kiss between boy and girl signified a blossoming romance, now it may portend nothing more than palship. Men in America rarely kiss their own kind, but women are apt to plant a peck on each other's face. As often as not, this

This couple show how to miss kiss while dancing.

"kiss" harks back to the Prussian method of "dry" hand kissing, as it involves little more than a dusting of cheek to cheek and two puckered pops into thin air. H. L. Mencken belittled the practice: "When women kiss it always reminds one of prize-fighters shaking hands."

Whence comes all this face-to-face contact in a land once noted for its puritanical attitudes? In part, show business is responsible, particularly the movies and television. The long languorous embraces on the silver screen that Rudolph Valentino bestowed on his leading ladies in the 1920's may well have begun metamorphosing the kiss into an acceptable form of contact among the unwed. And by 1943, who but the most reactionary could think any evil when, in the movie *For Whom the Bell Tolls*, wholesome Ingrid Bergman lifted her face to meet Gary Cooper's and asked: "Where do the noses go?"

What the movies began, television sustained, bringing hours of

However disinterested Barbara Stanwyck and David Manners seem, Hollywood set a new smooching style.

electronically transmitted kisses—in situation comedies, dramas, movies, and even quiz shows—into millions of homes around the nation. Nor was real life neglected on the tube, which sent such

events as movie openings, award ceremonies, and presidential inaugural balls into the nation's living rooms, where ordinary folk could see the high and mighty cruising about with puckered lips, bestowing busses in all directions. In a land of equality what is okay for a cabinet officer must also be acceptable for Mary Jones.

Not that everyone approves of all this social kissing. Some believe that the prodigal bestowing of smooches debases the coinage, granting equal weight to meetings of mere acquaintances and the rendezvous of lovers. Still others discern the taint of sin in every peck on the cheek. They hurry off to their Bibles to hunt up scriptural damnations of kissing, only to find numerous positive references (with, of course, the exception of Judas' kiss of betrayal). They go on to point out that most biblical kisses were between people of the same sex and were bestowed as signs of peace and reconciliation. But even in the Bible not all kisses denoted mere friendship, as these lines from the Song of Solomon attest: "Thy lips O my spouse, drop as the honeycomb; honey and milk are under thy tongue."

Kissers are well advised to exercise caution. A number of ailments, including mononucleosis, strep throat, hepatitis, and in some rare cases even syphilis, can be spread mouth to mouth. Given these dour medical facts, it might be well to recall Oliver Wendell Holmes' epigram: "The sound of a kiss is not so loud as that of a cannon, but its echo lasts a great deal longer."

America actually ate tomato ketchup because most thought the plant was poisonous. In Virginia even Thomas Jefferson, an agricultural innovator of considerable distinction, had a hard time convincing his neighbors that tomatoes would not kill them. Gradually, however, the fruit won converts, and once deemed edible it caught on everywhere. By 1876 Henry J. Heinz was busily at work, making and selling tomato ketchup in corked bottles whose long necks, so familiar today, were designed to deter discoloration.

Today tomato ketchup is America's most popular condiment and has appropriated the very meaning of the word. Nonetheless, one cannot help dreaming: how would a hamburger taste with a splash of mushroom or lobster ketchup?

KITCHEN "A good kitchen," wrote Mrs. Isabella Beeton in the 1861 edition of her classic *Book of Household Management*, should be "sufficiently remote from the principal apartments of the house, that the members, visitors, or guests of the family, may not perceive the odour incident to cooking, or hear the noise of culinary operations."

One wonders what Mrs. Beeton would have made of a popular magazine that not long ago devoted 47 glossy pages to the proposition that kitchens should be "sociable." Its point was well buttressed by a gallery of pictures of wall-to-wall upholstered kitchens, kitchens in the round, kitchens that open onto a pool, and even a psychedelic kitchen.

That kitchens should be "sociable" is hardly a new idea. For thousands of years, they were not only the social center of the house but usually the only room in it. In fact, some archeologists believe that the earliest houses were simply constructions of animal skin and bone set over a central hearth.

From the beginning, the keeper of the hearth has almost always been a woman. To be sure, men sometimes lent a hand. Homer relates that Achilles was handy at roasting meat, and the Bayeux Tapestry, which gives a richly detailed view of 11th-century life, depicts a group of men preparing a banquet. But far more often, and especially in everyday homes, it was the women who wrestled with the spits, burned themselves on the cauldrons, and cleaned up the dishes.

Nor has the manner in which they performed altered much over the years. Looking at old engravings and paintings of medieval kitchens, Renaissance kitchens, Restoration kitchens, colonial American kitchens, and even Victorian kitchens, one mostly perceives changes in costume.

There has never been any shortage of praise or encouragement for women's work. "Nothing lovelier can be found in Woman," wrote John Milton, "than to study household good." William Alcott's *The Young Housekeeper*, published in 1838, announced: "A principal aim of this book has been to elevate the important profession for whom it is written. . . . The duties and destinies of the housekeeper are too important to be misunderstood." Another popular text, *The Hearthstone, or Life at Home, a Household Manual*, flatly stated: "The home in which the kitchen is neglected is not a healthy or a happy home."

Despite all these inspirational sentiments, actual technical progress seemed only rarely to enter by way of the kitchen door. The World's Columbian Exposition of 1893 in Chicago, for example, displayed a fully electric kitchen. Yet it was only recently that kitchens caught up with the 20th century. But once they did, they did so with a vengeance. In a typical year, for example, some 3.6 million American families spend an average of $4,500 each remodeling their kitchens.

It would be pleasing to think that husbands were behind this culinary renaissance in behalf of

Washing, cooking, and grinding. In India, West Pakistan, Dibai, and a U.S.S.R. Mongolian Kirghiz caravan, kitchens may vary and culinary techniques differ, but the hard work of preparing foods goes on forever.

their wives, but the national rush to more "sociable" kitchens corresponds with an increase in male interest in cuisine.

This may be coincidence. But it is also possible that anthropologist Margaret Mead knew what she was talking about when she observed: "In every known human society, the male's need for achievement can be recognized. Men may cook or weave or dress dolls or hunt humming-birds, but if such activities are appropriate occupations for men, then the whole society, men and women alike, votes them as important. When the same occupations are performed by women, they are regarded as less important."

KNIFE, FORK, SPOON For tens of thousands of years, clear up to the Renaissance, people generally ate like savages—seizing food with their bare hands and tearing meat off the bones with their teeth. As late as 1897, British sailors were forbidden to eat with knives and forks because it was considered unmanly.

Although flint blades found in Europe and Asia indicate that knives have been used for at least 35,000 years, these early instruments almost certainly were used to hack up food and not to eat with. The first spoon was probably the cupped hand. But with the advent of fire and cooking, Stone Age people, to avoid being burned, devised spoons of seashells, stone, bone, baked clay, and finally wood. The word "spoon" comes from the Old English *spōn*, denoting a chip of wood.

Eating with forks was not in vogue until the Byzantines did so about 900 A.D. Even then most people continued to use their hands, which accounts for an entry in a 13th-century book of etiquette, advising the eater not to put "thy fingers into thine ears," or scratch any "foul part" of the body while dining.

During the Middle Ages, knights considered it proper to spear food from serving dishes with their knives—the same knives they used for hunting. After watching his dinner guests stab food with their knives and then pick their teeth with the points, Cardinal Richelieu of France ordered all knives in his household to be ground round. In 1669 the French government outlawed pointed knives altogether.

Spoons were used most often to retrieve small pieces of "spoon meat" from common serving dishes. The morsels were eaten on a trencher, a flat piece of bread that served as a

The knife, fork, and spoon helped transform this royal trencherman, George IV, into a corporeal success.

kind of absorbent plate. (At the end of the meal, a diner might eat his trencher, throw it to the dogs beneath the table, or give it to the poor waiting outside.) Welshmen often gave their sweethearts wooden spoons carved with affectionate mottoes, and eventually "spooning" became synonymous with courting.

In the early 1600's Tom Coryat, an Englishman, noted with astonishment that Italian diners were offended if someone touched "the dish of meate with his fingers." Instead, the Italians used small two-pronged forks made of silver, steel, or iron. Those who failed to use their forks, Coryat wrote, were "brow-beaten, if not reprehended in wordes."

Coryat brought a fork back to Queen Elizabeth. She was so delighted that she had others made in gold, coral, and crystal. Although eating with forks became a fad at court, commoners regarded their use as an affectation. One preacher sermonized that it was "an insult to Providence not to touch one's meat with one's fingers."

Slowly the furor quieted, and nonaristocratic Englishmen began to wield forks at table. Many forks were ornately made and were carried by the wealthy in fine leather cases when they dined out. Often, on accepting an invitation to dinner, a gentleman or lady sent a servant ahead with knife, fork, and spoon. In France the duc de Montausier became one of the first hosts to provide forks for his guests. About 1700, he entertained a party of 100 and placed a silver fork at each table setting. Most forks were two-pronged, but four prongs became more common in the 1800's.

Imagine feeding a baby with a jingly spoon that encourages banging. This pap spoon was created in 1698.

During colonial times the City Tavern in Philadelphia was the first American restaurant to offer forks to its patrons. Most Americans, however, went on eating with knives until the Civil War. Then they began using forks—for almost everything. Special models were manufactured for the consumption of fish, oysters, and desserts.

No one knows when or why Americans (at least right-handed Americans) adopted the habit of switching their forks to their left hands when cutting food, then switching back. Right-handed Europeans normally keep their knives in their right hands and their forks in their left. Americans are also "variant" when it comes to eating fresh fruit. Proper Europeans eat peaches and pears with knife and fork; Americans use their fingers.

 Around 900 B.C. the Greeks adapted Phoenicia's symbol lemedh *to write the "L" sound. We use the Roman form.*

LAWN There is an old joke about a visiting American lady who asked the gardener at one of England's stately homes how he managed to produce such perfect, carpetlike lawns. "It's easy, Madam," he replied. "We use only the best seed, water frequently, and roll them for 350 years."

He might have added these instructions, which appeared in a book published in 1613: "To fit a place for this manner of greene plot . . . there must be cast great quantity and store of turfes of earth full of greene grasse, the bare earthe part of them being turned and laid upward, and afterward danced upon with the feete . . . that within a short time after, the grasse may begin to peepe up and put forth small haires." Obviously, the mistake most of us have been making is laying sod green-side up.

Strictly speaking, there is no single plant called grass. The word actually refers to an entire botanical family, the Gramineae, which numbers some 5,000 species, including corn, oats, rice, sug-arcane, bamboo, and citronella. All share certain structural characteristics as well as the unusual faculty of growing from the bottom up—that is, new leaves appear at the base, not at the tip. Older ones wither and turn yellow at the top, which explains why grass can be—indeed, for appearance' sake, must be—mowed repeatedly.

Grass seeds possess another interesting quality, though a frustrating one for homeowners with bald spots on their lawns. They are able to travel great distances, sometimes with man's help, then take root where they drop. Bluegrass, for instance, is a native not of Kentucky but of Europe. It apparently crossed the Atlantic as part of the cattle fodder brought by 17th-century French missionaries. Bermuda grass is believed to have come from Africa in the holds of slave ships, where it was used for bedding. Some weeds, too, were a late and unintentional importation. Broad-leaf plantain, for example, which had been unknown in the New World, was christened "white man's foot" by Indians because of its shape and source.

"Country gentlemen will find in using my machine an amusing, useful and healthful exercise," wrote Edward Budding when he applied, in 1830, for a patent on the world's first lawn mower. It was a marked improvement over the instrument then in use—the scythe—though generations of country gentlemen, and their suburban descendants, have come to wish that Budding had designed his machine with a small, energetic boy attached to the handle. A substantially improved American mower, the "Archimedean," was awarded first prize at the Paris Exhibition of 1878. The smallest model sold for under $10. A hundred years later, one manufacturer

Dance performances by young women and girls dressed up as Graces, dryads, and other nymphal spirits were once a regular attraction at upper-class lawn parties.

was selling a machine to do basically the same work—for $1,250.

Today, there are more than 20 million acres of lawn in the United States, or between 1 and 2 percent of the total land area. Their planting and upkeep support a billion-dollar-a-year industry and demand uncountable hours of unpaid weekend and evening labor. Aesthetically acceptable, if artificial, substitutes do exist, however.

Why, then, man's enduring attachment to lawns? When our ancestors left the trees some 2 to 3 million years ago, it was probably in the shortgrass savannas of East Africa. According to one biologist, perhaps our stubbornness in growing and maintaining grass is an attempt to recreate our earliest ancestral settings.

LAWYER There is a story about a doctor who struck up a conversation with a stranger at a cocktail party. "You know," he said, "one of the hazards of parties such as this one is that as soon as people find out what I do they insist on describing their symptoms to me."

"That's no problem," the other man said, "just give them your office card and explain firmly that free advice is worth every cent it costs." Two days later, the doctor received a bill for $500 for professional services. The stranger he had talked to turned out to be a lawyer.

Alone among professions, lawyers seem to divide humanity into two groups: themselves and nonlawyers, and nonlawyers would quickly identify with that doctor. Shakespeare voiced a strong antilawyer emotion in *Henry VI, Part II*, in which one of the characters proposes: "The first thing we do, let's kill all the lawyers." Charles Dickens spoke for all nonlawyers everywhere when he observed in *Bleak House*: "The one great principle of the English law is, to make business for itself. There is no other principle distinctly, certainly and consistently maintained through all its narrow turnings." Warren E. Burger, Chief Justice of the U.S., was also concerned when he warned: "We may well be on our way to a society overrun by hordes of lawyers, hungry as locusts . . . in numbers never before contemplated."

Shysters have bled their clients time out of mind.

Daumier's "After the Hearing" illustrates the adage "In a thousand pounds of law there's not an ounce of love."

Hostility to the legal profession is almost as old as the profession itself. Under the Roman code, individuals involved in a legal dispute could choose to be represented at their trial by an advocate, but a specific law—the *Lex Cincia*, passed in 204 B.C.—prohibited anyone from accepting money or a gift for pleading a case. Nonetheless, lawyers apparently continued to demand and receive fees, occasioning a subsequent regulation requiring both parties before trial to take an oath that they had not given or promised any sum of money to their advocates. As Roscoe Pound, distinguished lawyer and former dean of the Harvard Law School, noted in his *The Lawyer from Antiquity to Modern Times*, "Every Utopia that has been pictured has been designed to dispense with lawyers." Robespierre and Lenin, both lawyers, made it a point to abolish the legal profession after their successful revolutions in France and Russia, respectively. In each case the attempt proved vain.

In the American colonies, popular opinion of lawyers was made clear from the start. The Fundamental Constitutions of Carolina declared it a "base and vile thing to plead for money or reward." In Massachusetts the Body of Liberties permitted anyone who could not plead his own cause to retain someone to assist him, "provided he give him no fee or reward for his pains." Both Massachusetts and Rhode Island prohibited lawyers from serving in their colonial assemblies. Frenchman J. Hector St. John de Crèvecoeur, author of *Letters from an American Farmer* (1782), described American lawyers as weeds "that will grow in any soil that is cultivated by the hands of others; and when once they have taken root, they will extinguish every other vegetable that grows around them." Colonists added their own sentiments: a bird with a particularly long bill became known as a lawyer-bird, and a species of particularly slippery fish was named the lawyer-fish.

Despite such unpromising beginnings, the profession grew and thrived. Of the 56 signatories of the Declaration of Independence, 25 were lawyers, as were 31 of the 55 members of the Constitutional Convention. Nearly two-thirds of American presidents have been lawyers, as are approximately three-quarters of present-day senators.

The first law school in the United States was founded by Thomas Jefferson at the College of William and Mary in 1779. Currently, there are more than 145 accredited law schools in the nation. Together, they turn out more than 30,000 graduates a year who join a profession that numbers some 460,000 practitioners—roughly one for every 500 potential clients. (By contrast, the ratio in England is about one to 1,000; in Japan, one to 10,000). To help provide employment for them, legislative bodies, from city councils to Congress, enact some 150,000 new laws every year—a burst of activity that, according to humorist Goodman Ace, is creating a profitable new legal specialty known as "ambivalence chasers."

For their part, clients are helping out by hauling each other into court at the drop of a hat—or a football. Not long ago, during a game between the St. Louis Cardinals and the Washington Redskins, a St. Louis receiver caught, bobbled, and eventually dropped a pass in the end zone. After a brief huddle, the officials ruled that he had held the ball long enough to score a touchdown. Angry Washington fans filed suit in federal court to have the decision reversed.

Already delicate, relations between lawyers and nonlawyers are bound to be affected by the recent Supreme Court decision permitting lawyers to advertise their services. Although this advertising may take various forms, a certain Major Hopkins who practiced in Arizona during the 1890's has left a useful precedent. "Come to Major Hopkins to get full satisfaction," ran one of his ads, "I win nine-tenths of my cases. . . . Embezzlement, highway robbery, felonious assault, arson and horse stealing don't amount to shucks if you have a good lawyer behind you. . . . Out of 11 murder cases last year, I cleared 9 of the murderers. Having been in jail no less than four times myself, my experience cannot fail to prove of value to my clients. Come early and avoid the rush."

LIBRARY Libraries are much older than books as we know them today. The first libraries, established for scholars and officials some 4,000 years ago in Mesopotamia and Egypt, housed collections of hard-baked clay tablets (inscribed with cuneiform writing) and papyrus scrolls. The excavators of one Egyptian library found its "card catalogue"—a list of all the scrolls it contained—carved on the walls. It is reported that above the

The form, color, and atmosphere of the House of Commons Library make it the quintessential bookhouse.

door of another ancient Egyptian library there appeared the inscription "Medicine for the Soul."

The first public library was probably opened in Athens in the 6th century B.C. Before that, much of Greek literature, including the *Iliad* and the *Odyssey*, existed only in the memories of bards, like Homer. Often when a bard died his stories vanished with him. Thus libraries furnished a permanent repository for the accumulation of human knowledge, though from ancient times to the present day they have too often been destroyed, most frequently by wars, invaders, and fires. When Julius Caesar burned the harbor of Alexandria in 47 B.C. (during his liaison with Cleopatra), the flames damaged many of the 700,000 papyrus scrolls in what was then one of the world's largest libraries.

The great libraries of antiquity also competed with one another, occasionally with beneficial results. Even before Caesar's attack, Alexandrians were fearful that a library in Pergamum (in what is now Turkey) would surpass their own. As a result, they cut off the supply of papyrus to the city. Not to be deterred, the citizens of Pergamum substituted parchment, made from dried animal skins, for papyrus. It turned out to be a superior product, for it could be used on both sides, cut into pages, and bound into books. By the end of the Roman Empire, public libraries filled with

Bound volumes: in this 18th-century Florentine library books were chained to guard against thievery.

books as well as scrolls were common throughout Italy and other parts of Europe.

Many ancient libraries had common features. Most faced the east, so that the morning sunlight would increase illumination and dry up nighttime dampness, which played havoc with papyrus and parchment. Rolls usually were stored on shelves or packed vertically in cylindrical boxes according to subject. Tags identifying the works were left exposed for ready reference.

Libraries grew in number during the early Christian era because Christians aspired to literacy so that they might read religious documents and the Scriptures, and sought as well to preserve pagan works. Many medieval monasteries maintained scriptoria, where monks laboriously copied manuscripts by hand. One of the most important monastic libraries, situated at Monte Cassino in central Italy, has survived wars, earthquakes, fires, and even aerial bombardment. In 1944 the Allies warned the monks before their attack so that precious books and other treasures could be sequestered.

Knowledge of papermaking, transported to Europe from the Muslim world, accelerated the quest for information during the Renaissance. In Florence the Medici family hired agents to seek out Greek and Latin texts. The family housed their discoveries in museumlike libraries and hired artists, including Michelangelo, to decorate the buildings. The invention of the printing press in the mid-15th century hastened the spread of knowledge and the growth of libraries.

Perhaps the greatest library in the New World was assembled at Maní, in Mexico, by Mayan scholars long before the Spanish Conquest. There, in hieroglyphic characters painted on rolls of flattened vegetable fiber, existed the greatest concentration of knowledge in the Americas. Then, in the mid-16th century, a zealous Franciscan monk found the library and because the codices, he wrote, "contained nothing [but] lies of the devil, we burned them all. . . ." Only three Mayan books survived. About that time the Spanish started what has become the oldest library in the New World, one that continues to function at the University of San Marcos in Lima, Peru.

In 1833 the citizens of Peterborough, New Hampshire, built the first public library in the United States. In the late 19th century steel magnate Andrew Carnegie launched some 2,500 public libraries, with the proviso that local communities provide sites and maintain facilities.

Although the number of volumes a library possesses gives some indication of its greatness, the value and the rarity of a collection are also important. At least 11 libraries in the world contain more than 4 million volumes, including four in the United States—the Library of Congress, the New York Public Library, and the libraries at Harvard and Yale universities. Others are the British Museum, the Bibliothèque Nationale in Paris (each containing more than 6 million volumes), the Biblioteca Nazionale Centrale in Florence, the National Library of Peking, China, and three libraries in the Soviet Union. Since World War II, modern libraries have also collected films, tapes, punch cards, cassettes, discs, microfilms, and even holograms.

LICENSE PLATE By 1901 there were enough automobiles on New York's roadways to cause the state to rule that they had to be registered. In those days the car owner stamped a number on a piece of leather or wood and stuck it somewhere on the vehicle. Since then a perpetual battle between uniformity and regional or private expression has been waged across the face of the license plate. Sizes, for instance, once varied so greatly from state to state that car manufacturers were not sure where to mount the tail lights. That problem was resolved when the 6-by-12-inch plate became standard.

The spirit of states' rights has viewed plates as "billboards" to advertise what each area has to offer. Georgia's once bore a glittering peach made of thousands of tiny glass beads; Alaska's has a Kodiak bear; Indiana's, the silhouette of a racing car; Wyoming's, a cowboy and a bucking bronco. With the advent of slogans, however, not all citizens are willing to parade their state's motto without some editing of their own. New Hampshire tags offer a choice: "Live Free or Die," but when one resident taped out the slogan, objecting that

Personalized license plates: fitness king Jack La Lanne and bandleader Lawrence Welk pose with theirs.

he would rather be alive and in jail than dead, the judge accommodated him with 15 days in prison. Some years ago, to preserve the hardworking image of his fellow Mainers, author Kenneth Roberts blotted out that state's slogan, "Vacationland."

Since most of the states issue personalized plates, or "vanities," for a fee, wit enlivens the highway. Boxer Rocky Marciano once had a KO on his plates, and actor Ernest Borgnine came up with BORG9. A California almond grower advertises with NUTS 2U, a dentist with SAY AH, and a favorite among Volkswagen owners is LUV BUG. Lest the messages on the plates verge on the blasphemous or the scatological, most states employ a license-plate censor, whose job is to turn down anything offensive, even if it is spelled backward or disguised in a foreign language. A Minnesota application for HORNY was granted, however, when the owner could show that the car sported several unusual horns.

Many plates are made by convicts in state prisons, and even they sometimes get in the game. More than one car owner has received his new plates to find, scrawled on the wrapper, "Help! I am being held here against my will."

Light fantastic: using a portable generator and rope, the Edison Company staged this remarkable march through the streets of New York in 1884.

LIGHT BULB Efforts to cast out darkness by electric lighting were under way at least 50 years before Edison devised the first practical light bulb. In Paris, the city of light, blazing carbon lights (illuminated by the arcing of an electric current between two carbon rods) were used to spot enemy troop movements during the Battle of Paris in 1870. Before that they had been employed for theatrical effect at the Paris Opera. Powered by wet cells or even primitive dynamos, these harsh lights consumed lots of electricity and burned out fast, all the while emitting noxious gases. As a result, most nightlife occurred in the glow of flickering gas jets in the city or in the gleam of kerosene lamps in the country.

Nonetheless, when Edison promised, in 1878, to perfect an electric light "having the mildness of gas" in six weeks, the principles of the incandescent filament lamp were at hand. Carbon was the preferred material, having the highest known melting point of any element; and it was known that a filament contained in a vacuum tube would be

Lightheaded: this 1890's device helped a doctor see and poke all at once.

consumed less rapidly. Yet every filament that was tried burned through almost at once, and the equipment for creating vacuums was still undergoing technical refinement.

Undaunted, Edison and his team went ahead, trying some 1,600 different filaments, including hair from an assistant's beard, before they made the discovery that cotton thread glowed, and would continue to glow, for 40 hours. It had taken 14 months—not six weeks—to arrive at this conclusion. In the weeks that followed, passengers on trains that passed Edison's laboratory marveled at the warm light pouring from his windows.

Today filaments are made of tungsten, a metal with the remarkable melting point of 6170° F. Coiled, then coiled again, a 21-inch filament half the thickness of a human hair ends up measuring only five-eighths of an inch. On this precious thread hangs the light of the modern world. Or so it did until the fluorescent lamp, which uses less electricity, was developed, along with the even more efficient mercury-vapor and sodium-vapor lamps. These are used mostly for lighting streets.

Vandalism remains a problem for all public lighting, however. To prevent the theft of light bulbs in city subways, General Electric makes a maddening little bulb that, unlike all other bulbs, screws in counterclockwise. Thus a thief can only use his booty in a subway socket.

Light and wisdom have long been allied concepts, and cartoonists still use light bulbs to signal the arrival of bright ideas. Today's newest bulbs include those that emit "black," or ultraviolet, light, which can detect ringworm, minerals, underground water, and even art forgeries. The ozone lamp kills odors, and other lamps, providing a kind of synthetic sunlight, can hasten the growth of plants and induce chickens to lay more eggs. In the century since Edison brought light to rural and urban darkness, man has carried its glow down to the bottom of the sea and up to the surface of the Moon.

LOAN Said Artemus Ward, with a touch of the wry, "Let us all be happy and live within our means, even if we have to borrow the money to do it with." It is well known that money cannot buy happiness, but most of us borrow a lot of it in our lifetimes while we chase a sense of well-being. As of 1977, Americans' outstanding installment credit loans totaled more than $185 billion, not including home mortgages. The largest single category of installment loans, about $65 billion, arises from the American passion for owning automobiles.

Generally, when a loan is granted, it means that the lender has confidence in the borrower's capacity and willingness to return the money, plus in-

Electric streetlights brightened the world overnight. Here, a lighted Tokyo street in 1883 in full glory.

terest, at a certain future date. Credit managers probe the "Three C's of Credit": Character, Capacity, and Capital. Some add a fourth C—Conditions. A borrower who looks good when measured by the first three C's can still default on his

---

people

The Perspiring Genius

Thomas Alva Edison's beliefs and habits were those of a crackpot and a bum. Rats lived happy and undisturbed in his laboratory; he often slept in his clothes, because he believed that changing or taking them off induced insomnia; he thought Richard Wagner was Jewish; he was a disastrous husband and father; he all but starved himself to death because he believed that food poisons the intestines; his own company in Europe coined the cable name "Dungyard" for him. But he invented or contributed significantly to the telephone, the phonograph, the mimeograph, the incandescent lamp, the motion picture, the heavy-duty electric generator, the storage battery, and about 1,000 other devices or processes. Beyond doubt he was the greatest inventor of the American Age of Invention.

Coming from a Middle Western family that can be called extraordinarily ordinary, Edison as a young man showed signs of being an accident-prone, possibly men-

tally deficient misfit. Hardly out of babyhood, he burned down his father's barn. Beginning at 12, he worked as a newspaper hawker on trains, then as a railroad telegrapher. At 15, he blew up a telegraph station while experimenting with a battery. At 16, he forgot to set a danger signal, causing a train to be derailed. At 19, he signed his first contract for an invention and was on his way.

A madness for invention was in the air at the time of Edison's young manhood, when he did his greatest work. Invention was seen as a profession for the ambitious, just as, say, corporate management is today. By his middle 20's, Edison was already the nation's leading inventor of printing telegraph devices and was involved in enough corporate tangles to make one's head spin. Not only pure scientific curiosity drove Edison on. He was explicit on the point: "Anything that won't sell, I don't want to invent."

The story of the electric light is well known; what is less well

known is that, with constant encouragement from Edison, the process of invention was followed in newspapers in the U.S. and Europe like a sporting event, long before Edison's success. When he was ill, bulletins on his condition were printed almost hourly, and editorial writers clucked over how he was burning himself out with overwork.

Rumpled and tireless, he lived on five hours of sleep a night most of his life. As a grand old man, Edison's directness made his statements memorable. When asked whether he exercised, Edison scoffed, "I use my body just to carry my brain around." To him we owe the canny observation that genius is "one percent inspiration and ninety-nine percent perspiration." The practical Edison put his trust in hard work. Had he not logged more than 1,000 experiments to get the light bulb? "Remember," he said, "nothing that's good works by itself. You've got to make the damn thing work."

The usurer of yesteryear has been replaced by today's loan shark, who has gangsters as his collection agents.

loan if general business conditions deteriorate.

America is no longer a country of small towns, so the method of determining a person's suitability for a loan has changed from personal judgment to automatic rating systems. For example, Sears, which uses such a system in about 25 percent of its stores, has discovered that a person's occupation, considered alone, is not a good indicator of whether a loan will be repaid. A high-income doctor, for example, may receive a lower credit score than a mechanic of modest means. Among the reasons why: a high-income person in his middle years may be stacking up possessions, and debt, more rapidly than an older borrower who is getting by on a lower income.

For all the care that lenders lavish on cutting their credit losses, anomalies do appear in the system. For instance, a pharmacist in California collected credit cards as a hobby. He had more than 800 in his name. Although he earned about $27,000 per year, he could have run up debts of $9.3 million in a month while staying within the credit limitations on all of his credit cards. And one New York lawyer decided that he would permit installment payments on the fees he got for bankruptcy cases.

Although Shakespeare warned, "Neither a borrower nor a lender be," virtually all of us are acceptably both, a far cry from the prevailing attitude in the Middle Ages, when all lending at interest was prohibited by canonical and civil law throughout western Christendom. In fact, medieval usurers risked being burned at the stake after the Council of Vienne (1311), which issued a declaration that if any person obstinately maintained that there was no sin in demanding interest, he would be punished as a heretic. Both approaches vary from those in Babylon and Sumer, where priests functioning as moneylenders were making loans 5,000 years ago.

LOCK AND KEY When the prophet Isaiah declared, "And the key of the house of David will I lay upon his shoulder," the place where large keys were importantly displayed, he may have been referring to the key that opened the oldest type of lock known—the pin-tumbler or Egyptian lock. Remains of a 3,000-year-old contraption have been found on a door of a palace at Khorsabad, in modern-day Iraq, but Egyptian bas-reliefs depicted this type of lock as early as 2000 B.C.

These locks operate by means of pins that engage the bolt and prevent it from being moved. When the key, which looks like a toothbrush with pegs instead of bristles, is inserted, the pegs lift the pins, and the bolt can be thrown, or turned.

The ancient Greeks used a more primitive lock. Theirs was a bolt located on the inside of the door. The key, a curved piece of metal, was pushed through the keyhole and manipulated to free the bolt. The Romans introduced iron locks and a type known as the ward lock. The wards, or baffles, were simply projections inside the lock that interfered with any key without slots closely matching the wards. Ward locks were common until the 18th century. (The Romans also developed locks so small that the key could be worn on a finger as a ring.)

Ward locks, however, were easily foiled. Any picklock could insert a blank key coated with wax and turn it against the wards to make a perfect impression from which a duplicate key could then be made. In 1778 Robert Barron, an Englishman, devised a lock with two tumblers that made pick-

Through the ages every improvement in locks has spawned a better breed of picklock; escape artist Harry Houdini, above, was one of the best.

ing the lock more difficult. This principle is still used in most modern locks. Just six years later Joseph Bramah, another Englishman, patented a lock with a cylindrical key that stymied even professional picklocks.

Locks today might be entirely different if Linus Yale, Jr., had been a better portrait painter. But after a few years of dabbling with paints, he forsook the art and became a locksmith like his father. Yale gained a measure of notoriety in the 1850's when he picked model after model of the Parautopic Lock, then considered one of the best on the market. To add insult to injury, Yale often locked the locks so they could not be unlocked even with their own keys.

In 1861 Yale patented the cylinder lock, which revolutionized the industry. Although based on the principle of the pin-tumbler lock of the Egyptians, Yale's improved version could be used on a door of any thickness (eliminating the need for massive keys). Yale locks were the world's first mass-produced *unidentical* products.

Today locks are almost unbelievably sophisticated, and the conventional key has been made all but obsolete, at least in principle. Some locks employ electronic components and can be unlocked only by keys that bear invisible magnetic codes, similar to a tape recording, or by small cards, which are actually electric circuits that trigger small radio transmitters inside the lock. One new lock has no key at all. It can be unlocked only by the sound of its owner's voice.

people

The Bramah Locksmith

About 1790, London locksmith Joseph Bramah hung a handsome 4-inch iron padlock in the window of his shop with a message engraved on its face: "The Artist who can make an Instrument that will pick or Open this Lock, shall Receive 200 Guineas the Moment it is produced. Applications in Writing only." It was a large boast for a Yorkshire plowboy who had come to the big city on foot from his home 170 miles away 18 years earlier. Although he began work as a cabinetmaker, Bramah was soon pursuing his love—inventing—and in 1784 patented the lock named after him. His design was the first of a kind to arrange the slides, which prevent the bolt from being thrown, in a radial pattern. However, when competitors tried to keep business away by a smear campaign, Bramah improved his invention, and the lock with the challenge printed right on it was born.

Bramah's challenge stood for 60 years, long after the inventor died in 1814. In 1817 one "artist" worked on the padlock for a week and then gave up. In 1851, at London's Great Exhibition in the newly completed Crystal Palace, a New York locksmith named Alfred Charles Hobbs decided to try his hand. Hobbs worked on the lock a few hours a day for a month. He then summoned the representatives of the Bramah company to show them their lock with the hasp open.

Hobbs had indeed picked the lock, but he had also started what the newspapers referred to as "the Great Lock Controversy." Because Hobbs had taken so long and used so many tools, many believed that he had only demonstrated the lock's virtual impregnability. Also, the Bramah firm had unwisely furnished Hobbs an older model lock mounted on a piece of wood rather than on a door or an iron chest.

No one knows if Hobbs—or anyone else—could have picked the more up-to-date model of the Bramah lock or one that had been mounted conventionally. In spite of the defeat, Joseph Bramah's lock designs are still being used, and he is remembered for other inventions, including the hydraulic press.

The letter "M" may have originated as a hieroglyphic symbol representing the crests of waves and meaning "water."

MAGAZINES Few institutions in our national life have exerted greater influence on styles, tastes, and customs, raised more public issues, identified more villains, and created more heroes and heroines than magazines.

Their beginning, however, was anything but auspicious. Benjamin Franklin is frequently credited with publishing the first magazine in the Colonies—*The General Magazine, and Historical Chronicle*. In fact, he was second by three days to Andrew Bradford's *The American Magazine*, which died after three issues. It has been speculated that while Franklin was postmaster of Philadelphia he permitted postriders to deliver his own magazine but tried to keep his rival's publication out of the mails. Nonetheless, Franklin's magazine collapsed after half a dozen issues.

In part, these and other early failures were due to high prices and low numbers of subscribers. In some cases a year's subscription cost the equivalent of a working-man's weekly wages. In any event, by 1800 nearly 100 magazines were being published in the United States, and George Washington noted that they were "easy vehicles of knowledge, more happily calculated than any other, to preserve the liberty, stimulate the industry, and meliorate the morals of an enlightened and free people."

Pulp power: when this issue appeared, Weird Tales *was years old.*

Bright, innovative Mc-Clure's *launched the age of 10-cent magazines.*

had helped bring about the war) *Harper's Weekly* sent a staff of writers and artists to cover it.

Franklin's *General Magazine* had published the first American political cartoon. However, *Harper's Weekly* demonstrated the full power of the medium. The magazine's target was William Marcy Tweed, boss of New York's corrupt Tammany Hall political machine, and its weapon was the remarkable talent of cartoonist Thomas Nast. Even Tweed recognized the danger. "I don't care so much what the papers write about me," he reportedly said, "my constituents can't read; but, damn it, they can see pictures!" Despite repeated attempts to stop the magazine's sale, he was defeated, arrested, and eventually died in jail.

There have been many gifted magazine editors. One of the first was a 40-year-old New Hampshire widow, Sara Josepha Hale, who, to support herself and her five children, became editor in 1828 of a slim pamphlet entitled the *Ladies' Magazine.* Sensitive to the marital climate of the time, she advised that every husband "may rest assured that nothing found in these pages shall cause her [his wife] to be less assiduous in preparing for his reception or encourage her to 'usurp station' or encroach upon the prerogatives of men." Then in issue after issue she fought quietly for women's education and opportunity. She continued to edit her magazine (renamed *Godey's Lady's Book* after a merger) until 1877 and, by editorial proxy, helped raise two generations of American children.

Meanwhile, other periodicals flourished. *Leslie's* pioneered pictorial journalism, sometimes rushing to press by dividing a picture into segments and giving these to waiting crews of engravers. The *National Police Gazette* appeared in 1845 and promised its readers "a most interesting record of horrid murders, outrageous robberies, bold forgeries, astounding burglaries, hideous rapes, vulgar seductions, and recent exploits of pickpockets and hotel thieves." In 1852 *The National Era* serialized a book called *Uncle Tom's Cabin,* and when the Civil War exploded (the book's appearance

Seeing is part of believing—and of growing up.

One of the most colorful figures in American magazine journalism was a Dutch immigrant, Edward Bok. At the ripe age of 26, Bok was hired by Cyrus Curtis in 1889 to edit the *Ladies' Home Journal.* Though a bachelor at the time, Bok was convinced that "in thousands of cases the American mother was not the confidante of her daughter," and he set out to remedy the situation. He initiated a column entitled "Side Talks to Girls," which he wrote under the pseudonym of Ruth Ashmore. Sample advice: "Learn to say no. There is in that little word much that will protect you from evil tongues." At a time when women were beginning to go into business, he took the negative view: "To be in an office where there are only men has never yet done a single girl any good; and it has done harm to thousands. . . . I know whereof I speak." He commissioned series of articles on "Unknown Wives of Well-Known Men" and "Clever Daughters of Clever Men." But he also persuaded Rudyard Kipling, Mark Twain, and Sir Arthur Conan Doyle to write for the *Journal,* along with Grover Cleveland, Benjamin Harrison, William Howard Taft, and Theodore and Franklin Roosevelt.

By 1900 some 5,500 magazines were being published in the United States. While recuperating from wounds incurred in World War I, a former promotion writer, DeWitt Wallace, occupied himself by condensing magazine articles—a skill that he had long thought might lead to a career. In 1920 Wallace made his idea a reality; he put together a magazine and sent copies to leading publishers, but none was interested. He decided on another approach, soliciting subscribers through the mail, and it worked. Working with his wife-to-be, Lila Bell Acheson, and borrowed capital of $1,300, he assembled a pocket-size, unillustrated magazine, cleanly printed but on less than the best stock. The first issue, published in February 1922, went to 1,500 charter subscribers. Currently, the same magazine—the *Reader's Digest*—appears in 15 languages and is read each month by 100 million people around the world.

In 1922 two recent Yale graduates, Briton Hadden and Henry Luce, raised $86,000 and the following year started a publication they decribed as a "newsmagazine." They called it *Time*. Two years later a World War I veteran, Harold Ross, persuaded backers that there was room for a bright, humorous weekly—*The New Yorker*.

Magazines, which have caused so many changes in the pattern of American life, have also been affected by change. The popularity of television was certainly responsible for the temporary disappearance of some magazines and the appearance of new ones. Yet not everything that seems new in magazines really is. One of the standard attractions promoted by a number of magazines is a center-fold portrait of a nude woman. In 1899 every issue of *Truth* magazine, a 25-cent monthly subtitled "A Journal of Society, the Clubs, Sports, Drama and the Fine Arts," offered its readers a full-color portrait of a beauty—with clothes.

MAIL Much of the credit for our modern postal system can be given to a man who never set foot inside a post office. His name was Rowland Hill. In the 1830's Hill came to the conclusion that volume was the key to a cheap postal system. To prove his point, he argued that the cost of sending letters in England, and by extension in America, was too high and therefore people were avoiding writing letters. For his genius, he was awarded an honorary doctor's degree from Oxford, was named a Knight Commander of the Bath, and after his death was buried in Westminster Abbey.

Politics and the post office have long been linked. The rulers of the Roman Empire had their *cursus publicus,* a highly efficient mail system that connected Rome and its far-flung provinces. Throughout its history, America has mixed political loyalty and post-office sinecures. Even before the founding of the Republic, Benjamin Franklin was eager to reap the benefits of a job with the postal service. In 1753 he and William Hunter, printer of the Virginia *Gazette,* were appointed

Postman: in the marshy Landes region of France, mailmen use stilts.

jointly by the British crown as the postmasters general of the American colonies. Franklin sought not only the prestige of a royal appointment but an opportunity to increase the circulation and advertising of his own newspaper. Though fired by the British for his support of the colonists' cause, he was appointed as America's first postmaster general. President Andrew Jackson (1829–37), who introduced the spoils system, rewarded party workers with post-office jobs. When his own postmaster general objected, Jackson moved him to the Supreme Court and continued to find his postmasters among other party supporters.

The franking privilege, free use of the mails, was once a refuge of political rascals. In the mid-1800's one U.S. senator declared that his horse was a political document, fastened his frank to its bridle, and sent the animal home free of charge—to all except the taxpayers.

In 1847 the U.S. post office handled six pieces of mail per year for every American citizen; by 1977 the average had climbed to 427. On a typical day the U.S. postal service handles almost half as much mail as the rest of the world combined—over 92 billion pieces. That is enough to fill 440,000 railroad boxcars strung between San Francisco and Boston. Rural carriers alone cover more than 2 million miles a day, or about the equivalent of four round trips to the Moon. De-

Strange bedfellows: in the 1971 London mail strike the "Devil's Henchmen" delivered YMCA mail.

spite these impressive statistics, many customers still wonder whether the postal service works as well as it could. For instance, a letter mailed from the new Senate Office Building in Washington took three weeks to find its way to the old Senate offices just across the street from it. For its part, the post office points to its record on misaddressed mail, which postal employees call "nixies." One such, addressed simply to "S.O.B., Washington," was delivered accurately to muckraking columnist Drew Pearson.

MAP Most of us have examined reproductions of old maps with their fanciful creatures and puffy-cheeked faces representing the winds. As we have done so, some part of our mind notes that cartography has come a long way since the creation of those ancient charts. And so it has. It is nevertheless humbling to learn that in the United States in 1954 only six states had 100 percent topographic map coverage.

The word "map" comes from the Latin word *mappa*, which means "napkin," "cloth," or

people

Riders of the Pony Express

The Pony Express was in existence only 19 months, and it died a financial failure. Yet as a dramatic manifestation of the opening of the American West, it has no rival. Almost every trip produced an adventure, and in their brief gallop for glory the riders of the Pony Express delivered 34,753 pieces of mail between Missouri and California—and most of them on time.

The Central Overland Pony Express Company was born in adversity on April 3, 1860. Its founder, William H. Russell, was in deep financial trouble, and his dramatic promise of 10-day mail service between St. Joseph, Missouri, and Sacramento, California, was his way of getting out of it. Russell's stagecoach and freighting company, Russell, Majors & Waddell, had been carting supplies to the U.S. Army during its 1857–58 campaign to assert federal authority over rebellious Mormons. Attacked by Mormons and hampered by severe winter weather, the company incurred heavy losses, which the Army refused to reimburse. If, thought Russell, he could prove that the central overland route was faster than the southern route then in use, government mail subsidies would surely be forthcoming to bail him out of trouble.

On the day the prairies first heard the drum of Pony Express horses, a rider named Johnny Fry left the St. Joseph terminal two hours behind schedule because

the mail from points east was late in arriving at the railway depot. Another rider, nearly 2,000 miles away in Sacramento, started on time, and pounded to meet him. Riding in relays, the men and horses made the connection in fewer than 10 hours.

The Pony Expressmen and the horses they rode were picked to exacting specifications. A rider had to be young and of small build yet show great endurance, courage, and maturity of judgment. The horses were sturdy animals, chosen for stamina and bought at a price that was often four times the market rate. These hardy horses had much to do with the fact that the Pony Express lost only one man during its months of operation, despite the hazards of weather and several attempts by Indians to interfere bloodily with the mail service. The Pony Express horses were simply faster than Indian ponies, as rider Nick Wilson found out when Indians jumped him between Shell Creek and Deep Creek, Utah. Fueled by grain, Wilson's horse outran the grass-fed Indian ponies. And in the case of the rider who lost his race with the Indians, his pony delivered the mail alone.

Buffalo Bill Cody was 15 when he became a Pony Express rider. Tough and courageous, Cody once rode for 322 miles when no relief riders awaited him at the post. The record for the longest continuous ride, however, belongs

to "Pony Bob" Haslam, who covered 380 miles in about 36 hours with a total of 9 hours' rest along the way. The Paiutes were in a killing mood during that ride. Haslam expected fresh mounts at the Pony Express way stations ahead of him, but the Indians had raided a number of stations and scattered the stock, and he had no choice but to flog his horse and keep going.

At the end of his eastbound run, Haslam found the relief rider unwilling to face the Paiutes. So Haslam got a fresh horse and made the trip himself. He slept at the next destination, and then made the return trip, carrying the westbound mail. It may be that still another Pony Express rider made a longer continuous ride—340 miles in 24 hours. But he probably did it on a bet, without Indian harassment, and he arrived fast asleep in the saddle.

Although the Pony Express earned as much as $1,000 per trip, it was not enough to carry the expense of 190 stations, 80 riders, and 500 horses. It cost the company about $16 for every piece of mail it delivered, and it got back only about $3 per letter. Although Russell had not expected to make his mail service profitable right away, losing $13 per letter was a fierce drain. And then the transcontinental telegraph made the Pony Express irrelevant. On November 20, 1861, the last rider handed over his mail.

"sheet." From earliest times maps have been a call to travel, adventure, and, occasionally, confusion. Most American students learn in school that Columbus ignored the conventional wisdom of his time—that the earth was flat—and sailed forth to discover America. Yet the idea that the earth was round flourished long before Columbus. The ancient Greeks conceived of the earth as a sphere, a theory widely accepted in Greece by the 4th century B.C. Claudius Ptolemy, the Greco-Egyptian geographer, astronomer, and mathematician, finished his atlas about 150 A.D., mapping as far north as Denmark and including a large chunk of Africa to the south. The Middle Ages replaced the rudimentary science with piety, and cartographers put Jerusalem in the center of the world map and east at the top. This was because the Garden of Paradise was believed to lie to the east, or orient, which explains the derivation of the word "orientation." Mapmaking made its greatest strides in the age of exploration when the roving mariners tried to explain where they had been and how to get there again. The first maps of Columbus and Magellan, which held the promise of enormous wealth in the New World, were so valuable that most disappeared from the archives of Seville, Spain. The modern science, however, could not develop until the end of the 17th century after the invention of the sextant, an accurate clock, and other measuring instruments.

The most accurate map is a globe. The Mercator projection on flat maps distorts the real world the farther it moves from the equator. Greenland appears larger than South America, whereas the latter is actually eight times larger.

The accuracy of maps—and their corresponding inaccuracies—have produced large revenues and great costs for humankind. Today, mapmaking is an expensive undertaking. Major mapmakers fight a never-ending battle against cartographic inaccuracy. For example, U.S. post-

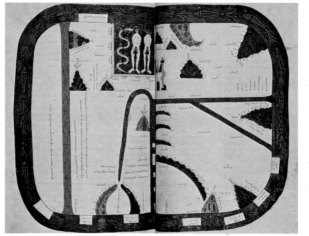

Limited edition: a 12th-century map of the world.

masters receive some 15,000 cards a year from Rand McNally & Company alone, asking for updated information on population. One reply noted succinctly: "Eastman, Okla., all gone; schoolhouse moved, stores burned."

As a practical matter, most of the maps we use do not depict the whole world. They show us only a part of it—the way across a state, or, supplemented by guidebooks, the best way to travel and where to stay on arrival. Such advice is not really new. The Romans, for example, had the *Tabula Peutingeriana*, a parchment more than 22 feet long that depicted the Roman road system. It also showed inns along the way, including a small colored picture that told the traveler what he might expect in the way of services when he reached his destination.

MARRIAGE When the Virginia Company set out to wrest riches from the New World in the early 1600's, it advertised first for young bachelors to found its settlements. But as a company agent wrote, "the Plantation can never flourish till . . . wives and children fix the people on the Soyle." The company was soon advertising in England and Ireland for young women ready to travel and follow the urgings of Genesis to be "fruitful and multiply . . . that thou mayest be a multitude of people." Although the passage says nothing about the institution of marriage, for thousands of years people of most cultures have insisted on formally entering that honorable estate before they reproduce.

The notion that a man and a woman should be in love before marrying is considerably more recent. The word "wed" originally meant the money, livestock, or other property assigned by the groom to the bride's father. Similarly, we tend to use the word "wedlock" to mean an indissoluble union, but to the Anglo-Saxons, who invented it, all it meant was a pledge and

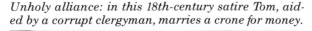

Unholy alliance: in this 18th-century satire Tom, aided by a corrupt clergyman, marries a crone for money.

Tying the Knot

The modern wedding has very little to do with religion. Most of the customs associated with it owe much more to the earthy practices of our ancient ancestors.

Marriage by capture is the oldest form of family formation. It consisted of an ardent groom stealing a bride from a neighboring tribe and hiding out with her until her family and friends got control of their tempers. The first honeymoon, then, was less an idyll than a practical attempt on the groom's part to stay out of harm's way until the bride and her family became reconciled to the new arrangement.

Anthropologists have speculated that the ancient problem of stealing a bride who was likely to resist fiercely led the first suitor-thief to take a few friends along to help carry her off. According to one theory, these hardies were the forerunners of today's best man and ushers, and they were there to provide muscle, not moral support. Often enough, they tied the bride up and fled with her as her tribesmen, in angry pursuit, hurled spears, stones, and other objects after them. The practice of tying shoes to the bumper of the honeymoon car may well come from an older English practice of throwing shoes at the groom for taking the bride away. Although the shoe has various symbolic values in different cultures, including being a lucky piece and a symbol of power, the idea of throwing a shoe is reminiscent of those ancient objects thrown in anger. It is much more certain that the ties that bound the early captive brides evolved over centuries from actual bindings, to symbolic restraints around the bride's waist, legs, or wrist, to the wedding ring. The ring was the product of a slightly more civilized view of how a couple should get together—marriage by purchase.

"Chairing the bridegroom" at a Scottish soldier's wedding. Parliamentary winners also used to be "chaired" through streets.

The bride was still seen as a piece of property, but now she was bought, not stolen. In some societies wedding rings were a token of purchase.

There has been much difference of opinion over the centuries about the correct finger on which to wear a wedding ring. Our current custom of slipping it on the

Nevada offers opportunity for those who would try the wisdom of "Marry in haste and repent at leisure."

third finger (thumb excluded) probably comes from the ancient Greeks. Their first, faulty dissections of the human body led them to believe that a particular vein, the *vena amoris*, ran from that finger straight to the heart. In one of the very few ancient customs that even hint of romance, the Greeks thus nodded to the connection between marriage and love. With the Greeks, the Romans believed that a finger so closely linked with the heart had special properties. They called the third finger "the medicated finger" and stirred mixtures and potions with it.

A modern American bride, on marrying for the first time, typically wears a white gown, and the popular supposition is that the color symbolizes the purity and chastity she is about to give up. The truth is, any bride can wear white with a straight face because the original symbolism of white had to do with joy, not abstinence. In Japan, white is also an appropriate color for mourning, and Japanese brides wear it to show that with their marriage they are "dead to their parents."

During the American Revolution, red became a popular color for bridal gowns because red stands for rebellion. Spanish peasants have no trouble wearing black to their weddings, and green is a popular color in Norway.

Although white originally stood for joy, not chastity, many cultures have been fussy about the bride being a virgin. In Morocco, for example, a workingman will pay $70 to $100 for a virgin bride, and only $30 for a widow or divorcée. Just before the turn of the 20th century, it was reported that Arab girls could be repudiated by their husbands if they were not chaste, and a clear finding of premarital intercourse allowed the fathers or brothers of the bride to cut her throat.

But if chastity has been a premarital goal across the centuries, reproduction has been the postmarital preoccupation. The rice we scatter over the bride and groom is a fertility symbol, and other, earlier cultures used wheat in the same way. The Jews of Morocco lob raw eggs at the bride so that she will bear as easily and often as a hen. The earliest wedding cake, which was probably a loaf of barley bread, was cooked up by the Romans. The groom broke some over the bride's head, symbolizing both the loss of her virginity and the submissive nature of her role in marriage. The early Anglo-Saxons confronted the bride and groom with a mound of small, hard biscuits. The newlyweds were supposed to exchange kisses over the stack. If they succeeded, prosperity and fecundity were theirs.

Relatively few cultures believe that a wedding is a time for simplicity. There were those who felt that the $62,000 wedding of President Lyndon Johnson's daughter Lynda Bird was gaudy and typically Texan, but it was a simple affair compared to some. Attila the Hun, well known for his in-

A Hindu bride and groom meet at her home and place garlands around each other's neck: hers is of flowers; his, of something almost as ephemeral—money.

temperate ways, died suddenly in 453 after his wedding to a Gothic damsel. Historical gossip has it that the king perished from guzzling too much mead. Charles Durande, a wealthy Louisiana plantation owner during the days of slavery, put on a ceremony for his two daughters that may be

"A damnably serious business," John P. Marquand wrote of marriage, and these Laplanders seem to agree.

the last word in excess. He ordered a shipload of spiders from China and released them in the trees that stood along the mile-long road to his mansion. The spiders draped the trees with their webs. From California, Durande ordered up hundreds of pounds of silver and gold dust, which were delivered by courier. Using hand-operated bellows, Durande's slaves festooned the lacy spider webs with the dust, and produced a sparkling canopy under which 2,000 guests marched to an altar Durande had built in front of his mansion.

In a novel attempt at setting a dowry for his daughters, one 18th-century Englishman promised them their weight in halfpence. It was a brave thing for a man with 11 chunky daughters to do. The reediest of the girls collected 50 pounds, two shillings, and eight-pence. She was much luckier than a bridal candidate in some Algerian tribes or among the aborigines of Nicaragua. These groups are not overkeen about chastity, so the young girls are expected to earn their dowries—by prostitution.

gift at the time of betrothal. So the earlier practice of marriage had more to do with economics, including the idea of the bride as property, than with romantic love. Indeed, crusty Ambrose Bierce clearly did not believe the idea that love ruled the home when in the 19th century he wrote a definition of marriage: "A community consisting of a master, a mistress and two slaves, making in all, two."

Most of the rules of marriage have been set by men. Polygyny, the practice of having more than one wife, has been quite common in the history of marriage. An Egyptian pharaoh not only had a queen, or "great wife," but a harem as well. Polyandry, the estate of a woman having several husbands, is exceedingly rare, and has most often showed up not as a sign of liberation but in societies that murdered girl babies and so ran short of brides. Over the centuries, both forms of plural marriage have lost ground before the trend to monogamy, which is one person, one spouse.

Most marriages begin on the presumption that they will last. Gypsy men, however, begin married life after agreeing to this injunction: "Swear you will leave this woman when you discover you no longer love her!" An American, Glynn de Moss Wolfe, apparently held the record for loving women and leaving them. He was married 19 times to 17 women. But Theresa Vaughan of England reportedly had 61 husbands—without polygamy.

In Brooklyn, Hasidic men enjoy a ritual wedding dance.

MATCHES Alchemy was a reputable but feckless profession. Not one practitioner discovered how to make gold from base metals, but in 1669 alchemist Henning Brandt discovered the chemical element phosphorus and its flammable properties. Because the price of phosphorus was about $250 an ounce, it was little more than a source of parlor entertainment for the very rich, who amused themselves by watching the substance burst into flames.

In 1827 a British druggist, John Walker, brought out a wooden match that became known as the "lucifer," from the Latin meaning "bringer

of light" but also one of the names for the devil. When a lucifer was pulled through a folded piece of abrasive paper, the chemically treated tip would ignite, producing a shower of sparks and a noxious puff of smoke that smelled like rotten eggs. Eventually, white phosphorus proved to be a health hazard. Workers in match factories contracted "phossy jaw," a necrosis that attacked bones and

19th-century match boys—and girls—peddled their wares for pennies.

resulted in disfigurement and death. Murderers and suicides had already discovered the effectiveness of white phosphorus. In 1911 the Diamond Match Company took the industrial and social danger out of matches by substituting the harmless sesquisulfide of phosphorus.

Of the 550 billion matches manufactured in the United States annually, about 500 billion are paper matches in books. Nearly all matchbooks carry advertising, for the obvious reason that an advertiser has a chance to flash his message 20 times, one for each strike. The earliest matchbook advertisement, in 1889, announced the virtues of New York's Mendelson Opera Company. A single hand-lettered matchbook carrying that message survives, and it is insured for $25,000. The Soviet government uses matchbooks for solemn socialist messages, and during World War II Gen. Douglas MacArthur air-dropped 4 million matchbooks to promise the people of the Philippines: "I shall return." A relatively new match, the Stop Lite, burns only for 15 seconds and is self-extinguishing. It is a safety measure, but it also ends the risk of lighting three cigarettes on one match. One superstition against doing so grew out of the Boer War, when soldiers thought that three-on-a-match gave the enemy too much time at night to aim.

MILK Milk has been called the perfect food. Although it is not, milk is so fundamental to the human diet that one guess is that man started milking animals during Pleistocene times, about a million years ago.

When English-speaking people say "milk," they are using a word that comes from ancient Sanskrit, and they usually mean cow's milk. In many other cultures the source of milk may be the buffalo, goat, reindeer, sheep, mare, or even yak. Indeed, a favorite milk product, Roquefort cheese, is made from the milk of the Larzac sheep of France. Cow's milk, however, remains the overwhelming choice among Americans and the foundation of a $12 billion industry.

Milk is 87 percent water; it is for the other 13 percent that it has been designated the perfect food. One reason is that milk contains what scientists call "complete" proteins. These proteins are all the amino acids essential to man for creating blood and tissue, and they occur in the necessary amounts. Milk is also an important source of calcium and phosphorus. But cow's milk only approximates perfection as a baby food and is not as good as mother's milk. Skim milk, having less fat, is generally better for adults than whole milk is.

"Went out to milk and I didn't know how," the line goes, but she does.

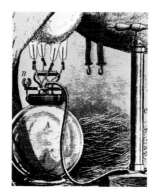

One asks if this beats hand milking—especially if one is the cow.

Before refrigeration, the best way for people to obtain fresh milk was to keep cows. Even then, there were wide variations in quality, for the health and diet of the milk-producing cow are crucial. For instance, if a cow eats wild onions, or even inhales their odor, the milk she gives will have an oniony flavor. There appears to be no basis for the charge, however, that thunderstorms can sour milk, though they often occur during hot weather, which can turn milk sour. Such concerns are trivial today because milk production is thoroughly controlled.

The modern dairy cow is bred to be a milk producer, and if she does not produce, she goes to the slaughterhouse. (The record for a single cow in a year is 55,660 pounds of milk.) A cow's diet

people

The Swedish Matchmaker

Ivar Kreuger, the greatest entrepreneur in the history of the world match industry, was a fabulous charlatan. Born in Sweden in 1880, he died in his bachelor apartment in Paris of self-inflicted gunshot wounds 52 years later. However, he became Sweden's most famous international industrialist, controlling three-quarters of the world's match market, and moved as well into gold, iron, real estate, movies, and finance.

But the Wall Street crash of 1929 shattered Kreuger's financial empire. When he escaped his creditors by committing suicide, he left behind companies worth a quarter of a billion dollars less than their financial statements indicated, and personal debts amounting to an additional $250 million. Eventually, his creditors received 21 cents on the dollar. Kreuger was a mountebank of matchless proportion.

Observers of Kreuger during his lifetime attributed his low-key life-style to modesty. He traveled alone. He carried his own luggage. He rarely gave interviews to the press. He dined alone or with a few trusted aides. Like the American millionaire-recluse Howard Hughes, he feared germs and greeted women with a kiss on the wrist, not the hand. He also was in horror of becoming overweight. Like William Randolph Hearst, Kreuger accumulated possessions ranging from great paintings to garish junk.

He treasured articles that gave him long service: he used one Gillette razor for 32 years. With even greater passion, he cherished secrecy—one of his slogans was "Silence, more silence, and still more silence." His employees at his Swedish Match Company signed documents promising that they would reveal nothing of company business.

In a rare instance of candor, Kreuger once told a friend, "I've built my enterprise on the firmest ground there is—the foolishness of people." He regularly read the biographies of great American industrial buccaneers; he studied John D. Rockefeller's construction of oil monopolies.

Kreuger was 16 years old when he graduated from high school, with the help of considerable cheating. Because he was highly astute in the nuances of mathematics and finance, and the laws of his day were undemanding about financial disclosure, Kreuger was able to create a maze of assets, incomes, banks, and loans that never existed. In one instance, he personally supervised the forgery of almost $140 million in Italian government bonds and notes, signing the finance minister's name with his own pen.

If not for the financial crash of 1929, Kreuger might never have been found out, for he had an especially insidious way of handling business: "You can flatter a man so much that you'll be ashamed of yourself, but never enough to make him ashamed of *him*self."

and activity are rigorously regulated, and she is milked by machine. In fact, she is more likely to stroll on a paved lot and eat from portion-controlled troughs than to graze a pasture. She even has her calves without actually meeting a bull—by artificial insemination. About 1,000 bulls can keep 12 million dairy cows calving. Calves are important because a cow will not give milk until the first calf appears.

The biotechnical drive to develop a perfect milk-producing cow has paid handsome dividends. In 1945 it took 27 million cows to produce milk for roughly 140 million Americans. Today only 11 million provide all the milk we need.

Full team ahead: decades ago, dogs helped deliver milk.

people

Mr. Gail Borden

In what he referred to as the "downhill side of life," Gail Borden perfected, in 1853, the process of manufacturing condensed milk. By then he had already been a farmer and cattle rancher, a newspaper publisher, a teacher, a surveyor, and a sometime inventor.

Borden's first interest in concentrating foods ended in failure, though some observers described it in stronger terms. Noting the difficulty the pioneers had in transporting food, he produced a "meat biscuit." It consisted of an extract of 11 pounds of meat mixed with flour and pressed into a two-pound loaf. The product won him a gold medal at the London Exhibition of 1851, but

Little did Borden guess that in mid-20th century his name would become synonomous with a bovine family.

little praise from the consuming public. Frederick Law Olmstead, the landscape architect and writer, traveling through Texas, tried one of Borden's biscuits and fed it to the birds. He wrote that he would "decidedly undergo a very near approach to the traveler's last bourne, before having recourse to it."

Returning from the London fair by ship, Borden noticed sickly children and asked the captain why they were not fed milk. The captain replied that the cows in the hold were too seasick to give milk. Such was the beginning of a revolutionary idea. Fortunately, Borden was not aware of the opinions of contemporary scientists, who decreed that condensing milk was impossible. His first attempts at concentration by boiling produced evil-tasting, burned broths. A breakthrough came when he journeyed to New Lebanon, New York, to visit the Shaker religious community there. He found the Shakers using vacuum pans to condense fruit juices and sugar, and he borrowed one. After a number of experiments, he found the right procedure and applied for a patent. It took him three years to get one, with the U.S. Patent Office protesting that he had accomplished nothing new. The intercession of the editor of *Scientific American*, Robert

MacFarlane, and another distinguished scientist, Dr. John Currie, finally carried the day for Borden.

Borden's first condensed-milk company was undercapitalized, however, and collapsed when consumers were slow to buy. His second plant, which opened a year later in Burrville, Connecticut, might have failed as well had Borden not chanced to sit next to Jeremiah Milbank on the train one day. Milbank was a financier and wholesale grocer, and he agreed to put up the money to give Borden's business financial staying power. At the same time, New York newspapers were beginning to print scandalous stories about "swill milk" (produced by cows fed on residue from distillers), which contained almost no butterfat. A worried public soon became receptive to Borden's product, and Borden, realizing the importance of cleanliness, set rigid standards for the farmers who sold him raw milk. It was the Civil War that finally made Borden's fortune. Condensed milk had been drunk on the battlefield, and when soldiers came home they educated the public to its virtues.

Borden is buried in New York's Woodlawn Cemetery. The epitaph which appears on his tombstone: "I tried and failed; I tried again and again, and succeeded."

MIRROR It is easy to understand why mirrors have always been associated with magic and the supernatural. How long was it, for instance, before early man, seeing his reflection in a pool of water or a gleaming slab of mica, finally realized that he was examining his own countenance—and not the visage of some bizarre creature?

The ancient Chinese made good use of such reflective magic, placing concave pieces of polished brass on their doors so that marauding spirits would frighten themselves away. The Japanese used mirrors to perform an entirely different function, holding them before suspected criminals during intense questioning to detect guilt in their facial expressions.

In addition, they believed that at the dawn of time the sun goddess, having become angry, had stalked off into a cave, thus plunging the world into darkness. No promise—or threat—could bring her back, until finally a resourceful maiden thought to hold a silver mirror before the mouth of the cave. So enthralled was the goddess by her own reflection that she sallied forth for a closer look. Instantly, she was barred from reentering the cave, and the sun again shone over the Empire of Japan.

The ancient Greek mathematician Euclid removed much of the mystery surrounding mirrors by working out the optical laws that govern their function. Archimedes, the story goes, applied these laws to the construction of concave mirrors. When a Roman fleet attacked his native city of

Alluring image: in this tapestry (c. 1500), a virgin tries to trap a unicorn with its reflection.

Syracuse, he concentrated the sun on these mirrors to set the approaching ships on fire. In the 2nd century B.C., Ptolemy II ordered a giant mirror built atop the great lighthouse at Pharos so that enemy ships might be spotted when they were still miles out at sea.

Hundreds of years later, in 1668, Sir Isaac Newton built the first reflecting telescope. Today, its modern descendant, the 200-inch Hale telescope at Mt. Palomar in California, contains the second-largest, most perfect mirror ever constructed. Weighing 14.5 tons, it was ground to a tolerance of nearly a millionth of an inch. With the telescope, astronomers are able to study celestial bodies countless millions of light-years away in deep space.

Yet legend and literature abound with accounts of more wondrous—if less believable—mirrors, including one fashioned by Vulcan that could reveal the present, past, and future. Merlin, the magician, presented King Ryence with a mirror capable of exposing secret plots, treasons, and projected invasions.

According to one of Chaucer's *Canterbury Tales*, Cambuscan, the king of Tartary, possessed a mirror that warned him of approaching ill fortune. Reynard the Fox had a mirror, too, in which he said he could see what was happening a mile away. And Oliver Goldsmith, the Irish writer, described a unique sort of Chinese mirror, one so powerful that it could reflect the mind and its thoughts.

One of the most useful of all mirrors, however, appeared in the *Arabian Nights* and was presented to Zayn A'l Asnam by a sheik so that he might find a pure maiden. All that was required of the prince was that he stand in front of the mirror and think of a likely young woman. If she was pure, the mirror would remain clear; if she was not, the mirror would darken.

One of the principal truths behind these legends is that mirrors do not lie, even if the truth is disagreeable. A magnificent, ivory-encased Italian mirror that once belonged to Leonardo da Vinci and is now in the Louvre expresses this reality as follows: "Complain not of me, O Woman, for I return to you only what you give me."

This long-standing reflective flaw, however, was corrected—at least in part—in 1974, with the creation of the Select-A-Size mirror. As the patent explains, the upper part of the mirror is designed to provide normal reflection, while the lower portion is curved and can be adjusted to make a viewer appear as thin as he or she wishes. Buyers include physicians and psychologists who want to provide their patients with encouraging "after" views of themselves—ahead of time.

MOBILE HOME Is a mobile home a vehicle or a house? If it is private property, sprouts orange trees and TV antennae, but sits on someone else's land, how should it be taxed? In some states owners pay a motor-vehicle tax; in others, a personal-property tax. Some purchases of mobile homes are financed like cars; others, through the Federal Housing Administration and Veterans Administration, are financed like houses.

Once classified as "recreation vehicles," mobile homes for decades were exempt from uniform building and even safety codes, a situation that changed drastically when the Department of Housing and Urban Development recognized the obvious: few mobile homes ever go anywhere after they are delivered. For mobile homes, once so expressive of the American tradition of "moving on," are no longer very mobile.

Available now in bolt-together double-wides, complete with carports, fold-out rooms, air conditioning, laundries, rustic siding, and even "exposed beams," they are just too much for a car to move. As a result an owner must sometimes pay a professional trucker hundreds of dollars to haul his mobile home to a lot just a few miles away.

In the Sahara, nomads turn their camels into highly mobile homes.

Trailers, declared one early manufacturer, would never be used as homes. "The lack of privacy and room," he said, "would soon have the average family at one another's throats." Seen as playthings for the wealthy, trailers with fold-down bunks and gas stoves were hitched to expensive cars and dragged over the new roads of the 1930's to "See America." William K. Vanderbilt had one, dubbed a "land yacht" because of its luxurious appointments.

World War II, with its endless shortages, turned trailers into trailer homes. Only a third as much critical material was needed to house a family in a trailer as in a frame dwelling or apartment. Soon enough, trailers became assembly-line housing for thousands of workers and were widely used as mobile headquarters and field hospitals abroad. And when the postwar marriage boom coincided with the postwar housing shortage, trailers helped

This 1937 trailer came equipped with a chauffeur, air conditioning, and Missouri license plates.

fill the void. Although years ago many trailer parks were open litter-strewn eyesores on the landscape, today a large number of them have been transformed into landscaped, planned towns for the retired, with post offices, pools, and even recreation directors.

Whole mobile towns have bloomed practically overnight in Middle Eastern oil fields and Alaskan logging camps—only to be trucked away later to other sites. One developer in St. Paul, Minnesota, actually stacked three mobile homes on top of each other, thus creating the first upwardly mobile, mobile-home high rise—and perhaps it goes without saying that he added terraces.

MONEY It is not known where money as we know it—coins and bills of standardized value—originated. Most accounts date the innovation to the kingdom of Lydia in about 700 B.C. Lydia's most famous ruler, King Croesus, may have minted the first pure gold coins in the 6th century B.C. What is certain is that not long thereafter, about 540 B.C., Polycrates of Samos was found guilty of dealing in counterfeit coins.

Despite this aberration, which no amount of ingenuity or punishment has as yet been able to eliminate, money must count as one of mankind's most useful inventions. And in his attempts to overcome the impracticality of bartering systems, man has employed a wondrous variety of money substitutes, including salt, cheese, tea, wood, leather, velvet, and even silk. Some primitive societies favored feathers, others used beetles' legs or bits of tufted string,

In Peru the paymistress for next year's fiesta banks on her neck.

made from the fur of fruit-eating bats. Today, in Fiji, one of the islands of the South Pacific, porpoise teeth are still an accepted form of currency among some of the inhabitants. Natives in need of extra funds drive schools of porpoises into shallow waters, where some of the porpoises smother in the mud, and then extract their teeth. On the Pacific island of Yap, millstones served as money until World War II. Stones of small denominations had a hole carved in their centers so that the owner might roll them around on a wooden axle. Large denominations, measuring a dozen feet across and weighing several tons, were displayed outside their owners' homes, indicating high social and economic status.

In many societies, cattle have served as a form of money. The word "pecuniary," meaning concerned with or related to money, comes from *pecu*, the Latin term for "cow." "Chattle" and "capital" are derived from the same Latin stem as cattle. A "fee," payment for professional services, comes from the Old Norse word *fe*, meaning "cattle." Even today coins have heads and tails.

Probably the oldest form of money is the cowrie shell, a small, delicately tinted mollusk native to the shores of the Indian and Pacific oceans. Cowries have been found in Cro-Magnon graves dating from 20,000 B.C., and in the Neolithic ruins of Nineveh. Marco Polo described their use by Chinese merchants. Cowries were used as currency in Africa well into the 19th century, and in certain parts of Southeast Asia they were an accepted medium of exchange until the start of World War II. In fact, when the Japanese invaded New Guinea in 1942, their troops carried cowrie shells in such quantities that the island's economy was dangerously disrupted. Three years later the Russians did much the same in their sector of occupied Germany, printing up billions of worthless reichsmarks and distributing them to Red Army troops.

Early Greek coins not only facilitated trade and commerce but were objects of great beauty, as rival cities and states vied to produce the most attractive designs. Corinth, for example, minted silver coins bearing the likeness of Pegasus, the legendary winged horse, while Athens produced coins from a mixture of gold and silver that were etched with the Athenian owl.

Soon statesmen learned that coins might serve them twice—as the medium of their wealth and power and as an effective form of self-advertising. Ptolemy I of Egypt initiated the practice of putting imperial faces on money, and virtually every ruler of every country has followed his example.

The fact that their faces may appear on coins, however, has never deterred needy rulers from debasing them, if necessary. The emperor Nero, for

---

Money Talks

In the 16th century, when Europe was flooded with coins of questionable value, a rich silver mine was discovered in St. Joachimsthal in what is now Czechoslovakia. The ruler of the valley where the mine lay issued silver coins, which, because of their reliability, became highly prized. One could depend on a "Joachimsthaler," or "thaler," as the coin came to be called by all who used it.

Ten thalers—in English "dollars"—eventually became something quite different in America: a "sawbuck," because of the shape (X) of the Roman numeral for 10.

A "fin," meaning five dollars, is a corruption of the German *fünf* or Yiddish *finnif*. Actually the term was used in England in the mid-19th century as slang for a five-pound note. One of the coins in circulation in colonial America was the Spanish piece-of-eight—a silver coin that was frequently hacked into eight parts, each eighth being worth around 12 cents at that time. Its memory lingers on: a half dollar is sometimes called "four bits," and a quarter dollar "two bits."

The word "money" itself owes a debt to the Romans, who established their first mint, in 269 B.C., in the temple of Juno the Adviser, or *Juno Moneta* in Latin. Coins are coins because, before the advent of presses, their design was imprinted with a wedge-shaped tool known as a *cuneus*.

Keeping a budget, a form of financial self-discipline most people admire even if they do not practice it as well as they might, dates from medieval times, when French merchants carried their money in little bags known as *bougettes*. Sticking to a budget relates to another medieval practice whereby an Italian moneychanger transacted his affairs at a special bench, or *banco*. If in the course of his dealings he became insolvent, it was said that his bench was broke, or *rotta*, making him "bankrupt."

---

instance, reduced the silver content of Roman coins by 10 percent, under the pretext of making them more durable—and pocketed the difference. His high-living successors continued the practice until finally less than 2 percent of the metal in the coins was silver. England's Henry VIII, a compulsive spender, issued coins made of copper and thinly plated with silver. Daily wear soon exposed his fraud and earned Henry the nickname "Old Coppernose."

The expansion of international trade in the 17th century revealed other shortcomings of coined metallic money: it was heavy to transport in quantity, and once stolen it was impossible to identify. Both difficulties were dealt with by the introduction of bank notes or deposits, instruments that could be exchanged for a given amount of gold or silver at specified places. They in turn led to the institution of paper money, checking accounts, and, in time, credit cards.

Still to come, some suggest, is a universal charge-it card. Such a card would be issued to every child at birth and used to charge everything from diapers to homes, cars, vacations—and funerals. After burial, everything would be toted up and paid for from the deceased's estate.

MOTORCYCLE To outsiders, motorcyclists are often either all good or all bad. On the one hand, there was the clean-cut military courier speeding across the pockmarked war zone, his dispatch bag filled with intelligence reports that might change the tide of battle, intent on getting through despite the shells bursting around him. On the other hand, there was the slack-jawed, inarticulate hipster in "sawed-off" jacket and boots, whose joy was to terrorize respectable small-town folk. This less charitable view, though equally stereotyped, was enshrined in popular culture by the 1953 film *The Wild One*, based on a 1947 incident when 4,000 motorcyclists ran riot through Hollister, California.

In the wake of the movie, the public suddenly became acutely aware of the rumble and roar of motorcycle gangs—outlaw clubs (they did not belong to the American Motorcycle Association) including such loosely organized groups as California's "Hell's Angels," New Jersey's "Gooses," and the District of Columbia's "Pagans." Dressed in leather and sporting Nazi-style helmets and insignias, they roared up and down the roadways, tight-jeaned girlfriends pressed close behind the black-jacketed drivers at the controls.

Though relatively few serious crimes have been proved against members of motorcycle gangs, there is no doubt that they revel in the image of violence. The leather jackets and pants emblazoned with metal studs may offer a degree of protection in spills, but they are also symbols of havoc. And what of the Nazi emblems? The cyclists claim they are apolitical. "The swastika means don't mess around with us," explained one.

Probably the best-known motorcycle daredevil is the stunt cyclist Evel Knievel, who rose from a career of petty theft, swindling, and safecracking to celebrity status for his death-defying leaps while astride a motorcycle. Dressed in red-white-and-blue leathers, Knievel has stormed up ramps at speeds over 80 miles per hour to soar over 20 cars lined in a row and has jumped 141 feet over the fountains in front of a Las Vegas resort.

If Evel Knievel represents one perception of the motorcyclist, a new and very different image has also emerged. In large measure, this stemmed from the energy crisis, which led people from all walks of life—brokers, teachers, housewives—to take to the motorcycle saddle as a means of reducing gasoline bills. Some purchased traditional, high-powered cycles, but the trend appeared to be toward a little two-wheeled, motorized vehicle all but unknown in the United States until the mid-1970's—the moped. About the size of a bicycle, the vehicle has a small motor (about half as powerful as that of a lawn mower) and pedals: hence the name moped.

While the moped's use is curtailed by bad weather because of its relatively poor traction, perhaps most limiting of all is the fact that it is infinitely more dangerous than it looks. About 17 percent of all vehicular-related deaths in France involve mopeds, and a California policeman has remarked that moped drivers are all but guaranteed a hospital stay should they become involved in even a minor collision. As one Florida expert put it, the moped "will go fast enough to get you in trouble, but not fast enough to get you out."

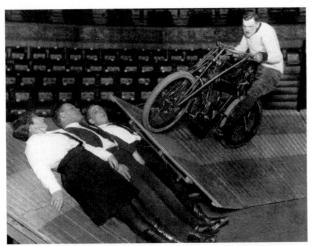

Flying finish? Looks can be deceiving, but in this publicity shot the participants seem to be fatally fixed.

MOVIE A battle-scarred Western desperado raises the muzzle of his trusty pistol, aims it directly at you, and fires. Such was the last shot of the first movie smash of all time, Edwin S. Porter's *The Great Train Robbery*, and audiences in 1903 loved it. Over and over they trooped back to storefront theaters to see the bad guys take over the telegraph office, rob the train, and be run down by the virtuous posse, all in 11 minutes.

In 1889 Thomas Edison and his assistant, William Dickson, devised the first practical motion-picture machine, dubbed the "Kinetoscope." Edison's laboratories also contributed the idea of a filmstrip perforated at equidistant intervals, allowing the film to run smoothly past the Kinetoscope's lens. Edison's "peep show" device was widely used until 1896, when it was superseded by larger projectors. By 1915 Hollywood was cranking out an impressive number of motion pictures, and poet Vachel Lindsay was moved to write these words of prophecy: "Edison is the new Gutenberg. He has invented the new printing."

Music has charms: a violin and organ accompany Gibson Gowland and his burro during the making of Greed, *a silent film directed by Erich von Stroheim.*

The product of the new medium, however, was more than good and bad guys and breathtaking action. It was craggy heroes, hectic comedians, swooning damsels, and malevolent villains. But who were they? Until 1910, producers kept the names of their actors and actresses totally secret, fearing (rightly enough) that publicity would turn actors into stars, who would demand higher salaries. But as adoring letters poured into studios begging to know the identity of the "Man with the Sad Eyes," or the "Poor Waif," producers realized that more fans (short for "fanatics") meant more money, and the star system was born.

people

"History Written in Lightning"

Imagine a movie in which the actors move but the camera never does. Imagine a movie in which the head and feet of every actor are included in every shot—no close-ups. Imagine a movie with no long shots, flashbacks, or cutaways. This is how our earliest silent films looked—very much like plays filmed head-on. The art was awaiting the great director D.W. Griffith, who developed the expressive cinematic techniques that taught movies how to move.

David Wark Griffith wanted to be a writer. To support himself he became an actor, first for a traveling company and later for the young Biograph film company. When Biograph asked Griffith in 1908 to become a director, he nearly turned the offer down. He made Biograph promise that he could go back to acting if he flopped as a director. In a few years, however, Griffith had made Biograph a leader in the nascent film industry. When he left the company in 1913 (having made an ambitious four-reel film that almost broke the firm), Griffith had directed more than 450 films—and took out a full-page ad in a newspaper to say so. More

important, he had been hunching his way toward new camera and editing techniques that would express the emotions of his stories.

Before him lay the film for which he is best remembered, the epic social drama of the Civil War and Reconstruction, *The Birth of a Nation*, released in 1915. It is flawed by Griffith's prejudiced Kentucky-bred view of blacks as wicked and Klu Klux Klansmen as noble. But the bad press and even the race riots that the movie incited in 1915 are less important today than such filmic innovations as intercut scenes to build tension and crowded panoramic battle scenes. President

D.W. Griffith looked like a star director; boy at his right, Ben Alexander, later played in TV's Dragnet *series.*

Wilson said of *The Birth of a Nation* that it was "history written in lightning."

Most silent "flicks" jiggled on to the accompaniment of pianists following music sheets labeled, for example, "Hurry No. 2 (for scenes of great excitement, duels, fights, etc.)" For *The Birth of a Nation*, however, Griffith issued a special score culled from well-known pieces, perhaps the first example of a thematic, coordinated film score.

Lillian Gish, one of the great acting talents developed under Griffith, reported that so staunch was his Victorian sense of womanly modesty that he was shocked to hear of an actress who had taken off her stockings in a film. "Doing such things before the camera!" he exclaimed. "How can I compete with that?"

He made other films—some good, some not so good. When sound came to movies, Griffith took up the challenge. He made two unsuccessful talkies before retiring in 1931. He ended his career bankrupt and mostly forgotten by the industry and art to which he had given its fundamental vocabulary.

By 1910 that sturdiest of Hollywood staples, the Western epic, was bravely getting under way.

The first movie stars were more than that: they were members of a pantheon of movie types that would live for generations. Notable among them were Douglas Fairbanks, the dashing hero; Mary Pickford, the ingenue; William S. Hart, the honest cowboy; Theda Bara, the vamp; and, of course, Charlie Chaplin, the tramp. In 1916 the tramp and the ingenue were locked in an oft-headlined struggle to determine who would receive the first million-dollar contract.

Traditional guardians of culture and aesthetics found movies disreputable from the start. As early as 1908, all New York movie theaters were closed during Christmas week. Movies, some said, incited criminal, even salacious, acts. One Chicago doctor testified that movies gave children Saint Vitus's dance. Others concluded that because silent movies portrayed courtship at relatively high speed, young people would become "fast." Had not some

Evil was never more blatantly portrayed than by the hirsute villains who regularly popped up in silent films.

adolescents admitted that they had learned to kiss by watching Douglas Fairbanks?

Movies, as Edison had once dreamed, finally found their voice. *The Jazz Singer*, made in 1927 with Al Jolson in the starring role, was the first real talking movie. In it, Jolson was only supposed to sing, but being an irrespressible ad-libber, he managed to drawl, "You ain't heard nothin' yet"— the first, and perhaps most prophetic, of all movie lines.

Motion pictures launched the era of mass entertainment, uniting millions of people in common language and experience. Though in the United States television reduced attendance from 4 billion paying customers in 1949 to 1.6 billion in the later 1970's, the impact of the movies in terms of laughter, tears, mores, fads—and money—has always been awesome. Nearly a half century ago, for example, when Clark Gable whipped off his shirt and strode around bare-chested in *It Happened One Night*, undershirt sales plummeted so disastrously that manufacturers begged Gable to appear in his next film with his shirt on.

MUSTARD Farmers in the time of Christ marveled that the tiny mustard seed, the smallest known to them, could produce such a flourishing plant, sometimes 10 feet tall. (Modern farmers calculate that an acre will yield as much as 1,000 pounds of seeds.) No wonder that Christ in his parables likened the mustard seed to the kingdom of heaven and to the power of faith itself. So hardy is the plant that Spanish missionaries marked the Mission Trail in California by strewing mustard seeds, Hansel-and-Gretel style, to show the way from mission to mission. Near some of those missions that still survive, the mustard plants continue to bloom.

Mustard has been used, in one form or another, for some 3,000 years. The ancient Chinese favored it as much as do modern Chinese restaurant diners. Mustard seeds were found in Egyptian pyramids, and the Greeks and Romans used mustard as both a condiment and a medicine. Pythagoras recommended it for scorpion bites and depression, and Roman historian Pliny the Elder reported its efficacy for reviving swooning, hysterical females.

From ancient times until quite recently, mustard baths and plasters were used to break up chest colds and ease the pain of gout and rheumatism. If it works at all, it is because mustard contains an irritant that stimulates circulation. John Evelyn, who wrote a 17th-century book on salads, waxed rhapsodic on the salubrious effect of mustard, claiming it to be of "incomparable effect to quicken and revive the Spirits, strengthening th

Memory, expelling heaviness, preventing the Vestiginous Palsie."

Though the debilitating and often fatal mustard gas used in World War I was not made from mustard (it smelled like it), it did contain a chemical called sinigrin, found in mustard in small amounts, which caused severe lung damage.

The seeds of the mustard plant originally were ground like milled pepper at the table and sprinkled on food. The Romans mixed it into sauces, having discovered that water brings out the hot flavor. Today we know that an enzyme becomes active when powdered mustard is combined with water, but the mixture soon goes flat unless it is cut with vinegar. French author Anatole France noted: "A tale without love is like beef without mustard, an insipid dish," and French cooking would certainly not be the same without mustard. King Louis XI liked it so much that he always brought his own mustard pot with him when invited out to dinner. Mustard was awarded its own coat of arms by Louis XIV, and one of the popes at Avignon fussily appointed his nephew "mustard-maker to the Pope." The very word "mustard" comes from the French by way of the Latin word *must*, denoting the juice of unfermented grapes, with which powdered mustard was often mixed.

Gourmet writer James Beard calls the spicy stuff that Americans smear on hot dogs "ballpark" mustard. Fans like it so much that in one year at New York's Yankee Stadium alone, they consumed more than 1,600 gallons of the condiment plus 1,000,000 individual packets. Most modern mustard is a blend of "white" or "brown" hulled and powdered mustard seeds, the brown being the spicier. National tastes vary from the dark, sweet mustard of Germany to the hot sharpness of Colman's English mustard to the many creamy varieties of French Dijon. After all, not all blends equally cut the mustard for all dishes.

 "N" has always appeared with "L" and "M;" together they may have made the Latin elementum, *meaning "alphabet."*

NAIL Someday, space-age adhesives may make them obsolete, but for now American manufacturers ship some 280,000 tons of nails every year. There are special nails for just about everything—for wallboard, roofing, masonry, flooring, upholstery, horseshoes, and even miniature spikes made with model-railroad hobbyists in mind. Nearly 300 kinds of nails are manufactured, including double-headed and headless. Some nails have diamond needle, chisel, duckbill, and blunt points. Most nails are made of steel, although aluminum alloy, brass, copper, copper alloy, and stainless steel are also used.

In all, nails have served civilization for about 5,000 years, since Sumerian artists first used bronze nails to attach copper sheets to wooden statues. In colonial America families gathered around small forges in bad weather and made nails. Today's nail-making machines, fed from large wire coils, are capable of stamping out more than 700 nails a minute.

The claw hammer is probably used more frequently than any other tool to drive—and pull—nails, but most nails are set by gun nailers, equipped with machine-gun-beltlike clips. (With a hammer, the more blows used to drive a nail, the better it will hold.) The shape of nails, however, has resisted modernization: most designs are more than 15 years old, and many are ancient.

NECKTIE The tie is the one article of male apparel that does not have a single practical purpose. And is there a man who has not complained about the silly and uncomfortable thing, only to don one again the next day? The answer to the mystery of the tie clearly lies in its symbolic value. Even in this age of casual attire most of the so-called white-collar classes still wear ties on social occasions as well as to work, perhaps to signal their place in those ranks. Men who encase themselves in the same blue, gray, or brown uniform every day lavish time and attention on the selection of a—usually more colorful—necktie.

Most men in Western cultures knot a tie for formal gatherings like weddings and funerals as if to punctuate the occasion. A boy's first necktie has become a rite of prepuberty, signaling a move from infancy to full-fledged boyhood. The priestly collar, with no accommodation for a necktie, in part symbolizes a disdain for things of the world. In Frederic Wakeman's *The Hucksters*, one of the earliest fictional accounts of life along Madison Avenue, the hero, on his way to an important interview, stops to spend most of his money on an

J.C. Leyendecker's ads were nearly as famous as the collars they sold.

expensive but "sincere" necktie, presumably arming himself with self-confidence.

For many years the male guests of a night-club in Paris could be compelled by the hostess to stand up and sing a song. If they refused, or failed to perform to her satisfaction, she would cut their ties off with a large pair of scissors. The raucous laughter occasioned by this forfeit left little doubt that the act stirred unconscious emotions among the men.

Laborers and farmers for countless eons have

The necktie party, which acquired its name in Las Vegas in 1882, became a favorite Hollywood cliché.

worn a cloth or rag around their necks to absorb perspiration and keep off the sun. But as an article of fashionable dress, the necktie can trace its origin, and its more formal name, "cravat," to the decorative cloth worn around the neck and knotted in front by Croatian mercenaries who served in the armies of King Louis XIV. Attracted by its cocky flair, French aristocrats adopted the cravat; it vanished after the French Revolution but returned early in the 19th century. Styles varied

words

What's In a Name?

To know a man's name, primitive people believed, was to have a piece of him, like a lock of his hair, which was very useful in composing effective curses.

No syllables define us more intimately than our names. Parents have unwittingly blessed or cursed their offspring with the good and bad poetry of their appellations. Puritans, eschewing popish saints' names, would call a child "Hew-agag-in-pieces-before-the-Lord" or "Job-rakt-out-of-the-ashes." A baby born out of wedlock in 1609 was dubbed "Flie-fornication," and another, "Misericordia adulterina." A fellow in 18th-century Rhode Island was named "Through-much-tribulation-we-enter-the-Kingdom-of-Heaven Clapp." And the brother of "Praise-God Barebone of London" was cheerfully dubbed "If-Christ-had-not-died-for-thee-thou-would-have-been-damned Barebone." He shortened it to "Damned Barebone."

Nowadays we name a lad William Smith to distinguish him from all other Smiths, but in 16th-century England he was named Smith to distinguish him from all other Williamses. Medieval villagers knew each other on a first-name basis until after the Norman Conquest. Surnames did not become established until well into the 15th century. When Henry V decreed in 1413 that a person's occupation and dwelling be listed on all writs, the clerk (Clark today) might put down Thomas, "atte water" (he lived near the pond); or John, "milne" (near the mill); or Richard, "William's son"; or James, "carter" (he hauled stuff). Our Baxters were bakers, our Baileys bailiffs, our Wellses lived near a well, and thus surnames drifted into use.

Many Jewish last names such as Rosenthal (rose valley) or Greenblatt (green leaf) are thought to reflect the longing of ghetto dwellers for the countryside. Today, the most widely held name in the world is not Smith, but Chang, the name of some 85 million Chinese. Many last names are patronyms: Simons is the son or child of Simon, Fitzpatrick means the son of Patrick, and O'Malley is the grandson of Malley. All this patriarchy so bothered feminist Toni Zimmerman that she changed her name to Zimmerwoman.

One queer old practice was that of giving the same name to each boy in the family. One Scotsman named all 14 of his sons Charles Edward. Two brothers in Oklahoma were named Younger Stringer and Older Stringer, only the older was Younger and the younger Older. Twins have sometimes fared just as badly: one pair was named Charlie and Extra Charlie; another, Jeru and Salem, so the parents could piously shout "Jerusalem" when calling them in for dinner.

Americans have a commemorative streak, a kind of chauvinism that occasionally gets visited upon offspring. ("Chauvinism" comes from Napoleon's superpatriotic adjunct Nicholas Chauvin.) Thus we have had born to us: States Rights Jones, E. Pluribus Ewbanks, and K.N. Bill (for the Kansas Nebraska Bill) and his sister Missouri Compromise. Invasia was named for the World War II invasion of France, and a boy, 54° 40′, which stood for the 1856 dispute over the Oregon bor-

according to one's profession or disposition. Romantic men took to wearing the flowing ties affected by the poet Byron. More sober males chose to wear tightly wound neckpieces. For those who could not make up their minds, a book called *Neckclothiana or Tietania* (1818) offered a choice of more than 20 styles including *à l'Americaine*, which had a raffish, casual look. Beau Brummel, the greatest of the century's dandies, spent hours tying his cravat. The high point was the final knotting, often performed before an audience. For less fussy men, the 1897 Sears Roebuck catalogue offered ready-tied silk neckties at 19 cents apiece, or six for a dollar.

Although it may seem at first like a fairly simple proposition, the modern necktie is a bit of engineering clever enough to have earned its inventor, Jesse Langsdorf, a patent in 1920. It con-sists of four separate pieces of cloth, each of which is cut on the bias in order to prevent twisting or corkscrewing. To permit the tie to be knotted and pulled into place, the inner seam is slip-stitched and the thread allowed to hang within the thinner end. If that thread is pulled or cut short, the entire tie will almost inevitably come apart.

Some time ago tie manufacturers discovered that two-thirds of their annual sales were made at Christmas—a finding that encouraged them to actively support the movement to establish Father's Day. What happens to those neckties is anybody's guess. Some years ago two enterprising young men advertised: "Mail us one to six ties you are sick of. You'll receive pronto same number of handsomely cleaned different ties we got same way. Then you pay postman $1." Within six months they had received 17,000 neckties.

---

der. But is Moon Orbit Zappa a male or a female?

No doubt, however, of the gender of Alice, Emma, Ann, and Lucy—except that these names were originally for men only. Anna, for instance, was a king of East Anglia in the 7th century. Nowadays, though female Bobbis are respectable, Clarence and Harvey inevitably draw ridicule. In 1965 the much-maligned Harveys organized to stop TV commercials from portraying Harvey as a bumbling boor. Clarences had done the same decades earlier, when the mere mention of the name drew guffaws from vaudeville audiences.

But who will protect people with such fanciful soubriquets as those collected by John Train in his book *Remarkable Names of Real People*? These are all authentic: Charles Adolphe Faux-Pas Bidet, the Baroness Gaby Von Bagge of Boo, Hugh Pugh, Horsey de Horsey, I.O. Silver, Madonna Ghostly, John Senior, Jr., Warren Peace, Reverend Canaan Banana, T. Hee, Rosetta Stone, and Violet Organ.

"Names and Natures do often agree," wrote one John Clarke in 1639, which may explain the awful aptness of Cardinal Sin of Manilla; Preserved Fish of New Bedford, Massachusetts; Mr. Groaner Digger, undertaker; I.C. Shivers, iceman; Ronald Supena, lawyer; and a New Orleans criminal named Mr. Vice.

Some people overcome the nominal burden of their birth certificates by adopting pseudonyms, a practice with advantages for the Jerry Lewises of the world who do not feel funny as Joseph Levitch, moonlighting writers, and crooks on the lam. Others do not escape. Studies show that young men with unusual names like Oder, Lethal, or Vere are more likely to flunk out of Harvard than John or William, and that grade-school essays written by Karen, Lisa, or David get marked consistently higher by teachers than the same essays signed by Elmer, Bertha, or Hubert.

According to a British poll, John is seen as trustworthy and kind; Robin, young; Agnes, old; Matilda, unattractive; and Ann, nonaggressive. Percival's and Isadore's virility is in question, but James and Michael are as masculine as Wendy is feminine. Gordon works hard but without success, and Phil and Al are winners. The unusual name is far more of a psychological burden to men than it is to women, which may be why John has been, and remains, the Western world's most popular name for boys. Still, Efrem Zimbalist, Felix Frankfurter, and Judge Learned Hand were very successful in their fields.

Names are so basic to identity that a man with multiple personalities will use a different name for each: here are signed drawings by two of many selves of the same deranged person.

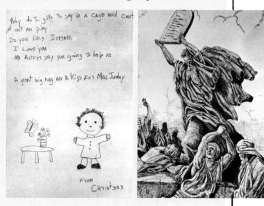

NEON The gaudy, pulsing signs that so changed the look of America during the last half century owe their existence not to American ingenuity but to two English chemists and a French inventor. In 1898 Sir William Ramsay and Morris Travers, while conducting experiments with what is known as liquid air (air under pressure at very low temperatures), discovered the existence of a colorless, inert gas. They christened the gas "neon"—after *neos*, the Greek word for "new"—and then abandoned it in pursuit of more interesting gases. A few years later, however, physicist Georges Claude in Paris found a use for the new gas: he sucked air from a glass tube, replaced it with neon, then passed an electric current through the tube. The tube glowed a bright orange. Claude recognized the potential of his discovery and went on to develop the neon sign.

The cool, compelling color of neon first shone in America in 1922, when a Los Angeles car dealer put a sign on display. From miles around people came to witness its glow. The novelty wore off quickly, however, as neon signs, manufactured under Claude's patent, winked to life in commercial districts throughout the country.

Not surprisingly sign makers refined their techniques, and signs became steadily more elaborate and colorful. A drop of mercury added to the gas, for instance, changed its color when electrified to brilliant blue. In the years following World War II, more than 3,500 neon-sign makers worked to color the American night. All were craftsmen to a degree, because each sign had to be handmade. The first step was to draw a full-size outline of the sign on asbestos, then heat glass tubing until it could be formed to fit the pattern. Next electrodes were melted into the ends of the tube, and finally the sign was filled with gas.

In the 1930's an indoor rival of neon light appeared—the fluorescent tube. Filled with mercury vapor, its inner surfaces coated with a fluorescent substance, the tube pulsed white when electrified, and the long slender lamps became permanent fixtures in most offices and many homes. Because it uses less electricity than neon and conventional bulbs, fluorescent light seems likely to survive its more spectacular outdoor counterpart. During the energy crisis in the early 1970's many signs went dark. Today there are fewer than 250 neon-sign makers in the U.S.A.

But as some of the larger signs began to fade out, a group of artists in the 1960's decided to protect what an MIT professor termed "the palette of a stupendous new civic art." The glass tubing that once lit up the barrooms and bus depots of America is now likely to be a collector's item or a museum "sculpture."

NEWSPAPERS In 1680 Lord Chief Justice Scroggs of England issued an opinion about whether the press should be regulated. He and his fellow judges announced: ". . . to print and publish any news books or pamphlets of news whatsoever is illegal; . . . it is a manifest intent to the breach of the peace, and they may be proceeded against by law for an illegal thing." Although his views did not prevail, Justice Scroggs was correct in a sense. Newspapers have been a breach of the peace many times, as they go about their triple duties. They are to inform a community about its affairs, make public the laws that govern it, and cover the news of its industry and commerce.

The first newspaper publisher was Julius Caesar. The *Acta Diurna* ("Daily Doings") appeared in Rome about 60 B.C. On a series of white tablets called albums were written the news of the city and the empire, and Roman crowds pushed and shoved to read them. In China, metropolitan gazettes appeared about 600 A.D., although the Chinese did not call them that. The word "gazette," now almost generic for any kind of newspaper, comes from *gazetta*, a small Italian coin that was enough to buy a paper in the mid-1500's. The birthplace of one of the earliest news sheets is Germany. In 1502 a *Newe Zeytung* appeared, and Germany led the world in the proliferation of new papers.

Hard news: in China, posters are regularly used to spread the news.

Newspapers were relatively slow in getting started in America, partly because of the British government's attitude toward them and partly be-

In Patna, India, a teacher reads the morning newspaper in Hindi to a group of junior high school students.

Joseph Pulitzer

Pulitzer Prize-winner, 1975: integration in Louisville.

Joseph Pulitzer became one of the most famous names in American journalism because he was thwarted in his ambition to become a soldier. Born in 1847 in Hungary, he grew to manhood with poor eyesight and an unimpressive physique, and was rejected by the Austro-Hungarian Army, Napoleon III's Foreign Legion, and British recruiters for the Indian Army. Finally, he managed to join the Union Army toward the end of the Civil War, but probably never saw combat. After the war ended in 1865, he went to St. Louis. He studied law there, working on the side, then took a position as a reporter on the St. Louis *Westliche Post* which he eventually bought on credit. In the end he owned two St. Louis papers, the *Dispatch* and the *Post*, and made them one, the *Post-Dispatch*. By 1883 he was rich and powerful.

In New York at that time, Jay Gould, king of the railroad speculators, was losing money on the New York *World*, and Pulitzer bought it for $346,000. He blanketed the city with reporters, and they turned up sensational stories that sold newspapers. A crusader, Pulitzer attacked Tammany Hall, powerful corporations, and those responsible for the barbarous treatment of immigrants at Ellis Island. He also believed that stunts helped build circulation. For one, he sent journalist Elizabeth Cochrane, under the name of "Nelly Bly," racing around the world to beat Phileas Fogg's record of "around the world in 80 days." She did.

Throughout his life Pulitzer was plagued by ill health, including dyspepsia, headaches, a detached retina, insomnia, and depression. He died in 1911, but not before he had provided the money for the founding of the prestigious Columbia School of Journalism. His New York paper, the *World*, folded in the Great Depression, but the St. Louis *Post-Dispatch* remains. Once, when attacked for his sensational approach to journalism, Pulitzer summed up his passion for mixing love trysts, murder, and moralizing with these words: "I want to talk to a nation, not a select committee."

cause the first colonial towns were small and insular and had little need for broadcasting information. The first American newspaper came out in Boston in 1690: it was to be a monthly periodical titled *Publick Occurrences Both Forreign and Domestick*. In his first issue publisher Benjamin Harris censured the French king for immorality and criticized the Mohawk Indians, friends of the British, for their brutal treatment of French prisoners. Having no license to publish, the paper was promptly closed down.

The constant argument about newspapers is how they go about their business. Almost any bit of news is an inconvenience to someone, so the charges of sensationalism, of enriching themselves by the misfortunes of others, have haunted newspapers from the beginning. The virulent age of "yellow journalism" took place in New York City in the late 1890's, when two giants of journalism, Joseph Pulitzer and William Randolph Hearst, collided in a battle for circulation. They stole each other's reporters and editors, and vied mightily to print the most titillating news.

On the basis of excess, Hearst won, for there is considerable evidence that he provoked the Spanish-American War by printing tricked-up stories of Spanish atrocities in Cuba. The artist Frederic Remington was sent by Hearst to Cuba to make sketches of the atrocities. He wired Hearst: "Everything quiet. No trouble here. There will be no war. I wish to return." Hearst wired back: "Please remain. You furnish the pictures and I will furnish the war."

Yellow journalism suffered a setback with the assassination of President William McKinley. He had been slow to order U.S. intervention in Cuba, and one editorial in the Hearst papers said of him: "If bad institutions and bad men can be got rid of only by killing, then the killing must be done." In the wake of McKinley's death, Hearst was accused of being anti-American. His response was to rename his New York paper the *American-Journal*.

The newspapers of the world have traditionally been a proving ground for writers who later achieved some measure of literary or other fame. Daniel Defoe, author of *Robinson Crusoe*, went to jail for satirizing the Church of England. In Germany, Goethe and Schiller worked as journalists. Benjamin Franklin, at the age of 16, was writing the popular "Silence Dogood" letters in his brother's paper. Alexander Hamilton and Thomas Jefferson each used a newspaper to attack the other. In later years Stephen Crane, author of *The Red Badge of Courage*, worked as a war correspondent, and Mark Twain covered special events for Hearst. Winston Churchill was a journalist during the Boer War. Even Theodore Roosevelt was a reporter. He was responsible for calling reporters who exposed corruption "muckrakers," after "The Man with a Muck-rake" in *Pilgrim's Progress*. Roosevelt also figured in a famous newspaper error when the Chicago *Examiner* published an X-ray of what purported to be the wound in Roosevelt's chest, sustained in an assassination attempt in Milwaukee. The X-ray had been stolen by a reporter from the hospital laboratory. Enterprise journalism came to naught when the reporter was told by a physician friend: "What you printed was a picture of a six-month-old fetus."

Perhaps the most enduring adage of the newspaper business was coined by John Bogart of the New York *Sun*. He instructed a young reporter: "When a dog bites a man, that is not news, because it happens so often. But if a man bites a dog, that is news." The notion of bite, of journalism as weaponry, had already occurred to Napoleon. He said, "Three hostile newspapers are more to be feared than a thousand bayonets."

NUMBERS Why is the number 13 considered so unlucky that many Manhattan skyscrapers ignore the existence of the 13th floor? Why are the houses in France numbered 12, 12½, 14? Why does a 13th dinner guest bode evil? Triskaidekaphobia—fear of the number 13—has resulted in numerous superstitions. They have evolved from an ancient belief that 12 was a perfect number and the addition of 1 disrupted that state. The rightness of 12 was written in the heavens, where each year the 12 constellations of the Zodiac wheeled overhead in order, telling men when to plant and when to harvest. The labors of Hercules were 12; 12 gods dwelt on Mt. Olympus; there were 12 tribes of Israel, 12 Disciples, and 12 days of Christmas. And at the Last Supper, Judas was the ominous 13th guest.

The Greek philosopher Pythagoras thought that in numbers lay the meaning of the universe. He and his followers assigned symbolic meaning to numbers, a practice more mystical than mathematical but irresistible to numerologists from the Middle Ages on. Pythagoreans regarded all even numbers as feminine and all odd ones as masculine. Number 1 was identified with reason, God, unity, and the sun; 2 meant divisibility, opinion, sociability, and the moon; 3 had many meanings; 4, imagined as a square, stood for solidity and foundation, as in the 4 seasons, the points of the compass, and the Evangelists; 5 was associated with fire, love, and marriage; 6 was perfect, being the sum of 1, 2, and 3; it represents Creation, accomplished in 6 days. The Pythagoreans called two numbers "friendly" if each were the sum of

the divisors of the other (220 and 284, for instance). Such numbers were considered so friendly as to be positively aphrodisiac by some, who wrote them on digestible pellets and swallowed them.

Number 3 is in a category of its own. Some people regard it as a universal concept of the human mind. Sacred trinities are found in Egyptian and Hindu religions as well as in Christianity. And since it takes two people to make a new one, 3 is the number of fertility and the family. Our words "tree" and "three" have the same root. To Pythagoreans, 3 was special because it was the sum of 1 (heavenly unity) and 2 (earthly diversity), and thus stood for all of reality. Poseidon's trident; the three sons of Noah from whom mankind descends; the many fairytale kings with 3 sons or daughters; past, present, and future—all suggest the potent influence of 3 on the imagination. Also, 3 mediates between dualities, as in Hegel's theory of logic as "thesis, antithesis, and synthesis." Freud's theory of personality as ego, superego, and id may well echo the father of psychoanalysis' subconscious understanding of the universal regard for the number 3.

Good things come in threes, they say, as well as bad things. Except, of course, four-leaf clovers. Legend has it that they grew plentifully in Paradise, and Eve took one with her when she and Adam were evicted.

Despite the fact that mathematics has given us, for better or worse, our modern world, the highjinks of numerology are still popular with gamblers, followers of the occult, and even mathematicians. Did Shakespeare work on the King James translation of the Bible? Certainly, says a numerologist, and here is the proof. The 46th word in the 46th psalm is "shake." Count back to the 46th word from the end (excluding amen) and you come to the word "spear." When the King James Version was completed in 1610, Shakespeare was 46 years old.

The life of composer Richard Wagner is absolutely enveloped in 13's. There are 13 letters to his name, he was born in 1813, the sum of which is 13. He wrote 13 great works. *Tannhäuser*, for instance, was completed on April 13, 1845, and first performed in Paris on March 13, 1861. He died on February 13, 1883, a year whose first and last digits make 13.

Number 7 has always been lucky, both to Pythagoreans and to gamblers. So on 7/7/77 bettors at The Meadows, a racetrack near Pittsburgh, naturally bet on the 7th horse in the 7th race, a nag called Speech Writer. Suddenly a bolt of lightning struck the tote board, demolishing it, and superstitious bettors withdrew their bets en masse. Too bad, because he won.

"O" traveled the usual route from Phoenicia to Greece to Rome. In Greece it was omikron, *the short "o" sound.*

OIL There is no doubt that oil—petroleum—makes the world go round. Motorists in the United States burn up about 300 million gallons of gasoline each day, and gasoline is just one of the by-products of the vast petroleum industry. For example, petroleum is the base of some 3,000 petrochemicals used in the production of synthetic fibers, in "miracle" fertilizers, and in a host of other products. Without oil, the bulk of the plastics industry would wither and die, public utilities would be unable to produce sufficient electricity to meet current needs, and nearly all forms of transportation would grind to a halt. Today, no nation can exist for long without a steady supply of petroleum.

It was in large measure to secure the oil output of Indonesia that Japan attacked Pearl Harbor in

---

people

A Bag o' Tricks

In the spring of 1977 the offshore well blew, spewing a deadly geyser of hot oil that fell into the chilly waters of the North Sea. Fireboats were called to the scene to soak the spouting oil and keep it from exploding into flames. On the deep-ocean rig itself, the *Bravo 14,* the crew worked furiously to seal the well, but to no avail. Minutes after the accident, all 112 of the rig's workers were fleeing for their lives. Almost immediately, an oil slick began to form, which would eventually extend some 37 miles and contain more than 5 million gallons of crude oil. The spill posed a dire threat to Norway's beaches and fishing grounds. It was then that the call went out for Paul Neal ("Red") Adair, the world's foremost practitioner of the deadliest of technological arts: extinguishing natural-gas and oil fires and capping runaway wells.

When Adair, a tough, red-faced 61-year-old Texan, arrived in Norway, concern was mounting among oil company and government officials. But to Adair it was just another routine disaster. He announced: "Don't worry . . . we'll get it. We got a bag o' tricks." And so he had. Using immense hydraulic-powered valves, called rams, he finally sealed the wellhead.

Adair's expertise was acquired over many decades and at a tremendous physical price. Once, after his pelvis and hips were shattered by an errant crane during a California oil fire, doctors said that he would be permanently crippled, but four months later he was back on the job, directing operations.

For Adair the pursuit of exploding wells began with a lucky break in 1939. A high school dropout, Red was working in the oil fields when a sudden blowout tossed him 50 feet into the air. Shrugging off the incident, he immediately got to his feet and resumed working. Watching was a man named Myron Kinley, the world's pioneer oil-field fire fighter, and he was so impressed that he immediately hired Adair. Over the next two decades the two men worked together constantly, capping runaway wells and "killing" oil-field fires all over the world. When Kinley retired in 1959, Adair went into business for himself. By then he was known worldwide as a man who was part daredevil and part superb technician, a combination crucial to killing and capping wells. In such work, high explosives are used to blow out a rig fire by depriving it of oxygen, and the explosives must be placed with exquisite care within a few feet of the flames. At a monstrous gas-and-oil fire in Algeria in 1961–62, generally considered to be the biggest in history, Adair directed operations. After months of preparation, he delicately maneuvered the boom of a giant tractor, on which hung a 550-pound explosive package within 2 feet of the roaring, flaming column. Seconds later Red ignited the charge and snuffed out the flame. Then the second and most dangerous half of the job began: capping the well against an upward pressure of 3,000 pounds per square inch. While working on the ruptured 13-inch well pipe, Red and his crew were drenched in gas: a spark could have killed them instantly. Finally, the eight-ton cap, suspended from ropes, was lowered in place. Red and his men hammered and bolted it to the top of the pipe, swinging brass hammers and wielding brass wrenches to avoid producing sparks. The cap was secured, and history's largest oil-field break was brought under control.

Such exploits have made Red Adair famous and rich, but hardly a good risk. "The greatest freedom I enjoy," he has said, "is the freedom from life insurance salesmen."

Using mud and explosives, Red Adair snuffs out oil-field fires.

1941, just four months after the United States froze Japanese credits and halted America's oil exports. And in 1973 when the Arab states, with the world's largest reserves of petroleum, banned exports of oil, the entire world economy felt the aftershock.

Yet oil was not always considered a necessary resource. The Indians of northwestern Pennsylvania skimmed the gummy stuff off streams and drank it down, thinking perhaps that anything that smelled so awful and tasted so bad had to have medicinal value. European farmers and lumbermen who came to settle in Pennsylvania in the 18th and 19th centuries were somewhat less enthusiastic about the petroleum than the Indians had been.

The newcomers cursed the mineral that seeped into their wells and bubbled up in their fields, contaminating both. Some tried to sell it as "Seneca oil," claiming it was a liniment good for both horses and men. Eventually, some who tried to burn the stuff discovered that it made an excellent illuminant, a substitute for the increasingly scarce and expensive whale oil.

In mid-19th century a group of speculators hired a former railroad conductor, Edwin Drake, gave him the bogus title "Colonel," and sent him to Titusville, the center of Pennsylvania's oil country. His job was to find oil in great quantities. Despite his inexperience in the field, Drake, a man of intelligence and imagination, hit upon the notion of drilling for oil. With the help of "Uncle Billy" Smith, Drake brought in the world's first oil well on August 27, 1859. His success generated an oil rush and turned the once sleepy hamlet of Titusville into a raucous boomtown known as "Sodden Gomorrah."

For about the next 40 years, the oil industry grew and prospered, though its principal product was still kerosene, used chiefly as an illuminant. By 1900, in the United States alone, some 37,000 oil wells were in operation and together produced 137,000 barrels a day. But as the new century dawned, two things happened that would change the nature of the oil industry. The first was the development of the internal-combustion engine, which ran on gasoline. The second was the dis-

covery of vast pools of oil beneath the soil of Texas. On January 10, 1901, just outside of Beaumont on a low rise called Big Hill, a group of diggers working under the direction of an Austrian-born engineer, Anthony Lucas, struck paydirt. As Lucas' drill bit the substratum, 1,160 feet down, there was a tremendous roar, followed by a shower of rock heaved up by pressure from below, and then a spurt of oil, followed by spectacular geysers that shot over the top of the 84-foot-high drilling derrick. This was Spindletop, the first real gusher, and it blew out 80,000 barrels a day before it was capped. The age of oil had burst upon mankind.

As greater reserves of oil were found in various parts of the United States, in Canada, Russia, Southeast Asia, Latin America, and most important, the Middle East, the world became increasingly dependent on this mineral. As for the future, some studies predict exhaustion of the world's reserves within a century. Consequently, major oil companies have taken some of their drilling equipment to sea, probing the ocean floor for new resources of gas and oil. At the same time the search for new forms of energy—solar, thermal, wind—to name just a few, is receiving worldwide attention.

OPINION POLL In 1938 only 8 percent of the American people believed that Hitler had no further territorial ambitions in Europe, and 84 percent favored registration of pistols and revolvers—so reported the three-year-old Gallup Poll, the "granddaddy" of opinion polls in the United States. While the public's recorded ideas about Hitler may have influenced America's diplomatic stance prior to the declaration of war, the citizenry's attitude toward stricter handgun control has yet to sway Congress. But decision makers at least were made aware of what people thought.

Formal opinion polls did not exist until the 1930's, but they have become increasingly important, particularly in politics and business. With no scientific way to gauge the mood of the populace, 18th-century rulers were often startled to learn of public sentiments via boycotts, demonstrations, or riots. Today, widely reported polls warn leaders of pervasive distrust of government, shrinking support

Super Ball? Actually the thing is the end of a rubberized fuel container belonging to the U.S. Army.

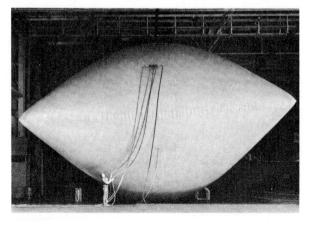

of organized labor, or a reluctance to support the open use of marijuana.

How accurate is the polling operation? In a typical survey, 1,500 people are interviewed in a sample computer-picked to approximate the desired population mix. The pollsters divide the country into 150 to 300 sections. Starting off on a randomly selected but premapped route, interviewers knock on doors, seeking interviewees. Along with answers to specific questions about political choices, opinions about products and institutions, or attitudes toward social and economic issues, these accommodating souls provide personal information about age, income, family size, religion, and education. The data are compared with census figures to make sure that the sampling is a microcosm of society as a whole—if that is what is desired.

Top polling organizations shun telephone interviewing when canvassing public opinion because it injects a bias against the poor and prohibits in-depth questioning. Although accuracy tends to increase in proportion to the number of interviews, the addition of thousands or even millions of persons has very little effect after the first 500 interviews. The Gallup Poll boasts a remarkable record. Since the 1936 presidential election, their final figures for national elections have deviated on the average by only 2.3 percentage points from the actual election returns. An impressive performance, despite the 1948 Dewey-Truman gaffe that Gallup and most other pollsters committed. The margin for error has been dropping steadily since 1936, and in the period of 1970–76 it was slightly more than one percent.

Nevertheless, critics fear that people will shift their votes because of poll results and that leaders will follow public opinion rather than try to mold it. Professional opinion researchers respond that there is no scientific proof that voters switch because of polls, and they warn against placing too much reliance on their projections. Emphasizing their faith in the democratic process, George Gallup averred: "Polls are designed to be highly accurate, but not perfect. If we were perfect, then we could do away with elections."

A greenhouse director fondles a 4-pound Ponderosa lemon. Those at right will be about 3 pounds.

The "discovery" of citrus was important enough to inspire this allegory about its arrival in Europe.

ORANGES "Oranges and lemons/Say the bells of St. Clement's./ . . . When will you pay me?/ Say the bells of Old Bailey./ When I grow rich,/ Say the bells of Shoreditch," goes an English nursery rhyme. So great was the value placed on the citrus fruits imported from southern Europe that even the bells of London pealed out a lively trade in the commodity. Introduced in northern Europe in the 1500's, the luscious orange was the fruit of kings, for only monarchs could afford the shipping costs. In the legends of ancient Greece, however, oranges, "the golden apples of Hesperides," were for the gods alone until the hero Hercules stole the fruit.

The first-known mention of oranges appeared in a Chinese book written about 500 B.C. From the mild climate of southern China, the cultivation of oranges spread throughout Asia, along the east coast of Africa, and to the Mediterranean basin. Columbus brought the orange to the Caribbean in 1493. Tradition has it that Ponce de León, the Spanish explorer, introduced the fruit to Florida in 1513, where it has flourished ever since. Today Florida produces far more oranges than does any other region on earth. Thousands upon thousands of boxes filled with fruit and millions of cans of frozen concentrated juice are exported annually from the state, and what was once the fruit of the gods has become the daily fare of common folk from Norway to Argentina.

Most Florida oranges are processed into frozen juice. One writer on assignment in Florida was dismayed to find that no restaurant could provide him with the fresh-squeezed variety. The disappointed scribe was forced to purchase a hand squeezer and press his own pulpy juice. Yet there is hope for the true citrus-fruit fancier—that is, if he happens to live in a climate suitable for citrus cultivation. With proper knowledge of budding and grafting, he can produce a single tree that will yield oranges as well as tangerines, grapefruits, limes, lemons, and even kumquats—a tree putting forth a fantasy of delights that would have thrilled even the gods on Mt. Olympus.

The original sign for the "p" sound looked like a crook, but was named by Phoenicians pē, *meaning "mouth."*

PACKAGING A truism that animates America's supersalesmen in the worlds of advertising and marketing holds: it is the package rather than the product that causes the consumer to plunk down hard cash at the checkout counter. One has but to wander the aisles of a well-stocked supermarket to be convinced of the truth of this adage, for the variety of packaging designs far exceeds the variety of goods.

Gone are the sturdy wooden barrels that held nails, beans, or pickles, which customers themselves could shovel out and give to the clerk. And soap bars that once were wrapped in papers on which were printed in no-nonsense letters the manufacturers' names are now likely to be encased in fancy cardboard boxes. Even the vegetable and fruit bins have a new look. Where once they overflowed with apples, onions, or tomatoes—an arrangement that permitted the customer to squeeze and poke to determine freshness—now there are apt to be neat rows of produce-filled boxes, the glow of their contents enhanced by the light-reflecting plastic wrap that covers all.

Does it work, this emphasis on packaging? According to marketing researchers, it could hardly work better. A survey of nearly 7,000 consumers revealed that about 30 percent made impulse purchases and that most did so because they were attracted by the appearance of the merchandise. Well then, what kinds of displays attract customers? Color, evidently, plays a major role. For example, some experts believe that a bluish-white package conveys the idea of cleanliness about detergents, while pastel shades in general suggest refinement and sophistication. But this is not always the impression the seller wishes to convey. Coffee is often packaged in cans that are colored in rich reds or browns, and on jars of instant coffees the same colors predominate, for buyers apparently associate these hues with hearty flavor.

As is evident during even the most casual perusal of the nation's stores, the art of packaging and the science of mass psychology are now inextricably joined. But this is no marriage of recent vintage. For many decades, French perfumers have known that a scent's appeal is greatly enhanced by the cut-glass vial in which it is held. In Japan there is a centuries-old art form called *tsutsumu* that is dedicated to the creation of simple yet elegant handmade wrappings for such humble fare as eggs and fish—wrappings that at once delight the eye and tempt the palate.

All this packaging may sell goods, but it creates problems, too. The millions of tons of packaging—glass, metal, paper, wood, plastic—manufactured every year turn to garbage. Packagers are making tentative steps toward recycling, but their forte remains the development of new products. The retort pouch, for example, a "flexible can" of plastic and aluminum, can be packed with anything that metal containers can, stacked on shelves, and heated in boiling water. Because in the processing the contents are heated in a fraction of the time needed to heat the contents of cans, the food is better tasting, and packagers think that pouched foods will eventually replace canned and frozen kinds. When one firm tested beef Stroganoff and chicken cacciatore in such containers in the late 1970's,

Tsutsumu, *the old Japanese packaging craft, is also art.*

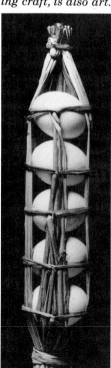

A Turkestani melon vendor wraps each fruit in a protective fiber casing.

they ran into a major snag: they could not keep up with the demand. A colander bag now allows the cook to serve hot, nongluey rice even when dinner is delayed, and housewives can put food sold in plastic-coated paperboard trays right into the oven.

One of the great merchandisers in American business was Raymond Loewy, a Frenchman who came to the United States after World War I and established himself as an industrial designer. Even as a youth, Loewy seemed to have a unique flair for design, so much so that as a private in the French Army he insisted on a uniform of his own creation. During the war his dugout was renowned as the most elegant shelter on the western front. The sleek, streamlined look of today's automobiles owes much to Loewy's pioneering efforts in the 1940's. But the humble cigarette pack most dramatically sustained Loewy's belief in the primacy of package over product. During World War II he reworked the Lucky Strike package, changing the color from green to white ("*Lucky Strike* Green Has Gone to War") and emblazoning the pack, front and back, with the cigarette's original trademark: a tricolored bull's eye. Shortly, sales increased by 20 percent.

PAIN There is no precise scientific definition of pain, yet we all know it when we feel it. But all people do not experience pain in the same way. For example, women in the so-called developed nations, such as the United States, apparently feel more pain in childbirth than do women in developing countries, such as the nations of Africa. The difference is cultural. We are "not the land of the stiff upper lip," as one pain expert put it, so women are permitted to feel more pain and consequently do. Similarly, studies have shown that people from cultures that value stoicism, such as those of northern Europe, experience less physical suffering than those from cultures that permit greater expression of emotion. These and other studies make clear that there is a strong psychological ingredient in a person's perception of pain.

Some individuals, for reasons yet to be fully explained, do not feel pain at all. These "painless people" live in danger, for hurting is the body's warning signal, calling attention to a condition that needs to

Those who have suffered gout will find James Gillray's etching (1799) neither funny nor exaggerated.

be remedied. A person unable to feel pain, for instance, might place his hand on a hot stove without noticing and sustain a severe burn.

Medicine traditionally has divided pain into two categories, acute and chronic, although neurologists can classify more than 100 different types. Acute pain is the alarm clock going off, as when we cut a finger or break a leg, and it can be expected to go away eventually. Chronic pain endures. In the United States victims of chronic back distress book 18 million appointments at doctors' offices every year, and headache sufferers account for another 12 million. One expert on pain estimates that we lose $50 billion a year to chronic pain in health care, lost productivity, and insurance compensation. We spend $1 billion on analgesic drugs for severe pain, and another $1 billion on ordinary painkillers.

Despite the knowledge that some pain is psychological in origin, dolorologists (pain specialists) have begun to treat all physical aches as real, as they are to the persons feeling them. "The overwhelming majority of chronic-pain patients need to have their whole lives examined," asserts a doctor in the pain clinic at the University of Washington in Seattle. (At least 20 clinics devoted to relieving chronic pain have been established in the U.S. since the mid-1960's.) The understanding is that patients often pamper themselves or are pampered by their families, so the approach to a cure can involve working with the attitudes of the patient and his family as well as with his body. In one clinic, sufferers are not allowed to mention their problems unless specifically asked in a consultation. They are weaned from drugs and encouraged to exercise as soon and as much as possible. They may also be taught biofeedback and self-hypnotism and receive acupuncture treatments along with more conventional therapy.

Regrettably, there is enough pain in the world to keep physicians busy, and so it has always been. The ancient Greeks used opium, derived from the poppy plant, as a painkiller, but the problem was that it was addictive. The same was true of morphine, derived from opium 2,000 years later, in 1805. Its discoverer named the drug after Morpheus, the god of dreams. Heroin, another derivative of opium, followed. But heroin is so addictive that it has no legal medical use in the U.S. Other methods of alleviating

Prometheus bound: a symbol of pain's grip.

pain have been found. When Governor George Wallace of Alabama developed severe back pain after being confined to a wheelchair, his physicians installed a "transcutaneous nerve stimulator," which sent a weak electrical current into the area over a portion of his spinal cord. It helped. The use of electrical current to block pain is not new. In 43 A.D., a Roman doctor used electricity-generating fish to fight pain, although the fish sometimes gave off enough electricity to kill the patient. There is strong evidence that the body manufactures its own painkillers, called endorphins. They resemble artificial painkillers chemically, and some are addictive. Researchers are hoping that others are not, because we then would be closer to the final solution to pain: a cheap, safe painkiller that works every time.

PAJAMAS Before climbing into bed, men and women in medieval times usually tied on a snug nightcap, took off their clothes—and that was that. On cold winter nights, however, they kept on the shirts they had worn during the day. Not until the Renaissance was much distinction made between day smocks and night smocks. By the 1600's, however, it had become the custom for an engaged couple to give each other fancy nightclothes with matching caps. Lest nights be steamy, one writer advised, "Let your night cappe have a hole in the top through which the vapour may goe out."

Did she don these duds for sleeping or partying?

People keep trying to take the loose, comfortable nightclothes out of the bedroom and set them up as daywear. In Queen Anne's time, a vogue among ladies for wearing nightgowns in the street caused public concern until a murderess was induced to appear for her execution in her nightgown, which swiftly quelled the fad.

Until well into the 1800's, men as well as women snuffed the candles in a shoulder-to-ankle garment that made women look cuddly and men look ridiculous. But in the 1870's British colonials brought back a new type of nightwear from India. Called *pājāma*, meaning "leg clothes" in Hindi, these loose-fitting trousers with sashed tops gave boudoir distinction to men at last. Lounging pajamas seemed to go well in the 20th-century with central heating, the electric light, the radio, and the cocktail shaker. "The nightgown," wrote a fashion commentator of the 1920's, "was an early-retiring garment, while the modern pajama goes to bed rather late." And when Valentino, the romantic idol of early movies, appeared in lounging pajamas, every wife demanded that her husband have a pair. The boyish flappers took up pajamas gleefully, giving adult "pajama parties" to which everyone came in gay stripes and prints.

In Buenos Aires in the 1920's it was illegal to appear coatless, so in the hot summer of 1929 a brief craze of men going to work in their coatlike pajama tops swept the city. And in Chicago in the same year, haberdashers trying to liberate men's summer dress marched through downtown streets in pajamas. But in the long run it has been the women (and their designers) who have taken pajamas out to dinner, bringing the comfort of bedclothes into high fashion.

PANTS In China women wore trousers. In ancient Egypt men wore skirts, as they did in Scotland. And in Turkey the sultan's harem girls wore pants. But for centuries in Europe and America, the man in the family wore the pants, while his wife wore skirts. Men and women both wore loose-fitting garments until Asian horsemen, who spent much of their time in the saddle, adopted a costume more practical for that occupation—the ancestor of the modern pair of pants. The custom of wearing pants spread throughout northern Europe, and when Julius Caesar landed in Britain in 55 B.C., he was struck by the vividly colored trousers worn by the natives. But most Romans were not impressed, and for a time they continued to wrap themselves proudly in tunics and togas, considering pants contemptible garments suitable only for slaves and barbarians.

Throughout the centuries ordinary men continued to wear trousers, while the upper classes switched their attire with the changes in fashion. In the Middle Ages the rich wore tunics and tights. In the 18th century they wore tight knee breeches. By the end of the century pantaloons, loose-fitting breeches, were in fashion. They were named after Pantaleone, an Italian stock comic character who

Rosa Bonheur, 1893. Skirts made her painting trips impossible, so Paris police allowed her to wear pants.

always wore baggy pants. (Our word "pants," which comes from "pantaloons," always appears in the plural, since pants are double, like trousers and scissors.) After the French Revolution, tight breeches loosened, and as the 19th century progressed, trousers came into style for all men. But trousers were not accepted easily in some upper-class circles. In 1814 the duke of Wellington was refused admission to his club because he was wearing trousers instead of knee breeches.

Recently, history has repeated itself. Women have been refused admission to fashionable restaurants for being so unladylike as to wear pants, though the precedent for women wearing pants was set more than a century ago. At that time a few women's liberationists, most notably Amelia Bloomer, who gave her name to a startling new pantaloon-like costume called the "bloomer," shocked America by wearing pants. Women's liberation, however, has not progressed as fast as the acceptance of women in trousers has. Now even the most conservative women wear them, as the most conservative men have done for centuries.

For want of a horse: the world went pantless until Asians made riding garb. Above, Mongol polo players.

PAPER "It shoes newe bookes, and keepes old workes awake," wrote poet Thomas Churchyard, Gentleman, in his 1588 paean to paper. Though paper still "shoes newe bookes," its capacity to keep "old workes awake" has diminished. Like many articles of civilization, paper—at least the sort commonly used by publishers for the last century—will self-destruct within 30 to 50 years. Thus much of the written record of this period—novels, short stories, essays, histories, biographies, and even documents and business and private papers—unless they are reprinted, microfilmed, or computer-stored, of course—are in danger of crumbling and turning to dust.

The culprit is the decay built into the chemistry of paper itself. Almost all paper used for printing is made from wood pulp, and much of it contains an acid that is released over the years and eats away at the paper. Even high-quality sheets that do not release acid are only marginally less suicidal, as they are coated with a compound called alumrosin that gives off sulfuric acid and inexorably consigns its host to dust.

It was not always so. There was a time when paper would last for hundreds, and in some cases even thousands of years. Indeed, from the beginning of the Christian era through the mid-19th century, paper was made of fibers—most often of macerated rags—and was coated with gelatin, which helped to preserve it.

Perhaps paper suits did not catch on because they disintegrate in rain.

The word "paper" is derived from *papyrus*, a writing material made by the ancient Egyptians, who scraped out the inner bark of the papyrus plant and pressed the fibers together into thin sheets on which court scribes could set down the Pharaoh's activities. By 3000 B.C. papyrus was in wide use. In time, the sheets were rolled into scrolls and stored in repositories that served as libraries. Wherever papyrus grew in the civilized Mediterranean world, it became the primary medium of literature. But papyrus did not grow everywhere, and the peoples who had scant access to it had to find some other medium. The Hebrews of biblical times, and the Persians as well, made use of animal hides, which were readily available to them. The processed skins were called "parchment" and became by medieval times the writing surface of choice.

Much earlier, however, according to traditional accounts, the inventor of paper as we know it was Ts'ai Lun, a eunuch in the court of the Chinese emperor Ho-Ti. In 105 A.D. Ts'ai Lun conducted a great experiment. He macerated the wet inner bark of trees, along with pieces of hemp, old rags, and fishnet, spread the pulp evenly and thinly on a drying frame, and produced a surface suitable for receiving inks and paints. This material was cheaper than the sheets of silk his countrymen were accustomed to using.

A craftsman in Kyoto, Japan, adds touches to a paper shrine.

Though the use of paper soon spread through China's neighboring regions, a millennium would pass before techniques of papermaking reached the Western world. The purveyors were the Arabs, and they learned Ts'ai Lun's secret only through the accident of war. In 751 A.D. a battle between Arab and Chinese soldiers near the central Asian city of Samarkand left two Chinese papermakers in the hands of the Muslim victors. The craftsmen, making the best of a bad thing, set up shop in Samarkand, and the Chinese secret of papermaking was out. By that time Muslim power had expanded westward to North Africa and Spain, and so went the papermaker's trade. Lacking the mulberry bark that was the primary ingredient of Chinese paper, the Arabs turned to linen and hemp for their basic raw materials. By the middle of the 12th century, Europe's first paper mill had opened in Moorish Spain, and from there the art spread throughout the continent.

The invention of the printing press in the 15th century increased the demand for paper. But the proliferation of books and newspapers in the wake of the Industrial Revolution created a shortage of rags for papermaking. So severe was the shortage in the United States by the mid-19th century, for example, that papermakers actually imported linen wrappings from Egyptian mummies. But progress of a sort was on the way. On January 14, 1863, a Boston newspaper proudly proclaimed itself to be made entirely from wood-pulp paper. Fine linen and cotton papers all but disappeared after that, and at about the same time, animal gelatins for sizing were replaced by alum-rosin.

Paper-base products have been used for an amazing variety of items—from houses to throwaway clothing—and paper for books is but a tiny fraction of the production of mills. Yet the most vital use of paper remains, at least for now, what it always was: a material on which to inscribe the record of man's accumulated knowledge.

PAPER CLIP Unbend and consider the lowly paper clip. Its primary uses are legion—from cleaning fingernails and charred pipes, to securing ties and suspenders, to masquerading as poker chips in office card games, to being twisted and broken viciously during tense phone calls. Twenty percent of all clips, however, are used to hold papers, or so states a legendary and perhaps apocryphal report attributed to Lloyd's Bank of London. The report declines to track the whereabouts of clips fired into space by rubber bands, or fashioned into chains, or transformed into wearing apparel. One office girl, for example, accumulated 40 pounds of clips and then made them into a dress.

The forerunner of the paper clip, a fastener of wax and ribbon, appeared in the 13th century, when paperwork was all but nonexistent. The modern "gem" clip, that thrice-twisted triumph of wire and human ingenuity, was invented by the British around 1900 to help keep a grip on the paperwork involving the empire.

Contemporary paper clips start life as part of a 19,000-foot coil of rusty, recycled steel, which is high in carbon, an element that gives clips their staying power. The wire then is stretched, bathed in acid, coated with tin or copper, twisted, and fired out of a machine at the rate of more than 200 clips a minute.

In 1974 something of a national emergency occurred when a scarcity of raw materials created a shortage of paper clips, and office workers were forced to scrape their pipes and attach their papers by other means. The nation's largest paperclip purchaser? The United States government, of course, which uses (and loses) 10 percent of all clips produced in this country.

PARKING METER There is something about a parking meter than can rouse the rebel in the most conforming breast, turn an honest man or woman into a petty felon, and bring out the brute in the mildest of people. With its insatiable appetite for coins and inexorable clockwork, the parking meter is just one more tax—a levy, in effect, for parking beside a public curb already paid for with taxpayers' funds. Invented by Carl C. Magee

Wornout welcome: parkers who overstay their time in Osaka, Japan, are chained to the meter till they pay up.

inserted her gold wedding ring in a meter slot.

Besides meter cheaters, there have been meter thieves, too. In New York some robbers have done it the hard way, slicing off meters with a pipe cutter. A boy in Houston had a better idea. He found that he could suck coins up to the slot, hold them with his teeth, and remove them with his fingers—until the police caught up with him.

At least some nongovernmental good has come of the parking meter. According to one story, policemen sometimes put in coins for delinquent parkers, especially during the holiday season. A little note points out the good deed and suggests that the police association children's fund gratefully accepts all contributions. The policemen find that returns on their investment are very good.

In spite of the public's obvious discontent, the parking meter is here to stay. It represents one more skirmish in the long war between the bureaucracy and the citizenry over traffic control. The war dates back at least as far as Julius Caesar's time, when the dictator banned private chariots from the streets of Rome during business hours. (State vehicles, of course, were exempted.) Caesar would have approved the latest wrinkle in parking meterology: a built-in sensor that automatically turns the clock to zero when the car beside the meter pulls away before its time is up. This will put an end to the old ploy of finding and using time left ticking on a meter.

and introduced on the streets of Oklahoma City in July 1935, the parking meter has been the target of bricks and bats and lock picks, manipulated by professional burglars, and the cause of at least one statewide referendum to ban their use, successfully launched by a North Dakotan who objected to paying a one-dollar fine for overstaying his curbside welcome.

Consider the fury that must have animated one wealthy Minnesota matron as she sat in her limousine on a subzero night and cruised the streets of her hometown. The car stopped at meter after meter, and her chauffeur stepped into the cold. Waterfilled syringe in hand, he injected each coin slot, freezing 30 of them before the local constabulary confronted the malefactors.

Many less ingenious, but no less incensed, parkers have taken their revenge by stuffing the machines with whatever came to hand. In the mid-1960's, after the introduction of the pulltop can, city officials all over the United States complained of finding coin boxes full of metal rings. Chicago amassed the largest collection—the yield there was some 74,000 in one month. Can manufacturers reluctantly redesigned the pulltab but not without complaining that, aside from the fact that it would cost millions, the fault lay with the meter makers. The machines, in fact, have accepted as payment objects as diverse as paper clips, toothpicks, earrings, religious medals, and buttons. There was one woman, perhaps meaning to solve two problems at once, who

Meter feeder: a reindeer grazes on in Anchorage, Alaska, while a man buys him standing room.

PASSPORT For centuries governments have issued passes of safe conduct to travelers—in forms ranging from letters of confidence drawn on papyrus to rings bearing the royal seal—but the use of passports as compulsory documents of travel is largely a 20th-century phenomenon. The Roman emperor Augustus anticipated the language of today's passports by 2,000 years with his certificates of travel: "If there be anyone on land or sea hardy enough to molest [the traveler], let him consider whether he be strong enough to wage war with Caesar."

The first American passport was issued on July 8, 1796, to Francis Maria Barrere, "a citizen of the United States having occasion to pass into foreign countries about his lawful affairs," and was signed by Secretary of State Thomas Pickering. Most early American passports were simple sheets of paper issued by local authorities and notaries. They were not mandatory, but most travelers carried them. A Texan likened his passport to his pistol: "You didn't want it often, but when you did want it, you wanted it very badly." In 1856 the responsibility for issuing passports was given to the U.S. secretary of state exclusively rather than to notaries and local authorities. In 1914 photographs replaced written descriptions of the bearers, and in 1926 the passport was transformed into a hardcover booklet.

Today's standard passport of 24 pages is held by some 13 million Americans. To obtain one, people need to present proof of citizenship and identity and two photographs taken within the past six months and pay a modest fee. Passports are required for visits to most foreign countries, the most notable exception being Canada.

people

Passports from Nowhere

"Let me tell you one secret of such so-called successes as there have been in my life. It was to burn my boats and demolish the bridges behind me. Then there is no choice but Forward!" So spoke Fridtjof Nansen (1861–1930)—Norwegian oceanographer, zoologist, artist, and explorer—near the end of a life marked by incredible scientific and humanitarian achievements.

A physically powerful man, 6 feet 2 inches tall, with blond hair and chilling blue eyes, Nansen became world famous, first as an Arctic explorer of extreme courage and incalculable resource. Born on a farm outside Oslo, Nansen had a passion for the wilderness, and he despised cities, where, he said, "men incessantly rub against each other until they become round, smooth ciphers." And so in 1888 Nansen, three Norwegian sportsmen, and two Lapp guides set out on an incredible journey—the crossing of Greenland from east to west, with no base to return to in the east. In making the journey in less than two months, Nansen and his band gathered invaluable scientific data for weather forecasting throughout the North Atlantic.

Nansen's next adventure involved a unique method of reaching the North Pole. Concluding that "a current flows at some point between the Pole . . . [and] the east coast of Greenland," he planned to ram a specially built and equipped vessel into the ice field north of the Siberian islands and allow the ship to freeze there.

In three to five years, he reasoned, the ship would emerge near Greenland after having passed near the Pole or crossed it. His vessel was designed with a round hull so that it would rise above the ice and not be crushed. His wife christened it the *Fram*, the Norwegian word for "forward." Nansen and 12 handpicked sailors and scientists set out in September 1893. Early in the second year of the icebound voyage, Nansen realized that the *Fram* would not reach the Pole, so with a single companion and three sleds and

Fridtjof Nansen as a young man

dog teams, Nansen left the *Fram* some 360 miles south of the Pole. In less than a month Nansen and his partner traveled to within 226 miles of the Pole, farther north than any explorer had ever gone. But southerly currents and movement of the ice made further progress impossible. After living through the Arctic winter in a hand-built stone hut, they were rescued by an English exploring party in the spring of 1896. In Au-

gust, Nansen reached Norway, followed shortly by the *Fram*.

Back home and now world famous, Nansen left his scientific research in 1905 to become head of Norway's successful move to win its independence from Sweden. At the end of World War I the already embattled League of Nations did what Norway had done in time of crisis: it called on Nansen. He was to negotiate with Russia for the release of thousands of sick and starving prisoners of war. Acting as a private representative of the nations involved, Nansen succeeded in getting 427,000 prisoners released. The League of Nations thought that repatriation would cost $200 for each prisoner; Nansen did the job for $8.60 per person. Called in again to help the needy—1.5 million refugees wandering through Europe as a result of the Russian Revolution—Nansen arranged to resettle most of the displaced persons, in many cases providing food and jobs. He even solved the lack-of-passport problem in the spirit of his credo, "Forward," by issuing his own "Nansen certificates." Eventually 52 governments came to honor these unique documents, which bore, instead of a government seal, the profile of Fridtjof Nansen. In 1922 Nansen was awarded the Nobel Peace Prize. Characteristically, he gave away the money, part of it for the rehabilitation of Greek refugees. Nansen was still looking forward when he died: one of his final dreams was to cross the North Pole in a zeppelin.

Cascades of pasta hung out to dry serve as a backdrop for the proudly posed employees of an Italian pastificio.

PASTA Thomas Jefferson introduced pasta to a tiny group of Americans. Returning in 1789 after a tour of duty as ambassador to France, he brought home a spaghetti-making machine and served small steaming portions of pasta to family and friends at Monticello. Pasta, however, was not produced commercially in the United States until 1848, and not until the introduction of durum wheat late in the 19th century did it become popular. Americans tried pasta, liked it, and began to consume it at a prodigious rate.

A popular belief is that Marco Polo introduced pasta to the West when he returned from China in 1295, but perhaps he has been given credit for too much. At least 11 years before his trip, according to records of that time, the Romans were eating ravioli, and fettuccine is more ancient than that. But even the Romans may not deserve credit, for many cultures have legends about its beginnings.

A Laotian woman employs an ingenious device to make rice noodles.

Whatever its origins, pasta has aroused controversy. At least one pope published regulations about its quality, and several physicians launched campaigns against its consumption. In the 1930's a political supporter of Mussolini began his own anti-pasta campaign. Calling it "anti-virile," he wrote, "Spaghetti is no food for fighters." Probably he was right, for all over the world pasta is a true food of contentment for peace-loving folk.

Poetic Pasta

According to the National Macaroni Institute, pasta comes in 150 different shapes, but that is only an estimate. All it takes to change the tally is a fillip of imagination on the part of a pasta maker. The Italians, glorying in their melodic language, are responsible for naming the various shapes. "We make poetry with our pasta—flowers, stars, seashells, beautiful twirls, and elegant twists," rhapsodized one proud countryman.

The names of some of the smallest pasta, the tiny bits of noodles that can be sprinkled in soup, translate as "little cupids," "angel's hair," "maidenhair fern," "little mushrooms," "lily of the valley," "apple seeds," or "little boots." Spaghetti, the most ubiquitous of pastas, means "little cords" or "strings"; linguine, narrow and flat, means "little tongues"; and vermicelli, a thin spaghetti, means "little worms."

The following guide may help diners to decipher an Italian menu the next time around. Bucatini is hollow, like macaroni, but thinner than spaghetti. Cannelloni, or "large reeds," is a pasta wrapping for a variety of stuffings. Farfalle means "butterflies," and the American counterpart is called "bows." Fettucine translates as "small ribbons." Lasagne, wide and flat, is used for baked dishes. Manicotti, or "small muffs," are tubes for stuffing, and ravioli, or pasta squares, are also for stuffing. Rigatoni are large pasta tubes with grooves, and tortellini are "small twists."

PEANUT Today when people hear the word "peanut," many think of Jimmy Carter, the Georgia peanut farmer who rose to become President. A generation ago they thought of George Washington Carver, the great black scientist, born a slave, who made the lowly peanut a mainstay of the South's economy. When children hear the word "peanut," however, they have visions of treats—sweet peanut brittle, chocolate bars filled with crunchy peanuts, and bags of peanuts in the shell sold at circuses and ball games. But above all in the United States they probably think of peanut-butter-and-jelly sandwiches, that staple of the American child's diet.

Americans yearly eat more than 4 pounds of peanut butter per capita, accounting for 55 percent of U.S. peanut production. Some like it chunky, some like it smooth, and some become hysterical when it sticks to the roof of the mouth (a fear called "arachibutyrophobia," from the botanical name of the peanut, *Arachis hypogaea*, and from the Latin word for butter). Cavils aside, Americans consume more peanuts than do any other people. Peanuts are used in soups, breads, cakes, salads, and even beverages. Thanks to the pioneering research of Carver and his successors, peanuts also go into the manufacture of ink, shampoo, linoleum, fabric, soap, paint, axle grease, and even nitroglycerin. Though the peanut is also grown widely in China, India, West Africa, and in South America, where the plant originated, in those areas it is used mostly to make cooking oil.

Peanuts and peanut butter are among the most nutritious foods known to man. Astronauts ate peanut-butter-and-jelly sandwiches on their trip to the moon. One peanut-butter sandwich, a glass of milk, and an orange make a meal that is almost perfectly balanced nutritionally, with the peanuts supplying large quantities of protein. That is because the peanut is a member of the protein-rich legume family, like beans and peas, and not a nut.

Like other legumes, the peanut grows on a bush. Its pods, peanuts in shells, which are the fruit of the plant, grow underground. Fields of peanut bushes cover thousands of acres in Southern states, most notably in Georgia, which annually produces almost a million pounds of peanuts, more than twice as many as any other state.

The Indians of South America cultivated peanuts at least 2,000 years ago, and pottery jars shaped like peanuts have been found in tombs of the Incas. The Spaniards brought peanut cultivation to Europe, and soon thereafter the plant reached Africa. Slave traders fattened captives for the auction block on a diet of peanuts. African slaves introduced peanuts to the American South, where they were dubbed "goober peas" and considered suitable only for slaves and poor folks.

During the Civil War, however, Yankee troops in the South munched peanuts on their long marches and sang a tune popular among their Southern brothers about eating goober peas. They brought the habit back home with them, and the peanut became a national staple. But its popularity reached a peak only after 1890, when a St. Louis doctor got the bright idea of grinding peanuts into a smooth paste suitable for invalids, and peanut butter was born.

PEN The prolific consumer society of post–World War II America was heralded not by shiny automobiles and whirring air conditioners but by a more modest device: the ball-point pen. In its 1945 incarnation, however, the pen sold for the far-from-modest price of $12.50.

The ink was barely dry on Japan's surrender documents when a Chicago promoter, Milton Reynolds, began mass-marketing an adaptation of a ball-point pen invented just a few years earlier by a Hungarian living in Argentina. (As early as

In this 9th-century manuscript illumination, St. Mark dips his pen before continuing to set down his gospel.

1888 an American, John Loud, had obtained a patent on a similar device.) In October 1945, when a New York department store announced that it had a supply of these newfangled writing devices, long lines of customers waited patiently outside, and the store sold some 25,000 pens in a week. After all, it was rumored, the pen could write underwater. This tale was given substance when a store set up a display in which a pen was shown writing under water. One of Reynolds' competitors became so incensed that he launched an advertising campaign for a nonexistent "rocket" pen. Among the pen's many functions, said the manufacturer, was its ability to "spotweld, melt locks, etch letters in solid concrete [and] remove superfluous hair. . . ."

But could Reynolds' ball point do so prosaic a thing as write on paper—on dry land? Not very well, apparently, for the chromium-steel balls stuck, the "leak-proof" cartridges leaked ink into thousands of pockets, and the ink itself, when applied to paper, had a tendency to smear. In just seven months no fewer than 104,643 dissatisfied customers returned their hard-won purchases, and the ball-point pen seemed headed for oblivion. Eventually, however, the bumps in the ball point were smoothed out, and prices plummeted to a highly reasonable 19 cents for utilitarian models.

Found everywhere today—even underwater—the ball point is a worthy descendant of the first pens developed in ancient times to inscribe signs, symbols, hieroglyphs, and letters on clay and wax tablets, and papyrus. These first pens were sharpened reeds, and styluses made of metal, bone, or ivory. Indeed, reeds and then quills—shaved to a fine point—remained man's primary writing instruments until well into the 19th century. As early as the mid-17th century, however, the precursors of the fountain pen, complete with built-in ink tank, made their appearance. By the early 19th century, metal nibs were challenging the dominance of the quill. Still, as late as the 1850's, American schoolchildren were expected to make their own pens, using a penknife, of course, to sharpen the goose quills. Then in 1884 an American, Lewis Waterman, devised the first effective fountain pen. This premier model was filled by eyedropper and had a feed bar to maintain a steady flow of ink. With various improvements, the fountain pen remained for decades the writing instrument of choice and a favorite gift for graduations and birthdays.

Today a new type of pen has captured the public's fancy: soft-tipped markers with inks in rainbow hues and points ranging from superfine to thick. The fountain pen now serves as a status symbol for some executives. As for the ball point, a variant has been developed that would gladden the heart of Milton Reynolds. Styled for the needs of astronauts, this new point can write in gravity-free environments and at any angle, even upside down. Its applications here on earth seem a bit limited, but it is certain that promoters somewhere are working on plans to persuade the public that happiness requires a pen that its owner can use while floating around freely in his personal space satellite.

PENCIL Few items have been so mislabeled as the lead pencil. Traditionally, the only lead in pencils has been the traces of that metal in the paint used to color the wood casings. The core that forms the writing point contains no lead at all but is rather a mixture of graphite and clay. The more graphite, the softer and darker the point. Yet the word "lead" does have a historical relevance. The Romans made rules on papyrus scrolls with lead discs and then used a tiny brush, called a *pencillus*, to write across the lines they had made.

Cavalier by Ingres

A lot of talent and simple pencil and paper resulted in artist Ingres' sketch of Mrs. Vesey and daughter.

According to most sources, the pencil had its origins in a fierce rainstorm in 1564 that uprooted an immense tree in Borrowdale, England. In the cavity the townspeople discovered a vast supply of pure graphite, thought at the time to be a form of lead. In the next year, 1565, a German-Swiss naturalist, Konrad von Gesner, reported that he was using pieces of graphite secured in a wooden holder as an implement for making notes and sketches. Whether this was the world's first pencil is not known, but it was certainly among the earliest.

Since Gesner's day, billions of pencils have been produced. In the United States alone, more than 2 billion are made annually, or almost 10 pencils for every American. Ever since the invention of the first practical typewriter in the 19th century, the demise of the pencil has been widely predicted, with renewed prophecies of doom every time a new communications tool or calculating device is made available to the consumer. But through it all, pencil makers the world around have endured and even prospered.

Today's typical pencil contains enough graphite to trace a 35-mile-long line or write no fewer than 45,000 words. With but two pencils, a sufficient supply of paper, and a dash of inspiration, an author can write a novel or an artist can fill a gallery with sketches—all for a few dimes.

PENICILLIN During World War I a young bacteriologist, serving as a lieutenant in Britain's Royal Army Medical Corps, looked at the face of death and, like so many of his colleagues, cursed the impotence of his science. Hundreds of soldiers, some of them with only minor wounds, were condemned by infections that sent death-dealing

Penicillin certainly cannot cure every ill, but many of these children would have been freed from this dreary 19th-century hospital ward by the wonder drug.

bacteria coursing through their bloodstreams. "Surrounded by all those infected wounds," said Alexander Fleming many years later, "by men who were suffering, dying without our being able . . . to help them, I was consumed by a desire to discover . . . something which would kill those [disease bearing] microbes. . . ." That desire launched Fleming on a scientific search that culminated in the development of penicillin: the world's first antibiotic, the first of the miracle drugs that kill off hosts of life-destroying bacteria, without dangerous side effects in most cases.

For Fleming the war was a goad to action, and through the 1920's he worked in his London laboratory culturing various strains of harmful bacteria as he sought a chemical means of destroying them. Yet when the first victory came, it was chance as much as hard work and genius that made the triumph possible. One day in 1928, while discussing his work with a colleague, Fleming's eye wandered over to a petri dish filled with a bacteria colony. The dish had been left open and had become contaminated by some airborne spores that had settled in and formed a mold around the edge. Nothing unusual there; such molds often formed on petri dishes. But something about this particular dish caused Fleming to give it a second look. At the point where the mold and the bacteria colony met, the microbes were dying off. "What had formerly been a well-developed staphylococcus colony," he later wrote, "was now but a shadow of its former self."

Over the next weeks, Fleming cultivated this apparently amazing fungus, encouraging its growth in a broth and extracting from it droplets of what he at first called "mold juice" to test

against various forms of deadly bacteria: streptococcus, staphylococcus, gonococcus. In each case the microbes died on contact with the mold juice. But what would this agent do to the human body? Would it kill the patient as well as the disease? So certain was Fleming that the fungus was benign that he drank some in solution and, as he anticipated, suffered no ill effects.

Eventually Fleming identified the mold as *penicillium notatum*. But when, in 1929, he read a paper on this seeming wonder drug to his fellow medical researchers, he failed to impress them with his findings. Perhaps his paper lacked literary merit, or perhaps his colleagues were deficient in imagination. In any case, Fleming's paper was consigned to the musty stacks of medical-research libraries.

A decade later in one such library at Oxford University, two other researchers—Dr. Howard Florey and Dr. Ernst Chain—came upon it. Fascinated by Fleming's work, and believing the author of the paper was dead, they began conducting their own experiments with the mold *penicillium notatum* and soon proved out all of Fleming's claims. Though they found that the mold was highly unstable and produced precious little antibacterial material, they were able to extract enough penicillin from the fungus to test the drug, first on mice infected with staphylococcus germs and then on a few humans similarly afflicted.

By then it was 1940, and Britain was at war again with Germany and fighting for its very existence. Though the new drug had the potential of saving hundreds of thousands of war wounded, Britain had neither the facilities to spare nor the manpower to devote to this will-of-the-wisp that was still a laboratory curiosity. No one knew how to stabilize the mold or to culture it in the vast quantities necessary to reproduce enough life-preserving antibacterial material to make it a truly viable drug. In 1941 Florey traveled to the still-neutral United States, where he enlisted the support of America's great drug concerns. Many months passed before a commercially useful *penicillium* mold was successfully produced, and additional months passed before the drug was refined and delivered to the world's battlefields.

By 1945 U.S. drug companies were producing enough of the antibiotic to treat 7 million patients each year. At last, killer ailments like blood poisoning, strep throat, venereal diseases, and scarlet fever were brought under control—all vanquished by an extract from a common mold. As for Alexander Fleming, recognition finally came his way. In 1944 he was knighted by King George VI, and in the following year he shared, with Florey and Chain, a Nobel Prize.

PENSION The first pensions were looked upon by employers and employees alike as rewards for years of faithful service, and not as a means of support for workers too old or ill to hold their jobs. It was not until the late 1800's that any government tried to create pension systems that were formal, relatively universal, and reliable. In 1881 the German political leader Otto von Bismarck put forth a proposal for social insurance, leaving little doubt about his motive for doing so. "Whoever has a pension for his old age," he said, "is far more content and far easier to handle than one who has no such prospect."

Bismarck's labor was not one of love for the German worker. He simply wanted to underwrite as much social serenity as possible. Bismarck's proposals were denounced, of course, as radical. Nonetheless, he was able to pass a national pension system, to be paid for by employers and employees, though he failed in his attempts to make the German government a contributor as well. Bismarck's ideas have since been copied in various forms by some 90 countries.

The first formal pension plan in the United States was launched in 1875 by the American Express Company. The country's largest old-age insurance program, however, commonly known as Social Security, is not really a pension at all. Its full name is now the Old Age, Survivors, Disability and Health Insurance Program, and its political father, President Franklin D. Roosevelt, had no intention of founding a pension system. He simply wanted American citizens to have a financial cushion against poverty, old age, and illness.

Despite substantial increases in Social Security benefits since 1935, it is a frugal person indeed who is capable of living on them today. In all, payments average less than $3,000 per year for each person. Nonetheless, since Social Security is compulsory, about 90 percent of the U.S. labor force pay into the program, and one estimate is that two-thirds of all private industrial employees will retire on Social Security alone.

Most people do not stay with one employer long enough to become eligible for private plans, and only relatively few private pension funds are "fully funded." Neither is Social Security, and indications are that this gigantic system may be in for trouble at about the time the century turns. The reason is that the American population is growing steadily older. In 1977, for example, the number of beneficiaries paid by Social Security amounted to about 27 percent of the active work force. Some experts believe that by the year 2030, beneficiaries will constitute about 42 percent of the active work force. In short, there will be fewer and fewer workers to pay more and more benefits to an in-

Poor folk have always counted on children for old-age care: the more, the better. This American pioneer family undoubtedly needed each other for company too.

creasing number of retirees. Because of this, many active workers are taking advantage of personal retirement plans that permit the banking of some income without taxation during each year. As time passes, such funds earn interest and increase in value. And when the owner of a plan retires and starts drawing out money saved, he may pay taxes at a low rate because his retirement income will probably be substantially less than his salary while he was working. Such funds today represent one of the brighter strands in the tangled financial patchwork that so often blights one's golden years.

PEPPER In the first decade of the 5th century A.D. the barbarian Visigoths, under their chief Alaric, swept down into Italy through the Alpine passes and laid siege to the imperial capital of Rome. As his troops screamed out their bloodcurdling war cries just beyond the city's walls, Alaric set forth his demands for lifting the siege. Aside from the usual booty—vast quantities of gold and silver and bolts of silk—the great warrior demanded from, and was given by, the terrified Romans 3,000 pounds of pepper.

Gold, silver, and silks. Certainly all these were hard to come by, and the loss of such wealth must have occasioned profound regret among the Romans. But 3,000 pounds of pepper was a deprivation almost beyond measure. For centuries before that, Rome's intrepid seamen had cast off from Red Sea ports, sailed through the Gulf of Aden, and crossed the storm-tossed Indian Ocean to the Malabar Coast of India, where they exchanged the goods of the West for the pepper of the East. It was for the most part an unprofitable trade for

Pick a peck: the tedious task of pepper gathering is depicted in illumination from French Book of Wonders.

Rome. The historian Pliny claimed that the empire was losing the equivalent of $25 million a year in Oriental barter. But Rome's aristocracy would not be denied its portions of pepper, for ownership of the spice had become a status symbol. The host who seasoned his roast fowl with a pungent peppery sauce could bask in the certainty that his guests counted him a man of taste and substance.

Originally, pepper was sought in the West more as a medicine than as a seasoning. As far back as 400 B.C. the Greek physician Hippocrates recommended it as a treatment for female complaints, and a century or so later the botanist Theophrastus wrote of pepper as an antidote for hemlock poisoning. In those times and for hundreds of years thereafter the routes to India, through Central Asia, were controlled by bands of Arabs who acted as middlemen in the pepper trade and charged extortionate prices for the spice. Even after the Romans opened the sea route to India, pepper continued to bring high prices in the markets of the Western world, and the outflow of gold to the Orient helped to debase the currency on which the economic stability of the empire depended.

The fall of the Roman Empire ushered in startling changes in many aspects of Roman life, but through the Dark Ages and medieval times pepper retained its value. It was in fact as good as gold and often replaced precious metals as a medium of exchange. Dowries, taxes, and rents were sometimes calculated in peppercorns, and many a landlord preferred payment in the spice than in the coin of the realm. For centuries Genoese and Venetian merchants in the India trade maintained a monopoly over Europe's pepper supply, and it was

partly to break that monopoly that mariner Vasco da Gama of Portugal rounded the Cape o Good Hope in 1498 to open a new sea route to the Orient. Christopher Columbus had had much the same purpose when six years earlier he sailed westward from Spain, hoping to find yet another route to Asia. He came upon the Americas instead

So anxious were Columbus and succeeding explorers to associate these new lands with the Orient that they blithely gave the name "pepper" to all the hot spices they found in the Americas— such as ground cayenne and chili—despite their dissimilarity to the true Asian varieties. But the "peppers" of the New World were no substitute for the real thing, and by the 16th century Holland was fiercely contending with Portugal for control of the Spice Islands of Indonesia. By the end of the 17th century, England, through the agency of Britain's East India Company, was wresting control of the lion's share of the Oriental pepper trade. In 1672 a young New England-born clerk, Elihu Yale, arrived in India to take a position with the British East India Company. Over the following years, Yale made a fortune in the pepper trade, much of it apparently secured by defrauding his employers. He later gave a small portion of this pepper money to a struggling Connecticut college, which showed its appreciation by changing its name to Yale.

PERFUME Since the dawn of history women and men have succumbed to the powerful allure of perfume. The Magi carried frankincense and myrrh to the Christ Child. The ancient Chinese perfumed their robes and burned incense at funerals. The earliest fragrances generally used took the form of incense because ways had not yet been found to preserve the oils from flowers. The word "perfume" is derived from the Latin words *per* meaning "through" and *fumare,* "to smoke."

Shakespeare has Cleopatra sailing down the river Cydnus to meet Mark Antony in a barge with sails "so perfumed that the winds were lovesick with them." Crusaders wore it into battle to bring them luck. Catherine de Medici ordered her chemist to concoct as many scents as there were varieties of flowers in southern France and thereby laid the foundation for the French cosmetics industry. Today, in the United States alone, the billion-dollar fragrance business supplies not only perfume and cologne in infinite variety but scents for everything from air fresheners to shaving cream to laundry detergents.

Modern fragrances are created from a mixture of natural or synthetic oils, giving a scent its character. Natural oils from the rose and the jasmine

Stripping: eyed by foremen, Algerian women strip leaves from lemon verbena for perfume distillation.

are two especially valuable ingredients. It takes about 1,225,000 roses to produce just one pound of the best oil, and extracting one quart of pure jasmine oil requires 1,760 pounds of flowers. Various materials are used to fix, or hold, the fragrance. The best fixatives are derived from animals: civet from the scent glands of the civet cat; musk from the male musk deer, native to Central Asia; castor from the beaver; and ambergris from the intestines of whales.

Since the 17th century French perfumes have been the most prestigious. Great perfume dynasties like Houbigant and Guerlain date from the late 18th century. Today, however, some of the most popular fragrances are those launched more recently by French dress designers: Arpège by Lanvin, Joy by Patou, and Chanel No. 5 by Coco Chanel. Each would agree with Napoleon's per-

Sorting: men also look on while women and girls in Grasse, France, sort through cloud banks of roses.

fumer, who wrote: "All the resources of our art have been employed to obtain those fragrant elements, the gifts of Flora, which, when skillfully garnered, compensate us for the absence of flowers and seem to make them live once again as one of our greatest joys."

PLASTIC Somewhere in America there probably is a man with an implanted plastic valve in his heart, who works in a building supported by plastic beams, who wears plastic shoes, and who writes with a plastic pen. He probably also carries a sandwich to work in a plastic bag or eats in a restaurant and pays for his meal with a plastic credit card after asking the waiter, "Do you take plastic?" The answer is almost certainly yes, for these days almost everybody, whether he likes it or not, takes plastic.

Plastic "environment" allows immune-deficient child to get outside.

Mankind went from the Stone Age to the Bronze Age to the Iron Age and then to the Steel Age. Now we are in thick of the Plastic Age. In all, the United States produces about 29 billion pounds of plastic each year. By 1983 plastic production is expected to equal the combined production of all metals—at least in volume, if not in weight—for plastic is a lightweight material. And this is one of its great virtues. Another is that plastic is very strong and durable and can be made in any color. It can also be molded into any shape. In addition, plastic can be hardened or used soft; it can conduct electricity or be used for electrical insulation. And so it is, quite uncontestably, the century's all-round miracle material.

Plastic is made from a number of substances, including cellulose, coal, certain plant oils, and petroleum derivatives (which play a part in 99 percent of all production but use only about 2 percent of each barrel of crude). From these raw materials feedstocks called monomers are produced, which are then turned into giant molecules or polymers, tiny by human standards but huge compared with ordinary molecules consisting of only a few atoms. These giant molecules bond together to form a material that becomes pliable at easily attainable temperatures, in the range of

249

This plastic place was created by a designer appropriately named Chrysalis. It is an inflated double dome.

300° to 480° F. The material becomes "plastic" in the original dictionary meaning of the word ("capable of being shaped or formed; pliable") like putty. Thus it can be heated, put into a mold, and shaped to whatever form is desired.

Although plastics are a modern development, the idea of molding material is not. In colonial America, animal horns and hooves were sometimes ground, mixed with other substances, then molded. Often the product that resulted was used to make lantern windows, which is why we sometimes encounter the old word "lanthorn" for lantern. The forms used to mold these "plastic" products were the direct ancestors of the enormous molding machines used today.

The plastics industry was born in 1869 when an American, John Hyatt, mixed a chemical made from cotton with nitric acid and camphor to form a new product he called Celluloid. In a short time Celluloid came to be used for men's stand-up shirt collars, for babies' rattles, for toys and packaging, for combs and film, and even for windshields—first on buggies and then for Model T Fords. Hyatt's work was pursued by others, both in America and abroad. The Quaker Oats Company, for example, developed plastics from oat hulls. And scientists made plastic buttons out of casein, derived from skim milk mixed with other substances.

The Plastic Age really began during World War II. Polyethylene, today's most widely used plastic, was developed during the war as an insulating material for radar cables. Thermoset polyester, another wartime product, became a popular boat building material a decade later. And ABS (acrylonitrile-butadiene-styrene) now goes into the manufacture of refrigerator liners, safety helmets, pipe, and luggage.

Dozens of kinds of plastics were put to thousands of uses. Almost every home in America today contains at least a hundred objects—from toothbrushes to telephones—made from plastic.

PLAYING CARDS

The devil invented playing cards, or so St. Bernardine of Siena thought in the 15th century. Because they appeared in Europe in the 1300's, however, the facts suggest that playing cards must have been imported from the Orient, where they had been known since before 1000 A.D. Legend has it that a Chinese emperor invented playing cards to enthrall his favorite concubine, an explanation that is probably as valid as any.

Pursuing St. Bernardine's view, the Puritans of the Massachusetts Bay colony outlawed all cards, linking them, not unreasonably perhaps, with gambling and idleness. Playing cards, however, had arrived in the New World considerably earlier with Columbus' sailors. According to one account,

when a ferocious storm struck the explorers' ship, the guilty sailors tossed their cards overboard to appease God. But when they arrived safely in balmy San Salvador, they missed their cards and fashioned new ones out of dried leaves.

These rawhide playing cards provided diversion for Apache Indians.

George Washington played cards even during the Revolution, though records indicate that he was only a middling player—he lost more than he won. Perhaps the best player of the many who have resided in the White House was President Eisenhower. He was reportedly so good at bridge that he might have been a top tournament player. When the invasion of North Africa lay stalled in November 1942 because of fog, Eisenhower sat down and played bridge with his officers until the fog lifted.

The 52-card pack that Eisenhower shuffled and dealt in those historic hours is in itself a history book. Though the 56-card Oriental deck

Play a round: circular cards go in and out of fashion. On these from India (1840), people denote number value.

had but three suits, Europeans adopted four, each representing one of the four estates of medieval society—the church, nobles, merchants, and peasants. From the French came the suit symbols we use today. Hearts represented the shields of the knights of the church; pikes (called spades by the English) were the lances of the nobles; diamonds symbolized the special tiles that paved merchant exchanges; and the clover leaf and shepherd's staff denoted the life of the peasantry.

Mora photographed a fortune-teller bedecked in the tools of her trade.

Later, clover signs came to be called clubs.

Face cards, originally painted in full figure, resembled famous historical rulers. On French cards, which became popular throughout Europe, the king of spades was the biblical King David; the king of clubs, Alexander the Great; the king of diamonds, Julius Caesar; and the king of hearts, the Frankish king Charlemagne. Jacks represented famous squires, and their garb is that of the landed aristocracy of 16th-century England. Tradition indicates that Sir Launcelot was represented by the jack of clubs, and the French knight La Hire, Joan of Arc's loyal companion, by the jack of hearts. The jester survives from early Italian playing cards, which included a wild card known as "The Fool," a pasteboard that may have symbolized the folly of playing cards at all.

Not surprisingly, card players are a superstitious lot. One must not, for instance, touch one's elbow to a two of spades, or let a black ace fall on the floor, or sing while playing, or play on a bare table. Those actions bring bad luck, without question or explanation. The ill fortune associated with the ace of spades, however, does have an explanation. In the 18th century the English government made the ace of spades the duty card. The Commissioners for Stamp Duties collected a tax on every new pack of cards issued, a transaction that was duly noted on the ace of spades. Those who failed to pay were fined, but the punishment for forging an ace of spades was death.

Originally, playing cards had blank backs, which made them useful for scribbling on. Parts of *The Beggar's Opera*, by John Gay, and all of the hymn "Rock of Ages" are said to have been first transcribed on the backs of cards. In colonial America playing cards were also used as calling cards, invitations, and tickets of admission.

Though some now turn to them in hope of monetary reward, cards may actually have served as the first paper money used in North America. In 1685 the French king's representative in Quebec ran out of coin to pay his troops. Hastily, he called in all playing cards, signed them, cut them in fourths, and declared them instant money.

PLYWOOD AND VENEER The idea behind plywood—the gluing and pressing of several layers of wood into rigid sheets—is at least 3,500 years old and was born of luxury craftsmanship and perhaps a little chicanery. Ancient Egyptian artisans were among the first to cut thin strips of wood (veneer) and glue them to cheaper, less decorative woods. Thus the best woods could be extended without diminishing the weight, strength, and apparent richness of the finished product.

The Romans carried the idea of veneering even farther, experimenting with different cuts along and across the grain to create exotic patterns. Such patterns came to be known by the natural images they brought to mind—"the spots of the leopard," "the swarm of bees," or "the stripes of the tiger," for example.

The use of veneers, including the art of marquetry, the creation of elaborate designs in veneer with wood, shell, or ivory inlays, varied over suc-

Marquetry in room reassembled from an Italian palace consists of walnut, oak, beech, and fruit woods.

ceeding centuries as tastes changed. Today veneering remains the prime means of finishing wood. In the 19th century, with the introduction of machine-driven cutting tools, modern plywood made its appearance. America's growing piano industry was the first to use plywood on a large scale. A multilayered sandwich of sheets or plies, usually set so the grain of one runs counter to the grain of the next and bonded under heat and pressure, plywood is actually stronger than steel of the same weight. It also has greater stability and is more resilient than conventional woods.

Plywood proved its worth in the manufacture of dozens of items, including automobile running boards, doors, drawers, curved furniture, boat hulls, and even airplane components. But only in 1934, with the addition of synthetic waterproof glue, did plywood become tough enough to withstand the rigors of outdoor exposure year after year. As a result, the demand for exterior-grade plywood soared. Today there are about 350 plywood mills in the United States, producing some 20 billion square feet of plywood a year. In terms of boards, that translates to 625 million standard-size sheets, each of them 4 by 8 feet and ⅜-inch thick—that would be enough to floor over more than 400 million football fields.

POLICE Criminals have always been with us. Fortunately, most of the time the law enforcers have not been far behind, although in ancient Rome the poet Juvenal carped that "bolts and padlocks and bars will never keep out all the burglars."

In early 19th-century England, crime control was mostly in the hands of "thief-takers" who were paid for each criminal they apprehended.

Dragged out: the trick of disguising policemen as women is not new. A peculator was thus apprehended in 1872.

Mounted in a canoe, a member of a world-famous police force pursues his man; according to legend he'll get him.

"No prisoner, no pay" was the system they operated under, and it encouraged corruption. Some cities, like Liverpool, with a population of almost a quarter of a million, had no police except for a few night watchmen.

In 1829 Sir Robert Peel got Parliament to establish an official police force with regular pay, blue uniforms, a rattle to call for help, and a billy club or stick labeled "Police Officer." These London policemen constituted the first modern police force in the world. Peel's police headquarters was located next to a medieval palace called Great Scotland Yard, and though the headquarters was moved the central command post of the London police is still known as Scotland Yard.

Early in the 19th century New York's police force was made up of various and sundry groups of men who usually held other jobs as well. There were the "Leatherheads" who wore old-style firemen's hats, the Bellmen, the Toll Takers, the Lamplighters, the Polls Watchers, the Night Watch, the Day Watch, a few marshals, and a small detective force. But in 1845, with the passage of the Municipal Police Act, all 800 of them became policemen, appointed for one year at an annual salary of $500. The brass star, worn over the left breast, was their only official identification until 1853, when uniforms became compulsory. In 1855 the Chicago police department was created, and officers were given blue uniforms as well as brass stars. By the 1860's the idea of a regular police force had reached the West Coast. In San Francisco the police wore uniforms, and in the then-small town of Los Angeles a six-member police force was established. In 1896 New York's police commissioner Theodore Roosevelt established a special force of bicycle police who could

What's the Color of an Old Penny?

To be a policeman is to be a target. Along with sticks and stones, and bullets and bombs, policemen have been cannonaded over the years by a special assortment of nonlethal but often very infuriating missiles—nicknames. Some, like "blue bottle" and "blue belly" (for the large-bodied, bluish fly), "bandog" (for bloodhound), "arm" (as in arm of the law), "elbow" (as in elbowing through a crowd), and "finger" (as in pointing accusingly), are no longer au courant. But others retain all the vim and vinegar they have been splattering on "goms" (short for gumshoe) and "frogs" (for police ebullience in pouncing on offenders) for years. The term "bull," for example, as in "harness bull" (a uniformed policeman) and "cinder bull" (a railroad detective), dates from a 19th-century Spanish Gypsy word for policeman—*bul*.

The terms "cop" and "copper," probably the most widely used of all police sobriquets, have tangled roots. They may be derived from an old English verb, "cop," meaning to catch or hold, or from the large copper buttons sported by early 19th-century London officers (who are still known as "bobbies" and "peelers" because their force was organized by Sir Robert Peel), or from the nickname of the mayor of Chicago in 1858, John C. Haines, who was called "Copper Stock" as a result of his spectacular dalliances in the copper market. "John," by contrast, comes directly from *gendarme*, the French word for policeman, but is followed by different surnames in different countries: "John Law" (United States), "John Dunn" (Australia), and "John Hop" (New Zealand).

The appellations "flatfoot," "flatty," and "crusher" all pay tribute to the aching architecture of the patrolman's roving feet. The term "fuzz" dates from the 1920's and may be a corruption of "feds," which in its turn is short for federal narcotic agents, or "fussytail," a term for a demanding person. "Pig," perhaps the most provocative of all police pejorations, is more than a century old, dating from the 1840's. At that time, the word was applied mostly to police informers and stool pigeons who were paid to squeal on their criminal brethren and thus avoid the pen.

1830's: original bobbies accoutred in "chimney-pot" hats, tight collars.

give any fleeing criminal a good chase. New York also had a special squad of "Star Police" who were identified by their copper badges.

Another important reform that had taken place under Peel, as important as uniforms and regular pay, was the institution of a system of police record keeping. In that sense police technology was born at the same time as the modern police force.

When photography was sufficiently developed, policemen began to photograph criminals and the scenes of crime. Many of the advances in police technology were developed in Europe. Various types of fingerprints were classified by an Englishman, Sir Francis Galton, a cousin of Charles Darwin, and the system was adapted for police work. (Some of the police "advances" rest on ancient foundations. The Babylonians, for example, had recognized the value of placing fingerprints on their clay writing tablets to guard against forgery.) In 1882 in France, Alphonse Bertillon began identifying suspects by using measurements of various parts of the body. Police crime laborato-

ries, working with blood samples, were first established in France. Americans also made important technological innovations. As early as 1845 the New York police used the telegraph. By 1880 Chicago police were able to call for help or report crimes on telephones installed at strategic locations along their routes. The first police car was put on the road in Akron, Ohio, in 1899.

August Vollmer of Berkeley, California, is generally considered the father of the 20th-century U.S. police force. During Vollmer's term as Berkeley's police chief in the first decades of this century, his methods of crime control gave Berkeley the distinction of having the nation's lowest crime rate. Vollmer was responsible for introducing the lie detector, crime laboratories, radio patrol cars, police schools, and first-aid courses for policemen. And he initiated the first college course in criminology, at the University of California in 1916.

American police departments have also been notorious dens of corruption. One 19th-century New York detective took in nearly $500,000 in payoffs from operators of illegal gambling houses and the madams of the city's fanciest brothels. Similar situations have occurred repeatedly in U.S. cities, and the figure of the policeman filching an apple from an indignant but powerless fruit vendor is a stock character in American cartoons.

With modernization and increasing professionalism, corruption has diminished. More and more new officers have studied police work in college. Though those instruments of power, guns and nightsticks, still have to be used, they have been supplemented by modern tear gas, tranquilizing darts, and other devices that immobilize but do not permanently harm malefactors. Crime has not been wiped out, and it probably never will be, but in the past century the police have made some strides in controlling it, helped by computers and other technological advances.

POTATO Exploring high in the Andes, too high for corn to grow, the Spanish conquistadores found Peruvians cultivating a small yellow-flesh tuber called *papa* and decided that it was "a dainty dish even for Spaniards." The vegetable was not only tasty but portable and long-lasting, for the Peruvians had developed a method of preserving potatoes by freeze-drying them at high altitudes outdoors. When the looting conquistadores began to ship silver back to Spain, they sent along potatoes (or *patatas*, as the Spaniards called them) as ship's stores. Overall, the potato was perhaps a more valuable find to the world than all the silver in Peru.

Ironically, the potato of South America took almost two more centuries to reach North Amer-

Violent rioting accompanied the potato blight in Ireland in the 1840's. Mass emigrations followed.

ica, and then by a circuitous route—from Spain to Italy to northern Europe to Bermuda to the Virginia colonies. Related to the deadly jimsonweed and henbane, the potato for many years was accused of causing everything from tuberculosis to leprosy. Scottish divines thundered from the pulpit that it was the forbidden fruit because it was not mentioned in the Bible.

In an effort to popularize potatoes in France, Marie Antoinette appeared at a ball with a wreath of potato flowers in her hair. Behind this stroke of advertising genius was Dr. Antoine Auguste Parmentier, a chemist and nutritionist whose research showed that the potato could replace grain as a source of food in times of scarcity and famine. To arouse curiosity among reluctant farmers, he posted a military guard around his experimental field but removed them at night. Just as he had hoped, the farmers sneaked into the plot and stole the plants.

As the chief food of the poor the potato succeeded—perhaps too well because some people, like the Irish in the 1840's, lived on them almost exclusively. A small plot could feed a family with six children and a pig and a cow to boot. Safe underground, the crop could survive the looting and trampling of endless armies. But in 1845, in the space of a few weeks, potato plants all over Ireland turned black, and the disease then spread to Europe. In the world's most devastating potato blight to date, over a million Irish starved. The Great Potato Famine altered the population of the United States, bringing thousands of Irish, Germans, and Poles to these shores.

In today's weight-conscious society, potatoes are often shunned as fattening. They are not, says the American Medical Association. One medium boiled potato contains between 70 and 100 calories (without butter), less than a serving of cottage cheese or an apple. And it is filling, since about 7? percent of the vegetable is water. High in vitamin C and minerals, and one of the least expensive of all staple foods, the tuber of the Andes is the world's most important vegetable.

PRINTING As early as the end of the 2nd century A.D. the Chinese had at their command the three basic elements of printing—paper, ink, and the notion of the woodblock on which images and word characters could be carved for transposition to another surface. But not until about 700 A.D. did they put them together to produce what may be called printed material—a Buddhist charm. One charm led to many, and in 868 an entire Buddhist tract was printed in multiples from a succession of unique woodblocks.

A typesetter in Peking, China, understandably pauses before his myriad choices.

with the Chinese. The first books printed from wood carvings were called *donats*, after Aelius Donatus, whose Latin grammar, along with religious works, was the most widely selling text of the day.

Around 1423 a Dutchman known as Coster made the first trial runs of movable wooden type. Though he needed far fewer symbols than the Chinese language required, the carved letters were so small and fragile that they wore out quickly and new ones had to be cut. As a result, no two carvings of the same letter were identical. Almost simultaneously, master metalworkers created a complicated process that resulted in a relief plate used to print in multiples.

Johann Gutenberg, a goldsmith by training, is generally credited with being the first European to print a full-scale book using a combination of movable metal type cast in molds and a printing press. Unfortunately, he neglected to print his name in any of the works ascribed to him, and there are enough questions about the details of his life and printing operation to cloud his claim to this honor. The so-called Gutenberg Bible, or "42-line Bible" (after the uniform number of lines in each printed column), is believed to have been completed in Gutenberg's workshop in Mainz, Germany, in 1455. Printed in Latin in Gothic type, it had hand-painted illuminations in the margins. One copy of the edition belonged to Cardinal Mazarin, in recognition of which it is also known as the Mazarin Bible. Forty-seven other copies identified as the work of Gutenberg are currently recorded in public and private collections. In 1978 three of the Bibles sold for $1.8, $2, and $2.4 million, respectively.

After the time of Gutenberg, improvements in Western printing methods came at an ever-quickening rate as printers found themselves hard pressed to keep up with the demand of the new literate class for Bibles, scientific works, histories, literature, and newspapers.

The 19th century produced numerous advances in the mechanization and eventual automation of printing (though with scarcely any reduction in messiness of the operation or the daubing of ap-

Movable type, separate characters that could be used over and over in different texts and different combinations, was introduced sometime after 1041. A clever commoner, Pi Sheng, cut characters in soft clay and fired them in an oven. Then he assembled the hardened characters as text on an iron plate smeared with turpentine, resin, wax, and burned paper ash, locked the pieces tightly together with what was called an iron fence, and warmed the plate from below until the sticky mixture took hold. Finally, he laid a wooden board across the face of the characters to make sure that none stood higher than any other. With that the printing block was ready for inking and printing. After the job was done, type could be recovered and used elsewhere by reheating the plate and plucking off the characters.

Revolutionary as Pi Sheng's invention was, it scarcely affected traditional printing methods in China. Since the written language contains about 80,000 characters, most printers found it easier to cut new symbols into woodblocks as needed than to keep a huge inventory. (The Koreans, however, adopted the Chinese movable-type concept, switching from clay to cast bronze. History records that King Htai Tjong ordered his printers to make a 100,000-piece set in 1403.)

Meanwhile, Europeans were still becoming accustomed to the novelty of paper, which they had learned to manufacture in the 12th century. And while the Koreans were busy casting new typefaces, Westerners were just learning the art of woodblock printing. Not until early in the 15th century did European technology catch up

The Printer's Devil

Though printing continued to be a small hand-craft operation for several centuries following the invention of the printing press, more efficient techniques led to the creation of specialized jobs within the shop. One helper was known as the "printer's devil." Several charming explanations have been advanced for this colorful title. Joseph Moxon, writing in *Mechanical Exercises* in 1683, proposed the theory that "the Press-man sometimes has a Week-Boy to Take Sheets, as they are Printed off the Tympan: These Boys do . . . commonly black and Dawb themselves: whence the workmen do jocosely call them Devils; and sometimes Spirits, and sometimes Flies."

Another legend holds that the celebrated printer Aldus Manutius (1449–1515) employed a black African as helper in his shop in Venice. As blacks then were all but unknown in that part of Europe, the people of Venice were uneasy at the sight of this stranger in their midst and began to look upon him as an evil spirit. Wishing to end speculation and put the citizens at ease, the good printer issued the following statement: "I, Aldus Manutius, printer to the Doge and the Holy Church, have this day made public exposure of the printer's devil. All who think he is not flesh and blood are invited to come and pinch him."

prentices). Relief or letterpress printing continued to be the chief method of transmitting word to page. Then intaglio and planographic or lithographic techniques were developed, as were continuous rolls of paper, rotary presses, improved inks, color printing, and mechanized casting of type and composition. Finally, the advent of computers and magnetic tape, making it possible to compose 1,000 characters per second, or 3.6 million per hour, portends a new era for the industry. And eventually lead, ink, and ultimately the press will become relics.

In the not-too-distant future, newspapers and other written material may routinely be transmitted as electronically coded information, by phone lines or radio waves, into our homes where devices hardly more complex than television sets will translate them into words and "print out" copies for home consumption. Futurologists conceive of a time when the individual will become a subscriber to a variety of electronically transmitted magazines, book series, journals, and other services, like one giving information about available merchandise of various sorts, that will issue forth quietly and cleanly from a box in the living room. Fundamentally, the notion is no more remarkable than Pi Sheng's movable type or Gutenberg's press.

PURSE Before coins and bills became a common medium of exchange, no one had much need of a purse. Ladies in the Middle Ages simply attached whatever articles they needed—scissors, comb, keys—to their low-slung girdles, or belts. When the Crusaders returned from the East wearing little coin purses called *amônières*, both men and women found them useful accessories, but no more, for carrying alms for the poor.

In time the money pouches became elegant purses fashioned of embroidered damask or velvet, often decorated with silk tassels or bells. Dangling on a long string tied to the girdle, they inspired a

A 17th-century English cutpurse demonstrates his skill.

profession of "cut purses," who separated wearer and money with one deft swipe of a knife.

There could be no pickpockets until there were pockets, a development that came about early in the 17th century when pockets (in today's sense) were thrust deep into puffed breeches. Up to that time, men had buckled a *gipcière*, a flat pouch with an ornate metal frame, onto their belts. England's Henry V had a "pocket" made of purple velvet and trimmed with gold; he pawned it in 1415 to finance a French expedition.

The word "purse" comes from the Latin *bursa*, meaning "oxhide," and derivations include both pursers and bursars, as well as the Paris Stock Exchange, the Bourse. The "pocketbook," however, may have originated when women began putting little purses into their pockets.

Through the ages, women have tried to look composed while fumbling with long skirts, trains, purses, babies, fans, opera glasses, and gloves. Handbags were meant to help: they were slipped over the fingers or wrist of the skirt-swishing hand in order to leave one hand free. During World

Home-pun Humor

"There is no kind of false wit which has been so recommended by the practice of all ages, as that which consists in a jingle of words, and is comprehended under the general name of Punning," wrote the acclaimed 18th-century English essayist Joseph Addison in a disapproving tone. "It is indeed impossible to kill a weed, which the soil has a natural disposition to produce. The seeds of Punning are in the minds of all men; and though they may be subdued by reason, reflection, and good sense, they will be very apt to shoot up in the greatest genius that is not broken and cultivated by the rules of art. Imitation is natural to us, and when it does not raise the mind to poetry, painting, music, or other more noble arts, it often breaks out in Puns and Quibbles."

Plays on words often involving homonyms (words that sound alike or are spelled alike but have different meanings), puns have enjoyed alternating periods of fashionability and opprobrium in virtually every language. They were celebrated as a verbal art form by Aristotle and Cicero, given the royal stamp of approval by King James I, and employed prominently in the plays of Shakespeare. (Dr. F.A. Bather, a Fellow of the Royal Society, was so thoroughly submerged in his study of Shakespeare's puns that he made a statistical survey of their frequency per hundred lines of dialogue and came up with such scores as *Comedy of Errors*, 2.08; *Much Ado About Nothing*, 1.42; *Titus Andronicus*, 0.15, for a grand career total of 1,062 puns.) Oliver Wendell Holmes called puns a form of " 'verbicide'—violent treatment of a word with fatal results."

Old puns such as the Bard of Avon composed with almost every breath frequently go unappreciated by modern readers who are not familiar with Elizabethan social history. But new puns rise up to take their places daily.

Some pungent examples of wordplay heard in recent times:

Broadway is the street of ham and aches.

Acrimony—another name for marriage, sometimes called holy.

The famous TV star Cleo the basset hound was sometimes required to play the piano, but listeners rated her Bach worse than her bite.

Bilious is the feeling you get when you open your mail on the first day of the month.

A divorcée is a woman who gets richer by decrees.

The Tower of Babel was a din of iniquity.

A mixed grill is an ecumenical inquisition.

Flattery is like soft soap; 90 percent lye.

Lamb stew is much ado about mutton.

Caught chasing girls in a convent, the intruder was charged as a *nun sequitur.*

Once the punning habit has taken hold, few practitioners of the art are totally satisfied with one-liners like those above; whole tales—shaggy dog stories—are constructed as prologues for well-honed punch lines. Take, for example, the story about the traveler in Africa who fell ill. He summoned a witch doctor, who examined him carefully, then presented him with a leather thong. "Bite off an inch of this thong every day," the witch doctor pre-

scribed. "Chew it carefully and at the end of a week you'll be as good as new." When he returned a week later, however, he found the traveler sicker than ever. The witch doctor demanded, "How come?" The traveler answered weakly, "The thong is ended, but the malady lingers on."

Or consider the sad tale told of the court jester. His fate perhaps provides a warning for all punsters. It seems that the king's jester punned incessantly until the king, in desperation, condemned the jester to be hanged. However, the king had second thoughts, thinking that after all a good jester was not easy to find, and sent a messenger posthaste with a royal pardon. Arriving at the gallows as the jester stood with the rope already about his neck, the messenger read the king's decree: The jester would be pardoned if he would promise never to make another pun. The jester could not resist temptation, however. He cackled out, "No noose is good news." And they hanged him.

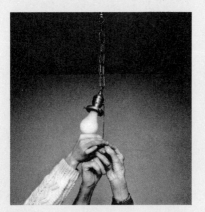

Play sans words: assault and battery; many hands make light work.

War II, shoulder bags appeared as part of female military uniforms because no woman could salute smartly while dangling a purse in one hand. But the real change in handbags came when woman herself changed. *Vogue* magazine, attempting to organize the modern working woman, featured a mid-1970's bag that was an "office-on-the-go." It contained makeup, keys, hairbrush, wallet, glass-

Quiz Shows: Some Had All the Answers

Born on radio and brought to overripe maturity by television, the quiz show and its siblings, the panel show and the game show, have become staples of programming, constituting one of the most listened to and watched kinds of entertainment ever devised. The basic idea grew quite naturally out of the early mind-teasing games and spelling bees that Americans played in school and at home. One of the very first shows to capture the public's imagination was called *Dr. I.Q.*, and it featured the doc-

tor as a "mental banker," who posed questions to volunteers in the audience. His assistant's call, "Doctor, I have a lady in the balcony," became a household phrase, as did the doctor's ringing acknowledgment of a right answer, "Give that man 20 silver dollars!"

Dr. I.Q.'s questions were fairly easy, and the radio audience had the pleasure of competing vicariously and occasionally congratulating themselves for their astuteness. In 1938 the first of the "egghead" quiz shows appeared. Called *Information Please*, it was a panel show that put such polymaths as Franklin P. Adams, John Kieran, and two guest experts each week on the firing line. *Information Please* reversed the usual format in that the public was asked to provide the questions—the harder the better—and watch the experts squirm. The panelists themselves were encouraged to go farther than simply answering the questions—they were expected to be witty along the way, as in this exchange between guest panelist John Gunther and master of ceremonies Clifton Fadiman. Fielding the question "Who is Reza Pahlevi?" Gunther hesitated, then answered, "The ruler of Persia. "Are you shah?" queried Fadiman, to which Gunther responded, "Sultanly."

Information Please soon spawned a short-pants version known as the *Quiz Kids*, a program that recruited precocious youngsters for its panel. Typical of the kinds of questions these juvenile geniuses thrived on was this literary number puzzler

posed by interlocutor Joe Kelly: "Divide the number of Ali Baba's thieves by the number of quins (short for quintuplets), add the horsemen of the Apocalypse, and subtract the number of days it took to make the world."

"Five," said 14-year-old Cynthia Cline in an instant. "I beg to differ," interjected 13-year-old Virginia Booze. "The answer is six," she declared, explaining in detail that there were forty thieves, which divided by the five quins gave eight, plus four horsemen made twelve, minus six days for the creation of the world, which left six, not five, as the total. "For on the seventh day He rested," announced Virginia, understandably triumphant.

The quiz kids each received a $100 war bond for their appearances, and listeners whose questions were chosen were given portable radios. Other shows were equally modest in their prizes: *Take It or Leave It*, for example, had as the ultimate test of a contestant's ability a "$64 question." In the early 1950's, when television adopted the quiz format, cash awards grew enormously, and audience excitement rose with them. Shows like *The Big Surprise, The Big Payoff, Break the Bank, Strike It Rich*, and *The $64,000 Question* gave enthralled viewers a chance to dream of overnight wealth and instant glory.

The $64,000 Question was the prototype, and it was so successful that at one time it commanded 85 percent of the TV audience. The basic gimmick of the show, sponsored by Revlon, the cosmetic company, was to hold a contestant over for several weeks

Hollywood squares, rear view. Sets got fancier, prizes lower after scandals.

es, address book, credit-card case, briefcase, calculator, camera, tape recorder, and, in case one needed it, a regular handbag.

About that time some men decided that their pockets were no longer spacious enough. They were not so desperate as to return to the *gipcière*, and they did not call it a purse, but a purselike bag unmistakably hung from one shoulder.

First $64,000 winners: Father-and-son team confer in tension-adding "isolation booth" before correctly spieling off a menu from a royal banquet.

while he or she won ever-larger sums of money, and the suspense built. Contestants were picked for their encyclopedic knowledge in a particular field along with everyday qualities—a Bronx shoemaker who knew grand opera, a Marine captain who knew about haute cuisine—that viewers could identify with. As the stakes grew higher, they performed their feats of "memory" inside a glass-enclosed "isolation booth," and they agonized over their answers with some 50 million viewers looking on. Revlon was rewarded with a 200 percent increase in sales during the show's first year.

But the success of *The $64,000 Question* and its spinoffs—which represented in their peak years a $100 million annual investment in production costs and purchase of time—led in a very real sense to their downfall. To keep audience involvement at a peak in an increasingly competitive market, producers began "warming up" contestants who were favorites of the viewers with discreet clues to the questions—and answers—they might encounter under pressure.

In 1958 a disgruntled standby contestant on *Dotto* discovered that the show's producers had given advance cue cards to a contestant and complained to the Federal Communications Commission. Then a winner on *Twenty-One* reported a "fix" on that show. Finally, one of the best-known winners of all, Charles Van Doren, went before an investigative committee in the House of Representatives and disclosed that he, too, had been helped—while winning $129,000 on *Twenty-One*. Almost overnight, disillusionment on the part of viewers and fear of public controversy on the part of sponsors brought the world of the quiz show tumbling down. Though game shows reappeared in the mid-1960's, the stakes they offered were consistently lower and their rules against fixing considerably more stringent.

These junior geniuses awed their elders with their wide range of knowledge and quick recall, earning the enduring animosity of their less-gifted contemporaries.

QUILT Among purely indigenous American craftworks, none excites more interest today than the patchwork quilt. Not that the notion of quilting is uniquely American. The ancient Chinese made padded clothing out of layers of stitched-together fabric; and Europeans of old slept under coverlets whose "counterpoints"—the stitches used to tack interior padding in place—were frequently worked in elaborate linear patterns. What was, and is, distinctive about American quilting is the patching—the careful utilization of scraps of variegated fabrics to create the ornamental, multicolored tops of coverlets.

American patchwork was not, initially, an intricate expression of exuberant color sense. It was born of adversity and necessity. For many years new yard goods were expensive and in short supply, and patching was an ingenious if time-consuming means of recycling bits of worn-out clothing and fabric. As a result, one of the favorite "patterns" used was no pattern at all. Called a Crazy Quilt or occasionally a Hit-or-Miss, it had the overall look of cracked porcelain and imposed few if any limitations on the types and colors of the materials used by the patchmaker.

Gradually, however, quilters developed favorite patterns, and working and reworking them became a form of recreation, a chance to demonstrate one's artistry in a world that provided few opportunities for creative expression.

Patchwork quilts usually were produced in two separate steps: first came the patchwork top, made all on one's own, then the quilting "bee." In this, a communal effort, several women gathered about a frame and sewed top, padding, and backing together with neat pattern-transcribing stitches while enjoying each other's company. A female child was introduced to the art and expected to have at least a dozen tops completed by the time she reached courting age. After marriage she would continue to hone her skills as she marked important occasions in the life of her family with ceremonial quilts. Bridal quilts, for example, frequently displayed stylized hearts or lover's knots within their overall patterns. A Mourning Quilt included bits of the departed's clothing. A Friendship Quilt (also, Album Quilt), often the work of several patchmakers, revealed favorite pattern blocks and the signatures of the sewers.

Even the pitfalls and passions of social history found their way into quilts—Drunkard's Path recalls the temperance crusades of the 19th century, and Whig's Retreat examines party politics on the eve of the Civil War. Delectable Mountain, on the other hand, refers us to the legendary landscape made famous in *Pilgrim's Progress*; and Lemon Star pays homage to Jean Baptiste LeMoyne, one of the founders of the French colony of Louisiana. In all, there were dozens of basic patterns and hundreds of variations on them.

Nowadays, old quilts are more likely to be found on museum walls than on country bedsteads, and some of the rarest have been sold for $10,000 only to be locked away in vaults by collectors. Though few quilts were dated when they were created, patterns, fabrics, and dyes provide specialists with enough clues to establish age and provenance. As for new quilts, there are still lots of Americans with the patience and interest to keep the craft alive, creating a handmade record of our time for generations to come.

"Quilting Party" by Henry Bacon (1872): three generations join to create a beautiful covering from scraps.

Quilting is still a group effort. Here members of the Big Creek Sewing Co-op of W. Va. stitch and chatter.

RENDERINGS: The Craftsman's Art

Body and mind, hand and eye: these are the twins of creation and
from their interaction come works that fuse life's main preoccupations—
clothing, the home, food—with beauty and turn everyday things into
extraordinary objects. The magnificent black-marble tabletop, above,
exquisitely inlaid with semiprecious stones, and the objects that glitter
and astound on the pages that follow all attest to the skill of the hand,
the creative fire of the mind. Yet which dominates, which controls?
From what source does creation flow? Even now scientists are certain
only that without the inquiring hand the brain would not possess the
extraordinary powers it uses so uniquely. The fine craftsman who is
also the maker of everyday things, whether he be a Scythian goldsmith
or a designer of geometric chairs, orchestrates hand, mind, and eye to
lift everyday things beyond the realm of the ordinary. As G.K. Chesterton wrote, ". . . a thing constructed can only be loved after it is
constructed; but a thing created is loved before it exists."

Aesthetic Comforts

"The meanest artisan," wrote Samuel Johnson, "contributes more to the accommodation of life than the profound scholar." And it is in the home, around the hearth, Johnson might have added, that the renderer's labors have proved most accommodating. For over the centuries the furnishings that elevate and add comfort to human existence—tables and chairs, beds and cupboards—have become the palette-domus of man's accomplishments, utilitarian tributes to his knowledge, wealth, sense of beauty, and even his belief in magic. The wood-and-bead crocodile stool below, for example, is a symbol of virility and immortality among Bamileke tribesmen in North Africa.

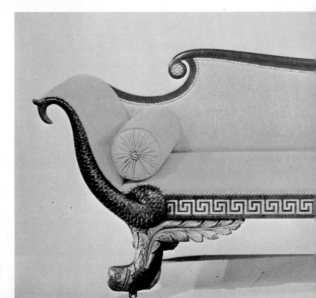

Cupboard, 1820, Finnish.

Reproduction of an 18th-century French chandelier.

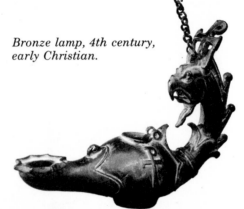

Bronze lamp, 4th century, early Christian.

Variegated marble tabletop, 1st century A.D., Roman.

Stool, early 20th century, Cameroonian.

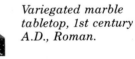

Dresden lacquer desk, 1740, German.

Cupboard, 18th century, French.

Worktable, early 19th century, American.

Painted bed, c. 1850, Swiss.

Spiderweb Tiffany lamp, late 19th or early 20th century, American.

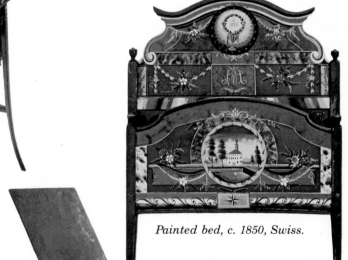

Chair, c. 1920, German.

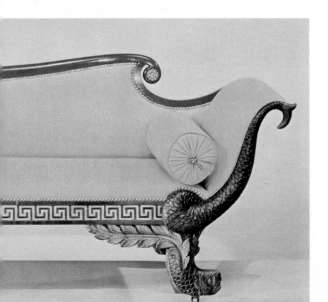

Empire-style sofa, c. 1820, American.

Personal Adornment

Protecting and decorating oneself: surely these fundamental concerns—one elemental, the other aesthetic, egotistical, and quintessentially human—are irresistibly reflected in the lines and colors of the objects of bodily adornment shown on these pages. What better example than the suit of fluted armor shown below, as tailored and elegant as the finest garment and yet capable of turning aside arrow and lance with functional ease? A comb that is an ancient jeweler's masterwork, a belt buckle alive with a dragon's coils, a cap of lacy filigree—each individual work is an example of a common-place thing transformed, and each attests in its artistry to the truth of the craftsworker's litany: the useful can be beautiful, the beautiful useful.

Silver air purifier,
20th century,
Dahomeyan.

Vest, 20th century, American.

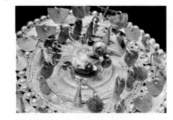

Detail of golden
earspool disc
(top), 2nd century
to 8th century
A.D., Peruvian. Bottom, gold combs,
4th century B.C.,
Scythian.

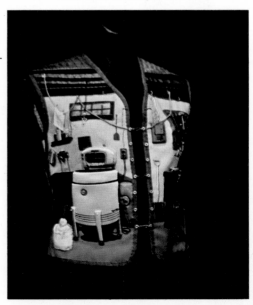

Maximillian armor, 1525, German.

Gold belt buckle,
2nd century B.C.,
probably Chinese.

Envelope-style bag, 20th century, Philippine.

Embroidered silk cap, 18th century, French.

Cheyenne Indian legging moccasins, early 20th century, American.

Gold snuff-box, 18th century, French.

Feather and ivory fan, 18th century, Dutch.

Kimono, 20th century, Japanese.

Mirror, 3rd to 1st century B.C., Egyptian.

265

Gustatory Accouterments

The fine craftsman, unlike the "use" or "production" craftsman, whose labors produce functional things, courts beauty with his craft. And in no other setting, has he shone more brightly than at the table, enhancing in crystal, silver, and porcelain man's exchanges over wine and food. From the gleaming crenulations of the silver wine fountain below to the flowing sculpture of the Cellini salt dish at the right, it is clear that the artistic craftsman's creations are a good match for the most formidable triumphs of kitchen and vineyard.

Salt by Benvenuto Cellini, 16th century, Italian.

Table fountain, late 14th century, French.

Brass candle-holder, 15th century, German.

Silver spoon, late 16th century, Italian.

*Nautilus cup, 1660,
Italian.*

*Bronze wine vase, c. 771
B.C., Chinese.*

*Porcelain coffeepot, 19th
century, French.*

*Earthenware platter, c.
16th century, French.*

*Point d'Angle-
terre lace, mid-
18th century,
Flemish.*

*Porcelain teapot,
18th century, English.*

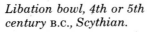

Porcelain rabbit tureen, 1775, English.

*Ivory mug, 1676,
German.*

*Libation bowl, 4th or 5th
century B.C., Scythian.*

The Need to Decorate

The barbarous and nomadic Scythians, some experts believe, created tiny golden objects because they had no walls to embellish, no temples to fill with icons. The irrepressible human need to color, organize, and decorate is what joins the multiplicity of objects on these pages. As Joseph Conrad wrote, there is something "beyond mere skill; almost an inspiration which gives to all work that finish which is almost art—which *is* art."

Clock, 18th century, French.

Battersea enamel box, 1750's, English.

Bamboo picnic basket, 19th century, Chinese.

Wooden and ivory chest, 16th century, Italian.

Painted cart, 20th century, Costa Rican.

Vase, 20th century, Mexican.

Duncan Phyfe tool chest, late 18th to early 19th century, American.

Bark painting of kangaroos, 19th century, Australian.

Leather book cover, late 16th century, Italian.

Jeweled box cover, late 17th to early 18th century, Chinese.

Tapestry screen, 16th century, Belgian.

Copper weather vane depicting an Indian with a bow, late 19th century, American.

Originally a crude drawing of a face, the letter "R" may have gotten its name from the Semitic word for head—resh.

RADIO On Christmas Eve 1906, shipboard operators off the coast of New England, accustomed to the chatter of the telegraph, suddenly heard a man's voice speaking through their earphones. The voice read the Christmas story from the Gospel of St. Luke, music was heard, and then the voice wished everyone a merry Christmas. Canadian inventor Reginald Fessenden, speaking from his laboratory on the Massachusetts coast, had quietly completed the first radio broadcast.

Both Fessenden (who had labored with Thomas Edison) and the American Lee De Forest were working toward a wireless telephone, but they had also begun to dream of voice radio, a system that might, as De Forest put it, be "a means by which opera can be brought into every home; someday the news, and even advertising." Working with theories developed by a German physicist, the Italian Guglielmo Marconi had perfected the wireless telegraph and in 1901 had spanned the Atlantic with a signal. But the possibility of reassembling electromagnetic wave impulses into clear speech or music became practical only with De Forest's invention of the audion, a triode vacuum tube that received and amplified signals. Despite the availability of the tube before World War I, radio broadcasting for the most part remained the plaything of amateurs, energetic hams whose sets were often no more elaborate than cereal boxes wound round with copper wire.

The hobby, however, became popular enough to tempt Westinghouse to promote the sale of receivers through not-to-be missed programming. Thus on November 2, 1920, with the financial support of Westinghouse, ham operator Frank Conrad went on the air to announce the returns of the Harding-Cox presidential election. Broadcasting from station KDKA in Pittsburgh, his "up-to-the-minute" returns thrilled the public, and commercial radio became an overnight success. By

In World War II even nomads in the French Camel Corps listened to NBC broadcasts.

Sound effect? During a broadcast of the radio program "Lights Out," actors build atmosphere by falling down.

1923 more than 700 stations, set up in barns, kitchens, and stores, were operating. And General Electric was selling 11 million sets a year to an eager public, though many cost as much as $275 and had to be sold on the installment plan.

Radio was immediate, intimate, and allowed the listener to fill in details with his imagination. It penetrated the heart of rural America, bringing the voices of presidents (Harding was the first to use the medium), the ruckus of political conventions, and the roar of prizefights into living rooms in some of which kerosene lamps still flickered. "From the beautiful Bamboo Room of the Hotel Belton in the heart of downtown Des Moines," the sound of big bands thrummed out across the prairies in the 1930's. On more than one occasion, radio—and the men who tended it—performed heroically. When the dirigible *Shenandoah* went adrift one dark night in 1924 in a storm that destroyed the radio tower at its air base, station WOR in New York staged a dramatic rescue—by radio. Asking listeners to call in if they heard the vessel's motors humming overhead, station operators carefully plotted the dirigible's course, then communicated it back to the crew, who had no idea of their position. By this method they talked the ship back to base; at first light, it landed.

Two vital concepts put radio on its feet financially, and both passed intact to television. In 1922 a New York real estate firm bought the first 10 minutes of airtime, to advertise the pleasures of living at Hawthorne Court. From that moment the profit—and irritation—levels of radio rose considerably. American Telephone and Telegraph pioneered the network system of stations in 1923 but retired from the broadcasting business three years later, to be followed in 1926 by the 19 stations (including AT&T's WEAF) of the National Broadcasting Company and in 1927 by the 16 stations of the Columbia Broadcasting System. In but a few years radio had become big business, a hard-sell, mass-culture medium, different in content and profitability from the government-funded systems of England and the Commonwealth.

So pervasive was radio advertising that the most addictive form of drama was named for what it sold. Some called them "washboard weepers"; the world knows them today as "soaps." Soap operas began in Chicago about 1930 as economical time fillers, and by the end of the decade a housewife could listen to seven straight hours of romance, nervous breakdowns, amnesia, brain tumors, kidnappings, and illegitimate babies and, if

she had any energy left, still do the ironing. So involved were listeners with programs that when a character on *Big Sister* married, the studio was swamped with truckloads of wedding gifts. When a tot was lost on another series, calls poured in reporting his whereabouts. As one devoted listener put it, "I can get through the day better knowing they have sorrows too."

Of the writers behind these formula heartthrobs, none were so successful as Frank and Anne Hummert. With 67 shows a week on the air, they resorted to the factory system: the Hummerts outlined the plot, and a stable of writers filled in the lachrymose dialogue. Suspense, of course, was the key; and emotion, the lock. One heroine managed to take 17 days to get through a revolving door because flashbacks prevented her from making the move; others languished on and on in romantic indecision, while still others lingered at death's door for months at a time.

By 1950 television had captured a large share of

people

Mr. Broadcasting

His mother wanted him to be a Talmudic scholar; his father, a merchant. Instead, David Sarnoff became the most dynamic, foresighted figure in the history of American broadcasting, a communications genius whose career spanned the airwaves from the days of the Marconi wireless to the era of color television.

Two days after he arrived in the United States from Russia in 1900, nine-year-old David was peddling newspapers. He never stopped working. Early jobs as a telegraph operator for American Marconi took him to the Arctic aboard ship, to a lonely station on Nantucket Island (where he read a complete technical library), then to a wireless station atop Wanamaker's department store in New York.

There, on April 14, 1912, he picked up a faint message: "S.S. *Titanic* ran into iceberg. Sinking fast." Sarnoff called newspapers and bent every effort to establish contact with ships near the *Titanic*. When President Taft ordered all other stations off the air, the 21-year-old operator became the nation's only link with

the scene of the heart-rending disaster. Slowly, the names of survivors taken aboard the rescue ship *Carpathia* began to trickle in. Not until the list was complete did Sarnoff abandon his post: he had been at his key for 72 hours.

In 1916 Sarnoff submitted a historic memo to his boss at American Marconi: "I have in mind a plan of development which would make radio a 'household utility' in the same sense as the piano or phonograph. . . . in the form of a simple 'Radio Music Box.' " No one paid any attention, however, until after the Radio Corporation of America absorbed American Marconi in 1919 and Sarnoff tried again. This time, determined to dramatize the enormous potential of radio, he broadcast a blow-by-blow description of the 1921 Dempsey-Carpentier prizefight. Sarnoff's equipment held until Dempsey delivered a knockout blow, then burned out. No matter; Sarnoff had made his point.

Under Sarnoff's guidance, RCA founded the National Broadcasting Company in 1926 to promote

the radio and its programs. Decade after decade, he pioneered technical and programming advances. A music lover, he broadcast live opera from the stage of the Metropolitan in New York, and in 1937 he formed the NBC Symphony Orchestra under the baton of Arturo Toscanini. Just as he had foreseen the future of radio, so was he a leader in the development of television. In February 1939 Sarnoff made the first experimental telecast from the unfinished New York World's Fair grounds—"Amos 'n' Andy" in blackface makeup. Technically, TV was ready, but the world was not. The new medium had to wait for the end of World War II.

After serving as General Eisenhower's communications expert in Europe, Sarnoff returned from the war with the rank of brigadier general. As chairman of the board of RCA for 24 years, he led NBC from black and white to color. "General Sarnoff," he was called, but to the world of radio and television this stocky, quiet-spoken prophet might more appropriately have been addressed by the title "Mr. Broadcasting."

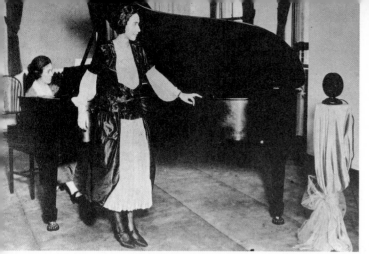

Early radio studios had a homey look; above, the "studio" facilities at WEAF New York in the 1920's.

radio's evening audience along with much of its talent, its sponsors, and its formats: the quiz and variety shows, the serial, and the situation comedy. But radio proved to be both durable and adaptable. It survived, and both the number of sets sold and stations in operation increased.

The technology that brought us Jack Benny and The Lone Ranger has advanced, too, producing radar and a remarkable array of radio telescopes. At Goldstone, California, for example, a project is afoot to eavesdrop in every corner of the sky on all possible frequencies by radio telescope in the hope of detecting other civilizations. If such things exist, and if they too are listening, what might they think of the bursts of energy radiating out from our tiny spot in space? Is it awesome or bizarre to think that the words of the characters along Allen's Alley, the voice of The Shadow, and Lowell Thomas' hearty "So long until tomorrow!" might still be resonating in the curve of time?

RAINCOAT Animal skins, worn with the hide side out, were probably among the first garments devised to turn back the rain. Aleut Eskimos added a hood to their rainwear, which was made from seal intestines stitched together, with feathers or fur stuck in the seams to plug leaks. In parts of the world where fur-bearing animals were less plentiful, people made raincoats of other materials. Asians wove raincoats of rice, straw, or reeds. Some of the straw coats were heavily thatched, giving wearers the appearance of moving haystacks. Polynesians made tapa-cloth garments from bark pounded thin and coated with sap that was water repellent.

South American Indians had the perfect material for waterproofing their clothes—liquid latex from rubber trees. Many Europeans made coats of thick wool, which did not need protective coating because the natural oil in the wool made the fabric water resistant. Scottish fishermen applied linseed oil to their heavy canvas hats and coats, thus creating waterproof "oilskin" slickers. (Similar slickers, dyed bright yellow and dabbed with snappy sayings like "Darn Mah Sox" and "Hya Butch," were the rage on American college campuses during the late 1920's.)

Spanish explorers in the New World recognized the value of latex as a waterproofing material and used it in making cloth coats and leather boots and pouches that were impervious to the elements. Rubberized rainwear eventually became popular in Europe, but the latex-coated garments were sticky in warm weather and brittle in cold. Charles Macintosh improved the situation in the early 1800's by sandwiching rubber between two pieces of fabric. Soon, Macintosh's fabric was adopted by Europeans for raincoats, some of which resembled ankle-length coats of armor. Later a "k" was added to the name of these coats, and people called them mackintoshes or just plain macs.

World War I revolutionized rainwear. U.S. doughboys fighting in the trenches of Europe needed protection from rain, without the heat and clamminess that rubber coats produced. Thomas Burberry, an Englishman, provided the answer—a raincoat of fine cotton-twill gabardine treated with chemicals so that it would repel water while providing adequate ventilation. The first trenchcoat was born, and it became the coat of the Allied fighting men. After the war civilian men and women adopted the coat, retaining even its shoulder gun straps and brass grenade rings.

Miracle fabrics, such as Dacron and polyvinyl chloride, spawned by World War II technology, enabled manufacturers to make coats thinner and lighter than ever before. Today, emergency raincoats made of thin plastic are small enough to be carried in pocket or purse. So popular has the raincoat become that even its name now seems obsolete, for raincoats are worn in cold and snow and on sunny days as well as in the rain.

Shepherds in Spain weave and wear layered straw raincoats like this.

RAZOR Napoleon, it was rumored, was terrified of shaving. One can scarcely blame him because, until the safety razor was perfected in the 20th century, getting a good shave was a time-consuming and sometimes dangerous affair. Not even an emperor was spared an occasional nick or gash delivered by a barber who brandished an unguarded steel blade. Gentlemen had to "feel up to shaving," and very few of them felt like it every day.

A long time before Rube Goldberg, an Englishman engraved this trenchant view of a steam shaving shop.

"Master Slave," a British device, provides the ultimate in grooming ease: a remote shave.

The hirsute male has been ridding himself of his whiskers off and on for thousands of years. Prehistoric cave drawings show men shaving with razors made of clam shells, shark's teeth, and polished flint. Central Americans Indians used obsidian, and some light-bearded North American tribesmen simply plucked out chin hairs with tweezers. Bronze, copper, and even gold razors shaved both the chins and heads of Egyptians.

To the Romans we owe the discovery that a wet beard gives a closer shave. Scientists now know that hairs expand as much as 34 percent when doused with warm water, making them more supple and easier to mow. Whenever man acquired new metallurgical knowledge he applied it to the whisker problem, but only the widespread use of steel made a really close shave possible.

However finely ground, the shaving edge of a razor gets bent and chipped with use. The flaws are invisible except under a microscope, but the bloody results are not. From the 18th century on, the finest steel edges came from Sheffield, England, and from Germany. Some of these long blades were handed down for generations. They had to be stropped constantly and honed frequently, but there are men who contend that no modern disposable blade gives as fine a shave.

When a French cutler, Jean-Jacques Perret, came back from the barber with a skin disease, he launched the long search for a safe razor. Borrowing from the principle of the carpenter's plane, Perret encased the blade in a wooden guard. In 1847 the English inventor William Henson set the blade at right angles to the handle. But these prototypes of the safety razor failed to solve the problem of how to keep a blade sharp. This perplexing situation awaited the genius of an American salesman who was obsessed with one idea: that of getting rich by making something that users would throw away.

King Camp Gillette knew it could be done. He worked as salesman for a company that manufactured bottle stoppers; people threw out the stoppers, and Gillette sold more. One morning, while staring grumpily at his dulled razor and thinking that he would have to take it to the cutler again for honing, the idea of the disposable razor struck him. "It seemed as though I could see the way the blade could be held in a holder. . . . already a finished thing and held before my eyes," he later wrote. "Fool that I was, I knew little about razors and practically nothing about steel."

He hired inventor William Nickerson, and in 1903 sold a total of 51 razors and 14 dozen blades. Within a few years Gillette's thin disposable blade was literally changing the face of America—at least the patriarchal, bewhiskered visage that had dominated the 19th century. Smooth chins made men look 10 years younger, wives were happier, and barbershops busier. By the end of World War I men were shaving at home, and by World War II they were doing it every day.

But all the credit does not belong to Gillette's cheap blade and good advertising. In 1928 Joseph Schick, a retired army colonel, had patented an electric shaver—a dry method that did away with suds, creams, brushes, and styptic pencils. Ever after, partisans of each method have bickered over which implement gives a better shave.

Any method of shaving, say dermatologists, is a trauma to the face, and the average male removes some 27½ feet of whiskers in his lifetime. Today, researchers have come up with stainless-steel coated-edge blades and efficient double-track razors that swipe the stubble twice. Surely Napoleon would have enjoyed shaving with a little battery-operated pocket razor at Waterloo.

Reducing Diets

To eat fat and stay thin has been a major, if intermittent, preoccupation of Western man and woman since the days of Rome. Perhaps it was the Romans who hit upon the most efficient, though least aesthetic, means of achieving those contradictory ends.

Consider, for instance, a banquet during the time of Roman Emperor Claudius I, when each guest was served generous portions of jellyfish, brains, tree fungi, sea urchins, roast deer, boiled ostrich, pork-stuffed dormice, boiled ham, flamingo, sweet cakes, and fricassee of roses. Clearly, such a repast was beyond the capacity of mortals, but to turn away a dish was both impolite and impolitic. So, when that overstuffed feeling caused discomfort, a senator's wife merely crooked her finger at an attendant. The servant rushed over, tickled the diner's throat, and in a trice the lady was disgorging her spiced sea urchins into a bowl kept handy for just that purpose. Then it was on to whole boiled turtle dove and roast parrot.

Not all Romans thought such conduct seemly and instead sought less direct means of overcoming the effects of gluttony.

Catch a falling star: this publicity shot employed planks and a rope.

The steambath, followed by a relaxing massage, was another favorite means of shedding extra pounds in imperial Rome.

For the contemporary gourmand, however, the most common way of restoring a svelte figure after months of gourmandizing self-indulgence is the reducing diet. Common? Yes! Popular? Not really. Humorist Art Buchwald expressed his feelings about calorie counting when he postulated that the word "diet" is derived from the verb "to die."

Because thinness and beauty are often equated, dieting has become an obsession with millions of people, or so the mountain of literature on the subject would suggest. As often as not, the titles reveal a desire to sugarcoat what is, after all, an exercise in self-denial. Readers are assured that they can "Daydream Those Pounds Away" while they "Eat and Grow Beautiful." For those of a cerebral bent, there is the "Think Thin and Get Thin" approach, and gluttons are promised they can lose weight while "Feasting on Fat."

For those who are unable to feast, dream, or think themselves thin and are unwilling to follow doctor-directed diets, there have been many shortcuts. These take the form of food supplements, low-calorie concoctions that supposedly contain most of, or even all, the basic nutrients needed to sustain life and vigor. Yet such diet aids are not unique to contemporary life; a nostrum called Allan's Anti-Fat was ballyhooed a century ago. This medication purportedly was made from the

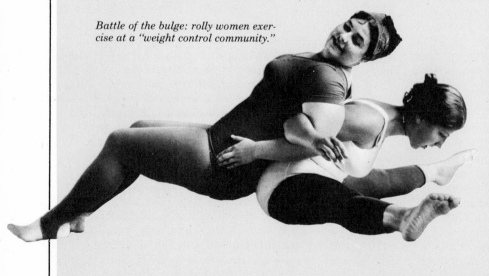

Battle of the bulge: roly women exercise at a "weight control community."

"concentrated fluid extract of sea lichens," and buyers were assured that it would keep the body from turning food into blubber.

Today's diets are sometimes just as spurious. There was a fad for liquid proteins, which in no time at all became a $40-million-a-year business before it fell victim to government warnings about their safety. Liquid protein, marketed under various brand names, was flamboyantly advertised as the "breakthrough of the century" by one manufacturer. Research, however, revealed that it was nothing more than a blend of slaughterhouse leftovers—hide, tendons, and bones—disguised by flavorings and fortified with amino acids. Its nutritional value was questionable. True, those who went on liquid-protein diets did lose weight, for that is a by-product of starvation. One manifestation of this desperation to lose weight was aptly called "The Last Chance Diet"; for some the liquid-protein diet was probably their last hurrah.

For those who want neither to starve nor to endure the rigors of a well-planned diet in solitude, there is yet another route to a slim and trim figure: the reducing spa, or "fat farm." Such places are not for everyone. Money is the passkey to these "resorts," which combine pampering with a strict dietary and exercise regimen that one visitor has likened to a Marine boot camp. A week at a reducing spa may run to more than $1,500, exclusive of tips.

Fat farms generally have names that suggest luxury or care giving: Golden Door, La Costa Spa and Country Club, and The Greenhouse, among others. More often than not they are located in a spectacular setting, such as the Maine coast, the Arizona desert, or at the foot of the sylvan hills of southern California. The decor

In a year Dolly Wager dieted away the equivalent of the weight of these sacks of coal—more than 300 pounds.

is sumptuous. The bedrooms are thickly carpeted, the furniture is luxurious, and the facilities—swimming pools, gymnasiums, saunas, and steam rooms—are

He filled the gap with 417 pounds.

the best that money can buy.

But if the setting is posh, life within the confines of a fat farm tends to be spartan, particularly when compared with the sybaritic styles that most of the patrons are accustomed to. For these patrons come seeking that will-o'-the-wisp the body beautiful, which usually requires shedding the weight of months of easy living. To achieve even the roughest approximation of that goal, they allow themselves to be pressed and pummeled by expert masseurs and masseuses and submit to exercise contraptions that resemble some medieval torture machines. And when they have worked up a healthy sweat in the gym, it's into the sauna, followed by a massage and then more exercise. Perhaps most important of all are the individually tailored diets. The dishes on which the thin sliver of lean meat is served may be of the finest bone china; the crystal from which mineral water is drunk may be imported from Ireland or France; the tableware may be solid sterling. But neither the elegant appointments nor the legerdemain of the chefs can satisfy the gnawing hunger. Small wonder that one patron, in a frenzy of appetite, was observed wolfing down her scanty portion of melon—rind and all.

That "thin is in" is no great news, of course. Thinness and beauty have been synonymous for several decades. Yet the lean figure, the small bust, and narrow hips have not always been regarded as exemplars of human, particularly feminine, beauty. At one time the "pleasingly plump" was the ideal. Westerners still refer to the ancient Greek statue of Venus de Milo as the standard of comparison. But a close and measured examination of this marble figure would reveal her to be a candidate for a fat farm.

Cube route: before the mass production of refrigerators, machines like this carved icebox ice from frozen lakes.

REFRIGERATION Almost every aspect of our daily life is affected by refrigeration. Not only foods but plastics, steel, cooking gas, printed matter, radios, tobacco, textiles, film, and drugs involve refrigeration in their manufacture or storage. Summer heat waves are made bearable by air conditioners, another leading use of refrigeration; and in hospitals, blood, bone, sperm, eyes, and even diseased organisms (preserved for study) and other biological materials are stored under refrigeration. In the treatment of some diseases, the entire patient may be cooled. Experiments have shown that refrigeration of humans may make possible the extension of life itself, by slowing the aging process. But the earliest use of refrigeration was to preserve food.

Centuries before the Christian era, mountain snow and lake ice, harvested during the winter, served to cool perishables. The Chinese stored ice and snow in cellars prior to 1000 B.C., and about 500 B.C. Egyptians and Indians made ice by setting water out of doors on nights that were cool (but still above freezing) and continually wetting the earthenware container, which was cooled further by evaporation. By the 1700's many commercial products were cooled and frozen by natural ice or snow mixed with chemicals to decrease the temperature to as low as –27° F (–32° C).

Natural-ice refrigeration grew to a major industry in the United States and elsewhere during the 1800's. River, pond, and lake ice was harvested with handsaws and horse-drawn equipment, stored in immense icehouses, and shipped in pine sawdust. Many homes had icehouses or cellars for storing ice, as well as iceboxes—lined with tin or zinc and usually insulated with cork or sawdust—in which food and beverages were kept cold.

In 1834 Jacob Perkins, an American living in England, received the first patent for a refrigeration machine. According to one story, helpers working with Perkins' refrigerator first produced ice one summer evening and were so excited with their success that they wrapped up the ice in a blanket and sped across London by cab in order to show it to the inventor at his home.

The machine that Perkins invented employed the same principles used in household refrigerators to this day. A volatile fluid (Perkins used ether) was compressed, allowed to evaporate to

Montreal, 1859: block ice could outlast August packed in sawdust, stored in windowless, wooden shacks.

produce the cooling, condensed, and returned to the compressor. His design incorporated a hand-turned compressor. The inventor broke into a sweat just demonstrating that it could make a few lumps of ice, and though he impressed his spectators, he aroused no interest in buying. Some advocates of natural ice argued that anyone who wanted to produce ice by artificial means was probably in league with the Devil, but Americans showed increasing interest in Perkins' invention. Deliveries of Northern ice to Southern ports were erratic (partly because of storms at sea), and Northern ice merchants quarreled with customers over credit arrangements and price, which was generally 10 cents a pound at Gulf ports.

The unpredictable delivery of natural ice had inspired one Southerner, Dr. John Gorrie, to invent his own ice machine to ensure that patients in his hospital in Florida would have relief from fevers. Gorrie's refrigerator, which both air-conditioned the hospital and produced ice, used compressed air as a coolant, and in 1851 he was awarded the first U.S. refrigeration patent.

By the turn of the century the switchover from natural to machine-made ice was well under way, with the proponents of each type arguing the supposed advantages of their product. In the end, mechanization did carry the day. That did not prevent home iceboxes from continuing to drip and smell bad. Spreading newspapers on the kitchen floor to protect it against the muddy boots and dripping burden of the iceman was a daily ritual in many homes.

Household refrigerators were introduced by manufacturers prior to World War I, and by 1920 more than 200 different makes were on the market. The compressor was usually driven by a belt from a motor that was located in the basement or an adjoining room because it was so noisy. In 1923 Frigidaire introduced the first self-contained household refrigerator. Today refrigerators are the most-used appliance in the U.S.; less than one percent of the nation's homes are without at least one. After World War II and the popularization of frozen foods, home freezers proliferated and are now in some 40 percent of America's kitchens.

Pie in the sky: diners relish the food and the view from the 107th floor of New York's Windows on the World.

RESTAURANT In 1765 an enterprising Frenchman named Boulanger conceived the novel idea of opening a public establishment where people could go at any time simply to eat soups and broths, which he called *restaurants*, meaning "restoratives." Over its door was inscribed an ungrammatical and slightly modified version of Christ's words in chapter 11 of the Gospel According to St. Matthew: *"Venite ad me omnes qui stomacho laboratis et ego restaurabo"* ("Come unto me, all ye that labor in the stomach, and I will restore you"). The idea, and the word, caught

on. Two years later the philosopher Denis Diderot wrote to a friend: "I went to dine at the *restaurateur's* place. . . . one is treated well there but has to pay dearly for it."

The French Revolution of 1789 launched res-

Marie-Antoine Carême

When Marie-Antoine Carême, one of 25 children born to an impoverished stonemason, was 11 years old his father took him to a tavern at the gates of Paris, fed him a last meal, and abandoned him to his own devices: "Misery is our lot. . . . Go, little one, perhaps some fine house will open its doors to you."

That house could well have turned out to be a cobbler's or a tailor's, but as Prosper Montagné, another celebrated chef, observed, "Destiny led him to a humble cookshop." Carême quickly mastered what there was to learn and moved on to become (in 1804, when he was not yet 21) *chef de cuisine* to Talleyrand, the durable diplomat whose table was reputed to be the finest in France.

Seeking to improve upon his native cuisine, England's prince regent—later George IV—summoned Carême to the elegant kitchens of the pavilion at Brigh-

ton, where he performed only too well. "You will kill me with a surfeit of food," his employer once complained. Carême replied, "My great concern is to stimulate your appetite . . . not to curb it." But the climate, at once rainy and bourgeois, depressed him. He returned to France briefly before accepting an offer from Czar Alexander I to manage the imperial kitchens, only to find Russian winters even more inhospitable than England's. He returned to Paris, where he took a position in the luxurious household of Baron de Rothschild.

Carême was extremely serious about his craft, which he associated with the five arts: "Painting, sculpture, poetry, music, architecture—whose main branch is confectionery." Indeed, his decorative *pièces montées* were architectural marvels of wax, glue, almond paste, pastry dough, and spun sugar that faithfully lived up to their titles of the *Ruins of Athens*

or the *Tower of Rhodes*. But he also created countless dishes, did away with the undisciplined gorging that until the 18th century had passed for formal eating (one banquet for 100 people called for 322 dishes, not including 66 salads and 30 sauces), and established the basis upon which *haute cuisine* still rests: the logical complementarity of carefully matched flavors and textures.

Carême died young; he was 48. It was said that he was burnt out by the flame of his genius and the heat of his ovens—possibly because he spent his days inhaling the noxious fumes emitted by the charcoal-fired kitchen ranges of his day. According to one story, his last words were spoken to a favorite pupil. "My boy," the great chef said, "the *quenelles de sole* were splendid, but the peas were poor. You should shake the pan gently, all the time, like this." He moved his hand back and forth on the sheet and died.

In Ethiopia the well-to-do, despite their white robes, use rounds of unleavened bread to eat traditional stews.

taurants as a popular institution, by simultaneously depriving legions of chefs of private employment in noble houses and creating a class of *nouveaux riches* able to afford the pleasure of eating out. By 1804 Paris could boast of more than 500 restaurants.

Quantity as well as quality seems to have been the order of the day. Dining out at Véry's, the novelist Honoré de Balzac once managed to put away a plate of Ostend oysters, a dozen lamb cutlets, a duckling with turnips, a pair of roast partridges, *sole à la normande*, as well as hors d'oeuvres, fruits, and unspecified quantities of wines and liqueurs. And best of all he had the bill sent to his publisher's office for payment.

Before long, however, another abiding institution—the food critic—arose to point a disapproving finger at such undisciplined gluttony. The greatest of his time—possibly of all time—was Anthelme Brillat-Savarin, who habitually carried small game birds in his overcoat pockets until they reached the perfect degree of gaminess. ("The discovery of a new dish," he wrote, "does more for the happiness of mankind than the discovery of a star.") Another was Grimod de la Reynière, who claimed, "A well-made sauce will make even an elephant or a grandfather palatable."

France produced not only discriminating critics but masterful chefs. Auguste Escoffier was one of the finest. He was also the author of the *Guide Culinaire*, which includes nearly 3,000 of his recipes. It is said that Escoffier once prepared a meal for Kaiser Wilhelm II of Germany so flawless that that monarch was moved to ask, "How can I repay you?" "By giving us back Alsace-Lorraine," the Frenchman replied.

The first restaurant in the United States was opened in Boston in 1794 by a French immigrant named Jean-Baptiste Gilbert Payplat. His soups and cheese fondue were much admired, but one

wonders how the sensible citizens of the home of the bean and the cod reacted to another of his innovations: the truffle.

The restaurant did not come of age in America until after the arrival in 1832 of a 19-year-old Swiss named Lorenzo Delmonico. Two of his uncles, who had already established themselves in New York, created the first of the Delmonico restaurants. In 1831 they imported a French chef and dumbfounded the carnivorous New Yorkers with carefully prepared exotic vegetables such as endive and eggplant. (To assure their supply, the Delmonicos started their own 200-acre farm in Brooklyn.) But young Lorenzo had more ambitious ideas. He created a seven-page menu offering a bounty of game, meat, and fish. New dishes were invented such as lobster à la Newburg and a delicious concoction of creamed chicken. The latter had been christened in honor of a favored patron named Keene but fumbled its way onto the menu as chicken à la king.

Delmonico's became a New York institution, with a succession of 11 restaurants bearing that name; the last of them closed on May 21, 1923. No visit to the city, whether by the Prince of Wales or such luminaries as Charles Dickens, William Dean Howells, or Mark Twain, was complete without a Delmonico's banquet. The house's most serious competition would come from a former caterer named Louis Sherry.

Sherry's acquired a reputation for a more risqué sort of soirée, which Delmonico's had prudishly

At the MaiKai Restaurant in Hawaii, the fruits of sea and land mix in the pungent jumble of a luau.

discouraged. There was, for instance, "the awful Seeley dinner" given by Herbert Barnum Seeley, a nephew of the great showman, for 20 of his high-living chums. The *pièce de résistance* was a tabletop dance by Little Egypt, whose abbreviated costume had scandalized audiences at the Chicago World's Columbian Exposition of 1893. For this occasion she simplified it still further to just black lace stockings and high-heel shoes. For dessert came the police and a horde of reporters who had been tipped off.

Legal, though of even more questionable taste, was the "Horse Dinner" given by C.K.G. Billings for 30 fellow members of the New York Riding Club. Guests ate their meal on horseback in the restaurant's fourth-story dining room. While one platoon of waiters passed around food for the human guests, another group served oats to the horses.

The greatest innovation in the art of eating out in America was probably the diner—not the chrome and neon-lighted structure forlornly marooned along the highway but the wheeled kind that clicked along the rails from New York to Chicago and points west. Every line had its proud specialties—terrapin stew on the Baltimore & Ohio, scrod and Cotuit oysters on the New Haven, broiled sage hen on the Santa Fe. The food was not only of the highest quality but incredibly inexpensive—75 cents or a dollar for a full meal. The reason for this largesse was that savage competition existed among the railroads, and shrewd officials used their dining cars to attract passengers. Indeed, the legendary Fred Harvey, who was in charge of catering arrangements on the Santa Fe, was reported to have fired a dining-car manager because his operation had been losing $500 a month and replaced him with a man who upped the deficit to $1,500. Something to ponder as one chews the plastic food that today is universally served at an altitude of 35,000 feet.

From restaurants *on* wheels, it is an easy step to restaurants *in* wheels. The transition was achieved in 1956 with the opening of the world's first revolving restaurant, located atop a 700-foot tower in Stuttgart, West Germany. An instant success, the idea was copied by similar establishments in Brussels, Rotterdam, London, Sydney, and Cairo as well as in a growing number of American cities. Taken as a group, these spinning dining salons have yet to make gastronomic history, but their engineering is something of a marvel. So delicately balanced are they that the Summit, which crowns a 50-story building in Sydney and can accommodate 330 diners at one time, is powered by only two ¾-horsepower motors. And even mechanical power can be dispensed with: on

the opening night of the Holiday Inn's revolving restaurant in Denver, the works became jammed by the thick carpeting. So the innkeeper himself pushed the restaurant around for an hour and a half to keep the party moving.

There have been some memorable meals in restaurant history, such as the "Dinner of the Three Emperors," served in Paris on June 7, 1867, at the Café Anglais to a

Paradoxical pig: this pigheaded food stand sold kosher corned beef.

group including the king of Prussia, Czar Alexander II of Russia, and his son, the future Czar Alexander III. The service used on that occasion is still on display at the world-famous Tour d'Argent. Another spectacular dinner was given on February 8, 1876, at San Francisco's Palace Hotel for the silver baron William Sharon by some of his happy colleagues in the Comstock lode. Not only did it consist of 10 courses and as many wines, but to make the occasion more festive the menus were engraved on solid silver plates.

The most famous, or infamous, meal of recent years was the $4,000 feast to which Craig Claiborne, a food editor for *The New York Times*, treated himself and a friend in November 1975. Having made the high bid on "a dinner for two" at a charity auction, they betook themselves to one of the best restaurants in Paris, where they ordered a meal of 31 dishes and proceeded to wash down nibbles of each with nine rare wines, an event reported on *The Times'* front page the following day. The general reaction to this performance was summed up, again in Latin, by columnist Harriet Van Horne: "*Edunt et vomant*" ("They have eaten and let them vomit").

An Egyptian lunch spot features monumental decor.

ROLLER SKATES The first man on record to invent roller skates, Joseph Merlin, decided to publicize his brainchild—in the early 1760's—by wearing a pair of skates to a fashionable masquerade party in London. His plan was to skate around the ballroom while playing a violin. Unfortunately, his musicianship was better than his skating, and he crashed into an expensive mirror, shattering it and his violin and seriously injuring himself. After Merlin's disaster, interest in roller skating remained slight for nearly three decades.

Then, in 1790, a Frenchman whipped up a *patin-à-terre*, or "ground skate," that attracted some attention in France and later in Germany. German ballet masters used similar skates to simulate ice skating in the ballet *The Artist, or Winter Pleasures* in Berlin in 1818. In the following year another Frenchman, Monsieur Petitbled, was granted the world's first patent for roller skates. Most skating, however, was still limited to stage productions or occasional outdoor demonstrations. This

Risking face and limb, a California skateboarder executes a dangerous downhill sidewinder maneuver.

changed dramatically in 1849, when the German composer Giacomo Meyerbeer created an ice-carnival scene for his opera *Le Prophète*, which featured an entire corps de ballet on roller skates. Highly successful, the opera toured the continent with its rolling stock, and by 1860 roller skating had become a fad in many European cities.

The modern roller skate might never have been

customs

The Battle on Roller Skates

The roller derby is a child of the grueling dance marathons and walkathons of the Great Depression. During the 1930's walkathon producer Leo Alexander Seltzer, a former Hollywood promotion man for silent movies, realized that the public was ready for something stronger—and racier. Noticing a magazine story extolling roller skating as the country's leading participation sport, Seltzer immediately began making plans to cash in on the craze. And on August 13, 1935, he launched the first roller derby, as he named the event, in the 12,000-seat Chicago Coliseum. The first derby was essentially a roller-skating race, but as more contests were held new rules were devised by spectators and even sportswriters, including Damon Runyon.

Speed is not the deciding factor in today's derbies, which at times resemble brutal free-for-alls on wheels. Opposing teams of five women and five men alternate in competition on a banked oval track (90 by 50 feet), during eight 12-minute periods. Only two

players (known as jammers) on each unit, are eligible to score—by streaking past members of the opposing team. Other team members, two blockers and one pivotman, try to prevent opposing jammers from scoring while they help the jammers on their own team. According to one expert, the basic strategy of the sport is simple, if intimidating: "Kill or be killed."

The bone-cracking action of roller derbies attracts some 3 million fans annually to arenas throughout the United States, from New York's Madison Square

Garden to San Francisco's Cow Palace. Nearly seven times as many fans may watch the melees on television. A star skater can earn about $40,000 a year as long as he or she stays out of the hospital. Injuries are frequent and may involve anything from a friction burn to a fractured pelvis or brain concussion.

Roller-derby fans frequently batter each other and even attack the skaters, but they all agree on one thing—women skaters are rougher, meaner, and more vicious than men. Women also tend to skate on with injuries that normally send their male counterparts to the hospital. Some women have continued to compete through the first five months of pregnancy. Occasionally, when substitutes for a unit are used up, a male skater may enter the female lists and limp off the worse for the experience. In one case, a male fill-in skater was knocked down, stamped on, and butted off the track by violent female opponents. As one sportswriter observed, "The ladies of the oval fear nothing in human form."

invented, however, had its inventor enjoyed reasonably good health. For shortly after the outbreak of the Civil War, James Leonard Plimpton, a Yankee furniture maker, moved to New York City and began ice skating in Central Park to improve his health. Unfortunately, it was an activity that he had to stop when spring came. And so, to make skating a year-round sport, Plimpton devised a new kind of roller skate and patented it in 1863. What made Plimpton's skate different was that it had cushioned mountings, so that the wheels might turn slightly when the skater shifted his weight, thus allowing him to "steer."

In New York traffic eight tiny wheels make more sense than reindeer.

Plimpton opened a number of roller-skating rinks to popularize his invention, and by 1870 skating was popular in much of the United States and in more than 20 other countries. However, skating was a pastime only the wealthy could afford; a good pair of skates and skating accessories cost about $20, a large investment for most people at that time. Around the turn of the century, manufacturers began to mass-produce roller skates, and the sport became available to the general public—which was ready for it.

Today the U.S. Amateur Confederation of Roller Skating lists more than 32,000 members, who regularly compete in speed, distance, and hockey contests. More than 1,500 roller-skating rinks across the country (some with costly light and sound systems) cater to weekend skaters. Roller derbies are a widely popular spectator sport, and roller skating may even become an Olympic event.

No one knows when the first pair of cast-off skates were nailed to a plank and made into a skateboard. But by the mid-1960's many manufacturers were producing factory models, and skateboards had become as popular as the Hula-Hoop once had been. The high accident rate (with injuries to one of every four skateboarders, according to some reports) virtually stopped the craze as quickly as it had begun. Then in the 1970's die-hard skateboarders in California discovered that soft urethane skate wheels gave them more control over their ships, and skateboarding was off and rolling again.

Experts now estimate that as many as 20,000 Americans take to the wheeled boards regularly,

At the Empire Roller Disco in Brooklyn, dancers prove that the disco beat really gets rolling on skates.

and at least 150 manufacturers turn out more than 300 different models—including some with steel runners for skating on ice—at prices up to $70. A true aficionado, however, may spend up to $200 for the components to roll his own. Skateboard parks, some costing as much as $1 million, have sprung up, dotted with moonscape-like cement hills, valleys, and tubes for the better display of the skateboarders' strut. Protective helmets and elbow and knee pads have made the sport safer. Nonetheless, the California State Highway Patrol continues to issue scores of traffic tickets for "reckless skateboarding."

ROPE Rope—without which the pyramids would not have been built, the oceans crossed, the West won, or Mt. Everest ascended—is now generally defined as cordage three-sixteenths of an inch thick or more. Its knotty history has been unraveled as far back as the Stone Age when, before man could spin or weave, he twisted plant fibers or sinew into cord for fishnets and traps.

Ropes have connected the beast to the cart and the arrow to the bow, and the Persian king Xerxes once used rope to connect Asia to Europe. On his way to invade Greece, Xerxes constructed two bridges across the Hellespont, each made up of more than 300 anchored vessels held in line by six great cables of flax and papyrus. The soldiers hopped from boat to boat and invaded Greece. When the Greeks defeated the Persians, they hauled home Xerxes' ropes and dedicated them to the gods.

The Greeks had a reputation for being superb tightrope walkers. "Those tightrope walkers," the Romans scornfully called all Greeks, but the entertainment was just as popular in Rome, where naked performers did their act high above the au-

Royal rope show: guildsmen demonstrate their skills for Sultan Murad III of Turkey in this 16th-century tableau.

dience. When a young aerialist fell to his death, the compassionate emperor Marcus Aurelius invented another use for rope: he decreed that a safety net should thenceforth be slung under the swaying tightrope acrobat.

Ancient Egyptian friezes and paintings illustrate the rope-turning process, which is essentially unchanged today: fibers are twisted (clockwise) into yarns, yarns are twisted (counterclockwise) into strands, and strands (clockwise again) into rope. This alternation of the twist is the secret that gives rope its cohesion and strength.

Until machinery took over the job, rope was made in open fields or long covered sheds called rope walks, where the rope was literally walked into existence. That method, also utilized by the Egyptians, prescribed that a man walk backward, slowly twisting the fiber as he went. The longest single piece of unspliced rope was made, however, by machine: it was 11.36 miles long.

The most valued organic ropes are made of abaca, sisal, jute, and hemp—fibers stripped from either the leaf or bark of plants. Horsehair, camel's hair, rawhide, and grasses have also been used. The greatest revolution in rope making came with the introduction of synthetics. Nylon, which was first used in rope for parachute shrouds, has an elasticity much appreciated by a falling mountain climber, a water-skier, or a roper snubbing a 1,000-pound steer. Nylon has twice

Jump Rope

Worldwide and centuries old, jump rope is hardly the dumb game that some small boys think it is. It was probably a boys' game once, back when girls were told to keep their ruffles clean. All it requires is a rope, although in Hungary plaited straw will do, and in Sweden a stiff piece of wicker is all right. Spanish kids have been seen jumping rope with leather strips, and Cherokee Indians with honeysuckle vines.

In Greece they use elastic; the two "enders" stretch it between their ankles, and the jumper has to perform intricate maneuvers in and out without touching the elastic. A game similar to that is played with a whole circle of kids. It is called American ropes, except that it is not played much in America. Actually, it is a Scottish version of a Chinese version of that Greek idea. But it is all jump rope just the same.

In the lore and lingo of the schoolyard, a "white sheep," or skilled jumper, might be tested by Double Dutch, a tricky game in which two ropes turn at once. Fast turning is known most widely as "pepper" or "hot pepper" (even faster), though in some regions it is called "bullets," "vinegar," "red hot bricks," "hot peas with butter," or "hot tamales." Whatever it is called, the pace is whipping fast.

Today, almost as many adults as children jump rope. Muhammad Ali jumped rope to get in shape before a fight; executives and old ladies and people who hate jogging jump rope for muscle tone and cardiopulmonary health. Doctors who have made Americans aware of the benefits of rigorous exercise equate 10 minutes of jumping rope with running a mile in the same time. A regular program of jumping rope, carefully graduated, can vastly improve the functioning of heart and lungs, lower the heart rate, and actually increase the number of blood vessels in the body. But to the girls performing out in the schoolyard, jumping rope is just good fun.

This World War II foursome leaped to loop the loop.

the strength of abaca and, like most synthetics, is resistant to decay from bacterial action. Today we have rope that floats (polyethylene), self-splicing braided rope, water-resistant Dacron, and even rubber rope. These synthetics haul space capsules out of the sea, lower instrument packs into the depths of undersea canyons, and hold supertankers securely moored during raging hurricanes.

But they cannot be used for the greatest feat of all—the Indian rope trick. In this legendary feat, rarely if ever verified by eyewitness, the itinerant Indian *fakir* throws a rope up in the air, where it miraculously stays. His young assistant then climbs the rope and disappears from sight. When the conjurer sternly summons him down from invisibility, the lad refuses to appear, so the angry *fakir* scurries up the rope, knife in teeth. From the upper regions fall bloody bits of the boy—first a hand, then a foot. The conjurer descends to the ground, and suddenly, out of the crowd, the boy appears intact once again.

ROSE "Rose is a rose is a rose," wrote Gertrude Stein, the high priestess of the Parisian art world from 1903 to 1940, but not everyone would agree. Among other things, a rose may be any one of 13,000 distinct varieties, with tiny buds the size of a button or lush blossoms that would hide a dinner plate. The colors range from pristine white to near black, with red, yellow, lavender, and pink in numerous shades in between. Some varieties creep along the ground, others climb walls nearly 50 feet high, and still others form deep, tangled hedges that are all but impenetrable. As for the accuracy of Shakespeare's line "a rose by any other name would smell as sweet," that would depend on the variety he had in mind. Some roses smell sweet indeed, others have a spicy odor, while at least one variety gives off a definite beery smell. And then there are even several kinds that are odorless.

This profusion stems from four varieties of wild roses that grew in ancient times. One of them, the *Rosa galica*, can be seen in a Cretan fresco paint-

---

words

Jump-Rope Rhymes

Passed from generation to generation, jump-rope rhymes are the poetry of motion—ritual chants full of romance, revenge, or just plain silliness. Francelia Butler, a scholar who has collected many of these rhymes the world over, speculates that jump-rope verses often express the unconscious conflicts of childhood. Within the circle of the thumping rope, the child experiences "a psychic loosening of emotional strictures, a way for unconscious elements of the personality to surface." Here, for example, are some about siblings:

I had a little brother,
His name was Tiny Tim.
I put him in the washtub
To teach him how to swim.
He drank up all the water,
He ate up all the soap,
He died last night
With a bubble in his throat.

Fudge, fudge,
Call the judge.
Mama's got a baby.
Ain't no girl,
Ain't no boy,

Just a plain old baby.
Wrap it up in tissue paper.
Put it on the elevator.

Justice for a mean big brother is the theme of this one:

Johnny over the ocean.
Johnny over the sea.
Johnny broke a milk bottle
And blamed it on me.
I told Ma. Ma told Pa.
Johnny got a lickin'—
Ha! Ha! Ha!

Do parents have the right to control a child's companions? Not according to this rhyme:

My mother said
I never should
Play with gypsies
In the wood.
If I should
She would say,
"Naughty girl to disobey." . . .
I wish my mother would
Hold her tongue.
She had a boy
When she was young.
I wish my father would
Do the same.
He had a girl

With an awful name.

Rebellious, maybe, but full of high spirits—like Salome:

Salome was a dancer.
She danced before the king.
She danced hanky-panky
And she shimmied everything.
The king said, "Salome,
You can't do that in here!"
Salome said, "Baloney!"
And kicked the chandelier!

Some rhymes are very old. This one has been traced back to Roman times:

All in together, girls.
No mind the weather, girls.
I spy a lark, sitting in the dark.

Equally mysterious and delicious to roll on the tongue is this singsongy lyric:

Intery, mintery, cutery corn,
Apple seed and apple thorn.
Wire, briar, limber lock,
Three geese in a flock
Sit and sing by the spring.
O-U-T spells out!
And the next jumper enters the magic circle of the rope.

ed some 34 centuries ago. This, however, is but a late bloom compared with a fossil found in America that blossomed 40 million years ago, and there is evidence that the rose evolved in Asia about 20 million years before that.

Over the centuries the rose has served as a symbol for a variety of things. In ancient Greece and Rome it was associated with love, a connection that has persisted. But in Rome it was also linked with secrecy and debauchery. According to one legend, a rose tied above a group of men seated around a table meant that their talk was secret, or *sub rosa*. And no lavish Roman dinner party was complete without roses. At one such affair the emperor Nero was reputed to have spent 4 million sesterces ($150,000) on the flowers. Perhaps it was at this orgy that a number of guests were smothered when an avalanche of rose petals fell on them from a balcony.

The link between roses and sensuality gave the flower a bad reputation in early Christian times. Not until pagan excesses dimmed from memory did the rose become a sign of purity associated with the Virgin Mary. It became a potent political symbol in 15th-century England, where for three decades the mighty houses of York and Lancaster bloodied the battlefields fighting for the crown under rose-emblazoned standards: the white rose for York, the red for Lancaster. The Wars of the Roses ended when Henry Tudor, a Lancaster, assumed the throne. Ever the diplomat, he wed a daughter of the rival house and with fine impartiality created a personal standard combining white rose petals with red.

Royalty has long been associated with roses. One of the most dedicated rose fanciers was Napoleon's empress, Josephine. Her rose garden at Malmaison near Paris boasted some 250 varieties. So great was her passion for the flower that even war could not interrupt her quest for the world's rarest specimens. Though her husband was at war almost perpetually with Great Britain, Empress Josephine's chief gardener, an Englishman, had a special dispensation from both governments to pass back and forth through the British blockade. Ships bound for France coursed the English Channel unhindered once it was known

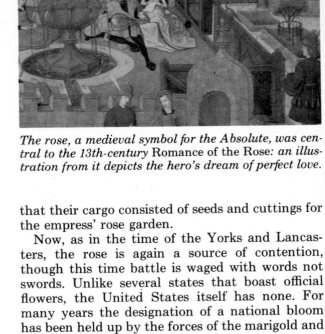

The rose, a medieval symbol for the Absolute, was central to the 13th-century Romance of the Rose: *an illustration from it depicts the hero's dream of perfect love.*

that their cargo consisted of seeds and cuttings for the empress' rose garden.

Now, as in the time of the Yorks and Lancasters, the rose is again a source of contention, though this time battle is waged with words not swords. Unlike several states that boast official flowers, the United States itself has none. For many years the designation of a national bloom has been held up by the forces of the marigold and the armies of the rose. Through it all, congressmen have procrastinated, fearful of incurring the wrath of either the rose or the marigold lovers. Perhaps in the end they will take a leaf from Henry Tudor's book and direct government artists to create a fantasy flower: half rose, half marigold, the world's first rosamari.

RUBBER When you break the stalk of a dandelion or a milkweed plant, the white fluid that oozes out is latex, the natural source of rubber. Some 2,000 species of plants secrete latex, but no one is certain why. The best guess is that latex is a waste product that plants store rather than eliminate. But if latex is worthless to plants, it is vital to man as one of a small group of materials upon which our industrial technology rests. Although two-thirds of the rubber produced in the United States is synthetic, derived from petroleum, that will never totally replace natural rubber. For example, the huge tires on large jet aircraft have to be made largely from natural rubber because it is less susceptible to heat buildup than synthetic rubber.

Men have known

Snappy shoes: the Mayans and other Latin American Indians used liquid latex to coat and protect their feet.

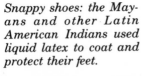

about natural rubber for centuries. In Hispaniola, Columbus found the natives playing games with rubber balls. Juan de Torquemada, provincial of the Franciscan order in Mexico, reported in 1615 that Mexican Indians tapped rubber trees to obtain latex, from which they produced an oil for treating diseases of the chest. Torquemada also noted that his fellow Spaniards tried to waterproof their clothing with rubber but that it was not sufficiently resistant to sun and heat. This quality of natural rubber, and its tendency to become stiff in cold weather, plagued rubber technologists until Charles Goodyear discovered the process of vulcanization in 1839.

One of the earliest words for rubber was *caoutchouc,* a creation of the Quechua Indians of South America. The term stuck until 1770, when a British mechanic, Edward Nairne, noticed that the material was good for rubbing out pencil marks. Joseph Priestley, one of the most distinguished chemists of the time, made the matter public in his writings, recommending that "rubbing" caoutchouc was better than bread crumbs for erasures, and it has been "rubber" ever since.

The story of rubber has its dark side. In the late 1800's, with the development of the rubber tire, the demand for natural rubber grew. Intensive human labor was necessary to locate the wild rubber trees, which grow only in the hot, damp climate of the equatorial zone, a belt about 1,400 miles wide. Native populations in South America, set to work searching for trees, were reduced to peonage. And in the Independent State of the Congo, which was actually a personal enterprise of King Leopold II of Belgium, the natives tapped rubber trees under force of arms. Since, reasoned Leopold, the land was his and the natives had no money, they could donate their labor in lieu of paying taxes. Leopold's foremen used the whip and held workers' families hostage against good performance. Rebellious workers sometimes had their hands chopped off and nailed to labor barracks as a grim warning to others. The exploitation of these tribes eventually caused a public outcry in Europe, and the Belgian legislature overruled Leopold and made the Congo a Belgian colony in 1908.

Henry A. Wickham, a coffee planter in Brazil in the 1870's, deserves much of the credit for making possible the commercial cultivation of rubber trees. He collected some 70,000 seeds of the *Hevea brasiliensis* tree and took them to England. Planted in Kew Gardens in London, enough of the seeds germinated to provide the stock for numerous rubber plantations across Southeast Asia, where the climate was favorable to their growth. By 1922 the area had become the world leader in rubber production. When the Japanese occupied it during World War II, the United States was spurred to develop a synthetic-rubber industry. The country might have had an easier time if the recommendations made in 1930 by a young army major had been followed. The officer had been assigned to study the guayule plant as an alternative to the conventional rubber-tree plant. Guayule grows in parts of Texas, Arizona, New Mexico, and California as well as in Mexico. His report urged that guayule plants in the U.S. be protected and reserved for strategic emergencies. Though his advice was ignored, Dwight D. Eisenhower went on to become a five-star general and president.

There may yet be a future for the guayule plant or some other latex-producing vegetation. About five gallons of petroleum go into making a synthetic-rubber tire, and oil prices could shoot up enough to make less efficient sources of rubber, such as guayule, relatively cheaper to use. Funded by the Ford and Firestone companies, in 1927 Thomas A. Edison set up a research company and selected a variety of goldenrod as the source of latex, hoping to ensure American independence in the commodity. The result was four extremely expensive tires for a Ford touring car. Failing health caused Edison to abandon further research.

RUG Over the years the words *carpet* and *rug* have come to have distinctly different meanings. Today, *carpet* refers to floor covering that can be bought in measured increments—by the foot, for instance—and then tacked down from wall to wall. *Rug,* on the other hand, usually refers to a piece of material, available in a broad variety of styles, that covers only a section of the floor.

In the West the idea of putting a fine, expensive rug on the floor to be tramped on is relatively new. Thick, woven fabrics or tapestries were usually used decoratively—and perhaps as insulation as well—as wall hangings or as bed and table covers. Before the beginning of the 18th century, only the most extravagant among the wealthy would have spread out a rug to walk on. Thus when an erring servant was summoned by his master for a proper upbraiding, he had to pass through his boss' carpeted chamber—hence

Iranian rugmakers wash their wares to brighten and fix colors.

Charles Goodyear

Charles Goodyear, whose name is all but synonymous with the word "rubber," was born in modest circumstances and died in abject poverty. What is more, he did not found the industrial giant that bears his name, and it was not even his idea to make tires out of rubber. This is surprising, for at various junctures in his life Goodyear imagined making almost everything of rubber. In all, he devoted nearly 30 unprofitable years to promoting and experimenting with rubber. Once he even asked: "Who can examine it, dwell in thought on the properties of elastic gum, without glorifying God?"

Goodyear was born in 1800 in New Haven, Connecticut, and his first task in life was to work as a partner in his father's small hardware manufacturing business. By 1830 the family concern had gone bankrupt. At the time, however, he was tinkering with rubber, though most felt that it was nothing more than a natural curiosity and thus of no major value. The United States had a small rubber industry, but it produced only boots, caps, and wagon covers. There were two very good reasons for this: in hot weather rubber decomposed into a foul-smelling mass, and when the temperature plunged in winter, it became hard and brittle. Goodyear believed he could change this, reasoning that some substance added to rubber might reduce or even overcome the problem.

In his first experiments, which took place in debtors' prison, he mixed ink, soup, cream cheese, witch hazel, castor oil, and anything else he could think of with rubber. Once, he tested a mixture of quicklime and magnesia, and produced a kind of white rubber that seemed much like leather. He trumpeted his discovery to the world, only to find that any acid, including a dash of lemonade, would rapidly dissolve the white substance. Later, puttering in his kitchen, Goodyear finally

Charles Goodyear had tried for years to find a way to stabilize rubber, but when he finally did discover the vulcanizing process it was quite by accident.

discovered the secret of vulcanization—which increases rubber's durability during temperature changes—when he accidentally spilled a blob of rubber and sulfur on the top of his stove. The year was 1839. After all his struggling and stretches in prison, Goodyear had the means to fully utilize rubber. The trouble was that no one believed him.

In all, it took Goodyear five years to find the money necessary to exploit his discovery. During that time, he was forced to sell his library, even his children's schoolbooks. A neighbor later recalled seeing Goodyear's children scrambling in the garden for half-ripe potatoes to eat. Tragedy struck as well, when Goodyear's two-year-old son died unexpectedly. Finally, in 1844, Goodyear received a patent for his vulcanizing process; it did not make him wealthy. Desperate for funds, he was forced to license the process cheaply to others.

Earlier, in England, Thomas Hancock, a chemist, had managed to obtain samples of Goodyear's new rubber. He noticed that one sample was dusty, and he sniffed sulfur. Goodyear's application for a patent in the United States was still pending when Hancock reinvented vulcanization in his own laboratory. He

even received a provisional patent two months before Goodyear's application reached England. The result was that American manufacturers bought licenses from Goodyear, and Europeans from Hancock. In America, Goodyear was forced into several expensive patent litigations. In one, he was successfully represented by Daniel Webster, who spent an hour preparing the case. Webster received $25,000 for his work, more by far than Goodyear had earned in any single year.

Finally, however, Goodyear was honored for his contributions. In 1855 Emperor Napoleon III of France awarded him the Gold Medal of Honor of the Paris World Exhibition and the Cross of the Legion of Honor. As it happened, Goodyear was on hand in Paris to receive them: he was serving a term in debtors' prison on the outskirts of the city.

In 1860, when Goodyear died in New York City, he was $200,000 in debt. Perhaps he had not been terribly troubled by the penurious course his life had taken, for he had said at one time, "The advantages of a career . . . should not be estimated exclusively by the standard of dollars and cents, as it is too often done. Man has just cause for regret when he sows and nobody reaps."

the expression "on the carpet."

The first rugs were probably animal skins, used by early man to protect against drafts and to keep down the cold and damp in his rude dwelling. However, the making of rugs and tapestries is one of man's most ancient crafts. Records show that carpet weaving was well established in China as early as 1300 B.C.

Although piled fabrics were popular in ancient Egypt, the pile carpet, with a thick raised surface, is thought to have originated in India about 1100 A.D. From there it spread throughout the Middle East. Hand-knotted pile is characteristic of most Oriental rugs, meaning simply rugs of Eastern origin. Each area developed its own variation on one of three basic patterns. One of the most remarkable Oriental rugs is the Ardabil Carpet, completed in 1540 for the mosque of Ardabil in northern Iran. The weaver devoted his entire lifetime to this masterpiece, which measures 34½ feet by 17½ feet and now hangs in London's Victoria and Albert Museum.

Not surprisingly, rug making reached its apogee in the East, an area rich in natural weaving materials—wool, cotton, and silk. Large workshops with 20 or more weavers feature a caller, who intones the design being carried out. According to the Koran and Muslim tradition, King Solomon owned a carpet of green threads. His magic flying carpet was so wonderful, the legend goes, that he could take along all his forces on it and tell the wind to carry them wherever he wished. To protect his entourage from the sun, a flock of birds flew overhead, forming a screen with their flapping wings.

Rug making was introduced into Spain at the beginning of the 8th century by invading Muslims. It became popular in Italy and later in France. The first government-sponsored weaving manufactory was established by King Henry IV of France in 1605. The weavers, set up in an old soap factory near Paris, produced soft-colored plush carpets known as *Savonnerie*, from *savon*, the French word for "soap." These contrasted with the nonpile tapestries produced at Aubusson in central France since the 16th century.

In 1840 a young Massachussets inventor, Erastus Brigham Bigelow, changed the handwork system of carpet making with the invention of a steam-driven power loom. It was capable of making a reversible, flat-weave carpet popular at that time. Within 10 years of his first invention, Bigelow created a machine that produced pile carpets, and the industry was changed forever. The first looms put out 27-inch-wide bands, which were then sewn together to make room-size rugs. Gradual technological improvements made possible wider looms that could weave carpets in widths up to 30 feet—hence the word "broadloom." The advantage of machine-made rugs was that they could be produced in volume and at a price that hand weaving could in no way match.

Weavers in a few areas of the world still produce handmade rugs for the commercial marketplace. There are the Alpujarra rugs of Spain; the shaggy wool rugs from the Scandinavian countries; the thick, high-pile Flokati rugs of Greece; the Indian rugs made by the Navajo and other tribes of the western United States; and the Orientals, which are made in various parts of Asia.

Over Baghdad, Douglas Fairbanks, Sr., unfurls the ultimate rug: it flies.

One of four sibilant sounds in Hebrew, shin became the Greek letter sigma, then the Etruscan and Latin "S."

SAFE AND VAULT Safe against what—that is the question. For King Cheops of Egypt, the problem was robbers. For his burial treasure he built a safe that measured 755 feet along each of its four sides and stood 481 feet high, with only two secret, sealed entrances. It took robbers 400 years to crack that pyramid.

Against fire, flood, foe, or friend, man has made, until recently, but small progress in protecting his valuables. An earthquake toppled the rich treasuries of Delphi; the library at Alexandria burned. And when Linus Yale, Jr., invented a combination lock with numerous possible number combinations, thieves simply memorized the numbers. By the 1800's companies were selling "fireproof safes." When much of New York City burned in 1835, so did many of the safes.

Today, even the ordinary householder can have a safe that is proof against fire (for records) or proof against thieves (for money), but rarely both at once. Bank vaults and safe-deposit boxes do protect against flames and felons. Solid steel, reinforced concrete, torch-resistant metals, and heat-

The Princes of the Profession

Thieves respect property," wrote G.K. Chesterton. "They merely wish the property to become their property that they may more perfectly respect it." No class of thieves has been more respected for its silk-gloved daring and expertise than safecrackers, the princes of the profession. In the long battle of wits between the makers and breakers of safes, the cracksmen have relentlessly tested—with drills, explosives, and even artillery—every new product on the market. In a sense, they have taught the safemakers their trade.

A few legendary safecrackers, like Herbert Wilson, were clearly geniuses. Wilson was a renegade minister turned thief, a thoroughly professional one. He meticulously apprenticed himself in a safe factory, studied welding, pored over government and manufacturers' pamphlets, and put together the best safecracking mob in the business. Since his overhead included getaway airplanes, Dictographs, custom-designed tools, and trick automobiles, only six-figure jobs, like knocking over Sinclair Oil, which he did, would make crime pay. For Wilson it paid to the tune of some $15 million before he was caught. And from time to time he remembered the poor Ontario church where he had worked in his more pious days by mailing them an offering from his ill-gotten gains. After 20 years in jail, Wilson went home to Canada and told the story of his exploits in *Collier's*.

The safemakers had barely made their creations gunpowder- and drill-proof, when nitroglycerin entered the picture. Wilson got his start in nitro, called "soup" in the business. Highly volatile, the stuff occasionally blew up the burglar along with the bank. One bumbler, plying his trade in a meat plant, buried the safe in hams to muffle the explosion.

The charge not only blew the safe, it blew off the roof, and hams rained into people's yards for blocks around. Another bunch used Oriental rugs worth thousands to insulate a safe that contained only $20.

Bank vaults with seamless doors into which thieves could not drip nitro rendered explosives ineffective. Made of steel, copperplated against torches, wired with alarms, and armed with combination time locks that automatically jam if tampered with, they forced burglars (night men) to become robbers (day men).

The famous Willie Sutton, known for his disappearances from several escape-proof prisons, developed his own style of robbery. Observing that anyone will open a door for a uniform, Willie "the Actor" rented a Western Union delivery boy's suit and gained admittance to a bank just as it opened. One by one, employees came to work and were told to sit in chairs lined against the wall. When the manager showed up, the job was as good as done.

Between jail and bank heists Sutton had to lie low. Once he took a $90-a-week job in an old-folks home on Staten Island while hiding out from the police.

After living quietly in Brooklyn he was finally nabbed, and the manhunt ended. The fuzz were exultant. "We've just caught the Babe Ruth of bank robbers!" they bragged to the papers. What they did not mention was that Sutton had sat patiently in the station house for an hour with more than $7,000 in cash and a loaded .38 in his pocket before anyone thought to frisk him.

The good ones, like Willie Sutton, had a way of making everyone else look dumb. Melville Reeves, "the skyscraper burglar" of Chicago, had that same classic confidence. "If you roll up your sleeves and put a pencil behind your ear, you can rob any office without trouble," he told the police. Reeves simply signed himself into a building at night, picked a lock or got a charwoman to open an office, and cracked safes at leisure. One of the tricks of the office burglar's trade is to stuff the loot in a stamped, self-addressed envelope, drop it down the mail chute, and leave the scene of the crime empty-handed.

Some of the best safecrackers are straight—manufacturers' men called in by frantic owners who have lost or forgotten their combinations. People still think that an expert safeman can lay his ear

Watchmen may fail, this 1870's ad crowed, but dual time locks do not.

to the lock, like the fictional Jimmy Valentine, and hear the tumblers drop in place. But Jimmy Valentine, with his sandpapered fingertips, came out of an O. Henry short story. Actually, the trick is impossible because combination locks do not work that way. The magic these experts use is more often simple psychology. They know, as knowledgeable burglars do, that most people base their combinations on personal numbers like social security or addresses or birth dates, or commit them to paper somewhere.

One day in 1929, a firm had been wired by its absent president to open the safe and sell every security in it before the stock market closed at 3 P.M. At 1 o'clock, responding to panic calls from employees who had their orders but not the numbers, the safe expert strolled in, poked around on the president's desk, and found a neat column of figures. He added them up, took the sum, and opened the safe, saving the firm a fortune on the very eve of the stock-market crash.

When President Roosevelt died without confiding the combination of his Hyde Park safe, the expert tried 30-04-33, a number based on the date of F.D.R.'s first inauguration—March 4, 1933. It worked. A burglar once had it even easier: he found the combination scrawled on top of the safe.

Some feel that the safecracker's crime is not against individuals but against the system; the challenge to his patience, wits, and technical know-how is an irresistible part of his calling. At least some safecrackers are nonviolent types who would not consider a face-to-face robbery.

This point was made by the extraordinary team that pulled off the biggest bank job in history—the $10-million "fric-frac" (as the French call it) of a wealthy bank in Nice, on the French Riviera, in

In the 19th century safecracking meant exactly that.

1976. The burglars, possibly 6 or as many as 15, gained access through a sewer under the street. In two months they had built a perfect tunnel from the sewer to the bank, 30 feet long, well braced, and reinforced with cement. It was even carpeted. Every scrap of dirt had been carefully removed.

Trial by fire: tests make safes safer.

On a Friday night the team punched into the vault, dragging an electric cable and a ventilation tube behind them. They were armed with crowbars, chisels, drills, hydraulic jacks, blowtorches, axes, jackhammers, and over two dozen acetylene tanks. All weekend, while commercial depositors dropped money down the chute directly into their hands, they camped in, drinking wine, cooking their meals, and thoughtfully rifling 317 safe-deposit boxes stuffed with Riviera jewels and cash. Before they loaded the loot on rubber rafts, they welded the vault door shut from the inside.

It took a while to open that door. When the bankers finally burst in on Monday afternoon, they were greeted with this proud, scrawled message: "Without weapons, without violence, without hatred." The message was signed with a peace symbol.

resistant insulation have made today's bank vaults virtually impregnable—a situation that has forced robbers to give up on vaults and concentrate on tellers. That bank vaults are indestructible was grimly proved when an American-made vault of the Teikoku Bank in Hiroshima survived intact after an American-made atomic bomb struck that city. The vault was only 300 yards from the center of the blast.

Civilization these days is mostly recorded on paper or film, and protecting our records and documents is probably in the long run more important than locking up money. The most valued documents in the United States, the original copies of the Declaration of Independence and the Constitution with the Bill of Rights, were stashed in Fort Knox, Kentucky, during World War II. They now repose in hermetically sealed glass cases filled with an inert gas in the National Archives building in Washington, D.C. Every evening they are lowered into a 55-ton vault below the rotunda that is designed to withstand fire, shock, temperature extremes, water, and nuclear explosion.

Modern nuclear warfare could be the ultimate safecracker despite the evidence of the Teikoku vault. In the late 1950's a group of Boston banks built a huge underground concrete bunker some 40 miles north of the city for storing their vital records. Near Albany, New York, another group of banks buried their records deep in a limestone cave to protect them against a nuclear holocaust.

SAFETY PIN, PIN, AND NEEDLE In 20,000 B.C., when chill winds blew off the glacial ice cap covering most of Europe, a crucial question before mankind was how to fasten a warm animal hide about a shivering body and not have to clutch it all the while. One could either hold the skin together with thorns or fishbones or poke holes through two sides and tie them together. The first solution led to pins (from the Latin *spina*, meaning "thorn"); the second, to needles. By the Late Ice Age, bone needles even had eyes, a design modification that passed intact to early Bronze Age metalworkers.

It was clearly a twist of fate that led someone to double a wire straight pin, then hook one end under a little bend in the other. Late Bronze Age graves from Greece to Denmark are full of such ancient safety pins—some complete with the springlike coil that creates tension in modern safety pins. The classical world of Greece and Rome transformed these rudimentary pins into ornate brooches, used to secure robes and mantles and to flaunt the wealth of their owners.

But in ancient Athens women preferred to bind their chitons with long stiletto-like straight pins. And when a single soldier staggered back to Athens from a losing battle with Aegina, the story goes that the women of Athens, unable to accept his cowardly escape, whipped out their pins and stabbed the soldier to death. A swift decree ended that particular straight-pin fashion.

In 14th-century Europe straight pins were in such demand that one French princess had 12,000 of them delivered to her wardrobe. In England a scarcity of pins drove the price up, and a special tax was levied to keep the queen in pins. Ordinary citizens, however, could buy pins in "open shop" only on January 1st and 2nd. The money that ladies set aside for their annual pin pilgrimage was called, of course, "pin money."

Oddly enough, the efficient safety pins of the Bronze Age were misplaced in the course of history, and so they had to be reinvented. Walter Hunt, a New York Quaker, did the job in the 1840's—in a

Safety first: Bronze Age straight pins were given a twist and hook.

decidedly offhand manner. Owing a friend some money, Hunt simply twisted up what we know as the contemporary safety pin and sold the patent rights to it to square his debt—all in three hours. Although he is sometimes credited with inventing the coil at the bend of the pin, as suggested above, the people of ancient Mycenae had wrapped it up centuries before.

SALAD In the opinion of the 19th-century French author and gourmet Alexandre Dumas, a salad should be served at that point in a meal when hunger is almost satisfied and the appetite is flagging. Dumas, like his countrymen, considered a serving of mixed greens or cold vegetables, lightly flavored with vinegar, olive oil, and certain herbs, to be an essential part of a civilized meal. Indeed, fresh crisp salad is as closely identified with France as the poodle, perfume, *haute couture*, and other manifestations of refinement. When, in the 1790's, revolutionary terror forced numerous French aristocrats to flee their homeland, several made a living as professional salad dressers, charging their English and American employers high fees for their services.

How did aristocrats learn so seemingly plebeian a skill as making, dressing, and tossing a salad?

Apparently salad making in the 18th century, like martini mixing today, had acquired a mystique that raised it from the mundane to the celestial. Thus one authority on food expressed his horror at the thought that a servant might be permitted to prepare a salad. The implication was that only the fine aesthetic sensibility of the host could guarantee success with so delicate an undertaking.

One of the earliest references in English to salads appeared in a book put together by Richard II's master cook in 1390. It gives directions for making a raw salad by combining greens, onions, parsley, sage, garlic, and olive oil. The final step: "Lay on vinegar and salt, and serve it forth." (Originally known as *sallet* or *salett*, the word "salad" derives from the Latin *sal,* or "salt.")

The foregoing Chaucerian salad would not be out of place in any French, Spanish, Italian, or Greek kitchen today. It is simply the basic Mediterranean salad, a combination of ingredients going back at least 2,500 years and probably a good deal more. To lettuce in particular, Greek folk tradition attached a very strange significance, which was taken up by the Pythagoreans and transmitted in medical and herbal writings until modern times. According to the tradition, lettuce—because it is "cold and moist"—has sedative and antiaphrodisiac effects. The Pythagoreans believed that sex could be seriously debilitating, especially during hot weather, and recommended complete abstinence throughout the "dog days" of summer. To make this easier, they prescribed that young people and married couples should eat salad daily in July and August—an internal cold shower, as it were. Their preferred lettuce was a variety similar to the present-day romaine, which the Pythagoreans nicknamed "eunuch." Salads were to be eaten in spring and fall as well, to counteract the presumed aphrodisiac effects of pepper and hot spices. The Mediterranean custom of eating salads spread northward during Roman and medieval times, and with it the folklore concerning salads as a regulator of desire. Thus, Shakespeare's phrase "salad days" (from Cleopatra's line in *Antony and Cleopatra*: "My salad days, When I was green in judgment, cold in blood") has long been proverbial for youthful inexperience, especially in sexual matters. In the same vein a 1533 English medical manual, *The Castle of Health*, recommends: "Young men shall eat salads of cold herbs." Likewise, Nicholas Culpeper's famous *Herbal* (1653) states that lettuce leaves wrapped round the testicles "abate bodily lust and repress venereous dreams." The celebrated metaphysical preacher Jeremy Taylor summed it all up: "A dish of lettuce and a clear fountain can cool all my heat."

Salad dressing: this remarkable portrait is the work of a 16th-century Italian artist named Giuseppe Arcimboldo.

In America the simple French-style salad has yet to triumph, though it seems to be gaining in popularity. The American tendency to improve on a good thing has led to salads and dressings that a purist would shun. Vinegar and oil mixed with ketchup is sometimes misnamed "French dressing" by its American proponents, and fruit salads are coated with sugary concoctions that include mayonnaise and a squirt of chili sauce. Yet the basic mixed green salad flavored with herbs, vinegar, and oil, or vinaigrette, is taking hold, with the support of nutritionists who believe that a salad a day is good for the body. The noted French gastronome Anthelme Brillat-Savarin (1755-1826) would have endorsed this claim for salad, which, he wrote, "freshens without enfeebling and fortifies without irritating."

SALT As much as air and as much as water, common salt—sodium chloride—is essential to life. Plants, which soak up salt from the soil, could not survive without it, and all animals, including man, would die of dehydration if they did not regularly ingest small amounts of salt. Strangely enough, this vital mineral consists of two elements that are anything but life supporting. Sodium is a metal that bursts into flames when placed in water, and chlorine is a gas that in pure form is deadly to both animals and plants. Nonetheless, from the union of these elements comes salt, a substance on which life depends and, though generally unknown now, on which empires have risen—and fallen.

Spilled Salt

Whether in myth, legend, or superstition, salt has always occupied a place of honor at the table of human belief. Consider, for example, the spilling of salt—which means bad luck—and its antidote, the throwing of a few grains over the left shoulder. One tradition has it that good spirits stand behind a person's right shoulder, bad spirits behind his left. Thus a few grains of salt tossed over the left shoulder will lodge, it is hoped, in a bad spirit's eyes and distract him from the evil he might be planning. A variation on this theme suggests that if the grains so thrown land on a dinner companion, the unfortunate recipient will be plagued by ill fortune.

Among the Scots it was a common practice to carry salt with newborns in order to ward off the evil spirits that might harm them. Such associations of evil tidings and spilled salt have even entered Christian lore, as an examination of Leonardo da Vinci's famous painting the "Last Supper" reveals. Jesus' disciples are gathered about Him, but in front of the traitorous Judas there appears an overturned saltcellar.

One theory holds that a society's access to salt may be the principal determining factor in its prosperity and even in the degree of freedom permitted its citizens. Where salt was scarce, the theory suggests, as in Germany during Roman times, heavy-handed rule prevailed, for strong men were needed to ensure equitable distribution of the commodity. On the other hand, where people had sufficient salt, as was the case in Britain, the need for omnipotent government was less, and freedom could flourish.

This view of history can be overstated, but there is no doubt that man and his social structures have always depended on salt. In some places and at certain times, the scarcity of salt made it almost as precious as gold. In the early civilization in the Sudan, for example, tribes of the south had access to gold mines, and those of the north were near salt deposits. As a result, traders from each region gathered at a central point and deposited the treasure of their homelands—the northerners carrying off gold and the southerners, salt. In ancient Rome each soldier and civil servant received a salt ration known as a *salarium* (from the Latin word for "salt"). Later, when money replaced the ration, it was still called a *salarium*—hence our word "salary." Thus "to be worth one's salt" was to be worthy of one's pay.

Though salt was in short supply in many pre-industrial societies, the problem was not so much locating deposits as creating technologies to harvest them. Solar evaporation of ocean water worked to some degree in coastal areas favored with hot sunny days. In other regions salt miners were subjected to unusually cruel treatment to keep them at their arduous labor.

Where there is a shortage of salt, government monopolies or taxes on consumption often exist. The salt tax in France—a tax from which the nobility was exempt—was an important contributor to fomenting the French Revolution. The British colonial government's salt tax in India led Mohandas Gandhi and his followers to march to the sea so that they might manufacture their own salt and evade the government's unfair exactions.

Most people think of salt as either a seasoning or a preservative. However, salt is also used in some 14,000 industrial processes and is essential in the manufacture of nearly every chemical product on the market. Among its many uses, salt is important in the production of steel, glass, leather goods, plastics, pharmaceuticals, and even of color television sets. It is second only to diamond as the hardest mineral known to man. For this reason, together with its capacity to melt ice and snow, salt is widely used in road building and maintenance in winter. It is also used by railroads to cool refrigerator cars and to control the formation of ice around railroad switches. Rock salt is used to freeze ice cream. In all, only 5 percent of the world's annual salt production goes

Sculptured out of salt, this chapel and its icons are part of an old Russian mine.

into the preparation and seasoning of food.

It is a measure of rising industrialization around the world that salt production has jumped by almost 100 percent since 1960. In 1970 more than 150 million tons of salt were carved from mines or evaporated from salt water, with the United States accounting for nearly a third of the total. It might be supposed that at this rate the world's salt supply will soon vanish. Fortunately, this will not happen, for unlike oil, the supply of salt appears to be virtually inexhaustible. The amount of salt in the oceans alone is estimated to be more than 100 million times man's annual needs. If all this salt were piled on the island of Manhattan, it would form a tower that would extend five-sixths of the distance to the moon.

SANDPAPER Sandpaper is not covered with sand and probably never was, although sea sand was a known abrasive. Modern technology no longer refers simply to sandpaper but to "coated abrasives," that is, any of a vast number of scratchy materials bonded to a flexible backing. From nature come grinders of flint, emery, and even crushed garnet, to which man has added synthetic abrasives hard enough to scratch glass and polish gems. There is scarcely a common object, from the delicate lip of a goblet to the gears of heavy-duty machinery, that has not been smoothed or precision ground in some way by coated abrasives. Fine sandpapers, for example, buff eggshells, hull peanuts, and even encourage alfalfa seeds to sprout by lightly scarring their tough outer shells. Other abrasives, infinitely rougher, can grind through two cubic inches of steel in less than four seconds.

The ancient Chinese flirted with the idea of abrasives when they glued crushed seashells to parchment and used the product for polishing. The Bible mentions a mysterious abrasive called *shamir* that helped Solomon build his temple without the use of iron tools. Hebrew lore held *shamir* to be a sort of magical worm capable of cracking glass by resting on it. More probably the abrasive was emery, an ancient substance still used in sandpaper and nail files.

SANDWICH Americans, it is estimated, wolf down some 300 million sandwiches a day—more than one per man, woman, and child—the addiction of a hungry nation in a hurry. Sandwiches were named, appropriately enough, for a gambler in a hurry—the debauched, incompetent John Montagu, 4th earl of Sandwich. An inveterate bettor, Sandwich spent entire days at the gaming table and would let his dinner grow cold rather than miss a play. About 200 years ago, during one of his round-the-clock sessions, he ordered his man to fetch him some cold beef between slices of bread and thus quickly fortified himself without the clutter of cutlery. Within a few years, all of England was eating "sandwiches."

Americans owe the earl another debt as well. As first lord of the admiralty, Sandwich managed to reduce the British Navy to a state of total confusion around the time that the American Revolution started—a contribution at least as significant as the munchable lunch.

Though sandwiches may have rescued the earl's name from infamy, it is unlikely that he was the only one to invent them. The idea is probably as time honored as bread and leftovers. French peasants customarily set off for the fields with cold meat wedged between generous slabs of black bread. Even the Romans nibbled layers of meat and bread called *offula*.

Tradition sometimes accords the invention of the sandwich to the great Rabbi Hillel, who in the 1st century B.C. bid his people eat bitter herbs and unleavened bread (matzoh) in memory of their days in Egypt. Passover feasts still include this type of brittle sandwich, which along with herbs may contain a mixture of chopped apples and nuts to represent the mortar that the Jews mixed for the Pharaohs.

Today, almost anything edible that can cut it between two slices of bread is a sandwich—from butter to chop suey vegetables to sunflower seeds to red licorice. It is no longer a humble snack.

SAW The fewer teeth a saw has, the faster it cuts; the more it has, the smoother it works. In the Orient sawteeth generally point backward, and the user pulls the saw to make the cut; in the Occident the teeth point forward, and the user pushes the saw. (The reverse stroke releases the sawdust.) Japanese saws look exactly like those of the ancient Egyptians. Both are in the form of a big curved knife with a notched edge and, as mentioned above, do their cutting "on the pull." Such a saw was doubtless the type used on the prophet Isaiah, who died when the hollow tree in which he hid from persecutors was sawed in two. The Egyptian saw was modeled on a stone prototype—the small, limited-purpose saw of flint used by cavemen. The Egyptians also had diamond-toothed saws for cutting stone, metal, and glass.

At different times and places a variety of other materials have been used to sunder things. The Tahitians made saws set with shark's teeth; the ancient Mexicans fashioned saws of chips of black

"Hold the Mayo"

Europeans have long regarded as uncivilized the American custom of grabbing a quick sandwich for lunch. But Americans have been civilizing the sandwich with gourmet distinction. Sandwiches can be found at every meal of the day and at after-theater parties. As such, they are a major national energy source.

What's in a sandwich is far more significant than what's in its name, of course, but sandwich fame has nonetheless become a sort of naming game. The venerable Stage Delicatessen in New York, a theatrical hangout, serves up mountainous sandwiches named for the famous. You can order a "Mohammed Ali," a three-decker with corned beef, pastrami, chopped liver, and Bermuda onion; or a "Shirley MacLaine," with lake sturgeon, Nova Scotia salmon, lettuce, tomato, and onion. The honor notwithstanding, Shirley MacLaine prefers plain chicken-and-tomato.

To laud the bread that frames the creations, the Wheat Flour Institute sponsors an annual sandwich recipe competition. The first winner, concocted in 1956 by the chef of the Rose Bowl restaurant in Omaha, was the "Reuben." Named for the old song that goes "Reuben, Reuben, I've been thinking," it is a grilled mix of corned beef, sauerkraut, and Swiss cheese on pumpernickel. A recent winner was the "Sweet and Sauer Burger," a hamburger topped with cranberries, sauerkraut, and chili sauce. No ingredient is too bizarre to be sandwiched into this contest: entries have included artichoke hearts, spinach, coconut, pineapple, and anchovy paste—though not necessarily all together under the same roof. Once a dessert sandwich won—the "Sweet Adeline," a harmonious melange of grilled prune cake, pastry filling, cream cheese, and whipped cream. It has yet to become famous.

America's ability to seize foreign ideas, add a bit of native sauce, and whip them into national cravings is well documented in the case of pizza. So, too, with the sandwich called variously a "hero" or "submarine" or "torpedo" (for the shape of the bread used to make it) or "grinder" or "hoagie" or "poor boy." It is best fashioned with a fresh Italian loaf packed with cold cuts, cheeses, lettuce, tomatoes, green peppers, oil, herbs, and little pickled things. Some call such a fabrication a "zep" (or "zeppelin"); and some, a "gondola." Heroic variations include such creations as the "Cinderella" (chicken cloaked in curried mayonnaise) and the "rich girl" (filled with lobster or crabmeat.)

---

volcanic glass; and the Caribs of the West Indies created broken seashell saws. Leonardo da Vinci developed a saw that could cut marble.

If your name is Sawyer, at least one yeoman who earned his living sawing wood adorns your family tree. The occupational title *sawyer* was first used in London about 500 years ago and supplanted an earlier term, *sawer*, with the same meaning. With the introduction of power mills in England during the 17th century, many sawyers felt that their jobs were threatened, and in 1768 a band of them tore a wind-driven sawmill to pieces. But like their machine-fearing brethren, the weavers of the early 1800's, the sawyers were powerless to stop progress. Today most of the sawing in the world is done by machine.

Only a silent-movie villain could set a saw to such evil slicing; only a hero could see saw and save sweetie.

SCALE The burdened human back probably provided the inspiration for the earliest scale. When man lugged a load of things suspended from a wooden shoulder yoke, his job was easier if the two baskets dangling from the beam were in balance. The combination of a yoke and two containers was the immediate precursor of the primitive balance scale. In fact, the word "balance" is from the Latin *bilanx*, meaning "two pans."

The first substance that man weighed with this clever device was gold. Goldsmiths were using balance scales and standardized weights when most of commerce was still done by barter. With the development of trade, however, scales entered common use. A system of weights known as shekels, minas, and talents was a way to

St. Michael weighed souls before leading them away; here Satan tips scales against an unworthy.

sure. Consequently, the measurements will be the same underwater as on the moon, a fact that makes the modern precision balance scale, which is accurate within 1/100,000,000th of a kilogram, invaluable to science.

Santorio Santorio would probably be amazed to find millions of modern men and women obsessed with the daily tabulation of their body weight. Indeed, until about 1920 the standard household scale was found in the kitchen. Thrifty housewives checked on the butcher's honesty and carefully weighed ingredients for their recipes. They weighed the baby, too. But most adults weighed themselves only for amusement, on the penny scales in drugstores or railroad stations. Fashion, in the form of a lean, flat-chested flapper, changed all that. Americans in the 1920's, wrote the *Journal of the American Medical Association*, succumbed to "a veritable craze for reduction, which has . . . driven women and young girls to a type of self-mutilation." With women anxiously weighing themselves as carefully as their forerunners checked the roast beef and the progress of their infants, the scale has now moved permanently into the bathroom.

measure a trader's honesty in the Middle East.

Since scales were the basis of fair trade, they also came to symbolize justice. The Egyptians believed that the human heart would be weighed after death to determine whether it was good or evil. According to the Egyptian Book of the Dead, in the vast Hall of Double Justice the heart was placed on the scales against a feather, symbol of truth. If the two pans balanced, the heart was good and the newcomer was welcomed by the god Osiris; if not, a monster stood waiting to devour the wicked organ.

Also known in the ancient world was a type of balance scale now called the steelyard. The common scale in doctors' offices, with a counterpoise that moves along a notched bar, is simply a modern steelyard. In the 16th century an Italian physician named Santorio Santorio, curious about the human body, built an enormous steelyard scale that was large enough for him to live in. By measuring the weight of his own body at different times of the day, he was able to determine how much weight was lost through excretion and perspiration. His experiments gave medicine a new, quantitative basis on which to study biological processes.

An equal-arm balance scale, unlike the spring or platform, measures mass and not weight. The object is balanced against another known mass without reference to gravity or atmospheric pres-

SCANDAL Everyone knows what a scandal is and can recognize one when it hits the newspapers, if only by the size of the type in the headlines. Its essential ingredients need not include philandering politicians and their glamorous friends. The simple public disclosure of a gap between what is expected of powerful, esteemed, and well-known persons or institutions and how they have been behaving will suffice. The revelation of the sins of the mighty often leads not so much to indignation or dismay as to the cynical observation, "So what? Everybody does it." Undoubtedly the scandal builds because so many secretly savor the public exposure of warts on the famous. And as newspaper publisher William Randolph Hearst early discovered, the more respected or powerful the participants, the more infamous the scandal.

The blackest scandal in the history of American sports involved the annual grand climax of what is still looked on as the national pastime. In 1919 the Chicago White Sox, considered one of the finest teams ever to take the baseball field, lost the World Series. Even before the first game, rumors were circulating that the players had conspired with a group of gamblers to throw the contest. A year later eight White Sox, including the great Joe Jackson, were indicted and eventually found not guilty. Even though complicity was never proved (he batted .375 and drove in six runs during the Series), "Shoeless Joe" Jackson, back-country boy from South Carolina, was a national hero and, accordingly, bore the brunt of history's unofficial verdict. People who cannot recall a single other fact about the scandal, including the name of the team that won the Series (the Cincinnati Reds), still remember the story about the street urchin who

In a 14th-century tapestry Arthurian courtiers, right, gossip as Lancelot and Guinevere embrace. The knight who introduced them seems to be blessing their affair.

came up to Jackson as he was leaving the grand jury that had indicted him and tearfully pleaded, "Say it ain't so, Joe."

There have been other sports scandals—involving college basketball players who did somewhat less than their best for old Alma Mater, world-class bridge players caught red-handed in the act of cheating at cards, stable owners and trainers surreptitiously switching race horses.

Another cherished American institution, the Soap Box Derby, was also beset with scandal. After the 1973 running of the annual race in Akron, Ohio, the judges, uneasy about the outcome, studied films of the heats in which the winning car had participated. They noticed that it consistently got off to a faster start than its rivals. An examination of the vehicle revealed an electromagnet hidden in its nose. X-ray study showed that a switch embedded in the car's headrest activated the magnet. The starting blocks used at the beginning of the race were made of steel, so that judicious use of the magnet would give the car a decisive advantage. Such engineering, the judges established, was beyond the abilities of the car's 14-year-old driver. It was the brainchild of his uncle, a prosperous sporting-goods manufacturer and leading citizen of Boulder, Colorado, who wanted desperately

Guilty or not, Joe Jackson was implicated in 1919 White Sox scandal.

to win the race. The Soap Box Derby, a national event for more than 40 years, has never been the same since.

Other scandals have been disclosed concerning seemingly trivial matters. One of these, "payola," involved the practice by record companies of bribing disc jockeys to play their songs on the air in preference to those of competitors. It is not likely that very many listeners detected the difference. Then there was the brouhaha over the purported autobiography of Howard Hughes, which turned out to be spurious but put its little-known author, Clifford Irving, in the limelight. Another scandal, far more serious, rested on the question, still unanswered, of how Harold Philby managed as a Soviet secret agent to become one of the senior officers in British intelligence.

Politics, with all its opportunities for exercising power, has proved to be a particularly rich field for scandal—especially with an alert opposition party looking on. Largely forgotten now are the depredations of William Marcy "Boss" Tweed and his Tammany Hall machine in New York, or the stewardship of Mayor Jimmy Walker, during which a man named Thomas M. Farley, who occupied the dim office of sheriff of New York County, managed in six years to save nearly $400,000 while receiving an annual salary of $8,500. The Teapot Dome scandal, named after the site of a U.S. naval oil reserve in Wyoming, showed that the kind of political enterprise that often leads to prison is not the exclusive property of a single political party. While serving as President Harding's secretary of the interior, Albert B. Fall in 1922 awarded leases to Teapot Dome fields and to the Elk Hill reserve in California, without benefit of competitive bidding, to two oil operators. Their chief qualification, it seems, was their willingness to lend large sums of interest-free money to Secretary Fall.

In the 1950's the electorate barely had enough time to simmer down after learning of the facility with which Maj. Gen. Harry Vaughan, President Truman's military aide, could procure free freezers for himself and his friends, when it was confronted with the disclosure that Sherman Adams, President Eisenhower's closest aide, had accepted a vicuña coat and an Oriental rug from a New England businessman.

On the strength of this record at least, money and power seem to tempt American politicians more readily than that hallowed lure, sex. There have been, to be sure, some exceptions, like the extramarital affairs that Warren Harding allegedly had while in the White House. More recently, the public has been treated to the antics of Representative Wilbur Mills of Arkansas and his frolicsome stripteasing friend, and of Representative Wayne Hays' "protégée" on Capitol Hill whose skills at her $14,000-a-year job with a congressional committee included neither shorthand nor typing. Both of these episodes, however, smacked more of low comedy than of scandal in high places. For some of the racier scandals of the century, the prize must be awarded to England.

On January 22, 1963, a young woman named Christine Keeler sold a story to the London *Sunday Pictorial* that would have made the most jaded newspaperman sit up and take notice. It involved a British cabinet minister married to a movie star, a clutch of bluebloods, a society physician with powerful friends and peculiar habits, a Russian spy, and, of course, her own sweet, innocent 21-year-old self. It seemed that she had been the mistress of John Profumo, secretary of state for war in the cabinet of Prime Minister Harold Macmillan and husband of movie star Valerie Hobson. Christine had met Profumo in 1961 during a midnight swim at the country estate of Lord Astor. The introductions had been made by Dr. Stephen Ward, whose circle of "friends" included Christine and several other equally attractive young ladies. Furthermore, Christine Keeler said she had also been the mistress of Capt. Eugene Ivanov, the assistant naval attaché at the Soviet Embassy in London.

Christine could cope with such double duty. What bothered her, she claimed, was that somebody was after her to wheedle some secret information—specifically, details about when the Americans were going to give nuclear weapons to West Germany—out of one of her boyfriends and pass it on to the other. So she decided she had better tell the world about it—for a price. Fearful of libel, *The Sunday Pictorial* decided not to run the story, but Christine had also been elsewhere along Fleet Street, and her tale reached the ears of the Labour opposition.

Questions were raised in Parliament. On March 22, Profumo stood up in the House of Commons and denied the accusations. With the press now in full cry, more details emerged, including the

Oscar Wilde believed in challenging rules; his homosexual affair titillated many but changed society little.

wholesale pandering of willing girls by Dr. Ward. Profumo resigned on June 4. Four days later, Dr. Ward was arrested for "living wholly or in part on the immoral earnings of prostitution." His trial lasted nine days and ended with a verdict of guilty. It was never handed down, however, because he committed suicide while the jury was deliberating.

In retrospect this scandal, like so many others, had been a case of much ado about nothing. No military secrets turned up missing. John Profumo, whose wife had magnanimously stood by him, redeemed himself by doing good works among the derelicts of London's East End. Christine Keeler vanished into the obscurity of two unsuccessful marriages. The essence of the affair—and of all scandals in general—was summed up in this anonymous limerick:

"What on earth have you done?" said Christine,
"You have wrecked the whole party machine.
　　　To lie in the nude
　　　Is not at all rude,
But to lie in the House is obscene."

SCISSORS A Bronze Age invention that remains basically unchanged to this day, the first scissors consisted of two blades linked by a C-shaped spring. Perhaps surprisingly, many such prototype scissors, roughly 3,500 years old, have been unearthed by archeologists all the way from Britain to China.

In legends, scissors have been associated with mortality. In Greek myth they are wielded by Atropos ("Inexorable One"), third of the three

Fates, who shears the thread of each mortal's life. In many folktales scissors bleed or cry out, portending a grisly end for someone.

Ancient Romans used pivoted scissors of bronze and iron as well as spring scissors. The Romans also invented sheep shears that could be managed with one hand, a design virtually identical to the type in use today.

Scissors for domestic use, however, did not become common until Elizabethan times, and even then they were a luxury item. Large-scale production of household scissors dates from 1761. In that

Old blades: woman presents to historical society president iron scissors that once signaled a yard-goods shop.

year an Englishman, Robert Hinchliffe, began to manufacture scissors from crucible cast steel, a process that produced stronger blades. Hinchliffe's new method was developed in the Yorkshire city of Sheffield, a cutlery center in the Middle Ages. Later Sheffield became world famous for the quality of its scissors and knives. Since the beginning of the 20th century, scissors have been made of stainless steel, which gives the blades a long-lasting edge. During World War II, however, bronze scissors were used in munitions plants to avoid accidental explosions from sparks.

The numerous varieties of scissors are named according to their use—for example, manicure, embroidery, and buttonhole scissors. In the hardware trade, implements of 6 inches or less are classified as scissors, while those that exceed 6 inches are called shears. Scissors and shears were once synonyms, and some country folk in England and Scotland still refer to all scissors as shears.

SCREW, NUT, AND BOLT Until the early 1800's, screws had the irregular charm of all objects crafted by hand—no two were precisely alike. So precious was the combination of a screw and a nut with threads that matched that people tied them together for fear of losing one. Screws and bolts were very similar, both stubbornly blunt-ended, so that anyone working with them had to first tap a hole with a gimlet. The craft had really not progressed much since the time of Archimedes, the Greek mathematician who first discovered the principle of the screw.

A screw is an inclined plane wrapped spirally around a cylinder. In order to bail out the Greek navy, Archimedes made a big, hand-cranked screw and enclosed it in a tube. It was a fairly good bilge pump, and the device, known as "Archimedes' screw" or the "water snail," is still used to move grain. Medieval torturers demonstrated their comprehension—and inhumanity—by inventing the thumbscrew, a device that slowly cracked a prisoner's bones as well as his resistance to questioning. A few screws were used in armor: in one type, the knight's breastplate was screwed on by an assistant before battle, and the wrench was attached to the suit. If he lost his companions—or worse, his wrench—the knight was in trouble.

Not until the Industrial Revolution did the clamor for interchangeable, precision parts set inventors to the task of making one screw exactly like another. It took Henry Maudslay, an English mechanic, 10 years to make a true and perfect master screw that would create equally true and perfect replicas. At last, any screw fit any bolt—of Maudslay's. But every other screw in England was different. Eventually, both England and America were forced to end the confusion by standardizing screw threads. Unfortunately, they went on different standards.

When American boys went "over there" in 1917 to fight the first mechanized war, the incompatibility of British and American screw specifications was a major inconvenience. In World War II it was nearly a disaster. British mechanics could not repair American bombers; they had the wrong screws. America lost 10 critical months trying to make a British engine here; the industry had to tool up to make British screws first. The Nazis, however, were worse off: a top German official reported that when Hitler ordered an expansion of armaments in 1942, the effort almost ran aground for want of sufficient screws.

In today's shrunken world, international standardization of threading devices and metal fasteners is of critical importance to trade, technology, and defense. Such standards can also simplify the life of the individual consumer. For example, if a tiny screw falls out of a piece of machinery imported from the other side of the world, it is now possible to replace it at home. Industry has come a long way since that unhappy day in 1904 when fire companies from nine neighboring cities stood by helplessly as Baltimore burned because not a one of them could thread the fire hoses they brought with them onto Baltimore's hydrants.

SERVICE STATION If you owned an automobile in the early 1900's and wanted to keep it running, you took your five-gallon gasoline can to the blacksmith's or the grocery store, where the fellow filled it for about 25¢ a gallon. Then you poured the gas into the tank through a funnel covered with a piece of chamois to filter out the "impurities." The storekeepers offered no service because they made more money selling kerosene. The major oil companies similarly were interested more in producing and marketing kerosene than gasoline.

But as the number of motorists increased, they took to driving directly to the oil-company warehouses, often backing up traffic for blocks as they waited in line. Historians cannot agree on the date or site of the first filling station, though a few were in operation as early as 1907. Standard Oil of Louisiana provided a glimpse into the future when it opened a gleaming facility in 1912 with 13 pumps, a ladies' rest room, and a maid who poured ice water to quench the thirst of waiting customers. Despite evidence that the age of internal combustion had arrived, gasoline was still hauled to the filling station by mules.

Bikini-clad attendants in a Maryland service station bring in business; the problem seems to be that it stays.

In the 1920's service stations became a permanent part of the American landscape. Vying to attract the motorist's dollar, oil companies built stations that resembled Greek temples, Chinese pagodas, or Spanish missions. They sold oil for every make of car, including the Jordan, the Gardner, the Rickenbacker, the Cleveland, and the Chevrolet. They stretched their porticos as wide as their smiles and put the boys in uniform. Most of all, they conducted bitter price wars. By 1929, at the time of the stock market crash, there were 26.5 million vehicles on the road, and in the midst of the Depression that followed, Will Rogers (whose radio program was sponsored by Gulf Oil) could remark: "We're the first nation in the history of the world to go to the poorhouse in an automobile." Service stations did a fairly good business during the Depression.

Today, the future of service stations looks oddly like the past. After a decade or two of hard-edged "icebox" architecture, regional coziness returned to station design. In New England, for instance, shutters and geraniums abound. Once, the village store sold more than gas, and so do modern highway stops and the motels, restaurants, trailer parks, and shops that attend them. One Southern truckstop, open 24 hours, even features a chapel.

Most of all, customers are pumping their own gas again. In today's self-service station gone is the guy who offers to wipe the windshield and check the oil and tires. Instead, the attendant is usually an indoor type. Feet propped on desk, he watches a video screen tally the sale while the customer fills his own tank—in the sleet. It is the supermarket approach to selling gas, and customers like it because they pay less. One industry observer predicts that during the 1980's, self-service stations will be pumping more than 50 percent of the nation's gas.

Some stations have no attendants at all. A primed pump takes your cash or credit card, makes change, and delivers what you paid for. But do not ask a computerized pump about the knock in your motor or directions into town; it is not programmed for that kind of service.

SEWING MACHINE The publisher of *Godey's Lady's Book* called it "humanity's most blessed instrument"—next to the plow. When Mohandas Gandhi told Indians to shun Western-made machinery in favor of simple tools, he nevertheless found merit in the sewing machine. "It is one of the few useful things ever invented," he said. Shops in Africa were selling sewing machines even before Stanley went searching for Livingstone, and the Wright brothers stitched the wings of the

first airplane on a Singer. Admiral Byrd took six machines with him to the South Pole. Yet the sewing machine, which has altered forever the way we dress, started out as the invention that no one, except inventors, wanted.

The issue from the first was automation. If a machine could sew, what would happen to tailors and seamstresses? The point was brought home violently to Barthélemy Thimonnier, a French

Careful! The new machine inspired imaginative repairs like this.

tailor who in 1841 had 80 machines whipping up uniforms for the French Army at 200 stitches per minute. The best a tailor could manage by hand was about 30 stitches. The result was that Thimonnier was nearly martyred when a mob of angry tailors burst into his shop and wrecked his machines. Again he started up; again the mob struck. He died a poor and discouraged man.

When New York inventor Walter Hunt improved the stitching machine by devising a shuttle and eyepointed needle that produced a practical interlocking stitch, his young daughter pleaded with him not to patent the invention because it would be "injurious to the interests of hand-sewers." Hunt complied. Though all subsequent machines used his concept, Hunt never earned a penny from his creation.

The chain of neglected geniuses extended to Elias Howe, who spent hours studying his wife's arm movements as she sewed in order to imitate them

Sewing machines freed many women from the drudgery of hand-sewing family clothes. For others it meant income, as for this group engaged in a "cottage" industry.

mechanically. (She was sewing for money, as Howe was too busy with his invention to support a family.) No one wanted Howe's expensive, somewhat clumsy machine when it appeared, and in despair he sold the patent to an English corset maker. He took his family to England, hoping to make a go of it working with the corset manufacturer. Unfortunately his plan failed, and Howe was so short of funds that he had to work on ship for his passage home.

By the time Howe returned to America, times were changing, and several makes of sewing machines were on the market. In 1850 Isaac Merritt Singer put out a machine that was, for the first time, truly practical. Singer's improved model sewed a continuous seam, even a curved one, and was easy to operate. After Howe had examined Singer's machine carefully, he sued him for $25,000.

Howe sued every other sewing-machine manufacturer as well, because they were all using ideas he had patented—and one another's as well. Soon manufacturers were suing each other in what became known as the great "sewing machine war" of the 1850's. The situation was impossible; the solution, inspired. Forming one of the first patent pools in American industry, the manufacturers agreed to share their ideas and a

Squirrely: a man got a patent on this two-thread sewer in 1857.

general patent fee, and get back to business. Howe was poor no longer.

Singer introduced a home sewing machine in 1856, but it cost $125 at a time when the average family income was $500 a year. Few husbands would invest so heavily simply to lighten a wife's traditional sewing duties. For centuries it had been taken for granted that wives and servants made and mended the family clothes, even if a family had 10 children.

Singer's partner, Edward Clark, a lawyer, made the great investment look small by initiating a "hire/sales" plan—the first installment plan in history. He also thought up the trade-in, offering $50 for old machines of any make. The used machines were then smashed. Another deterrent to selling sewing machines was the commonly held notion that women burst into tears when confronted with machinery. Singer installed pretty young ladies sewing calmly in store windows to prove otherwise.

Isaac Singer's personal style, however, sometimes made selling to respectable families difficult, since he gathered wives and spawned children with seemingly indiscriminate energy. In New York he drove a 9-horse yellow carriage that seated 31 and had room for a nursery and a small orchestra. Eventually, Singer retired in splendor to England. At his death, 24 children turned up to squabble over his millions.

As early as the Civil War, Singer agents were peddling sewing machines in Mexico and Uruguay, thereby making the company the first multinational firm in the United States. The sewer was making an impact in remote parts of the U.S. too. The colorful costume of Florida's Seminole Indians is attributed by some to the arrival of the sewing machine; before that, the Seminoles wore drab garb.

Ultimately, commercial sewing machines and reasonably priced ready-made clothing liberated women from the drudgery of needlework, and democratized fashion. But ready made is not always well made. With today's machines, some electronically programmed to perform a variety of special stitches at the touch of a button, home sewing may be an old way made new of restoring quality to one's wardrobe.

SHIPPING It was a banner day in the history of world shipping when a stately procession of steamships chugged through the new Suez Canal in 1869, cutting short the tortuous voyage around the tip of Africa. Yet as early as 2000 B.C. the ancient Egyptians had a canal of their own connecting a tributary of the Nile with the Red Sea. Egyptian trading vessels sailed along the coast of Africa, returning to the Nile laden with gold, ivory, ebony, and even baboons and monkeys for the amusement of the nobility.

For nearly 2,500 years this first canal, destroyed and rebuilt several times, linked the lively traders of the Mediterranean with the coveted silk and spice markets of the East. The Romans followed the route south, and about 50 A.D. they learned they could ride the monsoons straight across the Indian Ocean to India. By 160 A.D. they had shipping routes even to China.

During the early years of the Roman Empire, shipping reached a grand plateau. Warehouses at Ostia, Rome's port city, bulged with glass and corn from Egypt; building stone and dyed cloth from Syria; oil, wine, and truffles from Asia Minor; marble from Greece; and mica and furs from Africa. From Britain came oysters, geese, and prize hunting dogs. Roman ships, many of them bigger than those of Columbus' fleet (and indeed larger than others built well into the 18th cen-

Paper Patterns

When a tailor in 13th-century France devised a pattern made of thin wood, the Master Tailors' Guild was terrified. If patterns were to fall into the hands of dressmakers and seamstresses, who would pay for the services of master tailors? For nearly a hundred years thereafter the tailors' guild wisely discouraged patternmaking. But it finally gave in, and patterns became an important tool of their trade.

Full-scale paper patterns finally reached the hands of women in the 19th century, but they were utterly baffling. The Germans originated the idea, and some American magazines copied it. They printed as many as 15 different patterns on a single fold-out page, each with its own outline. The result was a discouraging maze of dots, dashes, and wavy lines. They came in one size, 36, and no instructions were included.

Ellen Butterick, for one, found it very tiresome. She wished fervently that she had a single pattern for a single garment, and said so to her husband. Ebenezer Butterick, a skilled tailor, immediately saw both the justice and the future of the idea. He devised a paper pattern for a man's shirt, and it was widely used in 1863 in their little town of Fitchburg, Massachusetts. Encouraged by his success, Butterick created patterns for boys' suits, and eventually, with women clamoring for like attention, he added dresses to his designs. Folded into envelopes with an instruction sheet, Butterick patterns were the first on the market that were sized and did not have to be cut out of magazines. Within eight years, the Butterick family was selling 6 million patterns a year.

America in the 19th century was hardly a classless society. Only wealthy women could afford to look wealthy, and the rest—well, one could tell at a glance who was not a lady. Ordinary women labored endlessly just to keep a family clothed and clothes mended. Butterick patterns and the sewing machine brought fashion to middle-class families for the first time. By 1900 lads in urban Brooklyn and rural Maine could be outfitted in a Butterick sailor suit similar to the one worn by little Prince Edward of England.

Today, computers have taken patternmaking a step further, eliminating those maddening adjustments necessary to adapt a standard-size pattern to the individual figure. A woman can feed her measurements into the computer and get back a printed, custom-tailored pattern as exquisitely designed for her form as anything the Master Tailors' Guild ever created.

tury) carried goods, soldiers, and travelers to every corner of the empire. The remarkable capacity of some of those vessels is perhaps best indicated by the fact that a single Roman ship transported a 500-ton obelisk (now in the Vatican) from Egypt to Rome.

The increase in commerce had made the sea-lanes safer for passenger traffic. Many of the travelers were wealthy citizens making the Grand Tour—to Greece for the Olympic Games, then to the Aegean Islands, a look at the sights of Egypt, and, finally, home with the Egyptian corn crop. In the great days of the *Pax Romana*, pirates did not hound the seaways—one of the few periods of nautical tranquillity before the 19th century.

Sailors have navigated by the North Star since the Phoenicians first crossed the Mediterranean. But in the days before the compass, medieval seamen are said to have considered the hog a fairly reliable navigational aid, because it was believed to know instinctively the direction in which the shore lay. Ships often carried hogs, and when in doubt a captain would heave one overboard, then sail off in whatever direction the hog decided to swim. Better by far was the compass, a 12th-century invention, though for many years its magnetic needle was regarded as magical and an instrument of the black arts. Even with a compass and an astrolabe—an early type of sextant—15th-century navigators commonly made navigational errors, sometimes missing the mark by as much as 600 miles. Modern navigational devices can chart a ship's position within five

The ungainly looking vessel below, the only seven-masted schooner ever, was built in 1902 as a last ditch try to make shipping more profitable by sail than by steam.

Saint of the Seaways

A politician needs a cause, and the fact that young Samuel Plimsoll, a coal merchant newly elected to the House of Commons in 1868, had none made him seem a dull fellow. Before long, however, he would have all of England concerned about the sorry state of British seamen and in the process become a saint of the seaways and incur the wrath of no less powerful a man than Benjamin Disraeli.

Certainly the sailors' plight cried out for a champion. Quite a few merchant-shipowners of Britain's mighty trading fleets had discovered that their ships were worth more on the bottom of the ocean than plying between ports. Rickety vessels went to sea so critically overloaded (and cynically overinsured) that the greenest sailor aboard knew he was a dead man. "Coffin ships," the sailors called them. From a fleet of 21 ships, one owner lost 10 in three years. The seamen, legally unprotected either by inspection or insurance and forbidden to leave their ships, frequently managed to get themselves jailed rather than risk a rendezvous with Davy Jones. The shipping interests, powerfully represented in Parliament, had little concern for the men.

With the instincts of a natural publicist, Plimsoll wrote an exposé entitled *Our Seamen.* In it he exhorted the reader to end "this manslaughtering; this widow-and-orphan manufacturing system." He also told tales of woe, mentioned names, and in the end got himself into libelous trouble with some honest shipowners. No matter: England was moved by his Christian zeal, and the safety of seamen became a popular cause.

To protect sailors against overloaded vessels, Plimsoll proposed doing what medieval Venetian traders had done in the time of the Crusades—to draw a mark, on both port and starboard, indicating the depth to which a vessel could safely be loaded. That such a reform had been put forward by a concerned shipowner named James Hall did not deter Plimsoll from high-handedly borrowing Hall's ideas and making them public. ("Plimsoll traded on your brains," wrote a sympathetic friend to Hall.)

As a result of Plimsoll's agitation, a law was passed in 1875 requiring shipowners to paint a circle bisected by a horizontal line on each side of a hull to mark the vessel's safe loading depth. Soon adopted by all nations trading with England, the mark is known even today as the "Plimsoll line." (Later, the English came to call sneakers "plimsolls." The association may have come about because the rubber mudguard on sneakers resembled a waterline.)

One dashing clipper ship was gratefully named for Plimsoll: on its bowsprit rode a frock-coated and top-hatted figurehead of the reformer.

A Builder

Young Henry John Kaiser was understandably in a hurry to make a living: the father of the girl he loved would give his daughter in marriage only if Kaiser were earning $125 a month, owned a house, and had $1,000 in the bank. Kaiser closed his little camera shop in Lake Placid, New York, and headed for Spokane, Washington, where he became a salesman for a paving contractor. He returned in a year's time to claim his bride, all conditions met.

But Henry Kaiser liked doing things that others considered impossible—completing the gigantic Hoover Dam two years ahead of schedule or turning out a third of the nation's wartime ships at the unheard-of average rate of one a day. "I'm a builder," he said, "and if you call yourself a builder you ought to be able to build anything." And build he did, including the Grand Coulee, Bonneville, and Shasta dams, the piers of the San Francisco–Oakland Bay Bridge, a cement business, a magnesium business, seven shipyards, Kaiser Aluminum, Kaiser Steel, the first American compact car (it failed), the Kaiser jeep, the Hawaii-Kai resort in Honolulu, and a bright pink mansion for himself at nearby Koko Head. Along the way, he spawned companies in mining, home building, insurance, agriculture, and airplane and washing-machine manufacture. Kaiser, said his disgruntled competitors, was just too ignorant to know what he could not do.

Though he had dropped out of school at 13, Kaiser had learned that "there's no money in a slow job." After the outbreak of World War II, when German U-boats were sinking Allied ships at a disheartening rate, he proposed to speed up ship production by using assembly-line techniques, unheard of in that time-honored craft. Whereas, traditionally, a vessel was built from the keel up in one place, in Kaiser's yards it was built in sections, which were then welded together. Any improvement suggested by a worker was given consideration: for example, some parts of the ship were built upside-down to save tiring overhead welding. When Kaiser turned out one Liberty ship in the record time of four days and 15 hours, the Navy brass stopped wincing at his habit of referring to the "front end" of a ship.

Jowly and genial, Kaiser in his heyday traveled 75,000 miles a year and kept in touch with his vast industrial empire by running up a $300,000 phone bill. He got along well with both labor and government—an innovation in itself. His belief in capitalism in those boom years was unbounded. If other industrialists faced the transition to a peacetime economy with misgivings, not so Henry Kaiser, whose head was aswarm with projects. "When you think," he said, "of China and all those countries—our business is to rebuild the world!"

In this mosaic from ancient Ostia, the famous Roman port, a worker moves a wine cask from a seagoing vessel to a riverboat; it served as a sidewalk ad.

miles at any point on the world's wide oceans.

Today every corner grocery store sells spices. Centuries ago, the procurement of these piquant flavorings, many of them native to the East Indies, was a complicated undertaking. Explorers from many nations set sail in small vessels to vie with their competitors. The mariners risked piracy and storms. They died in awesome numbers from the ravages of scurvy and tropical diseases, all for spices—cinnamon, nutmeg, mace, cloves. In search of a shortcut to these exotic products and other luxury goods, history was made, trade routes were forged, and Columbus found the Americas.

Behind much of this frantic activity, responsible for a great deal of the world's exploration and mapping, lay an odorous problem: bad meat. Because northern lands could not provide winter fodder, animals were slaughtered in the fall and had to be preserved by drying, salting, or pickling. In the days before refrigeration, spices were the only cure for the monotony and rank flavor of such meat, and for centuries they fetched exorbitant prices in the markets of Europe. After Vasco da Gama reached India in 1498, he returned home laden with luxuries and spices worth 60 times the cost of his long voyage.

The profits in modern-day shipping are rarely so grand, but neither are the risks. Ships today have become highly specialized, and many are built to accommodate truck-size containers or loaded barges or to handle "roll-on, roll-off" vehicles that can drive directly into their transoceanic parking spaces. For some of the new oil supertankers, even the Suez is now too small.

Oddly, the largest merchant fleet in the world today sails under the flag of one of the tiniest of African nations, Liberia, where low taxes make it profitable for large shipowners like the Greeks and the Americans to register their vessels.

SHIRT Interposed between his nakedness and the world, a man's shirt has served since earliest times to broadcast rank and status as well as to keep out the cold. So intimately connected are the shirt and the man that according to many ancient customs they are magically interchangeable. At one time, discarding a sick man's shirt at the crossroads was a way of casting out illness. Some believed that a successful lawsuit or immunity from projectiles could be guaranteed by a "charmed" shirt, which, to be effective, had to be sewn in a single night by a child under seven years of age. In the Middle Ages a pregnant woman could ensure giving birth to a strong baby if she wore its father's shirt, and many a grieving widow donned the blood-stained shirt of a husband fallen in battle to prove her undying love. Even today, when a man "loses his shirt," he loses some of his dignity along with his capital.

Shirts were first fitted with fancy collars in the 16th century; for the next three and a half centuries those persons concerned with fashion made the collar the focus of their creative energies. First came the "Spanish ruff," worn by Queen Elizabeth, her courtiers, and even her coachmen—a noble construction made of 40 yards of starched, pleated cambric propped up by wires. A hundred years later the shirt reached an ultimate in puffed and lace-trimmed finery, a creation so expensive that some noblemen had to sell property in order

An 1898 cover featured girls in the jaunty shirtwaists that dotted the era when women took up freer clothing.

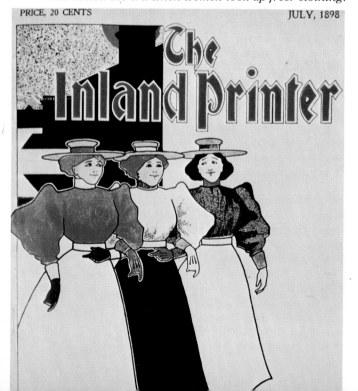

PRICE, 20 CENTS   JULY, 1898

The Inland Printer

to own one. One French courtier boasted that he was wearing "32 acres of the best vineyard property" around his neck. Cleanliness, however, was not often a prerequisite of fashion. A cavalier usually changed his frilly shirt once a month, which explains why gentlemen doused themselves liberally with scent.

Ruffled majesty: frills of England's Charles II bespeak his exalted rank.

Starch joined the tortures of vanity with the 18th-century dandy Beau Brummel, who did not like his shirt to wrinkle. In his day fashionable shirt fronts were so stiffly starched that they occasionally deflected a bullet, or so it was claimed, and more than one duelist could thank his shirt for his life.

In the 1820's a blacksmith's wife in Troy, New York, weary of washing her husband's shirts when only the collar showed grime, cut off the collar, washed, starched, and ironed it, and stitched it back on—thus inventing the first detachable collar. This discomforting style flourished for a full century. "Of all the absurd notions man has managed to hang himself with," wrote *Esquire* magazine, "the detached, starched collar stands as a singular monument to the extent of his foolishness." By 1900 some 400 styles of detached collars were being manufactured. The stiffest of them all was one that had been worn by the Victorians; it was made of steel glazed with white enamel.

The U.S. Army indirectly did in detachable collars. Doughboys returning from World War I remembered the comfortable army shirts with soft, attached collars, and revolted against the rigid grip of propriety. But it took the sport shirt to finally return to man the comfort he had known in the Middle Ages.

Fashion of the 1920's obsessively followed the lead of the Riviera rich,

In a 12th-century relief the resurrected cover up nakedness with shirts.

who adapted from Basque fishermen a lightweight knit shirt now called a polo shirt. The original polo shirt, however, had button-down collar points so they would not flap in the player's face during a hard gallop. John Brooks saw polo shirts in England in the late 19th century and sent some to his New York haberdashery. The Brooks Brothers button-down caught on; by 1914 the Yale Whiffenpoofs were proudly sporting button-down shirts from that men's store.

The casual, open-collar sport shirt was originally inspired by garb worn by the gauchos of Argentina. By the time the "Gaucho shirt" swept the country from west to east, men no longer felt like anarchists if they appeared in public without a jacket and tie. Today, a sport shirt is acceptable attire at cocktails, dinner, or the theater, and the only link to the once fashionable frills and flowing silk cravats is a classy label.

SHOE POLISH People have been wearing leather footgear since prehistoric times, a practice that has always required conditioning, staining, and polishing to make the leather long-lasting and shiny. Present-day shoe polishes do the whole thing at once; in the past the process involved separate steps and substances. For cleaning and conditioning, neat's-foot oil, mink oil, dubbin, and saddle soap long led the field. While leather has been dyed all colors in hundreds of ways since antiquity, the commonest stain for footwear has always been black.

Blacking was usually made of carbonized bone or vine twigs mixed with small amounts of sugar and vitriol (for chemical reactions yielding a rich, deep black) together with varying proportions of oil, glycerin, and wax. Inferior blacking included inexpensive ingredients, such as rancid lard, which were often smelly. But a good old-fashioned blacking was superior to any shoe polish now on the market. The blacking was nontoxic for both people and leather, and it could be spit-shined to a much higher, truly mirror-like, gloss than any of today's silicone-enriched waxes, liquids, or sprays.

SHOPLIFTING Shoplifting costs U.S. merchants millions of dollars. Estimates in the late 1970's put the amount at nearly $2 billion annually. The Federal Bureau of Investigation considers shoplifting to be one of the nation's fastest-growing areas of crime. About 4 million shoplifters are caught each year, but millions more make off with their booty, unapprehended.

Some of them are professionals. In South America there are schools that train shoplifters. Police

This expert lectures about and demonstrates rip-off tactics; later, clerks who spot her at work are rewarded.

report that thieves "educated" in Chile have stolen more than $150 million in merchandise in Miami, New York, Los Angeles, and other U.S. cities where they can blend easily into a large Spanish-speaking population. A shoplifting academy set up in California charged a tuition fee of $1,500; it boasted that its skilled graduates could "steal up to five women's suits while talking to a salesclerk."

Surprisingly, 75 percent of all shoplifters apprehended are ordinary, seemingly respectable folks who would never think of going to school to learn how to commit crimes; one in five comes from a high-income family. What makes people who would not steal elsewhere feel free to steal in stores? Many are acting out psychological problems. For them, "ripping off" clothing, jewelry, or phonograph records, some of the most commonly stolen items, probably satisfies an emotional need that is not being met in other ways. One report showed that shoplifting was a way of getting "kicks" and compensating for life's frustrations. Teenagers and college students often rationalize stealing by telling themselves that "the store will never miss it."

The average value of goods stolen by each shoplifter is, according to the F.B.I., $28.00 per item. Merchants are working hard to fight the crime wave. Every time you go into your local department store or supermarket, you are probably being watched. A television monitor or a two-way

The Boys of the Brigades

Temptations such as tavern singing, cheap theater, and low music halls, where boys and girls mixed together, were the first stepping-stone to sin and ruin, wrote a London reformer in 1875. Shoeshine boys, out on the streets at all hours and exposed to all sorts of people, were particularly susceptible. To save them, militants of the Reformatory and Refuge Union founded the "Shoe-black Brigades."

Many London shoeblacks were runaways who had come to the big city for fun and adventure. There they could mix freely with girls who had also run away from home and had inevitably ended up in an occupation considerably older and lower on the social scale than that of shoeblack. However, by joining a shoeblack brigade, a sensible boy could hope to save some money—and his soul—and rise in the world. Each brigade had its own shoeshine stations manned by brigade members dressed in "strong and decent" working-class clothes supplied by the Reformatory and Refuge Union. (Shoeblacks' garb traditionally had included a gaudy kerchief, light-colored trousers, and a jacket decorated with rows of brass and pearl buttons, resembling that of old-style street people still seen in British cities.)

Two-thirds of the boys' receipts had to be handed over to the Union. Half of that went for the work of the Union, and the other half was banked for the boy who earned them. The boys did not have much time to spend the third they were allowed to keep. They were kept busy—learning to read, playing cricket, marching, and tootling on fifes in the brigade bands. On Sundays they marched together to church and then marched home again to read religious tracts and sing hymns. Every morning they attended a 15-minute "family worship," which, it was hoped, would give them "something to think about during the day."

The Reformatory and Refuge Union did not intend its protégés to remain shoeblacks forever. Social promotion was the order of the day, then as now. Boys who did not go from the brigades to the navy could use the money that had been saved for them to secure a position as an apprentice (good jobs did not come free in those days) in some shop or firm where they could learn a trade and rise above the social class into which they had been born.

London's benevolent brigades showed what Victorian philanthropy could do to transform street scamps into honest workers; the shoeshine parlors of 19th-century New York City, if only occasionally, managed to do as much—and more. The brothers Rocco and Francisco Corresca were ragamuffins in the streets of Naples when a *padrone*, or labor agent, named Bartolo recruited them to join his cruelly oppressed brigade of young shoeblacks in the streets of Lower Manhattan. Bartolo kept the boys like slaves, gave them little or nothing from their earnings, fed them on scraps, housed them in a cellar, and clothed them in rags. He threatened to put them in jail if they ran away.

At length, Rocco and Francisco escaped to New Jersey, where a kindly Irishman employed them while they learned English. They managed to save enough money to open a shoeshine parlor in a cellar shopfront next to the Brooklyn Ferry. The rent was $20 a month. Customers paid 5 cents for a shine. The boys' independence enabled them to fix their own meals—but not for long. Customers complained of the garlic and onion on their breaths, and Mediterranean working-class fare had to give way to meals sent down by the widow upstairs for $3 a week.

The boys' original plan had been to save $1,000 apiece and buy a farm in Italy. But with prosperity came a decision to stay. The young men joined a neighborhood social club, played cards, and went to the theater. On Sundays they borrowed a horse and buggy from the grocer down the block and drove out to Coney Island for the day. Francisco fell in love with a girl whom he met at a picnic. Pleased with their personal lives, the brothers opened a chain of shoeshine parlors; long before they got their citizenship papers, the Correscas were well on the way to making their version of yet another American dream a reality.

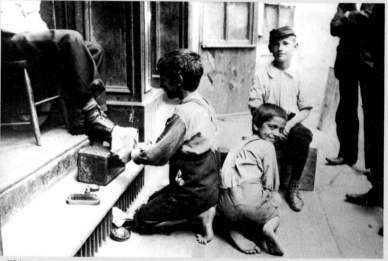

Shiny faces: smiles belie bootblacks' rough life; here, New York City c. 1890.

mirror allows employees to check on your movements to make sure that you do not slip any merchandise into your pocket. In many stores items of clothing are fitted with tags that trigger alarms if they are carried through doors.

But there are snags. Department stores, plagued by shoplifters who walk out of dressing rooms wearing two or three dresses under their own, have installed two-way mirrors and stationed detectives behind them to watch for thieves. Outraged customers, the innocent as well as the guilty, objected to being under surveillance while they were undressing. The mirrors were removed. Another problem for storekeepers involves the danger of apprehending someone for shoplifting, only to find that a mistake has been made. "One suit for false arrest," said a spokesman for a major chain of retail stores, "can wipe out the savings achieved through good security."

Nevertheless, storekeepers have not given up. One shoplifter was caught leaving a store wearing 10 bras, 20 pairs of pants, 15 dresses, and a coat. Amateur and professional thieves who escape cost merchants so much money each year that the problem cannot be ignored—by any of us, because the merchant's costs are eventually passed on to the innocent consumer.

SHOVEL The early American colonists, most of whom were farmers, had to depend on home-crafted shovels made entirely of wood. Only a few could afford expensive imports with metal blades shipped from England. In 1774, however, Captain John Ames of Bridgewater, Massachusetts, began making steel blades from local iron. He rigged up one of the first assembly lines, with 20 people working on each implement at various times. The company he founded is still the world's largest manufacturer of shovels.

Railroaders, especially coal stokers, took such pride in their tools that companies at one time issued illustrated booklets featuring the so-called veteran shovels. They were rated on durability and the number of miles they had logged (sometimes in the tens of thousands). Over the years, miners and railroad men began to balk at having to buy their own shovels, often at the company store, from wages as little as $1.85 a day. As a result of union demands, and studies of "scientific shoveling" which showed that workers were more efficient if they used the right shovel, large companies began supplying employees with tools.

Broadly speaking, the shovel category has included everything from 40-ton bulldozers for moving earth to delicate silver-headed ice-cream scoops. In the 1970's the plight of the cities engendered a new breed of shoveling device. The controversial New York City ordinance that decreed that dog owners must clean up after their dogs resulted in a spate of ingenious sanitary devices ranging from the 15¢ cardboard shovel to the $11 long-handled "pooper-scooper," which is equipped with a flashlight for night duty.

SIDEWALK At some point in the long-standing street war between the speeding wheel and the plodding foot, a thin line of compromise was drawn—a sidewalk. The Romans, who paved as much of the known world as they could, built raised sidewalks of stone in the streets of luxurious Pompeii so that pedestrians would not dirty their feet in the mud. And in Rome, after every profitable victory in war, emperor competed with previous emperor by adding to the city's covered walkways, or porticoes, where the citizens could stroll among shops away from the clatter of warhorses and the glare of the sun. History credits the Westminster section of London with constructing, in 1765, the first paved, curb-defined sidewalk after the disappearance of the lovely mosaic and paved walkways of the ancient world many centuries earlier.

Once there were sidewalks, people were not content merely to walk on them. On that narrow strip between the house front and the gutter, street performers juggled, gave Punch-and-Judy shows, pulled doves out of hats, jigged, and made music, while all around them lively crowds brawled, jostled, vended, and picked pockets. To protect a lady against such street ruffians and carriage splashes, the gentleman gallantly placed

New York's Fifth Avenue at noon on a nice day shows the psychological import of sidewalks to city dwellers.

himself on the outside of the sidewalk.

In the modern city, one group is always accusing another of taking up too much of the sidewalk. New Yorkers, for example, complain regularly about stepping over peacefully sleeping bums, about dodging speeding youngsters on skateboards, about unlicensed street vendors, about sprawling coffeehouses, about ladies of the night, about people thrusting flyers at them, and about around-the-block movie lines. Yet when these same people want a taste of city life, they go out onto the sidewalk.

In the suburbs few developers even bother to build sidewalks anymore because most everyone

Urban Oases

Differences in climate alone cannot explain why Rome has flourishing sidewalk cafés and London does not. Damp Copenhagen's Tivoli Gardens and Berlin's famous Kurfürstendamm are crammed with outdoor tables, but the streets of sunny Los Angeles are not. The difference is more profoundly one of attitude. In the European tradition the sidewalk café is a homey oasis at the heart of the urban throng, inviting the leisurely observation of one's fellowmen. For the price of a single cup of espresso or a glass of wine, one may sit for hours in convivial privacy, writing a novel, founding an art movement, or simply gaping at passersby.

Chilly Vienna is credited with inventing this urban ornament. In 1684, shortly after Vienna had resisted the Turkish invaders, a Serbian double agent was rewarded for his services with bags of coffee left behind by the Turks and given permission to open a coffeehouse. Other such establishments swiftly followed. At sedate sidewalk tables ladies chatted over frozen creams, but the inside rooms were only for men, who played billiards and talked politics amid clouds of cigar smoke.

Every great European city has had its so-called café society. At the famous Odéon of Zurich, Joyce wrote parts of *Ulysses*, the exiled Lenin bided his time, and Einstein read some of the 27 newspapers the establishment provided for its patrons. Famous men such as Casanova, Canaletto, Goethe, Byron, and Proust were sometimes customers of the café Florian in Venice. But because Paris is special, what happened in its cafés influenced the art, literature, and philosophy of the modern world.

The cafés of Montmartre harbored the Impressionist painters, and the cafés Flore and Deux Magots (where artist Gérard de Nerval occasionally turned up leading his pet lobster on a blue ribbon) became headquarters for the postwar Existentialists. On August 25, 1944, the Café de la Paix, once frequented by Maupassant, Zola, and Oscar Wilde, was digging out from bomb damage when a jeep pulled up outside. Could dinner be prepared for Gen. Charles de Gaulle, someone inquired. Paris had been liberated. In that hour, as joyous waiters scurried amid the wreckage, with some ham, salad, and potatoes that someone managed to find, civilization returned to Par-

Van Gogh captured the magic the outdoor café holds for the habitué.

is. Today the history that is such an integral part of these cafés has made them expensive tourist shrines, and one wonders how struggling artists and painters could have afforded them. Hemingway, at least, benefited from a favorable exchange rate.

Less famous are the small neighborhood cafés where workmen come for their morning and evening glass of wine. "A Frenchman is more faithful to his café than to his wife," revealed one Parisian. Cafés are the poor man's parlor, the local club, the student's other home. Many people receive their mail and phone messages there. According to café etiquette, heavy drinking is not permitted. When a customer orders another drink, the waiter leaves the first saucer and adds the next, as a tally. People may be crammed knee to knee, but no one overhears another's conversation. After three visits, you shake hands with the owner. If a woman has an escort, a man may smile at her only. If she likes him she will come back the next day, alone.

Sadly, today's cafés are threatened by urban ills. In Italy the fumes and noise of modern traffic have forced the closing of a number of open-air cafés. In New York, outdoor cafés have glassed in their slice of appropriated sidewalk against winter and the same urban poisons. People with heart and respiratory ailments are advised not to linger in open cafés because the carbon monoxide level may be 20 percent higher than indoors. It is time for another revolution fomented in, and for the sake of, sidewalk cafés.

Undulating walk: paving in Rio de Janeiro

goes everywhere by car. But mothers whose children walk to suburbia's schools want sidewalks back, even if it means the loss of a few prize bushes; walking in the road is too dangerous. Said one angry lawyer, arguing that older people had to take a cab in his town to travel a distance that would normally take them five minutes on foot, "It is against public policy to walk in Bellevue, because it tarnishes the city's image of affluence."

A modern cure for crowded urban sidewalks may be to keep the sidewalks moving. The first experiment in mechanized sidewalks (which operate rather like a horizontal escalator) took place at the 1893 World's Columbian Exposition in Chicago. Moving at its fastest (one mile in 10 minutes), the creeping sidewalk could convey 5,610 people at a time around the packed fairgrounds.

That particular idea lay dormant for half a century, but today London's Heathrow Airport, for example, has a network of moving walkways, which have also proved useful in shopping malls and sports stadiums. A few urban planners want to install moving sidewalks, with a slow-access lane leading to a faster lane, in the heart of cities, arguing that such a human conveyor belt could move 30,000 people across New York City in an hour—without bus fumes.

Some modern pedestrian walks, rising above clashing vehicular traffic, have ascended to the second-story level and left the vehicles churning in their own exhaust below. Minneapolis intends to connect most of its downtown area with covered, elevated walkways that will be heated in winter and cooled in summer. Atlanta has one 22 stories above the street, from which folks can take in the view as they walk along.

If elevated sidewalks are a mark of the future, one cannot help wondering if hot-dog wagons and ice-cream vendors will still be around. Will people be able to chalk huge pictures on them, as Parisian sidewalk artists do? Where will one find the street mimes, the steel drummers, the dog walkers? Where will children play hopscotch and roller-skate and play wall ball?

SIGN For thousands of years, in one form or another, signs have been telling people in concise terms what to do, where to go, and what to expect when they get there. Even before the invention of writing to express such ideas, there were glyphs— widely understood pictorial symbols scratched on cave walls and in the earth. By the time of the ancient Romans, a whole lexicon of picture signs existed, based on tradesmen's tools and goods. These symbols were commonly displayed on signboards to identify particular types of shops, and some of them have survived in modified form to this day.

For example, the branch or bush that hung over a tavern door in Rome was introduced to England by Julius Caesar's invaders. There it evolved into the "ale garland," displayed alongside the permanent tavern sign whenever a new batch of ale was on tap. The ale garland was also a signal to the "ale conner," or inspector, to drop by and put his stamp of approval on the brew. (Tradition relates that the conner arrived at his decision after pouring a little ale on the bench and sitting squarely on it. If, after the prescribed waiting time—presumably long enough to down several pints—his leather breeches stuck to the bench, the ale was pronounced fit.) Similar garlands of evergreen are still displayed in another onetime Roman outpost, Vienna, to identify wine taverns.

Other signs in long-standing use include various religious emblems, such as the cross, to mark houses of worship; heraldic signs or coats-of-arms to identify noble families, their estates, and possessions; the pawnbrokers' three golden orbs, a device purported to be adapted from the coat of arms of a noted Renaissance family, the Medici.

As towns and cities grew and the number of

words

Sidewalk Superintendent

When Rockefeller Center was being built, the story goes, John D. Rockefeller, Jr. was trying to get a better view one day of the fascinating proceedings on the other side of the wall fencing off the lot during excavation, and was told by a watchman to "keep moving, buddy." "Buddy" kept moving; but before long other excavation kibitzers found that neat peepholes had been cut for their convenience. Each gazer was even presented with a card announcing that he was now a member in good standing of the "Sidewalk Superintendents' Club." Printed on each card was the "club's" motto, an old Dutch saying, translated: "The best pilots stand on the shore." By popular demand, peephole service has become customary when any big structure is rising in New York.

Which way is up? An alert person can learn a great deal from the signs of his times—from where to get dentures for a guinea (c. 1900) to where to bed down.

tradesmen competing for business increased, the practice of using generic signs to designate simply "butcher" or "baker" or "candlestick maker" was no longer adequate. Shopkeepers began adding their names or some colorful phrase that would somehow make their premises memorable and more appealing than those of their competitors. They also took to displaying ever-larger and more eye-catching boards, even hiring the relatively expensive services of a professional artist to ensure notice. Inn signs consistently led the way in the development of handsome signboards.

But as people became more peripatetic, sign-makers and advertisers realized that they could improve sales by going out into the marketplace and enticing prospective customers to their places of business. With that, posters, broadsides, and freestanding billboards appeared in the United States—and ultimately the first legislation against their excesses. The sudden blossoming in the 1850's of patent-medicine signs—on cliffs, barn-sides, and finally a rock at Niagara Falls—caused that brief public outcry.

Not as Strange as They Seem

British inn and tavern signs traditionally have been among the most colorful of markers, with symbols and names that are amusingly incongruous and puzzling to the uninitiated. More often than not, their meanings can be traced through fractured English to historical, religious, or literary origins that once made sense. For example, the oft-used tavern name "The Bag o' Nails" probably derives from an earlier, more apt name, "The Bacchanalians." "The Pig and Whistle," showing, appropriately enough, a musical porker, is thought to be a combination of two Old English words, "pightle" and "wassail," suggesting a meeting place where revelries were held. "The Bull and Mouth" recalls Henry VIII's 1544 victory against the French at Boulogne's "mouth" or "harbor," and "The Pig and Carrot" traces to *pique* and *carreau*, French for the "spade" and the "diamond" of cardplaying.

Easier to translate are such satirical inn names and illustrated signboards as "The Man Loaded with Mischief," explained by the couplet: "A monkey, a magpie and a wife,/Is the true emblem of strife." The sign, which showed a beleaguered man under attack by all three troublemakers, must have provided solace to careworn customers bent on drowning their sorrows for a few hours. Another version of antiestablishment satire used repeatedly in the naming of 18th-century public houses was "The Five Alls," usually illustrated with a set of five portraits. As any Englishman of the time knew, they referred to the power structure of the society he lived in: a King—"I govern all"; a Bishop—"I pray for all"; a Lawyer—"I plead for all"; a Soldier—"I fight for all"; and a Laborer—"I pay for all." Colorful as the signs are to us, essayist Joseph Addison complained in 1710: "Our streets are filled with blue boars, black swans, and red lions . . . my first task therefore should be to clear the city from Monsters."

Colonists brought the English inn-sign tradition with them to America. Animal signs like this were popular.

Meanwhile, the great showman P.T. Barnum was writing another chapter in the history of sign-making. In the 1840's he placed a big gaslit sign above his museum on Broadway in New York—an idea he borrowed from amusement places. Legitimate theaters, bars, tobacco shops, and drugstores quickly followed suit, turning the old Madison Square area of Broadway into the well-lighted "Great White Way." Some 50 years later, in 1891, the first large electrically lighted sign made its debut at this Broadway crossroads: a consortium of businesses sang their own praises on a 60-by-68-foot billboard illuminated by 1,457 light bulbs. A few years later the sign was converted to advertise the "57 Varieties" of H.J. Heinz, with tomato red, pickle green, and several other startling colors of light bulbs flashing the company's name.

When the heart of Broadway moved uptown, electric signs were an essential part of the new glamour. Of all the gaudy glitter that lighted up the New York night, the Wrigley's spearmint gum sign reigned supreme from the time of its erection in 1917 to its destruction—to make way for a new skyscraper—in 1925. A full 200 feet long, five stories high, and studded with 15,000 varicolored bulbs, it presented a continuous flickering show of Wrigley's "spearmen" at play, framed between gigantic electric peacocks and a pair of illuminated fountains that seemed to spout real cascades of water. For many Americans in those innocent days the Wrigley sign was reason enough to go to New York.

Road signs, to aid travelers moving at fast speeds in unfamiliar territory, particularly drivers of newfangled automobiles, were also undergoing some major changes in those years. The British appear to have instituted the first system of traffic signs in 1903, and as it was based on glyphs or symbols rather than words, it was adopted as an international code six years later. About the only major country to resist standardization was the United States, where conflicting national, state, and local systems persist even now. But with a growing need for developing a universal code of symbols, affecting not only traffic but commerce, industry, and human services, the day will probably come when all of us are as comfortably conversant with modern sign language as our cavemen ancestors were with theirs. In a sense it will be an advance into the past.

SILVER The word "silver" usually brings to mind silver coins, tableware, jewelry, a trophy held aloft by a tired, happy athlete, or, if one is masochistically inclined, a dentist filling a cavity. Although all these represent common end-uses of

Silver palated: in India, those who want to feel sexier eat silver-foiled goodies—from chicken to ice cream.

the shiny metal, together they account for less than one-quarter of the annual U.S. silver market. By far the largest users of silver are manufacturers of photographic materials. But silver is also used to turn sunlight into electricity, to detect breast cancer, to kill some 650 different kinds of disease-causing organisms, to start cars, to operate computers, to keep jet engines working, and to repair damaged bones.

In the home, silver activates the morning alarm clock and, for better or worse, provides the reflection in a mirror. Silver was used to make the cooling unit of the refrigerator and the contacts in the electric coffee percolator. The television set contains silver capacitors. Electric watches and hearing aids work on silver batteries. The newest eyeglasses, which turn dark in sunlight and become clear indoors, contain silver. And even the polyester fabric used in clothing could not be produced without silver catalysts.

Silver owes its enormous versatility to a unique set of physical properties. It conducts electricity and heat, and reflects light, better than any other substance, and resists rust and corrosion. During World War II, for instance, the completion of the Manhattan Project—the building of the atomic bomb—was threatened by the need for 13,000 tons of metal to make heavy electrical conductors for an immense new power plant. Copper, which normally would have been used, was already in desperately short supply. Under a cloak of secrecy, which shrouded the entire project, silver—403 million ounces in all—was removed from the United States Mint, melted down, and cast into conductors. As the technicians who built it predicted, it performed admirably. Eventually, when copper again became available, the silver fittings were removed, melted down, and returned to the Treasury. Even after processing and seven years of use, only a fraction of one percent of the metal had been lost.

In space, silver-zinc batteries, which deliver more than 20 times the power of conventional batteries, have provided energy for many spectacular events. These batteries were used to operate the life-support systems of astronauts as they walked on the moon. Similar batteries powered the Lunar Roving Vehicles and sent the explorers' voices—and color TV pictures—back to earth.

Less well-publicized perhaps are the biomedical applications of silver. In addition to its other properties, silver is the most effective water-purifying agent known. It is used by more than a dozen international airlines to guard drinking water against diseases such as dysentery. NASA scientists selected a silver system to purify the drinking water aboard the space shuttle after testing 23 different methods. Their research only confirmed what ancient Greeks and Romans had known—silver keeps liquids fresh. And American settlers on the long voyage westward dropped a silver dollar into milk to delay spoiling.

Dr. Charles Fox of Columbia University demonstrated that a compound known as silver sulfadiazine is effective in the treatment of burns, long one of the most vexing of medical problems. And for many years doctors have been putting drops containing a solution of silver nitrate in the eyes of newborn babies to prevent infections that could lead to blindness. Surgeons often use silver wire, bands, and plates in their work. They have also discovered that a compound of silver and allantoinate is effective in preventing clotting and bacterial infection when used during the grafting of arteries and veins.

In addition, a modest amount of silver—about 17 million ounces a year—finds its way into solid silver bridal gifts and loving cups and baby rattles and tableware. In these forms it is called sterling. According to one story, the appellation goes back to the 13th century, when every duchy and principality in Europe struck its own coins. Among the most reliable coin makers were the free cities of the Hanseatic League, whose coins contained large proportions of silver. To the British they were known as coins of the "Easterlings." When, in the early 14th century, the king of England established a standard ratio for silver in English coins, the name "easterling" was used. Eventually it was shortened to "sterling." That ratio—925 parts per 1,000 of pure silver and the rest of copper, added for strength—is still maintained in sterling silver and is one of the very, very few standards that has not changed in the past 700 years.

Gold has always held a greater attraction for fortune seekers than silver—there is less of it and consequently it is more valuable. Out of the California gold rush came a great silver-mining find. During the mid-1850's prospectors became interested in the eastern slopes of the Sierra Nevada mountains. While looking for gold in a canyon of Mount Davidson in 1859, two miners hit the richest vein of silver ever uncovered: the Comstock Lode. It gave rise to Virginia City and turned a handful of paupers into millionaires.

SKIING More than a hundred ancient skis of pine or spruce have been unearthed in bogs in Finland and Sweden, most of which are believed to be between 4,000 and 5,000 years old. In northern Norway there is a 4,000-year-old rock carving of a skier who moves with the ease of a 20th-century ski bum—knees bent, feet slightly apart, planted firmly on extraordinarily long skis.

Today, skiing is primarily a recreational sport. Millions of people spend weekends and winter vacations on the slopes, and hordes more have taken up cross-country skiing. But in earlier times skiing was a necessity. In 950 A.D. King Haakon the Good of Norway found that the only way to collect taxes was to send out swarms of tax collectors on skis to his remote fiefdoms. Throughout most of Scandinavia ski troops were part of a country's military power. From the 15th to the 17th century, Finland, Norway, Sweden, Russia, and Poland regularly sent ski platoons into battle. In 1733 the Norwegians published the first ski manual; written in German, it was so comprehensive as to offer a 72-step rifle drill on skis.

By 1800 some Norwegians were taking up skiing just for the fun of it. When Norwegian emigrants arrived in America in the mid-19th century, they

Uphill work? Not when old Dobbin takes one ski riding, especially in a warm and comfy chair with runners.

These turn-of-the-century ski troopers seem to be paddling their way through air heavy enough to hold them.

brought the sport with them. "Snowshoe" Thompson and a hardy band of Norwegian-American gold miners had a great deal to do with launching the modern sport of racing on skis.

In 1855, when Thompson was 28 years old and looking for work in the California gold country, he saw an advertisement in the Sacramento *Union.* The ad offered a job to anyone who was willing to carry the mail back and forth over the 75 miles between Placerville in California and Genoa on the Nevada side of the Sierra Nevada mountains. Hired for the job, Thompson appeared with 9-foot 8-inch homemade skis. He took off across the mountains south of Lake Tahoe with some food supplies and a 50-pound sack of mail strapped to his back. Most of Placerville thought he was seriously deranged to attempt such a trip across "impassable terrain," but five days later Snowshoe was back in town with the return mail, having averaged about 30 miles a day.

As soon as the gold miners learned how a man could take to the hills on skis, they began organizing races and making bets on them—inveterate gamblers that they were. To increase speed, the miners "doped up" their skis with wax. Each man had his own special formula for the best stuff, but most concoctions used as primary ingredients beeswax, bacon fat, whale oil, or tallow, and a smidgin of bear grease.

America's first formal downhill ski races were organized at La Porte, California, at the mining camp ski-center. A "world's championship" meet, which took place in February 1867, featured a silver-studded belt, valued at $75, for the first prize in the men's finals. The Ladies' Club Purse of $25 went that year to a Miss Lottie Joy, who had "a pole under her arm, and just scooted down the track like an arrow to the mark."

SKYSCRAPER In 1890 the Pulitzer Building in New York rose to 14 stories, but at the expense of groundfloor space, because the bearing walls had to be nine feet thick. The true skyscraper owes its existence to all-steel-frame construction, which puts virtually no limitations on height. (An unbuilt design by Frank Lloyd Wright calls for 528 stories in a mile-high spire.) The other prerequisite for skyscraping was the "safety elevator," invented by Elisha G. Otis in 1854. The first building supported by a metal skeleton that was mostly steel was the 10-story Home Insurance Building in Chicago, designed by William Le Baron Jenney and completed in 1885.

The skyscraper's popularity derives from the demand for space in premium downtown areas of big cities and the desire of builders to maximize income from such expensive property. By the end of the 19th century, New York boasted 29 of the tall structures to Chicago's 16. Buildings now soar skyward in nearly every American metropolis, but the world's tallest are in those cities that gave birth to them: the towering twins at New York's World Trade Center (110 stories, 1,350 feet) are topped only by the 110-story Sears Tower, which looms 1,450 feet above the sidewalk on Chicago's famous Loop.

Mohawk Indians have played an important part in erecting this quintessentially American style of architecture. As early as 1714 an English

A place for everything: the University of Mass. library in bucolic Amherst seems a high-rise hallucination.

traveler noted of them: "They will walk over deep Brooks, and Creeks, on the smallest Poles, and that without any Fear or Concern. Nay, an Indian will walk on the Ridge of a Barn or House and look down the Gable-end, and spit upon the Ground, as unconcerned, as if walking on Terra firma." Scientists who have studied the phenomenon are unable to explain the Mohawk tribesmen's relative freedom from fear of heights, but it has helped make them widely employed as high-rise riveters.

Over the years skyscrapers not only have grown taller but have changed their looks in other ways. Imitations of such earlier architectural styles as Romanesque or Gothic, which resulted in gargoyles perching where only pigeons could see

people

A Building Profiled

The Empire State Building, for over 40 years the world's tallest building, is still New York City's leading tourist attraction, and those visitors familiar with a bit of the skyscraper's "biography" enjoy the tour even more than their blissfully ignorant companions.

Diverse factors determined the appearance of the building on Fifth Avenue between 33rd and 34th streets. In August 1929 its five financiers calculated that they could afford to build 36 million cubic feet; in fact, the Great Depression halved their estimated cost of $50 million to $24,718,000. A zoning law that required buildings to narrow as they rose forced its architects, Shreve, Lamb, and Harmon, to design from the top down; they created a series of setbacks that allowed the structure to rise legally on the two-acre lot.

A spire secretly constructed inside the Chrysler Building and elevated through its dome in 1930 brought it within 4 feet of the Empire's 1,050 feet. Consequently, after the Empire State Building was completed in 1931, the builders added a 200-foot mast for mooring dirigibles, then considered the coming thing in international travel. The first attempt to moor a blimp was futile. The second was disastrous—the craft upended, nearly killing its occupants, and the mast was converted to a tower with a 102nd-floor observation deck. The building reached its present height of 1,472 feet in 1950 with the installation of a 22-story television antenna.

Its construction took over 7 million man-hours, spread over one year and 45 days, including Sundays and holidays. During peak periods 3,400 men worked daily. They installed enough steel framing to build a double-track railroad from New York to Baltimore; 6,500 windows; 10 million bricks; 50 miles of radiator pipe and 70 miles of water pipe; and 3,500 miles of telephone and telegraph cable.

While it takes only 60 seconds to reach the 80th floor in one of the building's 73 elevators, it took the Polish Olympic ski team considerably longer to scale the internal heights by stairway in 1932. Upon reaching the 102nd-story summit, they were greeted by the Czech team who, unbeknownst to anyone, had entered the building a half hour earlier. Others have made the climb, including a fireman on a disability pension, but not many.

The building is a bustling place: 58,000 people work there, including a cleaning staff of 200.

Sporting Columbus Day colors

About 2 million tourists visit each year. Those who made the biggest impression were King Kong, who in a 1933 movie fantasy climbed the exterior while clutching Fay Wray, and a B-25 bomber cruising at 200 miles per hour that crashed into the building's 79th floor on July 28, 1945. Fourteen were killed, yet seven floors up, a messenger boy remained engrossed in his comic book.

The 102nd-floor observation tower is a good safe place to watch a lightning storm; the building's steel frame acts as a gigantic lightning rod, attracting bolts (19 during one storm) and grounding them harmlessly. During nighttime electrical storms, one can reach over the parapet, grab a handful of blue flame from the air, spread one's fingers, and watch the phosphorescence, called "St. Elmo's fire," dance between the tips. On dry days a little shuffling around in leather-soled shoes generates enough static electricity to give a loved one a crackling kiss that may be remembered for some time.

Colored floodlights, installed in 1976, make the building's top 30 stories glow against the night's black sky in glittering hues that reflect the season or the occasion. The building's distinctive Art Deco shape has gleamed autumnal orange and wintry ice-blue, and has been banded Christmas red and green and Bicentennial red, white, and blue. When the Yankees play for the pennant, it shines blue and white. (To prevent the deaths of migrating birds the lights are extinguished for a few days in May and September.)

Slang

"Slang," said poet Carl Sandburg, "is language that takes off its coat, spits on its hands, and goes to work." Vital, sardonic, and direct, slang is also somewhat less than respectable, a back-street peddler of hot goods continually restocking the "lingo." Most slang blows into town today and splits for the boonies or the boneyard tomorrow, but some of it goes button-down, joins the Establishment, and makes the scene permanently. When that happens, it is no longer called slang.

If yesterday's slang is today's standard English, it is equally true that most slang lasts about as long as a used paper plate. "Groovy" and "cool" are cold, and "way out" is out. When the scruffy insolence of slang makes it to Madison Avenue, it's had it—"zonked," "k.o.'d," "crashed." Slang that gets taken up gets used up. Who wants to be caught wearing knickers? Or the cat's pajamas? Gross. The pits.

Etymologists, who care where words come from, but only after they have arrived, have a hard time tagging slang in its winged flight. They are not sure, for instance, about the word "slang" itself, which might come from the Norwegian *slenja*, as in *slenja-namm* for "nickname" or

slenja-kjeften for "sling the jaw" (or abuse), or then again it might have been elided from beggar-(s'lang)uage or thieve(s'lang)-uage. "Sham," "banter," "bamboozle," "doggerel," "Cockney," and "Yankee" are all of uncertain origin, too, but it is nice having them around. "Nice," too, was once slang.

Slang words have a way of changing meaning even while you are using them. A "riot" in the 1950's was a "gas" (a funny person, an event), but "gas" meaning empty talk was current in 1847 and still is. "Soul" denoted a deep kiss in the 1950's; in the 1970's it stood for black style and sensitivity. "Bust" once referred to the feminine form, but in the 1930's it was black slang for "police raid"

Both "loonies" look "cracked."

or "arrest." "Heavy," a villain in the 1940's, meant serious or depressing in the mid-1970's.

"Funky," originally a dialect word meaning "smelly" was extended by jazz musicians of the 1940's to mean "earthy," "emotional," "having the qualities of the blues." The word was naturally associated with decrepit old music halls. Louis Armstrong referred to such a place as a "funky butt hall," and when nostalgia turned old into fondly remembered, funky turned mellow.

Historically, slang has emerged from subgroups who coined words because it was fun ("copacetic," "hootenanny," "pizzazz"), or because they needed a word where none existed ("rubberneck," "overkill," "mainline," "yesman"), or because they had good reason not to be understood ("The Man," "lam," "blow"). From thieves and prisoners, from circus and railroad workers, from students, soldiers, drug addicts, immigrants, and blacks, slang has mocked pretension and preserved the irony of the underdog.

H.L. Mencken, in his book *The American Language*, collected a rich stew of hobo words, some of which have survived. A "reefer" was not a marijuana cigarette but a refrigerator car. Hoboes called butter "axle-grease," pan-

them, gave way to gleaming, glass-wrapped slabs. Norman Mailer likened such edifices to boxes of "cleansing tissue propped on end [with] walls dead as an empty television screen," but many architectural experts considered them to be monuments of elegant simplicity.

Other critics have railed against the "inhumanity" of skyscrapers, which in their view isolate people from normal life in ways that are both physical and psychological. Most of the tenants who moved into the 100-story John Hancock Building in Chicago in 1970 disagreed. Not only did the complex offer them restaurants, bars, a grocery store, laundromats, cleaners, retail shops, and newsstands ("isolating" them in the bargain

from rotten weather), but some 15 residents commuted to their offices on lower floors by elevator. Most of the "cliff dwellers" found themselves enchanted with the view of kaleidoscopic cloud patterns floating about the building, the ice formations on Lake Michigan, or the magnificent summer lakescapes dotted with colorful sails or roiled with the angry waves of a squall. One harried executive, on returning to his aerie and looking out the window, marveled that "everything seems sort of small and the problems of the day disappear."

Others appear, though. One resident claimed that in the teeth of a violent Chicago windstorm the building sways so much that whitecaps appear in his toilet. (The experts say that no building

cakes "flat-cars," eggs "headlights," a small town a "jerkwater," and food "chuck." ("Chow" was from World War I.)

A special language like this, known only to initiates, is properly called cant or jargon. It becomes slang when the expressions spread more widely but are not yet colloquialisms.

The first recorded cant was that of the thieves of the Middle Ages, a motley code borrowed from German, Hebrew, Italian, and Gypsy words (they "gyp" you). The word "grease" for a bribe goes back to 1557, "hushmoney" to 1709, "lousy" to 1690, and "lip," "jug" (prison), and "sap" to the 1800's. American Prohibition added "big shot," "hideout," "to cut" (to dilute), "muscle in," and "take for a ride." The first "bogus" was a machine that made counterfeit coins.

Sports have made their own contribution to colorful language. From boxing comes "punchdrunk." "Off the wall" is a squash term for an unpredictable shot, and "one on one" is basketball talk. A "cheap shot," from football, is a tackle after an official blows his whistle to indicate that a play has ended.

The languages richest in slang are probably French and American English, but Americans, whose average vocabulary is estimated by some to be 20 percent slang, use it most frequently. Until the western expansion, most American slang was borrowed from the English, but the favor has since been returned. American slang now enriches or pollutes (depending on one's taste) most of the lively languages of the world. "O.K.," for example, is almost universal. Russian authorities may disapprove of comrades who say *kheppening* or *isteblishment*, but since "beatnik" was born of "Sputnik," it seems a fair trade.

The greatest number of slang words in English describe the great human concerns—sex, money, and drink, though mostly from a man's point of view. De-

"Big shots" toast one of theirs.

pending on your style, and the era, the women in a man's life were "chicks," "vamps," "birds," "gals," "broads," "old ladies," "dolls," "honeys," and the one and only "little woman." Before the Civil War, you could guzzle: "coffin-varnish," "mountain dew," "stagger-soup," "panthersweat," or "tonsil-paint," and get: "boiled," "canned," "cockeyed," "frazzled," "fried," "oiled," "ossified," "pie-eyed," "pifflicated," "plastered," "snozzled," or "stewed." Chug-a-lugging fraternity boys of the 1950's did most of that, but they also got "blotto," "stinko," and "bombed" out of their minds. Big deal. So what?

Which is like, man, part of the problem. Good slang, someone said, "has a real meaning. Bad slang has no meaning." And much slang has little nuance. A party that is either a "blast" or a "drag" leaves nothing to gossip about. In a few years the most current slang may be as dead as "twenty-three skidoo" and as leached of meaning as the once-decent words "fantastic" and "terrific." Then one can long for the good old frontier days, when no "robustious," "blustiferous" prospector would let himself be "horn-swoggled" or "flummucked" at a "conbobberation" by any "helliferocious, ripsniptious slangwhanger."

---

sways more than a few inches and that the effect of bending has other causes.) Relishing her privacy in the sky, a woman in the buff opened her curtains to let in the morning sun—and looked straight into the eyes of a window washer. Fortunately, she kept her cool and he kept his grip.

A recent innovation has been designed which has the potential of sparing sky-high curtain openers and window washers such rude surprises. Windows that used to take a team of two men 35 days to wash can now be cleaned by an automatic machine in seven. Once an operator positions it on tracks set in the face of the building and pushes a button, "Steeple Jac" can scrub and squeegee at the rate of five floors a minute.

SLEEP "Nature requires five,
Custom takes seven,
Laziness takes nine,
And wickedness eleven."

That is what poet John Milton said about sleep. Enrico Caruso, the great tenor, preferred to snooze surrounded by 18 pillows. Charles Dickens could only sleep in a bed that was aligned on a north-south axis. Benjamin Franklin slept in two beds each night, moving to the second when the first became too warm for him. Russian noblemen trying to doze had servants scratch their feet to produce a feeling of relaxation. Thomas Edison, Winston Churchill, and Napoleon may owe their greatness to the fact that they could only sleep fitfully. Marilyn Monroe, it was widely reported, slept wearing nothing but Chanel No. 5. And one wealthy French banker found that he could drowse only to the sound of young cultivated feminine voices chattering away in the background. And so he hired penniless princesses to surround his bed in their finery and prattle away.

Most of us spend a third of our lives sleeping, though no scientist has yet been able to explain why it is necessary or exactly what good it does us. Not long ago a psychotherapist, who obviously did most of his work at night, wrote a book in

customs

Night Music

"Laugh," observed the British novelist Anthony Burgess, "and the whole world laughs with you; snore and you sleep alone."

If this be true, then there must be millions of involuntarily isolated sleepers in the world, for it has been estimated that about one out of eight human beings is that most pestiferous of bedtime companions—a snorer. Some of the better-known snorers included Winston Churchill, who was once clocked in at 35 decibels (the sound of a drill going through a concrete wall produces only 70 to 90 decibels), Benito Mussolini, Plutarch, Lord Chesterfield, King George II, and King George IV. Twenty of the first 32 occupants of the White House snored, the most bombastic of whom was Theodore Roosevelt. Once, while in the hospital, he managed to keep awake nearly all the patients in one wing with his stentorian sonority.

The authority for this list of famous snorers is Dr. Marcus H. Boulware, a professor of speech pathology at Florida A. & M. University, who made snore research his life's work after his own nocturnal vibes led to the breakup of his first marriage. Scientists like Dr. Boulware have identified the basic cause of snoring, describing it as "an obstruction to the flow of air through the nose and mouth . . . when muscles at the back of the mouth (the velum, or soft palate, and the uvula) . . . relax and vibrate as air passes in and out."

This discovery, however, has not helped researchers find an effective cure. Boulware, for example, whose work has been supported by the Carnegie Foun-

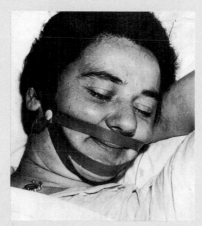
Muzzled: an antisnoring device

dation, has collected drawings and descriptions of some of the more than 300 antisnoring devices that have been registered at the U.S. Patent Office. Many are variations on a supportive theme—chin straps or other devices—intended to keep a sleeper's mouth closed. Others, more elaborate, are designed to prevent the snore-prone sleeper from as-

Fuzzled: tried snore inducers

suming the danger position: flopping over on his back. Unfortunately, their aggregate effect has been to demonstrate that it is quite possible to snore with one's mouth shut or while lying on one's side. At one time Boulware thought that he had his problem solved. "I've been working on my position for two years," he told an interviewer. "I prop my forearm under my chin. You do it for hours and hours, and after a while the subconscious mind takes over." Eventually, however, he conceded defeat: "You might say I've relapsed . . . I don't worry about it anymore."

Other treatments for which success has been claimed are considerably more drastic, ranging from surgery to the use of nasal tubes to autosuggestion and even to the elimination of salt from the diet—on the ground that salt retains fluids that swell the nasal passages. There is an ultimate, if fundamentally evasive, solution: earplugs for one's bedmate.

Throughout the literature on snoring, writers have almost always made the chivalric assumption that men were more likely to be snorers than women. Indeed, one legend has it that snoring originated as an attempt by primitive man to protect his mate from beasts of prey, his sounds being more terrifying than theirs, it is presumed. However pleasant a theory about such connubial concern may be, there is no proof that women snore less than men. In fact, Boulware says, children of both sexes snore, too. Individuals of both sexes among breeds of cats, dogs, and other animals also snore. Horses, he notes, can snore standing up or lying down.

which he claimed that sleep positions revealed the innermost secrets of the human psyche. The "royal" position—on the back, arms at sides, feet slightly apart—indicates security, self-confidence, and strength of personality. The "chain-gang" position—on a side, knees apart, and ankles crossed—reveals anxiety and the inability to enter into meaningful relationships. The prone position betokens a compulsion to overorganize one's daily life. The "water-wings" position—on the back, arms bent, and head resting on palms of hands—characterizes people who hide behind their intellectual powers. One of the most common, the "full fetal" position—on a side and tightly curled up or around a pillow—reveals a strong desire for protection and a central core around which to organize one's life. Or, possibly, a mild stomachache.

In a more scientific manner, researchers have demonstrated that sleep is far from the simple, restful activity it was previously thought to be. With the aid of devices such as the electroencephalograph, which measures brain-wave activity, they have shown that a sleeper passes through several distinct cerebral states during the night. The most unusual of them is accompanied by darting eye movements that occur—and can be detected—behind closed eyelids. This is called REM, for "rapid eye movement," and is marked by other bodily changes: brain temperature and blood-flow rise; sleepers suddenly stop tossing and turning; snoring ends and breathing becomes irregular, sometimes even halting completely for several seconds; the large muscles of the arms, legs, and trunk become rigid; and the muscles of the middle ear contract, as if the better to catch sounds. Periods of REM sleep occur regularly

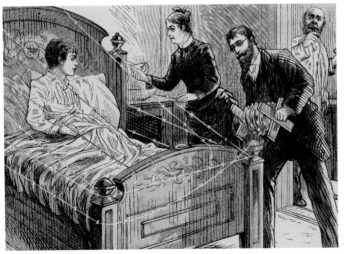

A hosteler patented this anti-somnambulism device; history does not say whether there were any takers.

from four to six times a night, at intervals of about 90 minutes and lasting from 10 minutes to an hour each. Almost invariably they are accompanied by dreams, many of them in color.

As much as the meaning of sleep itself, the significance of dreams has puzzled and intrigued men for thousands of years. The 4,000-year-old Chester Beatty Papyrus in the British Museum provides explicit guidance in interpretation: a dream

As likely as any: "Dream" by Suares

about the moon was thought to be good, while a dream about distant crowds meant impending death. Socrates believed that dreams were the voice of conscience. The Iroquois looked on them as commands to be followed. Voltaire dismissed them as a manifestation of overeating. Sigmund Freud saw dreams as the expression of repressed thoughts and therefore "the royal road to the unconscious." How best to interpret dreams, however, is still a matter of considerable debate among students of the brain's nocturnal meanderings.

What seems clear is that human beings need to dream. Laboratory subjects deprived of dreams—by the simple expedient of drugs that eliminate periods of REM sleep—quickly developed the classic symptoms of paranoia. When permitted to sleep again without drugs, all of them went on a "dream binge" of nearly pure REM sleep.

For some people, dreams serve a practical purpose as well. Robert Louis Stevenson quite literally "dreamed up" the plots of many of his stories, including *Dr. Jekyll and Mr. Hyde*. The golfer Jack Nicklaus reported that once, while in a slump, he dreamed about a new way of gripping his club, tried it, and improved his game. Many of us, however, are not that fortunate. For though we spend some five years of our life dreaming—about two hours a night—we tend in general to sleep through most of them.

SLEEPING PILL It is difficult to find anyone save drug companies who has anything very good to say about sleeping pills. Yet people continue to gobble them down at an astounding rate. In a typical year, for example, more than 40 million prescriptions, nearly half of which call for barbiturates, are written by doctors in the United

States alone. In addition, the U.S. Food and Drug Administration estimates that an equal number of barbiturate pills are sold illegally. On an international basis, sleeping pills and tranquilizers are the largest single group of prescription drugs sold.

One might suppose that the reason for the excessive popularity of sleeping pills is that they work. There is evidence that the exact opposite is probably true. Dr. Anthony Kales of the Sleep Research and Treatment Center at Pennsylvania State University compared the sleeping patterns of 20 insomniacs, of whom half were long-term users of sleeping pills and half were taking no medication at all. Observing both groups for several nights, he found that those who were taking pills slept as poorly as, or worse than, those who were not.

What happens is that regular pill-users often develop a dependence on, and then a tolerance for, the drug. As a result the pills not only do not convey them gently and soothingly into the arms of Morpheus, the Greek god of dreams, but cessation of medication often produces jitteriness, nervousness, and an inability to fall asleep—a condition that physicians call "drug-withdrawal insomnia."

It has been estimated that for every person addicted to heroin or other "hard" drugs, a dozen more are addicted to barbiturates, which include some types of sleeping pills. But since barbiturates, unlike heroin, are legal, one might suppose that the answer would be to increase dosage. The problem with this is that there is a very real limit to the amount of sleeping drugs the human body can tolerate at one time. Sadly enough, America's suicide statistics bear painful witness to this: one half of all suicides involve an overdose of sleeping pills.

In addition to the scores of sleeping preparations that can be dispensed only by prescription, there are a number of "sleep aid" products available on an over-the-counter basis. In general, they contain one of two drugs or both in combination: methapyrilene and scopolamine. Methapyrilene is an antihistamine originally developed for the treatment of allergies. One of its side effects is to cause drowsiness. Its other side effects include dizziness, lack of coordination, blurred vision, nervousness, anorexia (loss of appetite), frequent urination, and skin rashes. Scopolamine, which is derived from belladonna, is used under medical control to produce the state known as "twilight sleep." Most over-the-counter pills, however, lack enough scopolamine to have a significant effect of any kind, though excessive or prolonged use can produce outbursts of uncontrolled behavior.

Another chemical, according to preliminary

The makers of this inaptly named sleeping potion stated that two bottles had permanently cured insomnia.

studies, can also reduce the length of time it takes to fall asleep and even prolong total sleep time. It is called L-tryptophan, and thus far no prescription is needed to purchase it. In fact, since L-tryptophan is an amino acid and occurs naturally in certain foods, the chances are that there is some around the house. A very good source is milk—as in a warm glassful taken at bedtime.

SNEEZE Although the expression "not to be sneezed at" implies that people take sneezing lightly, this explosive act—a totally involuntary reflex of nerves and muscles—has long fascinated and frightened mankind. And even today it is not totally understood, though researchers have learned that the sneeze is surprisingly powerful, capable of launching infectious particles at speeds up to 50 miles per hour.

The ancient Arabs believed that Allah created the universe with a sneeze, while the Greeks held that Prometheus invented this most explosive of snorts. Some people considered sneezing to be a sign of God's favor, of luck, or even of sanity. The Romans thought that sneezing while making a decision would ensure the correct choice. In the 17th century Europeans took sneezing as a sign of good health rather than of impending infection,

Sneeze expels droplets at 100 feet per second.

319

Alone in a Crowd

The Lord Chancellor in Gilbert and Sullivan's *Iolanthe* described the plight of the insomniac with these restless words:

When you're lying awake
   with a dismal headache,
   and repose is taboo'd by
   anxiety,
I conceive you may use any
   language you choose to
   indulge in, without im-
   propriety. . . .
Well, you get some repose in
   the form of a doze,
   with hot eye-balls and
   head ever aching,
But your slumbering teems
   with such horrible dreams
   that you'd very much better be waking.

Unfortunately, it will provide little relief for most insomniacs to learn that they are not alone. Some 45 million Americans regularly suffer from the inability to sleep, and nearly three times that many have occasional problems getting a good night's sleep. Indeed, physicians report that insomnia is one of the most frequently cited medical complaints they hear.

One problem is that scientists, who have split the atom and rocketed a man to the moon, are still a long way from knowing what sleep is and how people can best attain it. In fact, they cannot even agree on the merits of the oldest of soporific bromides: counting sheep. Two Harvard psychologists, for example, reported on the pro side that counting sheep prevents the brain's right hemisphere, which controls mental imagery, from processing anxiety-provoking concepts while the left hemisphere, which controls rational thought, is kept busy counting. But another expert says emphatically: "Do not count sheep. Mechanical efforts require concentration, which is bad. . . . Let your mind wander to a relaxing scene, say a tranquil seascape."

Faced with the challenging task of imagining, but not becoming overly involved with, a distant beach and gently lapping waves, the incipient insomniac may seek mechanical assistance. For example, those who find noise distracting can install a Window Noise Repeller for $198, designed to screen out external noise with a specially built maze, or order a custom-made sound-proof bed for $1,500.

If, on the other hand, silence is the problem, a selection of records called Environments, at $6.98 each, will provide up to an hour of soothing vaguely outdoorsy sounds. For as little as $29.95, one can have a whole night of "white sound," which has been described as "a cross between an overworked air conditioner and a television set on the fritz." Failing that, there is a Japanese sleep-inducing pillow equipped with a tiny electronic device that produces a monotonous sound like that of raindrops.

Norman Dine made a career out of selling equipment to insomniacs. He once designed an "Ocean Bed," which consisted of an expensive fiberglass bathtub in which the sleeper floated in 100° F water made even more supportive by the addition of 25 pounds of salt. Dine also created a bed containing a massage unit, a device that generated lulling sounds, a source of tranquillizing ultraviolet radiation, a record that spoke soothing words, and mechanisms for regulating the

A Roman's wealth robs him of sleep.

temperature and position of the sleeper. If the problem of manning the controls kept the bed's occupant awake, he could until recently dial a New York number and be told, in a voice that was gentle without being sultry: "Hello, there, this is your Lullaby Lady. I'm so sorry you can't sleep. . . ."

In ancient Rome, some upper-class insomniacs would curl up in adult-size cradles and be rocked to sleep by yawning slaves, who perforce had sleeping problems of their own. Modern research has uncovered a housewife in Virginia who can only fall asleep to the hum of her hair dryer, and a man in San Francisco who, when unable to sleep, paints his face white and lies down in a coffin.

If these methods seem unappealing, as they undoubtedly will for most, the insomniac still has a number of options. He can, for instance, persuade himself that he is not suffering from insomnia after all. Most people, especially as they get older, simply do not need 8 hours of sleep a night. In addition, a study of 122 self-described insomniacs showed that most overestimated the time it took them to fall asleep and underestimated their total sleep time. They were suffering not so much from a lack of sleep as from anxiety about the sleep they thought they were losing.

Finally, there is this thought from authors Mary Eden and Richard Carrington, who point out that excessive brain activity—worry, fear, anxiety—is often the cause of insomnia: "Many of us have an entirely disproportionate sense of our own importance. . . ." They add, "When we reflect that life has existed on the earth for nearly two thousand million years, and even the longest-lived individual can scarcely expect to last for more than a century, we shall begin to appreciate the futility of magnifying any personal problem to the point where it can deprive us of sleep."

and hospital officials discharged patients who sneezed three times—a sure sign of recovery, they believed.

Most cultures, however, have associated the sneeze with malevolence, ranging from simple sickness to bad omens and even the breeze from Satan's wings. As a result, many have followed it with a benediction. The Hebrews held that the sneeze occurred at the moment in life closest to death, and responded with a prayer. They also claimed that when Eve offered Adam the fatal fruit, his response was immediate and precipitous: he sneezed for the first time and foresaw his own death. During plague periods the Romans perceived the sneeze as a dangerous symptom and quickly said, "Jupiter preserve you." Pope Gregory the Great reportedly originated the phrase "God bless you" for use during a particularly deadly 6th-century epidemic.

To the Hindus, sneezing represented the escape of evil spirits from the mouth. While bystanders quickly said "Live," the afflicted person evoked a blessing and snapped his fingers to prevent the unleashed demons from leaping down somebody else's throat.

Modern germ theory supports such Hindu concern, since sneezing does spread colds and other respiratory infections. Researchers, however, cannot always explain why certain people sneeze more than others. Sneezing can be a symptom of illness or a protective reflex designed to expel irritants such as pepper. Allergens, including pollen, fruit, or, in some cases, tomato soup, can also trigger the response. Some people actually sneeze at money (because of the ink and paper used), while others sneeze in response to bright light, cold, fear, anxiety, and even sex.

Tranquilizers, massage, surgery, and psychological counseling have all been used to treat prolonged or violent sneezing. However, none of these methods worked for June Clark, a Miami teenager who sneezed for 155 days, the longest siege on record. Doctors finally used mild electric shocks to help her, administering them after each spasm. And stop she did, helped by the same technique that people have been using for years to avoid the sneezes of others—aversion therapy.

SOAP "Soap has become a measure of the prosperity and culture of peoples. In any comparison . . . the richer and more cultured [people] will be that which uses more soap." So wrote the great German chemist Justus von Liebig in 1844.

From the vantage of human history, however, the notion of soap and personal cleanliness as bulwarks of civilization has been a sometime thing—

The Nostril Tickler

What do Catherine de Medici, Winston Churchill, and Babe Ruth have in common? Though the bond may be thin, and for some unattractive, they all tickled their nostrils with snuff, a form of powdered tobacco that is often fermented and scented—attar of rose, mint, musk, brandy, coffee have been popular. Sniffed in through the nose, snuff promotes sneezing, though connoisseurs frown on giving in to such primal explosiveness and say a deeper, more contained, quiver brings greater pleasure.

Cortés discovered snuff at the court of Montezuma and, along with other explorers of the New World, introduced it to Europe in the 16th century. Louis XIII of France advocated snuff over smoking, an attitude some medical specialists share, because snuff does not involve smoke inhalation and actually has less nicotine than cigarette tobacco. Some leaders, however, tried to suppress its use but were unsuccessful. Pope Urban VIII threatened in 1624 to excommunicate snuff takers. The czar of Russia in 1634 cut even more drastically at the nub of the problem, ordering that the noses of snuff users be amputated.

Snuffing rather than puffing enjoyed a heyday in the 18th century (when schools rife with pinching technique and etiquette flourished). Napoleon was a heavy sniffer, consuming four ounces or more a day (three a week is considered about average), despite unregal paroxysms of choking.

Snuff boxes were *de rigueur* in the 18th century and indicators of personal prestige as well. Some resembled fans, animal heads, pistols (for up-the-nose shots). The mistress of Louis XV had a different snuff box for each day of the year, though Frederick the Great outdid her with his private collection of some 1,500 boxes.

Today an estimated 6 million Americans dip and sniff "cowboy candy," as some call it. Joe Namath and Tom Seaver are snuff supporters, as are a number of other athletes. Outdoorsmen, factory workers, and students often carry their snuff, packed in flat round tins, in the hip pockets of their jeans, and the resulting faded circle has become something of a modern macho symbol.

highly prized in some eras and looked on with suspicion and even distaste in others. The Greeks and early Romans, for example, managed to get along quite well without soap. When they bathed, they scraped their skin with a knifelike instrument called a strigil. As for laundering, the Romans washed their togas in lye, steeped them in a brew of putrid urine, trod them underfoot for a bit, then rinsed them in plain water as a final touch. The urine provided not only a certain bleaching action but supposedly imparted to clothing some deterrent to gout. (The city's professional laundrymen came up with the clever idea of erecting public urinals to assure a steady, free supply of the washday miracle.)

Various other cleansers, including the lathering juices of certain saponaceous plants like soapwort, also were used, but it was not until the 1st century A.D. that soap was mentioned in written documents. The Romans were introduced to the niceties of real soap—a mixture of tallow (animal fats) and wood ashes (potash)—by the barbarian Gauls. The Gauls used it to keep their hair shiny, but the Romans noted that it had medicinal value in curing "scrofulous sores."

Soap slipped from favor again during the aptly named Dark Ages. Despite a marked rise in disease, it was widely held that filthiness was next to godliness, a practical means of mortifying the flesh. But beginning around the 10th century, soap began to make a comeback, particularly for personal bathing, among the wealthy classes. It has been gaining favor ever since.

Professional soapmakers, who were usually the same people who made candles, since both processes involved the rendering of fats and oils, began to appear in urban centers in the Middle Ages. But they produced a crude and harsh product until the second quarter of the 19th century.

Working themselves into a lather: an unknown French artist depicted the hard task of making soap at home.

Then, within a short time, large-scale soap manufacturing became one of the most competitive and fastest-growing industries both in England and America, with many kinds of soaps produced for many sorts of tasks. The first individually wrapped, standardized cakes of soap were manufactured in Newburgh, New York, about 1830. Weighing a pound each, they replaced hunks of soap that formerly were cut to order in the shop. Packaged soap powder came along 15 years later. Procter & Gamble's "floating" white soap was created by accident in 1878. It was given the inspired name "Ivory" when young Harley Procter heard his minister intone the words of Psalm 45: "All thy garments smell of myrrh, and aloes, and cassia, out of the ivory palaces, whereby they have made thee glad."

Almost from the start, soap-industry growth went hand in hand with that of the new advertising industry. Lever Brothers' Lifebuoy soap, for example, was transformed over several decades of provocative advertising from an antiseptic kept in the medicine cabinet, to a "health soap" to protect users during the influenza epidemic of 1918, to a battler against the dread "B.O." This catchy term for body odor became a part of the language almost immediately, and sales of the product quadrupled within a decade.

Soap has also given us such phrases as "soft soap" to describe unctuous words; the "Soap Box Derby" to denote a racing event for motorless cars originally made from wooden soap boxes; and the still-thriving "soap opera," which traditionally has promoted soap products to the accompaniment of long-running radio and television melodramas.

Today household soap and detergent sales in the United States exceed $2.2 billion a year and

Lather up: detergent pollution reached a high-water mark when foam bubbled onto the Appian Way in 1971.

average out to some 59.5 pounds of soap per capita. Some soaps are close relatives of the natural soaps of old, but many are of the synthetic detergent variety introduced in the 1930's. Synthetics generally have proved better cleansers because they work in hard (high mineral content) water as well as soft water. Conventional soaps react with calcium and magnesium salts to form bathtub rings and other scummy deposits. But detergents have also engendered massive problems in the environment. The first synthetics proved to be non-biodegradable; that is, their bubbles could not be destroyed by sewage systems, and therefore they went down the drain to create mountains of foam in rivers, lakes, and water-supply sources. More recently, the addition of other chemicals to break down detergents has created still other hazards. Perhaps the child who resisted washing hands "because they'll only get dirty again" and the Roman who was satisfied with strigil scraping were not that far from the mark after all.

SOUVENIR When it was announced that the luxury liner *Queen Mary* would be converted into a floating convention center, a Los Angeles entrepreneur figured that some people would probably like souvenirs from the doughty old ship. He arranged to buy nearly 70 tons of bits and pieces from the salvage company hired to strip the vessel. To his delight he found thousands of purchasers eager to pay $8.50 for a faucet, $3.50 for an engine-room bolt made into a paperweight, and $40 for a chamber pot converted to a planter. In all, he walked away with well over $1,000,000 on an investment of about $20,000.

Similarly, as the Metropolitan Opera company prepared to move to new quarters in Lincoln Center in New York City, opera lovers rushed to buy pieces of the old hall, including auditorium seats. To please the greatest number of souvenir hunters, the Met arranged to have its mammoth gold curtain cut into some 50,000 three-inch squares, which were then distributed to purchasers of a commemorative record album.

Even before returning Crusaders brought back

Something to remember me by: 19th-century English sailors gave "rolling pins" to fiancées before parting.

enough pieces of the "true cross" to erect a small village, travelers enjoyed collecting souvenirs of the places they visited. Today the fulfillment of this desire is a thriving business. The variety of wares that manufacturers and wholesalers offer is a tribute to man's ingenuity and greed—from plastic salt and pepper shakers shaped like animal heads to decorated plaques with witty sayings, such as "A wise monkey never monkeys with another monkey's monkey." Many manufacturers of spoons, dishes, key rings, ashtrays, and the like intentionally leave a blank space on their product so that wholesalers can suitably inscribe it. They have also learned to move fast: within 10 minutes after *Apollo 11* splashed down in the Pacific on its way home from the moon, Esso dealers in Italy were giving out Apollo shoulder patches with every purchase of gasoline; and the astronauts were still two days from the earth when a recording of the lunar landing was already landing on supermarket shelves.

Among the most prized of souvenirs are personal memorabilia, ranging from the sublime to the ridiculous. King Louis IX of France redeemed what was said to be the original Crown of Thorns (which the emperor of Constantinople had pledged to the Venetians as collateral for a loan) and purchased part of the true Cross and other relics. The king was so pleased that he decided to have a suitable shrine built to house the collection. In only 33 months, and at less than half the price Louis had paid for the relics, his workmen created Sainte-Chapelle, one of the glories of Gothic architecture in Paris.

At the other end of the scale, the story goes that Henry Ford, a friend and admirer of Thomas Edison, paid a small fortune for a sealed vial said to contain Edison's last breath. Spokesmen for the Ford Museum in Greenfield Village, Michigan, denied it, but they confirmed that Ford did buy Edison's gold teeth some 10 years after the inventor's death.

Because some souvenirs are not for sale, collectors have been known to take direct action. When, a few days after Gerald Ford became president, the town fathers of San Clemente, California, decided to take down the signs that described their city as "the home of the Western White House," they discovered that souvenir hunters had beaten them to every single one. And authorities in England's Sherwood Forest sadly report that the 1,400-year-old oak tree in which Robin Hood reputedly once sought refuge from the sheriff of Nottingham has been all but hacked to pieces by souvenir-hungry visitors.

Whether the removal of any portable item from a restaurant or a hotel constitutes souvenir hunting or something else is a question for patrons' consciences. Industry spokesmen, not wishing to plant the idea in people's minds, are reluctant to discuss the problem, but sources have estimated the "take" in the United States to be more than $500 million dollars a year. Much of it is in small pieces of tableware, which is why most restaurants do not set out butter knives or oyster forks. (Some of the finest hotels in the world, such as the Ritz in Paris, cut their losses by providing guests with cheap, simply marked ashtrays.) Occasionally, however, customers show evidence of downright enterprise. A restaurateur in San Francisco watched with mounting admiration as three lady diners expertly took apart a 12-inch-high silver table lamp and deposited the parts in their purses. When he delivered the check, he attached a second one for $100 for the lamp. They put the pieces back and left in a huff.

SPICE Saint Matthew's account of the gifts of the Wise Men—gold and two aromatic gum resins, frankincense and myrrh—is one of the most familiar passages in the New Testament. Spices are also mentioned frequently in the Old Testament. Indeed, the Garden of Eden is described as containing bdellium, another fragrant resin, obtained from a shrublike tree. In Genesis, Joseph's envious brothers sell him to a passing caravan of Ishmaelite spice merchants. The formula given to Moses for the oil to be used in anointing the tabernacle calls for cinnamon, cassia, and sweet calamus. The Queen of Sheba, when she visits Solomon, brings with her "camels that bare spices, and very much gold, and precious stones." And Muhammad, the prophet of another great religion, married a wealthy widow whose business was trading in spices.

In Elizabethan times, when pepper was sold by the individual grain, guards on the London docks had their pockets sewn up to ensure that they did not pinch spices. And in 1770 the French smuggled enough cinnamon, nutmeg, and clove plants from Dutch plantations in the East Indies to start their own spice-growing industry.

Today, too, when spices are available everywhere and even the rankest of novice chefs dispenses such exotica as coriander, cardamom, and turmeric, one spice remains that is nearly worth its weight in gold—saffron. For it takes about 14,000 dried stigmas—the female organ of the flower of the *Crocus sativus*—to make a single ounce of saffron. Fortunately for those who enjoy the spice's agreeable flavor and aroma, a tiny amount goes a long way, and it has not been necessary in recent years—as it was in Bavaria in

The Building Bread

Carpenter's gothic, a trim often called "gingerbread"

Not only is gingerbread probably the oldest of all sweet cakes, dating from a recipe that is now more than 4,700 years old, but it has long been associated with good times and festivities. Parents and children, for example, have been building and decorating gingerbread houses for centuries, though few have rivaled the one that was presented to Peter the Great, czar of all the Russias, when he was born. The gift was a faithful representation of the Kremlin, with every turret duplicated, and the outer wall was surrounded by squads of mounted soldiers.

Fancy gingerbread shapes, known variously as *pain d'épices, Lebkuchen,* or *panforte,* depending on where they are baked, originated in the great fairs of medieval Europe, which included stalls filled with fragrant gingerbread creations. Gingerbread cakes, decorated with gold leaf, were the reward that ladies of the court often bestowed on victorious tournament champions.

In England, gingerbread existed before the Norman Conquest. Both Chaucer and Shakespeare mentioned the artful cake in their works. Queen Elizabeth I was particularly fond of it, and her father, Henry VIII, swore by ginger as a remedy for the plague.

In this, Henry may have been influenced by the teachings of the Greek physician Dioscorides of the 1st century A.D., who in his *De Materia Medica* described ginger's warming effect on the stomach and its efficacy as an antidote to poisons. Indeed, for centuries ginger continued to appear in various medical and pharmacological formularies.

The inhabitants of the island of Rhodes, however, enshrined ginger in its ultimate gustatory niche. About 2800 B.C. they became famous in the Mediterranean area for the golden cakes they fashioned of flour, honey, and ginger. Even then, the taste and smell of the spice were its most beguiling characteristics. They still are today.

1444—to burn alive any merchant caught selling adulterated saffron.

Spices are by definition the aromatic parts of plants—bark, leaves, seeds, stamens, shells—that usually grow in the tropics. (Herbs, by contrast, are the leaves of temperate-zone plants.) To justify the exorbitant prices of spices—and to help discourage competition—early traders concocted lurid stories about the sources of their wares. According to one, as reported by the Greek historian Herodotus, cinnamon (which comes from the inner bark of various trees of the laurel family) was normally found in the nests of large birds on "mountain precipices which no man can climb." To get at it, hunters would set out great chunks of freshly killed meat. "They then retire to a safe distance and the birds fly down and carry off the joints of meat to their nests, which, not being strong enough to bear the weight, break off and fall to the ground. Then the men come along and pick up the cinnamon." At a quick trot, it is presumed, though Herodotus did not specify. Whether the story was believed or not, the price of cinnamon remained so high that when Nero wished to display his overwhelming grief at the death of Poppaea, his second wife, he ordered a year's supply of Rome's cinnamon to be burned at her funeral.

There seem to be strong affinities, occasionally odd ones, between geographic regions and spices. The Scandinavians, for instance, have been inordinately fond of cardamom ever since a Viking captain returned from Constantinople with a sample more than 1,000 years ago. The smell of cardamom fairly fills the streets of Oslo at Christmastime, and in Sweden its consumption per capita is 50 times that in the United States. When Cortés and his conquistadores arrived in Mexico in 1519, they discovered not only gold but also a delicious drink the native Aztecs called *chocolatl*. It consisted of powdered cacao beans and ground corn flavored with bits of the pods of a plant they called *tlixochitl*. Introduced into Europe, the drink became an instant success. One writer even noted that Spanish ladies were not content to drink several cups of it at home daily but insisted that the drink be served in church. The name of the drink has remained basically the same, but the other ingredient, *tlixochitl*, was barely pronounceable in European tongues, so the Spaniards renamed it—*vainilla*.

Vanilla, said to be the world's most popular flavor, has the additional distinction of being the Western Hemisphere's major contribution to world spicedom. A latecomer to the trade, the United States has nonetheless managed to make one heady contribution. Accounts differ as to the date of discovery, but it was certainly in Texas that an inquisitive chef found a way to extract the pulp of various ground peppers, add certain ingredients of his own choosing, and set the world on fire—with chili powder.

SPONGE Sponges have been harvested from the warm waters of the Mediterranean since the beginning of civilization, and used much as we use them today. Greeks and Romans scrubbed their houses with sponges; they whitewashed walls, cleaned floors, and padded their armor with them. Babies sucked on honey-soaked sponges. And when cups were in short supply, Roman soldiers dipped sponges into the common wine bowl and drank by squeezing the liquid into their mouths. The Bible tells that a Roman soldier comforted Christ on the cross with a sponge dipped in vinegar.

Prior to the 19th century, almost everyone thought that the sponge was a plant; hardly anyone realized that this exceptionally absorbent household item is really the skeleton of an animal. Dropouts from evolution, sponges have survived millions of years virtually unchanged. The most primitive of the multicellular animals, sponges have neither heart, lungs, nor brain. Though some grow to six feet, they are actually a cluster of cells so simple that biologists had to create a new subkingdom between the Metazoa and the Protozoa to accommodate them taxonomically.

Fish swim around a sponge tube, one of nearly 5,000 sponge species.

Most sponges taste and smell so bad that only a few fish will nibble on them. If smashed to bits, pieces of sponge will float away and regenerate in new locations. Scientists have tried to separate sponge cells by pressing them through cloth, only to watch them stubbornly regroup and form new sponges. Such cells can reproduce either sexually or asexually by a variety of means. Some are male, some female, some neither, and some both—true hermaphrodites producing sperm and egg in the same organism.

Sponges are at home in water—salt or fresh, cold or warm. Vivid colors and shapes characterize tropical sponges. Though many grow in such shallow spots that they can be hooked from an open boat, sponges have also been dredged up from a depth of 1,800 feet. Some deepwater sponges are pure white. Of the nearly 5,000 species known, only about 12 are commercially valuable.

The only sponges that get around at all owe their mobility to crabs, who use them for camouflage. One crab decorates its shell with a bit of sponge, which grows there. This sponge "suit" enables the crab to scuttle about protected from predators. A hermit crab that moves into an abandoned shell may also wake up one morning to find itself living in a sponge. The transformation occurs when a species of sponge encrusts and eventually dissolves the shell without disturbing the crab inside.

Other sea creatures use sponges as convenient—if deadly—condominiums. Into the delicate Venus'-flower-basket sponge, two tiny shrimps move; they become imprisoned in the sponge and die there. The glasslike skeleton of this sponge, with the two shrimps still inside, is a traditional Japanese wedding gift, symbolizing the marriage bond.

Today the popularity of synthetic sponges has vastly reduced sponge-fishing industries from the Dodecanese Islands of the Aegean Sea to Tarpon Springs, Florida. The sight of a brightly painted sponge vessel returning to port stinking of gurry and festooned with garlands of drying sponges is rare indeed.

But sponges may hold beneficial secrets for man. In the Middle Ages the ashes of burned sponges were used as medicine. The custom was not born entirely of superstition, for scientists have long noted that certain sponges are remarkably resistant to bacteria. One investigator kept a sponge in water for five years before it even began to break down. Today, numerous antibiotic substances are extracted from sponges, one of them used in the battle against leukemia.

STAPLER Staplers today play a vital role not only in putting a crimp in office paper blizzards but also in factories, homes, and increasingly in operating rooms. In the 19th century, however, users often cursed the clumsy cast-iron machines, which had to be loaded with individual staples. Later, staplers were built to accommodate a strip of 25 staples at a time, but to work such a device the user had to whack the contraption with a mallet. Finally, in the early 1900's, lever-action staplers solved the delivery problem—and the staple boom was on.

Today, powerful pneumatic staple guns quickly and efficiently perform many of the jobs that formerly required application of hammer and nails:

making furniture, mending fences, even assembling houses, sailboats, and cars. In addition, homeowners now use staplers to fasten upholstery, tack up curtains, assemble and affix screens, and erect room dividers. Artists staple canvases to frames, fishermen stake out their fish for cleaning with staples, and housewives clamp refrigerator bags with staples.

Surgical staplers, devised in 1922 by a Hungarian physician, improved in the 1950's by Russian scientists, and perfected in the 1960's by Americans, are being used more widely, for they reduce suture time and thus lessen surgical risk and speed recovery. Stainless-steel medical staples are also less likely to cause infection than silky gut, and their shape, in the form of the letter B, allows blood to continue to flow through tissue.

Dieters have used staples as substitutes for self-discipline, both internally and externally. In extreme cases of obesity, for example, surgeons sometimes close off the top of the stomach with staples, leaving naught but a small hole for food. The stomach hurts if the patient overeats. Some, on the other hand, prefer "staple puncture," the placing of a staple in the ear in the hope that it will defuse hunger pangs. Based on the acupuncturist theory that every region in the body has a sensitivity point in the ear, the method requires dieters to wiggle the staple instead of their mouths when the urge to eat arises.

STEEL Steel is not a specific metal but any of several different alloys of iron and carbon, usually with other elements mixed in. Although the word comes from the Teutonic *stah* or *stag,* meaning "firm" and "rigid," one form of steel is so soft that it can be bent by hand, whereas another is so hard that only a diamond can scratch it. Massive steel frameworks support skyscrapers, while delicate strands one-fiftieth the diameter of human hair are woven into space suits and static-free hospital gowns.

Almost everything we use or consume involves steel. A shoe may contain 62 pieces of the metal, and an average car over 100 different kinds of steel. The political and economic life of this country revolves to a great extent around the production and use of steel, on which, it is estimated, 40 percent of all industrial jobs rely.

Indians in Asia made steel as early as 1000 B.C., and Japanese master craftsmen fashioned swords of steel from the 13th century on. These were remarkable weapons, at once flexible, hard, and razor-sharp, composed of 30,000 steel layers. As a final step, the sword was coated with clay to different thicknesses, heated, and cooled in water so

Steely-eyed: this man's clothing protects him from the blasting heat.

that the many layers within this huge "sandwich" achieved different properties.

Because of the difficulty of and cost involved in creating it, steel was not widely used until Sir Henry Bessemer in the 1850's perfected the process of forcing air through molten iron to incinerate its impurities and make a more malleable metal. The Bessemer furnace might have been called the Kelly converter, for it was first invented by an American, William Kelly, whose "fireworks" were of such a revolutionary nature that he was nicknamed "Crazy Kelly."

The Bessemer or Kelly converter produced in about 15 minutes small quantities of steel from pig iron—iron ore that had been combined with limestone and coke in a blast furnace to extract the molten iron. (This was poured into a rectangular sand trough surrounded by smaller molds, an arrangement that reminded steelworkers of a sow with her litter.)

The open-hearth furnace, developed after the Civil War, eventually made vast quantities of steel and was capable of using scrap iron, though it took 10 to 12 hours to do the job. Not surprisingly, use of the Bessemer declined, while the open-hearth furnace became increasingly popular. By the 1880's steel had supplanted iron rails for the country's railroads and triggered an economic revolution. The booming demand for steel plows, farm tools, and oil and mining machinery, as well as for bridges and other kinds of construction, made America the largest steel-producing nation in the world by 1886, with an annual output of 2.9 million tons.

This was the time of the great steel barons: Andrew Carnegie, the immigrant bobbin boy who forged an empire of iron deposits, coalfields, and steel mills; and J.P. Morgan, who by 1901 controlled 161 plants capable of producing more than half the nation's steel. Steel put America on wheels, not only by building the body of the Model T Ford but also by providing the drills and pipes used to tap the oil that made it possible to operate cars at a reasonable cost.

In the three decades after 1900, steel production increased nearly sixfold. World War I sparked development of armor plate for military weapons.

Advances in metallurgy resulted in new and more varied alloys, including stainless steel. World War II, in a very real sense, became a "war of alloys," for new steels were vital for building bombers with engines that could withstand temperatures as high as 1200° F and as low as 65° below zero. The Russians requested and got specific alloys essential to the arms and armor spearheading their defense of Stalingrad.

Even today the steel industry continues to make stronger and lighter alloys to meet new demands and compete with other materials, such as plastics and aluminum, and less expensive steel from abroad. Lightweight steels allow cars to burn less gas and have helped make bicycles so popular that it is estimated that nearly half the U.S. population now rides regularly. Space exploration depends on new alloys for solid-fuel rocket casings and for pumps and valves in environmental-control systems.

Beneath the seas, gigantic steel cylinders house teams of underwater scientists in pioneer communities, and steel rigs probe for offshore oil. In medicine, tiny low-alloy "seeds" are injected into blood vessels and, guided by magnets, reach otherwise inaccessible tumors, which they help to destroy. And science has finally found a way to can "draft" beer—with filters made of steel wires so fine that they trap yeast particles.

The production of steel demands the use of millions of tons of dirty materials like iron ore and scrap iron, coal, and limestone. And while the industry has made progress in meeting federal regulations for clean air and water, massive environmental problems resulting from steelmaking remain. In tomorrow's world overcoming these obstacles may constitute the greatest challenge that the steel industry has yet to face—and solve.

STEREO March king John Philip Sousa saw little good in the mechanical reproduction of music, for he thought it would bring about "a marked deterioration in American music and musical taste, an interruption in the musical development of the country, and a host of other injuries to music. . . ." Despite his several aesthetic reservations, Sousa allowed his name to appear on band records to the end of his long life.

The legends about devices that could capture

The piano with a difference is actually a stereo.

and reproduce the human voice go back at least 3,000 years to a Chinese prince who supposedly owned a magical box into which he would speak messages to a friend. When the box was delivered to the other prince, he had only to raise the lid and a message would come forth. In 1632 a sea captain reported that natives of South Sea islands spoke into sponges and then squeezed them to hear their own voices. And in the 1650's the French author Savinien Cyrano de Bergerac foretold the phonograph and the use of earphones in his story of an imagined trip to the moon.

In late 1877 Thomas Edison turned fancy into fact. The first words he recorded were "Mary had a little lamb." They were etched on tinfoil wrapped around a drum; but the foil was awkward to handle, produced poor sound reproduction, and wore out after a few playings. The substitution of a wax cylinder for the clumsy tinfoil one made possible the recorded-music industry. Edison, who

One-man band: a disc jockey relies on a complex sound system to provide dance beat at a 1970's discotheque.

was partially deaf and unsophisticated about music, thought the phonograph would be used mainly as a dictaphone and an aid in education—and perhaps as a means of recording telephone messages. He did not foresee that the record industry would be the biggest result of his invention.

Stereophonic sound is a later improvement of Edison's brainchild. Before that became possible, the industry moved from the wax cylinder to the round, flat record and then to the long-playing disc, which was introduced commercially in 1948. Stereo appeared in the 1950's. It is two-channel sound, recorded by two or more microphones and broadcast through two separate speakers to give the sound greater depth and realism. With one-track music, the sensation is similar to listening with one ear. Stereophonic sound, however, was a successful attempt to reproduce music as we hear it with both ears, as if we were present when the music was being played. The early experiments to

In the Mood—or Not

Liberace's bejeweled fingers make the kind of music recorded for people put on hold.

Nobody knows exactly why music pleases or displeases us, how it arouses emotion or sets the feet to tapping, or what would happen if there was no music at all. Most people in the Western world today feel that music exists for their own pleasure rather than as part of some ritual such as a church service. That is possible partly because records and tapes have made music available to all of us, at any time we want it.

Even when we do not want it, music is increasingly part of daily transactions. Inflicted music can be big business, as it is for Muzak, America's largest purveyor of background music. Airlines play music to customers who are waiting for a reservation clerk. Music fills our waiting time in banks, supermarkets, elevators. Music wakes us up in the morning when our clock radios turn on. And in the streets the owners of transistor radios generously provide music for all within earshot.

People have even experimented with the effects of music on plants and animals. A St. Louis seed company once piped music into cornfields just to see how the corn would react; the growers felt the results were inconclusive. And in Tolleson, Arizona, meat-packers soothed their cattle with music from a local FM station. Reportedly, the cattle preferred classical and semiclassical music to vocals, rock, and opera.

A small but affluent band of jingle writers make music for advertisers, carefully synchronizing words and notes for maximum sales effect. Such a minitune can cost the advertiser $100,000, not counting the costs of putting the message on the air. Similarly, moviemakers allocate lavish budgets for film scores in the belief that the audience's response to a story may lie as much in the music as in the talent of the actors. Says one composer and advocate of movie music: "I'd love for them to see a movie once without the music."

So complete is the electronics revolution in music that nature lovers can summon birds from the wild for close-up study using recordings of bird calls. They can appeal to any bird, even a virtuoso like the winter wren, whose song can contain 130 notes in a seven-and-a-half second aria.

get two-channel recordings and reproduction equipment into balance frustrated musicians and engineers. They got a "ping-pong" effect, with the two speakers bouncing sound back and forth between each other. During one recording session Dimitri Mitropoulos, conductor of the New York Philharmonic orchestra, complained to the engineers: "I try to make the orchestra play together—and you pull it apart!"

Until the early 1900's, record labels did not identify the artist, and recording fees were low. The breakthrough came in Milan, Italy, when engineers of the Gramophone Company asked a young tenor to make some records. He agreed but demanded a fee of $480 for the 10-song session, exorbitantly above the usual payment of $2 or $3 per song. The company made $70,000 from those 10 recordings, and Caruso went on to receive more than $2 million in royalties during his lifetime. Though excellent for his time, his earnings do not approximate those of the all-time recording champions, the Beatles and Elvis Presley.

Caruso really worked hard for his money, for in those days a recording session was also an athletic event. The singer had to jump back and forth in front of the microphone to balance the high or loud notes with the soft ones. Caruso's valet would hover nearby with changes of clothing for the sweat-drenched artist. Exertion aside, early recording artists had to try for perfection in their performances. One sour note could mean repeating long passages of music because there was no way to remove the jarring note from the master record. The advent of magnetic tape, which allows even a fraction of a note to be snipped out and the desired sound spliced in, made recording much easier for artists and engineers. Tape cassettes now represent about 30 percent of all sales of recorded music.

In the future musical reproduction on records and tapes may well become obsolete, replaced by the computer and the laser beam. A music buff might be able to buy all the works of a popular artist on a recording the size and shape of a picture slide. The musical information would be etched on film by a laser beam. In theory, such a system would permit no distortion of sound whatsoever—a far but perfectly reproduced cry from the scratchy rumbles that Edison first heard.

STEREOTYPE You can always tell the villain: he's the one in the black hat. The fat man is to be laughed at. And how about the short guy on a blind date with the tall gal? Or the mother-in-law who moves in and rearranges the furniture? Or the henpecked husband, the spaced-out hippie,

the inscrutable Oriental, the jivey black man, the wicked scientist, the icy lady executive, the dumb blonde? Or the nice, befuddled suburban lady slamming her car into the garage door?

No one, of course, thinks in stereotypes all the time. But in that great central-casting office in our heads, the messy complexities of humanity often can be straightened out by being molded in certain images. There they lurk, ready to tell us who we are seeing a split second before we see them. Without that shorthand, that economy of outline,

Stereotypical male dancer: a bit lightfooted.

reality would probably be too confusing. And whether we approve or not, stereotypes are the language of advertising and TV, the staple of humor, and they represent little shreds of personal experience. When the stereotype prevents us from judging others on the basis of reality, it becomes the stuff of prejudice.

Take, for example, short people. According to a survey conducted by the University of Pittsburgh, short people tend to get a lower starting salary than tall people. What's more, tall people earn progressively more for every inch over 6 feet. According to the stereotype, short men are cocky, stubborn, and aggressive, while their tall counterparts are competent, bold, reliable—winners. (Tall, skinny men, however, are suspected of being nervous and pessimistic.) Yet this often unconscious prejudice, dubbed "heightism" by employment experts, cannot be legally challenged as can racism because it goes undetected even by those who practice it.

A he-man hefts railway wheels weighing 250 lbs.

Equally absurd is the image of fat people as lazy, oafish, or dumb. One employer an-

Early movies relied on such stock characters as an old-maid schoolmarm, a dunce, a whimpering coed.

nounced to a personnel agent that he did not want to see anyone who was fat or from Brooklyn because, he said, "they both steal." A successful singer who has been both svelte and fat in her career reports that fat women are seen as motherly types and considered sexually unthreatening by other women, who therefore trust them. Men tend to strike up brother-sister, palsy relationships. One survey found that over 40 percent of executives in the lower salary brackets were fat, but in the upper brackets, only 9 percent were corpulent—proof, perhaps, that stereotypes can become self-fulfilling prophecies.

Everyone dreads old age, but one statistical group that defies society's stereotype is the elderly. Surveys in the United States reveal that small children see the elderly as people who are "wrinkled, crippled, chew funny, and haven't any teeth," but they also see them as "friendly and kind." In a 1974 Harris poll, adults under the dread age of 65 saw those over it as lonely, ill, poor, and beset with feelings of uselessness. Yet for the large majority of the elderly the facts prove otherwise: only a fifth reported medical problems, less than a quarter worried seriously about crime, and only 5 percent were actually in nursing homes. Older workers are equal or superior to young ones on most counts, says the U.S. Department of Labor. In London the safest bus drivers were in the 60–64 age group. Most found their lives quite as interesting as ever before. The people who expressed the greatest dissatisfaction with their lives were those under 65.

Could it be the very energy of the old that gave rise to the bitter stereotype of the dynamic mother-in-law? Consulting with Sigmund Freud on the question, we find this analysis of his own mother-in-law: "Because her charm and vitality have lasted so long, she still demands in return her full share of life—not the share of old age—and expects to be the center, the ruler, an end in herself. Every *man* who has grown old honorably wants the same, only in a woman one is not used to it." Perhaps Freud would have preferred the Zulu way, where taboos say that a man cannot look directly at his mother-in-law and may communicate with her only through a third person.

Surely some stereotypes have their roots in eternal psychological tensions or cultural traditions. But the elderly not withstanding, people become in part what is expected of them. Thus stereotypes amplify themselves in the souls of women, blacks, and even artists—all groups that have been regarded as powerless or irresponsible.

One such destructive stereotype is the black "rhythm man," who "jess always singin' 'n shufflin' along." He never existed at all, contend black sociologists, but was born of the guilty white psyche. Certainly slaves sang—it got them through the day. Certainly blacks dance, but so do Greeks and Hasidic Jews. Only decades of research and reappraisal have saved contemporary blacks from seeing a childlike reflection in that false mirror.

Women, too, have been weeding laboriously in the vineyards of prejudice. Even very young children are not immune to forming rigid conceptions about the nature of society. One little boy, for example, was shown a picture of a man giving a bottle to a baby and then asked to describe what he saw. "A mother holding a baby," he answered. "Look again," urged the interviewer. "Oh," said the boy, "it's the grandfather." Other nursery-school children built a hospital of blocks. All the female figures were placed in beds; all the male figures were actively riding elevators and driving trucks. That school decided to have another look at its curriculum.

Some stereotypes have a way of sneaking up on us. Take, for example, the story of a man and his son who were involved in a terrible automobile accident. The man was killed instantly, and the seriously injured child was rushed to the emergency room of the nearest hospital. After a horrified glance, the surgeon who was summoned to care for the boy uttered: "I can't operate on that child. He is my son!" If you do not understand that story, you may be more influenced than you think by a very common stereotype. The story is not a supernatural tale; the surgeon was a woman.

The businesswomen most often relegated to playing the traditional "wifey" role by their bosses are secretaries. The Women Office Workers of New York have met the problem humorously by publicizing annual awards for the most absurdly demeaning tasks that secretaries are asked to perform. One had to take photographs of her boss before, during, and after he shaved off his mustache. She was further instructed to pluck out every gray hair that appeared on his head. Another woman arranged regularly for a messenger service to deliver to her boss' home materials that he had stolen from the office.

But women cherish their own stereotypes. One of them is that gentlemen prefer blondes. Not so, says a survey of New York college students. Brunet men consistently rated brunette women highest, and blond men cared equally for blondes and brunettes. Least favored were bleached blondes. After reading that one might think stereotypes run differently in California—if one nurtures the "typical Californian" stereotype.

These days, few organized groups will suffer demeaning stereotypes in silence, and pressure from such organizations has made TV, advertising, and publishers of children's books sensitive to avoiding them. A few years ago, however, Nabisco ran an ad promoting a new crunchy snack that showed it being devoured by a crotchety, old fuddy-duddy librarian. (We did not say she was female; you just assumed that.) Librarians, who include young people of both sexes, were aroused. They pointed out that Mao Tse-tung, Casanova, a Miss World winner, and a Playboy "playmate" were also librarians. Their suggestion that Nabisco use Chairman Mao to represent librarians in a new ad for the product was not acted on, however.

STOCK EXCHANGE In broad terms a "stock exchange" is a place where people assemble to buy and sell securities under a prearranged set of rules. By that definition there are about 138 stock exchanges in the world—10 of them in the United States. But for the majority of Americans—to the extent that they understand securities trading at all—the stock exchange means the New York Stock Exchange, the "Big Board." It is the symbol of Wall Street and of all that street of dreams implies about ambition, power, and money.

To "make a market" is to assure buyers and sellers that they will be able to buy and sell when they wish. The group of merchants and auctioneers that met under a buttonwood tree on Wall Street in May 1792 wanted to do just that. They agreed to get together daily at regular hours to buy and sell securities, and to deal only with each other. Among the first securities they handled were stocks in the U.S. government, issued to pay the costs of the Revolutionary War. That was the birth of the New York Stock Exchange.

Differences of opinion about the value of a par-

An even trade: to end the year, Canadian floor traders and office workers bombard each other with missiles.

ticular security are what make stock exchanges tick. J.P. Morgan, one of the most awesome barons of Wall Street, summed it up briskly for a young man who asked him what stock prices were going to do. Said Morgan, "They will fluctuate," and so they have ever since the first stock exchange came into being in Amsterdam in 1611.

Today, keeping track of the price fluctuations, enabling experts to quote the latest reconciliation of supply and demand in an instant, has made the New York Stock Exchange a massive communications machine. Five hundred thousand miles of teletype and telephone wires link the floor, the open trading area, of the Exchange with brokerage houses around the United States. Under the Exchange floor, 40 miles of pressurized aluminum tubes whisk plastic message containers around the giant chamber. Even the hasty notes that floor traders make to themselves during the day amount to a ton of rubbish to be swept up at night. The latest stock ticker system spits forth

The semi-staid Stock Exchange takes on a bizarre air at this turn-of-the-century "Christmas Carnival."

Outside the home of the Big Board, the Curb Exchange acted as an open-air market for freelance brokers.

tape that details market transactions at the rate of 900 printed characters per minute.

That system is the sophisticated descendant of a ticker-tape machine invented by Edward A. Calahan in 1867. Inadvertently, he became the godfather of the ticker-tape parade, the heaviest of which was held for astronaut John Glenn on March 1, 1962, following the first American orbital spaceflight. On that day 3,474 tons of paper rained down on the celebrants. Calahan sold his patent in 1867 for $100,000, a substantial sum in those days. Yet his machine had a way of breaking down. It was the job of a young man, then living temporarily in the boiler room of the Exchange, to repair it. Eventually the young man improved the ticker's performance so much that he was awarded $40,000. His name: Thomas Edison.

For a speculator in the stock market, speed is a key factor. Bernard Baruch, adviser to presidents, answered proudly to the name of "speculator," and he liked to tell a story that underlined the need for speed. In December 1916 he watched the ticker as it printed out a speech being made before the British Parliament by Prime Minister David Lloyd George. Lloyd George began a sentence: "The Allies will fight on to victory, but. . . ." Without waiting for the end of the sentence, Baruch snapped out an order to sell 25,000 shares of U.S. Steel. To him, the "but" in Lloyd George's sentence signaled a statement about the chances of peace breaking out, which would hurt America's munitions business and hence the price of U.S. Steel. That afternoon Baruch realized a profit of $500,000 not possible the next day.

In terms of colorful chicanery, the Exchange is not at all what it used to be. A layer of regulations prevents the manipulation of stock prices, once a

Bulls and Bears

Those who trade in stocks and bonds have a rich jargon all their own. Some elements of it come from the days when security markets were unregulated jungles, rife with sharp dealing. Other words and phrases are fairly modern. But even the most strategically situated of many Wall Street insiders have no idea where the most basic terms in their business come from.

Stock: A share of ownership in a particular enterprise. In Old English *stocc* meant "tree trunk," but how the term found its way to the heart of the securities business is now obscure.

Bond: This instrument of indebtedness derives from the early English *band*, a "fastening." Thus the issuer of a bond is bound or fastened to pay back whatever money he has borrowed.

Watered Stock: Daniel Drew, a notorious stock-market manipulator, also worked in the New York cattle business. Legend has it that before he actually sold cattle, he would deprive them of water, dose them liberally with salt, then let them gulp all the water they wanted just prior to weighing them. Thus a company is said to "water its stock" when it adds shares but adds nothing to its assets. Not surprisingly, watered stock dilutes the equity of all shareholders.

Blue-Chip Stock: The blue chip is often the most valuable in a poker game. A blue-chip stock is thought to be most reliable because of the solidity of the company that issued it.

Broker: The person who buys and sells stocks for others earned his name from the Anglo-French word *brocour*, meaning a person who broached, or opened, a keg of wine—a wine salesman. Eventually, the term "broker" came to stand for any middleman who bought and sold things.

Bear Market: A declining stock market. A person who believes the market is going to fall is called a "bear," and he is said to feel "bearish." Several stories suggest how this term might have come into being. One is that a bear fights by striking downward with its paws. Another involves an old saying about "selling the skin before you've caught the bear." This aptly describes a trader who is likely to sell short—that is, to sell a stock he does not have on the chance that when he is required to deliver he can buy the stock at a lower price and make a profit.

Bull Market: A rising stock market. Bulls toss their horns upward when fighting, and people who are optimistic about the future of the market are said to be "bullish." They buy in the belief that the stocks will increase in value.

Blue Sky Law: Such laws are for the protection of gullible buyers who might otherwise try to purchase—if offered to them by artful pitchmen—the Brooklyn Bridge, the Empire State Building, or even a chunk of clear blue sky.

common practice. To "corner the market"—to own all the available shares of a company—was once a Wall Streeter's dream. Now it is virtually impossible to accomplish. But it was not in the year the New York Common Council granted a franchise to Cornelius Vanderbilt's Harlem Railway. News of the franchise made the stock jump $25 a share. Utilizing as a ploy a trading mechanism known as "selling short," the larcenous councilmen agreed to deliver, in the future, 137,000 shares of Harlem stock at a fixed price. They repealed Vanderbilt's franchise, reasoning that Harlem stock would plummet well below the price at which they had agreed to deliver the stock. They would buy at the depressed price and make a fine profit. But as is always true of a short sale, the councilmen had sold stock they did not own. And as the old Wall Street couplet has it: "He that sells what isn't his'n,/Either pays or goes to prison." When the councilmen went to market to buy the stock they had promised to sell, they found none available. It all belonged to Vanderbilt, who had foreseen their evil plan and bought up the outstanding shares of his own company. He had cornered the market and consequently placed a high value on the shares he owned. Just to help out the short-selling councilmen, he allowed them to buy some of his shares for $179 each. That cost them—and earned Vanderbilt—nearly $5 million.

STUNTS There is one on every block: the kid who swallows live worms, swings upside down from the tallest tree, or coolly plunges downhill on a weaving skateboard—making jaws drop and mothers scream. Society adores a daredevil, and no one knows it better than the performer himself, urged on by the crowd and his own defiant spirit to trickier and more bizarre feats. To be "best" at something, to do what no one has ever done before, is every youngster's dream. The few who grow up lucky or skilled enough to succeed redefine the limits of the humanly possible. They tie the word "can't" in knots—and sometimes they die trying.

For more than a century, Niagara Falls was a mecca for daredevils. The legendary Sam Patch, who had an affinity for waterfalls, leaped about 125 feet into that swirl and thunder in 1829 and bobbed up alive. "Doing Sam-Patch" swept the East: "Multitudes would rush and jam/Just to get a sight of Sam," wrote one balladeer. Some said Sam was drunk before he leaped into the Genesee falls at Rochester, New York, and his body was not found until four months later. Many refused to believe that Sam was dead. One tale reported a Sam-sighting by a Yankee whaling

captain in the South Seas, who asked Sam how on earth he got there. "Why," said Sam, "I didn't get *on earth* here at all, but I came slap *through* it. . . . I went so everlasting deep, I thought it was just as short to come up t'other side."

Far more accomplished a performer was the great French tightrope walker Blondin, who sat down to supper at a table and chair balanced on a three-inch rope stretched between the United States and Canada, high over Niagara Falls. In the summers of 1859 and 1860, Blondin went across the rope backward, he went across blindfolded, and teetered over in the dark. At other times, he carried a man on his back and made the crossing on stilts. Blondin knew his stuff: he died peacefully in bed at 72.

For a time there was a mad fad for plunging over the falls in a barrel. Only three survived the ordeal: two came through with only bumps and bruises, but the third broke his jaw and both kneecaps. After recuperating 23 weeks in the hospital, he slipped on a banana peel and was killed. Today strict laws forbid plunges over the falls. Philippe Petit, a French tightrope walker, applied for permission to do what Blondin had done. His request became so mired in red tape that after two years he gave up. For his most famous feat, however, Petit asked no one's permission. Disguised as workmen, he and some friends calmly strung a cable between the twin towers of the World Trade Center in New York. Slowly, Petit inched out over the yawning city, while office workers gaped at his tiny figure teetering 110 stories up. Petit was an instant hero: he went on to top billing with the Ringling Brothers circus.

There is something about the World Trade Center, those bold slabs on the Manhattan skyline, that tempts people. The World Trade Center "was very appealing, very *vertical*," explained George Willig, the dashing young toy designer who took a walk there, straight up. Willig simply appeared one morning in 1977 and proceeded to crawl like a fly up the side of the vast South Tower, using specially designed mountain-climbing equipment that slotted into grooves made for window-washing machines. A police helicopter hovered nearby, but Willig did not

Some everyday stuntkids become stuntmen: here one hangs on by his toes.

need it. Later he admitted that "the challenging part was designing the devices, not the climb." Willig was threatened with a $250,000 suit, but he had given humankind such a pleasing triumph over that awesome structure that the mayor ordered instead a fine of $1.10—a penny for every floor.

What drives people to attempt such a difficult or preposterous adventure alone? Admiral Peary first reached the North Pole in 1909 with five other people, but in 1978 Japanese explorer Naomi Uemura did it alone. "If you accomplish something alone, there is much more satisfaction," he once said, which may also explain why he had previously sailed a raft solo down the Amazon and taken a

At 12 Alexander the Great broke the "untamable" Bucephalus, his famous mount. This Indian miniature depicts legendary exploration of the deep in glass barrel.

7,000-mile dogsled trip across the polar ice cap from Greenland to Alaska. Said a young Norwegian who spent five winters alone on an Arctic island, "When you are all alone, totally alone, there is no one else to take credit or blame."

Solitary adventure lures women as well as men. In 1978 New Zealander Naomi Jones became the first woman to sail single-handedly around the world—by way of the great capes of the southern seas. When her 53-foot sloop nearly capsized in the South Pacific, she righted the vessel and went on. Completing the 30,000-mile voyage in 272 days, she broke the record of Sir Francis Chichester. She had learned to sail only two years earlier. "I had a good boat," she said modestly.

Another hardy New Zealander took a radio receiver, a charcoal stove for cooking, and a pair of oars and shoved off in a rowboat to row from Valparaiso, Chile, to Samoa, a distance of some 6,000 miles. He made it in 10 months. Rowing a bathtub, however, is another matter. Bearing a

tubful of friendship letters from Americans to Russians, one zany set out across the frigid Bering Strait in a 4½-foot bathtub. When he found he was bailing more than rowing, he sent the letters off in an inner tube and turned back. After such feats what is left—walking on water? Walter Robinson claims he did just that. He sloshed the 50 miles of the Panama Canal straight across Central America on inflated foot pontoons. No one dared call him unbalanced.

Now that the seas and peaks of the planet have been conquered, the poles—flagpoles, that is—still offer a test of endurance, though a somewhat immobile one. Undoubtedly, no one will better the duration records of the early Christian ascetics. Saint Simeon Stylites, for example, lived on a small platform on top of a pillar for 35 years. Depression-era endurance records have long since been broken, for today's flagpole sitters have chemical toilets, TV sets, and radios for company. One lad of 18 was offered a salary by a used-car salesman if he would stay up a pole for 400 days. He did, even though the salesman left the scene and the money stopped coming up the pole.

To set records, adventurous young folks must dream up ever-wackier feats. A Louisiana fellow wins fame by catching a grape in his mouth at a distance of 252 feet. A gal yodels nonstop for a record-breaking 6 hours, only to find that someone else had already done 7½. A precocious kid develops arthritis by hopping 80,080 times on a pogo stick. A musician drums continuously for a marathon three weeks, only to find that no one was paying attention. A fellow spits a watermelon seed a distance of 59 feet 1½ inches and becomes a world champion in his category. It took an estimated 400,000 people to fly men to the moon. The seed spitter and the flagpole sitter are champions of trivia, perhaps, and there may be a lot of them, but each does perform his magic all alone.

SUBWAY There are more than 50 underground metropolitan mass-transit systems in the world today, most of them built in the 1960's and 1970's. The oldest, and probably one of the most comfortable, is in London. Opened in 1863, it provides riders with seats upholstered in plush tapestry and fitted with armrests. There are also, as on any proper railroad, cars reserved for smokers. Just how well it is built was demonstrated during World War II when the Underground, as it is called, became every Londoner's air-raid shelter.

The most efficient subway system, an awesome monument to Gallic logic, is probably the Paris Métro. It is so well laid out that, with the exception of a small area of the city, no Parisian lives more than a few short blocks from one of its 315 stations. Indeed, if you ask a resident of Paris what part of the city he lives in, chances are that he will respond by telling you his Métro stop. Inaugurated in 1900, the Métro has undergone continuous improvement, which includes the installation of sound-deadening rubber wheels and even rubber matting in passageways to muffle the thudding footsteps of hurrying crowds. The filtered air at many of the stations is purer than at street level. A new super-rapid line now whisks passengers through the heart of the city in 10 minutes, a trip that at rush hour is all but impossible to make by car.

For years the most glittering subway system in

Tunnel vision: this elegant passageway, complete with chandeliers, is part of the Moscow subway system.

the world was in Moscow. Built as a showcase of Socialist progress, neither money nor human life was spared in the construction. Russians still debate whether Lazar Kaganovich caused more deaths as leader of the purges of the 1930's or as minister of transport during the building of the subway with its constant cave-ins. There is no question, however, that the stations with their elaborate mosaics, chandeliers, marble floors, stained glass, and statuary dazzle foreign visitors. The fare, thanks to generous state subsidy, is pegged at a sensible 5 kopecks—about 7 cents.

The highest subway in the world, at 7,350 feet above sea level, was inaugurated in Mexico City in 1969. During the digging workmen uncovered an

people

Alfred Ely Beach

Looking out his office window at the hopelessly snarled traffic at Broadway and Chambers Street in downtown Manhattan, Alfred Ely Beach decided that something should be done about it. Beach's solution was far from ordinary, but Beach was hardly an ordinary man. Part owner and editor of the *Scientific American*, he was also an inventor, credited with a typewriter for the blind, a cable railway, and the pneumatic tube.

To relieve congestion in the streets, Beach decided that some of the traffic would have to be moved elsewhere, either above the thoroughfares or below them. A train system above ground would be impractical—too noisy and unsightly—so he resolved to build one underground. The year was 1866, and neither the gasoline nor the electric engine had yet been perfected, so Beach had to find a means of moving his train. Because a steam engine on the car would pour forth too much soot, he decided instead to use air. A surface steam engine powered a giant fan which pro-

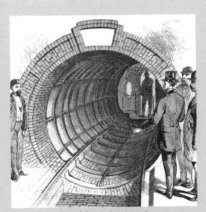

Beach's block-long subway

pelled a cylindrical 20-passenger car, snugly fitted inside a cylindrical tunnel. When the direction of the fan was reversed, the train was sucked backward to the point of origin.

The bigger challenge, however, was a political one. At that time New York's Tammany Hall and "Boss" Tweed controlled the granting of franchises. Beach refused to pay the political blackmail required, so he decided to build his subway in secret. He had applied for a permit to construct a small mail-carrying pneumatic

tube below Broadway, but he instructed his men to excavate a tunnel 9 feet in diameter and 312 feet long. Incredibly, the work was completed without incident or detection in just 58 nights. To make his subway attractive to passengers, Beach added a waiting room, complete with a fountain, some paintings, a grand piano, and even a goldfish tank.

The opening was a smashing success. "A Fashionable Reception Held in the Bowels of the Earth," reported a headline in the New York *Herald*. But in the end, Tweed was successful in delaying the necessary legislation until Beach's financial backers lost interest.

Indeed, the entire project was abandoned and completely forgotten until February 1912, when a construction crew digging a new subway line, to their collective astonishment, chopped through the wall of Beach's tunnel. There they found the elegant station and Beach's little train still standing on its tracks, but long gone were the top-hatted, frock-coated passengers.

A single-sex subway car, 1909, on the New York-New Jersey shuttle is guarded by an upstanding trainman.

vein as those in Mexico City: eels and other marine life at the New England Aquarium stop; a sports mural at the stop that serves the Boston Garden, the city's sports arena.

Other North American cities—Washington, San Francisco, Atlanta, Toronto, Montreal, and Edmonton, Alberta—have spanking new subway systems, but the best is yet to come: a proposed New York-to-Los Angeles system dreamed up by the American Association for the Advancement of Science. The so-called Planetran would cross the continent in 21 minutes, at speeds of up to 14,000 miles an hour. It would be magnetically suspended in a vacuum and powered by electromagnetic impulses. The projected fare for the trip would be $6. And for that you would probably have to stand and hang onto a strap all the way.

Aztec pyramid, which now forms part of the decor of one of the system's 45 stations. To help tourists and illiterate riders, a graphic designer developed signs to identify the stations—a crate of apples for the stop near the central market; a grasshopper for the Chapultepec Park station, which draws its name from an Indian word for that insect.

The unearthing of archeological remains, which was a substantial fringe benefit to subway builders in Mexico City, has frustrated their colleagues in Rome. Italian government regulations require that experts be allowed to study newly discovered artifacts before their removal. Since it is virtually impossible to turn over a shovelful of dirt under the Eternal City without coming up with some remains—classical, medieval, or Renaissance—and since experts are notoriously slow about making judgments, many observers fear that Rome's subway will never be completed. Still the problem is simpler than the one faced by subway engineers in Munich. They have had to remove—with utmost caution—unexploded bombs from World War II.

O. Henry referred to New York City as "Bagdad-on-the-Subway," and a song rhapsodized about a "helluva town" where "people ride in a hole in the groun'." Despite such recognition, one study has characterized it as "the most squalid public environment of the United States: dank, dingily lit, fetid, raucous with screeching clatter."

The oldest working subway in the U.S. was opened for service in Boston in 1897. It ran under Tremont Street, where, according to one observer, "during the afternoon rush hour the cars were packed so close together that one could almost walk from Scollay Square to Boylston Street on the car roofs." In its first year it carried more than 50 million passengers. Its successor, the Metropolitan Boston Transit Authority, not long ago blossomed out with decorations much in the same

SUGAR There are many types of sugars, including cane sugar, beet sugar, maple sugar, corn sugar, and palm sugar. The human predilection for the sweet substance, designated by the chemical formula $C_{12}H_{22}O_{11}$, finds ample expression in vernacular speech. The object of one's affection is likely to be "sweetheart," "honey," "sugarplum," or "sweetie pie." Since the mid-19th century sugar has meant "money," and lots of sugar has enabled some to enjoy *la dolce vita*. Any man getting on in years and well padded with cash can become a "sugar daddy" to a "sweet young thing." That which is sweet is so closely identified with that which is desirable that we even speak of the "sweet spot" of a tennis racket.

One of the earliest references to sugar is contained in a report by an officer who accompanied Alexander the Great on his campaign to India in

Mountains of sugar beets, about 280,000 tons of the 1960 crop, are shown being moved to a processing plant.

the 4th century B.C. "There is said," the report noted, "to be a reed which yields honey without the help of bees." But even before that time people had discovered their sweet tooth and found ways to satisfy it.

The reed mentioned in the document was sugarcane, and it is still the source for the largest portion of the world's supply of sugar. Believed to have been cultivated first in India, sugarcane was gradually introduced into western Asia, North Africa, and Europe. Christopher Columbus, whose mother-in-law owned a sugar plantation on the island of Madeira, thought it would grow well in the New World and brought some cuttings with him on his second voyage.

So well did the cane fare in its new home that it became responsible in large part for the traffic in slaves. The need for manpower to work the plantations grew markedly. Before 1600 fewer than one million black Africans had been brought to the New World. During the 17th century the number increased to 2,750,000, and by the 18th century it reached 7 million. Sugar in the form of molasses also formed one of the legs in the infamous triangular trade, which brought considerable wealth to American colonists. Shipped up from the West Indies to the Colonies, the molasses was converted into rum, which was then shipped to the Gold Coast of Africa, where it was traded for slaves, who were delivered to the West Indies. The availability of sugar at reasonable prices went hand in hand with the growing consumption of tea and coffee. In 1665 fewer than 88 tons of sugar were imported by England. In 1700 the figure stood at about 10,000 tons, and London alone could boast of 3,000 tea shops.

The cultivation of sugar beets, the other major source of the world's sugar, was largely the result of the Napoleonic Wars. After Adm. Horatio Nelson's fleet destroyed the French fleet at Trafalgar in 1805, Napoleon was faced with a British blockade that cut him off from supplies of sugarcane. He finally decided to offer a large prize for the development of a commercial method of extracting sugar from beets—a process known largely at that time as a laboratory curiosity. As a result 40 factories were established in France, producing millions of pounds of beet sugar a year, aided by the large-scale application of the recently invented steam engine.

In the United States the earliest widely used sweetening agent was maple sugar. Four times more of it was consumed annually 200 years ago than is today. It gave way gradually to brown sugar, which in turn gave way to white sugar when manufacturers persuaded housewives that refined sugar, which happened to be more profit-

A gust strong enough to power this sugarcane processor (early 1800's) must have been an ill wind for others.

able to make, was of higher quality and socially more correct. From that moment on, it was only a matter of time until brown sugar would reappear, as it now has, on the smartest hostesses' tables—in a small silver or crystal bowl as a special "gourmet" sweetener for coffee.

Americans consume sugar at the per capita rate of some 95 pounds a year—white or brown, powdered or crystallized. It is spooned into coffee or sprinkled over breakfast cereal, but the greatest amount—some 70 percent—is doled out by food makers. Sugar is not only put into soft drinks, baked goods, and canned fruits, where one might expect it, but also into soups, salad dressings, and mayonnaise. Indeed, it is difficult to find any processed food that does not contain sugar.

Sugar has many nonnutritional uses as well—in metallurgy, leather tanning, and the manufacture of paint, cement, embalming fluids, and phonograph records. None of them, however, makes much of a dent in the world's supply.

The reason sugar was rationed in the United States during World War II is that enormous quantities were needed to make the ethyl alcohol required to produce smokeless gunpowder. Patriots who cheerfully drank bitter coffee for the cause in those dim days may be interested to learn that it took an entire acre of sugarcane to make enough gunpowder for five shots from a 16-inch gun.

SUITCASE From the time man first packed his few belongings in a crude basket and carried it from place to place, luggage (from the verb "to lug") has become a necessity of life. One of the earliest cases was the portmanteau, which derived its name from French officers, who carried (*porter*) a prince's mantle (*manteau*) in a bag over the horse's back. The French also invented the overnight bag, a small portable trunk strapped to a larger trunk that could be detached and carried separately for a night's stay at a hostelry.

No one knows for sure why the hinged leather carrier popular in the 1800's, with separate compartments for clean and soiled linen, took its name from W.E. Gladstone, the prime minister of Britain under Queen Victoria. Perhaps it was because Gladstone traveled extensively and was also known for his obsession with moral cleanliness, which drove him to approach prostitutes and beg them to change their lives.

From soldiers on the move came various sacks for carrying provisions. The Danish *knappen* ("to eat") and *zac* ("bag") gave us the knapsack. A kit bag (named after the Dutch drinking tankard, or *kit*) was the English term for a knapsack, and it became popular in the United States during the Civil War. "Pack up your troubles in your old kit bag," advised a World War I song.

Americans moving westward transported their belongings in saddlebags slung across horses' backs or in small trunks with one side at an angle to fit snugly between the knees during the bumpy stagecoach ride. Northerners who after the Civil War milked the chaotic South for profit came to be known as "carpetbaggers" because many of them preferred carrying cases made from durable carpeting, which enabled them to travel fast and light.

The Jenny Lind trunk, ordered by P.T. Barnum for "the Swedish nightingale," combined a graceful form and sturdy frame. This attractive case,

Basket case: A Guatemalan woman is transporting some straw.

unfortunately, was superseded by the Saratoga trunk, a lavishly decorated monstrosity used by fashionable ladies to haul everything from mirrors and washbasins to writing tables as they traveled to the swanky New York State resort. Later, huge wardrobe trunks that resembled portable closets, with spaces for hanging garments and pull-out drawers, accompanied passengers on elegant transatlantic steamers.

The actress Elizabeth Taylor commonly embarked with 10 such trunks. She was also known to have packed 128 pieces of luggage for one journey, including the carpetbags trimmed with red leather that became her trademark. Cole Porter, who traveled with just about everything portable he owned, liked to tell a story of how one Italian in a small town explained to a friend that the mountain of bags was "Mr. Porter's orchestra."

Airline travel and regulations spurred manufacturers to streamline baggage designs: steamer trunks yielded to lightweight suitcases for easy carrying. People travel more now and buy more luggage—the average person today acquires three or four sets in a lifetime, compared with two sets half a generation ago. According to one manufacturer, Americans want suitcases that "look like what would be carried on a plane" even if they never board one.

While some status-conscious travelers buy designer bags with easily recognizable patterns, initials, and color combinations—Dior, Gucci, Vuitton, and Hermès among them—others feel that the mark of true chic is a carrier that is unidentifiable yet distinctive. The Marchesa Alessandro di Montezemolo found the perfect container for her paraphernalia—a sturdy black doctor's bag. Columnist Art Buchwald never leaves home without his combination typewriter-briefcase, and a European baron who developed a taste for dry martinis always carries a portable bar case.

Customs officials as well as fellow travelers eye expensive suitcases, but for different reasons. Spanking new cases either too heavy or too light for their size can tip off narcotics agents to illicit drugs. One agent claims that a particular make of suitcase widely advertised for its strength and pickproof combination locks "seems

Baggage check: a guard keeps a wary eye on but a modest amount of Elizabeth Taylor's famous luggage.

to be standard issue for narcotics smugglers."

Nearly every airline passenger who travels with any regularity has a long, involved story about lost luggage. Conductor Eugene Ormandy landed in Brazil for a scheduled concert, but his musical scores and dress suit as well as the rest of his things landed in Bermuda. The baggage of an entire planeload of passengers bound for Mexico City wound up the next day in Singapore, making for one very hostile group of tourists.

A couple reported to an airline in Omaha that one of their suitcases was lost but never showed up to claim it. Airline officials found that it contained $38,000, still in the wrappers of the Midwest bank from which it had been stolen.

Most airlines now use computers to track down "mishandled" (airlines' term) bags. Thefts from baggage-claim areas remain a problem, however, and the companies still pay millions of dollars a year for stolen, misrouted, or damaged articles. After a barrage of inflated and false claims, the airlines set legal limits on the amounts they are required to pay for reimbursements.

The logistics of replacing belongings have caused nightmares for many an airlines official. A woman visiting America for St. Patrick's Day refused to accept Irish whiskey from an American store, so the airline flew over three bottles from Dublin. Another line ordered replacements for three stray cheesecakes from a famous Broadway restaurant and flew them to Paris for a U.S. correspondent who had planned to use them for gifts.

One single night was crucial for the woman separated from her birth-control pills at a Charleston, South Carolina, airport. She became hysterical and threatened to hold the airline responsible for any child born. An airline clerk finally located a druggist who agreed to sell one pill without a prescription and sent a taxi for it.

SWIMMING Swimming is probably the most popular and healthful of all sports, since it rhythmically works most of the muscles without strain and develops grace and strength. Yet swimming does not come naturally to humans. Man is not built to move smoothly through the water. According to one authority on swimming, the human neck ideally should be a good six inches longer than normal and the thighs six inches shorter. Consequently, ever since man progressed from floating with the aid of an inflated animal bladder to swimming a cautious dog paddle, people have been learning the art and trying to improve it along the way.

An Egyptian hieroglyph for swimming, from about 2500 B.C., shows a man doing a form of crawl, an efficient stroke that was forgotten for centuries. The Greeks and Romans made swimming a part of military training, and Roman youths at the Campus Martius took dips in the nearby Tiber. After the fall of Rome, swimming seems to have declined in popularity.

The early recorded history of swimming is scanty. Most of what we know about swimming concerns the colorful figures it has attracted—some fictitious, some real. One of the best-known literary references to swimming is the story of Leander, who drowned traversing the Hellespont to reach his beloved Hero. Leander's admirer Lord Byron retraced his strokes and thereby contracted the "ague."

Among Americans it was reported that George Washington loved swimming, as did his compatriot Benjamin Franklin. The latter wrote a book on the subject and almost accepted an offer to open a teaching academy in England, where he was sometimes known as the "watery American."

Competitive swimming appeared in England shortly after the first indoor swimming pool was built in 1828. Racers used the breaststroke with the frog kick, until, more than a decade later, the still-decorous English sidestroke proved to be a faster way to move through the water.

The inspiration for most new strokes was the desire for increased speed. An early form of the modern freestyle stroke surfaced in the 1870's, when J. Arthur Trudgen, an English swimmer visiting South America, noticed that the Indians swam on their stomachs and alternated their arms

In a race against time and each other, hundreds of contestants swim the waters to Hong Kong Island.

Gratuitous advice: none of these play-it-safe waders seem to need the advice not to get in over their heads.

and alternating leg kick gasped, "Look at the kid crawling!" The modern classic racing style was born.

The first modern Olympic Games, in Athens in 1896, included swimming races. Over the years the Games have bred a number of idols. Gold-medal winner Johnny Weissmuller set records in 67 different events in the 1920's while engaged in competitive swimming and was later crowned Hollywood's Tarzan. After winning seven gold medals in 1972, Mark Spitz became the world's bestselling poster pinup person since Betty Grable.

In 1962 a 12-year-old girl beat Weissmuller's winning time for the 400-meter freestyle in the 1924 Olympics, and swimming times continue to shrink. This is due to improved training and longer workouts, and the growing number of amateur swimmers to pep up the competition.

The English Channel, a choppy, treacherous stretch of water, has challenged endurance swimmers over the years. The first man to swim the Channel was Matthew Webb, who accomplished this feat on August 24–25, 1875. He sipped beef bouillon and brandy and ate a little raw meat when he was not battling tides and jellyfish on his 21-hour, 45-minute journey. In 1926 Gertrude Ederle, the first woman to swim the Channel, did

over their heads. He failed to observe their legs, however, and the Trudgen stroke retained the old frog kick. Then in 1897 an Australian coach observing a 12-year-old boy from a Pacific island slice through the water with the overhand stroke

customs

The Beached Swimmers' Salvation

Before the Industrial Revolution, a white complexion suggested an aristocratic life of sheltered ease. But by the 1920's the tone of affluence had deepened, and a year-round bronze glow often indicated wealth and status. By the end of World War I sun worship was in full frenzy, and millions of dollars worth of suntan lotions began to pour into the market.

Effective sunscreens, however, were not developed until the crucial need to protect American troops fighting under the tropical sun arose during World War II. One scientist discovered that the red petroleum jelly used by veterinarians screened out the ultraviolet rays that cause sunburn. More sophisticated concoctions soon followed. Suntan lotions range in effectiveness from products containing zinc oxide, which filters out virtually all burning

and tanning rays, to those designed to moisten the skin and enhance tanning. Skin coloring and length of time already spent in the sun help determine the type of preparation each person needs. The federal government has pro-

One dime bought a 30-second hosing at this suntan lotion pump.

posed that all products be labeled according to the degree of protection they provide.

Among the zanier products spawned by the craze for sun-bronzed skin were preparations that provided a tan without sun (unfortunately, the lotion rubbed off on clothes, often streaked, and did not always blend in with the person's natural tan). A special concoction, introduced during the topless fad, promised to protect sensitive nipples.

Doctors hope that the sun-powered bronze age may be passing, because studies show that the tanned look is not really all that healthy. Overexposure to the sun hastens aging of the skin and speeds up the onset of wrinkles. It may also cause a precancerous condition known as solar keratosis and skin cancer as well, a disease that now affects some 300,000 Americans a year.

so in 14 hours, 31 minutes. She found the ticker-tape parades in her honor, medal ceremonies, and tours more stressful than the swim, and after two years in the limelight she suffered a nervous breakdown and then lost her hearing. In later years she taught deaf children how to swim.

SYMBIOSIS Give and take, the most basic of human exchanges, is expressed in myriad ways throughout the civilized world—in politics, in the marketplace, in marriage, and in the machinations of child raising. Even within the human body the process goes on, bacteria and human cells, organs, and neural systems sustaining and being sustained in magnificent mutuality. But it is in the world of plants and animals that the helpful give-and-take of existence reaches its most fascinating expression.

Such a mutually beneficial arrangement between different species is called symbiosis, a term coined by the scientist Heinrich de Bary in 1879. The term means "living together," and originally referred to parasitism (a relationship good for one partner but destructive for the other) and commensalism (an arrangement good for one partner alone) as well as a beneficial mutualism between species. Today, however, the word is most commonly used to describe those remarkable, natural collaborations from which both partners derive benefit.

Consider the little African bird with a hopeless fondness for the wax of honeycombs. To find a bee's nest is easy for the bird, but to break it open is impossible. For that job, claws are needed. Thus the bird faces an impossible choice: either give up honey or grow claws. It does neither; instead, it flies off in search of a honey badger or ratel, a tough-skinned mammal that adores honey but

In a mutually beneficial partnership, cattle egrets feed on vermin embedded in the hide of African buffalo.

rarely has the wit to locate a nest on its own. Then the honey guide (as the bird is called) sets up a tremendous fuss before the ratel's nose. Finally the beast gets the message, and together they set off for the nest—two oddly but professionally matched burglars intent on splitting the take.

Doctoring and dentistry are among the strangest symbiotic exchanges between large and small creatures. The fierce Nile crocodile, for example, gapes its jaws while a fragile plover hops into its deadly maw. The bird is not suicidal. It is hungry, and by pecking out the leeches that infect the crocodile's gums it does itself and its host a good turn. From its nonfeeding perch on the crocodile's back, the plover also acts as an early warning system. Similar relationships exist between the sharp-eyed tickbird and the nearsighted rhino, between the impala and the red-billed oxpecker, between the hippopotamus and a heron that com-

Workers: wood-eating termites digest cellulose in symbiosis with digestive-tract protozoans or bacteria.

The tropical sea anemone provides shelters to a colony of damselfish but will sting intruders to death.

Marine iguanas in the Galápagos Islands lounge in the sun as some lava crabs remove ticks from their hides.

panionably picks food particles from between the hippo's teeth.

The oddest of all cleaning rituals are performed beneath the seas. In tropical waters, brightly marked little fish set up "cleaning stations" near obvious landmarks such as coral reefs and wrecks. There they receive their "clients," baracudas, moray eels, and others, who lie quietly in the water while the cleaner fish nibbles away parasites and cleans wounds. One such full-time fish-powered service station can handle a clientele of up to 300 a day.

Underwater symbioses create strange bedfel-

A cleaner fish gets a nourishing meal in exchange for ridding its bucktoothed "client" of pesky parasites.

lows. The spreading tentacles of the sea anemone are poisonous, so the boxer crab wears two of them on its front claws, ready to jab at any predator. Amid the lethal thicket of arms of another kind of anemone, a damselfish will take up residence, safe from all other jaws. It always returns to its own anemone and, in what remains one of nature's mysteries, is somehow recognized by its host. The harboring anemone will tolerate its own damselfish, and even its mate and offspring, but will sting to death and devour others of the same species that wander near. In a complete symbiosis neither partner could exist without the other. The complex organization of creatures in a Portuguese man-of-war can survive only as a group. For the man-of-war, borne along by a sail bubble, poisonous tentacles dangling below, is actually a colony of a thousand different creatures clustered in specialized groups.

Even more dazzling perhaps is the sophisticated cooperation evidenced by ant colonies, some of which appear to mimic man's agricultural activities. Leafcutting specialists, for example, systematically denude a tree but do not eat its leaves. Snippet by snippet, the leaves are transported to large underground caverns, where they are chewed to mulch and used to cultivate edible fungi. Some farmer ants even keep herds of aphids, as men keep cows. When gently stroked or "milked" by an ant, the aphid exudes a drop of honeydew—ant ambrosia. The herding ants take tender care of their flocks and even carry aphids out to "pasture" on leaves. For the aphids it is not such a bad life.

On the pollinating services of bees, flies, and butterflies depends the health of much of the earth's plant life. Flowers, in fact, evolved their colors and fragrances in response to this relationship. Yet plants, in turn, would not fatten beef were it not for the bacteria in the intestines of a cow, which break down the cellulose in grass and permit the cow to digest it. Without the action of these microorganisms, found in all ruminants, or grazing animals, the cow would starve in clover.

Even the foolish and long-extinct dodo bird of Mauritius may once have been a symbiotic partner to a tree, as one scientist posits. For 300 years, almost precisely the time since the last dodo disappeared, the calvaria tree on Mauritius has not germinated. Such trees are all but gone now, but a few still produce thick-hulled seeds. Unfortunately, they never open. Assuming that the dodo must have abraded the seed hulls in digesting them, the scientist fed some calvaria fruit to a turkey. The recaptured seeds were then planted, and a few germinated. Thus perhaps even the dumb dodo had a place in nature's vast symbiotic show.

TECHNICAL GENIUS: *sum of its parts*

A pistol, an automobile, a bar of soap—single objects, everyday things. The first two are also complex mechanisms that evolve through many stages on the way to completion; the third is a folk concoction richly rendered by modern chemistry and technology.

The 19th century saw an incredible multiplication of new manufacturing methods, processes, and standards built on the accumulated technical wisdom of the ages. The century's prolific inventors teamed with others who learned to organize systems and collect the tools, including capital, needed to manufacture parts and assemble products for a burgeoning market. (The photograph above furnishes an example of the continuing accretion—and increasing complication—of industrial knowledge. A man, one of hundreds involved in producing a railroad car, inspects wheels.) On the following pages we examine a few things we take for granted, seeing some from the inventor's point of view and others as their makers see them, in all the lavish intricacy of their component parts.

The Beginnings

The glimmerings of many mechanical discoveries are lost to history, but by the Renaissance men of genius like Leonardo da Vinci foresaw the construction of such modern marvels as die presses and screws, flying machines and submarines. (Leonardo's drawing of a tank and a re-creation of it appear at bottom.) The scientific triumphs of the 1600's and ever-growing technology based on those principles eventually turned vision to reality. Though many of our important breakthroughs today are the result of well-financed team efforts, much of what we think of as commonplace sprang from the minds of men alone, improving and improvising on the ideas of their inventive forebears.

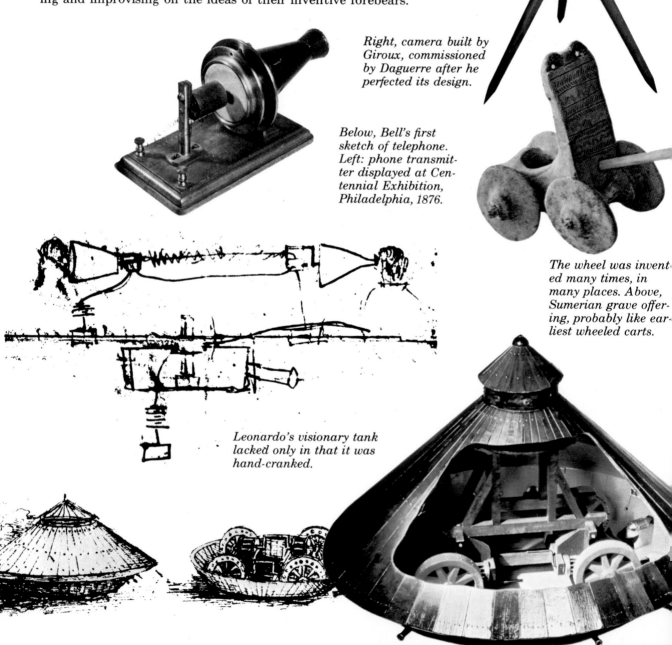

Right, camera built by Giroux, commissioned by Daguerre after he perfected its design.

Below, Bell's first sketch of telephone. Left: phone transmitter displayed at Centennial Exhibition, Philadelphia, 1876.

The wheel was invented many times, in many places. Above, Sumerian grave offering, probably like earliest wheeled carts.

Leonardo's visionary tank lacked only in that it was hand-cranked.

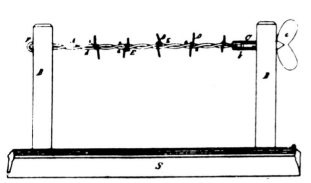

Patent drawing by J. F. Glidden, 1874. Invented after 1850, barbed wire changed the American West. By 1900 over 400 U.S. barbed-wire patents were held.

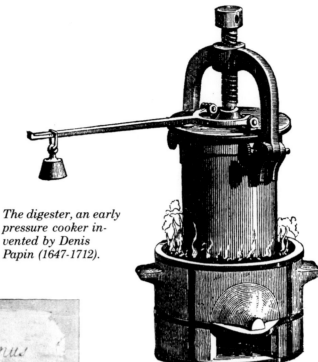

The digester, an early pressure cooker invented by Denis Papin (1647-1712).

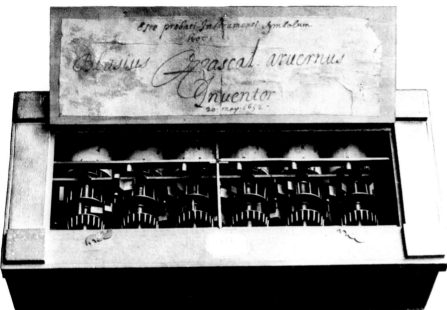

Adding machine invented by French philosopher and mathematician Blaise Pascal, c. 1644. Each gear advances a unit as the one to its right completes a cycle for addition, retreats for subtraction.

Chain pistol, 1866, forerunner of machine gun: never produced.

Threshing machine, mid-1800's: early models caused riots by English farm help put out of winter work by the machines.

Also-rans

Some wag has said, "Invention is the mother of necessity," which may be true enough of many things, like the telephone, in today's world. Unfortunately for the creators of the devices that appear on these two pages, their brainchildren did not give birth to urgent need. Patents, according to law, are supposed to be awarded to what is "novel and useful," but these gadgets indicate that such determinations may be equally impossible for inventor and patent officer alike. The perpetual-motion machine is an exception: the French Academy of Science refused to review any after 1775, and eventually the British and U.S. Patent Offices came to similar conclusions.

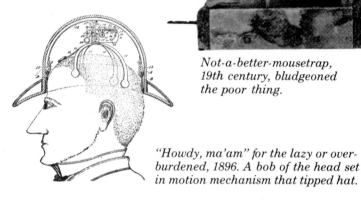

Not-a-better-mousetrap, 19th century, bludgeoned the poor thing.

"Howdy, ma'am" for the lazy or over-burdened, 1896. A bob of the head set in motion mechanism that tipped hat.

Corpse preserver, 1868, sported free air circulation, insulated walls.

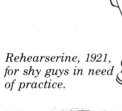

Rehearserine, 1921, for shy guys in need of practice.

A 19th-century inventor of this bustle-bulger did not addres the problem of sitting in a carriage or on a chair.

An English firm offered the pedi-bath in 1897, saying harder pumping induced a harder shower—and more sweat.

Fig. 1.

Decoy for duo, patented in 1897

Spring-driven roller skates appeared in 1901. One hopes the skater was also a steerer.

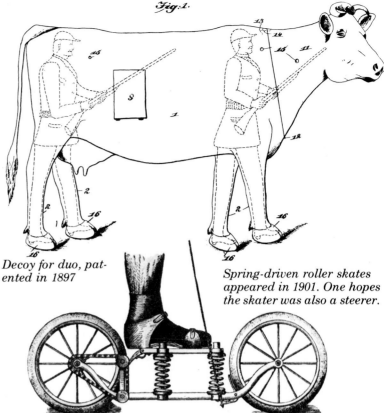

This ad appeared in 1882, although perhaps the cover was never manufactured.

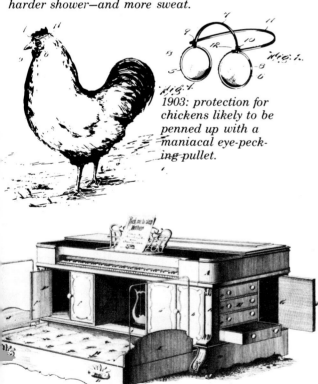

1903: protection for chickens likely to be penned up with a maniacal eye-pecking pullet.

Bedroom suite, 1866: insomniacs could play a lullaby with this bed, chest, sofa, and piano combo.

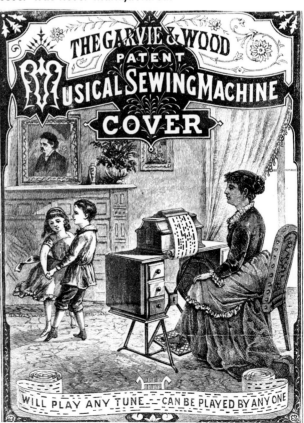

THE GARVIE & WOOD PATENT MUSICAL SEWING MACHINE COVER

WILL PLAY ANY TUNE — CAN BE PLAYED BY ANY ONE

Assemblage

Although philosophers and poets like to laud simplicity, most of the objects that play a part in—and yes, in many cases simplify—our lives are extremely complicated in their design and manufacture. When Steinway & Sons put together a filmstrip to illustrate the steps involved in building a piano, they found that they needed some 150 frames to hit the high notes. (Eleven of those are shown here.) Whether an item is as grand as a piano or as mundane as a toaster, it is an intricate assembly of various materials and parts. Those have already been processed by many hands before they meet in the finished product. Thus each new device is born in many stages.

The materials that go into a piano come from many sources, go through many refinements. At top right, steel is smelted in Pittsburgh. Right, Filipinos dress mahogany. Above, a downed elephant in Africa. Because of conservation efforts, keys are no longer made of ivory but rather from a fine plastic.

Men in one of 7 departments involved in making the cases for Steinways bend the rim for a small grand.

A skilled woodworker carefully places the veneer on the curved arm shape that has just been coated with glue.

Piano plates are single cast of iron. Here a workman grinds casting marks off a raw plate.

nvibrating string guides are inserted
the plate. The pattern indicates
w strings will run.

In this closeup, the spinning machine
turns copper wire onto the steel core
of a piano string.

Provided with finished strings, a
craftsman proceeds to string the
bass section of a concert grand.

inspector checks repetition assem-
es with a gauge indicating how much
ssure is needed to move a hinge.

A workman in the Grand Finishing
Department fits the action assembly
and the key frame into the piano.

To achieve the precision spacing required between the hammers, Steinway
utilizes a shank heating process.

*Blissfully unaware of all the work that went into their piano, Harry
Truman and Lauren Bacall enjoy a light moment.*

A coarse-sandpaper-covered wooden
file is employed by a craftsman to
give the felt hammers exact shape.

The positioning of lead weights in keys
produces the precise and equal down
pressure required on each one.

Industrial Art

"A tool is but the extension of man's hand, and a machine is but a complex tool. And he that invents a machine augments the power of a man and the well-being of mankind." So preached Henry Ward Beecher in the 19th century. Those who are replaced by machinery would take issue, whether they were English sawyers of the 1600's or are modern-day elevator operators automated out of a job. Others might add that no matter how sophisticated the tool, men are still crucial to its performance. However beautifully orchestrated a process is, its success still depends on the individual's skill. Photographs of people playing their parts constitute a unique kind of industrial art.

New England textile mill

Gangsaws cut stone slabs to architect's measurement.

Iron puddlers, Stalingrad, U.S.S.R., 1930.

Nikon workers take mandatory break.

Steeliners, Fort Peck Dam, Montana, 1937.

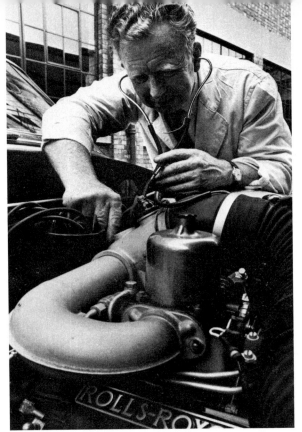

In a plant in England, a Rolls-Royce inspector listens to a new engine with a stethoscope.

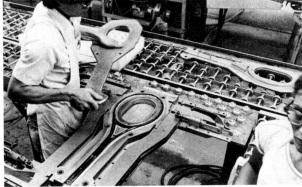

A worker fastens on the fiberglass-mold top plate before a tennis racket-to-be is "cooked" in a press.

A machine strips off ribbons of soap.

This view of an assembly line in a Chrysler plant in Detroit indicates the numbers of people and machines involved in turning out every automobile.

TABLE LINEN Fingers were made before forks, as the folk saying goes, and so were napkins. Noting the vagaries of dining in America in 1780, Baron Louis de Closen wrote: "Another peculiarity of this country is the absence of napkins, even in the homes of the wealthy. Napkins, as a rule, are never used and one has to wipe one's mouth on the tablecloth, which in consequence suffers in appearance." But in many other parts of the world napkins existed long before the 18th century.

Fragments of wool and flax found in Switzerland suggest that crude napkins were in use during the Stone Age. Wealthy Romans employed napkins in at least two ways: one was to protect the couch on which they reclined while dining;

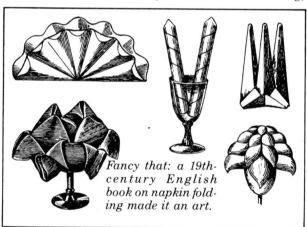

Fancy that: a 19th-century English book on napkin folding made it an art.

the other was as wrapping for specially favored foods to be taken home from a feast as a compliment to the host.

The Franks introduced an elegant twist in tablecloths. During Charlemagne's time, as one writer described it, the table "had more roses on it than a whole field. It was not an ordinary tablecloth that was covering it, it was roses; they chose something that flatters the sense of smell and covers the table at the same time, in preference to linen." But the Franks' vision did not catch on. For ennobling the festal board, nothing could surpass rich white linen. Collapsible tables were used in the Middle Ages, and since these amounted to little more than boards placed across supports, or trestles, coverings were first called "boardcloths." In the late 17th century a man might bring his own napkin, which was in the form of a bib, to a dinner party. The lady attending with him used a tucker, a cloth of muslin or lace, tucked into the neck of her dress. To wear one's "best bib and tucker," then, meant to be properly accoutred for a banquet.

Diarist Samuel Pepys wrote in 1668 that he was "mightily pleased with the fellow that came to lay the cloth and fold the napkins, which I like so well, as that I am resolved to give him 40s. to teach my wife to do it." Folding napkins into fancy shapes was a prestigious thing to do for several centuries. Giles Rose, chief cook to Charles II, showed how 26 different shapes could be created, including one that resembled "a pigeon upon her nest in a basket."

Such works of art were not meant to be used, only admired. Ironically table linen's centuries-old association with the gentry may be responsible for one of our humblest folk sayings. In Elizabethan times a man usually knotted his napkin around his neck. This was a struggle when he was also wearing a ruff, so that he often had a problem "making both ends meet."

TAXICAB In the Musée de l'Armée in Paris, which houses what may be the world's most comprehensive collection of military hardware, one of the proudest exhibits is an old, battered Paris taxicab. It was one of the more than 1,000 that were commandeered by the city's military governor in September 1914 and used to rush two infantry regiments to the front about 30 miles away during the first Battle of the Marne.

During World War II, 400 taxicabs—English ones this time—were requisitioned and fitted with machine guns for antiparatroop duty. An additional 2,000 London cabs were converted into a fire-fighting force; the cabs' great maneuverability and their drivers' encyclopedic knowledge of the city enabled them to respond to fires faster than conventional vehicles.

Beep, beep: hand resting cautiously on the horn, Frau Papp chauffeurs a carload of customers, 1908.

The first taxis to cruise the streets of New York City await riders outside the old Metropolitan Opera House.

This knowledge of the city is what still distinguishes London taxi drivers from their colleagues elsewhere around the world. To receive a license, a driver must undergo up to 18 months of training. During oral examinations, he must demonstrate familiarity with much of the 720 square miles of London and know most of the names of its 39,000 streets as well as the most direct route between any two of them. To complicate matters, for example, London not only has a Cambridge Circus and a Cambridge Square but also two Parks, two Places, two Drives, three Avenues, five Gardens, two Crescents, and 21 Roads all bearing the name Cambridge.

No such test exists in Tokyo, where most streets are unnamed. Not surprisingly, the city's 34,000 taxicabs—the largest fleet in any city in the world—are the subject of endless complaints, hor-

Two for the handwagon, 1884: the Chinese continued to use man-powered carts even in the 20th century.

ror stories, and angry letters to newspapers. Not long ago one newspaper, deciding to let the drivers tell their story, elicited a partial explanation for the mess. "Let me tell you," said one driver, "this is tough work. Most of us are from out of town. Because no native Tokyo man would be so foolish as to stay in such a job."

New York City, international gathering place for tourists, has 11,787 taxis, many dirty and as uncomfortable as the pitted roads they ride on. A maximum legal number was established in 1937 by a city administration fearful of congesting the streets with too many cabs. As a result a taxi medallion—the permit to operate a cab in New York—which originally cost $10, now sells for about $60,000.

According to legend, the bases of which seem at best obscure, most of the 40,000 New York City cab drivers—including a growing number of women—are a beguiling combination of political expert, natural philosopher, and sit-down comic. Such talents, however, are not always readily apparent to passengers, some 30,554 of whom filed complaints in a recent year. In an effort to improve this seamy record—and spawn some publicity—the president of one fleet arranged for Amy Vanderbilt, the etiquette expert, to address a group of drivers. One of her first rules of conduct had to do with the proper way to address a woman passenger. "Not," decreed Miss Vanderbilt, "as 'Hey, you' or 'Sugarplum.'" From then on, it was a rough ride all the way.

To some people taxicabs represent luxury transportation, to be indulged in by the affluent, rain-sodden, or indolent. In rebuttal, industry spokesmen point out that the 298,000 taxicabs in America annually transport some 3.4 billion passengers, more than twice the number carried by all forms of urban transit. Fleet cabs alone move nearly 40 percent more passengers than all rapid transit combined. In all, taxicabs log 12.2 billion miles a year, compared with a mere 2 billion for all bus and rail lines. Where all those taxicabs go when it sprinkles, however, industry sources have not as yet determined.

Essential and mobile though they may be, taxicabs are not a very efficient mode of transportation. For more than half its street time, the average cab is occupied by the driver alone. Many attempts have been made to improve this lonely and unrewarding situation. Often such attempts have involved some form of sharing, as in "jitney" operations—named after the slang term for the nickel. In 1915 more than 60,000 jitneys operated across the country. Unfortunately, they carried so many passengers that streetcar companies lobbied to pass regulations

Taxi!

In Hong Kong or Singapore, one might hail a *rickshaw*; in Jakarta, a *bemo*; in Kiev, a *droshky*; in the United States, a *cab*; and pretty much anywhere else in the Western world, a *taxi*.

1896: Horseless taxi

Londoners who depended on carriages for hire for their transportation had to be thankful for the day in 1834 when, according to some sources, Joseph Hansom obtained a patent on an ingenious and revolutionary vehicle. This was a two-wheeled closed carriage in which passengers could ride in privacy, enjoying the scenery rather than looking at the back of the driver who was now stationed in a little seat atop the rear of the vehicle. The Hansom cab was an improvement over an earlier type of carriage known as a "cabriolet," which was shortened to "cab."

The name "taxi" derives from "taximeter," a device invented by Wilhelm Bruhn in 1891 that combined a timing mechanism with a clever system of computing the distance traveled by a vehicle. So convincing was an early demonstration of Bruhn's invention, which took place in Frankfurt am Main, that a mob of outraged local cab drivers gave him a free ride—into the river.

The convergence of the two ideas—cab and taximeter—occurred in 1907, shortly after an American named Harry N. Allen was charged $5 by a New York cab driver who drove him from 44th to 58th Street, a distance of about three-quarters of a mile. Rightly enough, Allen reasoned that there might be many people who did not take cabs because of overcharging and haggling with surly drivers. He tested his theory by equipping a number of automobiles with taximeters and manning them with drivers in gray-blue uniforms trimmed with black braid. The uniforms are gone now, but the rest of Allen's scheme is very much with us.

Various systems of self-drive taxis have also been tried. One, started some years ago in Amsterdam under the name Witkar (White Car), employed electrically powered two-seat scooters. Participating members could pick them up at one station and drop them off at another. In 1972 in the French town of Montpellier, a company equipped 37 automobiles with special slot-machine devices that controlled operations. Members purchased plastic tokens that allowed them to drive at a cost of about 18 cents per mile. The plan had all the elements of success, save for one unforeseen difficulty. Rather than return the cars to a designated parking area, renters left them anywhere they wanted, making it extremely difficult for the next renters to find them.

TEA Tea is, after plain water, the most widely consumed beverage in the world. It owes its origin, according to a legend, to some sloppy housekeeping in the kitchens of the great Chinese emperor Shen Nung in 2737 B.C. It seems that while the imperial drinking water was being boiled—a common sanitary measure—some leaves from the burning branches fell into the open kettle. The aroma intrigued the emperor, and he insisted on tasting the brew.

Although tea was enormously popular throughout Asia, it did not make its appearance in western Europe until 1610, when the Dutch East India

A Tuareg tribesman takes a tea break in the Sahara.

that ultimately put most jitneys out of business.

However, a few still survive in the United States: in San Francisco, where they have been cruising Mission Street since 1916; and in Atlantic City, where they drive up and down Pacific Avenue. They can also be found, alive and packed with customers, in Caracas, Mexico City, Teheran, Istanbul, and Manila, where, in tribute to the vehicles first used, they are called "jeepneys."

Company imported a few jars of the precious leaves. Because of its exorbitant price, it predictably became the new craze of Dutch society. Predictably, too, medical authorities were wary. A learned Frenchman, Guy Patin, decried it as "the newest impertinence of the century." Some years later, when the British Isles threatened to float away on great waves of tea, the Reverend Dr. Hales demonstrated that if the tail of a suckling pig were dunked into a cup of hot tea, it would emerge hairless—a dramatic experiment that had no effect whatever on tea sales.

The British had had their first "cuppa" about 1650—coincidentally at the time that the beverage was introduced to the good burghers of New Amsterdam, the cozy Dutch outpost in North America. Despite its high price, tea became so popular that a London newspaper could soon report that tea was sold "almost in every street."

Catherine of Braganza, the Portuguese-born queen of Charles II, introduced tea drinking to the court in 1662, and more than a century later the duchess of Bedford started the custom of serving tea and cakes at five o'clock in the afternoon as a cure for what she called the daily "sinking feeling."

Tea drinking is now so much a part of life in Britain that its inhabitants consume more tea per person than those of any other country in the world. Not long ago, an eminent British industrial sociologist issued a 96-page report that defended the tea break as "fulfilling a function far beyond a mere rest pause." And when the government tried to install tea-vending machines in their offices, the 173,000 members of the civil servants union filed a petition of protest because "the machines just can't match the personal touch."

Never as popular a beverage in the United States as in England, tea nonetheless has left its imprint on the nation's history. Tea was one of the most important ingredients in the brewing of the American Revolution. Protesting the tax on

tea, on the night of December 16, 1773, colonists dumped 342 chests into Boston Harbor. The colonial cause was set.

But tea also helped to establish a worldwide reputation for Yankee-built ships, the clippers, which consistently out-raced all competition in bringing tea from China to the docks of London. One of them, the *Lightning*, traveled 436 sea miles in 24 hours, an all-time record for a sailing ship and matched only by the fastest of steamships.

In a 19th-century tea-curing shop freshly plucked leaves are carefully processed to make dried tea.

Tea also figured prominently in the development of one of the most American of institutions: the supermarket. The granddaddy of supermarket chains, The Great Atlantic & Pacific Tea Company, was established in 1869 on the premise that by purchasing staples such as tea, coffee, and spices in large quantities the store could pass on some of the savings to customers. Photographs of early A & P stores show that their sign was a huge gaslit "T" hanging over the sidewalk in front of the entrance.

The tea plant, *Camellia sinensis*, is actually an evergreen tree that grows to a height of about 30 feet in nature but under cultivation is pruned to a bushlike 3 to 5 feet. It thrives in warm climates where there exists the combination of rainfall averaging 90 to 200 inches a year and fertile and loamy soil.

An additional requirement for successful tea cultivation is a large and cheap labor force. A hardworking tea harvester can gather some 40 pounds of leaves a day, which will shrink to 10 pounds after processing. Although there are hundreds of varieties of tea on the market, all of them start out very much alike. "Black" tea, which accounts for some 97 percent of U.S. consumption, is allowed to ferment during processing. "Green" tea, more delicate and subtle in flavor, is unfermented, and "oolong" is slightly fermented and sometimes scented with flower blossoms.

The first patent for an individual tea bag was granted in 1896 to an Englishman named A.V. Smith, and today contains an average of approximately 35 grains of tea. Whether tea is dunked or steeped, one pound should yield approximately 200 cups. As for the person who indignantly refuses to do something "for all the tea in China," what he or she is passing up is something on the order of 600 million pounds of tea a year, all but 70 million pounds of which is consumed domestically.

TELEPHONE Some years ago a man climbed out on the ledge of a hotel window in New York and threatened to jump. Within minutes firemen had rigged up a net, teams of policemen were trying to reach him, and a hastily summoned priest was vainly pleading with him from an adjoining window. Then a quick-witted newspaperman reporter simply put in a call to the man's room. As soon as the telephone rang, the would-be suicide dutifully scrambled off the ledge to answer it.

At its simplest the telephone is an ingenious device that extends the range of human earshot. In a broader context, however, it has come closer than any other modern artifact to being an extension of the human body. Few sounds can more immediately generate feelings of hope, fear, relief, joy, or anxiety than the ring of a telephone. It has become, as writer John Brooks noted, "our nerve-end to society."

Yet the inventor of the telephone was neither a scientist nor an engineer. Indeed, as one of his unsuccessful rivals observed with some bitterness, "If Bell had known more about electricity, he never would have invented the telephone." What Alexander Graham Bell did know about was human speech and how it worked. Like his grandfather (who reputedly was the model for Professor Henry Higgins in George Bernard Shaw's *Pygmalion* and thus in the musical *My Fair Lady*) and

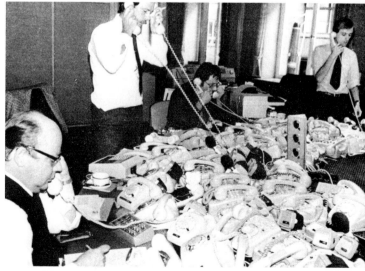

On the horns of a dilemma: brokers in Frankfurt trying to cope with the drop in the value of the dollar, 1977.

357

his father, Bell was a professor of elocution, but he was also a keen student of language. Once, while recuperating from an illness in Ontario, he passed the time by learning the language of the neighboring Mohawk Indians, becoming so fluent in it that he was initiated as an honorary member of the Mohawk tribe. The basic principle of the telephone—a vibrating membrane—came from another of Bell's inventions, an instrument to help deaf children to speak.

Few inventions have received more enthusiastic public acceptance or generated more awesome statistics than the telephone. The first commercial switchboard, connecting 21 customers, went into service in January 1878 in New Haven, Connecticut. By March 1880 there were 138 exchanges in the United States, serving 30,000 customers. Today there are well over 100 million phones, about two-fifths of the world's total, jangling some 500 million times a day.

Russians lag far behind the rest of the world in telephones—one per 15 citizens, compared with about one per 3 in Japan and Australia and one per 2 in Sweden, Switzerland, and Canada. Stalin had firmly refused to permit the establishment of a modern telephone system in the Soviet Union. "No greater instrument for counter-revolution and conspiracy can be imagined," he once said.

But the most patient, long-suffering telephone customers are in Great Britain, where one of every eight calls fails to go through and where lifelong friendships have probably been initiated by crossed lines—the random mixup of two conversations. The chanciest system may be in Egypt: Cairo businessmen have been known to

Stilted conversation: a conventional phone would not be much help.

The phone was once a means of communication for a sophisticated few.

fly to Athens in order to make their transatlantic calls.

Although Bell's original patent—number 174,465—withstood a number of challenges to become by far the most valuable one ever granted, much work has been done to improve upon his invention. The fringe benefits of this research have included such developments as the transistor, the laser, synchronous-sound motion pictures, high fidelity, and radio astronomy. Scientists at the Bell Telephone Laboratories, where all these advances were achieved, have collected an aggre-

Answerer and Questioner

"Mr. Watson—Come here—I want to see you." These words, spoken by Alexander Graham Bell on March 10, 1876, are well remembered and oft quoted as the world's first telephone conversation. But who was on the other end of the line? Thomas A. Watson was, and though he did not speak, he won distinction as the world's first telephone answerer.

Son of a livery-stable foreman in Salem, Massachusetts, young Watson left school at 14 and drifted for four years until, in July 1872, he found employment in a Boston electrical workshop. Part of the shop's business involved building models for inventors who had ideas but lacked the means or skill to execute them. One such was a young professor at Boston University, Alexander Graham Bell. It was to Bell that Watson, who had revealed an amazing capacity for tinkering, was assigned. The closeness of the two men's subsequent collaboration was remarkable, a circumstance borne out by the fact that Bell, in 1877, assigned to Watson a 10 percent interest in the newly formed Bell Company.

Such a hedge against adversity would have satisfied most men, but Watson remained restless and inquisitive. He visited the Continent, worked a farm in Massachusetts, and set up a machine shop to make marine engines. At the age of 40 he enrolled in the Massachusetts Institute of Technology to study geology. Responding to the navy's expansion program, he went into the shipbuilding business, where he lost most of his fortune. But he continued to travel, gave readings of poetry and plays, and, for a season, toured England as an actor in a Shakespearean company.

Bell and Watson held another historic telephone conversation—to inaugurate the formal opening of transcontinental telephone service on January 25, 1915. During the ceremony Bell, who was in New York, repeated his request of 39 years earlier. To which Watson, in San Francisco, finally replied, saying that he would be happy to comply but that it would take him a week to do so.

gate of some 20,000 patents as well as five Nobel Prizes. Presently on the drawing boards are: pocket-size, cordless telephones; a method of automatically forwarding calls to a designated number when the subscriber is away from home; a voice-recognition device that would permit subscribers to pay bills by issuing verbal "checks" on their bank accounts. A team of scientists is also working on the development of a display panel that would signal the number of the party who is calling, which would, of course, give the recipient who is up on his phone numbers the choice of either picking up the phone or letting it ring.

None of these, however, would solve the problem of the executive who, as a measure of his status, insisted on keeping two telephones on his desk. One day, both of them seemed to go berserk simultaneously. They would ring and ring, but each time he picked one up he would get nothing but a dial tone. All this made him so nervous that he failed to notice that he had put each receiver on the cradle of the other device.

---

customs

The Art of Answermanship

To the long list of life's minor contretemps can now be added the voice at the other end of the telephone line saying: "This is John Smith. I can't come to the phone right now, but if you leave your name and number when you hear the tone. . . ."

Once a status symbol of sorts, the telephone answering machine is fast becoming standard equipment in many American homes. Essentially a tape recorder, it can range in price anywhere from $60 for basic models to $1,300 for sophisticated ones. And thanks to modern technology, they are reliable and easy to install.

In fact, the machine's most serious drawback is that all too often callers, because of annoyance, resentment, or just plain "freezing up," fail to leave a message. To coax them into so doing, the art of "answermanship" has developed. Some people use a "cute" approach: "Hi there, I'm so-and-so's answering machine. He isn't here and I'm lonesome. Won't you talk to me?" Others, notably actors or writers, use more creative techniques: "I'm awfully busy right now translating *Beowulf*. But if you will leave your name and number. . . ." Success in this area, however, can be dicey, as one piano-playing machine user in Boston discovered. His "ragtime ditty" was so entertaining that he began receiving up to 300 calls a day from people who had no message but just wanted to listen. As a result, he decided to set up a company to sell prerecorded answering tapes—everything for the machine from a businesslike greeting to orchestrated production numbers with voice-overs.

Throughout the period of the answering-machine takeover, little attention has been paid to the poor caller who, suddenly finding himself talking to a robot, can think only of profane or obscene rejoinders—perhaps rightly so. But a possible alternative is to advise the machine's keeper to consult Holy Writ, specifically the Book of Isaiah, chapter 50, verse 2: "Wherefore. . . .when I called was there none to answer?"

TELEVISION After peering at a grayish, jittering image on a small screen in 1938, E.B. White wrote: "Television is going to be the test of the modern world." It just might, he thought, become an "unbearable disturbance." To some, television was worse than a disturbance; it was economic disaster. With sets entering American homes at the dizzying rate of a quarter-million a month in the early 1950's, movie theaters resorted to giving away china in hopes of luring back some of their patrons. Hollywood was in desperate straits. Newspapers and magazines grew thinner as advertising flowed to the new medium. Radio talked faster and faster to fewer and fewer listeners, and sports fans stayed home. Restaurant trade fell off, the deadest hour of all being precisely eight o'clock on Tuesday nights—when the Milton Berle show was on.

Like the word "television," which is half Latin and half Greek (from the Greek *tele* meaning "far" and the Latin *videre*, "to see"), the medium, too, has a dual, paradoxical nature. It influences everyone and pleases no one fully. If it has made of the world a "global village," it is also accused of

Camera-ready performers try to demonstrate the feasibility of TV transmission in a Philadelphia lab, 1935.

Set up: Mom need not miss a turn of the world.

destroying neighborhood and family life. Children have seen the sea bottom and the inside of the womb, yet television has taken a large share of the blame for America's shocking rise in illiteracy. Though reviewed as an art form, it is run, for the most part, as a business. Although it has brought ballet and opera to isolated communities, it is constantly excoriated for failing its potential, for developing instead, as commentator David Susskind once put it, into "a gigantic hokum, a huge comic strip."

Whatever television is, it is here, having leaped in one hypnotizing generation from the experimental broadcasts of the 1930's to that place in our lives once occupied by the family hearth, the neighbors, and the newspaper. Along with the automobile, it has been called one of the most influential social forces of the century.

The majority of Americans get most of their news from television. The typical American five-year-old has spent more hours in front of a TV set than a college student spends in four years of classes. Some estimates award to TV a quarter of America's waking life, though the total hours in which sets are on have declined slightly since 1973. Political candidates devote a good three-quarters of their campaign budgets to television advertising, perhaps because Americans own more sets than bathtubs.

In its great moments television creates shared experiences that cut across social, geographic, and ethnic distinctions. In 1951, for example, the co-axial cable spanned the continent, and Edward R.

customs

Is Anyone Listening?

Some time ago an American magazine tried to dramatize the extent of electronic snooping by concocting a "bugged" martini. The olive held a tiny transmitter that, with the aid of an antenna disguised as a toothpick, could pick up and broadcast indiscreet cocktail conversation over a distance of some 100 feet.

Unfortunately, another magazine spoiled the fun by pointing out that the liquid in the martini would distort the sound waves. Nonetheless, very effective bugs have been hidden in such innocent objects as cuff links, lipsticks, fountain pens, cigarette packages, picture frames, briefcase handles, wristwatches, and even toilet-paper rollers. Portable laser microphones and similar devices can pick up conversations held in closed rooms hundreds of feet away.

Nor does a snooper need the resources of a James Bond. A miniaturized FM microphone—the bug's basic element—can be purchased for about $10, and do-it-yourselfers can assemble their own bugs. "It's as easy to make one," says an expert, "as the old crystal set."

According to electronic-security specialists, the telephone remains "the greatest threat to privacy." Every telephone is linked to a local exchange by two wires. Anyone who knows how to find the right set of wires can tap a phone. Furthermore, the addition of a simple device known as a "hook-switch bypass" will turn the tap into a bug that can then pick up sounds and voices while the receiver is on its cradle. For more sophisticated eavesdroppers there are other gadgets, such as the "silver box," which permits

As a movie snoop Gene Hackman stoops to bugging a bathroom.

lines to be tapped from any place in the country; the "harmonica," which defeats most bug-locating equipment; and the "pen register," which keeps a record of what calls are made, to what numbers, when, and how often.

Understandably, no one knows for sure how many phone lines have been tapped and for what reasons. Judicial approval, of course, is required now for all *legal* wiretaps. According to the American Civil Liberties Union, some 150,000 to 250,000 people are now or have been "tapped" by the federal government or local police alone. How many others may have been subjected to industrial espionage, professional snooping, or the search for damaging information is anyone's guess.

One clue to the number may lie in the success of another recent device, known as the "cloak," a telephone receiver equipped with a special panel that lights up if the phone is being tapped. Despite the $3,500 price tag, the "cloak" is being unfurled with remarkable speed in many locations.

Murrow's feature program *See It Now* broadcast simultaneous live shots of New York's Brooklyn Bridge and San Francisco's Golden Gate Bridge—television's symbolic golden spike. The political debates of 1960 brought two presidential candidates together to confront each other in the nation's living rooms. The one who looked straight into the camera, John F. Kennedy, won. And in the greatest broadcast ever, television took the eyes of the world for a walk on the moon. As astronaut Neil Armstrong bounded joyously in and out of camera range, the signal bounded to Parkes, Australia, then to a communications satellite over the Pacific Ocean, from there to Jamesburg, California, where it went by wire to NASA's Mission Control in Houston, Texas, and from the Houston television station to New York—all in 1.3 seconds.

Not everything that happens on television is so well orchestrated. There was the time when comedian Jackie Gleason fell during a sketch and broke his leg on the show. There was the streaker who dashed naked across the stage in front of the cameras during the Academy Awards just as David Niven intoned, "The envelope, please." And in the most shocking piece of unrehearsed business, President Kennedy's accused assassin Lee Harvey Oswald was himself fatally shot directly on camera in 1963.

Showing your emotions on television may or may not win friends. Vice-presidential candidate Richard Nixon defended his right to keep a bit of payola, a dog called Checkers, and the nation forgave him. But when cameras came upon presidential contender Edmund Muskie weeping over an insult his wife had endured, viewers felt that his image was damaged.

"Image" is what viewers conclude from what they get to see, a factor that has graduated television from being a mere observer to an actual participant in changing political styles. When Kennedy entered the White House with the century's slimmest popular-vote margin, he moved to shore up support by inaugurating the first live broadcasts of presidential press conferences. President Johnson shifted the State of the Union address from its traditional noontime delivery to evening prime time, addressing not just Congress but the nation. When television was introduced into the Canadian Parliament, many image-conscious members rushed out to buy pastel shirts and get their hair done. Even terrorists have learned to manipulate events for the greatest possible TV exposure. Arab terrorists who seized OPEC headquarters in Vienna in 1975 refused to budge until the television crews arrived. One man, to get the attention of the president of the United States, held a diabetic hostage and watched the president promise to speak with him on a TV set he had traded for another hostage.

Television is so potent a social force that South Africa's government banned it from the racially divided nation until 1975, making South Africa the last industrialized nation to give in. The color sets were priced around $1,200, in order, some suspected, to prevent nonwhites from buying them. (At the same time in the United States color sets were being sold at less than half that amount.) Because of television's high production costs, smaller nations find it cheaper to buy American shows than to make their own. The result: *Kojak* is big in Cairo, and Finland sits down to *Bonanza*. Iceland, however, has declined to overwhelm its traditional culture with American-made images.

An increasing number of parents and educators could not help agreeing with Iceland's choice. Says media critic Marshall McLuhan, "The TV experience is . . . as addictive as any known drug." Children who have let the tube do their talking, moving, imagining, and socializing for them may be showing, according to a number of studies, such disturbing generational patterns as lack of problem-solving ability, inability to concentrate, and a built-in expectation that everything has to happen easily. Or they may just be zonked, like the four-year-old who was told by a robber who had tied up his mother, "Look, kid, go watch TV for a couple hours, huh?" The kid complied.

TV or not TV: an artist showed boys enjoying the tube before it existed.

TV, adds McLuhan, "is not a substitute for reality; but is itself an immediate reality." Like many other electronic devices revolutionizing our world, the thing is hard to talk back to. One could, like the football fan who fell in a rage when his team lost, take a .30-caliber carbine and shoot the TV. A religious sect in Lapland did better. Tired of the devilish ways of television, they bought up all the sets in the village and ritually axed them. A Texas group immolated a TV set doused with lighter fluid in a San Antonio street.

They may have acted too soon, since television has more up its sleeve these days than sitcoms, reruns, docudramas, and miniseries. Shoppers may soon be able to push a TV button and order, by universal charge card, products shown on the screen. Closed-circuit systems used in business, education, and medicine, surveillance systems from banks to satellites, sets that play games or tape a favorite show—all are uses to which television technology has already been adapted.

And if viewers do not go for any of those improvements, they might, suggests one Midwestern engineer, use the television set to predict tornadoes. According to Newton Weller, when the set is tuned in a certain way, it will glow eerily if a ground-level tornado is within a 15- to 20-mile radius. If that happens, warns Weller, take cover!

TENNIS Gentleman, scholar, and sportsman, Major Walter Wingfield was also a considerate weekend guest. To relieve his fellow guests in the country of endless games of croquet, he introduced an amusing lawn game played with a rubber ball and a paddle on an odd, hourglass-shaped court divided by a high net. The game proved a natural for mixed company: ladies could merrily pop the ball back and forth without risk to either costume or coiffure. When Wingfield won a patent on his original court design in 1874, he modestly disclaimed having invented the game, explaining that he had merely adapted for outdoor play the game of court tennis, popular among royalty as early as the 14th century. And since the Greeks and Romans had played something similar in a courtyard, he donnishly dubbed his game *Sphairistiké*, meaning "ballplaying" in Greek. The lawn game was an instant success. As for the name, wrote one wag, anyone could master it in six easy lessons. Most people gave up trying and simply sang out, "Sticky, anyone?"

Yet lawn tennis, as it more sensibly came to be

Wrapped up in the game: net, balls, and a little bit of the green.

called, was indeed a new game. Court tennis had anciently evolved from a fierce sort of handball, with tricky off-the-wall shots played off sloping walls behind each player. So popular was the game in the 16th century that there existed some 1,800 courts in Paris alone. Court tennis bequeathed modern tennis its mysterious 15-unit scoring system, proceeding from "love" or zero to 15, to 30, to 40, and to game. (In hundreds of years of tennis, the only real change in game scoring was to elide the third point, which should be 45, to 40.) No one has the foggiest notion how such a system originated, not even Antonio Scaino, who wrote the first book on tennis in 1555.

The term "love" may derive from the French word *l'oeuf*, an egg, which would represent zero. Some, however, think it originated with the English usage of "love" for "nothing," as in an 18th-century shopkeepers' expression: "Look for love and buy for money." Shakespeare's *Much Ado About Nothing*, for example, is about love. The term "deuce" comes from the French custom of saying, when tied at 40, *à deux*, meaning two points to game. "Let," a serve that nicks the top of the net, was once a common English word for an obstruction or hindrance.

Considerable question surrounds the origin of the name of the game, historically spelled some 20 different ways, varying from "tynes" to "tennysse" to "tinnis" (after the name of an Egyptian town noted for the cotton used in balls). The most logical kinship seems to be the French word *tenez*, which could mean "Take it!" or even "Get set! I'm about to serve!" If, as the theory goes, the command was regularly cried out in the course of the ancient game, it just may have stuck.

In its first balmy Victorian decade, lawn tennis was played every which way—with triangular, square, or shovel-shaped rackets, with nets of all heights, and balls of all weights. At times, three or four people played on a side—quadruples instead of doubles. By the time some tennis buffs persuaded the All England Croquet and Lawn Tennis Club of Wimbledon, England, to mount a tennis championship on its manicured greensward, the court at least had achieved its present dimensions. The first Wimbledon championship was handily won in 1877 by S.W. Gore, who later decided that

This lady of lawn tennis wears traditional garb that enables her to play gracefully but not too vigorously.

On Being Theatrical

Colorful expressions from the theater permeate our language, from the half-ironic "The show must go on!" to the rueful "That's show biz." Some of the more obvious terms that have entered common language are "stage presence," "stage fright," "showmanship," or being "stage struck," which can now apply to any profession.

We speak of "overacting" or "underplaying" a situation, giving a "command performance," or "taking stage center." "Upstaging" began in early theaters where the stages sloped toward the audience. An actor's position near the back of the stage not only placed him above his colleagues but forced them to turn toward him—and away from the audience—when they addressed him. Such an actor might also try to "steal the spotlight," or "limelight." A chorus girl who plays to the audience is sometimes called a "footlight Fanny."

A "ham" actor is one who exaggerates his role or plays for "gags" (from the Middle English *gaggen*, meaning, appropriately enough, "to suffocate" or "to choke"). The term "ham" probably comes from the pork lard which performers once used to remove their makeup or from the free hams occasionally passed out to lure audiences into a show.

Many of today's common expressions have vaudevillian roots. A "one-man show" refers to a variety act by a single performer, often a "quick-change artist" with a large repertoire. A "straight man" sets up his comical partner, as Bud Abbott did in his routines with Lou Costello.

"A one-night stand," originally a portable theater put up for an evening's performance, now refers to a different sort of transient engagement. In early theater, men played women's roles, or "drag" parts, in long costumes that dragged across the stage. Now the

term refers to men's or women's clothing when it is worn by the opposite sex.

When a show flops or "lays an egg," it is said to be a "turkey," probably because performances given during holiday, or turkey, seasons often played to overfed, snoozing audiences. A "turkey" can now also refer to a disastrous business venture or to a very doltish person.

Many phrases relate to the mechanics of the theater. The "deus ex machina" in ancient Greek theater was a god flown in by a crane to set things right. Today the term means any sort of external, resolving action. "Winging it," or improvising, originated with actors who had to rely on prompters—standing in the wings. Even the modern airport practice of flying "stand by" comes from the theater, echoing the stage manager's warning to the actors to "stand by" at their places before the curtain goes up.

The "set" in all its glory, painted by the Italian Giovanni Paolo Pannini in the 18th century.

tennis was "very monotonous." Frankly, he preferred cricket. A letter written to the Harvard *Crimson* agreed, commenting icily, "The game is well enough for lazy or weak men, but men who have rowed or taken part in nobler sport should blush to be seen playing lawn tennis."

But this view of the game did not last. Gore had early discovered that rushing the net was the key to a successful game. The next year, a tea planter visiting from Ceylon decided to counter this tactic and came up with the lob, which, in turn, inspired the overhead smash. Volleying suddenly turned tennis into a competitive sport that required strength, and from that point on mixed tennis seemed doomed to part company. "The volley

game," declared the American champion Richard Sears, "is not made for ladies."

The ladies, swathed in lawn-length skirts, petticoats, corsets, and even hats, were too encumbered to scamper after a ball, much less volley. Gentlemen, in roomy trousers and light shirts, were certainly freer to move. Then suddenly, a feisty lass from California named May Sutton appeared to challenge that matter of women and the volley. She volleyed. She smashed. She ran like the wind. She was not, some felt, too ladylike. May Sutton went to Wimbledon in 1905 and won the women's championship, the first non-English person to beat the English on their home grass. She was not, however, permitted to set foot on the

customs

Theatrical Superstitions

Almost every group has its superstitions, but probably none has more or holds them more strongly than theater people, whose serendipitous profession has long depended on the patronage of kings, the approval of crowds, and a dash of first-night magic where drama critics are concerned.

Most everyone knows enough not to wish an actor good luck on opening night, but to advise him instead to "break a leg." The Swedes and Germans offer more tangible support in obtaining this goal—a swift kick. The French discreetly whisper "*merde*," while Americans are assured of success if they manage to say the English equivalent while on stage. Falling during a performance supposedly ensures a long-running play.

Actors, like many of us, also believe that a hare's foot brings luck. Tallulah Bankhead carried

one that her father had given her, and when she died, it was buried with her.

The "don'ts" of stage lore, however, far outnumber the "do's"; and a neophyte actor who ignores any of them may become known as a "Jonah" and find that no one will hire him. Whistling in a dressing room is considered a disastrous activity, perhaps because of an association with being "whistled out," or sacked. "Three Blind Mice" and "I Dreamt I Dwelt in Marble Halls" are among the many tunes never to be hummed or sung in theater.

Seemingly innocuous objects often barred from a stage include peacock feathers, umbrellas (opening an umbrella or leaving it on the prompter's table is even more unlucky), real mirrors, jewels, and Bibles (painted ones are used). Many foods and drinks are also eschewed, and actors often

eat colored bread instead of eggs and drink iced tea instead of Scotch. Live flowers, too, are tabooed, though on practical grounds, because an actor can slip on their petals and flowers can aggravate hay fever.

Certain colors, it is also believed, can induce bad fortune. Green, although standard for the actors' lounge, or "green room," is studiously avoided elsewhere. One explanation is that intense green lights, known as "limes," often followed villains in melodramas, and an actor garbed in green was hard to spot. Most probably, however, the belief was encouraged by those in charge of lighting, for green scenery and costumes tend to look brown when lit. Violet, black, and yellow are avoided as well.

An entire play, *Macbeth*, is thought to bring bad luck. Traditionally, certain passages are never quoted backstage, and props and costumes used for the play are kept separate.

Even today some directors forbid actors to say the last lines of plays—called "tag lines"—at rehearsals. This may reflect yet another superstitious belief among people of the theater that it is better to leave certain things to chance—and retain spontaneity—than to challenge the gods by displaying total perfection.

Strolling players of the 16th century had their own rituals.

Three on three: the game of court tennis as it might have looked in the time of England's King Henry VII.

awesome Centre Court until her scandalously exposed arms were covered and her tennis dress, which revealed a glimpse of leg, was let down. She won—a vanguard figure in the long struggle of women athletes for equal recognition and, finally, equal pay. The battle had its symbolic victory when Billy Jean King in 1971 became the first woman athlete to break $100,000 in winnings.

J.M. Barrie once wrote: "What a polite game tennis is. The chief word in it seems to be 'sorry.'" Only a century after its birth, Major Wingfield's polite pastime has become an aggressive mass movement, a top-rated spectator sport, and, in the United States, a $600-million industry. Tennis madness peaked in 1974 when a full 16 percent of the population set out to perfect its backhand. Once limited to the aristocratic turf of estates and clubs, tennis now draws its concrete and composition-bred champs from every race and nation. But such is the charm of tennis—as sociable as it is fierce, as ancient as it is adaptable.

THERMOMETER Galileo charted temperature changes with a "thermoscope," a glass bulb the size of a hen's egg drawn into a long stem open at the end. The bulb was heated, and the end of the tube was placed in a container of water. As the bulb cooled and the heated air shrank, the liquid rose in the tube. In this way, Galileo was able to measure heat. Santorio Santorio, Galileo's colleague and the originator of the instrumental approach to medicine, affixed a graduated scale to the thermoscope, thereby making the device practical outside the laboratory.

Two major problems remained, however. The first, that the thermoscope also responded to changes in atmospheric pressure, was solved by Grand Duke Ferdinand II of Tuscany in the mid-17th century. He and other Florentine acade-micians depended on the skills of the local glass-blowers to fashion glass cylinders that sealed the liquids, such as wine or mercury, inside. The second, that there was no standard system of measurements, had to wait until 1724, when Gabriel Daniel Fahrenheit, a German instrument maker living in Holland, announced that he had set the freezing point at 32° and normal body temperature at 96°. Until that time, scales had been calibrated to everything from the melting point of butter to the temperature of the basement of the Paris Observatory.

In 1742 a Swedish astronomer, Anders Celsius, proposed a graduated thermometer, using 0° as the boiling point of water and 100° as the melting point of snow. That scale, inverted, is known as the Celsius scale.

Today thermometers perform a wide range of functions, from measuring temperatures inside and outside the home to monitoring and controlling industrial processes. Indoor-outdoor thermometers are often of the "filled-system" type, which are made of metal bulbs and capillaries filled with either a gas or a liquid. They are also used to control thermostats in ovens, furnaces, and air conditioners. "Bimetallic thermometers" most commonly activate wall thermostats. Two different metals are wound together and connected to an indicator. When the strip

Seventeenth-century "slow" thermometers: pretty but inaccurate

is heated, one metal expands more than the other, causing the pointer to move.

The too-familiar fever thermometer, which London hospitals first began using routinely in 1867, is the most widely employed medical instrument. Researchers have developed a new kind of disposable fever thermometer, thereby eliminating the need to sterilize. A series of numbered dots, each containing a chemical that turns blue at an increase in temperature, are displayed on a plastic strip, which is held in the mouth for about 30 seconds. By reading the numbers next to the blue dots, a person can tell at a glance the temperature of the patient.

An even newer temperature-measuring device depends on liquid crystals that change color at specific temperatures. Attached to a baby bottle, it lets you know when the milk is heated to the right temperature; wrapped like a collar around a wine bottle, the crystals assure the host that when he serves the wine to his guests, it has reached the proper temperature for bringing out the flavor.

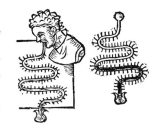

Early representation of Santorio Santorio's serpentine heat-measurer.

THREAD The art of spinning thread is woven into Greek mythology in the story of the three Fates, who control the thread of each man's destiny. Clotho holds the spindle on which the thread is wound at birth, Lachesis measures out its length, and Atropos snips it with her shears at the moment of death.

Until the late Middle Ages, when the spinning wheel was introduced into Europe, probably from India, thread was made in the West by the same tried-and-true method used by the ancient Egyptians. A ball of fibers—cotton, wool, or flax—was mounted on a stick called the distaff; the fibers were then pulled into strands, twisted, and wound as thread onto a spindle. "Distaff side" still means woman's work or branch of the family. Formerly, spinsters who spent too much time spinning ended up as "old maids."

By the early 1800's silk and linen thread manufactured in the Scottish city of Paisley was sold in loose hanks in stores. When spools were introduced they cost an extra halfpenny, which was refunded when an empty spool was returned. In those days cotton was considered inferior stuff, not fine enough for thread. But when Napoleon cut off Britain's supply of silk, the Scottish mills, forced to diversify, developed the first twisted cotton thread strong enough to compete with silk.

In the early 1800's John Mercer, a self-taught poor boy, landed a job in London as a chemist in the color shop of a fabric printer. This was the beginning of many years of smelly, steamy experiments that led Mercer to bring new and vivid colors to the English fabric industry.

In the early 19th century many scientific societies sprang up, through which practical and theoretical discoveries were exchanged with equal enthusiasm. A member of several of these, Mercer seems to have had a remarkable insight into matters that were beginning to change the world. Mercer's main interest, however, was the effect of certain chemicals on vegetable fibers, an investigation that led to the mercerizing of cotton. When cotton is subjected under tension to a solution of caustic soda, the fibers, he discovered, become permanently shorter, thicker, and tougher. The process, applicable to thread or fabric, also renders the cotton semitransparent and able to take a dye as it never did before. For this and other work Mercer was elected to the Royal Society, England's highest scientific honor, in 1852. His memorial is writ small on every spool of "mercerized" cotton thread.

There is in the world one wondrous thread that is older than other thread, as thin as air, and as strong as steel. Its secret rests with the spiders who spin it. Man has often attempted to appropriate this miracle thread, but, as one experimenter found, it would take 450 spiders to create a yard of usable thread. Spiderweb is used in optical instruments, such as the sights of certain large guns.

Industry has done better at creating synthetic threads of amazing variety and strength, in a myriad of colors. For example, there is now a basting thread that dissolves without a clue when the finished garment is cleaned. A "clue" also means a ball of thread, which is why master detectives have to unravel clues to solve a mystery.

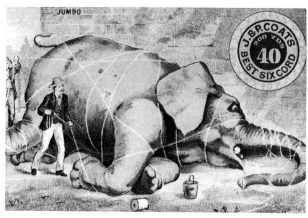

In a grand example of advertiser's hyperbole, this old ad trumpeted the strength of "best six cord" thread.

TIDE In no place in the world is the energy of the tides so impressive as in Canada's Bay of Fundy, between Nova Scotia and New Brunswick. There, twice a day, 100 billion tons of seawater bulge inland from the bay's wide mouth into ever-narrowing and shallower confines. Moving at 8 miles per hour over the long mud flats, the advance wave of the tide (known as a tidal bore) sounds like an approaching train. When the tide is high, the wharves perched on 50-foot pilings seem to be afloat and the fishing weirs to have vanished. During the great highs of the spring and fall equinoctial tides, a man who had left his clam rake on the flats would have to dive 60 feet straight

Ticket to Dream On

There is a story about a Frenchman, an inveterate player of the *Loterie Nationale*, who died and was duly buried in his finest suit. Sorting through his papers his widow came across a scrawled number, which had just won a large prize in the last lottery drawing. Unable to find her husband's ticket, she wrestled with her conscience, then ordered the body exhumed. Sure enough, tucked in an inside pocket was the precious ticket.

Critics could point to this incident as but another example of the base appeal of lotteries, but the practice of drawing lots to distribute something valuable has a long history and considerable biblical support. The Old Testament describes how the Lord instructed Moses to divide the Promised Land among the Children of Israel—by lot. One of the Proverbs teaches: "The lot causeth contentions to cease, and parteth between the mighty."

A lottery played a crucial role in Homer's *Iliad*. Unable to decide who should fight Hector, son of the king of Troy, the Greek heroes placed their names in a helmet and drew one out. Roman emperors frequently distributed prizes by lot, and Augustus added the fillip that was to guarantee lotteries their enduring prosperity: occasionally he required participants to pay for tickets.

From this mercenary maneuver it was an easy, if quick, shuffle to an equally fundamental law of lotteries: that a lottery's organizers are not required to pay out all of the money generated by ticket sales. Indeed, it is the very discrepancy between sales revenues and prize monies that has made lotteries such a popular way of raising large amounts of cash. In the late Middle Ages cities such as Bruges, Utrecht, and Ghent sponsored lotteries to pay for municipal improvements. But it was France's spendthrift king Francis I who took the broader and more venal view and

The French National Lottery in 1879 employed this elaborate apparatus.

established in 1539 the first national lottery. Elizabeth I of England followed suit in 1566. At her order, 40,000 tickets costing 10 shillings apiece were sold. The prizes—precursors of uncounted church and school raffles yet to come—consisted of "plate and certaine sorts of merchaundizes."

Fairly early in the game, lottery sponsors found that worthy causes helped spur ticket sales—perhaps because the idea helped to assuage guilt feelings about gambling. Thus, in 1627, a series of lotteries was licensed to help pay for a London aqueduct, and another later raised money to build the British Museum. In the American colonies, where lotteries were especially popular, drawings helped finance the construction of artillery batteries near Philadelphia, the reconstruction of Faneuil Hall in Boston, and the building of roads, bridges, and harbor facilities. Lotteries also helped pay for the buildings of a number of struggling colleges—Harvard, Yale, Columbia, Princeton, and William and Mary.

Not surprisingly, lotteries with their beguiling if statistically remote prospects of instant wealth have been enormously popular in many parts of the world. In Brazil, for instance, there are two national lotteries: the weekly federal lottery and the weekly sports lottery. In Mexico City the head-

quarters of the National Lottery for Public Assistance employs hundreds of workers to run the multimillion-dollar enterprise. Other countries have discovered that lotteries are an effective means of distributing scarce commodities without cries of unfairness or favoritism. In Argentina, when mortgage money was scarce, some 100 savings-and-loan societies organized monthly lotteries. The prize: the right to borrow. And in Japan, where luck-conscious citizens pay homage to no less than seven gods of chance, lotteries have been used to dole out everything from places in prestigious kindergartens to cemetery plots.

But money is what lotteries are all about, and the difference between what is taken in and paid out is of more than passing interest to ticket buyers. The French *Loterie Nationale*, more generous than some others, subscribed to a 60–40 ratio, with the 60 percent going back in prizes. Most of the state-sponsored lotteries that have blossomed in the United States since New Hampshire introduced the first in 1964 pay out only 45 percent. This constitutes a form of legal fast shuffle, according to some critics, who point out that illegal numbers games return from 60 to 74 cents on a dollar and the typical Las Vegas roulette table up to 95 cents.

Still, people do love a lottery, as was demonstrated not long ago by three enterprising psychologists. They selected a 22-mile stretch of road in Green River canyon, Utah, along which motorists and hikers had been working strenuously *not* to "Keep America Beautiful," and put up their own modest signs. These notified passersby that in exchange for every bag of litter collected they would receive 25 cents or a ticket in a weekly lottery that promised a $20 reward. The psychologists discovered that the volume of litter landing in trash cans increased dramatically.

down to retrieve it, or he could wait six hours for the water to recede and hope it was still there.

The eternal tides are not only lunar (and to some degree solar) but seem lunatic in their deviations from shore to shore. At Nantucket Island, a few hundred miles south of the Bay of Fundy, the tidal flux is no more than two feet. In Florida, Atlantic coast Miamians see two equal tides a day, but for residents at Pensacola on the Gulf of Mexico there is only one. At Key West, not far from Miami, fishermen adapt to mixed tides—two a day but of unequal highs and lows. These mixed tides (characterized by what oceanographers call a higher high or a lower high, or a higher low or a lower low) wash many of the world's shores.

Only recently has science caught the tide. Aristotle, aware that the moon affected the tide in some way, was said to have fallen into despair trying to discover why tides in the Euripos strait in the Aegean Sea behaved predictably for several days and then went into fits of ebbing and flowing 12 to 14 times a day. Not until Newton discovered the law of gravitation did the obvious attraction of sea and moon begin to make sense. Gravitation also explained what had long been another mystery: why, if the moon passes overhead once every 24 hours and 50 minutes, does the tide in most places rise twice—every 12 hours and 25 minutes? The answer is that just as the moon pulls the sea under it away from the earth, at a point exactly opposite on the globe it pulls the earth away from the sea, creating two tidal bulges on each side of the planet.

Every particle of matter on earth experiences some of the moon's pull: there are tides in the earth and the air as well, though they are barely perceptible to us. It is possible that earth tides, a

matter of a few inches, may play a role in triggering earthquakes.

Knowledge of gravitational attraction alone could not have solved Aristotle's problem about the strait of Euripos, since the tides at any single location are also affected by local factors, such as the shape and rhythm of oscillation in a particular coastal basin.

Today, tidal computers can take all these variables into account to predict future tides within minutes of accuracy—a service on which the world's shipping depends critically. But for centuries, seafarers had only local knowledge and their own experience to ride on. Julius Caesar, for example, accustomed to the minimal tides of the Mare Nostrum, had to learn the ways of the English Channel the hard way.

When Caesar and his troops invaded Britain, they landed near Dover during hard onshore winds. They anchored their transports and pulled the lighter galleys above what they supposed was the high-tide mark. Within hours, a great tide had pulled anchor on the transports and smashed them ashore, and most of the galleys lay smithered in surf. Bold Caesar, who had left the shipwright's tools behind in France, had to dispatch a galley to fetch them before repairs could even begin. These same tricky tides played a role in confounding the Spanish Armada and in discouraging both Napoleon and Hitler from risking an invasion of Britain by sea.

Poets have envisioned both natural law and apocalypse in the tides. Not far from where Caesar foundered, Matthew Arnold heard in the "melancholy, long, withdrawing roar" of the tide at Dover Beach the death of the old world view—in which man, god, and nature stood in unchanging relationship. He was righter than he knew, for scientists now say that the braking friction of the moon-driven tides has slowed the earth's rotation and will continue to do so. For instance, a clock started 100 years ago would now be 30 seconds fast. As the earth slows, the moon must speed up, slinging itself into a more distant orbit, until the month and the earthly day become equalized at about 47 current days, though billions of years from now. Then, as far as the moon is concerned, the rise and fall of the tides will cease altogether; both low and high tide will stand fixed in place as the earth turns but one cheek to the moon.

For the moment, however, the tides are "eternal," Homer's dread whirlpool Charybdis still churns in the Strait of Messina, across from the rock Scylla, occasionally tossing up an eyeless, phosphorescent fish of the deeps, and Poe's Maelstrom, an actual tidal whirlpool in Norway, still swallows a boatman now and then.

At low tide Little River, Nova Scotia, becomes a mere mudflat, but the high piers reveal the tide's power.

TOMBSTONE Of all the animal species, mankind alone buries its dead. How far back the custom goes is unknown, but evidence uncovered in the Shanidar cave in Iraq indicates that Neanderthal man practiced burial some 60,000 years ago and even laid flowers on the graves. "Mid the uneasy wanderings of paleolithic man," wrote sociologist Lewis Mumford, "the dead were the first to have a permanent dwelling: a cavern, a mound marked by a cairn . . . to which the living probably returned at intervals." A pile of stones, a single stone set upright—here, one could say, the spirit of one's ancestors abides. Probably the earliest tombstones were meant to placate those restless spirits or to seal the mouth of a cave or crypt from robbers.

The departed father and his family are forever united in this monument.

The style of the tombstone reflects the people. Vikings buried their chief with his boat, complete with supplies. But a humbler Viking had only the outline of a boat marked in fieldstones, though it sometimes stretched over 60 feet. In England the ground on the south side of a village church is frequently higher than on the north side, for in medieval times the dead were buried away from the shadow of the church in graves that were stacked practically on top of one another. The Devil lurked in shadows and, as everyone knew, appeared from the north. In Victorian times the north side of the church was reserved for persons who had committed suicide.

Victorians in America moved the village graveyard to the outskirts of town, and despite the preference of the age for ostentatious obelisks, angels, and crypts, a few 19th-century eccentrics managed to make a unique final statement. In Kentucky a wealthy old horse trader, the last of his line, had life-size statues made of his sisters, brothers, dogs, and even a deer and fox to keep him company at graveside. The Colonel himself was shown seated on his favorite hunting horse, Fop. There they stand today, the Wooldridge Monuments, an oddly unfriendly group, each staring stonily forward. In Buchanan, Michigan, a stubborn freethinker scandalized the town by unveiling prematurely a costly monument inscribed on the west face: "FREE SPEECH: The more Religion, the more Lying," and on the north face: "FREE RELIGION: The more priests, the more Poverty. Nature is the true God. Science the true Religion." The pious townsfolk defaced the monument; a few spat tobacco juice on it. When Joseph Coveney finally went to rest beneath those sentiments the controversy was forgotten, and the local paper noted only that he had been "a follower of Paine."

Tombstones of the famous and infamous alike risk the undying passions of the public. In London's Highgate Cemetery a huge bust of Karl Marx adorns his tomb. Many visitors come bearing flowers, but one whose philosophy was no doubt contrary to Marx's once deprived the statue of its nose. The Indianapolis tombstone of John Dillinger, the notorious bank robber, was chipped nearly to extinction by souvenir hunters, emulating, it would seem, his own skills.

One of the world's most extraordinary cemeteries, Père-Lachaise in Paris, is a crowded necropolis of the illustriously entombed. The remains of the medieval lovers Abélard and Héloïse lie there, and Colette, Balzac, Daumier, Proust, Modigliani, Chopin, Gertrude Stein, and Edith Piaf are among those eternally at home to callers.

Also buried there is the playwright Oscar Wilde, who scandalized England in his day by his homosexuality. Even his tomb, topped by a winged sphinx sculpture by Jacob Epstein, was not, in this Parisian Elysium, safe from English prudery. Shocked to discover that Wilde's sphinx was visibly male, two English ladies took a rock and broke off the offending parts. Rescued by a guard and taken to the office of the curator, they served for some years as paperweights.

The flag-draped casket of a French wine merchant stands before stone keg in which it will be interred.

Epitaphs: Parting Words

To those with a taste for it, graveyards are nice places to visit, not the least because they make good reading. Brushing away the lichen from an old headstone, one may come across an epitaph that, like a voice from the grave itself, roots the passer-by to his tracks. Some of the best inscriptions are found in New England graveyards that date from the 18th and 19th centuries, and not a few tell sad tales.

"Here lie Paul, Rachel, Amos, John and tiny Richard, put to an early death by the misability of sister Elizabeth to light a fire in the hearth." This angry epitaph, written before the truth-in-advertising laws, declares that the lady here interred "was fatally Burned . . . by the explosion of a lamp Filled with R.F. Danforth's Non-Explosive Burning Fluid." In Burlington, Massachusetts, another such unfortunate is entombed: "Here lies the body of Susan Lowder/Who burst while drinking Sedlitz Powder/Called from this world to Her Heavenly rest/She should have waited Till it effervesced." In Vermont the parents of a young boy had a similar complaint, this time for the doctor: "Behold the amazing alteration,/Effected by inoculation;/The means employed his life to save,/Hurried him headlong to the grave." A stone found in England makes a smugger claim: "Here lies the body of Thomas Procter,/Who lived and died without a doctor."

Where death's scythe harvested so many, second and even third marriages were not uncommon, and many were buried with their several spouses. New Englanders were wont to put the matter tersely: "Here lies a wife/Of two husbands bereft:/Robert on the right,/Richard on the left." No doubt the following was meant kindly: "She lived with her husband fifty years/And died in a confident hope of a better life." There is no ambiguity, however, in this touching tribute to a hap-py marriage: "We took sweet counsel together and walked unto the house of God in company."

Frontier America had its own roughhewn style of living and dying. Though many of the wooden headstones are lost, one can still read in Tombstone, Arizona, of poor "George Johnson/Hanged by Mistake." Tradition only preserves this: "Here lays Butch,/We planted him raw/He was quick on the trigger/But slow on the draw." Some elegant bits of tomfoolery adorn other stones in the Southwest—in Arizona: "Here

Early American tombstones, like this, were fraught with deathly symbolism.

lies/Lester Moore/Four slugs/From a forty-four/No Les/No more"; in New Mexico: "Here lies/Johnny Yeast/Pardon me/For not rising."

These wry epitaphs are exceptions, of course, in a long tradition of gloomy tombstone verse. Far more common is the darkly philosophic *memento mori* ("remember that you must die"), a meditation on the brevity of life. One above all was ubiquitous in early New England (its middle two lines appeared in French as early as 1376 on the tomb of Edward, the Black Prince): "Re-member me as you pass by,/As you are now, so once was I;/As I am now, so you must be,/Therefore prepare to follow me." Another early version appears in a British churchyard: "As I was, soe are yee/As I am, yow shall bee./That I had, that I gave,/That I gave, that I have,/Thus I end all my coste,/That I left, that I loste."

The epitaph, which challenges, as Ben Jonson wrote, "what man can say in a little," probably began with the Egyptians but entered Western literature with the Greek poets, who in writing some of the earliest, have left us some of the best. Here is the poet Theodoridas of Syracuse on a sailor: "I am the tomb of a mariner shipwrecked./Sail on:/Even while we died the others rode out the storm." Or this least puritanical of epigrams by Leonidas of Tarentum: "Remember Euboulos the sober, you who pass by,/And drink: there is one Hades for all men." The Greeks penned epitaphs for lovers, tyrants, children, and even pets. Tymnes wrote this for a stone for a dog: "Beneath me lies the white dog from Melita,/The faithful sentinel of Eumelos' house: living,/His name was Bully Boy; but now, in death,/His barking is hushed in the empty ways of night."

In modern times a few wits facetiously devised their own epitaphs. Columnist Walter Winchell offered: "Here is Walter Winchell—with his ear to the ground—as usual." When in the 1920's the magazine *Vanity Fair* asked a number of that decade's style-setters for their parting words, the elegant Alexander Woollcott responded: "Here lies Alexander Woollcott who died at the age of 92. He never had imitation fruit in his dining room." In the same article appeared W.C. Fields' famous and oft-misquoted epitaph: "Here lies W.C. Fields. I would rather be living in Philadelphia." His actual marker, alas, bears simply his name and dates.

TONSILLECTOMY For many people, being separated from their tonsils was part of growing up. Parents and doctors considered this surgical procedure not only a cure for but also a preventive against recurrent fever, sore throat, mouth breathing, and loss of appetite. At times, as was the case with six brothers and sisters in Oklahoma in the 1960's, if one child in a family developed infected or enlarged tonsils that warranted removal, all the other children were sent off to the hospital as well, just to get the tonsillectomies over with. By the early 1970's tonsillectomies were being performed on an estimated one million American children a year—or one operation every 30 seconds.

The removal of tonsils may be one of the most ancient forms of surgery. Records show that Hindu physicians performed tonsillectomies 3,000 years ago, using semicircular knives. In the centuries since, doctors have used a variety of tools to snip, snare, sear, and shear tonsils, including scissors, silver-wire lassos, hot needles, caustics, and miniature guillotines. Dr. Ambroise Paré of 16th-century France advocated the slow strangulation of tonsils, preceded sometimes by a tracheotomy; fights between him and his unwilling patients were frequent.

Usually the palatine tonsils are singled out for removal. A pair of oval lymphoid tissues at the back of the mouth, they are only one of several tonsils most of us are born with. The others include the lingual tonsils (on the back of the tongue and usually left alone) and the pharyngeals, or adenoids (at the back of the nose and often removed to cure or prevent ear infections or hearing problems). Although some adults may suffer from infected palatine tonsils, the tissue is at its most troublesome during childhood. Children may suffer the greatest discomfort between four and seven, because that is when the tonsils are at their largest and usually more susceptible to infections. At seven, however, children's tonsils begin to shrink and generally become trouble-free.

Because of this natural self-correction (which also happens with adenoids), many doctors believe that tonsils should be left in place in all but extreme cases of infection or swelling. Also, a growing body of research indicates that far from being idle, evolutionary leftovers, tonsils and adenoids are part of the body's early defense system against infections introduced through the mouth and nose, such as the common cold. One study explored the emotional effect that a tonsillectomy has on children and concluded that although the majority display no aftershock, some become negative, fearful, and have difficulty with family relations. Moreover, as in all surgery, there is always a degree of risk; of every 7,000 tonsillectomies, one patient dies of complications.

Tonsillectomies, after circumcision, are one of the most common reasons for the hospitalization of children. In 1978 a half-million American children underwent the operation, awoke from general anesthesia with a sore throat, and in most cases obeyed without demur their parents' admonition to eat a bowl of throat-soothing ice cream.

TOOTHBRUSH The toothbrush like so many other things, was probably invented by the Chinese, in this case in about the 15th century. But long before that, the Arabs used something similar—a fiber pencil, usually made from the Arāk shrub. Rich in sodium bicarbonate, the wood of the Arāk is an effective dentifrice. The Brahmins cleaned their teeth with cherry wood while facing the sun each morning as part of their religious ritual.

According to one story, the toothbrush first appeared in the West in England's Newgate Prison in 1780. There William Addis, a tanner charged with the crime of inciting riots, bored tiny holes into bones salvaged from suppers and filled them with bristles supplied by a guard. Later, out of prison, he set up a thriving business.

Apart from the convenience of the toothpaste tube and the addition of decay-preventing fluorides, modern science has done little to improve on early cleaning compounds such as calcium carbonate, bicarbonate of soda, salt, and chalk (used by George Washington).

Hippocrates' favorite concoction of burnt hare's head and three mice probably contained tricalcium phosphate, now considered too harsh for teeth. Pliny the Elder advocated burnt eggshells, which contain calcium carbonate, a mild abrasive.

Toothbrush drill: in 1919 students of an Alabama school proudly demonstrate proper brushing techniques.

Other early abrasives included pumice, emery, alabaster, coral powder, and trumpet shells.

We may laugh at—or be repulsed by—even more exotic early whiteners, such as powdered crab eyes, bat excrement, iron rust, and musk, or breath fresheners such as young men's urine. And yet not long ago many companies sold compounds that not only were useless but were made with dangerously strong abrasives and acids. Even today saccharin, an artificial sweetener that the U.S. government warns may cause cancer, is a standard ingredient in most toothpastes.

TOOTHPICK The earliest implement for cleaning the teeth was the toothpick. In 3000 B.C. the Sumerians carried gold picks attached to rings, which also held other toilet articles, and similar sets decorated apparel in Europe until well into the 19th century.

The Greeks and Romans picked their teeth with quills and with wooden toothpicks cut from the mastic tree, which they also used as chewing gum. Pliny the Elder claimed that porcupine quills firmed up the teeth but warned against vulture quills, which he believed soured the breath. The Muslims carried toothpicks for a second, unusual purpose—to repulse the Devil. And young ladies in Spain, who seldom took the toothpicks out of their mouths, could use them to ward off unseemly kisses.

The Japanese sold toothpicks at temples famed for dental healing, and these were frequently re-

Hang-ups: toothpicks are suspended from ancient Chinese toilet sets.

turned by pilgrims as testimonials to the success of their cures. Each season required a different kind of wood: willow in the spring, cherry in the summer, chestnut in the autumn, and mandarin orange in the winter.

In 19th-century Boston, wily toothpick manufacturers drummed up business by sending well-dressed gentlemen to expensive restaurants, where they created terrible scenes because toothpicks were not available. Their histrionics must have been effective; today 20 billion picks, mostly manufactured from the wood of the white birch, are sold each year in the United States.

Pick, pick, pick: the age-old toothpick has myriad uses. A Galápagos finch employs a thorn to grub for food.

TOURISM A guidebook reads: "As one ascends from the Piraeus . . . the most notable tombs are those of Menander and a cenotaph of Euripides without the body." Tourists who stumble through places with their noses in such enlightening matter might be encouraged to know that they are honoring an age-old tradition. The guidebook quoted was written by Pausanias in the 2nd century A.D. and accompanied Romans on their fashionable tours of Greece. It was just as crammed with mind-boggling detail as today's versions. Particularly fond of temples and battlefields, the educated classes of ancient Rome found travel educational.

A New Guinea chieftain makes quite a sight touring around London.

So, too, did the English aristocracy of the 18th and 19th centuries, who shipped their sons abroad for a year or two on what became known as the Grand Tour. Accompanied by a tutor, the young gentleman was supposed to improve his skill with languages, imbibe European culture, and return "finished." Eventually, entire families went on the Grand Tour, with their servants and 20 portmanteaus in tow and a good supply of spirits of sal-

Karl Baedeker

Steamboats had just appeared on the Rhine River when young Karl Baedeker arrived in Coblenz in the late 1820's to seek his fortune. Naturally, he boarded a steamboat, guidebook in hand, for the fine river cruise down to Mainz. The voyage past castles, vineyards, and historic towns was lovely, but Karl found his guidebook hopelessly lacking in information. A member of a family of booksellers, he bought rights to the guide and rewrote it. Thus began a German publishing tradition that was to make "The Baedeker" the indispensable traveling companion of sophisticated tourists in Europe and eventually the world.

Though Baedeker was neither the first nor the last to write travel guides, the unimpeachable accuracy and discreet charm of his works set such high standards that in time all travel books became known as "Baedekers."

Nothing was ever recommended in his detailed publications that Karl Baedeker had not personally witnessed and evaluated. And no tourist guided by his trusty Baedeker ever had to stumble into filthy accommodations or emerge from a cathedral unenlightened. To Baedeker, travelers also owe the system of rating attractions by one or more stars, an award for which innkeepers trembled as anxiously in Baedeker's day as they do for the three-star blessing of the *Guide Michelin* today. Not content to rate only travel and overnight accommodations, Baedeker also graded the great art of Europe. Thus his readers were informed that St. Peter's and the *Mona Lisa* were good enough for top rating—two stars—but that the Arch of Triumph and the works of Rembrandt rated only one. As practical as he was knowledgeable, Baedeker wrote of a certain European festival: "The torchlight procession presents a fairylike scene (beware of pickpockets)."

Karl Baedeker died in 1859, but his family-owned firm, publishing in several languages, survived two world wars, adding in the process superb maps and many new volumes to their remarkable series.

So closely identified was the name Baedeker with the great sights of Europe that when during World War II Germany bombed English monuments at Bath and Canterbury (in reprisal for English raids on Cologne and Lübeck), the attacks became known as the "Baedeker Raids." In a single night during the war, bombs also destroyed the valuable, long-accumulated files of the Baedeker firm then located in Leipzig. But with a small loan and a dream that Europeans might soon be visiting each other again, Baedeker's great-grandson began once more to publish the popular guidebooks. And as normality returned to Europe, so too did tourists, many of them carrying the familiar red and gold Baedeker.

miac on hand against the fits. A high point of the Grand Tour was wintering over in Rome, despite having to cross the Alps (mountains were not considered appealing until the Romantic age) and the need to cope with the mud and clouds of flies. Tutors were engaged for instruction in art and language, and chaperoned friendships were permitted to bud cautiously amid the ruins.

So eager were the island-bound English to get abroad that a young Baptist missionary named Thomas Cook decided in 1863 to mount the first packaged tour to Paris: four days for $36. In order to ensure safe conduct for his first tour group to the Nile, Cook had to negotiate treaties with local rulers. About the same time, a company called American Express ventured into the fledgling U.S. travel business. Making only $603 in four months, they withdrew from tourism for 57 years.

Ironically, war whetted the appetite of the average American for travel. Those of our boys who came back from "over there" sang saucy French songs and drank wine; later they returned, pointing out the sights to their families. World War II really awakened the folks of Main Street to European civilization, and the subsequent economic boom enabled many of them to experience the joys and discomforts of foreign travel.

Ally oop: a pyramid ascent was a must for tourists of yore, but it was hard on the portly and their porters.

Camera-slung and drip-dry clad, the tourist who fares forth to foreign places is known to economists as an "invisible export." Travelers and those who accommodate them constitute the largest single item in world trade and are a critical factor in the international balance of payments. Hearteningly, citizens of the world spend more to visit each other than to defend themselves against each other. Computer reservations and increased education and disposable income—and better accommodations—have made international travel more like a commute. Folks who once might have delayed until retirement a lifetime dream of

Japanese 19th-century painting sums up the reaction to foreigners then.

seeing the stained-glass windows of Chartres cathedral or sailing the fjords of Scandinavia are pressed by inflation to "fly now and pay later."

Though Italy has conquered the flies and France has made efforts to modernize the plumbing, one major problem for tourists has persisted—"Montezuma's revenge," also known as "Delhi belly." In 1976 a world health conference was summoned to see what could be done about it. Today, an antibiotic called doxycycline offers hope for at least a month's immunity against unfamiliar bacteria in exotic food. (One major result of tourism has been the international sophistication of the palate; until the 1950's the American staples were plain meat and potatoes.)

But tourism has its pitfalls, and those snapshots of happy travelers grinning from the Spanish Steps of Rome do not tell all. Along with death, divorce, and unemployment, vacation is listed high among the stresses of modern life. Some people panic when they are alone too much or together too much, are not working, or are removed

customs

Hand Out

A custom doubtless as old as small change, tipping is a financial necessity still thinly disguised as a social amenity. As such it creates endless anxieties for both tipper and tippee. The cabby, caddie, bellhop, and waiter, the redcap, skycap, chambermaid, and, of course, barber—all require tips. Some depend on tips for their livelihood. And despite the fact that figures as politically disparate as Eleanor Roosevelt, labor leader Samuel Gompers, and President Tito of Yugoslavia have disliked the custom enormously, most attempts to take up arms against the tyranny of itchy palms have met with failure.

"Tipping is not American!" declared signs posted in restaurants in 1905, and within a few years, the Anti-tipping Society, founded by harried traveling salesmen, had succeeded in outlawing tipping in six states—but only temporarily. Iowa's law was declared unconstitutional in 1919.

A relatively successful reversal of the tipping trend occurred in 18th-century England, when the demands of house servants for tips from guests became so relentless that even the queen complained. When a visitor arose to depart, the palm-outstretched line formed at the door: butler, groom, footman, maid, valet. One who slighted the line, known as the "vail," might find his horse lamed or gravy splattered on his breeches during future visits. Finally, the upper classes closed ranks against the vail, and by the 1780's it had been knocked down. In modern times only the commercial airlines have been successful in prohibiting gratuities.

The French word for tip is *pourboire*, meaning "for drinking"; in German it is *Trinkgeld*, or "drink money." In both cases custom called for the patron to offer the waiter a little something to buy himself a drink—which he often did. Not surprisingly this infuriated the waiters' wives, especially since most waiters got no salary, and they created such an uproar that the custom of automatically adding a percentage of the bill as a service charge

was devised to placate them.

The English word "tip" has been traced to 17th-century thieves' jargon, in which it meant "to hand something over," and also to the word "stipend," a small fee. A less likely source, though certainly an intriguing one, was the custom, prevalent in the coffeehouses of Samuel Johnson's day, of placing on the table a container labeled "To Insure Promptness"—TIP. Writing of dining with friends Dr. Johnson revealed, perhaps smugly: "I gave the waiter a penny; so that I was served . . . better than the rest, for they gave the waiter nothing."

From Dr. Johnson's penny it was a far monetary cry to the $100 bills that Diamond Jim Brady used to toss at hatcheck girls in the 1920's. And today, despite expense-account affluence, such big-time tipping is all but extinct—partly because no one seems to carry cash anymore. As the doorman of a swank New York club complained, "All they have on them is plastic."

from familiar comforts. Friends come to screams over croissants, children sulk in castles, and lovers backpack off into separate provinces. Not a few Americans, feeling sublimely protected by "our way of life," run afoul of the laws governing others' way of life and end up in jails. (In 1976 more than 2,400 Americans were held in foreign prisons on drug counts alone.) Other travelers find themselves the victims of such calculated misunderstandings as overcharging, and many more, reports American Express, simply lose their traveler's checks. As a policy since 1891, American Express refunds the loss if the numbers on the checks can be produced. One day, a man who had just been released from 10 years in a prison camp in Communist China walked into the Hong Kong office of American Express. When apprehended, he had been carrying $2,000 in traveler's checks, which his captors neglected to return. In the office the man whipped off his shirt, displaying on his chest the tattooed numbers of the lost checks. His money was promptly refunded.

Waited on hand and foot: 18th-century French noble-woman luxuriates in towels, status symbols of her class.

TOWEL Towels in the past were luxury items for the wealthy only. Most people dried their hands in the air or on their clothing. Although Europeans in the Middle Ages rarely bathed, records show that upper-class families did own towels. One generation after another of the wealthy ordered drying cloths, some so beautifully worked that they were more decorative than utilitarian.

In 1841 the French made by machine the first terry cloth, a name probably derived from the French verb *tirer* ("to draw"), referring to the method of raising loops up from the pile of a fabric. The French made silk terry, but in the late 1840's Samuel Holt of England machine-produced terry, based on samples of a Turkish fabric, from cotton. The first towels made on his machine went on display in 1851 at the Crystal Palace exhibition in London. Queen Victoria, who was presented one of Holt's towels, awarded the inventor a gold medal and also ordered six dozen "Royal Turkish towels" for her household. After Holt emigrated to the United States in 1863, he set up a factory in Paterson, New Jersey, and introduced his towels to Americans.

A half-century later, American towels were still basic white, matching the basic white bathroom. In 1925, however, manufacturers introduced colored dobbies (the woven band that gives the towel its finished look) in blue, yellow, and green. "Yarn-dyed" towels, made of colored yarn woven into the material, appeared in the 1930's.

Though machines enabled every man to towel himself down, the rich went one better—by means of monograms, long a status symbol among the wealthy. Milton Weigler of New York City, who began his art over 50 years ago, still lists the elite of the world, including every monarch in Europe, among his clients. Weigler designed the towels embroidered with the presidential seal for the White House. Decades ago Marjorie Merriweather Post asked Weigler to rip out the "P" in her monogram when she married Joseph E. Davies, and replace it with a "D," at a cost of $25,000. The whole process had to be repeated when she divorced Davies and married Herbert A. May. Winthrop Rockefeller requested that his bath linen be decorated with the pattern of his ranch's branding iron. In the 1970's King Khalid of Saudi Arabia paid Weigler $100 apiece for towels decorated with his country's crest.

It is easy to dry off these days, whether one chooses to employ a monogrammed *objet d'art* or a lowly paper towel (which would have been the height of luxury in the Middle Ages when paper was a valuable commodity). The latest public dryer—the wall blower—brings us full circle to primitive man shaking his hands dry in the air.

TRAFFIC LIGHT As best as anyone can recall, the world's first blinking red-and-green traffic signal stood on the corner of George and Bridge streets, near London's Houses of Parliament. The year was 1868, and the illumination was supplied by gas lamps. The signal had been put there to give some degree of protection to members of Parliament as they went to or from work because traffic on the two thoroughfares tended to be heavy. This installation marked one instance when concern for pedestrians' welfare above all else animated the designers of traffic signals.

Caution: this bird made its home in the yellow glow of a traffic light.

The first modern automatic four-way traffic lights, using red-yellow-green, were put up early in the 1920's, appropriately enough in the automobile capital of America—Detroit, Michigan. The purpose of the signals was to regulate what officials considered heavy traffic; for example, some 20,000 vehicles a day passed through the intersection of Detroit's Woodward and Michigan avenues. Who could have foreseen that half a century later the interchange of the Harbor and Santa Monica freeways in Los Angeles would be used by an average of 425,000 cars in a 24-hour period?

Over the years, engineers, computer experts, and even physicists have been enlisted to find ways to cope with the explosive growth of traffic. To measure the speed and volume of traffic, as well as the distance between vehicles, one system uses sensors embedded in city streets. This information, digested by a central computer, enables engineers to adjust the timing of traffic lights. To keep traffic moving, bus drivers in some cities can request by radio that lights ahead of them be turned green. If the computer decides that this will speed up traffic, the lights turn green; if not, the request is ignored.

Several cities have installed what is called a Traffic Pacer. It is a large electric sign that indicates the optimum speed (from 20 to 50 miles per hour) a motorist must maintain if he is to arrive at the next traffic signal while it is still green. Another device, intended to reduce driver confusion at complex intersections, is the Programmed Visibility Signal. The signal was designed to be visible from relevant lanes, even around curves, but appear dark to motorists in lanes not affected. And there is also something new for pedestrians: the Audio Pedestrian Signal. Intended for what its manufacturers call "the visually handicapped," it emits a signal that sounds like a bird call, which alerts pedestrians that it is safe to cross.

Back in the 1950's, while the rest of the world was wracking its brains to keep traffic moving, the canny mayor of Ludowici, Georgia, did just the opposite. The city sits astride a crucial intersection that until the advent of interstate roads fun-

neled thousands of Yankees to the playgrounds of Florida. For years, Ludowicians stoically endured the noise and fumes. Then they decided to put up a traffic light specially rigged to stay green for an infuriating 16 seconds only. Inevitably, out-of-town motorists shot that light, and inevitably they were caught by the town's three-man police force, waiting just on the other side. The lawbreakers could plead guilty and pay the $15 fine or plead not guilty and leave a $15 "bond" pending trial. In a good year it all added up to something upwards of $50,000 for Ludowici, or about four times the town's annual budget.

TRAIN "One had a sense then of distance rather than of space," wrote Alan Moorehead, the Australian writer, of the grand days of train travel, "of time used rather than of time saved." The cindery screech as a locomotive slid into the depot, the whistle and door sounds, the ceremony of boarding—few children today can imagine what complex excitements these events once aroused. Railroads spanned more than the continents; they bridged an awesome era of power and growth, from the early days of steam to the arrival of the space age. And now, because of financial problems and the popularity of other forms of travel, the haunting whistle of trains is gradually fading.

When men walked on the moon, some people worried that their presence would unhinge the tides. When the Liverpool to Manchester Railway opened for passenger service in England in 1830, people predicted that the smoke would kill the birds, the sparks would burn fields and houses, the ride would precipitate early labor in pregnant women, and, what was worse, railroads in general would destroy fox hunting.

Early coach travel was exactly that—a series of wooden coaches hitched behind a steam locomotive, each seating six passengers on upright padded seats. Some were open-sided, subjecting travelers

A train in a Paris station makes an unscheduled stop.

to gales of dust and cinders. Soon, English families of quality acquired private coaches, the better to protect their eyes, clothing, and dignity.

Democratic principles, on the other hand, were everywhere apparent in the design of early American railroad cars. Salesmen, senators, and tobacco-spitting cowboys shared windows that sometimes failed to work, babies' crying, and wood stoves. Mark Twain, for one, preferred this convivial mode of travel to the private compartments of European trains, where he might be trapped with a tendentious drunk. Passengers were frequently impressed to haul water or wood and sometimes, on a steep grade, to push. Newspapers printed timetables listing the departure times of

A painting of a 1st-class car in 19th-century England portrays the luxurious conditions available to the rich.

words

On the Right Track

Trains may no longer stop at every tank town in the land, but railroading, as a source of colorful expressions that have "made the grade" in common parlance, still slides smoothly and regularly over the tongue. Rail roads (originally two words) in England were at first grooved tracks for a string of horse-drawn wagons filled with coal. About the time the steam locomotive replaced the horse, "rail" joined "road and the world became unified." "Train" arrived in the United States from England a bit later on. Derived from the Latin *trahere*, meaning "to drag," it went west in the mid-19th century, as in wagon or mule train.

Competing with canalboats and stagecoach travel, the railroads began appropriating the language of their competition. "All aboard!" is nautical talk, as are "berth," "gondola," and "crew." From stagecoach terminology, trains rumbled off with "conductor," "station," "car," and "coach." But railroading coined as many terms as it pilfered. Sports fans who attend "doubleheaders" may not know that to railroad men the term denoted a heavy freight train pulled by a pair of locomotives. Or that to railroad men a "deadhead" was not an ignorant person but a passenger who, by special privi-

lege, rode for free. Later on, the term was applied to a freight car returning empty from a run—no profit in its passage either. For years a "milk train" was one that had an easy local run and route, but early milk trains operated as both expresses and locals. On main tracks, the milk train had the right-of-way because its contents were perishable. But in areas where farmers set out milk cans for pickup, trains stopped frequently.

They were thirsty engines, those steam locomotives, and they often pulled up for water at towns consisting of a water tank and little else. A crewman had to jerk a cable to lower the tank's nozzle to the boiler; hence, the term "tank town" or "jerkwater town." Normally, a passenger

could get off at an unscheduled stop if the conductor would signal the engineer; the obliging engineer would respond with two whistles—thus the "whistle-stop" was born. This expression entered the American political vocabulary when Harry Truman's surprising 1948 triumph was attributed, in part at least, to his whistle-stop campaign through small towns. Truman, clearly, was "on the right track."

Once on a track, it is hard to get off it, which explains why some people object to being "railroaded" into things. On a single line of track the only way for opposing trains to pass is for one to pull off onto a sidetrack. That means waiting, and even today, no one with a full head of steam likes to get "sidetracked."

The first locomotive in Indore, India, arrives under elephant power.

trains but never their arrival times, for those were often a matter of chance. One may understand why from the report of an English traveler whose train one day in 1859 passed a field of wild mushrooms. Suddenly the train ground to a stop, and out leaped the engineer and guard, followed by the passengers—to gather mushrooms. When everyone's hat was brimming, the train ambled off toward its scheduled destination.

By the centennial year of 1876, one could travel by rail almost anywhere in the United States, and as journeys became longer in egalitarian America, comfort inevitably became a question of class. In Europe all the crowned heads of state traveled in private cars. Napoleon III and Princess Eugénie, off to visit the emperor of Austria in 1867, roughed it in nine private coaches grandly appointed with crystal chandeliers, a writing desk, a Renaissance clock, a wine cellar, and a conservatory for the sustenance of fresh flowers.

Royal opulence, however, could not begin to match the ostentation of America's merchant princes. "Private varnish," the railroad companies called the financial barons' gilded mansions on wheels. George Pullman (who did not originate the sleeping car but did make it famous) had

Track record: a private automobile fitted with train wheels and cowcatcher ambles on Canadian tracks.

a palatial car that he proudly lent to princes and potentates. Soon enough the Vanderbilts and mining kings from the West were ordering up railroad extravaganzas of their own. Lush with carved mahogany paneling, deep-cut velvet upholstery, china, crystal, gaming tables, and heavy fringed draperies, these private cars gave their owners a greater sense of status than a Fifth Avenue mansion or a steam yacht. (They also encouraged instant credit wherever the owner of one stopped to do business.) An opera star had a solid silver bathtub in her car; a dowager explained that her gold bathroom fixtures were "economical" because they didn't have to be polished. The free-wheeling financier Jay Gould, himself a railroad potentate, always traveled with a French chef to produce ladyfingers and a cow in the baggage car to provide fresh milk to go with them. Mr. and Mrs. Leland Stanford had "his" and "hers" cars. Yet among the most sumptuous of all were "outshopped" (railroad parlance for outfitted) cars of Mexican dictators. Many of the

grandest, it is believed, ended their days south of the Rio Grande.

No such style attended American heads of state. Throughout the heyday of railroads, no U.S. president ever had an official car at his disposal. One was built for Lincoln but, sensitive to criticism that the style did not suit a man of the people, he never used it. (Mohandas Gandhi, for similar reasons, always traveled third class on Indian railroads.) Instead, railroad lines made private cars available for presidential use. Teddy Roosevelt was shocked to discover that he had accepted, during his first term, $100,000 worth of free railroad travel—a potentially embarrassing situation for an outspoken trustbuster.

Most travelers never saw the inside of a private railroad car. Yet in the first decade of this century, the peak years in passenger travel, crack lines in America and Europe achieved an excellence of appointment and service that transformed trains into grand hotels on wheels.

Of them all, the Orient Express, the first train—in 1883—to take passengers across Europe from Paris to Istanbul, has been most celebrated in fiction, film, and fantasy. Built exclusively for the luxury trade, it was, as one historian wrote, "a steam-powered self-indulgence," which numerous countesses and dukes rode merely to savor the delights it purveyed. Nonetheless, an extraordinary number of fictional murders occurred amid the opulent settings. And its passengers were indeed important if not always mysterious. Because travel *and* champagne *and* oysters occasionally loosen the tongue, spies often were aboard. On the Orient Express, it was never necessary to clamber down at various borders to process papers in a drafty shack; all such diplomatic dallying was handled on board by the *Chef du Train*, who probably spoke six languages. Each passenger was permitted 330 pounds of luggage, quite enough for the flowing skirts and rustling crinolines that clogged doorways and splashed over plush chairs. Yet Princess Pauline Metternich often delighted gentlemen travelers by appearing on the Express in an outrageously straight skirt. (Indeed, it was the exigencies of railway travel that helped to do away with voluminous skirts.) As superb as the food and wine were, officials clearly understood that the Marquise de Polignac would always bring along her own chef and a supply of estate-bottled wines, served by waiters dressed in morning coats, light-blue silk breeches, and white stockings.

So great was the romance of the Orient Express that when it roared into Bulgaria, King Boris often climbed into the cab and drove the train himself. He was, after all, absolute monarch of his realm, and there was nothing the engineers could do about it. Fortunately, King Boris kept the Orient Express on time, and his stops were remarkably and royally smooth. Like many luxury trains, the Orient Express was never quite the same after World War II; its great run finally ended in 1977.

The United States has also lost legendary lines. The Twentieth Century Limited, famed for its punctuality on New York-to-Chicago runs, during which each passenger received a fresh carnation and a morning newspaper; the California Zephyr; the Super Chief, with its pleasure dome and an Indian in full regalia to tell children about the West—all were victims of rising costs and the speed and economy of air travel. And with their departure went an epoch of ceremonious adventure, of personal yet detached inspection of the passing scene, and of an amiability of travel that neither the highway nor the airways will ever replace.

TRANSLATION Translation, the art of rendering the meaning of words from one language accurately and idiomatically into another, has ancient and vital roots. As one biblical scholar pointed out, it is extremely unlikely that Jesus Christ and Pontius Pilate spoke a common language. Thus the trial and interrogation that play such a crucial part in the Gospels must have been carried out with the help of a translator.

In modern times the translator—particularly one who is capable of providing simultaneous translation—has become an essential part of international exchange. It has been estimated that the Nuremberg war crimes trial, held after World War II, would have dragged on for another two years had it not been for its simultaneous English, French, Russian, and German translations. And when half the staff of translators at the United Nations failed to appear for work some years ago, in protest against their work load, eight of the day's scheduled meetings had to be postponed. Work load aside, their job is brutally demanding. One interpreter ruefully analyzed himself as "a man with a ruined liver and worse nerves."

Simultaneous translation is used today in about 85 percent of all international meetings—not just political but also scientific, cultural, commercial,

Chinese interpreters perform their nerve-wracking task at United Nations; translations into Arabic, English, French, Russian, and Spanish are also taking place.

and professional conferences covering every conceivable subject from the plight of whales to the future of heart transplants. Indeed, the first use of simultaneous translation occurred not at a political conference but at a meeting of the International Chamber of Commerce held in Washington, D.C., during the early 1930's.

Accuracy—conveying exactly the sense of a speaker's words—is the crucial test of any translation. According to one account, a simple mistake in translation may have been responsible for a catastrophic change in the course of history. It occurred in Japan during the last days of July 1945. The Allies, meeting in Potsdam, had issued an ultimatum for Japan's unconditional surrender. The Japanese emperor, who had already dispatched peace feelers, was disposed to accept it but needed the full support of his cabinet. On July 28 the Japanese premier announced to the press that the cabinet would follow a policy of *mokusatsu*—a word that has no exact counterpart in English but can mean either "to ignore" or "to refrain from comment." The second meaning is the one that was intended, but the translation supplied by the Japanese Domei News Agency used the term "ignore." *The New York Times* ran a banner headline that read: "Fleet Strikes As Tokyo 'Ignores' Terms." Nine days later an atomic bomb was dropped on Hiroshima.

There is a lighter side to the profession of translating. Ted Fagan, for three decades an interpreter at the United Nations, translated for many distinguished orators. One speaker, he recalled, complained about a certain nation playing with another like a cat with a mouse. Sensing that the speaker meant to imply something more than playfulness, Fagan translated the phrase as "a terrier worrying a rat." "But then," he added, "the speaker went on to have his cat and mouse climb a tree, leaving my terrier on the ground and me out on a limb." Puns and other plays on words are the bane of translators. One quick-thinking woman interpreter managed to solve the problem neatly, saying, "The speaker has just made a pun which cannot be translated. Please laugh. It would please him very much." To her relief the audience did just that.

Other problems can occur when a speaker also understands the language into which his remarks are being translated. Soviet Premier Nikita Khrushchev frequently used an earthy style of expression that his translator routinely tried to tone down. On one occasion, however, the premier listened to the translator and staunchly corrected him: "I did not say 'riff-raff.' I said 'bastards.'"

Computers, given their enormous memory capacities and lightning speed, might seem ideal instruments for translation, but most efforts to harness them have fallen short of perfection. In one noble attempt, a computer that had been programmed with 1,500 words of basic English and their Russian equivalents, was required to translate the expression "out of sight, out of mind." It promptly produced "invisible idiot." Thinking that such an expression was too abstract and that the machine might do better with something more explicit, the programmers tried again with the saying "The spirit is willing, but the flesh is weak." The machine chattered, blinked its little lights, and announced: "The liquor is holding out all right, but the meat has spoiled."

TYPEWRITER At least 51 men tried their hand at producing a typing machine before the first practical typewriter appeared on the market in 1874. As early as 1714 Queen Anne awarded Henry Mill a patent for "an artificial machine or method for the impressing or transcribing of letters," but no one knows whether it was ever built. In 1830 an American, William Austin Burt, came out with Burt's Typographer. It was basically a wooden box with a dial on the outside that activated a type frame inside. Other early contrivances resembled a permanent-wave machine, a birdcage, a loom, a pincushion, and even a baby grand piano.

In 1873 the inventor Christopher Sholes and his associates produced the first practical machine that actually wrote faster than clerks could pen words in long-

Veiled meaning: a Yemeni woman practices at her typing lesson.

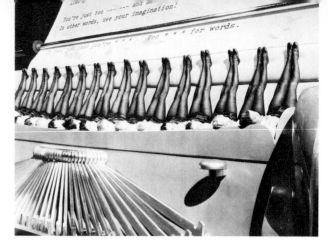
Tiptoe to the typer: Busby Berkeley chorines tap out some words to "You're just too. . .," in 1937 movie.

hand. Consequently, Sholes has been referred to as "the 52nd man to 'invent' the typewriter." He had tried out nearly 50 different models before succeeding. A favorite test phrase was the campaign slogan of presidential hopeful Ulysses S. Grant: "Now is the time for all good men to come to the aid of their party."

That same year E. Remington & Sons, manufacturer of firearms and sewing machines, bought Sholes' patent. In some ways Remington's "Type Writer" looked very much like a sewing machine, for it featured a foot-treadle carriage return and a black case with finely stenciled flowers. Many mechanical problems remained to be solved. Over the years the improvements included an attached carriage return, an arrangement of type bars that enabled the typist to see what he or she was writing, the addition of lowercase letters, and a ribbon that automatically reversed itself.

Sholes' keyboard remains in use today, although it almost seems programmed for inefficiency. Originally, the inventor had arranged the letters alphabetically, with the result that the keys jammed frequently. Instead of fixing the type bar, Sholes simply scattered the popular letters. In 1932 Dr. August Dvorak proposed a more practical keyboard with the most-used letters on the middle bar. Although the Dvorak board is available, opposition—mostly from professional typists and typing teachers—has prevented its adoption.

Mark Twain was enthralled with the typewriter, which he called a "curiosity-breeding little joker." Said Twain, it "piles an awful stack of words on one page. It don't muss things or scatter ink. . . ." His *Life on the Mississippi* was probably the first typed manuscript in American publishing.

Businessmen were slow to accept the new machines, especially since few people knew how to operate them. In 1881 the YWCA in New York City made history and caused an uproar by offering a training course in typing, which in the words

Mr. Typewriter

The title "Mr. Typewriter, U.S.A.," goes to a man named Martin Tytell, long the world's foremost expert on typewriters. For over 50 years, Tytell's company in New York City repaired, sold, and custom-designed more than 50,000 specialized writing machines.

During World War II, Tytell invented typewriters that could print in 16 languages; the polyglot machines were then parachuted to Office of Strategic Services personnel in occupied countries. Now United Nations delegates, university professors, and Arab princes, among others, purchase his machines to type in 145 languages, ranging from Persian script to Japanese. Tytell's other creations include a typewriter with card-suit keys for a bridge columnist, one with sex symbols for a museum botanist, and a keyboard composed entirely of different question marks for a customer who refused to answer the inevitable question: why?

Tytell's favorite occupation, however, is sleuthing. With his wife, Pearl, and son Peter, both handwriting and typewriter experts, he identifies counterfeit contracts, forged wills, and phony checks, and tracks down writers of threatening letters. According to Tytell, typewriting is a good deal easier to trace than handwriting. For one thing, machines wear differently, so that not only their make but their individual mechanical "fingerprints" can be identified. Also, typists give themselves away through idiosyncratic habits in spacing, punctuation, and grammar. The "Sherlock Holmes of typewriters" claims that he can even deduce a writer's level of education.

One case involved a letter sent to a young woman's rich father, accusing her of carrying on a "shocking romance" with an unemployed actor and suggesting that her father demand that they be wed. Tytell, not illogically, compared the note with some of the actor's love letters. Dashes instead of commas and broken exclamation points in both the accusatory and amatory missives nailed the young actor, who had hoped that a wealthy marriage might solve his financial woes.

Tytell was called in to examine documents and testify at the trial of Alger Hiss, the man accused of retyping secret documents and passing them on to a Communist agent, Whittaker Chambers. In helping the defense, Tytell actually constructed a typewriter identical to the famous Woodstock machine that Hiss was alleged to have used for the Pumpkin Papers, thus proving that typewriters could be forged as well as documents.

In another case, in 1976, Tytell showed that an electric plant in New Jersey had doctored its personnel records to mask discriminatory practices in hiring women. Because of Tytell's typographical expertise, the women sued the company for equal rights.

---

of one critic was "an obvious error in judgment by the well-meaning but misguided ladies of the YWCA." Women who until then had worked at low-paying jobs in factories, schools, or stores rushed to learn the trade, which offered a substantially higher salary and promised entry into the glamorous world of business. By the mid-1880's, 60,000 female "typewriters" (the word "typist" came later, and "secretaries" were all men) were seated at their machines in offices around the country.

In 1920 James Smathers invented the first electric typewriter suitable for office use. By the 1940's electric typewriters could space letters proportionately, an innovation that improved the legibility and look of the typed page. A printing element shaped like a golf ball with raised letters, numbers, and punctuation marks replaced the bars and moving carriages on many office machines in 1961. The element not only moves fast without sticking but can easily be changed for different styles of type such as italics, foreign-language alphabets, and dance-notation marks. Newspaper and magazine editors and businessmen can take advantage of the new memory typewriters, which are programmed to recall and revise previously typed material. The machine plays back the fresh copy error-free at 150 words per minute. As indispensable parts of the new business-machine complexes, there are sophisticated typing machines that can be programmed to prepare continuous business forms, send information via telephone, and even print out information which has been stored in computers. That is today—who knows what they will be able to do tomorrow?

With over 3,000 characters to choose from, this Chinese typist will average eight words per minute: 48-key Western machines afford an average of 120 wpm.

In the Roman alphabet "V" represented both a w and a u sound (as in Ivlivs—Julius). "U" evolved from it.

UMBRELLA Having sheltered lovers, soldiers, priests, queens, and statesmen, the umbrella and its sidekick, the parasol, have played so many symbolic roles that their practical function—shielding people from rain or sun—seemed at times to be almost secondary. The word "umbrella" comes from the Latin *umbra*, meaning "shade."

Ancient Egyptian carvings show pharaohs under ceremonial umbrellas, which were thought to convey power derived from heaven. A hieroglyph in the shape of an umbrella denoted sovereignty and also stood for a person's shadow, which held his regenerative powers.

The umbrella's bowl shape, reminiscent of the dome of the sky, lent the article religious significance throughout the Orient. In ancient China umbrellas, many of them made of gold cloth studded with gems, were often carried in processions as part of the ceremonial regalia. Twenty-four umbrellas preceded one emperor during his hunting forays. In Japan the mikado never stepped outside the palace without an attendant who carried a red sunshade, which was an emblem of absolute power.

A topiary artist shaped nature's umbrellas to resemble a man-made one.

In Greece umbrellas were held to shade priests and priestesses in holy processions. They were used to cover the dead during funerary rites, not to keep the flesh from putrefying in the hot sun but to protect sunlight from pollutants. And while women in Greece and Rome paraded under parasols, men who did so risked being called dandies.

Perhaps because of the feminine associations, Europeans ignored umbrellas until the 16th century when the clergy adopted the covering as a symbol of honor and dignity. The pope declared that no one could use an umbrella except those upon whom he conferred the privilege.

The French *parapluie* (which translates to "against the rain") became a fancy prop in the 18th century. Parisian ladies flirted under jaunty parasols decorated with tulle, lace, gauze, and even ostrich feathers.

The English at first turned a cold eye on the contraption. To Robert Louis Stevenson carrying

Umbrageous umbrellas: among the trappings of Ethiopian priests are extraordinarily gorgeous sunshades.

an umbrella proclaimed a lack of character, as only hypochondriacs, the very frugal, and the most respectable worried about getting wet. The status-conscious worried more that an umbrella proclaimed the lack of a carriage. The early models did not help to speed the umbrella's acceptance either. Consisting of whalebone ribs strung on a piece of wire and covered with oil-soaked cotton, they tended to be heavy, cumbersome, and only occasionally waterproof.

Despite early resistance to the umbrella, before long a plethora of styles appeared on the streets of London. Some people attached acorns to the handles, hoping that, since the oak was sacred to the god of thunder, it would protect them from lightning. Others preferred walking-cane umbrellas. Hollow handles held daggers, perfume, or writing materials, and some were even fitted with flasks to catch the drip. Others whistled when they were opened.

Military officers began to carry their "brollies" abroad to protect them from sun in India and Africa and from drizzle on the Continent. During the Napoleonic Wars, Lord Wellington carried a sword-stick umbrella and one of his generals, Sir Thomas Picton, rode into battle with a top hat, frock coat, and umbrella. The most notorious umbrella in history accompanied Neville Chamberlain to the ill-fated Munich conference in 1939 as a sturdy sign of British self-confidence. A Continental name for the umbrella is still a "Chamberlain," while the word is synonymous with bitter disillusionment to the English.

Today's sun worshipers have discarded the

parasol, but the umbrella has taken on bursts of color and designer styles and signatures. There are even disposable umbrellas, and see-through bubbles so the carrier can get a good look at the person he is about to impale.

UNDERWEAR The appalling fact that for centuries Europeans went largely unwashed explains why undergarments served for considerably more than keeping out the cold; they also protected outer garments from contact with the grimy body beneath. Regular bathing, which the classical world enjoyed, did not generally reenter civilized life until the late 18th century.

Before the Renaissance the underwear of king and peasant alike had little fashion appeal because no one was intended to see it. Appearing in an undergarment was a form of humiliation reserved for an adulterous woman while confessing her sin or for disgraced and vanquished foes. But with the unnaturally pinched waists favored by both Elizabethan men and women, undergarments assumed a new role as the very foundation of style. Women were bundled into three layers of petticoats, known charmingly as "the modest" (the outermost), "the rascal" (the middle), and "the secret" (the inmost). Next to the skin, the well-to-do favored linen or silk, not only for their softness but because these fabrics were less likely than wool to harbor lice.

For some 300 years (during the 1500-1800's), with the notable exception of the relaxed Napoleonic "Empire" style, women of fashion were mercilessly corseted above and crinolined below in demonic contraptions of steel, leather, and whalebone that sometimes took their breath away—a dangerous vanity that led to fainting and swoons and contributed to the generally held impression that women were a weaker sex. It was reported that women sometimes bound their waists so tightly that broken ribs and punctured lungs resulted. One sensible papa complained of his daughters' obsession with waist-cinching: "They are unable to stand, sit or walk. To expect one of them to stoop would

Appropriately embarrassed, a man models skivvies in fashion show.

be absurd." When one of them did stoop, "her stays gave way with a tremendous explosion and down she fell upon the ground." The good father added plaintively, "My daughters are always complaining of pains in the stomach."

What, ultimately, was under all that underwear? Shocking as it may seem, Englishwomen did not wear underpants until the late 1700's, and when they ventured to do so, their droopy "pantelets," demurely ribboned below the knee, were considered "immodest," since underdrawers were for men, not women. Fashion, however, took pantaloons in stride, and before long, lacy versions peeped out fetchingly below a swaying crinoline—which may explain why young men spent hours pushing young ladies on swings.

Men, too, have endured preposterous underpinnings for the sake of a slim waist or a well-turned leg. In the 1770's men with skinny shanks strapped padding onto their calves under tight breeches—no sillier, surely, than padding a bra. Men's corsets survived a long history into our day with little comment. During World War I the German Army actually issued corsets to paunchy officers. More recent rumors suggest that President Tito of Yugoslavia and Franco of Spain wore them, not to mention a goodly number of U.S. senators.

Until recently, men's underwear attempted little in the way of direct erotic appeal. Feminine undergarments, however, were often thought to be provocative—especially the corset. And who is to say that artful concealment did not once have its own allure? As the 18th-century poet John Logan wrote, "At times to veil is to reveal,/And to display is to conceal."

A Victorian lady's undergear caused her to be dressed by tong-wielding servants.

Abashed: because she seems to have under over? Or is it the checks?

Outerwear

"It's better than a bumper sticker," bragged a college undergraduate of his "Save the Whales" T-shirt. Said a New York woman, "When I get bored jogging, I read T-shirts; it keeps me going."

A onetime shy and sensible undergarment, the T-shirt became in the 1970's a mobile medium, a body billboard for proclaiming everything from the wearer's taste in beer, composers, and superheroes to ethnic jokes and risqué remarks. Brokerage firms and soup canners competed for chest space. Everyone from kids ("May the Force Be With You") to collegiate wags ("Drink Wet Cement—Get Really Stoned") to senior citizens ("Gray Power") could make a public statement simply by getting dressed.

American men adopted the T-shirt during World War I. Outfitted by the army in scratchy wool union suits, they discovered to their relief the short-sleeved French undershirt of silk and cotton lisle. It came to be called a T-shirt for its simple shape. In almost no time, the white T-shirt became a gentleman's essential undergarment, but Clark Gable in a 1934 movie nearly destroyed the undershirt business forever.

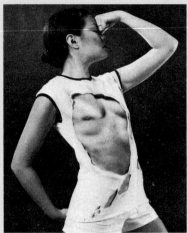

T-he: a trompe-l'oeil undershirt makes muscleman of a petite woman.

In *It Happened One Night*, Gable jauntily undresses a mere curtain away from a shocked Claudette Colbert. It was not the Gable strip that awed movie audiences but the bare fact that Gable wore no undershirt. Undershirt sales plummeted, to rally only briefly about a decade later when Marlon Brando slouched through *A Streetcar Named Desire* in a sexy T-shirt. Then, of course, undershirts went outer.

When Mrs. David Rockefeller turned up in a Superman T-shirt for the America's Cup Races in Newport, Rhode Island, the whimsical fashion had definitely made the scene. Though not quite everywhere, perhaps, as two Texas boys discovered when they wore their Farrah Fawcett-Majors T-shirts to school. The principal, who found the scantily clad image of the actress "vulgar," suspended them. Other students wore "smellies"—T-shirts that when scratched released strong odors of pizza or fish or chocolate or garlic. "When we all scratch together," boasted one teenager, "it stinks!"

From peace symbols to Watergate witticisms, T-shirts have played a visible role in politics. Even Uganda's onetime dictator Idi Amin decided to get in the act by ordering from Holland some 60,000 T-shirts emblazoned with his image. Rather than propagate Amin's self-expression, the Dutch workers expressed themselves by simply declining to fill the order.

T-shirts have even been involved in labor disputes. A worker was sent home for wearing a T-shirt with an obscene message on it, and the case went to arbitration. The decision was that the company did not have to put up with the vulgarity.

UNIFORM Elaborate uniforms call to mind an age of distinction and glamour. Consider the elegant Prussian officer of the early 19th century in svelte breeches and fringed epaulets, on his head an elegantly plumed hat. There he stands, hand resting lightly on sword, the cool pride of regiment in his bearing. Few looks today can equal that splendor. Indeed in our time uniforms are sometimes worn to deny distinction rather than confer it. The citizens and leaders of the most populous nation, China, for example, mostly go about in baggy, dark-colored trousers and jackets. In an age of democratized dress, splendor is somehow suspect, as President Richard Nixon discovered when he turned out the White House police in off-white and gold dress uniforms instead of their usual policemanly black. "Looks vaguely Lithuanian," cracked one critic. "Comic opera," said another. "Nixonian self-glorification," groused a third. The uniforms did not survive after Nixon's truncated second term.

And then in 1966 music star Mick Jagger of the Rolling Stones appeared on TV decked out in the musty finery of a Coldstream drummer's jacket. A whole funky generation followed suit, raiding attics and thrift shops to have the last laugh on uniforms. Many retired Brigadiers were so dismayed by these blasphemies that they complained to the British government, which rather than suffer mockery shredded its surplus uniforms to keep them off the market.

Short shrift indeed for the British red coat, whose famous scarlet, visible from a distance, had once saved England from invasion. According to one story, when Napoleon's forces landed in 1797 near Fishguard Bay in Wales, a group of brave

Welshwomen donned their traditional garb—red skirts and shiny hats. Seizing broomsticks for muskets, they immodestly flung their long skirts over their shoulders, and, white thighs flashing, advanced in rank in view of the astonished invaders, who fled, certain that the British Army had mustered to meet them.

Uniforms in warfare first served the practical purpose of distinguishing friend from foe in the heat of hand-to-hand combat. From the rise of national armies in the 17th century to the advent

Basic, black: were it not for Eve, we might all be wearing the same little nothing, underlining the irony of this photograph of a line of black-habited nuns.

of long-range artillery in the 19th, military garb took on increasing glamour, adding to the luster of nation, regiment, and soldier alike. But nothing makes so fine a sighting for long-range guns as scarlet coats and the gleam of a golden button. In the 20th century, therefore, most nations at war have outfitted their soldiers in drab colors, particularly khaki, intended not to distinguish but to camouflage the man in the field. The gold braid, what was left, swung from a hook in an officer's closet except for formal occasions.

Each of the letters "U," "W," "Y," and "F" was derived from the versatile letter "V."

VACCINE In the freezer of a government laboratory in Atlanta, Georgia, meticulously preserved at -94° F, lie some of the last known specimens of what scientists believe is an endangered species of infectious agent. No great regret accompanies its near demise, however, because the species in question is the virus that causes smallpox.

Smallpox was a killer for more than 3,000 years; the mummified body of the Egyptian pharaoh Ramses V has traces of its pockmarking ravages. Brought to the New World by Cortés and his conquistadores in 1519, the disease wiped out a major portion of the native populations and hastened the collapse of the great Inca and Aztec civilizations. In the early 18th century, for instance, 14,000 Parisians succumbed to the disease during one epidemic. In 1967 the United Nations World Health Organization set out to eradicate the disease from the face of the earth. In that year 131,000 cases were reported, and probably many more went unrecorded. Ten years later, in one of mankind's most remarkable achieve-

ments, WHO had nearly succeeded. Since the autumn of 1977, only three cases of smallpox have been reported. One of them occurred in nature, but the other two, in Birmingham, England, were attributed to sloppy laboratory procedures.

This remarkable accomplishment could not have been achieved without an effective vaccine. That is because the smallpox virus can live, so far as is known, only in human beings, and the vaccine creates an immunity against it. With no human habitat to occupy, the virus exists now only as an artifact in laboratory freezers, albeit a potentially dangerous one.

When Edward Jenner in 1796 demonstrated the effectiveness of the world's first vaccine (so named because it was derived from a cow, or *vacca* in Latin), he had not the least idea of how or why it worked. Neither did Louis Pasteur, who nevertheless developed vaccines against rabies and several other animal and human killers. It was not until 1890 that a German scientist, Emil von Behring, proved that immunity to certain diseases—specifically diphtheria and tetanus—depends on the presence in the blood of substances he named antitoxins. Behring showed that a vaccine, which contained a harmless, modified form of the disease-causing agent, stim-

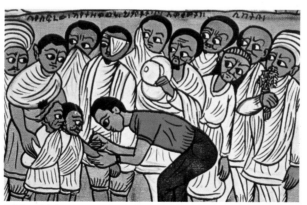

This Ethiopian poster is to encourage vaccinations, but those worried looks may have the opposite effect.

ulated the body into producing these antitoxins.

Armed with this knowledge, medical scientists devised vaccines against such diseases as whooping cough, typhoid fever, and cholera. By World War II the principle of vaccination had become so well established that one of the commonest laments uttered by draftees entering the armed forces was that Uncle Sam was turning them into pincushions. But as a consequence of such multiple vaccination and other medical advances, World War II was the first war in which infectious diseases claimed fewer casualties than the battlefield.

Of all modern vaccines, none was awaited with more eagerness or developed with more difficulty than that which would defend the body against polio. That disease, poliomyelitis, was not statistically a major health problem. In 1952, the peak year for polio, the U.S. Public Health Service reported 57,879 cases. But two factors greatly enhanced the drive to cure polio: the vast majority of its victims were young children, and the best-known American of his era was a victim of polio's ravages. Indeed the financial offensive against the disease—the March of Dimes—was launched in 1938 in the name of Franklin Delano Roosevelt.

Research difficulties appeared at once. Scientists found that polio was caused not by one but by three different viruses. More critically, even after they identified all three strains, researchers were unable to grow them in a safe medium or in sufficient quantities to produce vaccines. These obstacles were finally overcome in 1949. When the Nobel Prize was awarded in 1954, it went not to Dr. Jonas Salk or to Dr. Albert Sabin, who produced two different vaccines and whose names were closely linked with controlling polio, but to Dr. John Franklin Enders and his associates, who had cultured the poliomyelitis viruses. As Dr. Salk said, "Dr. John Enders pitched a very long forward pass and I happened to be in the right spot to receive it."

Less publicized but of far greater consequence to world health was the struggle to develop an effective vaccine against yellow fever. The disease was endemic to coastal Africa, South America, and the Caribbean islands, making forays into North America and Europe. Although often associated with the building of the Panama Canal, the disease is another longtime human killer. An epidemic of yellow fever in Philadelphia in 1793 claimed more than 5,000 lives in three months. Early in the 19th century an epidemic decimated an army of 25,000 men that Napoleon had sent to Haiti to put down an insurrection led by Toussaint L'Ouverture. One historian pointed out that this disaster so disenchanted the emperor with the

Edward Jenner

In artist's depiction, Jenner's shot is well attended.

Edward Jenner, a modest Gloucestershire country doctor, was both curious and observant—qualities that eventually enabled him to do a great deal for humanity. For years he had been aware while making his rounds of nearby farms that men and women who worked near cows seemed immune to the scourge of smallpox. He decided to test his hunch: on May 14, 1796, Jenner inoculated an eight-year-old boy named James Phipps with matter taken from a cowpox pustule on the arm of a milkmaid. Six weeks later he inoculated the boy again, this time with deadly smallpox. It had no effect.

News of Jenner's success spread even to the New World, where President Thomas Jefferson had himself and his family inoculated. Honors came quickly. In 1802 the British Parliament voted Jenner a grant of £10,000, and another of £20,000 in 1806. Although Britain and France were at war, Napoleon had a medal struck in Jenner's honor in 1804, and paid him the further compliment of making vaccination compulsory in the French Army.

But the sincerest praise came from Elizabeth, wife of Czar Alexander I and Empress of All the Russias. She was so enthusiastic about Jenner's discovery that she encouraged the inoculation of all her subjects. And at her command the first recipient of the vaccine, a boy named Anton Petrov, was formally given a new name—Vaccinov.

New World that he eventually sold the Louisiana Territory to the United States. As late as 1878, Memphis, Tennessee, was staggered by an outbreak of the disease, which claimed more than 5,000 victims and brought the city to a halt.

One of the frustrations of coping with outbreaks

of yellow fever lay in the mystery of its transmission. In 1900 a U.S. Army doctor named Walter Reed and his associates produced the answer: the disease was carried and spread by a mosquito, *Aëdes aegypti*. Armed with this knowledge another army doctor, William Gorgas, showed that the disease could be controlled by saturating mosquito breeding grounds with oil, thus killing the larvae. Then, in 1927, three research physicians proved that the disease-causing organism was a virus, and four years later a primitive vaccine was produced. Not until 1937, however, did Dr. Max Theiler of the Rockefeller Foundation in New York produce the 17D yellow-fever vaccine that has since been administered to millions of people.

VACUUM CLEANER For centuries cleaning was an aggressive art, and housewives, using salt, wet cornmeal, and even shredded cabbage to draw the dirt, wielded broom and carpet beater with a single word on their lips—attack. Then, in the 1900's, the cleaning tide turned toward a more useful principle—extraction. The architect of this change was an English engineer, Cecil Booth, who startled diners in a London restaurant with his bizarre behavior. For Booth suddenly began sucking the back of his plush chair, thereby proving to his satisfaction, despite coughing and

This lady looks calm enough, but it must have taken nerves (and muscles) of steel to run this early vacuum.

choking, that dirt could be removed by suction.

In 1901 Booth began manufacturing suction cleaning devices, known as Booth's Original Vacuum Cleaner Pumps, or "Puffing Billies." These were massive machines with their pumps mounted on horse-drawn carts. In operation they were manned by cleaning squads, who ran hose pipes into London stores, hotels, and houses of the wealthy with such zeal and ceremony that social matrons sometimes held drawing-room tea parties so that friends could observe them at work.

During World War I Booth received an emergency call to clean the Crystal Palace, a relic of London's 1851 Great Exhibition, where members of the Naval Reserve forces stationed inside were dying of spotted fever. Booth's machines hummed away and removed some 26 tons of germ-laden dirt, ending the epidemic. Booth was also called in to clean the great blue carpet at Westminster Abbey for the coronation of Edward VII. The results so impressed the heads of Germany, Russia, and France that they all wanted "Puffing Billies."

Because of Booth's work, the House of Commons eventually installed a centrally powered cleaning unit, consisting of hoses attached to tubes located throughout the building, which drew dust into containers. Similar systems later were scaled down for home use and even now are coming back into style.

It was a poor American inventor-turned-janitor with a hacking cough, however, who finally rescued the housewife from the endless drudgery of cleaning. The inventor was James Murray Spangler, and he developed an electrically driven portable machine to suck up the dust that provoked his cough. Later he sold his invention to a cousin's husband, William Hoover, whose sales methods not only made the machines famous but became as well a part of the image of the resourceful American common in the 1920's.

Teams of door-to-door salesmen, boosted by pep talks and rousing choruses of "The Hoover Song" ("All the dirt, all the grit,/Hoover gets it, every bit"), led the charge each morning to demonstrate the Hoover home models. Soon the country—and indeed much of the world—hummed to the revolutionary hymn of the vacuum cleaner.

VITAMINS The long and detailed entry on vitamins in a current encyclopedia concludes that scientists are hard at work trying to figure out exactly what each vitamin does in the body. Nonetheless, Americans spend over $1 billion annually on vitamins and food supplements, which they have been led to believe will control aging, ease the discomfort of colds, arthritis, and other ailments, prevent cancer, allay feelings of anxiety, and reverse the symptoms of schizophrenia.

An American biochemist of Polish extraction, Casimir Funk, coined the name "vitamin" in 1912. He believed that some chemical compounds were essential to sustain life—hence "vita"—and that these belonged to the "amine" group of chemicals. He was quickly proved wrong on this second count, and the final "e" was duly dropped. As to the first claim, additional research has tended to becloud the issue, because what is true for one organism may not be true for another. For instance, while vitamin C is essential to certain species including man, monkeys, guinea pigs, and a Persian songbird called the bulbul, other animals can get along without it—which is why we do not have to serve orange juice to cats. (Vitamin C, or ascorbic acid, has also proved useful in restoring old books, preventing rust, removing stains, waving hair, and reducing the effects of hangover in rats.)

Microorganisms that dwell in symbiotic harmony in the digestive tracts of cows and other ruminants produce sufficient amounts of B vitamins for their hosts' survival. Some animals are able to store fat-soluble vitamins in the liver for future needs. Adventuresome cooks should note, for instance, that polar-bear liver is so rich in vitamin A as to be toxic to man.

What can be said with assurance is that certain vitamins protect man against certain ailments. Sufficient daily amounts of vitamins A, B1, C, and D will prevent the onset, respectively, of xerophthalmia, beriberi, scurvy, and rickets—not exactly diseases that are emptying the nation's streets. Both the Food and Drug Administration and the American Medical Association insist that the recommended daily allowance established for these vitamins can be obtained in any normal balanced diet. When the FDA proposed in 1973 to regulate the sale of vitamins, several congressmen were deluged with more mail than they had received over any recent issue, including Watergate.

Our candy-vitamined kids will not need to suffer this potent diet supplement of old.

Consumers, eager to avail themselves of the benefits of vitamins, periodically discover new substances or new "cures." Some years ago the number one spot was held by vitamin E, a substance whose wide-ranging virtues were described at length in books with titles such as *Vitamin E for Ailing and Healthy Hearts* and *Vitamin E: Key to Sexual Satisfaction.* A druggist in Tulsa, Oklahoma, announced in an ad: "We know of no earthly use for it, but we have it for $4.99 per 100."

One of the most-publicized nutrition fads featured calcium permanganate, or B15. The list of diseases that this superpill allegedly helps to cure reads like the table of contents of a medical textbook: heart diseases, aging, senility, diabetes, gangrene, glaucoma, alcoholism, drug addiction, hepatitis, jaundice, allergies, dermatitis, mild poisoning, neuralgia, sciatica, neuritis, and minimal-damage brain dysfunction. Supporters point out that B15 is enormously popular in the Soviet Union, where it was officially sanctioned by the U.S.S.R. Academy of Sciences. Closer to home, Muhammad Ali's doctor claimed that the boxer owed his spectacular comeback in 1976 in part to the detoxifying blood-building properties of B15. Among the nonbelievers are many nutritionists and the FDA. The agency has made seizures of the product throughout the country and took measures in the courts to have it removed from the market.

Doctors are alarmed that people are applying the "chicken-soup" principle of medical therapy ("take some more, it can't hurt") to the taking of vitamins. Not long ago a mother brought her two young children to the Yale University School of Medicine. The two-year-old boy was losing his hair, was suffering from an enlarged liver and spleen, and could not walk. His sister's head was growing abnormally because the skull bones had begun to enlarge. Both recovered after doctors persuaded their mother to stop feeding them the massive doses of vitamins, including 25,000 units of vitamin A—12½ times the recommended daily maximum amount—she had been slipping into their morning porridge.

Past generations did not know about vitamins but sensed certain needs.

The letters "U," "V," and "W" are all related, "W" being the latest. Scribes used linked "V's" for the w sound.

WASHING MACHINE The world's first washing machine, if it may be called that, was a triumph of natural utilitarianism: a flat rock set by the side of a running stream. And the state of the art made small progress beyond such rudimentary lavation until 1780, when an Englishman named Rodger Rodgerson filed a patent for ". . . an entirely new machine called a laundry for the purpose of washing . . . in a much less expensive and laborious and more expeditious manner than any hitherto practised." The exact nature of his creation has been lost in the vortex of time. In 1797 an American named Nathaniel Briggs received a patent for a device to be used in "washing cloaths." According to some sources, what Briggs came up with was a type of washboard. In essence the flat rock had been moved into the kitchen. Nonetheless the laundry problem remained—back-wrenching, relentless. So bad in fact were things that prospectors in California during the Gold Rush of 1849, outnumbering women a dozen to one, were sometimes driven to send out their shirts to be washed—to China.

The idea of assembling an automatic washing machine was on the minds of many inventors. An early motor-driven washing machine powered by a 10-horsepower engine was assembled in 1851. Twelve years later another hard-thinking inventor came up with a belt-driven mechanism that tumbled clothes about in a cylinder of soapy water, a departure from the friction principle of getting clothes clean. By 1875 about 2,000 patents for mechanical washers had been granted in the United States. The most commonly used models, however, still required the use of a pair of chapped, inevitably female, hands. To deduce that washday was considerably less than joyful, one had but to peruse the names that inventors gave to their mechanical creations: "Housewife's Darling," "Pastime," "Woman's Friend," "Kill Kare," and "Hummer." They may have helped, but according to Mrs. Isabella Beeton's *The Book of Household Management*, published in 1861, laundry remained a week-long grind: "The laundry-maid should commence her labours on Monday morning. . . . Early on the following morning the fires should be lighted. . . . Thursday and Friday, in a laundry in full employ, are usually devoted to mangling, starching, and ironing."

The modern age of the washing machine dawned with the invention of a self-contained electric machine in the first decade of the 20th century. In 1922 Howard Snyder placed a circular plate studded with four vertical fins at the bottom of a tub and attached it to a drive shaft. The result was an agitator-type washer. The running stream had been brought into the kitchen. Although most home washing machines still use agitators, the fully automatic machine that, once activated, knows when to wash, when to rinse, and when to spin-dry, is a far cry from these early models.

Most people have been content to use their washing machine for its original intended purpose, but some have been more clever and imaginative. For instance, under the headline "Washing Machines Defy Nazis," *The New York Times* reported in 1941 that German occupation forces in Holland had seized all privately owned butter churns in order to centralize the industry. Dutch farmers sabotaged the plan by making butter at home in American-made washing machines.

In postwar times, a laundromat operator in Los Angeles found an appropriate way to celebrate the gala opening of a new branch on Sunset Boulevard: he used one machine as a martini mixer.

One of the staples of the local diet on Johnston Island, some 700 miles from Hawaii, is octopus. It is delicious and plentiful but was hard to tenderize—until a laundromat opened and women found they could do the job by running a bucketful of octopus through the wash cycle.

Laundry al fresco: she may not have been a city slicker but this plainswoman was clearly in the vanguard of believers in newfangled, labor-saving devices.

WATCH If a watch is distinguished from a clock primarily because the former is portable, then the honor of designing the first watch belongs to a German locksmith named Peter Henlein—but only on a technicality. Henlein's watch, completed about 1500 after two years of tinkering, was drum-shaped, stood six inches high, and was constructed entirely of iron. It was driven by a coiled spring, and its lone hand had a tendency to creep ahead or lag behind by an hour.

Further efforts at miniaturization produced models that a lady could wear on a sturdy chain around her neck. One of the most famous of these

This 17th-century crystal-cased Swiss watch was also fancy jewelry.

was owned by Mary Queen of Scots. It was in the shape of a human skull and bore the inscription: "The impartial foot of pale Death visits the cottages of the poor and the palaces of kings"—a sentiment that was not only grim but prophetic as well.

The first timepiece that might deserve to be called a wristwatch was presented to Queen Elizabeth I, Mary's archrival, about 1581. It consisted of "an armlet of gold, all fairly garnished with rubies and diamonds and having the closing thereof a small clock," but it still had only a single hand. The technical problem of mounting two hands on one shaft was not solved until 1676. Thereafter, however, improvements proliferated. In 1704 a Swiss watchmaker bored holes in tiny jewels and used them as watch bearings to reduce friction. (Switzerland had become the world center of watchmaking in the middle of the 16th century, and by the end of that century the craftsmen had formed a watchmakers' guild.) The first self-winding watch, generally thought of as a modern invention, was patented in 1780.

Watches became popular in the 19th century and were generally carried about in the pocket. Men did not wear wristwatches for fear of being thought effeminate. But stigma began to fade toward the end of the 19th century when, as the story goes, the German Navy ordered wristwatches for its officers so that they would not have to fumble for their pocket watches while striding a slippery deck. Military pocket watches vanished in World War I. One can hardly imagine a group of mud-spattered officers, tensely crouched in a trench, reaching for their fobs at the command, "Gentlemen, synchronize your watches."

Human nature being what it is, it was not likely that, having perfected an eminently useful timepiece, inventors would simply leave it alone. Wristwatches were equipped with alarms, with multizone faces, with calendars, with calculators. A patent has even been issued for a wristwatch that "functions by means of coupling a miniature speaker to a solid-state memory." When it is 11:43, it will not only show you the time but in a mechanical voice will announce it as well.

In recent times thinness has become one of the most prized characteristics of a wristwatch. Not long ago a Japanese manufacturer produced a watch that was a mere 2.5 millimeters thick and about the size of a silver dollar. The seven that were offered for sale cost $5,000 each. The Swiss, stung in their national pride, hurried to the drawing board and came up with the Delirium I, only 1.98 millimeters thick and roughly the size of a newly minted dime. At $4,400 it was something of a bargain.

The newest fad to sweep timekeeping is the digital watch, either the light-emitting diode (LED), which tells time at the touch of a button, or the liquid-crystal diode (LCD), which gives a constant reading but does not glow in the dark. Originally priced at about $300 to $400, these watches have become so popular that one manufacturer brought out a model costing the inelegant sum of $9.95.

Price aside, the digital watches have come under criticism as still another example of mass dehumanization. One critic noted that by fragmenting time into moments it denies man the "spatial relationship" of the day's cycle. Another complained of reducing time to "red numerals, balefully gleaming like hot little ingots fresh from the open hearth." And a mother pointed out that future generations of children, already robbed of the need to read by television, and of the need to add or subtract by calculators, would grow up unable to tell time on a clock.

This last danger, at least, has been averted. One of the leading makers of digital clocks has come up with a new device called an analog Time Indicator. Priced between $275 and $325, it features a 120-segment liquid-crystal display arrayed like a spoked wheel. A lithium–manganese dioxide battery activates the crystals in such a manner that they seem to sweep around the face, looking for all the world like the hands of a watch.

WEATHER Nothing so reminds technological man of his dependence on nature as the weather, that global caul in which we live and move and complain. When snow gags cities, when hurricanes snap communications or hurl a river down Main Street, we are likely to be as awestruck· as any primitive man was by the colossal energies around us—and with good reason. The earth experiences some 44,000 storms a day; in a single hour, lightning flashes 360,000 times. In the United States alone, tornadoes and flash floods each kill anywhere between 100 and 200 people a year. Though our Faustian science can now peer into the birth of a cyclone or analyze the ions of the thunder god, it cannot, in the end, keep cellars from flooding or guarantee the wheat crop.

The energies of the weather astonish man's mind. In one hour on a hot afternoon, 5.5 billion gallons of water evaporate from the Gulf of Mexico. A single fluffy cloud can hold up to 1,000 tons of moisture. A summer thunderstorm is capable of expending as much energy as a dozen or so atom bombs. One thunderstorm in coastal Providence, Rhode Island, strewed still-flopping fish over a quarter of an acre; another rained crabs and periwinkles by the bagful on Worcester, England—a city 40 miles inland. Tornadoes can whip winds of up to 250 miles per hour into a funnel anywhere from 50 feet to a mile and a half wide; one lifted an entire railroad coach with 117 people aboard and set it down 80 feet away in a ditch. Another neatly swiped a glass jar of pickles and abandoned it, intact, 25 miles away.

Dog and man alike tremble when lightning strikes, but few people are aware that a flash of lightning strikes up rather than down. The electri-

---

customs

Weather Lore

If bats fly into the house, if cows refuse to go to pasture, if a cat licks its fur against the grain, if geese meander, donkeys bray, or a pig carries straw in its mouth, then, sure enough, it is going to rain.

For centuries before official weather reports were commonplace, country people read the signs of impending weather in the life around them. Sensitive to the turn of a leaf or the time of day the spider spun its web, they wove their observations into a body of folk knowledge that was passed on from generation to generation. Grandma always said that frogs sing loudest before it rains—and who was wiser than she?

In Germany, Austria, and Switzerland, some people kept a frog and a little ladder in a jar half-filled with water. If the frog stayed in the water, rain was coming; if it clambered up the ladder, the day would be clear. Leeches were reputed to be so sensitive to changes in the weather that a Dr. Merryweather proposed in 1851 that the British government set up leech-bottle weather stations along the British coasts.

Crickets have been called "the poor man's thermometer" because they give the accurate temperature in degrees Fahrenheit. Here is the formula: count how many times a cricket chirps in 15 seconds and add the number 37.

The better to be remembered, weather lore was often rhymed. "Swallows fly high: clear blue sky;/Swallows fly low: rain we shall know." Or "When gnats swarm in January, the peasant will have an empty granary." Or "A rainbow in the morn, put your hook in the corn; A rainbow at eve, put your head in the sheave." Generally, the most accurate weather rhymes relate to the sky, for as Virgil wrote, "The sun who never lies,/Foretells the change of weather in the skies."

The most famous of these rubrics—"Sky red in the morning/Is a sailor's sure warning;/Sky red at night/Is the sailor's delight"—is based on sound observation.

Since the prevailing winds in the Northern Hemisphere are westerly, a red sky (indicating dry weather) on the western horizon in the evening indicates that good weather is coming. "A circle around the moon,/'Twill rain soon" is sometimes accurate because the effect is caused by ice crystals in a high layer of cirrostratus clouds that may indeed presage rain.

On the other hand, anyone who purports to predict the harshness of a coming winter from the thickness of onion skins or squirrels' tails or the width of the black stripe on a woolly bear caterpillar is reading the past, not the future. About as useful a piece of weather lore was passed on by a wise old Eskimo of the forest who always knew when a harsh winter was coming. His secret sign was that the white man gathered much wood.

The British artist George Cruikshank illustrated the phrase "raining cats, dogs, and pitchforks" in 1835. A vendor (back, left) sells cat and dog meat.

cal stresses set up by the negative particles in the cloud create faintly luminous ionized channels, which branch downward until they meet the positive charges of the ground. There is a sudden flow of charge through the ionized channels that heats the air to temperatures three times greater than the current flow at the surface of the sun, and in the process excites a blaze of light.

On a global scale, weather changes are created when the restless atmosphere, at least 5,600 trillion tons of it, is stirred to action by the sun's radiation. Warm, moist air of the equatorial zones rises and flows to the poles, from which cooler winds, skewed in their path by the earth's rotation, flow back to fill the gap. Add seasonal variations in the sun's angle, the interplay between

customs

Weather Forecasting: Necromancy or Science?

Each day the U.S. National Weather Service (part of the National Oceanographic and Atmospheric Administration) receives 40,000 global surface observations, 1,500 upper-atmosphere readings, 2,800 messages from airplanes, reports from ships and balloons, and hundreds of satellite photographs and temperature readings of the atmosphere. A giant, sophisticated bank of computers sorts the mass of information and twice a day comes up with a national weather forecast, which is further refined by regional forecast offices throughout the nation. Yet on February 5, 1978, a blizzard that cost an estimated $1 billion in damages to businesses and property and more than 50 human lives tore into the Northeast with a fury all the more devastating because its severity was unexpected.

Why do the weather forecasters get it wrong so often? Simply because man's knowledge and the reach and analysis of his observations are not yet able to cope with phenomena as complex as the weather. The region, then the hemisphere, then the great rhythms of our global atmosphere—the scale of these ascending and interrelated factors, set against the short history of past records, leaves too many gaps and creates chances for error. Despite the armory of intelligent hardware hurled into the task worldwide, the data are insufficient for anyone to expect perfection in prophecy, particularly in long-range forecasts. "Anyone who says he can tell you more than a few days ahead of time

what the weather is going to be is practicing necromancy," said M.I.T.'s Jule Charney.

A better question is how the weathermen get the short-term forecast *right* as often as they do. In colonial days no network for coordinating weather observations existed, though Thomas Jefferson, with his curiosity about things meteorological, kept temperature records even on the day the Declaration of Independence was adopted. The invention of

90°: Scripps' FLIP (floating instrument platform) tips for forecast data.

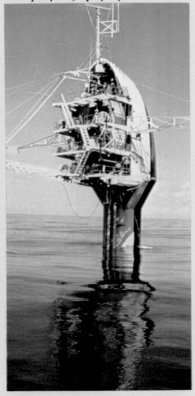

the telegraph gave rise to telegraphic weather services, which made possible the gathering of simultaneous data in different regions. Not until the 1930's was the upper atmosphere sounded, and not until after World War II was there any such thing as global forecasting, finally made possible by the use of radar, rockets, satellites, and computers developed during and since.

Progress in forecasting is expressed in humble terms: today's 24-hour forecast is more accurate than a 1960's 12-hour forecast. What that progress means in terms of lives, property, and dollars saved is incalculable. In 1900, for example, decades before weather satellites could plot with reasonable accuracy the path of tropical storms, a hurricane lashed into the coast of Texas at Galveston and killed 6,000 people. Parts of the city were starting to fill with water when the warnings to evacuate were heard.

True, weather forecasters are not always right. They may never be. But in 1979 the 147 nations of the Global Weather Experiment launched an ambitious program to glean, for the first time, an annual record of worldwide weather data. The $500-million program coordinated observations from scores of measuring devices, including satellites, aircraft, ships, high-altitude balloons, and drifting instrument buoys, in places where records have never before been taken. Such efforts one day may result in more accurate estimates of when to sow and when to reap and when to carry an umbrella.

land and sea, between mountains and plains, and the long-term characteristics known as climate take on those quirky local accents known as weather. Taking the long view, climatologists like to make us aware that weather existed long before humans were around to define it. And weather clearly has played a fateful role in human history.

England had the prevailing westerlies to thank for the the defeat of the Spanish Armada in 1588. Claiming an upwind advantage, the light British

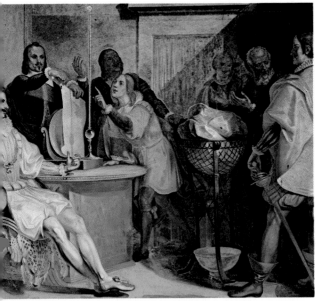

A gathering at Florence's Experimental Academy (1657-1667) determines whether cold reflects like heat.

warships outmaneuvered the more cumbersome Spanish vessels. Had those westerlies failed or shifted and pushed the Spanish fleet to windward, the language of the British Isles might be Spanish. In his long exile Napoleon had time to ponder the role of weather in the defeat of his imperial designs. So muddy was the field before the Battle of Waterloo that Napoleon elected to delay his attack six hours—just enough time for Prussian reinforcements to arrive in support of the British. The result, Napoleon's final defeat, is history.

The destructive seasonal typhoons of Japan resulted in Japan's historic independence from China. Twice the 13th-century emperor Kublai Khan sent ships and troops against the little Japanese islands, and twice the onslaught of the typhoon wrecked the ships of the invaders. Japanese remember the storm that spared them as the *kamikaze*, or "divine wind." Late in World War II, when Japan was again desperate to stave off defeat, this honorable name was given to the Japanese suicide pilots who deliberately drove their bomb-laden airplanes headlong into Allied vessels.

Studying the earth's weather history from tree rings and sea bottom, from fossils and soils, climatologists have come up with some startling theories about a few classic mysteries of history. The sudden end of the Mycenaean civilization, suggested one climatologist, may be attributable to severe drought. Drought may also explain the disappearance of the Mesa Verde cliff dwellers, who lived in the southwestern United States until the late 1200's. Northern Europe between 900 and 1130 experienced a climate much balmier than today's, so that vineyards flourished in England. This warm spell may help explain the burst of Viking energies that led to the colonization of Iceland and to exploration as far as North America. And was it a sudden failure of the seasonal monsoons that destroyed the remarkable civilization of the Indus River valley of eastern Pakistan and northern India in 1700 B.C.?

Weather has been held accountable for no less than the rise of civilization itself. Some historians, meteorologists, and other scientists claim that the tropics breed apathy, but the tumultuous north temperate zone, where polar air conflicts with tropical air, poses challenges to human survival that require vigor and resourcefulness—qualities that mark civilizations of Europe, Asia, and North America.

Next to deciphering the past, climatologists also debate the future of the earth's weather. If the sun's heat increased by 30 percent, all life would cease; if it decreased by 13 percent, a layer of ice a mile thick would encrust the earth. What they cannot predict is the effect of the newest wrinkle in the earth's 4.5-billion-year history—man. The debate centers around the increased amounts of CO_2 and dust pouring into the atmosphere from land clearance, industry, and the consumption of fossil fuels. If CO_2 traps sunlight in the upper atmosphere, in what is known as the "greenhouse effect," the result could be a heating of the earth. On the other hand, the dust particles we are pumping into the air could reflect back a portion of the sun's heat into space and lead to a general cooling. In either scenario technological man becomes a factor in his own forecast.

WEEDS Ralph Waldo Emerson, who preferred to look on the bright side of things, described a weed as "a plant whose virtues have not yet been discovered." And a botanist once devoted an entire book to the defense of weeds, pointing out that, among other good works, they return essential minerals to depleted topsoil, serve as useful indicators of soil conditions, and some of them make good eating. All these benefits, one suspects, caused few if any changes of heart among back-weary farmers and gardeners, to say nothing of hay-fever sufferers.

Botanically speaking, there is no such classification as weed. A weed is a weed because man says so. According to a dictionary, a weed is "a plant considered undesirable, unattractive, or troublesome; especially, one growing where it is not wanted." This definition

Beauty is in the eye of the beholder: poison hemlock is lacy but lethal.

not only betrays man's hostility toward the plant but also imputes an evil perversity to the likes of plantain, amaranth, nutsedge, and mullein.

Man's rejection of certain pesky plants is based on their double nature: a weed reseeds itself at an astonishing rate, and then, naturally, it "grows like a weed." A single tumbling tumbleweed, for example, can release more than 6 million seeds as it tumbles along. The small seeds of peppergrass have a gluelike coating; when moistened with dew the seeds adhere to the feet of birds, to be carried and dropped over hill and dale. Crabgrass has defeated nearly every attempt to destroy it: not only does a single plant produce up to 50,000 seeds, but the very act of digging or yanking it out of the ground only serves to spread them. A single ragweed plant can fill the air with 8 billion grains of pollen, each about one-fifth the diameter of a human hair. But the champion is the water hyacinth: in a single growing season 10 hyacinths can give rise to more than 600,000 plants and form a mat of closely intertwined vegetation that weighs 180 tons and covers a whole acre.

Against this runaway fecundity, man has deployed just about every weapon at his command. He has attempted to drown weeds by flooding his fields with water and to parch them to death by draining the ground. He has tried to smother them with plastic, to kill them with chemicals, and to burn them with flame throwers. He has even enlisted the aid of other forms of life against them. Some years ago California farmers imported from Australia quantities of a certain beetle that reputedly had an insatiable appetite for a particular breed of weed that was choking their crops. More recently, scientists in Florida stocked some of the state's rivers with certain fish from the Amur River in the Soviet Union in hopes that they would devour some of the noxious weeds.

And, not long ago, two scientists reported that some varieties of cucumbers kill weeds by releasing toxic chemicals into the soil, a first step toward producing a natural herbicide.

The acceleration of man's war on weeds is probably the consequence of an increasingly overcrowded and overpopulated planet. In earlier centuries weeds such as lungwort, milk thistle, foxglove, and bittersweet were prized for their therapeutic properties. (Just a few years ago, researchers isolated a substance in bittersweet called betasolamarine that appears to inhibit growth of tumors.) Weeds were also a rich food source. Amaranth seeds, ground and baked, were a staple food of Indians of America. (An analysis of the nutrients in lamb's quarters, a common garden pest, shows that one ounce contains 20 percent of the recommended daily allowance of protein, all the allowance of calcium, five times that of vitamin C, and more than six times that of vitamin A.)

The war continues, but its outcome is not much in doubt. The ancient Roman city of Pompeii emerged reasonably intact from the molten lava that completely buried it nearly 2,000 years ago. Now, however, it faces a greater threat. Italian authorities in charge of its preservation reveal that the buildings are being weakened and broken up by unchecked masses of weeds, which thrive in the volcanic soil. Chemical killers cannot be used, as they would damage frescoes and mosaics. Digging up the weeds by hand is prohibitively expensive. Perhaps eventually the war on weeds at Pompeii will be waged by the killer cucumber.

WINE No one knows who conceived the genial idea of pressing the juice from grapes and letting it ferment. Archeologists have found remains of grapes—stems and seeds—in prehistoric caves. Ancient Babylonians must have been drinking wine—and adulterating it—more than 4,000 years ago. The Code of Hammurabi, one of the oldest surviving bodies of laws, specified that a wine seller who gave short measure was to be thrown into the water. Wine's ancient origin is also borne out in the Bible, for after the Flood "Noah began to be a husbandman, and he planted a vineyard: And he drank of the wine, and was drunken." That is the first of many mentions of wine in the Old Testament. In the New Testament nine books have references to wine, including St. Paul's admonition to Timothy: "Drink no longer water, but use a little wine for thy stomach's sake."

It seems that this advice has been enthusiastically followed by millions. Some 6.4 billion gallons of wine are sold annually, or about 8 bottles for

The Wisdom of Wills

"'Where there's a will there are relatives.' But where there's no will at all there are even more," wrote financial columnist Sylvia Porter. At least 50 percent of Americans die intestate, thereby forfeiting to the impersonal wisdom of the state their right to dispose of their worldly possessions as they please. President Lincoln, though he was a lawyer, never bothered to write a will.

Obviously, a will constructed with sound legal advice is the best kind, but in the absence of other documents, wills that were scribbled on a visiting card, a hospital chart, even on a bridge score card have been declared valid. A blind woman wrote hers with a pen that, unbeknownst to her, had run out of ink. A handwriting expert deciphered the impressions left in the paper by the empty pen, restored her words, and the will was declared valid. Unwitnessed but clear enough was the message a farmer scratched on the fender of the tractor under which he was pinned. "In case I die in this mess, I leave all to the wife." He did die, and the testament in steel was honored.

Among Margaret Nothe's effects when she died in 1913 was her book of handwritten recipes. The last part of her recipe for "Chili Sauce Without Working" reads: "Chop tomatoes, onions and peppers fine, add the rest mixed together and bottle cold.... In case I die before my husband I leave everything to him."

Wills require no special legal jargon, only that the language be clear enough to avoid confusion. The kindly uncle who left his niece an annual income for "as long as she remains above ground" no doubt assumed that his wishes were obvious. But when the niece died, her husband simply laid her to rest in a mausoleum above ground and went on collecting her income—legally. Though the story may be apocryphal, it illustrates the point.

A testator's desire to do good to others—in a vague sort of way—has given lawyers some expensive headaches. In 1949 a grisly old prospector named James Kidd disappeared in the mountains near Globe, Arizona. Fifteen years later his will was discovered; it left $297,000 worth of stocks and bonds for "proof or research of a human soul which leaves the body after death." One hundred and thirty-nine claimants, from mediums to psychics to representatives of medical institutions, clamored for the funds as convincingly as they could, attempting to prove his thesis. And if confusion reigned, no wonder. The court first decided to award the money to a group of neurologists, but the final recipient of this tidy sum was the American Society for Psychical Research.

A number of eccentrics, on the other hand, have been all too specific in the stipulations attached to their posthumous largesse. A wealthy New York tailor in the 1880's left everything to his nieces and nephews except 71 pairs of pants, which he directed to be sold at auction. No one was permitted to mend, clean, press, or otherwise fuss with the pants before the sale. After the auction, stories began to circulate of the lucky buyers who had each discovered, sewed into a trouser pocket, a thousand dollars.

Some folks relish exercising control over others even after death. In the 17th century a pious lady who wanted a solemn funeral left a goodly legacy to the priests of her church on the condition that no smiles erupt during the service. The mass began. One young priest got a twinkle in his eye. Another looked away and covered his face. Infectiously, the giggles turned to uproarious laughter. A court determined, humanely, that "the absurdity of the prohibition was in itself a provocation to violate it."

The distinguished British philosopher Jeremy Bentham left his fortune to London Hospital, with the single wish that he be permitted to preside over board meetings. For 92 years Bentham's well-dressed skeleton sat in its glass case in the board room. The minutes of each meeting duly noted his presence adding after his name, "not voting."

Usually the dearly departed has only generous concern for a surviving spouse, but take the poet Heinrich Heine. He left all his assets to his wife, but only *if* she remarried. The reason? "Then there will be at least one man to regret my death," the poet added spitefully. Equally honest was the French merchant who died a bachelor in 1610 and bequeathed a tidy legacy to the woman who 20 years earlier had refused his marriage proposal—in gratitude for her good sense in leaving him a happy bachelor.

Reading the will, with its attendant smirking, sulking, and sniping satirized.

Window Dressing

Mannequins, as anyone who window-shops may have noticed, are no longer the dummies they once were.

The notion of displaying clothes more or less as they would look on a person is surprisingly recent. The first lifelike mannequin made its appearance in Paris at the Universal Exhibition of 1894. The early models were usually fashioned from wax, with demure expressions and large breasts. Shrouded in the fashion of the day, the rest of each store-window lady was left to the viewer's imagination.

The first plaster models made the scene in the 1920's. They were sturdier and much heavier than mannequins made of fragile wax. Eventually fiberglass, plastic, and clay became the materials of choice. Over the years, both the measurements of mannequins and their facial expressions—aloof, exquisite, sophisticated, naive, homely, aggressive—have mirrored the temper of the times. Today's most common proportions for synthetic women are 32-24-34, dispersed along a body measuring 5 feet 10 inches to 6 feet 2 inches, with impossibly long legs and size 6½-B feet.

The modern mannequin began to take shape when Dan Arje, a noted display designer, was visiting a model factory and with the help of a companion poked navels into some mannequins on the production line. "Most of our navel artwork was erased," he recalled, "but a few stayed in, and now navels are here to stay."

After navels came other realistic innovations such as freckles, human-shaped noses, and, as a concession to those see-through blouses, breasts tipped with nipples. How far the trend has gone was unwittingly demonstrated by a New York City police sergeant who raided a go-go bar near Times Square and tried to arrest, on charges of indecent exposure, two scantily clad mannequins.

The situations have also changed. A store in Los Angeles showed a beach scene in which a male mannequin triumphantly held up a bikini top belonging to a female mannequin, who had her back discreetly turned. And for a Christmas display a New York store prepared a window in which 10 masked mannequins and a maid were shown at a party. With

Amsterdam's red-light district features a come-hither window display.

each passing night the clothes were changed slightly, so that by New Year's Eve the maid's uniform was coming undone and the male partygoers had taken off their tuxedo jackets as if about to get more intimate.

And, as an example of how reality eventually catches up with illusion, a store in downtown Washington, D.C., showed in its 16-foot-high windows a group of live female models who occasionally changed their outerclothes in full view of passersby.

every man, woman, and child in the world. One out of every 130 acres of cultivated land on earth is devoted to vineyards, and one person in a 100 derives his or her livelihood from the growing, making, or selling of wine.

Wine has been lovingly praised by a group of writers as disparate as John Keats and John Wesley, Napoleon and François Villon, Ernest Hemingway and Elizabeth Barrett Browning. It is also the sole subject of a 650-page book published in seven languages under the auspices of the United Nations Food and Agricultural Organi-

A sip of sweet wine and the lady wants more.

zation and containing, among other information, 329 definitions of commonly used terms to describe the taste of wine.

The ancient Greeks drank wine, and coated the insides of porous clay storage jars with resin. Their modern counterparts add a bit of the resin to their wine, giving retsina its characteristic taste. The Romans drank wine at almost every occasion, although they customarily diluted it with water. They were well aware that good wine, properly aged, acquires an excellent flavor. And, most importantly, they introduced the growing of wine grapes in their province of Gaul.

There, the vineyards of Burgundy and Bordeaux were already producing wine by the 1st or 2nd centuries A.D. (Burgundy is bottled in the familiar slope-shouldered container. Bordeaux, in the straight-shouldered bottle, is called "claret" by the British.) The emperor Charlemagne, who was crowned in 800 A.D., owned his own vineyard. Corton-Charlemagne, a first-rate wine, was named in his honor.

In the monastic life of the Middle Ages, wine was made for sacramental use, but it was consumed on other occasions as well. The Rule of St. Benedict, compiled around 530 to guide the management of monasteries, allowed one pint of wine a day, or more at the discretion of the prior, to any monk who reported himself sick. Monasteries were also allowed to sell some of their output. So attractive was this trade that when the wily monks of Carbonnieux decided to peddle their wine in the Turkish market, where Muslim rule dictated abstinence, they labeled it "Mineral Water of Carbonnieux."

The practice of mislabeling the contents of wine bottles survives into the present. Not long ago Italians learned to their horror that the 12 million gallons they had appreciatively gulped down as Frascati, a popular light, dry wine grown on the hills southeast of Rome, was a concoction of water, grape dregs, molasses meant for cattle feed, and artificial coloring.

And, in a scandal that shook the wine establishment and probably caused sommeliers in some of the world's great restaurants to search suspiciously through their cellars, eight French wine merchants were found guilty of fraudulently passing off cheap wine as vintage stuff. When inspectors raided the warehouse of one company, they found vats of wine that had insultingly been labeled: "Can be used for Beaujolais in the United States." A similar French fraud was attempted a few years later.

Eventually the culprits paid out more than $2 million in punitive taxes, but at least they were spared the punishment meted out in 1362 to a London wineseller caught selling "sour or corrupt wine": he was forced to drink as much of it as he

Celebratory sipping, 1905: bridesmaids lift glasses in traditional—though unusual for women then—champagne toast.

could, and the rest was poured over his head.

One inducement to mislabeling is that the demand for wine far exceeds the supply. Among white Burgundies, the one generally conceded to be the greatest is Le Montrachet, which according to one wine lover was "to be drunk on one's knees with head bared." But the vineyard of Montrachet is small, only 19 acres, and the proprietors sensibly keep a quarter of the yield for themselves. Wines costing $4 or $5 a bottle a few years ago can fetch $30 and more today. Older vintage wines tend to be more expensive. A record $18,000 was paid at a recent auction for a bottle of Château Lafite 1864. To be sure, the bottle was a jeroboam, which is the equivalent of 4 ordinary bottles, but the cost still comes out to about $700 a glass.

The fortunate guests who shared the contents of that bottle, at a charity dinner in Memphis, Tennessee, were not only treating their palates to a rare experience but also doing something good for their health. St. Paul's advice, it seems, was even sounder than he knew. It had long been known that wine has antibacterial properties, but two Canadian scientists have also demonstrated that it is effective against a number of viruses, including those that cause polio and herpes.

The bilateral letter "X," particularly suited to computer language, originated with the ancient Greeks.

X RAY For the children present, it was an unforgettable party. Their host, Professor Wilhelm Roentgen, president of the University of Würzburg, had a trick to show them. Between a cathode-ray tube and a cardboard screen, he placed a wooden box. Could the children guess what was in the box? He switched off the light, and suddenly they saw on the cardboard the image of a set of weights which had been placed inside the box.

The astonished youngsters were among the first people in the world to witness the penetrating power of a mysterious new electromagnetic wave that Roentgen had discovered only weeks earlier. While exploring the properties of cathode rays, Roentgen had noticed an eerie glow across the darkened laboratory. A piece of cardboard painted with chemicals was fluorescing. Whatever materials Roentgen placed between the electrically charged tube and the cardboard—metal, rubber, wood—the "ray" penetrated; everything, that is, except lead or glass made with lead. While holding up a sheet of metal, the professor was startled to see the image of his own hand reflected on the

Leftovers: an X ray revealed forceps from surgery 20 years earlier.

cardboard. The darker shadows within were his living bones, visible to the eye for the first time.

In science and mathematics, an unknown quantity is expressed by the letter X. Publishing his astounding news in a scientific paper in 1896, Roentgen explained in a footnote, "For brevity's sake I shall use the expression 'rays,' and to distinguish them from others of this name, I shall call them 'X rays.'"

Similar to light or radio waves, X rays are electromagnetic waves, invisible themselves but having a frequency so short that the rays go through many materials opaque to light. They penetrate metal and bone less readily than flesh and muscle, which is why, when X rays travel through the body to expose a photographic plate, the bones appear as a paler shadow on the negative. Roentgen quickly understood what a boon to medicine his X ray might be; what he could not have predicted was the general hysteria with which the public received the news that man had been rendered transparent.

A New York professor suggested that X rays could save time for his anatomy students by projecting anatomical drawings directly onto their brains. A temperance leader was certain that any alcoholic who could look inside his body and see the awful degeneration caused by demon liquor would instantly give it up. Prophets came forth to say they had X-rayed the soul, and rumors flew that X-ray spectacles would soon be on the market. Acting swiftly to defend the intimate privacy of the body, a New Jersey legislator moved to outlaw the use of X rays in "opera glasses or similar aids to vision." A London firm did a brisk business in X ray-proof underwear for ladies.

The danger of X rays, however, lay elsewhere. Thomas Edison, with his usual instinct for making practical application of scientific knowledge, developed a remarkably good fluoroscope. At the Electrical Exposition in 1896 in New York, a proud assistant, Clarence Dally, repeatedly offered his arm to the ray, to the awe of observers. The result was serious burning, which convinced Edison to drop all experiments on X rays. In 1904 Dally became one of some 160 pioneers in X-ray technology to die of the cell destruction caused by radiation. Today, that very destructive power is applied carefully to destroy cancer cells.

Used widely in industry for precise measurements and analyses, and to detect flaws in parts that might weaken under stress, X rays have also turned their unblinking gaze of truth upon antiques and oil paintings, revealing some to be fakes, others to have been painted over. Under Gainsborough's famous "Blue Boy," for example, X rays saw another, earlier portrait of a man.

In the 1960's a group of dentists decided to X-ray the teeth of Egyptian mummies, whose ancient remains would have putrefied or turned to dust had they been unwrapped for study. The results were so startling that some of history had to be rewritten. There to view, for the first time in some 3,000 years, leaped the intact skeletons of queens and pharaohs, their mortal suffering still visible. Young Tutankhamen has a bashed skull, as if he had been struck on the head.

Others died either younger or older than historians had presumed, and Egyptian chronologies had to be recast accordingly. Clear genetic differences between dynastic rulers once believed to be related have necessitated the redrawing of ancient family trees. Poor old Ramses II, the X rays tell us, suffered terrible toothaches; his jaw is ravaged by abscesses. One ruler it seems had polio, a disease that was not finally more or less brought under control until the 20th century. Others suffered from arthritis and arteriosclerosis. Most startling of all was the revelation of a tiny mummy entombed with Queen Makare, long assumed to be her baby. X rays discovered that she had indeed died during or shortly after childbirth, but within the tiny shroud, to everyone's amazement, were the embalmed remains of a baboon.

The Romans used the letter "Y" when transliterating words that were borrowed from the Greek.

YAWN Hippocrates believed that intense or prolonged yawning heralded fever. In Finnish tradition a yawning horse foretold rain. A yawn has been called a silent shout, and a stifled yawn is a sign of protest recognized around the world. Yet a yawn is not always a sign of boredom. The involuntary reflex is nature's way of providing beneficial exercise to correct an oxygen deficiency and is one of the first acts of a newborn baby. A good yawn sends breath rippling from the diaphragm, pumping oxygen into the lungs and eventually into the blood and often stretching shoulder and neck muscles as well, thereby releasing tension and toning the body.

By sending blood to the brain, yawns can either relax one for sleep or wake one up. Yawns may also be self-induced just by going through the motions of yawning. One Japanese manufacturer of transistors claimed to have increased productivity considerably by instituting 30-second yawn breaks among his factory workers. At a signal the women raised their hands and yawned in unison.

Sometimes continuous yawning indicates diseases of the central nervous system. Records show that in 1888 one 15-year-old patient yawned nonstop for five weeks. More often, however, a stuffy room or a variety of emotions besides boredom can stimulate the reflex.

Acute anxiety can lead to yawning, as it did for a public speaker who was driven to see a doctor because he yawned each time he stood before an audience. The doctor prescribed breathing exercises before a speech, which both calmed and cured the man. Frustration or fear can often produce an intense desire to sleep (as observed in soldiers just before a battle) and bring on yawning as a kind of displacement sleeping. Darwin observed that baboons about to engage an enemy often yawn, and speculated that humans conceal feelings of aggression by the same act.

Psychological research confirms that yawning is highly contagious. Trained yawners sent to libraries and churches sparked outbreaks of yawning, and two-thirds of the students who were shown a film of a girl yawning reported that they either yawned too or felt the urge to do so.

Scientists studying rats observed that younger ones yawned more than older ones, and males more than females. So far these tendencies have not been confirmed among humans.

In spite of increasing data on the wide range of reasons for yawning, the act continues to be the butt of jokes and anecdotes—for example, the only time some married men ever get to open their mouths is when they yawn.

The story is told of magazine editor Harold Ross, who had been cornered at a party by a bore for an hour. Pointing to a yawning guest at the other side of the room, he whispered to his droning companion, "I think he's been eavesdropping."

YOGURT Persian men ate yogurt because they believed it would restore their hair, and their wives rubbed it on their faces because they thought it would remove wrinkles. Romans considered it the elixir of life. The biblical Abraham served it to his guests. The great Arab physician

Gapers galore: all mammals perform this mini-exercise, which stretches muscles, increases oxygen intake.

Avicenna was certain it promoted sexual desire. Today Americans consume some 300,000 tons of it, or 1.2 billion 8-ounce containers, a year.

The hope that yogurt will benefit a bulging waistline, however, may be as vain as earlier expectations, for a container of low-fat yogurt has approximately 150 calories, the same as an 8-ounce glass of whole milk. Yogurt with fruit, however, can contain almost as many calories as a serving of banana cream pie. The real secret of yogurt's enduring fame is that it tastes good.

Taste was not uppermost in the mind of Russian scientist Elie Metchnikoff, who was convinced that human beings hastened their own death by permitting "wild," putrefying bacilli to multiply in the intestine. He had heard that men and women in Bulgaria often lived 100 years or more, and theorized that they owed their longevity to consuming vast quantities of yogurt, a Bulgarian staple. At the Pasteur Institute in Paris, Metchnikoff examined the cultured milk under the microscope and discovered the presence of hordes of rodlike bacteria, which he named *Lactobacillus bulgaricus*. In the expectation that these helpful organisms would chase away the "wild" bacteria, Metchnikoff consumed heroic quantities of yogurt daily, but he died in 1916 at the age of 71, young by Bulgarian standards.

Today we know that when milk is mixed with two microorganisms—*Lactobacillus bulgaricus* and *Streptococcus thermophilus*—milk sugars are transformed into lactic acid, and yogurt results. The man often credited with yogurt's present-day popularity is Isaac Carasso, who in 1929 was making his "Dessert of Happy Digestion" at a Paris plant named after his son Danone. In 1942 Carasso's son and family friends opened a business in New York. Not until the 1950's, however, when touring Americans returned from the Continent with a taste for wine and yogurt, did yogurt sales take a noticeable upward turn.

ZIPPER The first "Zipper" was a rainy-day boot and not a fastener. The B.F. Goodrich Company, which made the galosh, was selling it in 1923 under the name "Mystik Boot," but Goodrich's president, Bertram G. Work, was uncomfortable with the label. It lacked zip. And there Work had it. The popular "Zipper Boot" was born, but the public seems to have missed the point. People referred to the boot's opening and closing device as a "zipper," and so it has been called ever since, however and wherever zippers are used.

It was a unique idea, and its inventor struggled to perfect it with no clear idea of what use it had or what human need it would fill. W.L. Judson, a Chicago inventor, got his first patent on what he called a "clasp locker or unlocker" in 1893. The plodding name was bad enough, but worse, Judson's device did not work well. And no machinery was available that could spew out the slide fasteners cheaply enough. Judson solved part of the manufacturing problem with his 1905 fastener, which was punningly called the "C-curity." But clothing manufacturers showed little interest because it meant a change in their manufacturing methods—even if the C-curity were not stiff, clumsy, and likely to pop open unbidden. It was Judson's lot to be the father of a brilliant idea that he could not personally make work. His obituary charitably stated that he had been "closely allied with the mechanical advancement of the country for forty years."

The advancement of the slide fastener, however, was the work of Gideon Sundback, an engineer brought to the Automatic Hook and Eye Company to work the bugs out of Judson's idea. After several tries Sundback in 1913 produced a practical "hookless" fastener using interlocking metal teeth, but the firm (renamed the Hookless Fastener Company) still had the problem of persuading manufacturers to use it. The first breakthrough came in 1917, when a

An eye-opener: the original Judson fastener, 1891, also used hooks.

money-belt maker saw an opportunity to help sailors carry their cash safely. Peddling zippered money belts along the waterfront, he gave impetus to the fastener market.

Then another mundane product, the tobacco pouch, brought a new surge to sales of slide fasteners. Marketed as the Locktite Tobacco Pouch ("Keeps Tobacco Right" No Strings—No Buttons), it put the struggling Hookless Fastener Company on surer footing. Then came the galosh. In a 1921 letter, B.F. Goodrich asked if Hookless could deliver 170,000 fasteners "within the near future." That was more than Hookless' entire output in 1920. With "walker squads" of company clerks slogging through the Goodrich plant to test the qualities of the galosh, Hookless was on the way to becoming a big business. By the time the Great Depression had paupered people across the country, Meadville, Pennsylvania, the Hookless headquarters, could brag that it was the town the Depression missed.

Though it started as a technological bafflement, the zipper has become a commonplace. One New Jersey entrepreneur built a comfortable business on repairing and replacing zippers. And when John Glenn roared into orbit in 1962, he wore 13 different zippers. The device is now with us from birth to death, on sleeping garments for babies and as the final fastening on burial shrouds.

ZOO It has been reported that when the bachelor Prince Rainier of Monaco was courting movie actress Grace Kelly he outdistanced other suitors by personally showing her around his private zoo. A shrewd move, but it was hardly the first time that a collection of wild animals had been used to flaunt one's position in the world.

The first so-called formal zoo was assembled for just that reason by an Egyptian queen, Hatshepsut, who usurped the throne in the early 15th century B.C. Her collection of animals presumably included wild leopards, exotic monkeys, and a strange long-necked spotted beast known as a camelopard.

In the 4th century B.C., Aristotle helped pioneer the systematic study of animals. He persuaded a former student to provide him with living samples of unfamiliar species. Since the student was Alexander the Great, who went on to conquer much of his known world, the collection of animals was impressive indeed. In his *History of Animals*, Aristotle classified and described some 300 species of vertebrates, about as many as can be found in a well-stocked modern zoo.

For the next 2,000 years, however, the show of wealth superseded science. Potentates great and small collected wild animals—the stranger the creature, the more desirable. Ptolemy II owned a rhinoceros and a snake that reportedly measured 45 feet—probably a python. Emperor Augustus brought to Rome the first tigers ever seen there. Henry III of England collected an even rarer prize: a polar bear. And when Cortés and his men came to Montezuma's court, the emperor showed them his menagerie and a most curious exhibit—cages of deformed human beings, including dwarfs and bearded women.

A tête-à-tête between a zoo keeper and an orangutan.

In time, many royal or ducal palaces in Europe acquired menageries. Pope Leo X established one, complete with elephants and lions, inside the Vatican. At Schönbrunn Palace in Vienna, Queen Maria Theresa, wife of Emperor Francis I, liked to breakfast in a small pavilion where she could watch zebras and camels grazing. And at Versailles, Louis XIV had the unsightly cages of wild animals surrounded by shrubs and flowers, thus originating an idea that professional zoo managers would later revive.

Zoos, like museums, "went public" around the time of the French Revolution. Emperor Joseph II decided in 1765 that the Viennese citizenry should be allowed to share in the pleasure his mother had enjoyed. The Schönbrunn Zoo still exists and is one of the finest in the world.

The first zoo in the United States opened in Philadelphia in 1859, and still draws enthusiastic crowds. Indeed, the 200 zoos in the United States annually attract some 115 million visitors, almost double the combined attendance at all professional baseball, basketball, and football games. Zoos are also irresistible magnets for children: truant officers learned long ago that the local zoo was the first place to check for students playing hooky.

Running a modern zoo is a complex, expensive enterprise. For example, an elephant eats his way through some $3,000 worth of fodder in a year. Meat prices being what they are, it costs around $1,800 a year to feed a tiger.

There is also the problem of catering to finicky appetites: mimosa or eucalyptus leaves for koalas; mice, mealworms, and roaches for birds; raw snakes for king cobras. The Lisbon zoo not long ago decided, as an economy measure, to stop feeding shrimp scraps to its flamingos, and the beautiful birds lost their brilliant pink color.

Animal medical care is an awesome problem. The San Diego Zoo, one of the most modern and spectacular in the world, maintains a 10,000-square-foot Jennings Center for Zoological Medicine with an X-ray room, surgical theaters, a recovery room, an isolation ward, and an intensive-care unit for critically ill animals. Among operations performed there and at other zoos are cesarean sections and hernia repairs. Viennese veterinarians have corrected the prolapsed uterus of a warthog. In Rotterdam, an African ground hornbill with a broken beak was fitted with a plastic one, and in the Tokyo zoo a favorite old donkey was treated to a set of false teeth—at a cost of about $2,000. Since animals in zoos are apt to suffer from boredom, officials at the Copenhagen zoo purchased a farm where their charges are periodically sent "to get away from it all." And the Frankfurt Zoo installed televisions in the gorilla cages. It remains to be reported which programs, if any, the animals prefer.

Once merely a source of amusement, zoos have begun to play a serious role in bionomics. It is estimated that in nearly four centuries some 94 species of birds and about 36 species of mammals have disappeared from the face of the earth and that many more species face extinction. Zoos and zoo officials have assumed the responsibility for preserving the endangered species and, where possible, reintroducing them into nature.

Breeding captive wild animals creates special problems. A month before Raji, the female Indian rhinoceros at the National Zoological Park in Washington, D.C., was to give birth, it was deemed necessary for the staff at the zoo and a battalion of 100 volunteers to set up a round-the-clock watch. It was worth it, for on the 487th day after breeding, the baby, which weighed in at 125 pounds and was named Patrick in honor of Daniel Patrick Moynihan, then the U.S. ambassador to India, was the first Indian rhinoceros born live in the Western Hemisphere.

Some species, especially cats, wolves, and gorillas, are so fertile that zoos have experimented with various contraceptive measures such as pills and vasectomies. It was reported that one lioness grew a mane after a hormone treatment. For

Oh, give me a home . . . : seemingly unperturbed by gaping intruders, elephants roam their like-home habitat, one of many such open areas featured in the San Diego Zoo.

and will, for instance, tell the keeper of a lonely male pygmy marmoset in Washington's zoo that there is an equally lonely and potentially affectionate female pygmy marmoset pining away in Kansas City.

Why are these efforts at rescue necessary in the first place? The Bronx Zoo in New York City makes its position clear about not only the importance, but the fairness, of saving endangered species. In one of its buildings hangs a sign that reads: "This animal . . . is the only creature that has ever killed off entire species of other animals." The sign is not mounted on one of the animal cages but below a mirror—since keeping humans in zoos is frowned upon.

scarcer animals, there is a computerized mating service entitled ISIS (International Species Inventory System), which has its headquarters in Apple Valley, Minnesota. ISIS lists the availability of some 42,000 animals in 110 zoos around the world

---

people

Menagerie to Zoo

Gottfried Claas Hagenbeck, a fishmonger in Hamburg, Germany, had an arrangement with certain local fishermen whereby they were obliged to bring him everything they caught. One day, the catch included six young seals that had gotten entangled in the fishing nets. Hagenbeck borrowed his wife's laundry tubs, filled them with water, and put the seals on show, charging visitors one shilling for a look. This venture was so successful that he added other animals—goats, polar bears, hyenas, monkeys, talking parrots—and quadrupled the price for viewing the exhibit.

Of the fishmonger's six children, Carl showed the greatest interest in his father's menagerie, and in 1859, at 15, the boy took over the running of the business. From this humble beginning he built the largest, most spectacular trade in wild animals the world has ever known. When still in his 20's, he arranged for the importation of perhaps the largest consignment of animals ever to set foot in Europe. One of his best customers was the American circus owner P.T. Barnum, who came to deal exclusively with Hagenbeck. The animal acts that Hagenbeck brought to the World's Columbian Exposition in Chicago in 1893—including a lion riding on horseback—proved to be a sensation of the show. In 1906 he supplied 2,000 dromedaries to the German government for use in their restive African colonies. But above all, he stocked zoos the world over with some of their rarest animals.

Despite the widespread belief that animal dealers are evil instruments for the enslavement of wildlife, Hagenbeck loved the living products of his commerce. "I desired, above all things, to give the animals the maximum of liberty," he once said, "to exhibit them not as captives . . . looked at between bars, but as free to wander from place to place within as large limits as possible."

On May 7, 1907, he turned this wish into reality with the opening of his extraordinary zoo in Stellingen, a suburb of Hamburg. Barless enclosures and settings were created to resemble the animals' native habitats, lions and zebras were free to wander around what could have been the African veld. In the "Polar Panorama," Arctic bears and other animals of frozen lands lounged comfortably. The proper depth and width of all the moats separating these animal kingdoms had been scientifically determined by Hagenbeck and his assistants.

Though in most cases they took many decades to accomplish, today Hagenbeck's revolutionary ideas are in effect in zoos all over the world, and his original zoo in Hamburg, rebuilt after World War II to repair air-raid damage, is still one of the great tourist attractions of Europe.

ACKNOWLEDGMENTS

The editors wish to express special appreciation for invaluable help in research to the following individuals and organizations and their staffs:
Merle Thomason, Fairchild Costume Library; Fashion Institute of Technology, Library Media Services; William A. Luke, Publisher, Friendship Publications, Inc.; Edwin H. Fisher, Ithaco; Philip James; Walter C. Pitman III, Lamont Geological Observatory; Donald J. Summar, Librarian, National Association of Watch and Clock Collectors Museum, Inc.; Margaret Rae Lonergan, Chief, Lynne Marie Fiorisi, Sylvia Grosse, Josefina Grundtner, Reader's Digest Editorial Magazine Stacks.

TEXT CREDITS

53 BUSMAN'S HOLIDAY, condensed from *Unusual Words and How They Came About* by Edwin Radford, The Philosophical Library, Inc., 1946. **74-75** COAL, origins and habits of the miners, condensed from *Pennsylvania Songs and Legends* by George Korson. Copyright 1960 by George Korson. Reprinted by permission of The Johns Hopkins University Press. **142-143** FISHING, condensed from "The Sport of Fishing: The Lure of Failure," TIME, 1974, by Stan Kanfer. Reprinted by permission from TIME, The Weekly Newsmagazine; Copyright Time Inc., 1974. **160 & 163** GRAFFITI, condensed from "Salient Scratchings," *MD Medical Newsmagazine*, June 1978. **201** PECK AND PECK, two lines from "Diamonds Are a Girl's Best Friend." Copyright © 1949 Consolidated Music Publishers, A Division of Music Sales Corporation, New York. All Rights Reserved. Used by permission. **209** THE PERSPIRING GENIUS, adapted from a review, "Also Known as Dungyard," by John Brooks of *A Streak of Luck*, by Robert Conot, in *The New York Times Book Review*, February 25, 1979. © 1979 by The

New York Times Company. Reprinted by permission. **229** (column 1, paragraph 2) WHAT'S IN A NAME?, adapted from *Remarkable Names of Real People* compiled and annotated by John Train. Copyright © 1977 by John Train. Used by permission of Clarkson N. Potter, Inc. **243** POETIC PASTA, adapted from *The Complete Book of Pasta* by Jack Denton Scott. Copyright 1968 by Jack Denton Scott. By permission of William Morrow & Company and Raines & Raines. **257** HOME-PUN HUMOR, puns used adapted from *Crosbie's Dictionary of Puns* by John S. Crosbie. Copyright © 1977 by John S. Crosbie. Used by permission of Harmony Books. **283** JUMP-ROPE RHYMES, rhymes condensed from "Over the Garden Wall/I Let the Baby Fall," by Francelia Butler in *The New York Times Magazine*, December 16, 1973. © 1973 by The New York Times Company. Reprinted by permission. **315** SKYSCRAPERS, Norman Mailer quotation adapted from "Cities Higher Than Mountains," *The New York Times Magazine*, January 31, 1965. Used by permission of the author and the author's agents, Scott

Meredith Literary Agency, Inc., 845 Third Avenue, New York, N.Y. 10022 and © 1965 by The New York Times Company. Reprinted by permission. **317** NIGHT MUSIC, based on Dr. Marcus H. Boulware, referred to in various sources and in *Snoring: New Answers to an Old Problem*, by Marcus H. Boulware, Ph.D., American Faculty Press, 1974. **317-318** SLEEP, sleep positions based on "What Your Sleeping Positions Reveal About You," by Nancy Axelrad Comer, *Mademoiselle*, March 1977. Courtesy *Mademoiselle*, Copyright © 1977 by The Condé Nast Publications Inc. **320** ALONE IN A CROWD, lyrics condensed from *Iolanthe* in *Plays and Poems of W.S. Gilbert*. Copyright 1932 by Random House, Inc. Reprinted by permission. **320** ALONE IN A CROWD, Mary Eden and Richard Carrington quotation adapted from *The Philosophy of Beds*. Copyright © 1961 by Mary Eden and Richard Carrington. Reprinted by permission of G.P. Putnam's Sons and Hutchinson and Co., Ltd., London.

PICTURE CREDITS

The editors are grateful for the important contributions of these individuals and organizations and their staffs in picture research: The Bettmann Archive; Black Star; Esther Bromberg, The Museum of the City of New York; Bruce Coleman Inc.; Editorial Photocolor Archives; Eugene Keesee, Photo Trends; The Granger Collection; Adelaide Hechtlinger; Magnum Photos; The New York Public Library, Picture Collection; Robin Raffer, Culver Pictures; Sapan Engineering Co.; UPI; Wide World Photos.

Front cover: (sandwich) New York Public Library, Picture Collection; (spoon) Courtesy of an anonymous private collector; (clock) Courtesy of the Henry Francis duPont Winterthur Museum; (sewing machine) Courtesy of Kennedy Galleries, Inc., New York; (juke box) Courtesy of Back Pages Antiques, photo by Mario Ruiz; (coin with computer chip) Dan McCoy/Rainbow; (necktie) The Arrow Company; (divan) The Metropolitan Museum of Art, Friends of the American Wing Fund. **1** Museum of Fine Arts, Boston, Maria Hopkins Fund. **2** (chairs) Office of Charles and Ray Eames; (bootblacks) The Bettmann Archive; (barber pole) Museum of the City of New York; (ape and man) Argus Africa/Photo Trends; (parachute) Perri. **3** (chariot) David Lees; (egg crate) New York Times Pictures; (ice-cream cones) The Bettmann Archive; (skateboard) Craig Aurness/Woodfin Camp & Associates; (golfer) UPI. **7** Courtesy of The Prudential Insurance Company of America. **8** Dorothy Gray, Ltd.; mannequin photographed by William Sonntag; Cascarets ad from the Collection of Business Americana, Smithsonian Institution; Shir-Gar ad from "Those Were the Good Old Days" © 1959 by Edgar R. Jones, reprinted by permission of Simon & Schuster, a Division of Gulf & Western Corporation; *remainder* from the New York Public Library, Picture Collection and the Adelaide Hechtlinger Collection. **9** Smith Brothers; Sears, Roebuck and Company; Carter's ad from the Museum of the City of New York; *remainder* from the New York Public Library, Picture Collection and the Adelaide Hechtlinger Collection. **10** Arthur Murray, Inc., *bottom left* Collection of Business Americana, Smithsonian Institution; *top right* from "Those Were the Good Old Days" © 1959 by Edgar R. Jones, reprinted by permission of Simon & Schuster, a Division of Gulf & Western Corporation; *remainder* from the New York Public Library, Picture Collection and the Adelaide Hechtlinger Collection. **11** *top left* 3-M Corp.; *top right* The Clark Grave Vault Company; *bottom left* The Adelaide Hechtlinger Collection; *bottom right*

Courtesy of American Standard, Inc. **12** A.&F. Pears, Ltd., London; Ford Motor Company; Dana Perfumes Corp.; Courtesy of Clairol; Listerine ad from Warner-Lambert Company; Ivory Soap ad courtesy of Procter & Gamble; *bottom left to right* Registered trademark of the Wm. Underwood Co., used by permission; Castle & Cooke, Inc.; Courtesy of Purex Corp.; Gerber Products Company; Registered trademark of Ralston Purina Company; the Quaker Oats Company; Courtesy of Uniroyal, Inc., from John W. Ripley Lantern Slides. **13** *top left* © 1967 Henry S. Levy & Sons, Inc., used by permission of Doyle Dane Bernbach; *top center* General Foods; *top right* New York Public Library, Picture Collection and the Sanforized Company; *middle left* Reprinted by permission of Simon & Schuster, a Division of Gulf & Western Corporation, and courtesy of Volkswagen of America, Inc.; *center* The Green Giant is a registered trademark and is used with the permission of the Green Giant Company; *middle right* Maidenform, Inc., and The Coca-Cola Company; *bottom left to right* Registered trademark of Sun Maid Growers of California; Standard Brands; Illustration used with permission of Western Publishing Company, Inc.; the CAMPBELL KID is a registered trademark of Campbell Soup Company and is reproduced by permission of its owner; Courtesy of Morton Salt Division of Morton-Norwich. **14** *left top to bottom* © 1970 Miles Laboratories, Inc.; Thomas J. Lipton, Inc.; Colgate-Palmolive Company; Procter & Gamble; Serutan ad from the J. B. Williams Company, Inc.; Barbasol ad courtesy of Pfizer, Inc.; *center* © 1978 The Pillsbury Company. Reproduced with permission of The Pillsbury Company. Both the character and "Poppin Fresh ®" are registered trademarks of The Pillsbury Company; *middle bottom* Used with permission of Ralston Purina Company; *right top to bottom* Hertz Rent-a-Car; Avis Rent a Car System, Inc.; Colgate-Palmolive Company; Procter & Gamble. **15** The Bettmann Archive. **16** *left* Rudy L. Klaiss; *right* Carrier Corporation. **17** *top to bottom* Musée de l'air; Brown Brothers; Musée de l'air;

Bibliothèque Nationale, Paris. **18** UPI. **19** National Library of Medicine, Bethesda, Maryland. **20** The Granger Collection. **21** Courtauld Institute Galleries, London. **23** Culver Pictures. **24** *top* Painting by Jackson Lee Nesbitt reproduced by permission of the Curators of the University of Missouri; *bottom & 25* Edward Malsburg. **26** Collection of John Chaputian. **27** *top* Editoriale Corriere della Sera; *bottom* Culver Pictures. **28** Ellen Warner/Black Star. **29** *top* The Huntington Library, San Marino, California; *bottom* Museum of the City of New York. **30** *top* Yale Center for British Art, Paul Mellon Collection; *bottom* Royal Museum of Fine Arts of Belgium. **31** Museum of the City of New York. **32** *top* Courtesy of the Boston Public Library, Print Department, McGreevy Collection; *bottom* Topps Chewing Gum, Inc., from the collection of Alexander Scott Mathews. **33** The Bettmann Archive. **34** The Gold Information Center. **35** Kohler Co. **36** Madeline Grimoldi Archives. **37** Reprinted from "Space, Time and Architecture" by Sigfried Giedion, by permission of Harvard University Press. **38** © 1970 Esquire Magazine. **39** New York Public Library, Picture Collection. **40** *top* Reprinted by permission of the Publisher, Thomas Nelson, Inc., from the book "The Bicycle: That Curious Invention," © 1973 by Stephen and Sybil Leek; *bottom* International Human Powered Vehicle Association, Photo by Bruce Sargeant. **41** *left* Reproduced by kind permission of Debenhams Limited; *right* Photofile Ltd. **42** Museum of Fine Arts, Boston, Charles Henry Hayden Fund. **43** Caulfield & Shook Collection, University of Louisville Photographic Archives. **44** Raeburn L. Van Buren. **45** Reprinted from The Saturday Evening Post © 1962 The Curtis Publishing Company. **46** Shostal Associates; *bottom & 47* Courtesy of Parker Brothers. **48** American Bowling Congress. **49** John Chao. **50** Illustration by Trina Schart Hyman from "The Bread Book" by Carolyn Meyer © 1971 by Harcourt Brace Jovanovich, Inc.; reproduced by permission of the publishers. **51** Advertisement courtesy of the Kellogg Company. **52** *left*

Granger Collection. **226** Private Collection. **227** The Arrow Company. **228** The Granger Collection. **229** Collection of Hank Reichard. **230** *upper* Marc Riboud/Magnum Photos; *bottom* Bernard Pierre Wolff/Magnum Photos. **231** Michael Coers/The Courier-Journal and The Louisville Times. **233** UPI. **234** Goodyear Tire & Rubber Company. **235** *left* The Bettmann Archive; *right* UPI. **236** *left* New York Times Pictures; *right* Reprinted from "Baskets as Textile Art" by Ed Rossback with the permission of Van Nostrand Reinhold Company. **237** The Granger Collection. **238** *top* The Bettmann Archive; *bottom* Culver Pictures. **239** *top left* The Bettmann Archive; *right* The New York World Journal Tribune; *bottom left* Courtesy of the Victoria and Albert Museum. **240** John Launois/Black Star. **241** Wide World Photos. **242** The Granger Collection. **243** *top* Culver Pictures; *lower* Paul Fusco/Magnum Photos. **244** Reprinted from "Eureka!" by Edward de Bono with the permission of the London Sunday Times. **245** Fogg Art Museum, Boston. **246** The Bettmann Archive. **247** Solomon D. Butcher Collection, Nebraska State Historical Society. **248** Bibliothèque Nationale, Paris. **249** *top left* The Bettmann Archive; *right* UPI; *bottom* The Granger Collection. **250** *top* Environmental Communications; *center* Museum of the American Indian, Heye Foundation; *bottom* New York Public Library, Picture Collection. **251** *top* Culver Pictures; *bottom* The Metropolitan Museum of Art, Rogers Fund. **252** *top* painting by Arnold Friberg © Northwest Paper Company; *bottom* Culver Pictures. **253** Reprinted from "The Victorians" by George Perry & Nicholas Perry with the permission of Viking Press. **254** New York Public Library, Picture Collection. **255** Henri Cartier-Bresson/Magnum Photos. **256** The Bettmann Archive. **257** Reprinted from "Punography" by Bruce McMillan with the permission of Penguin Books. **258** Courtesy of NBC. **259** *top* UPI; *bottom* Culver Pictures. **260** *left* Shelburne Museum, Shelburne, Vermont; *right* Linda Bartlett/Photo Researchers. **261** Editorial Photocolor Archives. **262** *upper left* Collection of the Door Store, Washington, D.C., photo courtesy of the National Air and Space Museum, Smithsonian Institution; *bottom left* Tribal Arts Gallery, New York; *upper center* The Metropolitan Museum of Art, Gift of Mr. & Mrs. J.J. Klejman; *bottom center* The Metropolitan Museum of Art, Rogers Fund; *top right* Private Collection; *bottom right* The Metropolitan Museum of Art, Friends of the American Wing Fund. **263** *top left* Private Collection; *middle left* Collection of Hugh and Jeannette McKean; *center* Courtesy of the Henry Francis duPont Winterthur Museum; *top right* Editorial Photocolor Archives; *middle right* Private Collection; *bottom right* Kunstsammlungen zu Weimar, DDR, Sammlung des Bauhauses. **264** *left* From the Collection of the John Woodman Higgins Armory Museum, Worcester, Massachusetts; *center top to bottom* Museo del Oro, Lima, Peru; Lee Boltin; Private Collection; *top right* John Reader; *bottom right* Julie: Artisans' Gallery Inc., New York. **265** *top left* American Museum of Natural History; *top center* Courtesy of the Museum of Fine Arts, Boston; *bottom left* Eliot Elisofon; *right top to bottom* Museum of the American Indian, Heye Foundation; The Metropolitan Museum of Art, Gift of Mr. & Mrs. Charles Wrightsman; The Metropolitan Museum of Art, Gift of Mrs. William Randolph Hearst; The Brooklyn Museum, Charles Edwin Wilbour Fund. **266** *upper left* The Cleveland Museum of Art, Gift from J.H. Wade; *top right* Kunsthistorisches Museum, Vienna; *middle right* Smith College Museum of Art, Northampton, Massachusetts, Gift of Mr. & Mrs. Stanley Marcus; *bottom* The Metropolitan Museum of Art, Rogers Fund. **267** *left top to bottom* Editorial Photocolor Archives; The Metropolitan Museum of Art, Gift of Julia A. Berwind; Lee Boltin; *center top to bottom:* Dmitri Kessel; The Metropolitan Museum of Art, Gift of Elizabeth L. Townsend Booth in memory of Mary Townsend White and Mrs. John Pomeroy Townsend; Courtesy of the Victoria and Albert Museum; *right top to bottom:* Private Collection; New York Public Library, Picture Collection; Liechtenstein Gallery, Vienna. **268** *top left* Courtesy of the Field Museum of Natural History, Chicago; *center* Private Collection; *top right* The Metropolitan Museum of Art, Gift of the Samuel H. Kress Foundation; *middle right* Editorial Photocolor Archives; *bottom left & right* Jane Latta. **269** *left top to bottom* The New-York Historical Society; Courtesy of the Victoria and Albert Museum; Courtesy of the Shelburne Museum, Shelburne, Vermont; *top middle* Courtesy of the Museum of Primitive Art; *top right* Henry Groskinsky; *bottom right* Private Collection. **270** *top* Courtesy of NBC; *bottom* Culver Pictures. **272** *left* Culver Pictures; *right* Courtesy of Agrupación de Actividades Artesanas del Fad, Barcelona. **273** *left* Culver Pictures; *right* The Illustrated London News Picture Library. **274** *top* Culver Pictures; *bottom* Arthur Grace/New York Times Pictures. **275** *top* Syndication International/Photo Trends; *bottom* Wide World Photos. **276** New York Public Library, Picture Collection. **277** Burt Glinn/Magnum Photos. **278** *top* Brian Seed/Black Star; *bottom* Charles Moore/Black Star. **279** *top* Culver Pictures; *bottom* Nik Wheeler/Black Star. **280** *top* Craig Aurness/Woodfin Camp & Associates; *bottom* Photoreporters. **281** Philip Carter/Photoreporters. **282** *top* Reproduced from the 16th-century Turkish manuscript "Book of Festivals," courtesy of Du Magazine, Zurich; *bottom* Fox Photos. **284** *top* Reproduced by permission of the British Library; *bottom* Courtesy of Shell Oil Company. **285** Harry Redl/Black Star. **286** Goodyear Tire & Rubber Company. **287** The Bettmann Archive. **288** Reprinted from "The Lure of the Lock" by Albert A. Hopkins, courtesy of the Mechanics' Institute Library. **289** *top* Culver Pictures; *bottom* Reprinted from "The Lure of the Lock" by Albert A. Hopkins, courtesy of the Mechanics' Institute Library. **290** Naturhistorisches Museum, Vienna. **291** Courtesy of Skoklosters Slott, Uppsala, Sweden. **292** Sovfoto. **293** New York Public Library, Picture Collection. **294** Culver Pictures. **295** Museo Civico, Padua. **296** *top* Pierpont Morgan Library; *bottom* Culver Pictures. **297** Culver Pictures. **298** UPI. **299** Wide World photos. **300** *top* New York Public Library, Picture Collection; *bottom* International Museum of Photography at George Eastman House; *right* Smithsonian Institution. **301** Reprinted from "Are Clothes Modern?" by Bernard Rudofsky, published by Paul Theobald and Company. **302** Courtesy of the Mariners Museum, Newport News, Virginia. **303** Editorial Photocolor Archives. **304** *top* The Granger Collection; *bottom left* Joseph Martin/Scala/Editorial Photocolor Archives; *bottom right* Basle Cathedral. **305** Wide World Photos. **306** The Bettmann Archive. **307** Private Collection. **308** The Bettmann Archive. **309** Nicholas DeVore/Bruce Coleman Inc. **310** *left top to bottom* Charles Gatewood/Magnum Photos; Cornelle Capa/Magnum Photos; Elliott Erwitt/Magnum Photos; *right top to bottom* Elliott Erwitt/Magnum Photos; The Bettmann Archive; Burk Uzzle/Magnum Photos; *bottom right* Courtesy of the Victoria and Albert Museum. **311** UPI. **312** Culver Pictures. **313** *top* Culver Pictures; *bottom* University of Massachusetts at Amherst. **314** Courtesy of the Empire State Building. **315** The Bettmann Archive. **316** Culver Pictures. **317** The Bettmann Archive. **318** *top* "Dream" by Jean-Claude Suares from "Art of the Times," published by Universe Books; *bottom* The Bettmann Archive. **319** *top* The Bettmann Archive; *bottom* Wide World Photos. **320 & 321** The Bettmann Archive. **322** *top* The Bettmann Archive; *bottom* UPI. **323** Private Collection. **324** James R. Holland/Black Star. **325** M. Timothy O'Keefe/Bruce Coleman Inc. **327** *top* Paul Fusco/Magnum Photos; *bottom* From "The Things I Love" by Liberace. © 1976 by Liberace. Used by permission of Grosset & Dunlap, Inc. **328** *left* Michael A. Norcia/Sygma; *top* From "The Things I Love" by Liberace. © 1976 by Liberace. Used by permission of Grosset & Dunlap, Inc. **329 & 330** The Bettmann Archive. **331** *top* UPI; *bottom* Culver Pictures. **332** The Bettmann Archive. **333** Culver Pictures. **334** The Metropolitan Museum of Art, Gift of Alexander Smith Cochran. **335** *top* Culos/Sygma; *lower* Culver Pictures. **336** *top* Culver Pictures; *bottom* Wide World Photos. **337** New York Public Library, Picture Collection. **338** *top* Jane Latta; *bottom* UPI. **339** UPI. **340** Culver Pictures; *bottom* UPI. **341** *top* A.J. Deane/Bruce Coleman Inc.; *bottom left* John Gerard/DPI; *bottom right* R.N. Mariscal/Bruce Coleman Inc. **342** *top* Jen & Des Bartlett/Bruce Coleman Inc. *bottom* Allan Power/Bruce Coleman Inc. **343** John Launois/Black Star. **344** *left top to bottom:* Smithsonian Institution; Library of Congress; Reproduced by courtesy of the Trustees of the British Museum; *right top to bottom:* British Crown Copyright. Science Museum, London; David Lees; IBM Corporation. **345** *top left* The Granger Collection; *top right* Ann Ronan Picture Library; *middle* Photo by Boyer/H. Roger Viollet; *bottom left* Reprinted from "Eureka!" by Edward de Bono with the permission of the London Sunday Times; *bottom right* Bill Ray. **346** *upper left* Bill Ray; *middle* U.S. Patent Office; *top right* From the collection of the Mercer Museum of the Bucks County Historical Society; *remainder* The Bettmann Archive. **347** *top left* Scientific American, 1897; *lower & bottom left* U.S. Patent Office; *top & upper right* The Bettmann Archive; *bottom right* Smithsonian Institution. **348** *top right* Marc Riboud/Magnum Photos; *middle left & right* Culver Pictures; *remainder* Courtesy of Steinway & Sons. **349** *bottom left* UPI; *remainder* Courtesy of Steinway & Sons. **350** *left* Margaret Bourke-White, Life Magazine © 1930, Time, Inc.; *top right* Erich Hartmann/Magnum Photos; *bottom right* Margaret Bourke-White, Life Magazine © 1930, Time, Inc. **351** *top* J.-P. Laffont/Sygma; *bottom* Margaret Bourke-White, Life Magazine © 1937, Time, Inc. **352** *top left* Mike Andrews/Black Star; *top right* AMF Incorporated; *middle right* Owen/Black Star; *bottom right* Bob Benyas/Black Star. **353** *left* American Heritage Publishing Co., Inc.; *bottom* Culver Pictures. **354** *top* Museum of the City of New York, J. Clarence Davies Collection; *bottom* New York Public Library, Picture Collection. **355** *top* New York Public Library, Picture Collection; *bottom* Explorer. **356** New York Public Library, Picture Collection. **357** *top* Editorial Photocolor Archives; *bottom* UPI. **358** *top* UPI; *bottom* Culver Pictures. **359** UPI. **360** *top* Syndication International/Photo Trends; *bottom* Culver Pictures. **361 & 362** Culver Pictures. **363** Editorial Photocolor Archives. **364** Bibliothèque Municipale, Cambrai. **365** *top* Culver Pictures; *right* Istituto e Museo di Storia della Scienza, Florence. **366** *top* The Granger Collection; *bottom* Museum of the City of New York, Print Archives. **367** Culver Pictures. **368** Photo Trends. **369** *top* Lisetta Carmi from Camera Press/Photo Trends; *bottom* Illustrated London News. **370** From "Early New England Gravestone Rubbings" by Edmund Vincent Gillon, Jr., published by Dover Publications. **371** Library of Congress. **372** *left* Alan Root; *top right* The American Museum of Natural History, courtesy of Dr. Erwin H. Ackerknecht, New York; *bottom right* Syndication International/Photo Trends. **373** Culver Pictures. **374** Tsuneo Tamba Collection, photo by Bradley Smith. **375** The Wallace Collection, London. **376** *top* Wide World Photos; *bottom* Editorial Photocolor Archives. **377** *top* Crown Copyright, National Railway Museum, York, England; *bottom* New York Public Library, Picture Collection. **378** Culver Pictures. **379** United Nations. **380** *top* Culver Pictures; *bottom* UPI. **381** Ian Swift from Camera Press/Photo Trends. **382** *left* Werner Wolff/Black Star; *right* Brian Seed/Black Star. **383** *top* Radio Times Hulton Picture Library; *bottom* Culver Pictures. **384** Wide World Photos. **385** *top* René Maltête/Black Star; *bottom* John Moss/Black Star. **386** Culver Pictures. **387** Brown Brothers. **388** *top* Culver Pictures; *bottom* The Adelaide Hechtlinger Collection. **389** Culver Pictures. **390** *top* Maurice Robert Collection. **391** Culver Pictures. **392** Scripps Institution of Oceanography, University of California, San Diego. **393** Editorial Photocolor Archives. **394** New York Public Library, Picture Collection. **395** Courtesy of the Boston Public Library, Print Department. **396** *top* Michael Freeman; *bottom* David Herman from Annan Photo Features. **397** Museum of the City of New York. **398** UPI. **399** *top left to right:* Les Wilson from Camera Press/Photo Trends; Marc & Evelyn Bernheim/Woodfin Camp & Associates; Syndication International/Photo Trends; *lower right* UPI. **400** Reproduced with the permission of Talon Division of Textron Inc., the original zipper manufacturer. **401** Argus Africa/Photo Trends. **402** K.W. Fink/Bruce Coleman Inc.

Efforts have been made to contact the holder of the copyright for each picture. In several cases these sources have been untraceable, for which we offer our apologies.

Index

In some cases only items of major interest about important subjects are entered.

A

Abacus, 82
Abbott, Bud, 363
Abplanalp, Robert H., 16
Abrasives, 293
  as dentifrices, 372–73
Absinthe, 29
Acacia, 42
Acetylsalicylic acid, 22–23
Acheson, Lila Bell, 213
Acronym, 15
Acta Diurna, 230
Action Comics, 24, 80
Actors
  language of, 363
  superstitions of, 364
Adair, Paul Neal ("Red"), 233
Adam and Eve, 21, 73, 154, 232, 321
Adams, John, 30
Adams, Samuel, 30, 78, 124
Adams, Sherman, 297
Adams, Thomas, 66, 78
Adding machine, 345
Addis, William, 371
Addison, Joseph, 257
  on signs, 310
Adenoids, 371
Adhesive, 157
  bandage, 15
Adidas, 145
Adobe, 52
Adventurers, 333–34
Advertising, 7–14
  by department stores, 106
  music and, 328
  packaging and, 89, 236–37
  radio and, 270–71
  signs for, 310
  soap industry, 322
  television and, 359, 360
Aerosol can, 16
Aesculapius, 119
Aesop, 120
Aga Khan III, 43
Agamemnon, 39
Aged, 384, 399
  pensions and, 247
  stereotyping of, 330
Ailurophobes, 61
Air conditioning, 16–17
Air door, 126
Airline baggage problems, 339
Airmail, 18
Airplane, 17–19, 252, 392
Air purifier, Dahomeyan, 264
Alaric, 247
Albret, Jeanne d', 156
Alchemy, 157, 158
Alcohol
  as cold cure, 80
  in medicine, 128, 129
  terms relating to drinking, 168
Ale garland, 309
Aleichem, Sholom, 67
Alexander, Ben, 225
Alexander I (of Russia), 277
Alexander the Great, 37, 251, 303, 334
  animal study and, 400
  beards and, 36
  ice cream and, 188
Alexandra, boudoir of, 132
Alexandria, library of, 206
Alfred (of England), 72
Ali, Muhammad, 388
  doll, 125
  jump rope and, 282
  sandwich, 294

Allan's Anti-Fat, 274–75
Alloys, steel, 326, 327
Aluminum, cast, magnification of, 185
Alum-rosin, 239
Ambergris, 249
Ambulance, 19
American Express, 247, 373, 375
American Telephone and Telegraph, radio and, 271
Amin, Idi, 384
Amsterdam red-light district, 396
Amulets, 197
Analog computer, 83
Ancestry, 154–55
Anemone, 341–42
Anesthetics, 20
  dentistry and, 104
Angling, 142–43
Anne, Queen, nightgowns and, 238
  typewriter and, 380
Annulment, 117
Answering machines, telephone, 359
Ant colonies, 342
Antibiotics, 246, 374
  first, 132
  sponges and, 326
Antihistamines, 80
Antiperspirants, 105
Anti-Tipping Society, 374
Antitoxins, vaccines and, 385–86
Antony and Cleopatra, 291
A & P, 357
Aphrodite, 22, 45
Apollo, 163
Apple, 21–22
"Appleseed," Billy, 20
Arabian Nights mirror, 221
Arachibutyrophobia, 243
Arãk, 371
Archimboldo, Giuseppe, 291
Archimedes, 221
  screw of, 298
Architecture
  service station, 299
  skyscraper, 314–15
Ardabil carpet, 287
Arden, Elizabeth, 165
Argentina, lotteries in, 367
Aristophanes, 29
Aristotle
  animal studies of, 400
  and optics, 55
  tides and, 368
Armor, Maximillian, 264
Armstrong, Louis, 315
Armstrong, Neil, 361
Arnold, Benedict, 124, 128
Arnold, Matthew, 368
Artemis, 43
Arthur, King of Britain, 36
Artisans, 261–69
Arts, the five, 277
Ascorbic acid, 388
Asepsis, 21, 173
Asphalt surfacing, 171
Aspirin, 22–23
Assemblage (manufacture), 348–52
Assembly line, 23–24
  automobile, 352
  shipbuilding, 302
  shovel, 307
Astrolabe, 72, 302
Astronauts, 244
  clothing of, 74, 158
  souvenirs and, 323
  on television, 361
Atome, 41
Atomic clocks, 73
Atropos, 297–98, 366
Attic, 24
Attila the Hun, 121, 217
Auction, 24–26
Audion, 270
Audio Pedestrian Signal, 376
  fire department of, 140
  lottery and, 367
  travel certificates of, 241
Augustus (Caesar), 84, 401

Australia
  aborigines in, 148
  tea ceremony in, 356
  telephones in, 358
Automat, 78, 139
Automation
  printing and, 255–56
  sewing machine and, 300
Automobile, 26–28, 171, 177, 252, 360
  commuting by, 81
  diesel, 115
  gasoline and, 299
  insurance for, 192
  license plates for, 207–208
  loans and, 209
  manufacture of, 352
  registration of, 207–208
  service stations and, 299
  steel in, 326
  train wheels on, 378
Aviators, 17, 18
Avon, 90
Aztecs
  chocolate and, 68, 69
  smallpox and, 385

B

Babbage, Charles, 83
Babylon, Hanging Gardens of, 152
Bacall, Lauren, 349
Backgammon, 46
Bacon, 29
Bacon, Francis, 147
Bacon, Henry, 260
Bacon, Roger, 136
Bacteria, 118
  body odor and, 105
  penicillin and, 246
  symbiosis and, 341, 342, 388
  tooth decay and, 104
  yogurt and, 399
Bacteriology, 176
Baedeker, Karl, 373
Bag, 256–59, 265
"Bag and baggage," 189
Bakers, 50
Balance scale, 294–95
Ball jar, 58
Balloon, 28–29
  ambulances and, 19
  high altitude, 392
  hot air, 92
Ball-point pen, 244, 245
Balzac, Honoré de, 108, 278
Bandages, adhesive, 15
Band-Aid, 15
Bank
  robberies 288–89
  vaults, 287, 290
Bankhead, Tallulah, 364
Bankruptcy, 223
Bar (tavern), 29–31, 309–10
Bara, Theda, 90, 226
Barbed wire, 10, 345
Barber and Barbershop, 31, 164
Barber-surgeons and dentistry, 103
Barbiturates, 318–19
Bar Mitzvah, 43
Barnstorming, 18
Barnum, P.T., 311, 338, 402
Barrie, J.M., 265
Barron, Robert, 210
Bartolo, 306
Baruch, Bernard, 332
Bary, Heinrich de, 341
Baseball, 31–33
  cards, 24, 32
  scandal (of 1919), 295–96
Basket, Chinese picnic, 268
Baskin-Robbins, 191
Bastet, 61
Bathing suits, 41
Bathroom, 33–35, 175
Baths, public, 33–34
Baths of Caracalla, 33, 34
Bathtubs, 33, 34–35, 176
  gold, 34, 158
Battersea enamel box, 268

Battery, 35–36, 209
  silver-zinc, 312
Battle Creek, Michigan, 50–51
Bavay, France, 170
Bayer and Company, 23
Bayeux Tapestry, 143, 202
Bdellium, 324
Beach, Alfred Ely, 335
Beano, 42
Beard, 15, 36
Beard, James, 227
Beards, 15, 36, 273
Beatles (musicians), 165, 328
Bear market, 332
Beatty, Papyrus, 318
Beatus, St., 215
Beauty marks, 89
Beauty shop, 165
Bed, 36–38
  day, 65
  hospital, 173, 174
  insomnia and, 320
  painted Swiss, 263
  piano, 347
Bedclothes, 38, 173, 174
Bedsprings, 38
Beecher, Henry Ward, 22
Beer, 30, 38–39, 167
  draft, canning, 327
Beethoven, Ludwig van, 163
Beeton, Isabella, 144, 202, 389
Beets, sugar, 337
Beggar's Opera, The, 251
Behring, Emil von, 385
"Believe It or Not," 60
Bell, Alexander Graham, 357–58
Belladonna, 319
Bellamy, Edward, 92
Bell Telephone Laboratories, 358–59
Belt, 39, 256
Bentham, Jeremy, 395
Bergerac, Savinien Cyrano de, 328
Berkeley, Busby, 380
Berkeley, California, police force, 253
Berle, Milton, 359
Berlin Adlon Hotel, 176
Bernardine, St., 250
Berry, duc de, 54
Bertillon, Alphonse, 253
Bessemer furnace, 327
Best man, 216
Bible. *See also* Genesis.
  abrasive in, 293
  Gutenberg, 255
  inns in, 174
  on Joseph's ring, 197
  Leviticus on marriage, 117
  libraries and, 207
  mustard seed in Parables, 226
  quotations from,
    Isaiah, 210, 359
    "milk and honey," 188
    on plague on Egypt, 176
    Song of Solomon, 201
    spices and, 324
  sponge in, 325
  theater superstitions and, 364
  translations of, 232, 379
  wine in, 325
Bibs, 353
Bicycle, 40–41
  commuting and, 81
  roads and, 171
Bidding, auction, 24–26
Bifocals, 137
Big Board, 331
Bigelow, Erastus Brigham, 287
Bikini, 41, 396
Billboards, 310, 311
  T-shirts as, 384
Billy "Appleseed," 20
Binet, Alfred, 193
Bingo, 41–42
Binoculars, 42
Biofeedback, 237
Biograph, 225
Bionomics, zoos and, 401
Bird calls, recording of, 328
Birds
  honey guide, 341

influenza and, 191
tool-using, 372
Birdseye, Clarence, 147
Birth control, 42, 44–45, 339
Birthday, 43
Birth of a Nation, The, 225
Birthstones, 197
Bismarck, Otto von, 247
Bittersweet, 394
Black (color), 44, 149, 364
Black Death (plague), 128
in London, 111, 118
Blacking for shoes, 305
Blackmail, 44
Black Maria, 44
Blacks, stereotypes of, 330
Blacksmiths, 40
Blackstone, William, 20
Blenders, 144
Blind date, 45
Block, Herbert, 60
Blondes, stereotyping and, 331
Blondin, 333
Bloodletting, 31
Bloomer, Amelia, 239
Bloomer girls, 40
Bloomers, 40, 239
Bloomingdale's, 107
Blue, 132
"Blue Boy," 398
"Blueblood," 54
Blue-chip stock, 332
Bluegrass, 102
Blue sky law, 332
Boardcloths, 353
Board games, 45–46
Bobbies, 253
Boccie, 48
Boeing airplanes, 18, 19
Bogart, Humphrey, 71, 107
Bogart, John, 232
Boleyn, Anne, 117
Bolts, 298–99
Bombers (aircraft), 18
Bonbon, 56
Bond, definition of, 332
Bonheur, Rosa, 239
Bonsack, James Albert, 71
Bonwill, G.W.A., 104
Books, 79
cover for, leather, 269
library, 206–207
Bootblacks, 306
Bootlegger, 168
Boots, 145, 146
zipper, 400
Booze, 168
Booze, Virginia, 258
Bordeaux (wine), 396
Borden, Gail, 58, 220
Boris (of Bulgaria), 379
Boston
fire fighting in, 140
first U.S. restaurant, 278
hotels in, 34–35, 175, 176
subway system, 336
Boston Cooking School, 85
Boswell, James, 112
Bottles, 47, 202
Bottomry contract, 192
Boulware, Marcus H., 317
Bouquet de corsage, 105
Bowl, Scythian libation, 267
Bowling, 47–48
Boxes, decorative, 268, 269
Brady, Diamond Jim, 374
Brain activity, sleep and, 318, 320
Bramah, Joseph, 211
Brand name, 168
Brando, Marlon, 196, 384
Brassiere, 49
Bread, 49–50
theater superstitions and, 364
Breakfast cereal, 50–51
Brenner, David, 82
Breuer, Marcel, 65
Brick, 51–52
Brides, customs concerning, 216, 217,
218
Brillat-Savarin, Anthelme, 278, 291

Broadcasting
radio, 270–72
television, 359–62
Broadcloth, 72
Broker (stock), 332
Bronx Zoo, 402
Brooks, John, 357
Brooks Brothers, 305
Broom, 52
Browning, Elizabeth Barrett, 396
Browning, Robert, 156
Brueghel, Pieter, the Elder, 95
Bruhn, Wilhelm, 355
Brummel, Beau, 229, 304
Bryn Mawr College, 79
Bubastis, 61
Bubble gum, 32, 67
Bucatini, 243
Bucephalus, 334
Buchanan, Michigan, monument in,
369
Buchwald, Art, 338
on dieting, 274
Buckle, 39
gold Chinese, 264
Budding, Edward, 204
Budget, 223
Buffalo, African, 341
"Bug bomb," 16
Bugging, 360
Bulgaria, yogurt and, 399
Bull (policeman), 253
Bullet, shock waves of, 185
Bull market, 332
Bun, hamburger, 166
Bundschuh, 145
Bunny hug, 102
Burberry, Thomas, 272
Burger, Warren E., 205
Burgess, Anthony, 317
Burglary, office, 288
Burgundy (wine), 396, 397
Burials, 369, 370
rites of, 148–49
societies for, 192
Burke, John, 154–55
Bus, 52–53
Bushmen, tea ceremony of, 356
Busman's holiday, 53
Bustle-bulger, 346
Butler, Francelia, 283
Butter, 53
Butterick, Ellen and Ebenezer, 301
Buttons, 53–54, 250, 385
on men's jackets, 194, 195
Byrd, Admiral Richard Evelyn, 300
Byron, George Gordon, 229, 308
Byzantium, 143
gardens of, 152–53

C

Cabs, 353–55
Cacao bean, 68–69, 325
Caddies, 158
Caesar, Julius, 15, 206, 238, 251
Calendar and, 54, 55
newspaper of, 230
tides and, 368
traffic ban by, 241
Café, 308. *See also* Restaurant.
Caffeine, 76
Cairo, hospital of, 172–73
Cake, 49
fried (doughnut), 126–27
gingerbread, 324
Calcium permanganate, 388
Calculator, 83, 390
Calculus, 82
Calendar, 54–55, 390
California, University of, 78–79
Calling cards, 134–35
Calvaria tree, 342
Camellia sinensis, 357
Camembert cheese, 65
Camera, 43, 55–56
Giroux's, 344
Camphene, 130
Canada, 361

coal in, 75, 234
stock exchange in, 331
telephones in, 358
tides in, 366
Canals, 301
Cancan, 102
Cancer, research, 76
skin, sunlight and, 340
tobacco and, 71
X rays and, 398
Candleholder, German, 266
Candy, 56–57, 69
Fanny Farmer, 85
Canneloni, 243
Canning, 58–59
draft beer, 327
World War II and, 146
Cans, 16, 236, 241
collections of beer, 39
Cant, 316
Cap, embroidered French, 265
Caproni bomber, 18
Caracalla, Baths of, 33, 34
Carat, 110
Carbolic acid, 21
Carbonated drink, 59
Carbon dioxide, weather and, 393
Carbon lights, 208
Carbon tetrachloride, 130
Carbonnieux, 397
Cardamom, 324
Cards
calling, 134–35
credit, 91–92, 210, 224
greeting, 161–62
playing, 250–51
Carême, Marie-Antoine, 277
Caricatures, 60–61
Carlson, Chester F., 130–31
Carnegie, Andrew, 207, 327
Carob tree, 110
Carpet, 285, 287
Carpetbagger, 338
Carriages, taxi, 355
Carrington, Richard, 320
Cart, painted Mexican, 268
Carter, Jimmy, 243
Cartography, 214–15
Cartoons, 59–61, 254
animated, 80
comic strip, 79–80
magazine, 212
Caruso, Enrico, 316
recordings of, 316
Carver, George Washington, 243
Casanova, 44, 69, 308, 331
Cash register, 61
Cassatt, Mary, 42, 94
Castor, 249
Catalina, 66
Catherine of Aragón, 117
Cats, 61–63, 141, 391
Egyptian beliefs about, 44, 61–62
Catsup (ketchup), 200, 202
Cattle, 219–20, 223
Caxton, William, 113
Cellini, Benvenuto, salt dish by, 266
Cells, battery, 35
Celluloid, 250
Cellulose, 249
Celsius scale, 365
Cement, 84
Cemeteries, 369, 370
pet, 121
Ceramics, 63–64, 267
Cerci, 75
Cereal, breakfast, 50–51
Cesium clocks, 73
Chain, Ernst, 246
Chair, 64–65
German, 263
"Chairing the Bridegroom," 216
Chamberlain, Neville, 382
Chamber of Commerce (international),
379
Chamber pot, 34, 35
Chandelier, 18th-century, 262
Cha-no-yu, 356
Chaplin, Charlie, 23, 226
Charge cards, 91–92

Charivari, Le, 61
Charlemagne, 36, 38, 167, 251
as a student, 78
wine and, 396–97
Charles I, ice cream and, 188
Charles II, 166, 304
Charles VI, 123
Charles VIII, 126
Charms, 197
Charybdis, 368
Chastity, 217
Château Lafite, 397
Chaucer, Geoffrey, 29, 221
Chauvinism, 228
Cheese, 65, 242
Roquefort, 65, 218–19
Chefs, 277, 278
Chenille, 72
Cheops, 287
Cheshire cat, 63
Chess, 46, 83
Chesterfield, 65
Chesterton, G.K.
on creations, 261
on thieves, 288
Chest of drawers, 65–66
Chests, antique, 268, 269
Chevrolet brothers, 27
Chewing gum, 66–67, 104
baseball cards and, 32
Chicago fire (1871), 141
Chicago White Sox scandal, 295–96
Chichester, Francis, 334
Chickens, 34, 67–68, 152, 156, 209
eye protector for, 347
Chicle, 66
Chiffon, 72
Childbed fever, 173
Chili powder, 325
China
aged in, 43
coal in, 75
colleges in, 78
eyeglasses in, 137
laundry in, 389
National Library of Peking, 207
newspapers in, 230
orange cultivation in, 235
paper and, 240
pasta and, 243
peanuts and, 244
perfume and, 248
printing and, 254–55
silk and, 73–74, 169
taxis and, 354
Chinaware, 64
Chinese, 28
brassieres and, 49
book on oranges, 235
carpet weaving and, 287
clothing of, 238, 260, 384
dice, 112
divorces, 119
doctor dolls, 122
flags of, 143
mirrors, 221
mustard and, 226
playing cards and, 250
refrigeration and, 276
Shar-Pei dogs, 120
surname, most common, 228–29
tea and, 356
toothbrush and, 371
typist, 381
umbrellas and, 382
Chintz, 72
Chocolate, 68–69, 325
Baker's, 57
Chopine, 144
Christie, Agatha, 107–108
Christmas cards, 161, 162
Chromium, 69
Chrysler plant, 352
Churchill, Winston, 37, 47, 120, 231, 321
cat of, 63
cigars and, 70
snoring of, 317
Churchyard, Thomas, 239
Churning of butter, 53
Cicero, 102

Cider, apple, 22
Cigar, 69–70, 71
Cigarettes, 71–72
  baseball cards with, 32
  machine, 78
  packaging of, 237
Cinchona, 129
Cincinnati fire department, 141
Cinderella's slipper, 157
Cinema. See Movies.
Cinnamon, 325
Citrus fruits, 235–36
Civet, 249
Claiborne, Craig, 279
Claret, 396, 397
Clarke, John, 229
Claudius II, 161
Clay
  bricks from, 52
  ceramics and, 63–64
  envelopes from, 135
  mannequins of, 396
  tablets of, 206
Cleaning
  dry, 130
  symbiotic, 341
  vacuum, 387
Cleansers, 322, 323
Cleopatra, 88–89, 197, 248
  jewelry and, 197
  party and, 43
Clergy, clothing of, 156, 166, 382
  wine and, 397
Cleveland, Grover, 212
Climate, 391–93
Clipper ships, 357
Clock, 72–73
  Dutch, 26
  18th-century French, 268
  stocking, 172
Closen, Louis de, 353
Cloth, 73–74
  envelopes of, 135
  names of, 72
  towel (terry), 375
Clothes
  artistically created, 264–65
  fads, 138
  mannequins for, 396
  paper patterns and, 301
  railway travel and, 378
  washing machine for, 389
Clotho, 366
Clue, 366
CO₂, weather and, 393
Coaches, railroad, 376–77, 378
Coal, 74-75, 249
  mining, 114
Coat. See Jacket, Raincoat.
Cobb, Irvin S., 168
Coca-Cola, 59
Cochineal, 132
Cock and Bull, 29
Cockfights, 67
Cockroach, 75–76
Cocksure, 168
Cocktails, 31
Cocoa, 69
Code of Hammurabi, 394
Cody, Buffalo Bill, 214
Coffee, 76–77
Coffee break, 76
Coffeehouse, 77
  sidewalk, 308
Coffeepot, porcelain, French, 267
Coin-operated machines, 77–78
  opposition to, 356
Coins, 82, 222–24, 241
  silver, 312
Coitus interruptus, 44
Coke, 74
Cold, common, 80–81
Cold cream, 89
Colesberg Kopje diamond fields, 109
Collars, 195, 304
College, 78–79
  law, 206
  police work in, 254
Color film, 56
Colors. See also individual colors.

dye, 131-32
  superstitions about, 364
  of thread, 366
Colosseum, cats in, 63
Columbia Broadcasting
  System, 271
Columbia University, 367
Columbus, Christopher, 57, 215, 303
  crackers and, 91
  orange and, 235
  pepper and, 248
  playing cards and, 250
  rubber and, 285
  sugar and, 337
  tobacco and, 69
Combs, 164
  Scythian gold, 264
Comic books, 24
Comic strip, 79–80
Common cold, 80–81
Commuter, 81–82
Compass, 302
Compurgation, 200
Computers, 82–83
  animal mating by, 401
  dates arranged by, 45
  medical diagnosis by, 120
  patternmaking by, 301
  printing and, 256
  traffic lights and, 376
  translation of languages by, 380
  typewriters and, 381
  weather forecasting and, 392
Comstock Lode, 312
Concrete, 84
Condom, 44
Cone, ice-cream, 188
Conestoga, Pennsylvania, 70
Conner, ale, 309
Conrad, Joseph, 268
Consanguinity tables, 154
Contact lenses, 137
Contraception, 42, 44–45
Conveyor belts, 23
Cook, Thomas, 373
Cookbook, 84–86
Coolidge, Calvin, 162
Cop (policeman), 253
Copying devices, 130–31
Corduroy, 72
Cork, 86
  bottle stoppers, 47
Corn flakes, 51
Corpse
  preserver for, 346
  rituals for, 148–49
Corresca, Rocco and
  Francisco, 306
Corsets, 40, 383
Cortés, Hernán, 321, 401
  chocolate and, 68, 325
  smallpox and, 385
Cosby, William, 105
Cosmetics, 88–90
  advertising of, 8–9
  drugstores and, 129
Costello, Lou, 363
Cotton, 74
  thread, 366
Couch, 65
Court tennis, 362, 365
Cowpox, 386
Cowries, 223
Cows
  dairy, 219–20
  as money, 223
  smallpox vaccination and, 385
Cozy, tea, 356
Crab apples, 21
Crabgrass, 394
Crabs
  sponges and, 326
  symbiosis of, 341, 342
Cracker, 90–91
Cracowes, 144
Craftsman's art, 261–69
Crane, Stephen, 231
Crapper, Thomas, 34
Cravat, 228, 229
Crawl (swimming), 340

Crayons, 91
Credit, 209–10, 378
Credit cards, 91–92, 210
  universal, 224
Cremation, 148
Crespi, Giuseppe Maria, 98
Crèvecoeur, J. Hector St.
  John de, 205
Crickets, temperature and, 391
Crime (and criminals)
  bank robbery, 288–89
  cant of, 316
  police and, 252–54
  shoplifting, 305, 307
  typewriters and, 381
Crocodile, 341
Crocus sativus, 324
Croesus, 222
Crossword puzzle, 92
Cruikshank, George, 391
Crusaders, 36, 37, 39, 248, 256
  baths and, 33, 34
  belts and, 39
Crystal Palace (Exposition, 1851), 133,
  211, 220, 375, 387
Cucumbers, 394
Cullinan Diamond, 110
Culpeper, Nicholas, 291
Cup
  drinking, 77, 127
  measuring, 85
  Nautilus, 267
Cupboards, antique, 262, 263
Curb Exchange, 332
Currency, 222–24
  gold and, 157–58
Currie, John, 220
Curtis, Cyrus, 212
Curtiss, Glenn, 17
Customs agents, 338–39
Cycling, 40–41
Cynotherapy, 121
Cyrano de Bergerac, Savinien, 328

D

da Gama, Vasco, 248, 303
Daguerre, Louis, 56, 344
Dagwood Bumstead, 79, 80
Dalí, Salvador, 69, 100
Damselfish, 341–42
Dance, Nathaniel, 96
Dancing, 102
Dante Alighieri, 126, 128
Daredevils, 333–34
Darrow, Charles, 47
Darwin, Charles, 112
  and cats, 63
  on yawning, 399
Data-processing machine, 82–83
Dating, blind, 45
Daumier, Honoré, 61, 95, 173, 205
Davenport, 65
David, biblical king, 251
Davies, Joseph E., 375
da Vinci, Leonardo, 16, 137, 150, 167,
  292
  automobile and, 26
  saw of, 294
  tank of, 344
Davis, Bette, 71
Davy, Humphry, 20
Daybed, 65
Days, names of, 54–55
Dead, rituals for, 148–49
Deadhead, 377
De Beers, 109, 110
Decimal system, 101
Decoy, bovine, 347
Defoe, Daniel, 231
Degas, Edgar, 91, 97, 194
de Gaulle, Charles, 65, 167
Delaroche, Paul, 56
de Léon, Ponce, 235
Delicatessen, 101
  sandwiches, 294
Delmonico, Lorenzo, 278
de Medici, Catherine. See Medici,
  Catherine de.

Denim, 72, 196
Dentifrices, 371
Dentistry, 31, 101, 103–104
Dentures, 104–105
Deodorant, 105
Department store, 105–107
  shoplifting in, 305, 307
Desk, Dresden (1740), 263
Detective story, 107–108
Detergents, 322
Detroit, Michigan, traffic
  lights in, 376
Deuce (in tennis), 362
Deus ex machina, 363
Deux Magots, 308
Devil. See Satan.
"Devil's advocate," 190
Dextrin, 88
Dextrose, 88
Diable, Le, 121
Diamonds, 108–10, 195, 197, 198, 227
Diary, 111–12
Dice, 112
Dickens, Charles, 29, 63, 170
  on lawyers, 205
  sleep and, 316
Dickinson, Levi, 52
Dickson, William, 225
Dictionary, 112–14
  crossword puzzles and, 92
Diderot, Denis, 277
Didrikson, Babe, 159
Diesel, Rudolf, 114, 115
Diesel engine, 114–15
Diets, reducing, 274–75
Digital computer, 83
Digital watches, 390
Dillinger, John, tombstone of, 369
Dine, Norman, 320
Diner, 279
Dining
  artistic accoutrements to, 266–67
  etiquette, 134, 203, 204
  fast-food, 139–40
  linen for, 353
  reducing diets and, 274–75
  utensils for, 203–204
Dioscorides, 324
Dirigibles, 17
  skyscraper mooring of, 314
Dirks, Rudolph, 79
Discount store, 115–16
Dishwasher, 116, 118
Disraeli, Benjamin, 303
Distaff, 366
Ditto, 130
Divan, 65
Divorce, 117
  vending-machine, 78
Dr. I.Q., 258
"Doctor ladies," 122
Dr Pepper, 59
Doctors, 118–20
  in epitaphs, 370
  jargon of, 195
Dodge brothers, 27
Dodo, 342
Dogs, 40, 86, 87, 120–22, 141, 391
  attacks by, 125
  epitaph for, 370
  experiments on, 178
Dokhmas, 148
Doll, 122–25, 165
Dollhouses, 122
Dolorologists, 237
Donatus, Aelius, 255
"Doonesbury," 79
Door, 125–26, 252
Door-to-door sales, 124–25, 387
Doré, Gustave, 62
Doubleday, Abner, 31–32
Doubleheader, 377
Doublet, 195
Dough, 49–50
Doughnut, 126–27
Douglas Aircraft, 18
"Down and out," 189
Dowry, 217
Doxycycline, 374
Doyle, Arthur Conan, 107, 212

D'Oyly Carte, Rupert, 175
Drag roles, 363
Draisine, 40
Drake, Edwin, 234
Drake, Francis, 74
Dreams, 318
Dressing, salad, 290, 291
Drew, Daniel, 332
Drinking, terms relating to, 168
Drinking vessel, 127
Drinking water, 127–28
Drought, 393
Drugs, 128–29, 132
  advertising of, 8–9, 12
  anesthetic, 20
  aspirin, 22–23
  injection of, 178
  legislation on, 129
  painkilling, 237
  penicillin, 245–46
  silver used in, 312
  sleep-inducing, 318–19
  vaccine, 385–87
Drugstore, 128–29
Dry cleaning, 130
Duccio, 97
Dudley, Robert, 102
Dumas, Alexandre, 108,
  on salads, 290
Dummies, window, 396
Dundes, Alan, 160
Dungarees, 72
Duplicating, 130–31
Durande, Charles, 217
Duryea, Charles and Frank, 27
Dust, 131, 377, 387, 393
Dutch
  butter making, 389
  clocks, 26
  gardens, 153
  golf, 158, 159
  spices and, 324
"Dutch courage," 168
Dutch East India Company, 355–56
Dvorak, August, 380
Dyes, 131–32
  hair, 89, 164
  shoe polish and, 305
  thread, 366

E

Eames chair, 64
Earp, Wyatt, 30, 104
Earspool disc, Peruvian, 264
Earth (planet)
  outer space view of, 186
  slowing of rotation of, 368
Easter egg, 68
Eastman Kodak, 56
Eating. See Dining.
"Eating crow," 190
"Eating one's hat," 170
Eavesdropping, electronic, 360
Eddy, Mary Baker, 35
Eden, Mary, 320
Ederle, Gertrude, 340–41
Edison, Thomas, 209
  fluoroscope and, 398
  "last breath" of, 323
  light bulb and, 208
  motion pictures and, 225, 226
  phonograph and, 328
  rubber research by, 285
  sleep and, 316–17
  souvenirs and, 323
  talking doll and, 124
  telephone and, 171
  ticker-tape machine and, 332
  X rays and, 398
Education, college, 78–79
Edward I, 74
  highwaymen and, 170
Edward, the Black Prince, 370
Egg, 68
  theater superstition against, 364
  unique view of, 180
Egrets, cattle, 341
Egypt, 31, 33, 36–37, 38, 39

beer of, 39
burial customs in, 148, 155
canal in, 301
cats and, 44, 61–62
cosmetics and, 88–89
dancers in, 91
glassmaking in, 155
gluemaking in, 157
hospital in, 172–73
libraries in, 206
locks in, 210, 211
mummies of, 21, 148
paper and, 398
rope making in, 282
saws in, 293
swimming in, 339
telephone system in, 358
timekeeping and, 72
umbrellas in, 382
Einhorn, Albert, 104
Einstein, Albert, 184, 308
Eisenhower, Dwight D., 142
  card playing by, 250
  rubber and, 285
  scandal under, 297
Elderly. See Aged.
Electricity
  battery and, 35–36, 312
  Edison's experiments with, 209
  ironing and, 194
  light bulb and, 208–209
  pain alleviation and, 238
  signs using, 311
  silver conduction of, 311–12
Electroencephalograph, sleep and, 318
Electrolyte, 34, 35
Electromagnetic waves, 398
Electronic snooping, 360
Electron microscope, images
  produced by, 179, 180, 183
Elephant, 377, 402
Elevator, 176, 133–34
Eliot, Charles W., 79
Elizabeth I, 89, 132, 324
  bath and, 34
  beard tax and, 36
  bed of, 37
  dancing by, 102
  epitaph of, 149
  forks and, 203
  hosiery of, 172
  lottery and, 304
  shirts and, 304
  teeth of, 105
  watch of, 390
  wigs and, 164
Elizabeth (of Russia), 386
Emerson, Ralph Waldo, 151, 393
Empire State Building, 314
Enders, John Franklin, 386
Endorphins, 238
Energy
  air conditioning and, 17
  coal and, 75
  garbage and, 151
  oil and, 233, 234
Envelope, 135–36
Epidemics, 191, 385–86, 387
  spotted fever, 387
Epitaphs, 149, 370
Epstein, Jacob, 369
Eraser, 136
Escoffier, Auguste, 175, 278
Eskimo Pie, 188
Espadrillas, 145
Ether, 20, 104
Etiquette, 134–35
  cab drivers and, 354
  dining, 134, 203, 204, 277
  sidewalk café, 308
Euclid, 221
Euripos strait, tides in, 368
Evelyn, John, 226
Evergreen oak, 86
Eyck, Jan van, 97
Eyeglasses, 136–37
Eye makeup, 88, 89

F

Fadiman, Clifton, 258
Fads, 138–39, 226, 238, 333. See also
  Gadgets.
  concrete canoe racing, 84
  dancing, 102
  dieting, 275, 295
  forks, 203
  nutrition, 388
  tennis, 365
  watch, 390
Fagan, Ted, 379
Fahrenheit scale, 365, 391
Fairbanks, Douglas, Sr., 226, 287
Fall, Albert B., 296
Fan, 16
  Dutch, 265
Farfalle, 243
Farley, Thomas M., 296
Farmer, Fannie Merritt, 85
Farsightedness, 137
Fashion dolls (babies), 123
Fasteners, slide, 400
Fast food, 139–40
Fat farm, 275
Father's Day, 162
Fat people
  Hippocrates on, 119
  in action, 274–75
  stereotyping and, 329–30
Fauchard, Pierre, 103–104
Fauchon, 101
F.B.I., 107
Feather, 170, 180
Feller, Bob, 33
Ferdinand II (of Tuscany), 365
Fertilizer, 86, 152, 233
Fessenden, Reginald, 270
Field, Marshall, 105
Fields, W.C., epitaph of, 370
Filaments, light bulb, 208
Filling station, 299
Film. See also Movies.
  color, 56
Filters, cigarette, 71
Fin (money), 223
Fingernail painting, 88, 90
Fingerprinting, 253
Firearms sales, 124
Fire fighting, 140–41
  oil-field, 233
  screws and, 299
Fish, cleaner, 341, 342
Fishing, 142–43
Fisk, James, 44, 124
Flagpole sitting, 334
Flags, 143
Flatirons, 194
Fleming, Alexander, 246
Fletcher, Horace, 138
Fletcherizing, 62
Flies, 176–77
Flint, Charles R., 66
FLIP, 392
Flip (drink), 168
Flore (café), 308
Florey, Howard, 246
Flu, 191
Fluorescent light, 230
Fluorocarbons, 16
Fluoroscope, 398
Food
  artistic accouterments to, 266–67
  concentrated, 220
  dieting and, 274–75
  fast, 139–40
  frozen, 146, 147
  packaging for, 236–37
  pouched, 236
  processor, 144
  restaurant, 277–79
  salad, 290–91
  sugar added to, 337
  weeds as, 394
Food critic, 278
Footwear, 144–46, 400
  shoe polish and, 305
Ford, Gerald, 323
Ford, Henry, 23, 26, 27–28
  Edison memorabilia and, 323
Ford cars, 23, 250

jokes about, 26
Forecasting, weather, 392
Forks, 176, 203–204
Fortnum and Mason, 101
Fountain pen, 245
Fox, Charles, 312
Fox, Herbert, 68
Fragrances, 248–49
France, Anatole, 227
Francis I (of Austria), 401
Francis I (of France), 36, 53, 367
Frank, Anne, 112
Frankfurters, 174
Franking, 213
Franklin, Benjamin, 54, 65, 121, 163,
  316
  advertising and, 7
  bathtub and, 34
  bifocals and, 137
  broom and, 52
  cartoon by, 61
  as fire fighter, 140
  garbage and, 151
  magazine published by, 211
  newspaper letters by, 231
  as pharmacist, 128
  as postmaster general, 213
  sleep and, 316
  stove invented by, 147
  swimming and, 339
Frascati, 397
Fraunces Tavern, 30
Frederick II, 128
Frederick the Great, 194
Freeman, Norman, 125
Freud, Sigmund, 70, 318
  on mother-in-law, 330
  on theory of personality, 232
Frick, Henry C., 74
Frigidaire, 277
Frontinus, Sextus Julius, 127
Frozen food, 146, 147
Fruit, citrus, 235–36
Fry, Johnny, 214
Fuller Brush Company, 125
Fundy, Bay of, tides in, 366–68
Funk, Casimir, 388
Furnace, 146–47
  steelmaking, 327
Funerals, 148–49, 395
  pet, 121

G

Gable, Clark, 226, 384
Gadgets, 150–51, 360
Gainsborough, Thomas, 95, 398
Galen, dentistry and, 103
Galileo, 42
  clock of, 73
  thermoscope of, 365
Gallup Poll, 234, 235
Galoshes, zipper and, 400
Galton, Francis, 253
Galvani, Luigi, 35
Gambling
  dice and, 112
  lottery, 367
  slot machines for, 78
Games, board, 45–46
Gandhi, Mohandas, 292, 299, 378
Gangsaws, 350
Garbage, 151–52
  packaging and, 236
  stock exchange, 331
Gardening
  lawn care, 204–205
  parlor, 177–78
Gardens, 152–54
  of Empress Josephine, 284
Garfield, James, 36, 155
Garth, Samuel, 195
Gasoline, 114, 130, 147, 153, 233
  as fuel in irons, 194
  shortages, 28, 41, 151
Gasoline engine, 27
Gas station, 299
Gaucho shirt, 305
Gay Deceivers, 49

Gay, John, 251
Geber, 168
Gelatieri, 188
Gemstones, 109–10, 197–98
Genesis, book of, 44, 215
Genealogy, 154–55
   X rays and, 398
General Foods, 51, 147
General Mills, 50, 51
George II, 317
George IV, 203, 277, 317
George V, 122
Gesner, Konrad von, 245
Getchell, Margaret, 106
Getty, J. Paul, 152
Ghee, 53
Ghiberti, Lorenzo, 126
Gibberish, 168
Gilbert (William) and Sullivan
   (Arthur), 320
Gillette, King Camp, 273
Gillray, James, 118, 237
Ginger ale, 59
Gingerbread, 324
Giroux, 344
Gish, Lillian, 225
Gladstone, William E., 338
Glass, 155–57
   drinking, 127
   hot plate, 150
   in syringes, 178
   indoor gardening and, 177
Glassmaking, 47, 136–37, 155
Glasses, eye, 136–37
Gleason, Jackie, 361
Glenn, John, 332, 400
Glidden, J.F., 345
Glider, 17
Gloves, 89, 156
   average size of, 167
Glue, 157, 252
Glyphs, 309
Godey's Lady's Book, 212
Godowsky, Leopold, Jr., 56
Goering, Hermann, 53
Goethe, Johann Wolfgang von, 128,
   231, 308
Gold, 157–58
   in dentures, 104
   scales and, 294
Goldberg, Rube, 80, 150
Golf, 104, 158–59
Gompers, Samuel, 374
Goober peas, 244
Goodhue, L.D., 16
Good Humor, 191
Goodrich, B.F., zippers and 400
Goodyear, Charles, 28–29, 105, 286
Gore, S.W., 362, 364–65
Gorgas, William, 387
Gorrie, John, 16–17, 276
Gout, 237
Gowland, Gibson, 225
Gozzoli, Benozzo, 60
Graffiti, 160, 163
Graham, Bette Nesmith, 136
Graham, Sylvester, 34, 90
Gramineae, 204
Grand Tour, 372–73
Grant, Ulysses S., 36, 70
   campaign slogan of, 380
Grapes, wine and, 394
Graphite, 245
Grass, 394
   lawn, 204–205
Grateau, Marcel, 164
Gravestones, 149, 369, 370
Graveyard, 369, 370
Gravitation, tides and, 368
Great Atlantic & Pacific Tea Company,
   357
Great Train Robbery, The, 224
Great Wall of China, 51
Greece, ancient, 38
   bathing in, 33, 34
   beds in, 37
   belts in, 39
   birthdays in, 43
   central heating in, 146

   coins of, 223
   cosmetics in, 89
   epitaphs in, 370
   gems and, 197
   hairstyles in, 164
   houseplants in, 177
   irons in, 194
   jump rope in, 282
   literature in, 206
   locks in, 210
   safety pins in, 290
   salads in, 291
   temples in, 24
   umbrellas in, 382
   wine in, 396
Greeley, Horace, 22
Green, theatrical superstition
   about, 364
Greenhouse effect, 393
Greenland, exploration of, 242
Greenwich Mean Time, 73
Greeting cards, 161–62
Gregory, Hanson, 127
Gregory XIII, 54, 55
Gregory I (the Great), Pope, St., 321
Grey, Zane, 104
Griffith, David Wark, 225
Grimm brothers, 113
Grog, 168
Guaiacum, 129
Guayule, 285
Guidebooks, 215, 372, 373
Guide Michelin, 373
Guild, button makers', 53–54
Guinan, Texas, 30, 171
Guitar, 163
GUM (Moscow store), 106, 107
Gunnysack, 72
Gunsmithing, 124
Gunther, John, 258
Guntram, 118
Gusmão, Bartholomeu de, 28
Gutenberg, Johann, 255

H

Haakon the Good, 312
Hackett, Buddy, 158
Hackman, Gene, 360
Hadden, Briton, 213
Hagenbeck, Carl and Gottfried Claas,
   402
Hair, hats and, 169
Hairstyles, 164–65
Hakluyt, Richard, 132
Hale, Sara Josepha, 212
Hales, Reverend Dr., 356
Hale telescope, 221
Hall, James, 303
Hallmark Cards, 162
Hamburger, 165–66
   fast-food, 139–40
Hamilton, Alexander, 231
Hamilton, L. H., 144
Hammer, 227
Hammett, Dashiell, 107
Hammurabi Code
   insurance and, 192
   wine and, 394
Hancock, Thomas, 286
Hancock Building, 315
Handbags, 256, 258–59
Handkerchief, 166
Hands, 144, 167, 257. *See also* Gloves.
Handshake, 134, 167
Hanging Gardens of Babylon, 152
Hansom cab, 355
Hanson, Duane, 100
"Happy Birthday to You," 43
Hard liquor
   terms relating to, 168
   rum and triangular trade, 337
   wakes and, 148
   See also Alcohol.
Hardart, Frank, 139
Harding, Warren Gamaliel, 176, 270
   scandals of, 296, 297
Harper's Weekly, 212

Harris, Benjamin, 231
Harrison Benjamin, 36, 155, 212
Harrison, George, 165
Hart, William S., 226
Harvard University, 79, 207, 367
Harvey, Fred, 139, 279
Hasidic Jews, 110, 218
Haslam, "Pony Bob," 214
Hastings, Battle of, 143
Hat, 169, 170
   tipping, 134, 346
Hatshepsut, 400
Hat trick, 170
Haughwout, E.V., 133
Haute cuisine, 277
Havana cigars, 70
Hays, Rutherford, 36
Hays, Wayne, 297
Headstones, 149, 369, 370
Hearst, William Randolph, 231, 295
   comic strips and, 79
Heating, central, 146–47
Heightism, 329
Heim, Jacques, 41
Heine, Heinrich, 395
Heinz, Henry John, 58, 59, 202, 311
Helen of Troy, 22, 45
Hellos, 171
Hemingway, Ernest, 396
Hemlock, 394
Hen. *See* Chicken.
Henlein, Peter, 390
Henna, 88, 89
Henriques, John, 198
Henry III, 166, 401
Henry IV, 132
   carpet manufacture and, 287
Henry VII, 37
Henry VIII, 44, 310
   bowling and, 48
   coin issue of, 223
   divorce and, 117
   drug compounded by, 129
   ginger and, 324
Henry, O., 336
   on safecracking, 289
Henson, William, 17
Herblock, 60
Herbs, 152, 325
Hercules, 232, 235
"Here's how," 31
Hermes, 163
Hero (Greek mathematician), 77
Hero (sandwich), 294
Hero and Leander, 339
Herodotus, 169
   on cinnamon, 325
Heroin, 237, 319
Heron, symbiosis and, 341
Herzogenaurach, 145
Hesiod, 16
Hicks, John, Jr., 118
Higgins, Henry, 357
Highgate Cemetery, 369
Highwaymen, 170
Highways, 29, 169–71, 215
Hill, Mildred and Patty, 43
Hill, Rowland, 213
Hillel, Rabbi, 293
Hinchliffe, Robert, 298
Hindu decimal system, 101
Hippocrates, 119, 191
   dentifrice for, 371
   dentistry and, 103
   pepper and, 248
   on yawns, 398
Hippopotamus, symbiosis and, 341
Hiroshima, 379
Hiss, Alger, 381
Hitler, Adolf, 18, 234, 368
Hobbs, Alfred Charles, 211
Hobson, Valerie, 297
Hofmann, Felix, 23
Hogarth, William, 30, 60
Hogs, 189, 391
   bacon and, 29
   garbage and, 151
   influenza and, 191
   navigation by, 302
Holbein, Hans, 96

Holland. *See* Netherlands, Dutch.
Hollerith, Herman, 82
Holliday, Doc, 104, 301
Hollywood, 225
Holmes, Oliver Wendell, 173
   on kissing, 201
   on puns, 257
Holmes, Sherlock, 107, 108
Holograms, 179, 183, 186, 187
Holt, Samuel, 375
Homer
   Charybdis of, 368
   Iliad of, 26
   lottery and, 367
Homonyms, puns and, 257
Honey badger, 341
Honey guide (bird), 341
Honeymoon, 216
Hong Kong Island swim, 339
Hooch, 168
Hood, Thomas, 29
Hookless Fastener Company, 400
Hookswitch bypass, 360
Hoover, Herbert, 142
Hoover, William, 387
Hope Diamond, 110, 198
Hopetown, South Africa, 110
Hopkins, Major, 206
Hopper, Edward, 99
Horn & Hardart Company, 78, 139
Horses, 10, 40, 41, 151
   as experimental animals, 178
   Pony Express, 214
Horsley, John, 162
Horticulture, 177–78
Hosiery, 172
Hospitals, 172–74
Hostess party, selling by, 125
Hot dog, 140, 174
Hôtel-Dieu, 173
Hotels, 174–76
   elevators in, 133, 134
   souvenirs and, 324
Hotray, 150
Houdini, Harry, 210
Housefly, 176–77
Houseplants, 177–78
Howard, Jane, 137
Howard Johnson's, 139
Howe, Elias, 300
Hsüan Tsung, 49
Hubschman, Herbert and Sidney, 116
Hudson, Edward J., 117
Hughes, Howard, 49, 296
Hugo, Victor, 108
Hull, Richard, 148–49
Humphrey, Hubert Horatio, 128
Hunt, Walter, 290, 300
Hunter, William, 213
Hurricane, 187, 392
Hush puppies, 87
Hyacinth, water, 394
Hyatt, John, 250
Hyperopia, 137
Hypodermic, 178

I

IBM, 82
Ibn Hayyān, Jābir, 168
Ibsen, Henrik, 128
Ice, refrigeration and, 276
Ice cream, 188, 191
Ice-cream soda, 59, 188
Idioms, 189–90
Idiots, 193
Iguanas, marine, 342
Iliad, 26
   lottery in, 367
Imbeciles, 193
Immunity, vaccine and, 385–87
Incandescent lamp, 208
Incas
   roads of, 169
   smallpox and, 385
Incinerators, 151
Incroyables, 138
Indian rope trick, 283
Indians, American

corn and, 86
dreams and, 318
headdress of, 169, 170
latex and, 145
peddlers and, 124
Pony Express and, 214
skyscraper building and, 313–14
smoking by, 69–70, 71
Indigo, 132
Indonesia, oil in, 232
Influenza, 191, 322
Information Please, 258
Ingres, Jean Auguste Dominique, drawings by, 245
Injections, medicinal, 178, 385–87
Inns, 29, 174–76
signs of, 310
Insomnia, 320
sleeping pills and, 319
Insurance, 192–93
Integram, 187
Intelligence test, 193–94
International Date Line, 73
Interpreters, 379–80
Intoxication, slang for, 316
Introductions, etiquette for, 134
Iolanthe, 320
IQ, 193–94
Iron (appliance), 99, 194, 389
Iron (metal)
filings, magnetized, 184
steel and, 326, 327
Iron puddlers, 350
Irving, Clifford, 296
Irving, Washington, 142
ISIS, 401–402
Ivanov, Eugene, 297
Ivory
dentures from, 104–105
piano keys and, 348
Ivory soap, 322

J

Jacket, 194–95, 385
Jackson, Andrew, spoils system and, 213
Jackson, "Shoeless Joe," 295–96
Jacob, Mary, 49
Jagger, Mick, 384
Jail-Breaker's Catechism, The, 69
James II and IV, golf and, 158
Jamestown Colony, 118, 156
Japan, 28, 33, 79
attacks Pearl Harbor, 233–34
auction bidding in, 25–26
bathing in, 34
commuting in, 81
hairstyles in, 164
invasion of New Guinea, 223
lawyers in, 206
lotteries in, 367
packaging in, 236
peace negotiations with, 379
swords of, 326
taxicabs in, 354
tea ceremony of, 356
toothpicks in, 372
typhoons and, 393
umbrellas in, 382
Jargon, 195, 316
Jars, Mason and Ball, 58
Jasmine, perfumes and, 248–49
Jay, John, 118
Jazz Singer, The, 226
Jeans, 195–96
Jeepneys, 355
Jefferson, Thomas, 30, 39, 155, 206, 231
clock invented by, 150
inoculation of, 386
meteorology and, 392
pasta and, 243
tomatoes and, 202
Jenner, Edward, 119, 385, 386
Jenney, William Le Baron, 313
Jennings Center, 401
Jenny Lind trunk, 338
Jerez, Rodrigo de, 69
Jericho, 128

Jerkin, 195
Jerkwater town, 377
Jesus, birthday of, 43, 55, 248
Jet engine, 19
Jewelry, 197–98, 264
Jigsaw puzzle, 198
Jingles, advertising, 328
Jitneys, 354–55
Joachimsthaler, 223
Joan of Arc, 251
John XXI, Pope, 103
John (policeman), 253
John, Elton, 137
John Hancock Building, 315
Johnson, Howard Deering, 139, 191
Johnson, Lyndon Baines, 217, 361
Johnson, Nancy, 188
Johnson, Samuel, 29, 50, 63
on artisans, 262
dictionary of, 113, 114
on tipping, 374
Johnston Island, 389
Jolly, Jean-Baptiste, 130
Jolson, Al, 226
Jonson, Ben, on epitaphs, 370
Jorn, Joe, 139
Joseph, 197
Joseph II, zoo of, 401
Josephine (of France), 117, 144
roses and, 284
Journal (New York), 79
Journalism, 230–32
pictorial, 212
yellow, 79, 231
Jouvin, Xavier, 156
Joy, Lottie, 313
Judas, 232
Juke box, 199
Jump rope, 282
rhymes for, 283
Jury, 199–200
Juvenal, 49, 252

K

Kaganovich, Lazar, 335
Kaffeeklatsch, 76
Kaiser, Henry John, 302
Kaldi, 76
Kales, Anthony, 319
Kamikaze, 393
Kato, Satori, 77
Katzenjammer, 168
"Katzenjammer Kids, The," 79
Keats, John, 396
Keeler, Christine, 297
Kegel; kegler, 48
Kellermann, Annette, 41
Kellogg, John Harvey, 51
Kelly, Grace, 400
Kelly, Joe, 258
Kelly, Mike, 32
Kelly, William ("Crazy"), 327
Kennedy, John F., 65
television and, 361
Kent, William, 153
Kentucky Fried Chicken, 140
Kerosene, 299
Kerr lid, 58
Ketchup, 200, 202
Key, 210–11
Keyboard, typewriter, 380
Key West, tides of, 368
Khalid, king of Saudi Arabia, 375
Khrushchev, Nikita, 380
Kidd, James, 395
Kieran, John, 258
Kimberley, South Africa, 109
Kimono, Japanese, 265
Kinetoscope, 225
King, Billy Jean, 145, 365
King Solomon's Temple, 126
Kinley, Myron, 233
Kinsey, Alfred, 160
Kipling, Rudyard, 212
Kirlian photography, 182
"Kiss," 163
Kissing, 201
Kissinger, Henry, 33

garbage of, 152
jeans and, 195
Kit bag, 338
Kitchen, 202–203
"Kith and kin," 189
"Klappers," 124
Knapsack, 338
Knievel, Evel, 224
doll, 125
Knife, 31, 144, 203, 204
Knights
armor, 264
credit usage by, 91–92
glove as token for, 156
Knud, Bishop, 176
Kodak, 56
Kohl, 88, 90
Korson, George, 74
Kraft, James L., 65
Kreuger, Ivar, 219
Kroc, Ray, 139
Kublai Khan, 393

L

Lace, Point d'Angleterre, 267
Lachesis, 366
Lactobacillus bulgaricus, 399
Ladies' Home Journal, 212
La Forge, Abiel T., 106
Lamb's quarters, 394
Lamps, 262, 263
Lana, Francesco de, 28
Lancelot, 251, 296
Land, Edwin, 56
Langsdorf, Jesse, 229
Language
acronyms in, 15
black in, 44
chickens and, 68
crossword puzzles and, 92
dictionary and, 112–14
dogs and, 120
eggs and, 68
graffiti, 160, 164
hats and, 170
hello, in, 171
idiomatic, 189–90
jargon, 195
liquor and, 168
money and, 223
of pasta, 243
police, 253
puns and, 257
railroad, 377
slang, 315–16
stagecoach terminology, 377
of stock exchange, 332
theatrical, 363
of toasts, 31
translation of, 379–80
Lanthorn, 250
Lapel, 194–95
La Porte, California, ski races, 313
Larrey, Dominique-Jean, 19
Lasagna, 243
Lasers
images produced by, 179,183
musical recording by, 328
Lasker, Albert, 7
Lassen, Kenneth and Louis, 166
Latex, 284–85
rainwear and, 272
Latter-day Saints, 154
Laundromat; launderette, 77, 389
Laundry, 322
machines for, 389
Lawn, 204–205
games, 48, 362
Law schools, 206
Lawyers, 205–206, 210
Lazenby, R.S., 59
Lead, pencils and, 245
League of American Wheelmen, 171
League of Nations, 242
Leander, 339
Leather, 47, 127
shoe polish and, 305
Leeches, weather prediction and, 391

Leeuwenhoek, Anton van, 103
Left-handedness, 167
Legumes, 244
Leibniz, Gottfried von, 82
LeMoyne, Jean Baptiste, 260
Lenin, Vladimir Ilyich 205, 308
Le Nôtre, André, 153
Lenses, 42
eyeglass, 136–37
Leo X, Pope, 401
Leonardo da Vinci. *See* da Vinci, Leonardo.
Leonidas of Tarentum, 370
Leopold II (of Belgium), 285
Leslie, Eliza, 84, 85, 200
Leslie's, 212
Leszczynska, Maria, 170
Let (in tennis), 362
Letterman, Jonathan, 19
Lettuce, 291
Levi's 195–96
Lexicographers, 113–14
Leyendecker, J.C., 227
Libel, 105
Liberace, 328
Liberia, 303
Librarians, stereotyping of, 331
Library, 206–207
genealogical, 154
university, 79, 313
License plate, 207–208
Lid, Kerr, 58
Liddy, James, 38
Liebig, Justus von, 321
Lifebuoy soap, 322
Light bulb, 208–209
fluorescent, 230
Lightning, 391–92
Lightning (clipper), 357
Light waves, photograph of, 186
Lincoln, Abraham, 30, 36, 84, 155, 395
detective story by, 108
railroad coach for, 378
Lind, Jenny, 338
Lindbergh, Charles A., 18, 60
Linde, Carl von, 115
Lindsay, Vachel, 225
Linen, 73
as contraceptive, 44
table, 243
Linguine, 353
Linnaeus, Carolus, 69
Liotard, Jean Étienne, 57
Lipman, Hyman L., 136
Liquid eraser, 136
Liquid-protein diet, 275
Liquor, terms relating to, 168
Lisbon zoo, 401
Lister, Joseph, 15, 21
Liszt, Franz, 70
Little, Anderson, 116
Little Egypt, 279
Little River, tide at, 368
Lloyd, Humfre, 103
Lloyd George, David, 332
Lloyd's of London, 193, 240
Loan, 209–10
Locks, 210–11
Locomotives, 376, 377
diesel, 114
Loewy, Raymond, 237
Logan, John, 383
Loggerheads, 168
London, 107
British Museum in, 207
cleaners in, 130
Great Fire of, 111, 140
hospitals in, 173, 365
mail strike, 213
sidewalks in, 307
subway system, 334
taxicabs, 353–54, 355
traffic light in, 375
London Exhibition of 1851. *See* Crystal Palace Exposition.
Loom, carpet-making, 287
Loos, Anita, 201
Lorelei Lee, 201
Lorillard Company, 70, 71
Lotteries, 112, 367

Loud, John, 244
Louis IX, memorabilia of, 323
Louis XI, mustard and, 227
Louis XIII, 36, 321
Louis XIV, 52, 53, 136
  beds of, 37
  cats and, 62
  dying statement of, 149
  footwear of, 144
  gardens of, 153
  Hope Diamond and, 198
  menagerie of, 401
  mustard and, 227
  plants of, 177
  wig of, 164
Louis XV, coffee and, 76
Louis Philippe, 61
Love (in tennis), 362
Lowe, Edwin S., 42
Lowell, William, 104
L-Tryptophan, 319
Lucas, Anthony, 234
Luce, Henry, 213
Lucifer. See Satan.
Ludowici, Georgia, 376
Luggage, 250, 337–39, 372, 378
Luks, George, 94
Lunar year, 54
Lupercalia, 161
Luther, Martin, 48, 126
Lutyens, Edwin, 122
Lydia, 222
Lyre, 163

M

Macadam road, 171
MacArthur, Douglas, 67, 218
Macaroni, 243
"Macaronis" (clothing faddists), 138
Macbeth, 364
MacFarlane, Robert, 220
Macintosh, Charles, 272
Macmillan, Harold, 297
Macy, R.H., & Co., 106
  patrol dogs of, 121
Madison, Dolley, 188
Madison, James, 38
Maelstrom, 368
Magazines, 211–13
  advertising in, 7–13
  electronic, 256
Magee, Carl C., 240
Maggots, healing and, 176
Magnetic tape, 329
Mail, 171, 213–14
  delivery on skis, 313
Mailer, Norman, 315
Maize, 86
Makeup, 88–90
"Making both ends meet," 353
Malta, Sovereign Order of, 172
Mangles, 194, 389
Mangold, Sylvia, 100
Manhattan Project, 311
Maní, Mexico, library of, 207
Manicotti, 243
Mannequins, 123, 396
Manners, 134–35
Manners, David, 201
Mannes, Leopold, 56
Man-of-war, Portuguese, 342
Mansion of Happiness, 46
Manutius, Aldus, 256
Mao Tse-tung, 331
Maple sugar, 337
Maps, 214–15
  dissected, 198
Marble Dry-Goods Palace, 106
Marcel, 164–65
Marconi, Guglielmo, 270
Marcus, Siegfried, 27
Marcus Aurelius, 282
Margarine, 53
Maria Theresa, 401
Marie Antoinette, 254
Mark Antony, 248
Marquetry, 251
Marriage, 117, 215–18

Marshall, Thomas, 70
Mary (of Burgundy), 109
Mary (of England), dollhouse of, 122
  hosiery of, 172
Mary Queen of Scots, 158
  hosiery of, 172
  watch of, 390
Mary Tudor (Mary I), 144
Marx, Karl, tomb of, 369
Mason, Chaytor, 151
Mason jar, 58
Masonry, 51–52
Mass production, 23–24, 211. *See also*
  Assembly line.
Matches, 218, 219
Mather, Cotton, 119
Mattress, 37, 38, 176
Matzoh, 293
Mauldin, Bill, 59
Mauve, 132
Maximilian I, 109
May, Herbert A., 375
Mayans, library of, 207
Mayer, Jean, 140
Mazarin, 255
McAdam, John Loudon, 170
McCarthy, Joseph, cartoon on, 60
McClure's, 212
McConnell, David H., 90
McDonald's, 139, 140, 166
McKinley, William, 231
McLuhan, Marshall, 131, 361
Mead, Margaret, 203
Meadville, Pennsylvania, 400
Meat, 165–66, 174, 293, 401
  spices and, 303
Medici, Catherine de, 156, 248, 321,
  ice cream and, 188
Medici family, 207, 309
Mellon, Thomas, 74
Memorabilia, 323–24
Menageries, 401, 402
Mencken, H.L., 31, 315
  on women kissing, 201
Mercator projection, 215
Mercer, John, 366
Mercerized thread, 366
Merlin, 221
Merlin, Joseph, 280
Mesa Verde cliff dwellers, 393
Meteorology, 392
Methapyrilene, 319
Métro, 334–35
Mexico City
  lotteries in, 367
  subway, 335–36
Meyerbeer, Giacomo, 280
Michelangelo, 196, 207
Michelin, Guide, 373
Microphone, bugging and, 360
Middlecoff, Cary, 104
Milbank, Jeremiah, 220
Milk, 53, 218–20
  condensed, 220
  cultured, 399
  tea and, 356
Milk train, 377
Mill, Henry, 380
Mill outlets, 116
Mills, A.G., 31–32
Mills, Wilbur, 297
Milton, John
  on sleep, 316
  on woman's role, 202
Milton Bradley, 46
Mimeograph, 130, 209
Mineral waters, 128
Mining, coal, 74–75
Minuet, 102
Mirrors, 89, 221, 364
  Egyptian, 265
Mitchell, John, 74
Mite, micrograph of, 181
Mitropoulos, Dimitri, 328
Mobile home, 222
Moccasins, 145–46
  Cheyenne, 265
Models (mannequins), 123, 396
Model T Ford, 26
Mohawk Indians, 313–14, 358

Molasses, 337
Mold
  microscopic view of, 183
  penicillin, 246
Monasteries
  houseplants of, 177
  libraries of, 207
  wine and, 397
Money, 222–24
  gold standard and, 157–58
  lotteries and, 367
  silver, 311–12
Moneylenders, 210
Money pouches, 256
Monogamy, 218
Monograms, towel, 375
Monopoly (game), 47
  underwater, 46
Monroe, Marilyn, 317
Montagné, Prosper, 277
Montagu, John, 4th earl of Sandwich,
  293
Montausier, duc de, 203
Monte Cassino, 207
Montélimar, 57
Montezemolo, Alessandro di, 338
Montezuma's revenge, 374
Montgolfier brothers, 28
Months, names of, 84
Montmartre, 308
Montpellier, France, 355
Montrachet, Le, 397
Monuments, burial, 369, 370
Moon, tides and, 368
Moonshine, 168
Moore, Marianne, 262
Moorehead, Alan, 376
"Moot point," 190
Moped, 224
Mora, 251
Morgan, J.P., 327, 331
Morland, H.R., 194
Mormons, 154
  rebellion of, 214
Morons, 193
Morphine, 237
Morton, W.T.G., 20
Moscow subway system, 335
Moses, Anna Mary Robertson
  (Grandma), 98
Mosquito, yellow fever and, 387
Mother's Day, 162
Mothers-in-law, stereotyping of, 330
"Motion-lotion," 195
Motion pictures. See Movies.
Motorcycles, 213, 224
Mount Olympus, 232
Mousetrap, 19th-century, 346
Movies, 209, 224–26
  cosmetics and, 90
  kissing and, 201
  scores for, 328
  television competing with, 359
Mower, lawn, 204
Moynihan, Daniel Patrick, 401
Muckrakers, 232
Mueller, Louis, 145
Mug (vessel)
  coffee, 77
  ivory German, 267
Muhammad Ali, 388
  doll, 125
  jump rope and, 282
  sandwich, 294
Muhammed, 324
Muleus, 145
Mumford, Lewis, 369
Mummies, X ray of, 398
Mummification, 148
  paper and, 240
Murray, James Augustus Henry, 113
Murrow, Edward R., 360–61
Music, 328
  answering machine tapes and, 359
  movies and, 225
  stereo and, 327–29
  stunts and, 334
Musk, 249
Muskie, Edmund, 361
Musonius, 156

Mussolini, Benito, 317
Mustard, 226–27
Mustard gas, 227
"Mutt and Jeff," 79–80
Muzak, 328
Mycenaeans, 393
My Fair Lady, 357
Myopia, 137
Mystery stories, 107–108

N

Nail, 227
Nail polish, 88, 90
Namath, Joe, 321
Names, 228–29
Nansen, Fridtjof, 242
Nantucket Island tides, 368
Napkins, 353
Napoleon I (Bonaparte)
  beet sugar and, 337
  canning and, 58
  divorce of, 117
  English invasion by, 384–85
  Jenner honored by, 386
  on newspapers, 232
  perfume and, 249
  shaving and, 273
  sleep and, 316–17
  snuff and, 321
  tides and, 368
  weather and, 393
  wine and, 396
  yellow fever and, 386
Napoleon III, 286
  railroad coaches of, 378
Nast, Thomas, 61, 212
Nathan's, 174
Nation, Carrie, 30
National Broadcasting Company, 271
National Cash Register, 62
National Police Gazette, 212
National Road, 171
Navigation, 302–303
Nearsightedness, 137
Nebula of Orion, 186
Necktie, 227–29
Needles, 290
  hypodermic, 178
Nefertiti, 88
Nelson, Horatio, 337
Neon, 230
Nero, 137, 223
  garden of, 152
  Poppaea's funeral and, 325
  roses and, 284
Nerval, Gérard de, 308
Nerve stimulator, 238
Nestlé, Charles, 165
Netherlands, the
  auctions in, 25, 26
  coffee-growing and, 76
New Guinea
  chieftain, 372
  Japanese invasion of, 223
Newspapers, 230–32
  advertising in, 7, 8–12
  comic strips in, 79–80
  crossword puzzles in, 92
  papermaking and, 240
Newton, Isaac, 128, 157, 221
New York City
  delicatessens in, 101
  shoe blacks in, 306
  subway system, 335, 336
  taxicabs of, 354
New Yorker, The, 61, 213
New York Public Library, 207
New York Stock Exchange, 331–33
Niagara Falls, daredevils at, 333
Nice, France, bank robbery in, 289
Nicklaus, Jack, 318
Nieman-Marcus, 106–107
Niépce, Joseph Nicéphore, 55
Nightclothes, 238
Nik-O-Lok Company, 78
Nikon workers, 351
Ninepins, 48
Nitroglycerin, safecracking and, 288

Nitrous oxide, 20
Niven, David, 361
Nixon, Richard, 155, 361
 White House uniforms and, 384
Noah, 232
No-Cal sodas, 59
Noise, insomnia and, 320
Noodles, 243
Norway, 242
 skiing and, 312
Nothe, Margaret, 395
Nougat, 57
Nova Scotia tides, 366–68
Novel, detective, 107–108
Numbers, 232
Nuts, 298–99
Nylon
 rope made of, 282–83
 stockings, 172, 184

O

Oak, evergreen, 86
Oatmeal, 50
Obesity. See Fat people.
Ochs, Adolph, 61
O'Connor, Frank, 85
Odéon (Zurich), 308
Offset duplicator, 130
Oil, 114, 233–34
 embargo, 116
Okykoeck, 126–27
Old people. See Aged.
Olds, Ransom Eli, 27
O'Leary's cow, 141
Olmstead, Frederick Law, 220
Olympic Games
 footwear in, 145
 swimming in, 340
Omnibus, 53
Oolong, 357
Opera glasses, 42
Opinion polls, 234–35
Opium, 237
Oppenheim, Meret, 100
Orangeries, 177
Oranges, 235–36
Orangutan, 401
Oraria, 166
Oriental rugs, 287
Orient Express, 378–79
Orion's Great Nebula, 186
Ormandy, Eugene, 339
Osiris, 295
Oswald, Lee Harvey, 361
Otis, Elisha Graves, 133, 313
Otto, Nikolaus August, 27, 114
Ouimet, Francis, 159
Outcault, Richard, 79
Overnight bag, 338
Oxford English Dictionary, 112–13
Oxygen, yawning and, 398–99

P

Packaging, 91, 236–37
 cereal, 51
 corn products in, 88
 of soap, 322
Pain, 20, 22, 23, 103, 104, 237–38
Painter, William, 47
Paisley, Scotland, 366
Pajamas, 238
Palamedes, 112
Palmer House, 176
Palomar, Mt., telescope at, 155, 221
Pandemics, influenza, 191
Panel shows, 258
Pannini, Giovanni Paolo, 363
Pantaloons, 238–39, 383
Pants, 238–39, 364, 395
Paper, 239–40
 clips, 240
 cups, 127
 printing and, 255
 towels, 375
Papin, Denis, 345
Papp, Fran, 353

Papyrus, 206, 207, 239
Parasol, 382
Parcheesi, 46
Parchment, 206, 207, 240
Paré, Ambroise, 15
 tonsillectomy technique of, 371
Paris (of Troy), 22, 45
Paris, France
 Bibliothéque Nationale in, 207
 busing in, 52
 court tennis in, 362
 hospitals of, 173
 hotels of, 174, 175
 lighting in, 208
 postal system in, 136
 sidewalk cafés of, 308
 siege of, 19
 smallpox in, 385
 stock exchange, 256
 subway system, 334–35
Parker Brothers, 46, 47
Parking meter, 240–41
Parmentier, Antoine-Auguste, 254
Par Puzzles, 198
Parry, William, 58–59
Parsis, 148
Pascal, Blaise, 82, 345
Passport, 241–42
Pasta, 243
Pasteur, Louis, 21, 385
Patch, Sam, 333
Patchwork, 260
Patent medicine, 8–9, 129, 388
Patents, 116, 344, 346–47
 for condensed milk, 220
 sewing machines and, 300
 for snoring devices, 317
Patin, Guy, 356
Patterns, sewing, 301
Patterson, John Henry, 61, 62
Paul, St., on wine, 394
Pauling, Linus, 80
Pausanias, 372
Payola, 394
Payplat, Jean-Baptiste Gilbert, 278
Peanut butter, 101, 243, 244
Peanuts, 243–44
Pearlroth, Norbert, 60
Pearls, 197
Pearson, Drew, 214
Peddlers, 124–25
Pedi-bath, 347
Pedigrees, 154–55
Peel, Robert, 252, 253
Pemberton, John S., 59
Pen, 244–45
Pencil, 136, 245
Penicillin, 245–46
Penn, William, 38
 trial of, 200
Pennsylvania coal mines, 74–75
Pensions, 247
Pepper, 247–48
Peppergrass, 394
Pepsi Cola, 32, 59
Pepys, Samuel, 111
 coffeehouses and, 77
 on table linen, 353
Perchloroethylene, 130
Percolator, 151
Père-Lachaise, 369
Perfume, 88, 89, 248–49
 as a deodorant, 105
Pergamum, 206
Perky, Henry, 50
Permanent wave, 165. See also
 Hairstyles.
Perpetual-motion machines, 346
Perret, Jean-Jacques, 273
Persia, Royal Road of, 169
Perspiration, 105, 209
Peruzzi, Vincenzo, 109
Peter the Great, gingerbread house
 of, 324
Petit, Philippe, 333
Petitbled, 280
Petticoats, 383
Petroleum, 114, 233–34. See also
 Oil.

Petroleum jelly as sunscreen, 340
Petronius, 155
Petrov, Anton, 386
Petzval, Josef Max, 56
Pharmacists, 128–29
Phenol, 21
Pheromones, 75–76
Philby, Harold, 296
Philip of Macedon, 143
Phipps, James, 386
Phomograph, 209, 327–29
Phosphorus, matches and, 218
Photography, 55–56, 311
 Kirlian, 182
Phyfe, Duncan, chest by, 269
Physicians, 118–20
 jargon of, 195
Piano, 347
 manufacture of, 348–49
Piazza del Duomo, 126
Picasso, Pablo, 94, 99
Pickering, Thomas, 242
Pickford, Mary, 226
Picklocks, 210–11
Picton, Thomas, 382
Piece-of-eight, 223
Pig
 bacon and, 29
 picture of, 189
 police pejorative, 253
Pig iron, 327
Pilots, airplane, 17, 18
Pil perpetuae, 129
Pilsner, 39
Pin, 290
Pin bowling, 48
Pinkerton agency, 107
Pin-tumbler lock, 210
Pipe smoking, 71
Pi Sheng, 255
Pistol, chain, 345
Placerville, California, 313
Plague. See Black Death.
Planetran, 336
Plantain, 204
Plants, 283–84, 393–94
 indoor, 177–78
Plastic, 249–50
 in dentures, 105
 eyeglass lenses, 137
 mannequins, 396
Plato, 72
Playing cards, 250–51
Plimpton James Leonard, 281
Plimsoll, Samuel, 303
Pliny the Elder, 35, 53, 226, 248,
 371, 372
Plover, 341
Plutarch, 317
Plymouth Colony, 86
Plywood, 251–52
Pocket, 256
Pocketbook, 256, 258–59
Poe, Edgar Allan, 107, 368
Poirot, Hercule, 107–108
Polaroid, 56
Police, 252–54
Police Gazette, 212
Polignac, Marquise de, 379
Poliomyelitis vaccine, 386
Politics
 scandals in, 296–97
 television and, 361
Polka, 102
Pollen, 182
Polls, opinion, 234–35
Pollution, environmental, 74, 151,
 152, 322, 323, 327
Polo, Marco, 174
 pasta and, 243
Polo players, 239
Polo shirt, 305
Polyandry, 218
Polycrates of Samos, 222
Polyethylene and polyester, 250
Polygyny, 218
Polymers, 259
Pompeii, 144, 152
 weeds in, 394

Pony Express, 214
Pooper-scooper, 307
Pop (soda), 86
Popcorn, 86, 87, 101
Pope, Alexander, 200
Poplawski, Stephen J., 144
Poppaea, 325
Porcelain, 35, 64
 antique pots of, 267
 in teeth, 105
Porta, Giovanni Battista della, 55
Porter, Cole, 167, 338
Porter, Edwin S., 224
Porter, Sylvia, 395
Porter, William Sydney, 128
Porticoes, 307
Portland cement, 84
Portman, John, 134
Portmanteau, 337, 372
Portuguese man-of-war, 342
Post, Charles W., 51
Post, Emily, 135
 on chewing gum, 67
 on "Hello," 171
Post, Marjorie Merriweather, 375
Postal system, 136, 213–14
Post-Dispatch (St. Louis), 231
Post Road, 171
Potato, 139, 254
Pottery, 47, 64
Pouch, retort, 236
Poulaines, 145
Poultry industry, 67–68
Pound, Roscoe, 205
Pourboire, 374
Powder, cosmetic, 89
P.P.C., 135
Prang, Louis, 162
Pratt, Samuel, 64
Pravaz, Charles Gabriel, 178
Prejudice, stereotypes and, 329
Premiums, breakfast-cereal, 51
Presbyopia, 137
Prescriptions, 129
Presley, Elvis, 163, 329
Press (newsmen), 230–32
Pressure cooker, 345
Prévost, Abbé, 123
Priestley, Joseph, 59, 136, 285
Princeton University, 367
Printer's devil, 256
Printing, 130, 254–56
Printing press, 137, 240
Privies, 33
Processors, food, 144
Procter, Harley, 322
Procter & Gamble, 322
Profumo, John, 297
Programmed Visibility Signal, 376
Prohibition, 30
Prometheus, 238, 319
Prontosil red, 132
Prophète, Le, 280
Protein, liquid, 275
Proust, Marcel, 86, 308
Pseudonyms, 229
Ptolemy I, 223
Ptolemy II, 221, 401
Ptolemy Claudius, 215
Puddlers, iron, 350
Puerperal fever, 173
"Puffing Billies," 387
Pulitzer, Joseph, 231
 comic strips and, 79
Pullman, George, 378
Puma (footwear), 145
Pumpers, fire, 141
Pun, 257
 translation and, 380
Punch, 60, 132
Punch cards, 82
Puritans, 89, 164
Purple, 131
Purse, 256, 258–59
 snatchers, 145
Puzzle jugs, 127
Puzzles
 crossword, 92
 jigsaw, 198
Pygmalion, 357

Pyle, Ernie, 120
Pyramid ascent, 373
Pythagoras, 37, 226
  numbers' meanings and, 232
Pythagoreans, salads and, 291

Q

Quackery, 119–20
Quaker Oats Company, 250
Quetzalcoatl, 68
Quele de bois, 168
Quill
  pen, 245
  tooth cleaner, 372
Quilt, 260
Quinine, 129
Quinone, 75
Quintus Maximus, 188
Quiz Kids, 258
Quiz shows, 258–59

R

Radford, Edwin, 53, 167
Radio, 270–72
  effect of television on, 359
  quiz shows and, 258
  transmitters, 211
Radio Corporation of America, 271
Radio waves, 256
Ragweed, 394
Railroads, 106, 376–79, 391
  commuting by, 81–82
  diesel engine and, 114
  diners of, 279
  influence on politicians, 171
  language of, 377
  private coaches on, 378
  stock, 333
  tools and, 307
Rain, 131, 391
Raincoat, 272
Rainier III (of Monaco), 400
Raleigh, Walter, 70, 123
  epitaph of, 149
Ramsay, William, 230
Ramses II, 398
Randolph, Cornelia, J., 177
Raphael, 137, 140
Ravioli, 243
Razor, 273
RCA, 271
Reach, Al, 33
Reader's Digest, 213
Recipes, 84–86
  bequest in, 395
Records, stereo, 328
Red, 132
  sky, 391
Redcoats, British, 384–85
Reducing diets, 274–75
Reed, Walter, 387
Reformatory and Refuge Union, 306
Refrigeration, 276–77
  spices and, 303
Refrigerators, 146, 250, 276–77
Refuse, 151–52
REM (rapid eye movement) sleep, 318
Rembrandt, 97
Remington, E., & Sons, 380
Remington, Frederic, 231
Renoir, Pierre Auguste, 94, 99
Restaurant, 277–79
  fast-food, 139–40
  sidewalk, 308
Retailing, 105–107, 115–16, 124–25, 299
  installment plan in, 300
Retort pouch, 236
Retsina, 396
Reuben (cartoonists' prize), 80
Reuben (sandwich), 294
Revere, Paul, 7, 30, 104
Revolving door, 126
Reynière, Grimod de la, 278
Reynolds, Milton, 244
Rhinoceros, zoo-born, 401
Rhinovirus, 81

Rhodes, Cecil John, 109, 110
Rhodes, island of, ginger and, 324
Richard II, 123
Richard the Lion-Hearted, 156
Rice, Grantland, 159
Richelieu, duc de 37
  knives and, 203
Riesman, David, 140
Right-handedness, 167
Rings
  key, 210
  ornamental, 197
  sealing, 91–92
  wedding, 216, 241
Ripley, LeRoy, 60
Ritty, James, 61
Ritz, César, 175
Roaches, 75–76
Roads, 40, 72, 169–71
Road signs, 311
Robbery, 241
  bank, 288–89, 339
Roberts, Kenneth, 208
Robespierre, 205
Robin Hood, 323
Rockefeller, Barbara "Bobo," 117
Rockefeller, Mrs. David, 384
Rockefeller, John D., Jr., 309
Rockefeller, Winthrop, 117, 375
Rocking chair, 65
Roebuck, Alvah, 125
Roentgen, Wilhelm, 397–98
Rogers, Will, 159, 299
Roller derby, 280
Roller mill, 50
Roller skates, 280–81
  spring-driven, 347
Rolls-Royce, plant inspection of, 352
Romance of the Rose, 284
Romans, ancient, 39, 41
  bathing by, 33, 34
  beds of, 37
  birthdays of, 43
  cosmetics and, 89
  eating by, 274, 353
  flags of, 143
  guidebooks of, 215, 372
  hairstyles of, 164
  heating systems of, 146
  highways of, 29, 168–69
  hospitals, military, of, 172
  lawyers of, 205
  libraries of, 206–207
  locks and, 210
  mail system of, 213
  money of, 223
  mustard and, 226, 227
  pearls and, 197
  pepper and, 247–48
  shaving and, 273
  shipping and, 301–302
  sidewalks and, 307
  signs of, 309
  wine of, 396
Rome, subway excavation in, 336
Roosevelt, Eleanor, 374
Roosevelt, Franklin D., 142, 212, 386
  safe of, 289
  Social Security and, 247
Roosevelt, Theodore, 17, 155, 170, 198, 212
  newspapers and, 231–32
  as police commissioner, 252
  railroad gift to, 378
  snoring of, 317
Roosters, 67, 68
Rope, 281–83
Roquefort cheese, 65, 218–19
Rose, 283–84
  perfumes and, 248–49
Ross, Betsy, 143
Ross, Harold, 213, 399
Rossetti, Dante Gabriel, 130
Rouge, 88, 89
Rowing stunts, 334
Rubber, 284–85
  balloons from, 28–29
  in dentures, 105
  erasing, 136
  Goodyear and, 286

rainwear and, 272
Rubinstein, Helena, 90
Rugs, 285, 287
Runyon, Damon, 28
Rush, Benjamin, 128
Russell, Jane, 49
Russell, William H., 214
Russia
  coal in, 75
  flag in, 143
  and the German economy, 223
  jeans in, 195
  libraries in, 207
  tea ceremony in, 356
  telephones in, 358
  traveling salesman in, 124
  vitamin B15 and, 388
Ruth, "Babe," 167, 174, 321

S

Sabin, Albert, 386
Sabot, 145
Saddlebags, 338
Sadirons, 194
Safecracking, 224, 288–89
Safes, 287–90
Safety pin, 104, 290
Saffron, 132, 324–25
Sailing stunts, 334
St. Bernard dogs, 121
St. Bernardine, 250
St. Louis Post-Dispatch, 231
St. Michael, 295
St. Paul, 394
St. Simeon Stylites, 334
St. Valentine, 161
Salad, 290–91
Salad days, 291
Salary, 292
Salicin, 22
Salisbury, James H., 165
Salisbury steak, 166
Salk, Jonas, 386
Salt, 222, 291–93
  as a cleaning agent, 371, 387
  superstitions and, 292
Salt dish by Cellini, 266
Saluki, 121
Samarkand, 240
Sand, George, 70
Sandals, 145
Sandburg, Carl, 163
  on slang, 315
Sanders, Harland, 140
San Diego Zoo, 401
Sandpaper, 293
Sandwich, 293, 294
Sanitarium, 51
San Marcos, University of, 207
Santa Anna, Antonio López de, 66
Santorio, Santorio, 295
  heat-measuring device of, 365, 366
Saratoga trunk, 338
Sargent, John Singer, 93
Sarnoff, David, 271
Sassoon, Vidal, 366
Satan, 218, 250, 295, 321, 369, 372
Savonnerie, 287
Saw, 293–94
Sawbuck, 223
Sawyer, 294
Scaino, Antonio, 362
Scale, balance, 294–95
Scandals, 295–97
Scopolamine, 319
Score, film, 225
Scotland Yard, 108, 252
Screws, 298–99
Scripps' FLIP, 392
Scroggs, Justice, 230
Scurvy, 140, 388
Sea anemone, 341–42
Seafaring, 302–303

Seals, 91
Seals, display of, 402
Sears, Richard, 125, 364
Sears, Roebuck and Co., 125
  credit system of, 210
Sears Tower, 313
Securities, 331–33
Seeley, Herbert Barnum, 279
Seersucker, 72
Selling, direct, 124–25
Seltzer, Leo Alexander, 280
Semple, William F., 104
Semur-en-Auxois, France, 73
Seneca, 34
Senufo, 149
Service station, 299
Seven, luckiness of number, 232
Sévigné, Madame de, 44
Sewing machine, 299–301
  musical cover for, 347
Shakers, 220
Shakespeare, William, 142, 197, 248, 291
  Bible and, 232
  on lawyers, 205
  on loans, 210
  puns and, 257
  on roses, 283
Shamir, 293
Sharon, William, 279
Shar-Pei dogs, 120
Shaving, 36, 273
Shaw, George Bernard, 357
  on death, 148
Shears, 298
Sheets (bed), 38, 174
Sheffield, England, 273, 298
Sherry, Louis, 278–79
Shipbuilding, 302
Shipping, 301–303
  tea trade and, 357
Shirt, 304–305, 364
Shoeblack brigades, 306
Shoe polish, 305, 306
Shoes, 144–46
  steel in, 326
  throwing of, at groom, 216
Shoeshine parlors, 306
Sholes, Christopher, 380
Shoplifting, 305, 307
Shor, Toots, 91
Shovel, 307
Shower (bath), 35
  pedaled, 347
Shreve, Lamb, and Harmon, 314
Sidetrack, 377
Sidewalk, 307–309
Sidewalk café, 308
Sidewalk superintendent, 309
Signals, traffic, 375–76
Signatures, 91
Signatures, Doctrine of, 22
Signs, 309–11
  electric traffic, 376
  neon, 230
  tavern, 309, 310
Silk, 73–74, 222
  stockings, 172
  thread, 366
  underwear, 334
Silver, 311–12
Simon, Théodore, 193
Simon and Schuster, 92
Simpson, James, 20
Singer, Isaac Merritt, 300–301
$64,000 Question, The, 258–59
Skateboard, 281
Skates, roller, 280–81
  spring-driven, 347
Skiing, 174, 312–13
Skin cancer, sunlight and, 340
Skin-care products, 89
Skirts
  bicycle and, 40
  tennis and, 364–65
  trains and, 378
Skyscraper, 313–16
Slang, 315–16
Slavery, 320
  Roman baths and, 33
  rubber trade and, 285

sugar trade and, 337
Sleep, 316–18
  yawning and, 399
Sleeping car, 378
Sleeping pills, 318–19
Slickenstones, 194
Slickers, 272
Sloan, John, 99
Slot machines, 78
Smallpox, 385
Smathers, James, 381
Smith, John, 156
Smith, "Uncle Billy," 234
Smoking, 69–72
Sneakers, 145, 146
Sneeze, 319, 321
  cold spread by, 81
Snoring, 317
Snowflake, 131
  photograph of, 184
Snuff, 321
  handkerchief and, 166
Snuffboxes, 265, 321
Snyder, Howard, 389
Soap, 164, 321–23
  machine stripper for, 352
Soap Box Derby scandal, 296
Soap operas, 271, 322
Social Security, 247
Socrates, 102
  trial of, 200
Soda, 59
Soda fountain, 129
Sodium chloride, 291–93
Sofa, 65
  bed, 37
  Empire-style, 263
Soft drinks, 59
Solar year, 54
Soliman's Water, 89
Solomon, flying carpet of, 287
Sotheby Parke Bernet, 25
Soul beer, 39
Sousa, John Philip, 327
Souvenirs, 323–24
Soviet Union. See Russia.
Spa, 128
  reducing, 275
Spade, Sam, 107
Spaghetti, 243
Spangler, James Murray, 387
Spanish Armada, 368, 393
Spanish flu, 191
Spanish ruff, 304
Speakeasies, 30
Sperm, birth control and, 42, 44
Sphairistikè, 362
Spices, 324–25
  in mummification, 148
  shipping and, 303
Spiderweb thread, 366
Spilsbury, John, 198
Spindletop, 234
Spinsters, 366
Spirit duplicator, 130
Spitz, Mark, 340
Sponges, 180, 325–26
Spoon, 85, 203
  silver Italian, 266
Spooning, 203
Sports, scandals in, 295–96
  language of, 316. See also
   individual sports.
Sport shirt, 304–305
Spray cans, 16
Sri Lanka, 142
Stage, language and superstitions of,
  363, 364
Stage Delicatessen, 294
Stalin, Joseph, 358
Standardization of parts, 23
Stanford, Leland, 378
Stanley Home Products, 125
Stanley Steamer, 26–27
Stanwyck, Barbara, 201
Stapler, 326–27
Starch, 88

reducing and, 274
Steam engine, 114
  automobile, 26–27
  coal and, 74
  fire pumps and, 141
Steam heating, 147
Steamer trunks, 338
Steel, 227, 326–27
  in skyscrapers, 313
  stainless, 69
Steeliners, 351
Steelyard (scale), 295
Stein, Gertrude, 283
Stein, Richard, 165
Steinway & Sons, 348–49
Stellingen Zoo, 402
Stencil, 130
Sterling, 312
Sterling Drug, Inc., 23
Sterne, Laurence, 55
Stereo, 327–29
Stereotyping, 229, 329–31
Stethoscope, 352
Stevenson, Adlai E., 61
Stevenson, Robert Louis, 318
  on umbrellas, 382
Stewart, Alexander Turney, 106
Stock, definition of, 332
Stock exchange, 24–25, 331–33
  Parisian, 256
Stockings, 172
Stogies, 70
Stonehenge, 55
Stool, Cameroonian, 262
Stores
  department, 105–107
  discount, 115–16
  supermarket, 357
Stoskopff, Sébastien, 95
Stoves, 147
Stow, John, 172
Strauss, Levi, 195, 196
Strigil, 322
Stunts, 333–34
Stuyvesant, Peter, 30
Stylites, St. Simeon, 334
Suares, 318
Sublime Porte, 126
Sub rosa, 284
Subway, 334–36
Sudarium, 166
Suez Canal, 301
Sugar, 336–37
  candy and, 56–57
  corn, 88
Suitcase, 337–39
Sulfonamide, 132
Sullivan, Arthur, 320
Sullivan, W.N., 16
Sun
  tides and, 368
  weather and, 393
Sundae, 188
Sundback, Gideon, 400
Sundials, 72
Sunglasses, 137
Suntan lotions, 340
Super Chief, 379
Superman, 80
Supermarket, tea and, 357
Superstitions
  cardplaying, 250
  salt and, 292
  theatrical, 364
  three-on-a-match, 218
Sûreté, 108
Surgery, 398
  on animals, 401
  barbershop, 31
  Paré and, 15
  staplers in, 326
  tonsillectomy, 371
Surnames, 228
Surrealists, 68, 100
Susruta, 120
Susskind, David, 360
Sutton, May, 364
Sutton, Willie, 288
Sweater girls, 49
Sweating, 105, 167

Sweets, 56–57, 69
Swift, Jonathan, 31, 37, 112
Swimming, 339–41
Switchboard, 358
Swords, 167, 326
Symbiosis, 341–42, 388
  sponges and, 326
Syringes, 178
Syrup
  corn, 88
  simple, 57

T

Table linen, 353
Tables, antique, 261, 263, 266
Tabula, 45–46
Tabula Peutingeriana, 215
Taft, William H., 36, 155, 212
Tailors, 300, 301
Take It or Leave It, 258
Talbot, William Henry Fox, 55–56
Talleyrand, Charles Maurice de, 76, 277
Tammany Hall, 61, 335
Tank, Leonardo's, 344
Tankards, 127
Tape recordings, 328
  telephone answering machine
   and, 359
Tapping, telephone, 360
Tarr, Jeff, 45
Tartar steak, 165
Tattoos, 89, 375
Taverns, 29–31, 38
  signs of, 309, 310
Taxes
  collection, 312
  salt, 292
  tea, 356
Taxicab, 353–55
Taximeter, 355
Taylor, Elizabeth, 197, 338
Taylor, Jeremy, 291
Tea, 355–57
  ceremony, 356
  as money, 222
  sugar trade and, 337
Teapot, porcelain English, 267
Teapot Dome scandal, 296
Teeth, 101, 103–105
  false, 104, 105
Teikoku Bank, 290
Telegraph, 104
  Edison and, 209
  Pony Express and, 214
  Sarnoff and, 271
  weather forecasting and, 392
Telephone, 176, 256, 357–59
  answering custom for, 171
  answering machine, 359
  cloak for, 360
  sketch of Bell's first, 344
  tapping of, 360
  typewriters and, 381
Telescope, 42
  glass of, 155
  images through, 186
  mirrors and, 221
Television, 359–62
  advertising on, 14
  future uses of, 361–62
  influence of, 360
  kissing and, 201
  movies and, 226
  politicians and, 361
  quiz shows and, 258–59
  Sarnoff, David, and, 271
  in zoos, 401
Telford, Thomas, 170
Temple, John, 118
Tennis, 362–65
  sneakers and, 145
Tennis racket manufacture, 352
Termites, symbiosis and, 341
Terry cloth, 375
Textile mill, 350
Theater
  language of, 363
  superstitions in, 364

Theiler, Max, 387
Theobromine, 69
Theodoridas, 370
Theophrastus, 248
Thermae, 34
Thermogram, 83, 181, 184
Thermometer, 365–66
Thermoscope, 365
"Thief catcher," 61, 62
Thieves. See Crime (and criminals).
Thimonnier, Barthélemy, 300
Thirteen, as unlucky number, 232
Thompson, "Snowshoe," 313
Thoreau, Henry David, 142
Thread, 366
  in light bulbs, 208
Three, significance of number, 232
Three Fates, 297-98, 366
Threshing machine, 345
Thumbscrew, 298
Thunderstorms, 391
Thurber, James, 31
Tiberius, 155–56
Tickbird, 341
Ticker-tape machine, 331–32
Tickets, lottery, 367
Tide, 366–68
Ties (neck), 227–29
Tiffany lamp, 263
Tightrope walkers, 281–82
  Niagara Falls and, 333
Tillie the Toiler, 80
Time, 213
Timing devices, 72–73, 390
Tin Lizzie, 26, 28
Tipping, 374
Titanic, 271
Tito, Marshal, 374, 383
Toasts, 31, 397
Tobacco, 69–72
  pouch for, zippered, 400
  snuff, 321
Toilet, 33, 34, 35, 63
  coin-operated lock on, 78
  public, graffiti and, 160
Tomato ketchup, 200, 202
Tombstones, 149, 369
  of dogs, 121
Tonsillectomy, 371
Tonti, Lorenzo, 138
Tontines, 138
Toothbrush, 371
Toothpaste, 371–72
Toothpick, 203, 360, 372
Tornadoes, 391
Torquemada, Juan de, 285
Torricelli, Evangelista, 28
Tourism, 308, 372–75
Towels, 375
Tower of Babel, 51
Traffic lights, 375–76
Traffic signs, 311
Trailers, 222
Train, John, 229
Trains, 376–79. See also Railroads.
  milk, 377
Translation of languages, 378–80
Transmitters, bugging, 360
Travel, 91–92, 168–71, 372–75
  airplane, 17–19, 339
  automobile. See Automobile.
  bicycle. See Bicycle.
  guides, 372, 373
  hotels and, 174–76
  luggage and, 337–39
  passports and, 241–42
  railroad, 376–79
Traveler's checks, 375
Travers, Morris, 230
Tremont House (Boston), 34–35, 175,
  176
Trench coat, 272
Trencher, 203
Trials, jury system and, 199–200
Triangular trade, 337
Triskaidekaphobia, 232
Trojan War, 22, 45
Trousers, 238–39, 364
Trudgen, J. Arthur, 339–40

Truman, Harry S., 167
  Bacall, Lauren, and, 349
  campaign of, 377
  scandal under, 296
Trunks, 338
  dugout, 65
Truth magazine, 213
Tryptophan, 319
Ts'ai Lun, 240
T-shirt, 384
Tsutsumu, 236
Tucker, 353
Tudor, Henry, 284
Tulips, 138
Tumbleweed, 394
Tungsten, 208
Tureen, English rabbit, 267
Turing Test, 83
"Turkey," 363
Turkish bath, 33
Turkish towels, 375
Turnkey, dental, 104
Turnpike, 171
Tutankhamen, 64, 398
  bed of, 36–37
  fad concerning, 138
Twain, Mark, 37, 212, 231
  on dogs, 122
  on golf, 159
  on jury system, 200
  railroad travel and, 377
  smoking and, 70, 71
  typewriter and, 380
Tweed (cloth), 72
Tweed, William Marcy ("Boss"),
  61, 212, 296, 335
Twelve, significance of number, 232
Twentieth Century Limited, 379
Twenty-One, 259
Twist (dance), 102
Two Guys, 116
Tymnes, 370
Typesetting, 255
Typewriter, 380–81
  erasers and, 136
Typhoons, 393
Tytell, Martin, 381

U

Uemura, Naomi, 334
Ultraviolet light bulbs, 208
Umbrella, 382–83
  superstition about, 364
Umpires, 33
"Uncle Henry," 92
Uncle Tom's Cabin, 212
Underground (London), 334
Underwear, 49, 364, 383, 384
Underwriter, 193
Uniform, 227, 384–85
Union of Soviet Socialist
  Republics. *See* Russia.
Unisex, 139
United Nations
  smallpox eradication and, 385
  translators, 379
Universities, 78–79
Urban VIII, 321
Urinals, 33, 322
Usurers, 210
Utensils, eating, 203–204

V

Vaccine, 385–87
Vacuum cleaner, 150, 387
Vail, 374
Valayer, De, 136
Valentine's Day, 161–62
Valentino, Rudolph, 201, 238
Valjean, Jean, 108
Valves, pressure-controlling, 16
Vanderbilt, Amy, 354
Vanderbilt, Cornelius, 333, 378
Vanderbilt, William K., 222
Van Doren, Charles, 259
van Gogh, Vincent, 97, 308

Van Horne, Harriet, 279
Vanilla, 325
Vanity Fair, epitaphs in, 370
Van Kannel, Theophilus, 126
Vase brigade, 140
Vases, antique, 267, 268
Vassar College, 79
Vaughan, Harry, 296
Vaughan, Theresa, 218
Vaults, bank, 287, 290
Vauquelin, Nicolas, 69
Veblen, Thorstein, 169
Velde, Adriaen van de, 159
Vending machines, 77–78, 340
Veneer, 251–52
Venereal diseases, 129
Venus, Willendorf, 123
Venus de Milo, 275
Vermeer, Jan, 99
Vernon, Edward, 168
Versailles
  gardens at, 153
  zoo at, 401
Vespucci, Amerigo, 128
Vest, American, 264
Vexilla, 143
Victoria, Queen
  diary of, 111
  hairstyles and, 164
  mauve and, 132
  towels of, 375
Vidocq, François-Eugène, 108
Vikings, burials by, 369
Vinci, Leonardo da. *See* da
  Vinci, Leonardo.
Vineyards, 396
Virgil, 391
Virginia Company, 215
Virginity, 217
Viruses, cold, 81
Vitamin C
  colds and, 80
  crystals of, 179
Vitamins, 254, 387–88
Voisin (bomber), 18
Vollmer, August, 253
Volta, Alessandro, 35, 36
Voltaire, 37, 318
von Stroheim, Erich, 225
Voronoff, Serge, 120
Vuelta Abajo, 70
Vulcanization, 29, 286

W

Wager, Dolly, 275
Wager of battle, 200
Wagner, Richard, 232
Wakeman, Frederic, 227
Walker, Jimmy, 296
Walker, John, 218
Wallace, DeWitt, 212–13
Wallace, George, 126, 238
Wall Street, 331
Walpole, Horace, 153
Walton, Izaak, 142
Waltz, 102
Ward, Artemus, 209
Ward, Stephen, 297
Ward lock, 210
Wardrobe trunks, 338
Ware, Frank, 198
Ware, Great Bed of, 38
Warhol, Andy, 100
  images of, 187
Waring, George E., 151
Warren, J.C., 20
Warren, Joseph, 104
Washing machine, 389
  coin-operated, 77
Washington, George, 7, 30, 36, 52,
  155, 371
  as a brewer, 38
  cardplaying and, 250
  dying statement of, 149
  as a fire fighter, 140
  ice cream and, 188
  on magazines, 212
  swimming and, 339

Waste disposal, 151–52
Watch, 24, 390
Water
  drinking, 127–28
  purification of, by silver, 312
Waterbugs, 75
Water clock, 72
Water closet, 34
Water hyacinth, 394
Waterman, Lewis, 245
Water snail (bilge pump), 298
Watson, Dr. John, 107
Watson, Thomas A., 358
Watt, James, 23
Waving iron, 164–65
Weather, 391–93
  forecasting, 362, 392
  lore, 391
Weather vane, antique, 269
Weaving, rug, 287
Webb, Matthew, 340
Webster, Daniel
  Goodyear defended by, 286
  poultry industry and, 68
Webster, Noah, 113
Webster's *Third New International
  Dictionary*, 113–14
Wedding, 216–17
Weeds, 393–94
Weight control, diets for, 274–75
Weigler, Milton, 375
Weihenstepan Brewery, 39
Weissmuller, Johnny, 340
Welch, Thomas, 104
Weller, Newton, 362
Wenson, William, 273
Westerlies, 393
West Indies, sugar trade and, 337
Wheat, 49–50
Wheel, 344
Whiskey, terms relating to, 168
Whistler, James, 132
Whistle-stop, 377
Whistling, superstition against, 364
White
  for mourning, 149
  wedding gown and, 216–17
White, Annie Randall, 135
White, E.B., 359
Whiteners
  skin, 89
  tooth, 372
Whitney, Eli, 23
Wickham, Henry A., 285
Wigs, 164
Wilde, Oscar
  scandal and, 297
  tomb of, 369
Wild One, The, 224
Wiley, Harvey W., 58
Wilhelm II, 278
Willendorf Venus, 123
William and Mary College, 367
Williams, James, 117
Williams, Roger, 119
Willig, George, 333–34
Willow tree, remedies from, 22
Wills, 395
Wilson, Herbert, 288
Wilson, Nick, 214
Wilson, Woodrow, 225
  women's education and, 79
Wimbledon, 362–64
Winchell, Walter, epitaph of, 370
Wind, 392, 393
Window dressing, 396
Window washing, skyscraper, 316
Windsor, Duchess of, 38
Wine, 122, 149, 366, 394, 396–97
  sidewalk cafés and, 308
Wine fountain, 266
Wingfield, Walter, 362
"Winging it," 363
Winthrop, John, 119
Wire, barbed, 345
Wiretapping, 360
Woad, 132
Wolfe, Glynn de Moss, 218
Women
  higher education for, 79

magazines and, 212
  slang about, 316
  stereotyping of, 330–31
  tennis and, 364–65
  typewriter and, 380–81
  waist-cinching by, 383
Wood, Alexander, 178
Woods, Rose Mary, 136
Wool, 73, 383
Woolf, Virginia, 121
Woollcott, Alexander, epitaph of, 370
Words. *See* Language.
Work, Bertram G., 400
World (New York), 79, 92
World Trade Center, 313
  stunts at, 333–34
Wren, Christopher, 178
Wright, Frank Lloyd, 177, 313
Wright, Orville and Wilbur, 17, 19,
  299–300
Wrigley, William, Jr., 66–67
Wrigley's spearmint gum sign, 311
Wristwatch, 390

X

Xenophon, 156
Xerography, 130–31
Xerxes, rope bridges of, 281
X ray, 104, 397–98
  images created by, 181, 184, 185
  Soap Box Derby scandal and, 296
  zoos and, 401

Y

Yale, Elihu, 248
Yale, Linus, Jr., 211, 287
Yale University, 22, 207, 248, 367
Yap, 223
Yawn, 398–99
Year, types of, 54, 55
Yellow fever, 386
Yellow journalism, 79, 231
"Yellow Kid, The," 79
Yoga, shoes and, 146
Yogurt, 399
Young, Chic, 79
YMCA, New York, 380

Z

Zaharias, George and Babe,
  159
Zahn, Johann, 55
Zenger, John Peter, 105
Zeppelin, 17
Zeppelin (sandwich), 294
Zeus, 119
Zinc oxide, 340
Zipper, 400
Zoo, 400-402